What Every Lawyer
Needs to Know About
IMMIGRATION LAW

EDITORS:
JENNIFER A. HERMANSKY
KATE KALMYKOV

CONTRIBUTING EDITORS:
WILLIAM S. JORDAN, III
ANNA WILLIAMS SHAVERS
JILL E. FAMILY

**Section of Administrative Law
and Regulatory Practice**

Cover design by Mary Anne Kulchawik/ABA Publishing.

Printed in the United States of America

18 17 16 15 14 5 4 3 2 1

Library of Congress Cataloging-in-Publication Data

What every lawyer needs to know about immigration law / Edited by Kate Kalmykov and Jennifer Hermansky.—First edition.
    p. cm.
Includes bibliographical references and index.
    ISBN 978-1-62722-543-4 (print edition : alk. paper)
    1. Emigration and immigration law—United States. I. Kalmykov, Kate, editor. II. Hermansky, Jennifer, editor.
    KF4819.W52 2014
    342.7308′2—dc23

2014023422

Discounts are available for books ordered in bulk. Special consideration is given to state bars, CLE programs, and other bar-related organizations. Inquire at Book Publishing, ABA Publishing, American Bar Association, 321 North Clark Street, Chicago, Illinois 60654-7598.

www.ShopABA.org

TABLE OF CONTENTS

Chapter 6
The Basics of Non-immigrant and Immigrant Visa Processing 77

ABOUT THE EDITORS

Kate Kalmykov is a shareholder in the Business Immigration & Compliance practice of international law firm Greenberg Traurig, LLP. She focuses her practice on the EB-5 Immigrant Investor program, with a decade of experience in the industry. She regularly works with developers across a variety of industries, as well as private equity funds, on developing new projects that qualify for EB-5 investments. She also counsels foreign nationals on obtaining green cards through individual or Regional Center EB-5 investments, as well as issues related to I-829 Removal of Conditions. She earned her BA, magna cum laude, from American University. Kate also earned her MA in International Affairs and JD from American University.

Jennifer Hermansky is an attorney in the Business Immigration & Compliance practice of international law firm Greenberg Traurig, LLP. She focuses her practice on employment-based and family-based immigration, with experience serving the health care, pharmaceutical, and real estate industries, as well as entrepreneurs, scientists, and researchers in scientific communities. Jennifer also concentrates on EB-5 immigrant investor visas. She counsels clients on the creation of new regional centers, amendments of regional center designations, and adoptions of developer projects by existing regional centers. She earned her BS, summa cum laude, and her JD, cum laude, from Drexel University.

William S. Jordan III is Associate Dean and C. Blake McDowell Jr. Professor of Law at The University of Akron School of Law, where he teaches Administrative Law. He received his BA from Stanford University and his JD, cum laude, from the University of Michigan. He serves as Chair of the Publications Committee of the Section of Administrative Law and Regulatory Practice of the American Bar Association.

Anna Williams Shavers is the Cline Williams Professor of Citizenship Law at the University of Nebraska College of Law, where she teaches, among other things, Immigration, Forced Migration, and Administrative Law. She received her BS from Central State University–Ohio, her MS from the University of Wisconsin–Madison, and her JD, cum laude, from xviii   *What Every Lawyer Needs to Know about Immigration Law*

the University of Minnesota. She was elected as the 2014–2015 Chair of the Section of Administrative Law and Regulatory Practice of the American Bar Association.

Jill E. Family is Professor of Law and Director of the Law and Government Institute at Widener University School of Law. Professor Family teaches Immigration Law, Introduction to Immigration Law Practice, and Administrative Law. She is a Fellow of the American Bar Foundation and was the 2010 Fellow of the National Administrative Law Judiciary Foundation. Professor Family served as a member of the governing council of the American Bar Association's Section on Administrative Law from 2011 to 2014. She received her undergraduate degree from the University of Pennsylvania and her graduate degrees from Rutgers University.

A NOTE FROM THE EDITORS

Immigration law is an integral part of our nation's rich history. It has shaped the cultural, political, and legal systems of the United States. It is a complex area of law, governed by statutes, regulations, federal and administrative court guidance, and guidance and adjudicatory policies from multiple administrative agencies. It is also a rewarding area of law, touching a wide range of organizations and individuals. Given the breadth of immigration law, it is likely a lawyer will encounter a client who also needs immigration law advice. Thus, it is important to understand how immigration law interacts with other practice areas, how to spot immigration issues for clients, and when to involve an immigration attorney for assistance with a client. We hope this book serves as a primer for understanding those issues.

1

WHAT EVERY LAWYER SHOULD KNOW ABOUT IMMIGRATION: WHO ARE THE PLAYERS?

Shoba Sivaprasad Wadhia[1]

INTRODUCTION[2]

For more than 200 years, immigration has been recognized as a federal responsibility and, pursuant to the "plenary power" doctrine, delegated to the legislative and executive branches of government.[3] Congress created the first immigration office in the U.S. Treasury Department in 1895 and identified the leader of this office as the "Commissioner-General of Immigration."[4] This office was titled the "Bureau of Immigration" and transferred to the Department of Commerce and Labor in 1903, and later

---

1. Professor Shoba Sivaprasad Wadhia is the Samuel Weiss Faculty Scholar and Clinical Professor of Law at The Dickinson School of Law at the Pennsylvania State University. She is the founder/director of the Center for Immigrants' Rights, an immigration policy clinic where students produce practitioner toolkits, white papers, and primers of national impact on behalf of client organizations. Prior to joining Penn State, Professor Wadhia was deputy director for legal affairs at the National Immigration Forum in Washington, D.C. She has been honored by the Department of Homeland Security's Office for Inspector General and Office for Civil Rights and Civil Liberties, and in 2003, she was named Pro Bono Attorney of the Year by the Arab-American Anti-Discrimination Committee.
2. The reader should check for any developments that have occurred since 2012.
3. *See, e.g,* Chae Chan Ping v. United States, 130 U.S. 581 (1889).
4. *See U.S. Immigration and Naturalization Service—Populating a Nation: A History of Immigration and Naturalization,* U.S. Customs and Border Protection, http://www.cbp.gov/xp/cgov/about/history/legacy/ins_history.xml (last visited Feb. 12, 2012); *see also* Judson MacLaury, *A Brief History: The U.S. Department of Labor,* U.S. Dep't of Labor (May 25, 2011), http://www.uscis.gov/portal/site/uscis/menuitem.eb1d4c2a3e5b9ac89243c6a7543f6d1a/?vgnextoid=e00c0b89284a3210VgnVCM100000b92ca60aRCRD&vgnextchannel=e00c0b89284a3210VgnVCM100000b92ca60aRCRD.

to the new Department of Labor in 1913.[5] It was not until 1940 that the immigration functions, by this time bundled into the "Immigration and Naturalization Service" (INS), were transferred to the Department of Justice. For the next several years, the INS operated under the Department of Justice.[6]

Over the years, the INS earned a reputation as a "bureaucracy" and was disparaged for having lengthy processing delays, long lines, and outdated operating systems. Along with the INS were a number of executive branch agencies charged with immigration functions, among them the Department of State, Department of Labor, and the Executive Office for Immigration Review (part of the Department of Justice). Following the tragedies of 9/11, the immigration bureaucracy was sharply criticized based on a reality that nearly every hijacker associated with the terrorist attacks entered the United States on a valid visa and remained without detection.[7] Together, the "red tape" reputation of the INS and the operational holes that enabled the hijackers to exploit the United States immigration system presented a real opportunity for policymakers to rethink the immigration structure. Following several months of deliberation, Congress passed the Homeland Security Act of 2002.[8] The HSA abolished the INS by statute and, effective March 1, 2003, created a cabinet-level Department of Homeland Security, the first "player" profiled in this chapter.

DEPARTMENT OF HOMELAND SECURITY

Several agencies within the executive branch play a role in administering or enforcing U.S. immigration laws. The Department of Homeland Security (DHS) is led by a secretary and is comprised of more than 200,000 employees and more than one dozen components.[9] The Office of the Secretary contains a number of officers responsible for a diversity of mat-

---

5. *See Our History*, U.S. CITIZENSHIP AND IMMIGRATION SERVICES (May 25, 2011), http://www.uscis.gov/portal/site/uscis/menuitem.eb1d4c2a3e5b9ac89243c6a7543f6d1a/?vgnext oid=e00c0b89284a3210VgnVCM100000b92ca60aRCRD&vgnextchannel=e00c0b89284a3210 VgnVCM100000b92ca60aRCRD.

6. *See id.*

7. *See* THOMAS R. ELDRIDGE ET AL., 9/11 AND TERRORIST TRAVEL: STAFF REPORT OF THE NATIONAL COMMISSION ON TERRORIST ATTACKS UPON THE UNITED STATES (Aug. 21, 2004), http://www.9-11commission.gov/staff_statements/911_TerrTrav_Monograph.pdf.

8. Homeland Security Act of 2002, Pub. L. No. 107-296, 116 Stat. 2135.

9. For an interactive organizational chart of the DHS, see U.S. DEPARTMENT OF HOMELAND SECURITY, ORGANIZATIONAL CHART, http://www.dhs.gov/xabout/structure/editorial_0644 .shtm (last visited Feb. 12, 2012).

ters, including immigration. These offices include the Office for Civil Rights and Civil Liberties, Office of the Inspector General, Citizenship and Immigration Services Ombudsman, and Office of General Counsel.[10] Among other functions, the Office for Civil Rights and Civil Liberties (CRCL) advises department personnel about civil rights and liberties matters; meets with a range of stakeholders whose civil rights and liberties may be affected; and investigates complaints alleging abuse and mistreatment by department employees, including immigration-related complaints such as conditions of detention, abuse of authority, and discrimination.[11] The Office of the Inspector General conducts audits, investigations, and inspections of DHS programs,[12] including immigration enforcement programs such as detention management, unaccompanied minors, and programs implicating local and state law enforcement.[13]

The United States Citizenship and Immigration Services (USCIS) acts as the "services" arm for immigration and processes applications for immigration and citizenship benefits such as family-based petitions; adjustment of status ("green card"); work authorization; asylum; and citizenship as well as benefits for victims of trafficking, crimes, and related abuses.[14] Many of the applications are processed by one of four regional Service Centers and/or the National Benefit Center.[15] Other offices within USCIS include the Administrative Appeals Office (AAO); Office of Citizenship; Fraud Detection and National Security; Office of Legislative Affairs; Office of Public Engagement; and the Refugee, Asylum, and International Operations Directorate (RAIO).[16] The AAO is an appellate

---

10. *See Office of the Secretary,* U.S. Dep't of Homeland Security, http://www.dhs.gov /xabout/structure/office-of-the-secretary.shtm (last visited Feb. 12, 2012).

11. *See About the Office for Civil Rights and Civil Liberties,* U.S. Dep't of Homeland Security, http://www.dhs.gov/xabout/structure/editorial_0371.shtm (last visited Feb. 12, 2012).

12. *See Office of Inspector General: What We Do,* U.S. Dep't of Homeland Security, http:// www.oig.dhs.gov/index.php?option=com_content&view=article&id=94&Itemid=63 (last visited Feb. 12, 2012).

13. *See, e.g., Office of Inspector General: Component: Immigration and Customs Enforcement (ICE),* U.S. Dep't of Homeland Security, http://www.oig.dhs.gov/index.php?option=com _content&view=article&id=24&Itemid=44 (last visited Feb. 12, 2012).

14. *See* U.S. Citizenship and Immigration Services, http://www.uscis.gov/portal/site /uscis (last visited Feb. 12, 2012).

15. *See USCIS Service and Office Locator,* U.S. Citizenship and Immigration Services, https://egov.uscis.gov/crisgwi/go?action=offices.type&OfficeLocator.office_type=SC (last visited Feb. 12, 2012).

16. *See Directorates and Program Offices,* U.S. Citizenship and Immigration Services, http://www.uscis.gov/portal/site/uscis/menuitem.eb1d4c2a3e5b9ac89243c6a7543f6d1a/?v gnextoid=de5a914c330dd110VgnVCM1000004718190aRCRD&vgnextchannel=de5a914c330 dd110VgnVCM1000004718190aRCRD (last visited Feb. 12, 2012).

unit within USCIS responsible for processing select appeals of applications and petitions decided by a USCIS adjudicator.[17] DHS may designate an AAO decision as "precedent" in which case the decision guides future cases and is binding on DHS employees. RAIO operates both the overseas refugee program and the affirmative asylum process.[18] USCIS employees are guided by the immigration statute, governing regulations, AAO decisions, and their own policies.[19]

Immigration and Customs Enforcement (ICE) is the law enforcement arm for immigration and has more than 20,000 employees.[20] ICE Enforcement and Removal Operations (ERO) has jurisdiction over a number of police functions, including the apprehension, detention, and removal of non-citizens.[21] ERO is also responsible for managing non-citizens in custody. On any given day, there are about 33,000 non-citizens in ICE custody. ICE Office of the Principal Legal Advisor (OPLA) is the largest legal program in DHS and also employs the trial attorneys responsible for pros-

17. *See The Administrative Appeals Office (AAO)*, U.S. CITIZENSHIP AND IMMIGRATION SERVICES, http://www.uscis.gov/portal/site/uscis/menuitem.eb1d4c2a3e5b9ac89243c6a7543f6d1a/?vgnextoid=dfe316685e1e6210VgnVCM100000082ca60aRCRD&vgnextchannel=dfe316685e1e6210VgnVCM100000082ca60aRCRD (last visited Feb. 12, 2012).
18. *See Refugee, Asylum, and International Operations Directorate*, U.S. CITIZENSHIP AND IMMIGRATION SERVICES, http://www.uscis.gov/portal/site/uscis/menuitem.eb1d4c2a3e5b9ac89243c6a7543f6d1a/?vgnextoid=e88514c0cee47210VgnVCM100000082ca60aRCRD&vgnextchannel=e88514c0cee47210VgnVCM100000082ca60aRCRD (last visited Feb. 12, 2012).
19. *See Laws*, U.S. CITIZENSHIP AND IMMIGRATION SERVICES, http://www.uscis.gov/portal/site/uscis/menuitem.eb1d4c2a3e5b9ac89243c6a7543f6d1a/?vgnextoid=02729c7755cb9010VgnVCM10000045f3d6a1RCRD&vgnextchannel=02729c7755cb9010VgnVCM10000045f3d6a1RCRD (last visited Feb. 12, 2012). USCIS's primary policy guidance is bound into a thick directory called the Adjudicator's Field Manual. *See Adjudicator's Field Manual—Redacted Public Version*, U.S. CITIZENSHIP AND IMMIGRATION SERVICES, http://www.uscis.gov/portal/site/uscis/menuitem.f6da51a2342135be7e9d7a10e0dc91a0/?vgnextoid=fa7e539dc4bed010VgnVCM1000000ecd190aRCRD&vgnextchannel=fa7e539dc4bed010VgnVCM1000000ecd190aRCRD&CH=afm (last visited Feb. 12, 2012). Asylum officers follow guidance contained in the Asylum Officer Basic Training Course. *See Asylum Division Training Programs*, U.S. CITIZENSHIP AND IMMIGRATION SERVICES, http://www.uscis.gov/portal/site/uscis/menuitem.5af9bb95919f35e66f614176543f6d1a/?vgnextoid=2a1d1a877b4bc110VgnVCM1000004718190aRCRD&vgnextchannel=f39d3e4d77d73210VgnVCM100000082ca60aRCRD (last visited Feb. 12, 2012).
20. U.S. IMMIGRATION AND CUSTOMS ENFORCEMENT, http://www.ice.gov/ (last visited Feb. 12, 2012).
21. *ICE Enforcement and Removal Operations*, U.S. IMMIGRATION AND CUSTOMS ENFORCEMENT, http://www.ice.gov/about/offices/enforcement-removal-operations/ (last visited Feb. 12, 2012).

ecuting non-citizens and representing the DHS in removal proceedings.[22] There are twenty-six OPLA offices around the country, each headed by a chief counsel.[23] ICE has created or updated a number of policy directives on immigration topics such as the exercise of prosecutorial discretion, detention standards, and the role of local law enforcement. In fiscal year 2011, ICE removed 320,000-plus non-citizens from the country.[24]

The Customs and Border Protection (CBP) presents a multifaceted mission of "keeping terrorists and their weapons out of the United States. It also has a responsibility for securing and facilitating trade and travel while enforcing hundreds of U.S. regulations, including immigration and drug laws."[25] On the immigration front, CBP officers are responsible for screening non-citizens that arrive at the border, airport, or seaport. CBP officers are authorized to admit, arrest, detain, or defer the inspection of a non-citizen. CBP officers are also responsible for identifying victims of human trafficking as well as arriving asylum seekers.

Noticeably absent from the DHS is a single leader in charge of managing and coordinating the varied immigration functions. In the congressional debates leading to the creation of DHS, some advocates and members pushed (unsuccessfully) for the creation of an "Immigration CEO" and a consolidation of the immigration functions into a single unit within DHS.[26] More than nine years since its creation, DHS remains a mammoth of an agency with a myriad of units that administer immigration.

DEPARTMENT OF JUSTICE

Housed inside the Department of Justice (DOJ) is the immigration court system known as the Executive Office for Immigration Review (EOIR). EOIR contains three components: the immigration judges housed under the Office of the Chief Immigration Judge; the appellate division known

---

22. U.S. Immigration and Customs Enforcement, Office of the Principal Legal Advisor (OPLA), http://www.ice.gov/about/offices/leadership/opla/ (last visited Feb. 12, 2012).

23. *Id.*

24. *ICE Total Removals through July 31st, 2011*, U.S. Immigration and Customs Enforcement, http://www.ice.gov/doclib/about/offices/ero/pdf/ero-removals.pdf (last visited Feb. 12, 2012).

25. U.S. Customs and Border Protection, http://cbp.gov/xp/cgov/about/ (last visited Feb. 12, 2012).

26. For an early analysis about the options for centralizing immigration policy following the creation of DHS, see David A. Martin, *Immigration Policy and the Homeland Security Act Reorganization: An Early Agenda for Practical Improvements*, Migration Policy Institute (Apr. 2003), http://www.migrationpolicy.org/insight/insight_4-2003.pdf.

as the Board of Immigration Appeals (BIA); and the Office of the Chief Administrative Hearing Officer, which is responsible for handling sanctions relating to employers who unlawfully hire unauthorized workers and other immigration-related employment practices.[27] Importantly, removal proceedings against a non-citizen commence once DHS files immigration charges with EOIR. At this juncture, ICE represents the U.S. government, the non-citizen charged with violating the immigration laws is identified as the "respondent," and the immigration judge presides over the hearing. Once an immigration judge renders a decision, either the government or the respondent may appeal the decision to the BIA or waive appeal. Select decisions by the Board of Immigration Appeals are published as "precedent" and considered binding law. By contrast, unpublished decisions by the BIA, immigration judge decisions, and EOIR policy memoranda and practice manuals are non-binding. The Attorney General is authorized to direct that a BIA decision be referred to himself and to reverse the decision.[28] The AG may also amend the regulations governing EOIR and, following 9/11, used this authority to increase the BIA's use of "affirmances without opinion" (AWO) and very short opinions by the BIA.[29] The number of such AWOs and short opinions has decreased in the last five years, but many of the policy questions remain the same, especially as they relate to the location of the EOIR and the authority of its judges. Though immigration judges and BIA members are guided by quasi-formal procedures contained in regulations and manuals produced by the EOIR,[30] they do not have the stature of Article III judges and instead are employees of the Department of Justice.

The Department of Justice houses a number of other units responsible for an immigration function. The Civil Division contains the Office of Immigration Litigation (OIL), an office responsible for "coordinating national immigration matters before the federal district courts and circuit courts of appeals."[31] In this capacity, OIL attorneys represent the U.S. government when a non-citizen has filed a petition for review of her removal order in a federal court of appeals. The Immigration and Nationality Act (INA) identifies the federal courts of appeals as the "exclusive means of review" for judicial review over cases in which a final order of removal

---

27. *Executive Office for Immigration Review Fact Sheet*, U.S. Dep't of Justice (Oct. 13, 2009), http://www.justice.gov/eoir/orginfo.htm.

28. 8 C.F.R. § 1003.1(h)(1)(i).

29. *Id.* § 1003.1(e)(4).

30. *See id.* § 1003.0; *Statistics and Publications*, U.S. Dep't of Justice, http://www.justice.gov/eoir/statspub.htm#Manuals (last visited Feb. 12, 2012).

31. *Office of Immigration Litigation*, U.S. Dep't of Justice, http://www.justice.gov/civil/oil/oil_home.html (last visited Feb. 12, 2012).

has been entered.[32] The Office of Legal Counsel (OLC) "drafts legal opinions of the Attorney General and also provides its own written opinions and oral advice in response to requests from the Counsel to the President, the various agencies of the executive branch, and offices within the Department."[33] One noteworthy OLC opinion issued in 1996 pertained to the role of law enforcement in immigration and opined, "Subject to the provisions of state law, state and local police may constitutionally detain or arrest aliens who have violated the criminal provisions of the [INA]. State police lack recognized legal authority to arrest or detain aliens solely for purposes of civil deportation proceedings, as opposed to criminal prosecution."[34] Following 9/11, the Attorney General declared that this opinion had been replaced with a statement that all state and local police have the "inherent authority" to enforce the federal immigration laws. The "inherent authority" doctrine sparked great controversy among immigration advocates and attorneys and unsurprisingly led to litigation, legislation, and administrative proposals that fall outside of the scope of this chapter.

The Department of Justice also houses a Civil Rights Division (CRD) responsible for enforcing federal statutes prohibiting discrimination on the basis of race, color, sex, disability, religion, familial status, and national origin.[35] The CRD became especially involved after 9/11 in monitoring hate crimes and related backlash against Arab, Muslim, and South Asian communities.[36] More recently, the CRD, through its Special Litigation section, filed lawsuits on behalf of the Departments of Justice, State, and Homeland Security against the states that enacted immigration legislation identified by the federal government as "preempted" by federal law.[37] Also within the Civil Rights Division is the Office of Special Counsel for Immigration-Related Unfair Employment Practices, responsible for

---

32. *See* Immigration and Nationality Act § 242(a)(5) (codified at 8 U.S.C. § 1252 (2012)) ("[A] petition for review filed with an appropriate court of appeals in accordance with this section shall be the sole and exclusive means for judicial review of an order of removal entered or issued under any provision of this Act. . . .").

33. *Office of Legal Counsel*, U.S. Dep't of Justice, http://www.justice.gov/olc/index.html (last visited Feb. 12, 2012).

34. *Assistance by State and Local Police in Apprehending Illegal Aliens*, U.S. Dep't of Justice, http://www.justice.gov/olc/immstopo1a.htm (last visited Feb. 12, 2012).

35. *Civil Rights Division*, U.S. Dep't of Justice, http://www.justice.gov/crt/index.php (last visited Feb. 12, 2012).

36. *See Initiative to Combat Post-9/11 Discriminatory Backlash*, U.S. Dep't of Justice, http://www.justice.gov/crt/nordwg.php (last visited Feb. 12, 2012).

37. *See, e.g., Department of Justice Challenges Alabama Immigration Law*, U.S. Dep't of Justice (Aug. 1, 2011), http://www.justice.gov/opa/pr/2011/August/11-ag-993.html.

enforcing the anti-discrimination provision contained in the immigration statute.[38]

DEPARTMENT OF STATE

The Department of State (DOS) contains a number of units responsible for immigration. Among these units is the Bureau of Consular Affairs, whose mission "is to protect the lives and interests of American citizens abroad and to strengthen the security of United States borders through the vigilant adjudication of visas and passports."[39] Consular officers employed by the DOS are responsible for issuing visas to non-citizens seeking to travel to the United States. Consular officers are stationed at U.S. Embassies, Consulates, and Diplomatic Missions.[40] In some cases, a visa will not be issued until the USCIS has approved a visa petition. Even if a visa petition is approved by the USCIS and a visa is issued by the DOS, it is CBP who is authorized to grant or deny entry at a United States port of entry, as described above.

Many immigration practitioners rely on the DOS Foreign Affairs Manual as a secondary source on how immigration and visa laws are interpreted and applied.[41] Another important document produced by the DOS is the Visa Bulletin, which is updated monthly and provides information about the wait times for immigrant visa categories that are subject to a quota under the immigration law.[42] The Visa Bulletin is organized to indicate the "priority date" the DOS is currently processing so that a non-citizen in waiting can plan his affairs accordingly. For example, if the Visa Bulletin indicates a date of May 2009 for spouses of lawful permanent residents, this means that the agency is processing applications that were initially filed in May 2009. Below is a sample of the Visa Bulletin for February 2012:[43]

---

38. *Office of Special Counsel for Immigration-Related Unfair Employment Practices*, U.S. Dep't of Justice, http://www.justice.gov/crt/about/osc/ (last visited Feb. 12, 2012).
39. *About Us*, U.S. Dep't of State, http://travel.state.gov/about/about_304.html (last visited Feb. 12, 2012).
40. *Websites of U.S. Embassies, Consulates, and Diplomatic Missions*, U.S. Dep't of State, http://www.usembassy.gov/ (last visited Feb. 12, 2012).
41. *See Foreign Affairs Manual*, U.S. Dep't of State, http://www.state.gov/m/a/dir/regs/fam/ (last visited May 19, 2014).
42. *See Visa Bulletin*, U.S. Dep't of State, http://travel.state.gov/visa/bulletin/bulletin_1360.html (last visited Feb. 12, 2012).
43. *Visa Bulletin for February 2012*, U.S. Dep't of State, http://travel.state.gov/content/visas/english/law-and-policy/bulletin/2012/visa-bulletin-for-february-2012.html (last visited May 19, 2014).

Family-Sponsored	All Chargeability Areas Except Those Listed	CHINA-mainland born	INDIA	MEXICO	PHILIPPINES
F1	22DEC04	22DEC04	22DEC04	22APR93	22MAY97
F2A	08JUN09	08JUN09	08JUN09	08MAY09	08JUN09
F2B	15OCT03	15OCT03	15OCT03	01DEC92	01NOV01
F3	01DEC01	01DEC01	01DEC01	01JAN93	22JUL92
F4	08SEP00	08SEP00	08SEP00	15MAY96	01NOV88

The Secretary of State also submits Country Reports on Human Rights Practices to Congress annually.[44] Adjudicators within USCIS, immigration judges, and Board of Immigration Appeals members within EOIR rely upon these reports when reviewing refugee-related claims such as asylum protection, withholding of removal, and protection under the United Nations Convention Against Torture. According to the DOS, the Country Reports on Human Rights Practices are based on information collected from U.S. and foreign government officials; victims of human rights abuse; academic and congressional studies; and reports from the press, international organizations, and nongovernmental organizations (NGOs).[45] The DOS also designates public and private entities to act as exchange sponsors in the J-1 program[46] and also recommends waivers for J-1 visa holders seeking a waiver to the immigration law's requirement that select J-1 visa holders return home for two years before being adjusted to a permanent status or changed to a temporary H or L visa status.[47]

---

44. *See Human Rights Reports*, U.S. DEP'T OF STATE, http://www.state.gov/j/drl/rls/hrrpt /index.htm (last visited Feb. 12, 2012).

45. *2010 Human Rights Report: Appendix A—Notes on Preparation of Report*, U.S. DEP'T OF STATE, http://www.state.gov/j/drl/rls/hrrpt/2010/appendices/154524.htm (last visited Feb. 12, 2012).

46. *See Overview—About the Exchange Visitor Program*, U.S. DEP'T OF STATE, http://travel .state.gov/visa/temp/types/types_1267.html#1 (last visited Feb. 12, 2012) ("The Exchange Visitor Program promotes mutual understanding between the people of the United States (U.S.) and the people of other countries by educational and cultural exchanges, under the provisions of U.S. law.").

47. *See Eligibility Information—Waiver of the Exchange Visitor Two-Year Home-Country Physical Presence Requirement*, U.S. DEP'T OF STATE, http://travel.state.gov/content/visas/english /study-exchange/student/residency-waiver/eligibility.html (last visited May 19, 2014); *Frequently Asked Questions—Waiver of the Exchange Visitor Two-Year Home-Country Physical Presence Requirement*, U.S. DEP'T OF STATE, http://travel.state.gov/visa/temp/info/info_5504 .html (last visited Feb. 12, 2012).

DEPARTMENT OF HEALTH AND HUMAN SERVICES

Housed inside the Department of Health and Human Services is the Office of Refugee Resettlement (ORR). Within the ORR, the Division of Unaccompanied Children's Services (DUCS) has jurisdiction over the custody and care of unaccompanied minors or "unaccompanied alien children" (UAC). UACs are defined as "children who: have no lawful immigration status in the United States; have not attained 18 years of age; and with respect to whom: (1) there is no parent or legal guardian in the United States; or (2) no parent or legal guardian in the United States is available to provide care and physical custody."[48]

DEPARTMENT OF LABOR

The Department of Labor (DOL) contains a number of agencies with jurisdiction over immigration. The Employment and Training Administration's Office of Foreign Labor Certification (OFLC) is a unit within DOL responsible for reviewing labor certification and labor condition applications submitted by U.S. employers in connection with temporary work visas and permanent labor certification programs.[49] Specifically, the OFLC is required to test the local labor market to ensure that there are no able, willing, and qualified U.S. workers to fulfill a particular job, and moreover confirm that approving the non-citizen for a particular position will not have an "adverse effect" on the wages and working conditions of similarly situated U.S. workers. In FY 2010, the OFLC processed 422,228 employer applications requesting 851,556 positions for permanent and temporary foreign labor certifications.[50] The DOL Wage and Hour Division (WHD) is responsible for reviewing the employer's wage to ensure that it complies with the wage requirements of the given job or work visa. Once an employer's application is approved or "certified," then a visa petition is normally filed with the USCIS. Even after the USCIS approves an employer-based petition, the non-citizen may need to "wait in line" if he falls in a category that is numerically or geographically limited and will

---

48. *Unaccompanied Children's Services*, U.S. DEP'T OF HEALTH AND HUMAN SERVICES, http://www.acf.hhs.gov/programs/orr/programs/unaccompanied_alien_children.htm (last visited Feb. 12, 2012).

49. *Office of Foreign Labor Certification*, U.S. DEP'T OF LABOR, http://www.foreignlaborcert.doleta.gov/ (last visited Feb. 12, 2012).

50. *Foreign Labor Certification Annual Report, October 1, 2009–September 30, 2010*, U.S. DEP'T OF LABOR, http://www.foreignlaborcert.doleta.gov/pdf/OFLC_2010_Annual_Report_Master.pdf.

normally have to apply for a visa with the Department of State. In other words, the DOL is often the "first stop" in an employment-based case that requires labor certification. The DOL website also contains a number of important resources such as decisions by the Board of Alien Labor Certification Appeals and the definitions of occupations recognized by the DOL.[51]

The Occupational Safety and Health Administration (OSHA) is a unit within DOL responsible for protecting workers from conditions that pose a risk of serious harm. OSHA requires that workers receive training about hazards in the workplace and have access to review the records of work-related injuries, among other rights.[52] OSHA also spells out specific responsibilities for employers to provide a safe workplace.

WHITE HOUSE

The White House also plays an advisory role on immigration. To illustrate, the Domestic Policy Council (DPC) "coordinates the domestic policy-making process in the White House and offers advice to the President. The DPC also supervises the execution of domestic policy and represents the President's priorities to Congress."[53]

THE LEGISLATIVE BRANCH

In 1952, Congress enacted the Immigration and Nationality Act (INA), which remains the key instrument for domestic immigration law. The INA has been amended many times, but its framework remains largely the same. Congress amends the INA by passing legislation that modifies a particular section or portion of the INA. For example, when Congress passed the Refugee Act of 1980, it established a statutory framework for U.S. asylum law that was codified in various sections of the INA. Importantly, the judiciary committees in the Senate and House of Representatives bear jurisdiction over immigration administration and

---

51. *See Immigration Collection: Board of Alien Labor Certification Appeals and Office of Administrative Law Judges*, U.S. DEP'T OF LABOR, http://www.oalj.dol.gov/LIBINA.HTM (last visited Feb. 12, 2012).

52. *About OSHA*, U.S. DEP'T OF LABOR, http://www.osha.gov/about.html (last visited Feb. 12, 2012).

53. *Domestic Policy Council*, THE WHITE HOUSE, http://www.whitehouse.gov/administration/eop/dpc (last visited Feb. 12, 2012).

enforcement.[54] Within the judiciary committees are the House Sub-committee on Immigration Policy and Enforcement[55] and the Senate Subcommittee on Immigration, Refugees, and Border Security.[56] In addition, the House Homeland Security Committee and Senate Homeland Security and Government Accountability Committee are responsible for oversight over the Department of Homeland Security. Importantly, these congressional committees play an important oversight function and over the years have scheduled oversight hearings on medical care in immigration detention, deaths in immigration custody, and the Executive Office for Immigration Review, among other topics. Members of Congress can also issue letters to executive branch agencies expressing concerns about or making requests on administrative immigration measures. For example, in April 2011, twenty-two Democratic Senators wrote a letter to President Barack Obama requesting that his administration exercise prosecutorial discretion favorable towards the individuals eligible for the DREAM Act.[57]

THE JUDICIAL BRANCH

While the "plenary power" doctrine is premised on the exclusive authorities of the "political" branches of government over the immigration function, the judicial branch continues to play a pivotal role in interpreting the legality of immigration laws. The INA identifies the thirteen federal circuit courts of appeals as the "exclusive" means for judicial review of final orders of removal.[58] Though Congress in 1996 stripped federal court review of immigration decisions that include, among other things, crimi-

---

54. *See* UNITED STATES SENATE COMMITTEE ON THE JUDICIARY, http://www.judiciary.senate .gov/ (last visited Feb. 12, 2012); UNITED STATES HOUSE OF REPRESENTATIVES COMMITTEE ON THE JUDICIARY, http://judiciary.house.gov/ (last visited Feb. 12, 2012).

55. *Committee on Judiciary Subcommittee Jurisdiction*, U.S. HOUSE OF REPRESENTATIVES COMM. ON THE JUDICIARY, http://judiciary.house.gov/index.cfm/subcommittees (last visited May 19, 2014).

56. *Immigration, Refugees and Border Security*, U.S. SENATE COMM. ON THE JUDICIARY, http:// www.judiciary.senate.gov/about/subcommittees#immigration (last visited May 19, 2014).

57. For a copy of this letter, see *Durbin, Reid, 20 Senate Democrats Write Obama on Current Situation of DREAM Act Students*, U.S. SENATE, http://durbin.senate.gov/public/index.cfm /pressreleases?ID=cc76d912-77db-45ca-99a9-624716d9299c (last visited Feb. 12, 2012).

58. Immigration and Nationality Act § 242(a)(5) (codified at 8 U.S.C. § 1252 (2012)) ("Exclusive means of review. Notwithstanding any other provision of law . . . a petition for review filed with an appropriate court of appeals in accordance with this section shall be the sole and exclusive means for judicial review of an order of removal entered or issued under any provision of this Act. . . .").

nal offenses, expedited removal, and discretionary decisions, additional language added by Congress in 2005 preserves deportation review by a federal circuit court if the case involves a "question of law" or a "constitutional claim."[59] Similarly, detained immigrants continue to bring habeas corpus challenges in federal district courts. Finally, the U.S. Supreme Court can choose to review an immigration case that falls within its jurisdiction, and more recently issued an opinion for the immigrant in *Judulang v. Holder*[60] while also agreeing to hear arguments around the constitutionality of Arizona's immigration law.

By no means exhaustive, this chapter outlines the numerous players involved in the crafting, administration, and implementation of immigration laws.

---

59. Immigration and Nationality Act § 242(a)(2)(D) (codified at 8 U.S.C. § 1252 (2012)).
60. Judulang v. Holder, 132 S. Ct. 476 (2011).

Appendix A

TABLE OF ACRONYMS AND WEBSITES

AAO: Administrative Appeals Office www.uscis.gov/portal/site/
uscis/menuitem.eb1d4c2a3e5b9ac89243c6a7543f6d1a/?vgnextoid
=dfe316685e1e6210VgnVCM100000082ca60aRCRD&vgnextchann
el=dfe316685e1e6210VgnVCM100000082ca60aRCRD

AWO: Affirmance Without Opinion

BIA: Board of Immigration Appeals
http://www.justice.gov/eoir/biainfo.htm

CBP: Customs and Border Protection http://cbp.gov/xp/cgov/home.xml

CRCL: Office for Civil Rights and Civil Liberties
http://www.dhs.gov/xabout/structure/crcl.shtm

CRD: Department of Justice Civil Rights Division
http://www.justice.gov/crt/index.php

DHS: Department of Homeland Security
http://www.dhs.gov/index.shtm

DOJ: Department of Justice http://www.justice.gov/

DOL: Department of Labor http://www.dol.gov/

DOS: Department of State http://www.state.gov/

DPC: White House Domestic Policy Council
http://www.whitehouse.gov/administration/eop/dpc

DUCS: Division of Unaccompanied Children's Services
http://www.acf.hhs.gov/programs/orr/programs
/unaccompanied_alien_children.htm

EOIR: Executive Office for Immigration Review
http://www.justice.gov/eoir/

ERO: ICE Enforcement and Removal Operations http://www.ice.gov
/about/offices/enforcement-removal-operations/

ICE: Immigration and Customs Enforcement http://www.ice.gov/

INA: Immigration and Nationality Act

INS: Immigration and Naturalization Service

OFLC: The Employment and Training Administration Office of Foreign
        Labor Certification http://www.foreignlaborcert.doleta.gov/

OIL: Office of Immigration Litigation
        http://www.justice.gov/civil/oil/oil_home.html

OLC: Office of Legal Counsel http://www.justice.gov/olc

OPLA: ICE Office of the Principal Legal Advisor
        http://www.ice.gov/about/offices/leadership/opla/

ORR: Office of Refugee Resettlement
        http://www.acf.hhs.gov/programs/orr/

OSHA: Occupational Safety and Health Administration
        http://www.osha.gov

RAIO: Refugee, Asylum, and International Operations Directorate
        http://www.uscis.gov/portal/site/uscis/menuitem.eb1d4c2a3e
        5b9ac89243c6a7543f6d1a/?vgnextoid=e88514c0cee47210VgnVCM
        100000082ca60aRCRD&vgnextchannel=e88514c0cee47210Vgn
        VCM100000082ca60aRCRD

UAC: Unaccompanied Alien Children

USCIS: United States Citizenship and Immigration Services
        www.uscis.gov

WHD: Department of Labor Wage and Hour Division
        http://www.dol.gov/whd/

2

A SELECTED HISTORY OF IMMIGRATION LAW AND ITS RELATIONSHIP TO MODERN IMMIGRATION LAW AND POLICY

Peter F. Asaad[1]

INTRODUCTION: THE FOUR PILLARS OF MODERN IMMIGRATION LAW

Today, there are four pillars of U.S. immigration law: family, employment, humanitarian interests, and diversity. That is, for foreign nationals to permanently reside in and eventually become citizens of the United States, they must be related to U.S. citizens or lawful permanent residents in specific ways, be employed by companies wishing to bring them to the United States for business purposes, be escaping specific types of persecution, torture, or other troubling circumstances addressed by existing laws, or they must be foreign nationals from countries not well represented in existing family- and employment-based immigration programs. U.S. immigration law was not always based upon these four pillars; in fact, race and national origin were major factors in determining who would be allowed to enter into, reside in, and become a naturalized citizen of the United States.

This chapter will examine legislative history to provide a greater understanding of existing statutes that govern the avenues of immigration to the United States today. The first part of the chapter will examine the

1. Peter F. Asaad is the founder and managing partner of Immigration Solutions Group, PLLC, where he represents individuals, families, and corporations in all immigration matters. For his work with domestic firms and multinational corporations, he assists in managing employee employment eligibility needs and develops effective streamlined immigration and compliance programs. He works closely with HR executives on day-to-day immigration matters, including temporary visa processing, permanent residency processing, corporate compliance policy guidance, consular processing matters, and immigration matters arising out of mergers and other forms of corporate reorganization. Mr. Asaad is a past president of the American Immigration Lawyers Association for D.C., Maryland, and Virginia and has been recognized by the American Bar Association "as one of the nation's leading litigators" in the field of immigration law and by the American Bar Foundation as a top lawyer in the field among the top one-third of one percent of the lawyers in Washington, D.C.

early years of immigration and nationality law when race and national origin were first introduced into the law, leading to a period of exclusion of Chinese nationals. The second and third parts of this chapter will examine the expansion of national origin exclusions to other nationalities, as well as other exclusions not based on race or national origin. The fourth part of the chapter will focus on the shift away from race- and national origin-based immigration to the modern immigration system based on family- and employment-based immigration. The fifth part of this chapter will examine the third pillar of modern U.S. immigration law based upon status as a refugee or asylee. Finally, the sixth part of this chapter will provide a brief overview of the fourth pillar of immigration law today that is based on a commitment to a diverse immigrant population, the exact opposite of U.S. immigration and nationality law in the early years of this nation.

THE EARLY YEARS OF IMMIGRATION AND NATIONALITY LAW: A STRONG FOCUS ON RACE AND NATIONAL ORIGIN

The first few acts of Congress on immigration and naturalization included the establishment of a naturalization process and statutes regarding the expulsion of enemy aliens. Each of these acts used race and/or national origin as the determining factors on who would be allowed to naturalize or enter the country.

In 1790, the first statute on naturalization was enacted and included only "free white person[s]."[2] The 1790 Act stated "[t]hat any alien, being a free *white* person, who shall have resided within the limits and under the jurisdiction of the United States for the term of two years, may be admitted to become a citizen thereof."[3] Several acts followed the 1790 Act in the early years of the nation to change the naturalization process in several ways, but the requirement of being a "white person" remained constant in the early years. Even when Congress acted to include the naturalization of "aliens of African nativity and persons of African descent" in 1870, the existing group of "free white persons" remained in the law and there was no mention of other individuals.[4] The "white person" requirement for naturalization remained in various statutes passed over the years, even as late as 1946.[5]

In addition to the naturalization acts, the U.S. Congress addressed the expulsion of certain foreign nationals in its early years. On June 25, 1798, the president was empowered to "order all such aliens as he shall judge

---

2. Act of March 26, 1790, ch. 3, 1 Stat. 103, 103 (emphasis added).
3. *Id.*
4. Act of July 14, 1870, ch. 254, § 7, 16 Stat. 254, 256.
5. Nationality Act of 1946, ch. 534, sec. 1, § 303(a)(1), 60 Stat. 416, 416.

dangerous to the peace and safety of the United States, or shall have reasonable grounds to suspect are concerned in any treasonable or secret machinations against the government thereof, to depart out of the territory of the United States."[6] Although this provision expired pursuant to the statute within two years,[7] another statute empowering the president with similar powers with regard to nonnaturalized aliens from nations with which the United States is at war, or engaged in hostilities, was enacted two weeks later and remains in our law today.[8]

While only "free white persons" and "aliens of African nativity and persons of African descent" were allowed to naturalize by 1870, there were no race- or national origin-based exclusions to simply enter the United States, nor were there other grounds of exclusion, such as those that can be found in the Immigration and Nationality Act (INA) today. In fact, in 1864, "An Act to encourage immigration" was enacted.[9] Pursuant to the 1864 statute, a commissioner of immigration was established who was empowered to create regulations to enforce contracts for labor by foreign nationals.[10] Furthermore, immigrants arriving after the 1864 Act were no longer compulsively required to be enrolled for military service.[11]

In addition to the act to encourage immigration, the United States and China entered into a treaty to promote the entry of Chinese immigrants in 1868.[12] In 1850, there were only 758 individuals in the United States who were Chinese. By 1860, there were 35,565 and that number proceeded to grow quickly through the next few decades with 63,042 in 1870, and 104,468 in 1880.[13]

The promotion of Chinese immigration to the United States ended suddenly in 1880 when the United States entered into another treaty with China to enable the United States to do the exact opposite of the Burlingame Treaty of 1868—to limit immigration of laborers from China.[14] The 1880 treaty stated:

---

6. Act of June 25, 1798, ch. 58, § 1, 1 Stat. 570, 571.

7. *Id.* § 6, 1 Stat. at 572.

8. Act of July 6, 1798, ch. 66, § 1, 1 Stat. 577, 577.

9. Act of July 4, 1864, ch. 246, 13 Stat. 385.

10. *Id.* § 1, 13 Stat. at 386.

11. *Id.* § 3, 13 Stat. at 386.

12. Additional Articles to the Treaty between the United States and China, July 28, 1868, U.S.-P.R.C., arts. IV–VII, 16 Stat. 739, 740–41 (Burlingame Treaty).

13. U.S. Bureau of the Census, *Region and Country or Area of Birth of the Foreign-Born Population, with Geographic Detail Shown in Decennial Census Publications of 1930 or Earlier: 1850 to 1930 and 1960 to 1990*, http://www.census.gov/population/www/documentation/twps0029/tab04.html (last visited November 13, 2011).

14. Treaty Providing for the Future Regulation of Chinese Immigration into the United States, Nov. 17, 1880, U.S.-P.R.C., 22 U.S.T. 817.

> Whenever in the opinion of the Government of the United States, the coming of Chinese laborers to the United States, or their residence therein, affects or threatens to affect the interests of that country, or to endanger the good order of the said country or of any locality within the territory thereof, the Government of China agrees that the Government of the United States may regulate, limit, or suspend such coming or residence, but may not absolutely prohibit it.[15]

Within two years, the Congress acted to execute this treaty with the Chinese Exclusion Act in 1882 which stated, "[I]n the opinion of the Government of the United States the coming of Chinese laborers to this country endangers the good order of certain localities within the territory thereof."[16] Therefore, the Act stated, "the coming of Chinese laborers to the United States be, . . . suspended; and during such suspension it shall not be lawful for any Chinese laborer to come, or, having so come . . . to remain within the United States."[17]

The 1868 Burlingame Treaty and the Chinese Exclusion Act also prohibited the naturalization of Chinese. Article VI of the Burlingame Treaty stated, "[N]othing herein contained shall be held to confer naturalization upon citizens of the United States in China, nor upon the subjects of China in the United States."[18] Executing Article VI of the Burlingame Treaty was Section 14 of the Exclusion Act of 1882 stating, "That hereafter no State court or court of the United States shall admit Chinese to citizenship."[19]

Although the Chinese Exclusion Act of 1882 banned Chinese laborers from immigrating to the United States, it did not prohibit other Chinese immigration. Article II of the 1880 treaty stated:

> Chinese subjects, whether proceeding to the United States as teachers, students, merchants, or from curiosity, together with their body and household servants, and Chinese laborers who are now in the United States, shall be allowed to go and come of their own free will and accord, and shall be accorded all the rights, privileges, immunities and exemptions which are accorded to the citizens and subjects of the most favored nation.[20]

---

15. *Id.* art. I, 22 U.S.T. at 817.

16. Chinese Exclusion Act, ch. 126, Preamble, 22 Stat. 58, 58 (1882).

17. *Id.* § 1, 22 Stat. at 59.

18. Additional Articles to the Treaty between the United States and China, July 28, 1868, U.S.-P.R.C., art. VI, 16 Stat. 739, 740.

19. Chinese Exclusion Act, ch. 126, § 14, 22 Stat. at 61.

20. Treaty Providing for the Future Regulation of Chinese Immigration into the United States, Nov. 17, 1880, U.S.-P.R.C., art. II, 22 U.S.T. 817, 817–18.

The Chinese Exclusion Act upheld Article II of the 1880 treaty, but it nonetheless required Chinese government-issued certificates of identity to enter the United States.[21]

The situation for Chinese immigrants deteriorated even further in 1888.[22] Although the 1888 act reaffirmed the 1882 act's provision that grandfathered in existing Chinese immigrants as legal immigrants,[23] if they departed the country, they could not return.[24] The Chinese Exclusion Act of 1882 was to expire within ten years pursuant to the Act, but it was extended for another ten years in 1892[25] and again in 1902, this time indefinitely,[26] until it was finally repealed in 1943.[27]

By 1890, the Chinese population in the United States had leveled to 106,468, just 2,000 more than in 1880, and by 1900 the Chinese population dwindled to 81,534 and eventually to only 43,560 in 1920.[28]

THE EXPANSION OF NATIONAL ORIGIN EXCLUSIONS BEYOND THE CHINESE AND THE INSTITUTION OF QUOTAS

Exclusions of immigrants based upon national origin dramatically increased in 1917 with the Asiatic Barred Zone Act.[29] Pursuant to the 1917 Act, most Asians were excluded from immigrating to the United States, including Indians and citizens of most of the islands around the continent of Asia. Prominent exceptions to this expansive exclusionary act included Japanese and Filipinos.[30] However, Japanese immigration to the United States had already been sharply curtailed through the 1907 Gentleman's Agreement, an informally negotiated agreement between the presidents

---

21. Chinese Exclusion Act, ch. 126, § 6, 22 Stat. at 60.

22. Act of Oct. 1, 1888, ch. 1064, 25 Stat. 504.

23. Chinese Exclusion Act, ch. 126, § 3, 22 Stat. at 59 (stating "[t]hat the two foregoing sections shall not apply to Chinese laborers who were in the United States on the seventeenth day of November, eighteen hundred and eighty, or who shall have come into the same before the expiration of ninety days next after the passage of this act.").

24. Act of Oct. 1, 1888, ch. 1064, § 1, 25 Stat. 504, 504.

25. Act of May 5, 1892, ch. 60, § 1, 27 Stat. 25, 25.

26. Act of April 29, 1902, ch. 641, § 1, 32 Stat. 176, 176.

27. Act of Dec. 17, 1943, ch. 344, § 1, 57 Stat. 600, 600.

28. U.S. Bureau of the Census, *Region and Country or Area of Birth of the Foreign-Born Population, with Geographic Detail Shown in Decennial Census Publications of 1930 or Earlier: 1850 to 1930 and 1960 to 1990*, http://www.census.gov/population/www/documentation /twps0029/tab04.html (last visited November 13, 2011).

29. Act of Feb. 5, 1917, ch. 29, 39 Stat. 874.

30. *Id.* § 3, 39 Stat. at 876.

of the United States and Japan in which Japan agreed to issue passports
to Japanese citizens bound for the United States *only if* they were "nonla-
borers, or are laborers who . . . seek to resume a formerly acquired domicile, to join a parent, wife, or children residing there, or to assume active
control of an already possessed interest in a farming enterprise in this
country."[31]

Just four years later, another bill dramatically limited immigration
with national origin quotas. Not only did the 1921 act reaffirm the 1917
act that excluded Asians, it limited the number of immigrants from each
country outside of the Western Hemisphere to only three percent of the
population of residents of that nationality already in the United States, as
determined by the 1910 census.[32]

Congress acted again in 1924 to limit and change the immigration
system.[33] This time Congress limited the total number of immigrants
to 150,000 per year.[34] It also adjusted the quota system already set forth
in the 1921 act by changing the number of immigrants allowed to enter
from each country from three percent to two percent of the population of
the foreign-born from that nation already in the United States during the
1890 census for the fiscal years prior to 1927.[35] For the fiscal years of 1927
and thereafter, the annual quota for each nationality became "a number
which bears the same ratio to 150,000 as the number of inhabitants in continental United States in 1920 having that national origin . . . bears to the
number of inhabitants in the continental United States in 1920."[36]

In 1940, a comprehensive bill was enacted which continued to
place racial limits on who could be naturalized. Section 303 of the 1940
act stated, "The right to become a naturalized citizen under the provisions of this Act shall extend only to white persons, persons of African
nativity or descent, and descendants of races indigenous to the Western
Hemisphere."[37]

---

31. U.S. Immigration Commission, Reports of, S. Doc. No. 61-747, at 584 (3d Sess. 1911).
32. Act of May 19, 1921, ch. 8, § 2(a), 41 Stat. 5, 5.
33. Act of May 26, 1924, ch. 190, 43 Stat. 153.
34. *Id.* § 11(b), 43 Stat. at 159.
35. *Id.* § 11(a), 43 Stat. at 159.
36. *Id.* § 11(b), 43 Stat. at 159.
37. Nationality Act of 1940, ch. 876, § 303, 54 Stat. 1137, 1140.

THE BIRTH AND EXPLOSION OF OTHER EXCLUSIONARY FACTORS

At about the same time Congress took up the exclusion of Chinese immigrants, it also began in 1875 to exclude immigrants from "China, Japan, or any Oriental country . . . [who] has entered into a contract or agreement . . . for lewd or immoral purposes."[38] In addition, the 1875 act excluded immigrants "who are undergoing a sentence for conviction in their own country of felonious crimes other than political . . . and women 'imported for the purposes of prostitution.'"[39] Grounds for exclusion not based on race or national origin were further expanded in 1882 to include any "lunatic, idiot, or any person unable to take care of himself or herself without becoming a public charge."[40]

In 1885, Congress broadened immigration restrictions by prohibiting "any person, company, partnership, or corporation . . . to prepay, or in any way to assist or encourage the migration of any alien . . . under contract or agreement . . . made prior to the importation or migration of such alien."[41] Furthermore, all such contracts were nullified and voided.[42] Exceptions included engaging foreigners already in the United States as "private secretaries, servants, or domestics," contracts with foreign labor exclusively for "personal or domestic servants," skilled laborers in new industries not yet established in the United States, if such labor could not otherwise be obtained, and artists, lecturers, and singers.[43]

The list of exclusions continued to grow in 1891 to include "[a]ll idiots, insane persons, paupers or persons likely to become a public charge, persons suffering from a loathsome or a dangerous contagious disease, persons who been convicted of a felony or other infamous crime or misdemeanor involving moral turpitude, [and] polygamists."[44] Furthermore, the 1891 act added to the 1885 act by excluding persons "whose ticket or passage is paid for with the money of another or who is assisted by others to come, unless" it was proven that he or she was not a contract laborer excluded in previously enacted statutes.[45]

---

38. Act of March 3, 1875, ch. 141, § 1, 18 Stat. 477, 477.
39. *Id.* § 5, 18 Stat. at 477.
40. Act of Aug. 3, 1882, ch. 376, § 2, 22 Stat. 214, 214.
41. Act of Feb. 26, 1885, ch. 164, § 1, 23 Stat. 332, 332.
42. *Id.* § 2, 23 Stat. at 332–33.
43. *Id.* § 5, Stat. at 333.
44. Act of March 3, 1891, ch. 551, § 1, 26 Stat. 1084, 1084.
45. *Id.*

By 1903, the exclusions list grew again to add the following classes: "epileptics, and persons who have been insane within five years previous, persons who have had two or more attacks of insanity at any time previously, . . . professional beggars, . . . [and] anarchists, or persons who believe in or advocate the overthrow by force or violence of the . . . United States."[46] In 1907,

> imbeciles, feeble-minded persons, . . . persons afflicted with tuberculosis, . . . persons . . . found to be and are certified by the examining surgeon as being mentally or physically defective, such mental or physical defect being of a nature which may affect the ability of such alien to earn a living, . . . [and] children under sixteen years of age, unaccompanied by one or both of their parents. . . .

were added to the list of existing exclusions.[47] By 1917 a literacy requirement was added: "All aliens over the age of sixteen years of age, physically capable of reading, who can not read" were excluded.[48] To enforce this latter provision, the 1917 law required immigration inspectors to perform literacy tests on those seeking admission to the United States.[49]

Exclusionary grounds grew substantially in the 20th century resulting in the large number in the INA today. For a general understanding of existing grounds of exclusion, see section 212 of the INA where most grounds of exclusions are located in the law today.[50]

THE SHIFT AWAY FROM RACE- AND NATIONAL ORIGIN-BASED IMMIGRATION TO FAMILY- AND EMPLOYMENT-BASED IMMIGRATION

The shift away from using race and national origin in immigration law began in 1943 when the Chinese Exclusion Acts were finally repealed.[51] Similarly, a bill to end exclusions of Indians was enacted in 1946.[52] The

---

46. Act of March 3, 1903, ch. 1012, § 2, 33 Stat. 1213, 1214.
47. Act of Feb. 29, 1907, ch. 1134, § 2, 34 Stat. 898, 898–99.
48. Act of Feb. 5, 1917, ch. 29, § 3, 39 Stat. 874, 877.
49. *Id.*
50. INA § 212(a), 8 U.S.C. 1182(a).
51. Act of December 17, 1943, ch. 344, § 1, 57 Stat. 600, 600.
52. Act of July 2, 1946, ch. 534, § 4, 60 Stat. 416, 417.

1946 act also amended the naturalization provision to include Filipinos, Indians, and Chinese, but the term "white person" remained in statute.[53]

Just a few years later, the McCarran-Walter Act of 1952[54] became the first comprehensive and significant piece of legislation after the 1924 Immigration Act and set the stage for today's INA.

While the quota system first enacted in 1921 remained intact in the 1952 act, the 1952 act changed the percentage used to determine the limit on the number of immigrants from each country. Instead of two percent in place since 1924, the 1952 act limited the number of immigrants from each country to only one sixth of one percent of the population of the foreign-born from each nation already in the United States during the 1920 census.[55]

Since the repeal of the Chinese Exclusion Acts in 1943 and the repeal of other statutes discriminating against other Asians in 1946, Asians were finally being treated equally under the immigration law. However, just six years later, the 1952 act moved the law back again on Asians by creating a special and very convoluted way to determine quotas for Asians, resulting in a very limited quota for Asian immigrants.[56]

Although Asian discrimination continued in the 1952 act and the quota system was still in place, there was a shift toward preferences of immigrants not based on race and national origin in the 1952 act,[57] thereby forming the basis of today's family- and employment-based preference systems.[58] The preference system under the 1952 act for each quota area for each year was as follows:

1. The first fifty percent were for quota immigrants "whose services are determined by the Attorney General to be needed urgently in the United States because of the high education, technical training, specialized experience, or exceptional ability of such immigrants and to be substantially beneficial prospectively to the national economy, cultural interests, or welfare of the United States";[59]

---

53. *Id.* sec. 1, § 303(a), 60 Stat. at 416.
54. Immigration and Nationality Act of 1952 (INA), ch. 477, 66 Stat. 182 (codified as amended at 8 U.S.C. §§ 1101–1537 (2006)).
55. *Id.* § 201(a), 182 Stat. at 175.
56. *Id.* § 202(b), 182 Stat. at 177.
57. *Id.* § 203(a), 182 Stat. at 178–79.
58. *See generally* INA § 203(a)–(b), 8 U.S.C. § 1152(a)–(b) (2011).
59. INA, ch. 477, § 203(a)(1)–203(a)(4), 66 Stat. 163, 178.

2. The second thirty percent were for "parents of citizens of the United States, such citizens being at least twenty-one years of age";[60]
3. The final twenty percent were for "immigrants who are the spouses or the children of aliens lawfully admitted for permanent residence"; and[61]
4. Any unused visas from the first three preferences would be for "the brothers, sisters, sons, or daughters of citizens of the United States."[62]

The biggest shift away from racial and national origin quotas came in 1965 when the quota system was finally abolished and replaced with a preference system very similar to the family and employment preferences in our law today. In fact, a provision was specifically included in the 1965 act that stated that, "No person shall receive any preference or priority or be discriminated against in the issuance of an immigrant visa because of his race, sex, nationality, place of birth, or place of residence."[63]

The following preference system in the following order was established in the 1965 act:

1. Twenty percent for unmarried sons and daughters of U.S. citizens;[64]
2. Twenty percent for spouses and unmarried sons and daughters of lawful permanent residents;[65]
3. Ten percent for "members of the professions," or because of their exceptional ability in the sciences or the arts will substantially benefit prospectively the national economy, cultural interests, or welfare of the United States;[66]
4. Ten percent for married sons and daughters of U.S. citizens;[67]
5. Twenty-four percent for brothers and sisters of U.S. citizens;[68]

---

60. *Id.*
61. *Id.*
62. *Id.*
63. Act of Oct. 3, 1965, Pub. L. No. 89-236, sec. 2, § 202(a), 79 Stat. 911, 911.
64. *Id.* sec. 3, § 203(a)(i)–203(a)(vii), 79 Stat. at 913.
65. *Id.*
66. *Id.*
67. *Id.*
68. *Id.*

6. Ten percent for "skilled or unskilled labor, not of a temporary or seasonal nature, for which a shortage of employable or willing persons exists in the United States,"[69] and

7. Six percent for those the Attorney General deems escaping persecution or catastrophe.[70]

While the national origins quota system was eliminated in the 1965 act, it was replaced with a Western Hemisphere limit of 120,000[71] and an Eastern Hemisphere limit of 170,000,[72] in addition to an Eastern Hemisphere per country limit of 20,000.[73] The per country limit of 20,000 was extended to Western Hemisphere countries in 1976.[74]

The final shift away from a national origin-based system came in 1978 when the hemispheric quotas were abolished and replaced with a total worldwide visa limit of 290,000,[75] later amended to 270,000, exclusive of refugees.[76] The per country limit was finally changed in 1990 to fully eliminate any preferences and/or discrimination by limiting every country to seven percent of the overall number of visas allotted to family- and employment-based immigrants,[77] a provision that persists in our law today.[78]

IMMIGRATION INTO THE UNITED STATES BASED UPON STATUS AS A REFUGEE OR ASYLEE

As explained in the prior two sections of this chapter, for citizens of countries not affected by the Chinese Exclusion Acts and the Asiatic Barred Zone Act, immigration to the United States was subject to no numerical limitation until the institution of national origin quotas in 1921. Thus, non-Asian foreign nationals suffering from persecution could enter the United States like all other immigrants did at that time without numerical limitation. Once numerical limits were introduced, legislation was needed to address urgent refugee situations around the world.

---

69. *Id.*
70. *Id.*
71. *Id.* § 21(e), 79 Stat. at 921.
72. *Id.* sec. 1, § 201(a), 79 Stat. at 911.
73. *Id.* sec. 2, § 202(a), 79 Stat. at 911–12.
74. Act of Oct. 20, 1976, Pub. L. No. 94-571, sec. 3, § 202(e), 90 Stat. 2703.
75. Act of Oct. 5, 1978, Pub. L. No. 95-412, sec. 2, § 202(c), 92 Stat. 907, 907.
76. Refugee Act of 1980, Pub. L. No. 96-212, sec. 202, § 211, 94 Stat. 102, 106.
77. Immigration Act of 1990, Pub. L. No. 101-649, sec. 102, § 202, 104 Stat. 4978, 4982–83.
78. INA § 202(a)(2), 8 U.S.C. § 1152(a)(2) (2012).

President Truman addressed the dilemma of resettling refugees in tremendous need and the constraining quota system when he issued a directive in 1945 to address the plight of European refugees, the result of World War II. In issuing the directive, President Truman stated:

> I consider that common decency and the fundamental comrade-ship of all human beings require us to do what lies within our power to see that our established immigration quotas are used in order to reduce human suffering. I am taking the necessary steps to see that this is done as quickly as possible.[79]

To do this, President Truman ordered the establishment of refugee assembly centers in Europe to expedite visas for refugees.[80] To address the existing law's exclusion of immigrants likely to become a public charge, he established a process for federal agencies to work with nonprofit organizations that would help support refugees left with nothing due to the war.[81] Although President Truman did not ask for an increase in quotas for refugees, he criticized attempts to place further limits on immigration:

> I am informed that there are various measures now pending before the Congress which would either prohibit or severely reduce further immigration. I hope that such legislation will not be passed. This period of unspeakable human distress is not the time for us to close or to narrow our gates.[82]

By 1948, Congress took its own steps to address the European refugee crisis with the Displaced Persons Act which allowed 202,000 refugees to be resettled outside quota limits over two years.[83] The act was amended in 1950 to increase the number of refugees to 341,000.[84]

In 1952, the Congress empowered the Attorney General to "in his discretion parole into the United States temporarily . . . for emergent reasons or for reasons deemed strictly in the public interest any alien."[85] Although

---

79. Statement and Directive by the President on Immigration to the United States of Certain Displaced Persons and Refugees in Europe, Paper 225, Pub. Papers 572, 573 (December 22, 1945).
80. *Id.* at 576.
81. *Id.* at 577.
82. *Id.* at 574–75.
83. Displaced Persons Act of 1948, ch. 647, § 3(a), 62 Stat. 1009, 1010.
84. Act of June 16, 1950, ch. 262, sec. 4, § 3(a), 64 Stat. 219, 221.
85. INA, ch. 477, § 212(d)(5), 182 Stat. 166, 188 (1952).

this provision provided tremendous flexibility to allow refugees to enter the country as parolees, it did not provide an avenue for paroled refugees to adjust status to become lawful permanent residents and be put on the pathway to naturalization. Thus, Congress acted to adjust the status of thousands of refugees resettled in the United States as parolees with the Hungarian Refugee Act of 1958[86] and the Cuban Adjustment Act of 1966.[87]

The 1965 Immigration Act was the first attempt to organize the flow of refugees into the United States. The act set aside six percent of the total number of visas for refugees who, pursuant to the 1965 act, were admitted as conditional entrants and, only after two years, allowed to become lawful permanent residents.[88] The act allowed for the resettlement in the United States of displaced individuals from communist countries, Middle Eastern countries, or individuals uprooted by natural calamity.[89]

The 1965 act was still not enough to address all the refugee situations around the world, particularly due to the limited number of visas in the act, only six percent of the 170,000 total number of visas, i.e., only 10,200 each year.[90] The Attorney General continued to use his parole authority to allow refugees to be resettled in the United States as a result of the refugee crisis surrounding the Vietnam War. This resulted in additional action by Congress to adjust the status of parolees surrounding the Vietnam War in 1977.[91]

In 1980, Congress finally moved from an ad hoc refugee system to codification of a detailed refugee system, much of which remains in the law today. Indeed, the Attorney General's parole power was severely limited with regard to refugees in the 1980 act. Section 203(f) of the 1980 act states:

> The Attorney General may not parole into the United States an alien who is a refugee unless the Attorney General determines that compelling reasons in the public interest with respect to that particular alien require that the alien be paroled into the United States rather be admitted as a refugee . . . .[92]

---

86. Act of July 25, 1958, Pub. L. No. 85-559, 72 Stat. 419.
87. Act of Nov. 2, 1966, Pub. L. No. 89-732, 80 Stat. 1161.
88. Act of Oct. 3, 1965, Pub. L. No. 89-236, sec. 3, § 203(a)(7), 79 Stat. 911, 913.
89. *Id.*
90. *Id.*
91. Act of Oct. 28, 1977, Pub. L. No. 95-145, § 101, 91 Stat. 1223, 1223.
92. Refugee Act of 1980, Pub. L. No. 96-212, sec. 202, § 203(f), 94 Stat 102, 108.

The 1980 act moved U.S. refugee law from a focus on refugees escaping communism, Middle Eastern countries, and/or natural calamity to a definition established by the United Nations.[93] The new definition was codified in Section 101(a) of the INA, a definition that continues today:[94]

> (A) any person who is outside any country of such person's nationality or, in the case of a person having no nationality, is outside any country in which such person last habitually resided, and who is unable or unwilling to return to, and is unable or unwilling to avail himself or herself of the protection of, that country because of persecution or a well-founded fear of persecution on account of race, religion, nationality, membership in a particular social group, or political opinion, or
>
> (B) in such circumstances as the President after appropriate consultation (as defined in section 207(e) of this Act) may specify, any person who is within the country of such person's nationality or, in the case of a person having no nationality, within the country in which such person is habitually residing, and who is persecuted or who has a well-founded fear of persecution on account of race, religion, nationality, membership in a particular social group, or political opinion.[95]

The 1980 act also required annual review of the refugee program, consultation with Congress, and annual adjustment of refugee ceilings.[96] For fiscal years 1980, 1981, and 1982, the refugee ceiling was 50,000.[97] For the years thereafter, "the number of refugees . . . shall be such number as the President determines, before the beginning of the fiscal year and after appropriate consultation, is justified by humanitarian concerns or is oth-

---

93. *Convention Relating to the Status of Refugees*, art. I, § A(2), 19 U.S.T. 6223 (Jan. 31, 1967), *available at* http://www.unhcr.org/3b66c2aa10.html (last visited December 1, 2011) (defining a refugee as a person who "[a]s a result of events occurring before 1 January 1951 and owing to well-founded fear of being persecuted for reasons of race, religion, nationality, membership of a particular social group or political opinion, is outside the country of his nationality and is unable or, owing to such fear, is unwilling to avail himself of the protection of that country; or who, not having a nationality and being outside the country of his former habitual residence as a result of such events, is unable or, owing to such fear, is unwilling to return to it.").

94. *See* INA § 101(a)(42), 8 U.S.C. § 1101(a)(42) (2012).

95. Refugee Act of 1980, Pub. L. No. 96-212, sec. 201(a), § 101(a), 94 Stat. 102, 102–03.

96. *Id.* sec. 201(b), § 207, 94 Stat. at 103–05.

97. *Id.* sec. 201(b), § 207(a)(1), 94 Stat. at 103.

erwise in the national interest."[98] The 1980 act also established the asylum process to grant refugee status to individuals escaping persecution who are already in the United States.[99] The general structure of this regularized refugee and asylum system remains intact today.[100]

THE FOURTH AVENUE OF IMMIGRATION INTO THE UNITED STATES: DIVERSITY VISA LOTTERY

Not only was there a major shift in eliminating racial and national origin discrimination in the immigration law in the middle of the twentieth century, as discussed in the previous sections of this chapter, there was a move in the later part of the twentieth century to ensure a diversity of immigrants with the creation of the diversity visa lottery program in 1990.[101] This program was specifically designed to increase immigration of foreign nationals from countries with low levels of immigration coming through the family- and employment-based systems.[102] The program provides 55,000 visas per year for foreign nationals from countries with low levels of admissions in the family- and employment-based immigration programs.[103]

The diversity visa lottery is essentially an immigration program established to accomplish the exact opposite of the race and national origin quota acts of the early twentieth century. While the quota acts limited immigration based upon existing immigrant populations in the United States, the diversity visa lottery specifically includes immigrants left out of other immigration programs.

CONCLUSION

When this country began, race and national origin were major factors in determining who would be allowed to immigrate and naturalize in the United States. As immigration and naturalization law became more fully developed through the years, it reflected changing perspectives on race occurring in the country. Immigration law has essentially moved from a race- and national origin-based system to one that is essentially race- and

---

98. *Id.* sec. 201(b), § 207(a)(2), 94 Stat. at 103.
99. *Id.* sec. 201(b), § 208, 94 Stat. at 105–06.
100. *See generally* INA §§ 207–208, 8 U.S.C. §§ 1157–1158 (2012).
101. Immigration Act of 1990, Pub. L. No. 101-649, sec. 131, § 203, 104 Stat. 4978, 4997–99.
102. *Id.*
103. *Id.* sec. 101, § 201(e), 104 Stat. at 4982.

national origin-neutral. The factors determining who is permitted to enter and naturalize today are specific relationships to family members of U.S. citizens and lawful permanent residents, labor needs of companies in the United States, and U.S. humanitarian interests. With the introduction of the diversity visa program in 1990, existing immigration law went even further by using national origin, not to prohibit or limit immigration to the United States as was done in the past, but instead to affirmatively promote immigration from countries under-represented in the family- and employment-based systems. Thus, the Immigration and Nationality Act today may be seen as an antidiscriminatory response to a historical immigration and naturalization system that discriminated based on race and national origin.

3

THE SOURCE AND SCOPE OF FEDERAL IMMIGRATION POWER

Anna Williams Shavers[1]

In May 2011, the Supreme Court, in a 5-3 decision in *Chamber of Commerce of the United States v. Whiting*,[2] upheld an Arizona law that requires all Arizona employers to verify the employment eligibility of all employees hired.[3] The eligibility is to be determined based upon each individual's immigration status and by using E-Verify, a voluntary Internet-based database created by the federal government to help employers verify the work authorization status of employees that are hired.[4] In addition,

---

1. Anna William Shavers is the Cline Williams Professor of Citizenship Law at the University of Nebraska College of Law. Professor Shavers joined the faculty of the University of Nebraska College of Law in 1989. She received her B.S. degree from Central State University in Wilberforce, Ohio and her M.S. in Business from the University of Wisconsin-Madison where she was elected to membership in the Beta Gamma Sigma Business Honor Society. She received her J.D. degree (cum laude) from the University of Minnesota where she served as Managing Editor of the Minnesota Law Review. She was admitted to the Minnesota bar in 1979 and the Nebraska bar in 1989. She currently serves as Chair of the American Bar Association (ABA) Section of Administrative Law and Regulatory Practice and as a Board Member of the Midwestern People of Color Legal Scholarship Conference, Inc., and formerly served as liaison for the ABA Administrative Law Section to the ABA Commission on Immigration and Secretary and Publication Chair of the ABA Administrative Law Section. She has also previously served as Chair of the AALS Section on Immigration Law, a Council Member and Immigration Committee Chair of the ABA Administrative Law Section, member of the ABA Commission on Law and Aging and member of the ABA Coordinating Committee on Immigration Law. She is a frequent national and international presenter on immigration and administrative law issues.
2. 131 S. Ct. 1968 (2011) (Justice Kagan was recused).
3. The Legal Arizona Workers Act of 2007, ARIZ. REV. STAT. ANN. §§ 23-211, -212, -212.01 (West Supp. 2010).
4. Originally known as the Basic Pilot/Employment Eligibility Verification Program, the program was renamed E-Verify in 2007. The program is administered by the U.S. Department of Homeland Security in partnership with the Social Security Administration. "The program started in California, Florida, Illinois, New York, and Texas (1997) with Nebraska joining in 1999. Congress authorized the expansion of the pilot program to employers in all 50 states in 2003." *The Forum for America's Ideas, E-Verify FAQ*, NATIONAL CONFERENCE OF STATE LEGISLATURES, http://www.ncsl.org/documents/immig/E-VerifyFAQ2.pdf.

the Arizona statute allows the superior courts of Arizona to suspend or revoke the business licenses of employers who knowingly or intentionally hire "unauthorized aliens."[5] The statute adopted the federal definition of "unauthorized alien" that is used in the Illegal Immigration Reform and Immigrant Responsibility Act of 1996 (IIRIRA).[6] Although the challenge to the Arizona law was based upon the argument that a specific piece of legislation, IIRIRA, had preempted state law, the case and the enactment of similar immigration-related laws by states and local governments has caused many to reflect more generally upon the power of the federal government in immigration matters.

Some of the state and local laws expand the rights of non-citizens and others contract their rights.[7] Most of this legislation has focused on the non-citizens who are not authorized to reside or work in the United States This has led to questions generally about the power of the federal government in immigration matters and whether this power preempts actions by state and local governments. While the Arizona statute was upheld on the basis that it was consistent with federal legislation and not preempted by that legislation, other proposed and adopted laws are much broader and raise issues of constitutionality.

The Immigration and Nationality Act (INA) is the comprehensive federal statutory scheme for regulation of immigration and naturalization.[8] As the name implies, the INA actually regulates two subjects: immigration and nationality. Immigration law is that body of federal law that determines the lawful residency of non-citizens in the United States. Nationality law, on the other hand, governs the acquisition, loss, and transmission of citizenship.[9]

A presumption that immigration law is the exclusive province of the federal government is the basis for challenges to the immigration-related state and local laws and other actions and requires an analysis of two

---

5. Ariz. Rev. Stat. Ann. § 23-211(11).

6. Pub. L. No. 104-208 through 104-231, 110 Stat. 3009-546 through 110 Stat. 3054 (1996), codified at 8 U.S.C. § 1101 *et seq.* and 5 U.S.C. § 552 note *et seq.* (1996).

7. The National Conference of State Legislatures reported that the trend for enactment of state and local immigration-related laws continues and in the first half of 2011, forty state legislatures enacted 162 laws and adopted 95 resolutions. Twelve additional bills passed but were vetoed by governors. http://www.ncsl.org/default.aspx?tabid=19897.

8. The Immigration and Nationality Act, or INA, was created in 1952. The 1952 act, also known as the McCarran-Walter Act, Pub. L. No. 82-414, 66 Stat. 163 (1952) (codified as amended at 8 U.S.C. § 1101 *et seq.*), collected and codified many existing provisions and reorganized the structure of immigration law. It has been amended several times.

9. Title II of the INA governs the admission and expulsion of non-citizens and Title III governs citizenship matters.

issues: (1) the source of the federal power over immigration and (2) the scope of that power.

THE SOURCE OF FEDERAL POWER OVER IMMIGRATION

Enumerated Powers

A traditional analysis of a question regarding the power of the federal government to enact laws in a particular field starts with the enumerated powers doctrine. This doctrine is based upon the theory that under the U.S. Constitution, the power that is delegated to the federal government by the people is enumerated in the Constitution. The Tenth Amendment is often cited for support of the limitations imposed upon the federal government by Articles I, II, and III. The Tenth Amendment states: "The Powers not delegated to the United States by the Constitution, nor prohibited by it to the States, are reserved to the States respectively, or to the people."

Article I, Section 8 enumerates a list of powers that the Congress is permitted to exercise. Congress is arguably prohibited from exercising powers not on the list.

Early Cases Challenging State Immigration Legislation

The power over naturalization is based upon an enumerated power in the Constitution,[10] but there is no enumerated power over immigration. Although the first act of Congress restricting immigration was not passed until 1875,[11] in the mid-nineteenth century, the Supreme Court was called upon to articulate the power of the federal government over immigration because of challenges made against state immigration restrictions. In the Passenger Cases decided in 1849,[12] statutes in New York and Massachusetts that required ship owners to pay a tax or fee for each passenger brought to the shores of the state from another country were challenged as unconstitutional. Five justices agreed that the statutes were void because such legislation was a federal matter and four justices held that the statutes were valid as "a fair exercise of the police powers of the State."[13]

---

10. Article I, section 8, clause 4, which authorizes Congress to "establish an uniform Rule of Naturalization."

11. Immigration Act of 1875, ch. 141, 18 Stat. 477. This law was passed primarily to exclude prostitutes and convicts but was provoked in part by anti-Chinese sentiments. *See* E.P. HUTCHINSON, LEGISLATIVE HISTORY OF AMERICAN IMMIGRATION POLICY: 1798–1965, at 66 (1981).

12. *Smith v. Turner* and *Norris v. City of Boston*, 48 U.S. (7 How.) 283 (1949), were decided as consolidated cases and are commonly referred to as the "Passenger Cases" and the fees charged as "head taxes."

13. *Id.* at 518 (Woodbury, J., dissenting).

In *Henderson v. Mayor of City of New York*,[14] the Supreme Court examined statutes of three states,[15] including New York's modified statute, and concluded the statutes were void because "transportation of passengers from European ports to those of the United States" is "a part of our commerce with foreign nations."[16] The New York statute required each ship captain to report information regarding each non-citizen passenger and to also post a bond for each such passenger. The Court added:

> We are of opinion that this whole subject has been confided to congress by the constitution; that congress can more appropriately and with more acceptance exercise it than any other body known to our law, state or national; that by providing a system of laws in these matters, applicable to all ports and to all vessels, a serious question which has long been matter of contest and complaint may be effectually and satisfactorily settled.[17]

In 1876, in *Chy Lung v. Freeman*,[18] at issue was a California statute that established a State Commissioner of Immigration and required a bond for all non-citizens landing from a foreign country that fit particular state-defined statutory classes. The plaintiff, Chy Lung, was one of several women arriving from China who were determined by the California Immigration Commissioner to be a "lewd and debauched woman," as designated in the statute.[19] As a result, the Commissioner required the ship's master to post a bond. After the shipmaster refused, the women were taken into custody and held until they could depart on their arrival ship. Chy Lung challenged the constitutionality of the statute. The Court again invoked the commerce power of Congress to hold that even if the state statute did not attempt to fully regulate immigration, it was void

---

14. 92 U.S. 259 (1875).

15. The Court consolidated a Louisiana case, *Commissioners of Immigration v. North German Lloyd*, 92 U.S. 259 (1876), with *Henderson v. Mayor of New York* and concluded that the Louisiana statute was similar enough to the New York statute that it did not need separate consideration, *id.* at 275, but issued a separate opinion regarding a California statute in *Chy Lung v. Freeman*, 92 U.S. 275 (1876).

16. *Id.* at 270. The Court distinguished its earlier decision, *New York City v. Miln*, 36 U.S. (11 Pet.) 102 (1837), where it found no conflict with the federal commerce powers because the required reporting of arriving non-citizens by ship masters was within the police powers of the state and did not interfere with commerce. *Id.* at 266.

17. *Id.* at 274.

18. 92 U.S. 275 (1876).

19. *Id.* at 277 (quoting C.1, art. 7, of the Political Code of California).

because it was an unconstitutional exercise of power that had been delegated to the federal government:

> The passage of laws which concern the admission of citizens and subjects of foreign nations to our shores belongs to Congress, and not to the States. It has the power to regulate commerce with foreign nations: the responsibility for the character of those regulations, and for the manner of their execution, belongs solely to the national government. If it be otherwise, a single State can, at her pleasure, embroil us in disastrous quarrels with other nations.[20]

The states were told by the Court that their actions attempting to regulate immigration violated the Supremacy Clause.[21] In support of this conclusion, the Court searched through several clauses of the Constitution for the source of the power.[22]

1. The Commerce Clause. Congress may "regulate commerce with foreign nations." U.S. Const. art. I, § 8, cl. 2 *The Passenger Cases*
2. The Import Duty Clause. Art. 1, sect. 10, subd. 2. "No State shall, without the consent of the Congress, lay any imposts or duties on imports or exports, except what may be actually necessary for executing its inspection laws. No State shall, without the consent of the Congress, lay any duty of tonnage." *Henderson v. Mayor of City of New York*
3. The Migration or Importation Clause. Article I, § 9, cl. 1 of the Constitution. "The Migration or Importation of such Persons as any of the States now existing shall think proper to permit, shall not be prohibited by the Congress prior to the year one thousand eight hundred and eight." *The Passenger Cases*
4. The Naturalization Clause. Article I, § 8, cl. 4 authorizes Congress "[t]o establish an uniform Rule of Naturalization." *The Passenger Cases*

---

20. *Id.* at 279.
21. U.S. Const. art. VI, cl. 2 (providing that "[t]his Constitution, and the Laws of the United States . . . and all Treaties made . . . shall be the supreme law of the Land"). *See Passenger Cases*, 48 U.S. (7 How.) 283 (1849).
22. *See* Stephen H. Legomsky & Cristina M. Rodríguez, Immigration and Refugee Law and Policy, 115–20 (5th ed. 2009).

5. The War Powers Clause. Art. I, § 8, cl. 11. "[t]o declare war." This clause is cited as a basis for federal immigration power on the theory that it includes the authority to prevent the entry and expel enemy aliens residing in the United States.[23]

6. The Necessary and Proper Clause. Art. I, § 8, cl. 18. "To make all Laws which shall be necessary and proper for carrying into Execution the foregoing Powers, and all other Powers vested by this Constitution in the Government of the United States, or in any Department or Officer there of Congress the power to pass all necessary and proper for carrying into effect the enumerated and all other powers granted by the Constitution." It has been argued that the Naturalization Clause, which gives the legislature the power to make a uniform process for becoming a citizen, implies the power to regulate immigration in context with the Necessary and Proper Clause.[24]

Federal Plenary Power over Immigration

When the federal government enacted the Immigration Act of 1882 to establish a tax on immigrants entering the country,[25] shipping companies challenged the legislation as a violation of the tax and spending power in Article I of the Constitution. Article I, Section 8, Clause 1 of the U.S. Constitution states: "The Congress shall have Power To lay and collect Taxes, Duties, Imposts and Excises, to pay the Debts and provide for the common Defence and general Welfare of the United States."[26] The companies argued the head tax was not for general welfare and common defense. The Supreme Court unanimously held in the *Head Money Cases*, decided in 1884,[27] that the legislation did not violate the tax and spending clause and further that the federal government had the power to enact immigration legislation under its commerce clause powers. Here, the Court found no need to look to other clauses of the Constitution. The Court noted that

---

23. *See* Korematsu v. United States, 323 U.S. 214, 245–46 (1944). *See generally* Sarah H. Cleveland, *Powers Inherent in Sovereignty: Indians, Aliens, Territories, and the Nineteenth Century Origins of Plenary Power over Foreign Affairs*, 81 Tex. L. Rev. 1, 90 (2002).

24. *See, e.g.*, Developments in the Law—Jobs and Borders: *V. The Constitutionality of Immigration Federalism*, 118 Harv. L. Rev. 2247, 2258 (2005) [hereinafter *Immigration Federalism*]; Ming-sung Kuo, *The Duality of Federalist Nation-Building: Two Strands of Chinese Immigration Cases Revisited*, 67 Alb. L. Rev. 27, 36 (2003).

25. Immigration Act of Aug. 3, 1882, ch. 376, 22 Stat. 214 (repealed 1974).

26. U.S. Const. art. I, § 8, cl. 1.

27. Edye v. Robertson, 112 U.S. 580 (1884).

all of the justices in the *Passenger Cases* had looked to the commerce clause as the source of power for federal power over immigration and suggested that it was only because Congress had not yet acted that four of the justices dissented.

The Supreme Court's modern approach to reviewing federal immigration actions can be traced back to its late nineteenth-century immigration opinions when it rejected the commerce clause theory in favor of a sovereignty theory. The Court first used the sovereignty theory as a basis for congressional power in immigration matters in *Chae Chan Ping v. United States* ("The Chinese Exclusion Case").[28] The Supreme Court concluded that notwithstanding there was a specific enumeration of power with respect to naturalization but not with respect to immigration, the inherent federal power over immigration was to be treated with as much judicial deference as the express federal power over naturalization. Instead of an enumerated power,[29] the Supreme Court determined that a more general principle of sovereignty provides the basis for congressional authority over immigration.[30]

This judicial recognition of the right of congressional control over immigration policy is based on the premise that the legislative branch has been delegated the authority that each sovereign state has to place unlimited restraints upon foreigners coming into its territory. The Supreme Court recognizes the plenary power[31] to legislate in immigration matters as "inherent in sovereignty, necessary for maintaining normal international relations and defending the Country against foreign encroachments and dangers—a power to be exercised exclusively by the political branches of

---

28. 130 U.S. 581 (1889). This case is commonly referred to as "The Chinese Exclusion Case," a reference that many find offensive both for its ethnic reference and its embodiment of the plenary power doctrine. *See, e.g.,* Louis Henkin, *The Constitution and United States Sovereignty: A Century of Chinese Exclusion and Its Progeny,* 100 HARV. L. REV. 853, 862–63 (1987) ("Chinese Exclusion—its very name is an embarrassment—must go.").

29. *See generally* Ming-sung Kuo, *supra* note 24, at 35–26 (noting that the Court could have implied Congress's power to regulate immigration and exclude aliens from "both the Necessary and Proper Clause and the naturalization power of Article I, section 8, clause 4").

30. *See, e.g.,* Fiallo v. Bell, 430 U.S. 787, 792 (1977); Kleindienst v. Mandell, 408 U.S. 753, 766 (1972); Fong Yue Ting v. United States, 149 U.S. 698 (1893); *see also* James A. R. Nafziger, *The General Admission of Aliens under International Law,* 77 AM. J. INT'L L. 804 (1983).

31. The Supreme Court has defined plenary power as the government's power that "may be exercised to its utmost extent [with] no limitations, other than are prescribed in the constitution." Gibbons v. Ogden, 22 U.S. 1, 196 (1824).

government."[32] Challenges to immigration legislation have been rejected based upon this plenary power doctrine.[33] As the Court stated:

> The power to regulate immigration—an attribute of sovereignty essential to the preservation of any nation—has been entrusted by the Constitution to the political branches of the Federal Government.[34]

In its continued expansion and extension of the sovereignty theory as a basis for federal power over immigration rather than an enumerated power, the Court has relied on its conclusion that "[t]he broad statement that the federal government can exercise no powers except those specifically enumerated in the Constitution, and such implied powers as are necessary and proper to carry into effect the enumerated powers, is categorically true only in respect to our internal affairs."[35]

THE SCOPE OF FEDERAL IMMIGRATION POWER

There now appears to be little disagreement that Congress has the power to establish an immigration law. To emphasize the plenary power status of federal power over immigration, the Supreme Court has stated that "it is important to underscore the limited scope of judicial inquiry into immigration legislation. This Court has repeatedly emphasized that 'over no conceivable subject is the legislative power of Congress more complete than it is over' the admission of aliens."[36] This plenary power classification has served to limit judicial interference[37] as well as state intrusion.[38]

---

32. *Mandel*, 408 U.S. at 765 (quoting government's brief).

33. *See, e.g., Fiallo*, 430 U.S. 787 (gender and legitimacy challenge); *Mandel*, 408 U.S. 753 (First Amendment challenge); Boutilier v. I.N.S., 387 U.S. 118 (1967) (sexual preference challenge); Fong Yue Ting v. United States, 149 U.S. 698 (1893) (race); *Chae Chan Ping*, 130 U.S. 581 (race).

34. United States v. Valenzuela-Bernal, 458 U.S. 858, 864 (1982) (citing Mathews v. Diaz, 426 U.S. 67 (1976)).

35. United States v. Curtiss-Wright Export Corp., 299 U.S. 304, 315 (1936).

36. *Fiallo*, 430 U.S. at 792 (citing Oceanic Navigation Co. v. Stranahan, 214 U.S. 320, 339 (1909)); *accord Mandel*, 408 U.S. at 766 (1972); Shaughnessy v. Mezei, 345 U.S. 206, 210 (1953) (the Supreme Court cases "have long recognized the power to expel or exclude aliens as a fundamental sovereign attribute exercised by the Government's political departments largely immune from judicial control").

37. *See, e.g.,* Hampton v. Mow Sun Wong, 426 U.S. 88, 101 n.21 (1976) (stating that "the power over aliens is of a political character and therefore subject only to narrow judicial review").

38. *See* Henkin, *supra* note 27, at 859 (stating that the Chinese Exclusion Case "ha[s] been taken to mean that there are no constitutional limitations on the power of Congress to regulate immigration").

What is disputed is the extent to which that grant of power makes laws which are based upon the immigration status of a non-citizen rather than the admission or expulsion of the non-citizen immune from state and local legislation.

Acceptance of a State and Local Role in Immigration

Despite the development of the plenary power doctrine, the courts, Congress, and executive branch agencies charged with the administration of immigration laws have recently allowed some state intrusion into the regulation of immigration. Some examples are described below.

The Courts

The E-Verity system that was at issue in *Chamber of Commerce of the United States v. Whiting*[39] had been created in 1996 by Congress to supplement and strengthen the restrictions contained in the 1986 Immigration and Reform Control Act (IRCA) and imposed upon employers with respect to the hiring of non-citizens who were not authorized to work in the United States.[40] Although the federal government had not made it unlawful to employ unauthorized workers until the enactment of IRCA, California had enacted a state statute in 1976 which prohibited an employer from knowingly employing an alien who is not entitled to lawful residence in the United States if such employment would have an adverse effect on lawful resident workers.[41] The Supreme Court rejected challenges to the California law and found that the law was neither an unconstitutional regulation of immigration nor preempted by the INA. In *DeCanas v. Bica* the Court confirmed that the power to regulate immigration is an exclusive federal power, but found that although the California law affected non-citizens, "[not] every state enactment which in any way deals with aliens is a regulation of immigration and thus per se pre-empted by this constitutional power, whether latent or exercised."[42] The Court also concluded that Congress had not included any provisions in the INA which precluded states from regulating under their police powers the employment of non-citizens who were not authorized to work in the United States. This opinion suggests, and the majority in *Chamber of Commerce*

---

39. 131 S. Ct. 1968 (2011).
40. Immigration Reform and Control Act (IRCA) of 1986, Pub. L. No. 99-603, § 274A(a), 100 Stat. 3359, 3360–74 (codified as amended at 8 U.S.C. § 1324a).
41. Section 2805(a) of the California Labor Code.
42. DeCanas v. Bica, 424 U.S. 351, 355 (1976). Although the Court did not find the California law was preempted, it reaffirmed its view that the "[p]ower to regulate immigration is unquestionably exclusively a federal power." *Id.* at 354.

confirms, that the first inquiry regarding a state or local law which affects non-citizens is whether the law is actually a regulation of immigration.

The 1986 enactment of IRCA contained language that presumably overrules *DeCanas* and expressly preempts state regulation of the employment of non-citizens:

> [A]ny State or local law imposing civil or criminal sanctions (*other than through licensing and similar laws*) upon those who employ, or recruit or refer for a fee for employment, unauthorized aliens.[43]

Congress

Congress has also participated in the allowance of state and local entities in immigration-related matters. For example, the meaning of the parenthetical in the above-quoted language from the INA was a major focus in the Court's discussion in *Chambers of Commerce*. The majority opinion noted that the language demonstrated that Congress intended for states to have a role in the regulation of the employment of non-citizens. Further support was found in the Court's analysis in *DeCanas* which discussed the 1974 amendments to the Farm Labor Contractor Registration Act,[44] and concluded that Congress intended for the States to have a role in the regulation of unauthorized workers.[45]

Another example of congressional acceptance of state and local intrusion is provided in the Personal Responsibility and Work Opportunity Reconciliation Act of 1996 (PRWORA).[46] This legislation restricts access by some legal immigrants to certain benefit programs and denies access by undocumented immigrants to many government-funded programs.[47] States were granted authority to determine immigrants' eligibility for state and local programs, subject to some exceptions,[48] as well as the right to restrict the eligibility of some otherwise qualified immigrants.

---

43. INA § 274A(h)(2), 8 U.S.C. § 1324a(h)(2) (emphasis added).
44. Farm Labor Contractor Registration Act Amendments of 1974, Pub. L. No. 93-518, § 2(3), 88 Stat. 1652, 1653 (codified at 7 U.S.C. § 2042(b)(3) (1976)), repealed by Pub. L. No. 97-470, Title V, § 523, 96 Stat. 2600 (1983).
45. *DeCanas*, 424 U.S. at 361.
46. Personal Responsibility and Work Opportunity Reconciliation Act of 1996, Pub. L. No. 104-193, 110 Stat. 2105 (1996) (codified as amended in scattered sections of 7, 8, 21, & 42 U.S.C.).
47. Title IV, Personal Responsibility and Work Opportunity Reconciliation Act of 1996, Pub. L. No. 104-193, 110 Stat. 2105 (see sections 401 to 412 limiting public benefits to undocumented immigrants).
48. 8 U.S.C. § 1622.

Executive Agencies

The Department of Homeland Security (DHS), pursuant to authorization in 287(g) of IIRIRA,[49] has entered into agreements, referred to as "287(g) agreements" with state and local law enforcement agencies, designating state and local officers to perform immigration law enforcement functions.

LOOKING FORWARD: STATE AND FEDERAL POWER

The scope of the federal government's power over immigration matters is likely to be subjected to judicial review based upon laws enacted by Congress as well as by state and local governments. The devolution of authority to states under PRWORA as well as the use of "287(g) agreements" and similar actions have been described as raising constitutional issues[50] and criticized as the granting of power to states that are best exercised by the federal government.[51]

State and local regulation of immigration has proliferated[52] because of the view that the federal government is not adequately confronting the

---

49. INA § 287(g), 8 U.S.C. § 1357(g).

50. *See, e.g., Roger C. Hartley, Congressional Devolution of Immigration Policymaking: A Separation of Powers Critique*, 2 Duke J. Const. L. & Pub. Pol'y 93, 94–95 (2007) (discussing the constitutional problems with PRWORA from a separation of powers perspective); Gilbert Paul Carrasco, *Congressional Arrogation of Power: Alien Constellation in the Galaxy of Equal Protection*, 74 B.U. L. Rev. 591, 635 (1994); Huyen Pham, *The Inherent Flaws in the Inherent Authority Position: Why Inviting Local Enforcement of Immigration Laws Violates the Constitution*, 31 Fla. St. U. L. Rev. 965 (2004); Litwin, Marissa B. Comment. *The Decentralization of Immigration Law: The Mischief of Section 287(g)*, 41 Seton Hall L. Rev. 399 (2011).

51. *See, e.g., Immigration Federalism, supra* note 24, at 2247; Howard F. Chang, *Public Benefits and Federal Authorization for Alienage Discrimination by the States*, 58 N.Y.U. Ann. Surv. Am. L. 357 (2002); Michael Wishnie, *Laboratories of Bigotry? Devolution of the Immigration Power, Equal Protection, and Federalism*, 76 N.Y.U. L. Rev. 493 (2001); Michael E. Fix & Karen Tumlin, *Welfare Reform and the Devolution of Immigrant Policy, in New Federalism—Issues and Options for States*, Series A, No. 15 (D.C. Urban Institute Press, Oct. 1997) ("Welfare reform gives states the power to shape the meaning of citizenship—a power that flows from the states' new authority to define the rights and benefits due to legal noncitizens.").

52. *See generally* Pham, Huyen & Pham Hoang Van, *The Economic Impact of Local Immigration Regulation: An Empirical Analysis*, 32 Cardozo L. Rev. 485 (2010); Cristina M. Rodriguez, *The Significance of the Local in Immigration Regulation*, 106 Mich. L. Rev. 567 (2008). *See also State Laws Related to Immigration and Immigrants*, National Conference of State Legislatures, http://www.ncsl.org/research/immigration/state-laws-related-to-immigration-and-immigrants.aspx.

challenges of immigration. Much of this regulation will be subjected to judicial review which will further define the scope of and limitations on federal immigration power.[53]

---

53. After this chapter was written, the U.S. Supreme Court decided in *Arizona v. United States*, holding, by a 5 to 3 majority, that three of the four disputed provisions in Arizona's Support Our Law Enforcement and Safe Neighborhoods Act, commonly referred to as S.B. 1070, were preempted by federal law and therefore invalid. Arizona v. United States, 132 S. Ct. 2492 (2012) (Justice Kagan recusal). The fourth challenged provision, Section 2(B) of S.B. 1070, which the Court held was not preempted, required police officers to make a "'reasonable attempt . . . to determine the immigration status' of any person they stop, detain, or arrest on some other legitimate basis if 'reasonable suspicion exists that the person is an alien and is unlawfully present in the United States.'" *Id.* at 2507, quoting ARIZ. REV. STAT. ANN. § 11–1051(B) (West 2012). Lower courts were left with the task of determining which state and local ordinances were intrusions into the federal government's power to regulate immigration. *See, e.g.*, Keller v. City of Fremont, 719 F.3d 931 (8th Cir. 2013) (held that ordinances requiring tenants to obtain occupancy licenses identifying their citizenship and immigration status were not preempted by federal immigration law), *cert. denied*, 2014 WL 833921, U.S., May 5, 2014.

4

ETHICAL ISSUES ARISING IN THE PRACTICE OF IMMIGRATION LAW

Mark J. Shmueli[1] and Tina R. Goel[2]

There are a myriad of sources for a new (or seasoned) immigration attorney to identify her ethical responsibilities including state rules of professional conduct, ethics publications from organizations such as the American Immigration Lawyers Association (AILA), and journal articles arguing the finer details of ethical conundrums. This chapter highlights some of the most pertinent and pressing rules that immigration attorneys grapple with on a regular basis.

---

1. Mark Shmueli is a private immigration law practitioner who focuses his practice on complex family, removal, and naturalization cases. Mark served on the Governor's Commission to Study the Impact of Immigrants in Maryland and was a coauthor of its 2012 final report. He also taught Immigration and Ethnicity at the University of Maryland in College Park in the fall 2011 semester. He is a regular guest on WPFW on immigration matters and recently appeared on XM satellite radio's Wilmer Leon Show. He currently serves on the media relations committee for the American Immigration Lawyers Association and in that role is a national spokesperson for AILA. He has authored several articles and opinion pieces, including a March 2014 coauthored editorial published in the Orlando Sentinel entitled "Republicans Must Embrace Inevitable Immigration Reform"; a two-part series on the historical context of comprehensive immigration reform in relationship to the current immigration reform bill, published in the August and September editions of the Maryland Bar Bulletin; and a chapter on the history of same-sex relationships in immigration law and the effects of recent Supreme Court decisions on DOMA and on immigration law. His other publications include "Protecting Immigrant Women: Benefits for Abuse Victims," MD Bar Journal, Sept./Oct. 2008; "One Nation, Divided by Immigration: State and Local Immigration Laws in the Absence of Comprehensive Immigration Reform," MD Bar Bulletin, October 2011 (coauthor); and "Pitfalls in the Bewildering Legal World of the 'Criminal Alien,'" MD Bar Journal, July/Aug. 2006.
2. Tina R. Goel is an attorney at the Law Office of Mark J. Shmueli. She practices all areas of immigration law, including appeals before the BIA, complex family-based and employment-based petitions, immigration court litigation, and naturalization. Ms. Goel was selected to serve on AILA's Military Assistance Program Task Force in 2013 and to be Vice-Chair of the WAS CIS Field Office Liaison Committee for the Washington DC chapter of AILA in 2014. She has previously written about the E-Verify program, the immigration implications of the fall of the Defense of Marriage Act (DOMA), and international trade.

45

This chapter uses the ABA Model Rules of Professional Conduct to analyze two significant areas where immigration practitioners find many of their dilemmas—duty to the tribunal and dual representation—and provides a short list of best practices for the immigration attorney today. In addition, this chapter briefly discusses the ethical obligations for criminal defense attorneys arising out of the Supreme Court's decision in *Padilla v. Kentucky*.[3] Ultimately, an attorney must be aware of her ethical obligations, be willing to take the time to consider the ethical ramifications of her actions, and be willing to grapple with the questions that arise as a result.

DUTY TO THE TRIBUNAL VS. CLIENT CONFIDENTIALITY

State bar associations maintain ethical codes of professional conduct that govern the actions of attorneys barred in the state as well as attorneys practicing on a limited matter within the state, at least partially fashioned upon the American Bar Association's Model Rules of Professional Conduct.[4] In an effort to self-regulate the ethics of the legal profession, the rules establish what an attorney "may," "shall," and "shall not" do. The ethical rules, taken together, provide that an attorney has a duty of good faith and fair dealing to the tribunals in which she practices that often directly conflicts with the attorney's explicit duty of confidentiality to the client.[5] In addition, federal agencies have also promulgated regulations under the immigration statutes to "prescribe standards of conduct and rules of procedure that are applicable to practitioners who appear before the Board, the Immigration Courts, and the [United States Citizenship and Immigration] Services."[6]

---

3. 559 U.S. 356 (2010).
4. *See, e.g.,* D.C. RULES OF PROF'L CONDUCT, *available at* http://www.dcbar.org/for_lawyers /ethics/legal_ethics/rules_of_professional_conduct/amended_rules/index.cfm; MARYLAND RULES OF PROF'L CONDUCT, *available at* http://www.courts.state.md.us/attygrievance/rules .html; NEW YORK RULES OF PROF'L CONDUCT, *available at* http://www.nysba.org/workarea /DownloadAsset.aspx?id=45804; CALIFORNIA RULES OF PROF'L CONDUCT, *available at* http:// rules.calbar.ca.gov/LinkClick.aspx?fileticket=8qtNkWP-Kjw%3D&tabid=476. *See also* ABA, MODEL RULES OF PROF'L CONDUCT, *available at* http://www.americanbar.org/groups /professional_responsibility/publications/model_rules_of_professional_conduct/.
5. *See, e.g.,* ABA MODEL RULES OF PROF'L CONDUCT R. 1.6, *available at* http://www.american bar.org/groups/professional_responsibility/publications/model_rules_of_professional _conduct/rule_1_6_confidentiality_of_information.html.
6. 65 Fed. Reg. 39513, at 39514 (June 27, 2000), *available at* http://www.justice.gov/eoir /vll/fedreg/2000_2001/fr27jn00R.pdf. *See also* 73 Fed. Reg. 76914 (Dec. 18, 2008), *available at* http://www.justice.gov/eoir/vll/fedreg/2008_2009/fr18dec08c.pdf. In the context of removal proceedings, INA § 240(b)(6)(C) establishes that the Attorney General may define by regulation "frivolous behavior for which attorneys may be sanctioned" and consider an

The Model Rules expressly prohibit an attorney from "knowingly mak[ing] a false statement of material fact" in representing the client to a tribunal, such as the USCIS, and require the attorney to "correct a false statement of material fact."[7] With regard to evidence, if the lawyer "has offered material evidence and [she] comes to know of its falsity, the lawyer shall take reasonable remedial measures, including, if necessary, disclosure to the tribunal."[8] The Model Rules establish the threshold as "knowingly," whereas immigration statutes specify penalties for knowingly "prepar[ing], fil[ing], or assist[ing] another in preparing or filing, any application for benefits under this Act, or any document required under this Act, or any document submitted in connection with such application or document, with *knowledge or in reckless disregard* of the fact that such application or document was falsely made."[9] This higher standard punishes a reckless disregard of falsity; a diligent attorney must ask herself what level of inquiry of the client and the evidence averts a claim of reckless disregard.

While knowingly submitting false statements is an extreme example of unethical behavior, a common question that arises is whether an application submitted is frivolous or whether further inquiry from the client would have illuminated a statement's falsity.[10] The rules are relatively clear that an immigration attorney is prohibited from submitting false

---

"administrative appeal of a decision or ruling . . . frivolous." *See also* 8 C.F.R. §§ 292.3, 1292.3; *id.* § 1003.102 (regulations establishing behavior deserving of a sanction by DHS and/or EOIR). The EOIR publishes a list of attorneys reprimanded under its rules. *See* EOIR, List of Currently Disciplined Practitioners, http://www.justice.gov/eoir/discipline.htm.

7. ABA, MODEL RULES OF PROF'L CONDUCT R. 3.3, *available at* http://www.americanbar.org /groups/professional_responsibility/publications/model_rules_of_professional_conduct /rule_3_3_candor_toward_the_tribunal.html; D.C. RULES OF PROF'L CONDUCT R. 3.3. *See also* D.C. RULES OF PROF'L CONDUCT R. 4.1 (discussing honesty with respect to "others").

8. ABA, MODEL RULES OF PROF'L CONDUCT R. 3.3, *available at* http://www.americanbar.org /groups/professional_responsibility/publications/model_rules_of_professional_conduct /rule_3_3_candor_toward_the_tribunal.html. ABA's Model Rule 8.4(c) also establishes that "[i]t is professional misconduct for a lawyer to engage in conduct involving dishonesty, fraud, deceit or misrepresentation." *Id.* R. 8.4, *available at* http://www.americanbar.org /groups/professional_responsibility/publications/model_rules_of_professional_conduct /rule_8_4_misconduct.html.

9. INA § 274(C)(a)(5) (emphasis added). *Compare* ABA, MODEL RULES OF PROF'L CONDUCT R. 3.3, cmt. 8 ("A lawyer's reasonable belief that evidence is false does not preclude its presentation to the trier of fact.").

10. *See* INA § 240(b)(6)(C) (establishing, in the context of removal proceedings, that the Attorney General may define by regulation "frivolous behavior for which attorneys may be sanctioned" and consider an "administrative appeal of a decision or ruling . . . frivolous"); *cf.* 8 C.F.R. §§ 292.3, 1292.3; *id.* § 1003.102 (regulations establishing behavior deserving of a sanction by DHS and/or EOIR).

statements about age, the time, manner, and circumstances of entry into the United States, and other biographical information.[11] Nonetheless, it is possible for an attorney to inadvertently submit a statement or document that she subsequently discovers to be false, e.g., a client affidavit depicting a course of events which the client later discloses is false. An attorney who allows a document to remain in the record without either withdrawing it or explaining its inclusion violates his obligation of candor to the tribunal and could face sanctions at worst and at the least risks his reputation with the court and USCIS or Immigration and Customs Enforcement (ICE).[12]

In circumstances involving the submission of false evidence or testimony, in D.C., the attorney is obligated to explain the harm of false documents to the client and convince the client to withdraw the document from the record. If the client is unwilling to withdraw the document, then the attorney must seek withdrawal from the case.[13] The D.C. Rule of Confidentiality ordinarily precludes a member of the D.C. bar "from disclosing such a fraud even if the client has refused to rectify it" because information that is gained confidentially from the client and would be detrimental or embarrassing must not be disclosed.[14] Under such circumstances, in withdrawing from the case, the attorney must be careful not to reveal the reasons for withdrawal to avoid harming the client;[15] a sug-

---

11. *See* MICHAEL MAGGIO, MATTER OF ETHICS, *in* ETHICS IN A BRAVE NEW WORLD 2 (AILA 2004).

12. *See supra* notes 5–6 and accompanying text.

13. *See* D.C. ETHICS OP. 219 (adopted July 17, 1991), *available at* http://www.dcbar.org/for_lawyers/ethics/legal_ethics/opinions/opinion219.cfm; *cf.* Cornell University Law School, Legal Information Institute, Topical Overview—Index of Narratives, *available at* http://www.law.cornell.edu/ethics/comparative/ (providing a step-by-step comparison of all state ethics rules).

14. *See* D.C. ETHICS OP. 219 (permitting disclosure "if regulations of the tribunal having the force and effect of law require that the fraud be revealed and the client is first afforded a reasonable opportunity to investigate and pursue any good faith challenge to the regulations"). The immigration regulations require "remedial measures," but do not mandate disclosure. *See* 8 C.F.R. § 1003.102(c). A practitioner who falls within one of the following categories shall be subject to disciplinary sanctions in the public interest if he or she "[k]nowingly or with reckless disregard makes a false statement of material fact or law, or willfully misleads, misinforms, threatens, or deceives any person (including a party to a case or an officer or employee of the Department of Justice), concerning any material and relevant matter relating to a case, including knowingly or with reckless disregard offering false evidence. If a practitioner has offered material evidence and comes to know of its falsity, the practitioner shall take appropriate remedial measures."

15. *See* Cornell University Law School, Legal Information Institute, California Legal Ethics: III. Advocate, *available at* http://www.law.cornell.edu/ethics/ca/narr/CA_NARR_3.HTM#3.3:600 (discussing California ethics opinions in which disclosing a client's perjury, without client consent, is prohibited).

gestion is to cite a difference of opinion in legal strategy and refrain from disclosing anything further.

It is the attorney's responsibility, as a counselor, to protect the client's interests—there is little more harmful to a client than a fraudulent document in the record. While an attorney's obligation to protect the client's interest is paramount, an attorney is obligated not to misrepresent material facts because such acts violate ethical rules and regulations.

DUAL REPRESENTATION

The nature of immigration law practice lends itself to conflicts of interest in numerous client representations because in a petition/application where there is a petitioner and a beneficiary the attorney simultaneously represents both parties. While the petitioner and beneficiary share the common goal of obtaining an approved petition, for example, an H-1B temporary employment visa petition, sometimes information shared by one party with the attorney gives rise to a conflict of interest. Because an immigration attorney must not subordinate the interests of one party to the other, the attorney may ultimately be forced to withdraw from the representation if the conflict cannot be resolved.[16] A conflict of interest, between a petitioner and a beneficiary, can arise in both employment-based immigration petitions as well as family-based petitions.[17]

In employer-sponsored immigration, conflicts often arise with respect to terminating the employer-employee relationship and the employer maintaining the employee in a manner consistent with the approved petition, i.e., with regard to salary and benefits. In the context of labor certification applications for immigrant visas, the employer must describe the position based upon the employer's actual minimum requirements for the position, rather than tailor the posting so as to enable the petition to proceed in a higher visa category in order to speed up the process. Nonetheless, the employee-client often asks the attorney to submit the petition to USCIS in a higher category than the employer-client has chosen. While it is possible to preempt some conflicts in the retainer agreement, by establishing, e.g., that the beneficiary of an employer petition will not be made aware of the employer's confidential business or tax information, it is

---

16. *See* ABA, MODEL RULES OF PROF'L CONDUCT R. 1.7, *available at* http://www.americanbar .org/groups/professional_responsibility/publications/model_rules_of_professional_conduct /rule_1_7_conflict_of_interest_current_clients.html; *id.* R. 1.8, *available at* http://www .americanbar.org/groups/professional_responsibility/publications/model_rules_of _professional_conduct/rule_1_7_conflict_of_interest_current_clients.html.

17. *See generally* BRUCE A. HAKE, DUAL REPRESENTATION IN IMMIGRATION PRACTICE, *in* ETHICS IN A BRAVE NEW WORLD (AILA 2004).

much more difficult for the immigration attorney to resolve the conflict that arises when the employer calls the attorney and wants to confidentially discuss methods of firing the H-1B employee or when the employee asks the attorney how soon he may quit or port his visa to another company. Any communication by one party without the other present has the potential to give rise to a conflict and the attorney is not permitted, without the consent of both parties, to advise either party as to how to deal with the other. Similarly, in family-based immigration, a conflict of interest can arise when the relationship between the petitioning relative and the beneficiary relative is not as strong as the application requires, often because one party is less committed to the relationship than the other. An affiant providing the affidavit of support whether she is the petitioner or a third party will sometimes not want the beneficiary to know his/her annual income and the attorney must either prevent this conflict by obtaining permission from both parties to keep information secret from the other or to recommend alternate counsel.

While some may argue that the attorney only represents one of the parties in a given petition (employer or family petitioner, but not employee or family beneficiary), it is important to bear in mind that the rules generally prohibit lawyers from giving legal advice to non-clients.[18] Therefore, in cases where the immigration attorney is receiving confidential information from the alleged non-client and advising him/her as to the ramifications of answering in the affirmative on an admissibility question, the practitioner is presented with a situation in which she must decide whether both the petitioner and the beneficiary are clients or whether she is giving advice to a non-client.[19] Regardless of whether or not required by state rules, a diligent attorney may be best served by seeking the consent of both of the parties at the outset of the representation; by sharing the services of one attorney, the clients are effectively waiving a portion of the attorney's duty of complete loyalty.[20]

---

18. *See* ABA, Model Rules of Prof'l Conduct R. 4.3, *available at* http://www.americanbar.org/groups/professional_responsibility/publications/model_rules_of_professional_conduct/rule_4_3_dealing_with_unrepresented_person.html.

19. *See* Hake, *supra* note 16, at 33–34.

20. *See, e.g.,* D.C. Rules of Prof'l Conduct R. 1.7, *available at* http://www.dcbar.org/for_lawyers/ethics/legal_ethics/rules_of_professional_conduct/amended_rules/rule_one/rule01_07.cfm. A diligent attorney must however consult his or her state rules as not all jurisdictions have adopted the ABA Model Rules of Professional Conduct. *See* ABA, Model Rules of Prof'l Conduct: Dates of Adoption, http://www.americanbar.org/groups/professional_responsibility/publications/model_rules_of_professional_conduct/alpha_list_state_adopting_model_rules.html.

PADILLA V. KENTUCKY: ETHICAL OBLIGATIONS FOR CRIMINAL DEFENSE ATTORNEYS

In March 2010, the Supreme Court of the United States held that the Sixth Amendment guarantee of effective assistance of counsel requires defense attorneys to provide competent advice to a non-citizen defendant regarding the immigration consequences of a criminal conviction.[21] When the immigration consequences are certain, the attorney must counsel the client that "deportation [is] presumptively mandatory" and when deportation is possible rather than likely, the attorney is required to inform the client "that pending criminal charges may carry a risk of adverse immigration consequences."[22] The Supreme Court, in discussing whether deportation is a direct or collateral consequence of a criminal proceeding stated that deportation is a "particularly severe penalty" and therefore, it is not entirely divorced from the criminal process.[23] Deportation is often more important to an alien criminal defendant than a jail sentence.[24]

At first glance, Padilla's effects appear localized geographically near the border, upon immigrants with legal status that is at risk of being lost due to deportation, or to those who have become "undesirable" because they committed severe felonies—but all of these scenarios are merely the tip of the iceberg.[25] With Immigration and Customs Enforcement (ICE) working with law enforcement in virtually every corner of the United States, it is not only the border states of Texas and Arizona in which criminal activity can lead to deportation. While immigrants who have legal status often have much to lose because of their ties to the United States, by accepting a guilty plea, an undocumented alien may forsake his/her claim to an otherwise legal status such as asylee or family-based petition beneficiary. Finally, even seemingly small crimes such as possession of 35 grams of marijuana for personal use can trigger automatic deportation.[26] Although many states had previously enacted laws requiring defense

---

21. Padilla v. Kentucky, 559 U.S. 356 (2010). *See also* INA § 101(a)(48) (defining conviction to include proceedings in which there is no judgment of guilt, but "the judge has ordered some form of punishment, penalty, or restraint on the alien's liberty").

22. *Id.* at 356. *See also* Office of Immigration Litigation, Immigration Consequences of Criminal Convictions: Padilla v. Kentucky (Nov. 2010), *available at* http://www.justice.gov /civil/docs_forms/REVISED%20Padilla%20v.%20Kentucky%20Reference%20Guide_11-8 -10.pdf.

23. *Padilla*, 559 U.S. at 366.

24. *Id.* at 368.

25. *See generally* TOVA INDRITZ, IMMIGRATION CONSEQUENCES IN CRIMINAL CASES AFTER PADILLA V. KENTUCKY, *in* CULTURAL ISSUES IN CRIMINAL DEFENSE (Linda F. Ramirez ed., 3d ed. 2010) (AILA reprint), *available at* http://www.aila.org/content/default.aspx?docid=35858.

26. *See* INA § 237.

attorneys to inform their clients of the immigration consequences of a guilty plea, this directive from the highest court of the land increases the obligations of the defense attorney.

BEST PRACTICES

- *Ethics:* Regularly consult the ethics rules for the state in which you are barred, in which you are practicing, and the rules provided in the INA and pursuant regulations. It is entirely possible that action that is consistent with one set of ethical precepts is inconsistent with the other two; in those cases, contact relevant board(s) of ethics and ask for guidance.
- *Document Retention:* Retain documents in a secure manner pertaining to a case for as long as required by law.
- *Vesting of Representation:* The attorney-client relationship needs no formal written agreement or payment of fees and can be implied from the conduct of the parties. The courts generally defer to the interpretation of the client as to the existence of the relationship. Therefore, at the end of every consultation, send a nonengagement letter, and at the end of every representation, send a disengagement letter.
- *Written Agreements:* Have a clear written agreement with the client defining the scope of the representation, fee payment schedule, and ensure the client understands the agreement.
- *Clear Communication:* Clients come with different levels of understanding of the immigration system and therefore, what is clear communication with one client may be much too complex and terminology-laden for another.
- *Explore All Reasonable Avenues:* Ensure that during the client intake appointment that you discuss the client's immigration history, how long the client has been in the United States, and whether any of the client's relatives are U.S. citizens. At least one state has reprimanded an immigration attorney for failing to explore an alternative form of relief that was available to the client.[27]
- *Open Lines of Communication:* In representing a petitioner and a beneficiary, it is essential to not assume that communications with one party (petitioner-relative/beneficiary-employee) are being conveyed to the other party (beneficiary-relative/petitioner-employer). As a corollary, because the attorney represents both parties, do not hesi-

---

27. *See* Attorney Grievance Commission v. Snyder, 956 A.2d 147 (Md. 2008) (stating that it violated Maryland ethics rules to fail to explore cancellation of removal as an option for a client who would have qualified).

tate in requiring both the petitioner and beneficiary to meet with you so that you can have first-hand confirmation of the nature of the relationship.

- *Confidentiality and Co-clients:* In a dual representation situation, discuss with your clients at the inception of the relationship that your duties to both parties places limits on your confidentiality with both of them.
- *Criminal Convictions:* Ask the client whether he or she was previously advised of the immigration consequences of being convicted and/or pleading guilty.[28]
- *Timeliness:* 1) File all applications and court documents in a timely manner; 2) contact clients in a timely manner so as not to fall prey to a claim of neglect.
- *Vicarious Liability:* The Model Rules provide that an attorney is liable for the conduct of attorneys he or she supervises as well as non-attorneys (e.g., legal assistants and paralegals).[29] Many attorneys depend heavily upon their paralegals and the attorney needs to keep in mind that he or she is ultimately responsible for any and all work product of the paralegal. While paralegals may assist lawyers with their practice of law, lawyers must be careful not to use support staff in a manner that results in the unauthorized practice of law, an activity strictly prohibited by ethics rules.
- *Ask for Help:* A practitioner cannot simultaneously be an expert in every area of immigration law—first, be willing to admit to yourself and your client that you need to do additional research and second, have a list of experienced professionals whom you can contact for advice. AILA members have access to experienced attorneys who freely share their expertise.
- *Withdrawal:* Be willing to take the final step of withdrawing from the representation if the client is unwilling to help in his/her own case or does not agree with your legal strategy.

---

28. In *Chaldez v. United States*, No. 11-820 (S. Ct. Feb. 20, 2013) (566 U.S. ___, 132 S. Ct. 2101, 182 L. Ed. 2d 867), the Supreme Court decided that *Padilla* would not apply to convictions that became final before March 31, 2010. However, some states have decided that *Padilla* does apply retroactively for convictions after April 1, 1997. *See, e.g.*, Denisyuk v. State, No. 45, slip op. (Md. Oct. 25, 2011).

29. *See* ABA, Model Rules of Prof'l Conduct R. 5.1, *available at* http://www.americanbar .org/groups/professional_responsibility/publications/model_rules_of_professional_conduct /rule_5_1_responsibilities_of_a_partner_or_supervisory_lawyer.html; *id.* R. 5.3, *available at* http://www.americanbar.org/groups/professional_responsibility/publications/model_rules _of_professional_conduct/rule_5_3_responsibilities_regarding_nonlawyer_assistant.html. *See also* Mark J. Newman & Russell C. Ford, Utilizing Immigration Paraprofessionals: The Ethical Considerations, *in* Ethics in a Brave New World 2 (AILA 2004).

- *Succession Plan*: Ensure that you have a succession plan in place to ensure that your cases are in capable hands in the event of your illness or death. Also make proper arrangements for a capable practitioner to handle your cases while you are on vacation.

CONCLUSION

Immigration attorneys stay abreast of laws that change with lightning speeds and become experts in one of the most complicated regulatory frameworks invented by the United States Congress. Regularly these attorneys battle issues of deciding what is relevant to an application and what would unnecessarily raise immaterial questions. With the plethora of resources available for the immigration attorney to seek guidance, including state offices of bar counsel, learned colleagues focused upon ethics, and published decisions and advisory opinions as to ethics questions, immigration attorneys are well-equipped to make the right decision and solve their ethical dilemmas. While knowledge of the applicable ethical rules leads to a tug-of-war within the mind of the immigration practitioner, it is important for the diligent practitioner to be aware of her ethical obligations, particularly those of confidentiality, candor to the tribunal and dual representation, and to seek guidance when he or she is unsure of the right course of action.

5

RIGHTS OF ALIENS IN THE UNITED STATES

Ofelia L. Calderon[1] and Christine Lockhart Poarch[2]

Here in the United States, there is a certain pride in the land of the free and the home of the brave. We cling to the idea that certain rights remain a viable part of our constitutional fabric in the United States, such as the right to be free from unlawful search and seizure, the right to effective assistance of counsel, and the freedom from unlawful detention. However, there are attorneys who believe that these rights are under assault for all Americans.[3] But if there is an apparent erosion of fundamental constitutional rights in our nation, the slow recession of protected rights for foreign nationals[4] in the United States provides the most apt illustration. Whether one examines the recent legislation aimed at undocumented immigrants in several states or the Board of Immigration Appeals latest opinion that immigrants are not entitled to *Miranda* rights when interrogated by Immigration and Customs Enforcement officers, the issue of what rights the law affords immigrants—documented and undocumented—is the subject of current debate.

The authors hope to explore and illustrate the most common applications of and limitations on the constitutional rights afforded documented and undocumented aliens in the United States. While this topic—alien's

---

1. Ofelia L. Calderón is a founding partner at Calderón, Racine & Derwin PLC in Arlington, Virginia. The boutique immigration firm handles all types of immigration cases with a particular focus on litigation matters.
2. Christine Lockhart Poarch is a partner at Poarch Law, a law practice in Salem, Virginia exclusively devoted to immigration practice.
3. Michael L. Vander Giessen, Comment, Berghuis v. Thompkis: *The Continued Erosion of Miranda's Protections*, 46 Gonz. L. Rev. 189 (2011); Alison Siegler, *The PATRIOT Act's Erosion of Constitutional Rights*, 32 Litig. 18 (2006); Sarah M. Bernstein, *Fourteenth Amendment—Police Failure to Preserve Evidence and Erosion of the Due Process Right to a Fair Trial*, 80 J. Crim. L. & Criminology 1256 (1990).
4. The authors use the term "undocumented" to consistently identify individuals who are in the United States unlawfully or without documentation. The term "illegal alien" has never been defined in U.S. Code or regulations, and while used frequently by ICE and various political and governmental agencies, the authors are of the opinion that the term "illegal alien" simply fuels further confusion about an already overwhelmingly complex matrix of immigration laws governing "legal" status in the United States.

55

rights—could include themes as esoteric as whether foreign nationals in the United States are part of the "people" protected by the Constitution's preamble and amendments,[5] or as mundane as the limitations on detainers, we hope that the scope of this article will yield the most practical application for criminal attorneys and other counsel who do not practice immigration law with regularity or at all. While the authors have opinions about what the law should be, the purpose of this article is to explain what the law is and in which direction the winds of alien rights are blowing today. For ease of use, the term "alien rights" is used throughout the article to denote the rights afforded the broad scale of different "aliens" from those who are undocumented and generally enjoy the fewest rights, to lawful permanent residents on the other end of the spectrum.

The chapter is divided into three sections. First, the authors explore the most common rights of aliens within the public and private forums to marry, own property, attend school and maintain driving licenses. Section II will explore the scope of rights afforded prior to and during detention, and Section III will discuss the most common rights provided to aliens in the quasi-criminal context of removal proceedings.

FUNDAMENTAL TENSION IN ALIEN RIGHTS

A Continuum of Rights

There is a public perception that alien rights follow a predictable continuum, with the rights of naturalized U.S. citizens existing on one end,[6] and the rights of those who are undocumented in the United States on the other,[7] with the rights of any individual alien being determined by the significance of the alien's connections to the United States. In fact, this perception—that the more ties an alien has to the United States, the more rights the alien may have—does not always hold true. As one article illustrates, "an alien who marries a U.S. citizen may lawfully enter and naturalize within three years and claim the full range of constitutional rights and

---

5. *See, e.g.,* United States v. Portillo-Munoz, No. 11-10086, 2011 WL 2306248 (5th Cir. June 13, 2011).

6. While naturalized citizens can, under certain circumstances, be stripped of their citizenship for certain crimes or fraud in procuring the naturalization, *see* Perez v. Brownell, 356 U.S. 44 (1958); Afroyim v. Rusk, 387 U.S. 253 (1967); Vance v. Terrazas, 444 U.S. 252 (1980), for the purpose of discussing alien rights, the article does not address the nuances of denaturalization.

7. Won Kidane, *The Alienage Spectrum Disorder: The Bill of Rights from Chinese Exclusion to Guantanamo,* 20 BERKELEY LA RAZA L.J. 89 (2010) (challenging the idea that the continuum of rights is consistent based on connection to United States).

privileges due to citizens," while "a thirty seven year old woman whose parents brought her to the United States at age one and lived in the United States ever since, will have no hope of claiming legal status and the full protection of the Constitution."[8]

This example—and countless others—disrupts the idea of an orderly "progressive continuum" in which the greater an alien's connections to the United States, the greater the scope of that alien's rights. Rather than following a simple calculus in which an alien's connections augmented by legal status equals greater rights, the determination of an alien's particular "rights" is based on a complex matrix of factors. This is obvious when one considers larger groups of similarly situated aliens, such as legal permanent residents or the undocumented population—the rights accorded these groups are not consistent member to member, but rather depend on each alien's prior contact with immigration and prior criminal conduct, as well as the individual alien's legal status.[9] The question of what rights the alien is entitled to is contrasted with the question of what rights he or she is limited to.

An example of this limitation can be found in observing legal remedies afforded during removal proceedings. Case in point: legal permanent residents are barred from a remedy called the 212(h) waiver if they have been convicted of a crime defined as an "aggravated felony" under the act, while an undocumented individual may qualify for the same remedy regardless of his "aggravated felony" conviction. This distinction between similarly situated groups has survived equal protection challenge again and again.[10]

In practice, the most fundamental tension in alien rights is between the scope of rights afforded to "even aliens whose presence in this country is unlawful," and the contrary deference afforded the federal agencies to interpret and implement immigration laws.[11] Because even the undocumented have rights, we begin with that premise, and hope to construct a moderately intelligible system based on modern jurisprudence from that simple starting point.

---

8. *Id.* at 120.

9. *Id.*

10. *See Martinez v. Mukasey*, 519 F.3d 532 (5th Cir. 2008) (holding that a statutory prohibition against waivers of inadmissibility under INA § 212(h) for certain LPRs who have committed "aggravated felonies," or have resided in the United States for less than seven years, does not apply to LPRs who obtained their green card through adjustment of status in the United States rather than by arriving on an immigrant visa). *See also Matter of Rosas-Ramirez*, 22 I. & N. Dec. 616 (B.I.A. 1999).

11. *See* Plyler v. Doe, 457 U.S. 202 (1982); *see also* Chevron U.S.A. Inc. v. Natural Resources Defense Council, 467 U.S. 837 (1984).

Even the Undocumented Have Rights

It is clear at the most basic level that "whatever his status under the immigration laws, an alien is surely a 'person' in any ordinary sense of that term" and is "guaranteed due process of law by the Fifth and Fourteenth Amendments."[12] That does not mean that the court is blind to alienage, however, or even blind to the nuanced difference between documented and undocumented aliens. On the contrary, depending on the context, one's rights under the U.S. Constitution begin and end with the question of whether the individual is a U.S. or foreign national and whether it is the federal government or states and localities making the rules. This is particularly evident in the arena of Fourth Amendment rights, described further in a later section.

The Federal Government Can Expand Alien Rights or Take Them Away

Because the federal government has the lion's share of the enforcement responsibility regarding who to let in and who to keep out, the federal immigration agencies are given wide berth by the Courts regarding the exercise of their administrative discretion.[13] Accordingly, the courts have consistently held that the federal government, because of its power to regulate immigration, can discriminate based on alienage.[14] In fact, when attacked on equal protection grounds, federal determinations that turn on alienage are often upheld, simply because the restriction or discrimination must bear only a rational basis to a valid governmental purpose in light of the federal government's plenary power in the area of immigration.[15] As Justice John Paul Stevens described in 1976, "in the exercise of

---

12. *Plyler,* 457 U.S. at 210 (citing Shaughnessy v. Mezei, 345 U.S. 206, 212 (1953); Wong Wing v. United States, 163 U.S. 228, 238 (1896); Yick Wo v. Hopkins, 118 U.S. 356, 369 (1886)).

13. *Chevron,* 467 U.S. at 864–66.

14. *See, e.g.,* Matthews v. Diaz, 426 U.S. 67 (1976) (holding that Congress could restrict alien access to federal medical insurance); *see also* Hampton v. Mow Sun Wong, 426 U.S. 88 (1976) (suggesting that when Congress or the president enacts a policy or program, the plenary power doctrine applies allowing the court to discriminate based on alienage). *But cf.* Graham v. Richardson, 403 U.S. 365 (1971) (holding that *states* violate the U.S. Constitution by discriminating against aliens in the distribution of welfare benefits).

15. *See, e.g.,* Lewis v. Thompson, 252 F.3d 567, 582 (2d Cir. 2001) (upholding, under the rational basis test, PRWORA restrictions on alien eligibility for state-administered Medicaid benefits); City of Chicago v. Shalala, 189 F.3d 598, 603–05 (7th Cir. 1999) (rational basis test also applied for state administered supplemental security income (SSI) and food stamps); Aleman v. Glickman, 217 F.3d 1191, 1197 (9th Cir. 2000); Abreu v. Callahan, 971 F. Supp. 799 (S.D.N.Y. 1997); Rodriguez v. United States, 169 F.3d 1342, 1346–50 (11th Cir. 1999); United

its broad power over naturalization and immigration, Congress regularly makes rules that would be unacceptable if applied to citizens."[16] Accordingly, the courts have upheld federal statutes that discriminate between U.S. nationals and non-nationals, as well as legal permanent residents and undocumented aliens.[17]

States and Localities Are Limited in Their Power to Curtail Immigrant Rights

On the other hand, the courts are not as permissive when states and localities begin to legislate in the immigration arena. Using the doctrine of preemption which, in simple terms, gives the federal government superior claim to legislate in the immigration arena, the courts apply strict scrutiny to state statutes challenged on equal protection grounds.[18] At the same time, the courts have upheld states' limited interest in what it defines as areas of political interest, and have allowed the states to constitutionally discriminate against legal permanent residents in areas

---

States v. Song, 1995 WL 736872, at *3 (S.D.N.Y. 1995) ("Although state laws that classify persons based on *alienage* are subject to strict scrutiny, *federal* laws that classify on the basis of *alienage* are subject only to *rational basis* analysis because of the immigration and foreign policy concerns inherent in the relationship between the *federal* government and aliens."); Cellswitch v. FCC, 511 U.S. 1004 (1994).

16. *Diaz*, 426 U.S. at 79–80.

17. In addition to those cases listed in footnote 14, see United States v. Lopez-Flores, 63 F.3d 1468, 1471–72 (9th Cir. 1995) (upholding a statute which operated such that "If either the alleged offender or the victim is a non-national, the Hostage Taking Act applies; however, if both the alleged offender and the victim(s) are nationals of the United States (and the offense occurred in the United States and each alleged offender is found in the United States) then the Act is inapplicable, unless the alleged offender sought to compel the government of the United States to do or abstain from any act.") *cert. denied*, 516 U.S. 1082 (1996); Hernandez v. United States, 516 U.S. 1082 (1996); Sudomir v. McMahon, 767 F.2d 1456, 1464 (9th Cir. 1985) (applying "not wholly irrational" standard to uphold denial of welfare benefits to asylum applicants because "federal classifications based on alienage are subject to relaxed scrutiny"); United States v. Ni Fa Yi, 951 F. Supp. 42, 44 & n.3 (S.D.N.Y. 1997); and Lopez v. Bergland, 448 F. Supp. 1279, 1282–83 (N.D. Cal. 1978).

18. *See, e.g.*, McGready v. Virginia, 94 U.S. 391 (1877); Patsone v. Pennsylvania, 232 U.S. 138 (1914) (limiting the rights of aliens to develop natural resources); Hauenstein v. Lynham, 100 U.S. 483 (1880); Blythe v. Hinckley, 180 U.S. 333 (1901) (restricting the right to devolution of property to aliens); Terrace v. Thompson, 263 U.S. 197 (1923); Porterfield v. Webb, 263 U.S. 225 (1923); Webb v. O'Brien, 263 U.S. 313 (1923); Frick v. Webb, 263 U.S. 326 (1923); Heim v. McCall, 239 U.S. 175 (1915); People v. Crane, 108 N.E. 427 (N.Y. 1915), *aff'd*, 239 U.S. 195 (1915) (denying alien's right to public employment); Ohio ex rel. Clarke v. Deckebach, 274 U.S. 392 (1927). *But cf.* Truax v. Raich, 239 U.S. 33 (1915) (holding that aliens do have the right to employment by private employers).

such as voting rights and eligibility for political office.[19] This limitation on states' rights to regulate immigration was not always the case,[20] however, and in recent years efforts to increase states' rights bear watching.

ALIEN RIGHTS IN THE PUBLIC FORUM

Public Education

Occasionally, the U.S. Supreme Court clarifies the rights of aliens within the public forum when it determines the constitutionality of invidious state statutes intended to target the undocumented populations living within a state's borders. The 1982 case of Plyler v. Doe was one such occasion, in which the United States Supreme Court struck down a Texas statute that withheld state funds for educating children who were not lawfully admitted to the United States and permitted local school districts to deny such students admission to their schools.[21] A majority of the U.S. Supreme Court held that this policy violated the Fourteenth Amendment because undocumented children are people "in any ordinary sense of the term," and therefore protected from discrimination unless a substantial state interest justified the differential treatment.[22] Despite the U.S. Supreme Court's clear language, states have continued to try to limit or otherwise qualify access to public education.[23]

Right to Maintain Driver's License

While there is some debate about what due process rights must be accorded in revoking a driver's license,[24] the determination of prerequi-

---

19. *See* Bernal v. Fainter, 467 U.S. 216 (1984); *see also* United States v. Arizona, No. 2:10-cv-01413-SRB (9th Cir. 2011), *available at* http://www.ca9.uscourts.gov/datastore/general/2011/04/11/10-16645_opinion.pdf.

20. *See* Gerald L. Neuman, *The Lost Century of American Immigration Law (1776–1875)*, 93 COLUM. L. REV. 1833, 1835–84 (1993) (exploring pre-1875 state and local immigration laws); *see also* ARISTIDE R. ZOLBERG, A NATION BY DESIGN: IMMIGRATION POLICY IN THE FASHIONING OF AMERICA, 74–76 (2006) (discussing state regulatory efforts).

21. Plyler v. Doe, 457 U.S. 202, 209 (1982).

22. *Id.* at 210.

23. *See* Kevin R. Johnson, *An Essay on Immigration Politics, Popular Democracy, and California's Proposition 187: The Political Relevance and Legal Irrelevance of Race*, 70 WASH. L. REV. 629, 646 (1995) (a discussion of California's 1994 ballot initiative to allow the state to screen the citizenship of public school students and to ban undocumented students from attending public schools).

24. *See* Kristen Davis, *Ohio's New Administrative License Suspension for Drunk Driving: Essential Statute Has Unconstitutional Effect*, 55 OHIO ST. L. J. 697 (1994); Jeffry S. Sheridan,

sites for issuance of a driver's license is historically the legislative prerog-
ative of the states.[25] The REAL ID Act and various proposed amendments
have tried to usurp this state power in the name of preventing terrorists from having licenses.[26] Whether initiated at the state or federal level,
restrictions on driver's licenses have had the deleterious side effect of
prohibiting licensure instead to countless undocumented aliens in the
United States.[27] In January 2008, the Department of Homeland Security
issued a final rule to establish minimum standards for state-issued driver's licenses and identification cards in accordance with the REAL ID Act
of 2005.[28] These regulations set standards for states to meet the requirements of the REAL ID Act, including: (1) information and security features that must be incorporated into each card; (2) proof of identity and
lawful status of an applicant; (3) verification of the source documents provided by an applicant; and (4) security standards for the offices that issue
licenses and identification cards.[29] Pursuant to the Department of Homeland Security's REAL ID regulation, states were to be in full compliance
with the REAL ID Act of 2005 by May 11, 2011.[30] A final rule issued March
7, 2011 changed that date to January 15, 2011.[31] Each state's mandate for
driver's licenses is beyond the scope of this article, but it bears noting
that as of 2009, 46 states either statutorily require proof of lawful presence
in the United States prior to granting a driver's license or have a similar
agency policy requiring such documentation.[32]

  In certain states, the effective date of the state restriction on driver's
licensing provides the best possibility for an undocumented alien maintaining a valid license. If the alien had a license prior to the effective date
of the act, he may be able to maintain that license without complying

---

Erika Burkhart Booth, *Revoke First, Ask Questions Later: Challenging Minnesota's Unconstitutional Pre-hearing Revocation Scheme*, 31 WM. MITCHELL L. REV. 1461 (2005).

25. *See, e.g.*, Travis v. Reno, 12 F. Supp. 2d. 921 (W.D. Wis. 1998); *see also* United States v. Snyder, 852 F.2d 471 (9th Cir. 2004).

26. Real ID Act of 2005, Pub. L. No. 109-13, 119 Stat. 302.

27. *See generally* Kevin R. Johnson & Bernard Trujillo, *Immigration Reform, National Security
after September 11, and the Future of North American Integration*, 91 MINN. L. REV. 1369, 1395
(2007) (discussing effect of Real ID Act § 202(b)–(d).

28. Minimum Standards for Driver's Licenses and Identification Cards Acceptable by Federal Agencies for Official Purposes, (January 15, 2008) (codified at 6 C.F.R. § 37).

29. *Id.* (codified at 6 C.F.R. § 37(I)(A)(7), (IV)(F)(1)).

30. *Id.* at Summary.

31. Minimum Standards for Driver's Licenses and Identification Cards Acceptable by Federal Agencies for Official Purposes, (March 7, 2011) (to be codified at 6 C.F.R. § 37).

32. *Overview of States' Driver's License Requirements*, NAT'L IMMIGR. L. CENTER, http://www.nilc
.org/immspbs/DLs/state_dl_rqrmts_ovrvw_2009-04-27.pdf (last visited November 1, 2011).

with the additional proof of legal presence.[33] On the other hand, the state licensure requirements defining proof of legal presence sometimes miss the nuance of legal status. For example, and individual who is lawfully present in the United States under withholding of removal—a form of relief permitted to individuals our government believes will be tortured upon return to their home country—is frequently refused a license simply because a state may interpret its "proof" of legal status requirement in such a way to prohibit that individual's licensure. The same result frequently occurs with a K visa holder who enters the United States as a fiancé of a U.S. Citizen and whose status is not clearly enumerated in the state's list of "legal status." In short, when the state tries to mimic in cold, hard regulation the complex and nuanced definitions inherent in determining legal status, there can be inappropriate exclusions and thus, refusals of the privilege or right of driving in this country.

Right to Marry

One particularly intimate rights issue that affects countless aliens is the refusal by county clerks to issue marriage licenses to individuals who cannot present either a federal Social Security number or some other documentation required by the state statute creating the clerk's authority to issue marriage licenses. This has raised the ire not only of immigrant advocates, but religious organizations such as the Catholic Legal Immigration Network and others who have crafted responses intended to provide guidance and offer correct information on the issue.[34]

The confusion arose, in part, because of a federal law enacted in 1996 called the Personal Responsibility and Work Opportunity Reconciliation Act (PRWORA) to make child support enforcement more effective.[35] As part of the plan, states were required to record the Social Security numbers for individuals applying for certain licenses.[36] In 1999, the Commissioner of the federal Office of Child Support Enforcement issued interpretative guid-

---

33. For example, in the state of Virginia, effective January 1, 2004, the Department of Motor Vehicles "will not issue an original license, permit, or ID card to any applicant who has not presented evidence that he/she is a citizen of the United States, a legal permanent resident, or an authorized temporary resident alien of the United States." Virginia Firearms Transaction Program, Virginia State Police, http://www.vsp.state.va.us/Firearms_VFTP.shtm (last visited November 3, 2011).

34. Undocumented Immigrants and the Right to Marry, Catholic Legal Immigration Network, Inc., http://www.archchicago.org/Immigration/pdf/Immigration/Undocumented Marriage.pdf (last visited Nov. 1, 2011).

35. *Id.*

36. *Id.*

ance in which the Commissioner held that "we interpret the statutory language in section 466(a)(13) of the Act to require that States have procedures which require an individual to furnish any Social Security number that he or she may have . . . not require that an individual have a Social Security number as a condition of receiving a license, etc."[37]

This confusion was further compounded by state statutory requirements that may require a Social Security number or a driver's license, access to both of which are limited by various state and federal laws. Without one or the other, many an alien was sent from the courthouse without the marriage license they came to obtain. The Southern Poverty Law Center has filed a lawsuit that challenges Alabama probate judges in 54 of Alabama's 67 counties who require a Social Security number to issue a marriage license.[38] Similarly, lawsuits may arise as states more ardently enforce vague statutory restrictions such as those surrounding most state marriage license laws and as more individuals are refused marriage licenses based on failure to provide documentation that their alienage and legal status prohibits them from procuring.

Parental Rights

Close behind the right to marry in the ranks of the most intimate and personal of rights is the right to parent one's children. While the best interests of the child reigns supreme in most juvenile and domestic relations courts, several well-publicized cases have brought to light a more sinister side of this discretionary balancing test. For example, when Encarnación Bail Romero was put in ICE custody after the plant where she worked was raided, her son, Carlos, was placed in the custody of an American family who immediately petitioned to terminate Ms. Bail's parental rights. While the Missouri Supreme Court reversed the decision and remanded for a new trial, other state courts have reached opposite findings.[39]

---

37. U.S. Department of Health and Human Services, Office of Child Support Enforcement, PIQ-99-05, Inclusion of Social Security Numbers on License Applications and Other Documents (July 14, 1999).

38. Case Docket: Linda Smith v. Reese McKinney, Jr., Southern Poverty Law Center, http://www.splcenter.org/get-informed/case-docket/linda-smith-et-al-v-reese-mckinney-jr (last visited November 3, 2011).

39. S.M. v. E.M.B.R. (*In re* Adoption of C.M.B.R.), No. SC91141, slip op. at 3 (Mo. Jan. 25, 2011) (en banc), *available at* http://www.courts.mo.gov/file.jsp?id=43941; Perez-Velasquez v. Culpeper Country Dep't of Social Services, No. 0360-09-4, 2009 WL 1851017 (Va. Ct. App. June 30, 2009); C. Elizabeth Hall, Note, *Where Are My Children . . . and My Rights? Parental Rights Termination as a Consequence of Deportation*, 60 Duke L. J. 1459 (2011).

Parents have a constitutional right to the care and custody of their children under the "parental rights doctrine."[40] A parent, to have his or her rights terminated, must generally be considered to be "unfit."[41] Clear and convincing evidence must support parental termination[42] because parental interests in children are "perhaps the oldest of the fundamental liberty interests recognized by this Court" and "as long as a parent adequately cares for his or her children (i.e., is fit), there will normally be no reason for the state to inject itself into the private realm of the family."[43]

Constitutional rights of parents are not limited to United States citizens because the constitutional protections of the Fourteenth Amendment extend to aliens as "persons" within the meaning of the Constitution.[44] As a result, there should not be any difference in the analysis between undocumented parents and U.S. citizens in terms of the application of these constitutional rights.

RIGHTS PRIOR TO AND DURING IMMIGRATION DETENTION

The Immigration and Nationality Act permits any immigration officer, without a warrant, to (1) interrogate any alien or person believed to be an alien as to his or her right to be or remain in the United States; (2) arrest any alien who in the officer's presence or view is entering or attempting to enter the United States in violation of any law or if the officer has reason to believe the alien is in the United States in violation of any law and is likely to escape if not arrested; or (3) board and search any vehicle to look for illegal aliens within a reasonable distance from the border.[45] The Code defines a reasonable distance from the border to be "100 air miles from any external boundary of the United States."[46]

Right to Be Free from Unlawful Search or Seizure

The Fourth Amendment of the United States Constitution provides that "[t]he right of the people to be secure in their persons, houses, papers, and

---

40. Meyer v. Nebraska, 262 U.S. 390 (1923); Pierce v. Society of Sisters, 268 U.S. 510 (1925); Troxel v. Granville, 530 U.S. 57 (2000).
41. Stanley v. Illinois, 405 U.S. 645 (1972).
42. Santosky v. Kramer, 455 U.S. 745 (1982).
43. *Troxel*, 530 U.S. at 69.
44. Plyler v. Doe, 457 U.S. 202, 210 (1982).
45. INA § 287(a) (2010).
46. 8 C.F.R. § 287.1(a)(2) (2010).

effects, against unreasonable searches and seizures, shall not be violated, and no Warrants shall issue but upon probable cause."[47] The Supreme Court has interpreted this to mean that law enforcement officers may not arrest a person without a warrant unless that officer has "probable cause" to believe that the person has engaged in some criminal activity.[48] Probable cause exists when "the facts and circumstances within [the officers'] knowledge and of which they had reasonably trustworthy information [are] sufficient in themselves to warrant a man of reasonable caution in the belief that an offense has been or is being committed by the person to be arrested."[49] In *INS v. Lopez-Mendoza*, the Supreme Court held that the exclusionary rule barring the admission of the evidence obtained through unlawful search or arrest does not apply in deportation proceedings.[50]

The Supreme Court has held that excluding such evidence would hinder the deliberately simple removal hearing system, would possibly suppress large amounts of information that had been obtained lawfully, and would "compel the courts to release from custody persons who would then immediately resume their commission of a crime through their continuing, unlawful presence in this country."[51] In the Court's view, the social benefits from excluding such evidence would be minor because exclusion would have little deterrent effect on future Fourth Amendment violations by immigration officials.[52] Notwithstanding *Lopez-Mendoza*, there is has been an increase in Fourth Amendment suppression litigation.[53] In *Lopez-Rodriguez v. Mukasey*,[54] the Court applied the exclusionary rule.

Due Process Rights

Fifth Amendment due process standards of fundamental fairness extend, however, even to deportation proceedings.[55] Accordingly, suppression of evidence may be appropriate in cases of egregious violations of Fourth Amendment rights or where the use of such evidence would be

---

47. U.S. Const. Amend. IV.
48. Illinois v. Gates, 462 U.S. 213, 245 (1983).
49. Dunaway v. New York, 442 U.S. 200, 208 (1979).
50. INS v. Lopez-Mendoza, 468 U.S. 1032 (1984).
51. *Id.*
52. *Id.*
53. Jennifer M. Chacón, *A Diversion of Attention? Immigration Courts and the Adjudication of Fourth and Fifth Amendment Rights*, 59 Duke L. J. 1563 (2010).
54. 536 F.3d 1012 (9th Cir. 2008).
55. Bridges v. Waxon, 326 U.S. 135 (1945).

in violation of the due process requirements of the Fifth Amendment.[56] Moreover, where the Department of Homeland Security violates its own regulations and protocol, the Court may suppress the evidence procured in the course of that violation.[57]

In *Garcia-Flores*, the BIA addressed the well-established principle in preservation of due process that an "agency of the government must scrupulously observe rules, regulations and procedures which it has established," and that when it fails to do so, "its actions cannot stand and the courts will strike it down."[58] While every violation may not result in the suppression of the evidence procured by that violation, the Court must rigidly protect against due process violations that result from the agency failing to comply with regulations and procedures "mandated by the Constitution or federal law."[59] It is still incumbent on an agency to observe its own rules, however, where the "rights of individuals are affected," regardless of whether those rules derive from constitutional mandate.[60]

The Circuit Courts of Appeal disagree regarding the standard of proof required in determining whether internal agency compliance results in suppression of evidence.[61] In general, the courts agree that the Respondent must demonstrate that the regulation was not adhered to and that the regulation was intended to benefit the respondent.[62] However, the courts disagree regarding whether the respondent must demonstrate that the violation prejudiced the respondent's interest in the outcome of the proceedings.

Scope of Immigration Detainers

Non-citizens who come into contact with state or local law enforcement (lawful or otherwise) generally enter immigration detention through one of the 14 different programs that connect ICE agents to state and local law enforcement agencies and operations, called ICE ACCESS "Agreements of Cooperation in Communities to Enhance Safety and Security." Of the 14 programs, there are three in particular that result in the most deten-

---

56. *Lopez-Mendoza*, 468 U.S. at 1050–51; Matter of Toro, 17 I. & N. Dec. 340 (B.I.A. 1980).
57. *See* Matter of Garcia-Flores, 17 I. & N. Dec. 325 (B.I.A. 1980) (disapproved of on other grounds by Montilla v. INS, 926 F.2d 162 (2d Cir. 1991)).
58. United States v. Heffner, 420 F.2d 809, 811 (4th Cir. 1969).
59. United States v. Caceres, 440 U.S. 741, 749 (1979).
60. Morton v. Ruiz, 415 U.S. 199, 235 (1974).
61. *Cf.* United States v. Calderon-Medina, 591 F.2d 529 (9th Cir. 1979); Waldron v. INS, 17 F.3d 511 (2d Cir. 1993) (declining to adopt third prong of *Calderon* test).
62. *See Calderon-Medina*, 591 F.2d at 531 (requiring a showing of prejudice) and *Waldron v. INS*, 17 F.3d at 518 (adopting a "no prejudice" approach).

tion of aliens: the Criminal Alien Program (CAP) of ICE itself, Secure Communities,[63] and 287(g) programs.[64]

Once an alien is in custody, ICE lodges Immigration Detainers to prevent release of removable aliens prior to immigration enforcement actions. An Immigration Detainer (Form I-247) is an advisory document issued by the Department of Homeland Security to the jail or prison holding the alien asking them to continue to detain the alien on behalf of ICE for a period of time to permit the alien's transfer to ICE custody.[65] The Board of Immigration Appeals has characterized a detainer as "merely an administrative mechanism to assure that a person subject to confinement will not be released from custody until the party requesting the detainer has an opportunity to act.[66]

Presumably such an administrative mechanism would mean that a non-citizen would not be affected by the existence of a detainer until he or she is released from confinement and the detainer is triggered.[67] However, as a practical matter, the alien is normally affected by the presence of the detainer because it may mean that they are ineligible for bond or work release. An alien may "fall to the detainer" upon the family's payment of a bond, after which the family is told that the individual cannot be released because of the immigration detainer holding them. In light of the high risk of losing the surety deposit if the family uses a bondsman, more and more magistrates are refusing to accept bond payments and sureties in cases involving aliens. More frequently, the alien "falls to the detainer" when his state or local sentence is completed.

Federal regulations specifically limit detention predicated solely on an immigration detainer to forty-eight hours, excluding weekends and federal holidays.[68] In practice, non-citizens have been held for many days, if not months, under the misapplication of Immigration Detainers. If ICE does not pick up the alien and transport them to an ICE holding facility

---

63. Secure Communities, Dept. of Homeland Security, U.S. Immigration and Customs Enforcement, http://www.ice.gov/secure_communities/ (last visited November 3, 2011). Secure Communities is a cooperative arrangement between ICE and state or local law enforcement communities to expedite and streamline issuance of detainers and transfer of non-U.S. nationals into ICE custody through the use of biometric technology provided by the federal government.

64. 287(g) agreements permit local non-immigration officers to arrest non-citizens on account of immigration violations. 8 C.F.R. § 236.1(b) (2010).

65. *Id.* § 287.7.

66. *See* Matter of Sanchez, 20 I. & N. Dec. 223, 225 (B.I.A. 1990) (citing Moody v. Daggett, 429 U.S. 78, 80 n.2 (1976)).

67. 8 C.F.R. § 287.7.

68. *Id.* § 287.7(d).

within the allowed time period, the jail lacks authority to continue the detention. In response to detainer abuse, the criminal defense attorney or other attorney should issue a demand letter to the jail advising that they are unlawfully continuing to hold the alien or file a habeas corpus action to permit the alien's release. In practice, however, most attorney action merely expedites the alien's transfer from state to ICE custody. Rarely does a habeas or other action result in the alien's actual release from the detainer or from jail.

If a correctional facility holding a non-citizen on a detainer does not contract with ICE to detain immigrants, ICE is supposed to assume physical custody of the non-citizen. In practice, this means ICE agents will relocate the non-citizen to an immigration detention facility. In this scenario, ICE physically picks up the subject of the detainer from a federal, state, or local jail or prison and, after processing, transfers him or her to an immigration detention center that is operated by ICE or holds detainees for ICE under a contract known as an Inter-Governmental Service Agreement (IGSA). The facilities authorized under such agreements are disclosed on ICE's website and the list is updated frequently, but not always concurrently with a new facility's authorization.[69]

Alternatively, a non-citizen may progress from criminal custody into immigration custody without changing location. This typically occurs at IGSA facilities where a jail contracts with ICE to house immigration detainees for the duration removal proceedings. Here, the filing of additional paperwork by ICE with the jail represents the transfer from criminal custody into immigration detention. Unlike an Immigration Detainer that authorizes a temporary custody extension, Form I-203A/B, "Order to Detain/Release Aliens," notifies a jail that an individual non-citizen is to be officially placed into ICE custody.

National Detention Standards

Law enforcement agencies and private companies that provide additional detention housing that contract with ICE to detain non-citizens are expected to meet the Performance Based National Detention Standards published in 2008[70] with respect to conditions of confinement. These detention standards are not codified, and are therefore not legally

---

69. Immigration Detention Facilities, Dept. of Homeland Security, U.S. Immigration and Customs Enforcement, http://www.ice.gov/detention-facilities/ (last visited November 3, 2011).

70. There are now 41 Performance-Based National Detention Standards that govern conditions of confinement for ICE detainees at ICE detention facilities, private-sector detention facilities contracted by ICE, and state or local government facilities used by ICE under intergovernmental contracts, http://www.ice.gov/detention-standards/2008/index.htm.

enforceable, but the standards apply at all facilities where ICE houses detainees.

Bond Determination

For a warrantless arrest, a non-citizen must be served with a Notice of Custody Determination (Form I-286) within forty-eight hours of entering ICE custody.[71] This determination informs the non-citizen as to whether ICE has decided to continue detention without bond, granted bond in a specified amount, or granted release on recognizance. Additionally, the Custody Determination will specify whether a charging document and arrest warrant will issue. Importantly, a caveat in the regulations suspends the forty-eight hour requirement "in the event of an emergency or other extraordinary circumstance in which case a determination will be made within a reasonable period of time."[72] No definition exists in the Code for "emergency," "extraordinary circumstance," or "reasonable period of time."

Unlike most criminal scenarios, not all aliens are able to secure their release through bond. Although the regulations state that at any time prior to a final order of removal, an individual detained by ICE can request that an immigration judge reconsider the initial custody determination reached by ICE,[73] the reality is different. These unlucky individuals are found at 8 C.F.R. § 1003.19(2) and include those subject to expedited removal proceedings,[74] aliens subject to "mandatory detention,"[75] and "arriving aliens." To illustrate, an "arriving alien" is defined at 8 C.F.R. § 1.1(q) as "an applicant for admission coming or attempting to come into the United States at a port-of-entry, or an alien seeking transit through the United States at a port-of-entry, or an alien interdicted in international or United States waters and brought into the United States by any means, whether or not to a designated port-of-entry, and regardless of the means of transport." This could mean an alien denied "admission"[76] at a port-of-entry or an alien entering without inspection. This term could include an alien who steps off the airplane and tells the CBO officer at the airport that they fear for their lives and wish to apply for asylum in the United

---

71. 8 C.F.R. § 287.3(d) (2010).

72. *Id.*

73. *Id.* § 1003.19(a); *id.* § 236.1(d).

74. INA § 235(b).

75. *Id.* § 236(c).

76. "Admission" is a legal term that is currently the subject of much litigation, but generally refers to a legal entry into the United States after being inspected by an appropriate DHS official. INA § 101(a)(13)(A); 8 U.S.C. § 1101(a)(13)(A).

States. Whichever circumstance gives rise to the application of the term "arriving alien," that alien is *not* entitled to a bond hearing before an Immigration Court.

Service of Charging Documents

Unfortunately, no law or regulation establishes a time frame in which written charges are to be served on a detained non-citizen. A 2004 DHS internal memo directs that detained non-citizens shall be charged within forty-eight hours of their arrest and served with a Notice to Appear (Form I-862) within seventy-two hours of such arrest.[77] Again, DHS delineates large exceptions to the time line, including "compelling law enforcement need" and "immigration emergency."[78] The Notice to Appear is also filed with the Immigration Court and states, among other things, the nature of the proceedings, the alleged acts that violated the law, the right to an attorney at no expense to the government, and the consequences of failing to appear at scheduled hearings.

RIGHTS DURING DEPORTATION (REMOVAL) PROCEEDINGS

As previously stated, the Department of Homeland Security holds broad power to subject those who are here without lawful authority to removal proceedings (previously called deportation and/or exclusion).[79] But even this authority to commence removal proceedings requires due process, the level of which is determined by the nature of the proceedings in light of past immigration history.[80] With that caveat, most individuals are entitled to notice of the deportation charges against them including the hearing time and place, effective assistance of counsel (detailed below) at their own expense, an interpreter, and the opportunity to examine the evidence and the government's witnesses against them. Any criminal

---

77. Memorandum from Asa Hutchinson, Undersecretary, Border and Transportation Security, to Michael J. Garcia, Asst. Secretary, ICE and Robert Bonner, Commissioner, CBP (Mar. 30, 2004), http://www.immigrationforum.org/images/uploads/iceguidance.pdf.
78. *Id.* at § I pt. C.
79. *See* INA § 101(a)(13) (consolidating what used to be known as exclusion and deportation proceedings into a solitary "removal" proceeding. It did not, however, change the fundamental distinction between exclusion and deportation).
80. Kaoru Yamataya v. Fisher, 189 U.S. 86 (1903) (in which the U.S. Supreme Court ruled that the INS could not deport someone without a hearing that meets constitutional due process standards).

defense practitioner is familiar with these rights in the criminal context, but in the removal context, these rights are more strictly curtailed.

Right to Notice of Charges

The Code of Federal Regulations requires that the Notice to Appear in Immigration Court, which is the charging document that commences immigration court removal proceedings, must include certain information, such as (1) the nature of the proceedings against the alien; (2) the legal authority under which the proceedings are conducted; (3) the acts or conduct alleged to be in violation of law; (4) the charges against the alien and statutory provisions alleged to have been violated; (5) notice that the alien may be represented, at no cost to the government, by counsel or other representative authorized to appear before the court; (6) the address of the Immigration Court where the alien must appear; and (7) a statement advising the alien that he must provide the court with any change of address.[81]

Right to Effective Assistance of Counsel

The Immigration and Nationality Act itself alleges to secure the right to counsel in immigration proceedings. Section 240(b)(4)(A) states that in any removal proceedings before an immigration judge and in any appeal proceedings before the Attorney General from any such removal proceedings, the "alien shall have the privilege of being represented, at no expense to the Government, by counsel of the alien's choosing who is authorized to practice in such proceedings." Notwithstanding or perhaps because of this statutory language, many individuals in deportation proceedings stand alone when facing an immigration judge.[82] Since the statute expressly states that individuals have right to counsel at no expense to the Government, there is no avenue for indigent aliens to obtain counsel. As a result, when faced with what has become an increasingly adversarial proceeding, only those either lucky enough to obtain the limited pro bono counsel available or those with sufficient funds to hire a private attorney are assisted in Immigration Court.[83]

---

81. 8 C.F.R. § 1003.15.

82. According to the EOIR, 57 percent of aliens whose cases were completed in immigration courts during fiscal year 2010 were unrepresented. DEPARTMENT OF JUSTICE, EXECUTIVE OFFICE OF IMMIGRATION REVIEW, 2010 STATISTICAL YEAR BOOK (2011).

83. *See, e.g.*, Escobar-Grijalva v. INS, 206 F.3d 1331, 1334 (9th Cir. 2000) ("Deprivation of the statutory right to counsel deprives an alien asylum-seeker of the one hope she has to thread a labyrinth almost as impenetrable as the Internal Revenue Code."); Castro-O'Ryan v. INS,

As noted in the title, the right to counsel does not end simply with the right to have an attorney or other representative stand at one's side during proceedings. There is the further belief that one is entitled to effective representation. In criminal cases, the standard for effective counsel is laid out in the landmark case of *Strickland v. Washington*.[84] That holding, recognizing a constitutional right to effective counsel and requiring a showing that the attorney's performance fell below an objective reasonable standard and that the defendant suffered prejudice (a reasonable probability that the outcome would have been different).[85] In the immigration context, that standard has never been applied.

Questions about the right to effective assistance of counsel were most recently raised by two separate attorneys general. In *Matter of Compean I*,[86] Attorney General Mukasey certified three cases involving ineffective assistance of counsel for consolidated review. *Compean I* held that the Constitution does not confer a constitutional right to effective assistance in removal proceedings. *Compean I* overruled the previous two cases, *Matter of Lozada*,[87] and *Matter of Assaad*,[88] which had laid out a framework for assessing the prejudice of lawyer error on an alien's case and rooted the right to counsel in the Fifth Amendment. In an unprecedented move, Attorney General Holder vacated *Compean I*, reinstated the framework of *Lozada* and initiated rule-making procedures "to evaluate the *Lozada* framework and to determine what modifications should be proposed for public consideration."[89]

---

847 F.2d 1307, 1312 (9th Cir. 1987) ("With only a small degree of hyperbole, the immigration laws have been termed second only to the Internal Revenue Code in complexity. . . . A lawyer is often the only person who could thread the labyrinth."); Biwot v. Gonzales, 403 F.3d 1094, 1098 (9th Cir. 2005) ("The proliferation of immigration laws and regulations has aptly been called a labyrinth that only a lawyer could navigate."); Leslie v. Att'y Gen., 611 F.3d 171, 181 (3d Cir. 2010) ("Many courts have recognized that 'our immigration statutory framework is notoriously complex.' E.g., N-A-M v. Holder, 587 F.3d 1052, 1058 (10th Cir. 2009); see also INS v. Nat'l Ctr.for Immigrants' Rights, Inc., 502 U.S. 183, 195 (1991) (referencing our 'complex regime of immigration law'). The complexity of removal proceedings renders the alien's right to counsel particularly vital to his ability to 'reasonably present[ ] his case.'"); Del Rey Tortilleria, Inc. v. N.L.R.B., 976 F.2d 1115, 1122 (7th Cir. 1992) ("[T]he federal immigration laws are exceedingly complex. . . . It is hard to believe that Congress wished to place upon an NLRB compliance officer . . . the responsibility of determining the alien status of an undocumented worker.") (quoting Local 512 Warehouse and Office Workers' Union v. N.L.R.B., 795 F.2d 705, 721 (9th Cir. 1986)).

84. 466 U.S. 668 (1984).

85. *Id.*

86. 24 I. & N. Dec. 710, 727 (A.G. 2009).

87. 19 I. & N. Dec. 637 (B.I.A. 1988).

88. 23 I. & N. Dec. 553 (B.I.A. 2003).

89. Matter of Compean (Compean II), 25 I. & N. Dec. 1, 2 (A.G. 2009).

Rule-making is incomplete at the time of this writing, but does not affect the authors' point which is simply that while perhaps questionable, the right to counsel (and a good one at that) appears to endure.

In addition to the right to have counsel in immigration proceedings themselves, there is also the question of the right to effective counsel as it pertains to aliens who face immigration consequences as a result of criminal proceedings. Prior to March 31, 2010, immigration consequences were considered collateral to the criminal conviction. After *Padilla v. Kentucky*,[90] the Court made clear that under the Sixth Amendment's guarantee of effective assistance of counsel, counsel must inform a client whether his guilty plea carries a risk of deportation.[91] In practice, the state and federal trial courts deciding the issue of ineffective assistance in the immigration context after *Padilla* have reached mixed conclusions, a quandary that relates back to the question of state versus federal treatment of immigration issues.[92]

Right to an Interpreter

Interpreters are provided at government expense to individuals whose command of the English language is inadequate to fully understand and participate in removal proceedings.[93] In general, the Immigration Court endeavors to accommodate the language needs of all respondents and witnesses.[94] The Immigration Court will arrange for an interpreter both during the individual calendar hearing and, if necessary, the master calendar hearing.[95] The Immigration Court uses staff interpreters employed by the Immigration Court, contract interpreters, and telephonic interpretation services.[96] Staff interpreters take an oath to interpret and translate accurately at the time they are employed by the Department of Justice while contract interpreters take an oath to interpret and translate accurately in court.[97]

---

90. For an additional discussion of *Padilla*, see chapter 19, "Immigration Consequences of Criminal Convictions: What Crimes and Criminal Activities Can Get Your Client into Trouble."

91. Padilla v. Kentucky, 130 S. Ct. 1473 (2010).

92. Steven Weller and John A. Martin, *Implications of* Padilla v. Kentucky *on the Duty of State Court Criminal Judges*, Center for Public Policy Studies, *available at* http://www.sji.gov/PDF/Implications_of_Padilla_for_State_Court_Judges.pdf.

93. IMMIGRATION COURT PRACTICE MANUAL § 4.11 (2009) [hereinafter MANUAL].

94. *Id.*

95. *See* 8 C.F.R. § 1003.22 (2010); MANUAL, *supra* note 91, § 4.15(o).

96. MANUAL, *supra* note 91, § 4.11.

97. *See* 8 C.F.R. § 1003.22.

Right to Examine Evidence and Cross-Examine Witnesses

Code section 8 C.F.R. 1241.14 permits the alien a "reasonable opportunity to examine evidence against the alien, to present evidence on the alien's own behalf, and to cross-examine witnesses presented by the Service," including the author of any "medical or mental health reports used as a basis for the determination" that an alien is dangerous. Although codified in the INA and interpreted in CFR, this right is also limited by the way in which removal proceedings are conducted.

The use of videoconferencing in removal proceedings illustrates this point. Many removal hearings involving detained aliens are conducted via videoconferencing.[98] This means that the alien is not physically present in the courtroom with the immigration judge, trial attorney, and perhaps his or her own attorney. Although determined by the Board of Immigration Appeals and some circuit courts as acceptable, the reality is that such proceedings appear to affect the quality of substance and procedure.[99] While videoconferencing is on the rise in all courts, use in immigration courts gives rise to concerns regarding client confidentiality and quality of presentation. A *pro se* alien watching his proceeding via video may not be able to see or hear accurately enough to properly cross-examine a government witness. A *pro se* alien on video may not be able to examine a document that DHS presents for the first time at trial. Even if represented, how does an alien convey to his attorney questions about such issues without informing the entire courtroom? Each of these issues raises important due process concerns about the conduct of removal proceedings generally.

CONCLUSION

The discussion above, including the most recent jurisprudence regarding an alien's right to effective assistance of counsel, demonstrates not only that alien rights are inconsistently preserved and protected by the courts, but also that even "fundamental" protections afforded aliens by law in the public forum or in the criminal and quasi-criminal removal contexts may be forsaken willfully or negligently without ardent representation and vigorous legal defense. While there is no question that aliens have

98. This is not the case in ICE facilities where there is an immigration court present such as York, Pennsylvania, Oakdale, Louisiana, or Krome in Miami, Florida.
99. Aaron S. Haas, *Videoconferencing in Immigration Proceedings*, 5 Pierce L. Rev. 59 (2006); *see also* Assembly Line Injustice: Blueprint to Reform America's Immigration Courts (Appleseed, May 2009).

certain legal protections, the question of which rights a particular alien possesses, who may exercise the particular right, and how to properly preserve the constitutional or other protection vary greatly from client to client. If nothing else, the authors hope that by pointing out the myth of a progressive, predictable continuum of alien rights, and by noting the inconsistent and irregular application of constitutional protections for aliens, that the legal community and other public service organizations will continue to do the truly meritorious work of aggressively protecting aliens' access to justice and demanding nothing less than the full measure of alien rights for individual clients.

6

THE BASICS OF NON-IMMIGRANT AND IMMIGRANT VISA PROCESSING

Stephen R. Pattison[1]

WHAT IS A VISA?

Any discussion of non-immigrant and immigrant visa processing must start with an understanding of what a visa is and what it is not. Since "visa" is nowhere defined in U.S. law or regulation, it is not surprising that this is not as simple as might be expected.

Black's Law Dictionary's definition of "visa" is instructive:

> **Visa.** An official endorsement made out on a passport, denoting that it has been examined and that the bearer is permitted to proceed. A recognition by the country in which the holder of a passport desires to travel of that passport's validity.[2]

An "official endorsement" can take many forms. For many countries, including the United States, it takes the form of a machine-readable foil containing the visa recipient's photograph and biographical details, as

---

1. Stephen Pattison is the owner of the law offices of Stephen R. Pattison, LLC. Steve has more than three decades of experience in immigration law and consular affairs. Bringing a depth and breadth of experience honed in private practice and working for the U.S. Foreign Service, Steve serves as an invaluable resource to clients in consular processing and business immigration matters. Prior to starting his own practice, Steve served as Senior Counsel to the firm of Maggio & Kattar in Washington, DC and was a partner in the firm Neazrath LLC in London, England, following a 28-year career in the U.S. Foreign Service. He served in consular sections around the world, including Beirut, Colombo, Bangkok, Bucharest, Brussels, and his last posting, Berlin, where he was Minister Counselor for Consular Affairs, the senior U.S. consular official in Germany. In Washington, Steve held positions with the Department of State that included the Bureau of Near Eastern Affairs and as country officer for Jamaica and the Bahamas in the Bureau of Latin American and Caribbean Affairs. He also served as head of the Coordination Division in the Visa Office within the Bureau of Consular Affairs.
2. BLACK'S LAW DICTIONARY, 1571 (6th ed. 1990).

well as information about the visa category. But for others (including the United States as recently as the early 1990s), visas are merely stamped in the recipient's passport. And in some instances, even today, a visa can be "endorsed" on a separate piece of paper separate from the recipient's travel document.[3]

"Visa" can also be used as a verb:

> **Visa:** v. tr. 1) to endorse or ratify (a passport); 2) to give a visa to (s.o.).[4]

This means that one can refer to someone as having been "visaed," that is, he or she has been approved by a government official to receive a visa. This can be confusing, but not necessarily misleading, because whether one is talking about a physical marker in a travel document or the process of receiving that marker, the significance is the same—it establishes that an individual traveler has received permission from a government official to travel to his or her country.

U.S. VISA IS PERMISSION TO SEEK ADMISSION TO THE UNITED STATES—NOT PERMISSION TO ENTER

Having a visa does *not* admit the traveler to the country whose officials granted it. This is a crucial distinction that many travelers, and a surprising number of attorneys, fail to recognize. A visa merely grants a traveler the ability to ask a border control officer to admit them to the country that issued the visa to him or her. It does not confirm admissibility, guarantee admission, or create or maintain legal status. Under U.S. law, U.S. Customs and Border Protection (CBP) officers at ports of entry determine whether to admit someone with a valid visa, and once admitted, that person's period of legal stay is determined by the I-94 stamp or entry endorsement in their passport, not the expiration date of their visa. Someone whose period of authorized stay has expired is no longer legally present in the United States, even if their passport holds a valid visa stamp.

---

3. Consular officers may not put visas in travel documents issued by the government of North Korea, and may also occasionally encounter applicants for whom the passport requirement has been waived. In such cases, consuls must instead place the visa foil on DS form 232, "Unrecognized Passport or Waiver Cases." *See* 9 U.S. Dep't of State, Foreign Affairs Manual § 41.113, Procedural Notes, and § 41.113 Exhibit II [hereinafter Foreign Affairs Manual].

4. American Heritage Dictionary of the English Language (4th ed. 2000).

APPLICABLE LAW AND REGULATION GOVERNING NON-IMMIGRANT AND IMMIGRANT VISAS

The Immigration and Nationality Act of 1952 (INA) is the fundamental U.S. statute governing immigrant and non-immigrant visas.[5] The INA is one of the most frequently amended federal statutes and ranks with the Internal Revenue Code in complexity. Not surprisingly, there is an extensive body of federal regulation that reflects this complexity. For purposes of our discussion of immigrant and non-immigrant visa processing, the relevant portions of the Code of Federal Regulations (C.F.R.) are Titles 8 (Subchapter B, Immigration Regulations) and 22 (Subchapter E, Visas).[6]

U.S. Consular officers,[7] who are charged with adjudicating non-immigrant and immigrant visas, also have access to another tool to aid them in interpreting and administering U.S. immigrant and non-immigrant law and regulation—Volume 9 of the Foreign Affairs Manual (9 FAM).[8] 9 FAM is part of a larger sixteen-volume compilation of the laws, regulations, and procedures governing the Department of State's operations both abroad and in the United States. While large portions of 9 FAM replicate the laws and regulations found elsewhere in the U.S.C. and C.F.R., there are also parts that are neither statutory nor regulatory but instead provide guidance to consular officers in processing and adjudicating various categories of visas. A careful reading of the relevant sections of 9 FAM can be very helpful in clarifying the decision-making process followed by an adjudicating consular officer in an individual visa case.

The laws and regulations of the United States governing the issuance and denials of visas are administered outside the United States by U.S. consular officers posted at U.S. embassies and visa-processing consulates around the world.[9] Consular officers adjudicate both non-immigrant and immigrant visa applications.

---

5. Immigration and Nationality Act of 1952, 8 U.S.C. §§ 1101–1778.

6. 8 C.F.R. §§ 100–499 (2010), 22 C.F.R. Parts 40–42.

7. See footnote 9, *infra.*

8. 9 FOREIGN AFFAIRS MANUAL, *supra* note 3, §§ 40, 41, 42, contain the regulations, procedural guidelines, and exhibits governing both non-immigrant and immigrant visa processing.

9. Consular officers are usually career members of the U.S. Foreign Service who have been granted consular commissions by the Deputy Assistant Secretary of State for Visa Services authorizing them to adjudicate visa applications at specific posts outside the United States to which they have been assigned. INA § 101(a)(1) (8 U.S.C. § 1101) defines a consular officer as "any consular, diplomatic, or other officer of employee of the United States designated under regulations prescribed under authority contained in this act, for the purpose of issuing immigrant or non-immigrant visas."

DIFFERENCE BETWEEN NON-IMMIGRANT AND IMMIGRANT VISAS

The INA is not particularly helpful in explaining the difference between non-immigrant and immigrant visas. The term "non-immigrant visa" is not even defined in the INA. Basically, all "aliens," as defined in the INA,[10] are considered to be immigrants unless they fall into the various categories listed in Section 101 (a)(15) of the INA.[11] Accordingly, aliens whose purpose for seeking entry to the United States falls under one of the categories in Section 101 (a)(15) cannot be immigrants. Instead, they are considered to be non-immigrants and require a visa in order to apply for admission.[12] In general, non-immigrants are presumed to be seeking temporary entry to the United States as opposed to permanent entry, which is the principle distinction between non-immigrant and immigrant visas, although it is also—and confusingly—the case that some categories of non-immigrant visas can be issued to persons who are seeking to enter the United States permanently.

By contrast, the INA does define "immigrant visa" as meaning "an immigrant visa required by this Act and properly issued by a consular officer at his or her office outside of the United States to an eligible immigrant under the provisions of this Act."[13] Immigrant visas, therefore, are the visas that consular officers are authorized to issue to aliens seeking to enter the United States *as immigrants* on a permanent basis.

WHO REQUIRES A NON-IMMIGRANT VISA?

The U.S. non-immigrant visa system is purpose driven—that is, it is the purpose for which entry is being sought that determines whether a visa is required and, if so, which category. There are several key exceptions to

---

10. *Id.* § 101(a)(3): "The term alien means any person not a citizen or national of the United States."

11. *Id.* § 101(a)(15) identifies aliens who are not immigrants by their purposes for seeking entry to the United States. The alphabetic subcategories of this Section from A to V correspond to the various categories of non-immigrant visas that can be issued by consular officers.

12. A significant exception to this requirement involves citizen of the 36 countries that currently are eligible for visa-free entry to the United States for temporary business and tourist visits for up to 90 days under the terms of the Visa Waiver Program. See footnote 13 *infra*.

13. INA § 101(a)(16).

this rule. The Visa Waiver Program[14] identifies citizens from a number of countries that have traditionally had very low rates of visa overstay as being eligible for visa free entry to the United States for certain business and tourist visits.[15] Because most entries to the United States are for business or tourism, this means that the large majority of travelers who are citizens of visa waiver countries do not require visas to be admitted to the United States.

Persons from all countries, including those participating in the Visa Waiver Program, whose purpose for seeking admission involves one of the listed criteria in INA § 101(a)(15) will require a visa, as well as persons whose business and tourist travel involves a stay of more than 90 days. There are some key exceptions to this requirement. Citizens of Canada do not require visas in most instances[16] and are authorized to seek admission at the port of entry for many non-immigrant purposes which otherwise would require them to have a visa. Citizens of the Bahamas are also authorized to enter the United States as temporary visitors for business and tourism without visas under a separate agreement that is not part of the Visa Waiver Program, while Mexican citizens who possess a Border Crossing Card are authorized to make visa free business and tourism entries across southern land and sea borders so long as they remain within a specific distance of the border itself.[17]

WHO REQUIRES AN IMMIGRANT VISA?

All persons seeking admission to the United States as permanent residents must first obtain an immigrant visa from a U.S. embassy or visa-issuing consulate. There are a few exceptions to this requirement. Persons

---

14. *See id.* § 217.

15. 9 FOREIGN AFFAIRS MANUAL, *supra* note 3, § 41.2 Exhibit II identifies the following countries whose citizens are eligible to enter without visas under the VWP: Andorra, Australia, Austria, Belgium, Brunei, Czech Republic, Denmark, Estonia, Finland, France, Germany, Greece, Hungary, Iceland, Ireland, Italy, Japan, Latvia, Liechtenstein, Lithuania, Luxembourg, Malta, Monaco, Netherlands, New Zealand, Norway, Portugal, Republic of Korea, San Marino, Singapore, Slovak Republic, Slovenia, Spain, Sweden, Switzerland, United Kingdom.

16. The only non-immigrant visa categories that Canadian citizens are *required* to obtain are the E treaty trader/investor visa, the K fiancee visa, the S visa for persons providing information about a criminal organization or enterprise or terrorist organizations or activities, and the V visa for certain spouses and children of LPRs whose immigrant petitions have been pending for three or more years.

17. 8 C.F.R. § 212(c).

who seek to enter the United States as the fiancées of a U.S. citizen, whom it can be presumed intend to remain in the United States as permanent residents, must first obtain a K non-immigrant fiancée visa.[18] And persons who have immigrant intent can nonetheless qualify for and be issued certain kinds of non-immigrant visas for which immigrant intent is not a bar to issuance, so long as their primary purpose for seeking entry is not to obtain permanent residence.[19] Such individuals, like K visa recipients, must apply to adjust their non-immigrant status to that of permanent residence after their admissions.

There are three categories of immigrant visas—family-based, employment-related, and diversity lottery. Family-based immigration visas are available to certain relatives of U.S. citizens and permanent residents. Depending on the relationships involved, these can be either immediate relative (for which there are no statutory limitations on issuances) or family preference (for which the numbers of visas that can be issued each year are limited by statute) visas. Employment-related visas are available for professionals, skilled workers, and other workers based on offers of employment or outstanding professional credentials, including certain kinds of investors.[20] Diversity visas are available to persons who participate successfully in the State Department's annual visa lottery draw.[21]

WHERE DOES ONE APPLY FOR A U.S. VISA?

U.S. immigrant and non-immigrant visas are issued by consular officers working in consular sections in U.S. embassies and visa-issuing consulates around the world. Nearly all U.S. embassies have consular sections

---

18. INA § 101(a)(15)(K). The fact that the K visa is actually a non-immigrant visa causes considerable confusion, especially as they are usually processed by the immigrant visa unit of a consular section.
19. *Id.* § 214(b), specifically exempts V and L visa applicants, as well as H visa applicants, other than those applying under the terms of the Chilean and Singaporean-U.S. Free Trade agreements, from exclusion for having immigrant intent.
20. Both family preference and employment-related immigrant visas are subject to an immensely complex scheme of annual allocation that is administered by the Department of State and takes into account worldwide, country-specific, and category specific limitations on the number of visas that can be issued each year. *See id.* §§ 201–203.
21. *Id.* §§ 201(e), 203(c). The diversity visa lottery makes 55,000 immigrant visa numbers available each year to persons from specified countries who have submitted an electronic lottery application. Lottery entrants do not have to have a qualifying family relationship or an offer of employment in order to be selected.

that process both immigrant and non-immigrant visas.[22] The use of the term "visa issuing consulate" highlights an important point, namely that some U.S. consulates do not provide any visa services at all.[23]

Persons who are applying for non-immigrant visas must be physically present and should be resident in the country or consular district where they are applying. A consular officer cannot put a visa foil in the passport of someone who is not physically present in his or her district— a subject that often comes up when a parent seeks to obtain a visa for a minor child who is not actually in the country where the application is presented. There is no statutory requirement that non-immigrant visa applicants must apply only in their country of residence. However, consuls have discretion whether or not to accept such "third country national" (TCN) visa applicants, and some consular sections will not accept out-of-country visa applicants due to space and resource limitations. Depending on the circumstances, exceptions can sometimes be made to this on a case-by-case basis. Applicants who are physically present but do not actually reside in the country or district where they are applying are frequently at a disadvantage at the visa interview because a consul in a country where the applicant does not reside is going to have a harder time evaluating that applicant's personal, economic, or professional ties to a residence in another country than would a consular officer working in the applicant's country of residence. For this reason, TCN applications should be discouraged and limited only to applicants with legitimate reasons for applying outside of their country of residence and clearly lack immigrant intent.

Immigrant visa applicants generally must apply for their visas at the embassy or consulate that has jurisdiction over their place of *residence* abroad. However, applicants who are present in but not normally resident in a consular district can apply for their immigrant visa at the consular section with jurisdiction over their location. Moreover, consular officers have discretion to accept an immigrant visa application from someone who neither resides in nor is physically present in their district.[24]

---

22. There are, however, some U.S. embassies which do not process immigrant visas and others that do not process either immigrant or most kinds of non-immigrant visas. This is often the case in countries where the political capital is not the commercial capital or the largest population center, such as Australia, Canada, or Brazil. A quick check of a specific embassy website will reveal the kinds of visa services provided by the embassy.

23. There is a growing trend towards eliminating non-immigrant visa processing in smaller consulates and centralizing immigrant visa processing in countries with more than one visa issuing consulate, such as Italy, where immigrant visas are processed in Naples, and Germany, where all immigrant visas are processed by the consulate in Frankfurt.

24. *See* 22 C.F.R. § 42.61. The Department of State may also direct a consular officer to

STEPS FOR APPLYING FOR A NON-IMMIGRANT VISA

The first step in the process of applying for a visa requires a determination of the purpose for which the applicant seeks to enter the United States in order to identify the visa category for which he or she must apply, as well as the preliminary steps that must be taken and the documents that must be acquired before the application can be presented. The complexity of U.S. visa law and regulation places uninformed visa applicants at a real disadvantage in addressing the question of why they seek entry to the United States. Most U.S. embassy and consulate websites will include brief summaries of the various non-immigrant visa categories, but there is ample room for confusion and error by applicants in identifying the visa category that fits their specific purpose for entry.

The twenty-two non-immigrant visa categories currently authorized under the INA can broadly be broken down into several categories: (1) government officials, or international organization employees and their families and staffs (A and G visas); (2) persons traveling for business or pleasure who require a visa to do so (B visas); (3) persons coming for training, education, or recognized exchange-visitor programs (F, J, and M visas); (4) persons in transit or crew members joining a ship or airplane (C and D visas); (5) persons seeking entry to invest or to perform certain kinds of authorized work (E, I, H, L, O, P, R, TN).[25] The role of counsel in assisting persons who wish to apply for entry to the United States, therefore, involves a careful preliminary analysis of the purpose for travel to determine under which non-immigrant visa category the intended activity can be performed, if at all.

In addition to the required visa, applicants for certain work authorizing non-immigrant visas, students, and exchange visitors must also obtain additional documentation before their visa applications can be processed. For example, most applicants seeking to enter the United States to work must receive prior approval from the U.S. Citizenship and Immigration Services (USCIS) division of the Department of Homeland Security in the form of an approved Form I-129 Petition for Non-immigrant Worker filed on his or her behalf by a prospective employer, before they can receive the

---

accept jurisdiction over the immigrant visa case of someone not present or residing in the consul's district. Applicants who are in the United States are usually considered to have been residents of the jurisdiction that they left to enter the country.

25. Of the remaining non-immigrant visa categories (K, N, S T U, and V) only the K fiancée visa is likely to be frequently encountered.

visa they require.[26] In each instance, failure to obtain the required documents prior to the visa interview will result in the visa being denied.

SCHEDULE THE VISA APPOINTMENT

Consular sections now only allow visa applicants to make electronic appointments, which enables them to manage their work flows more efficiently. However, for busy visa processing posts, the downside is the often lengthy delays before an appointment slot is available, especially during peak travel seasons. The State Department's Travel.state.gov website has information about appointment wait times for specific embassies and consulates.[27]

There are procedures for emergency and expedited visa appointments although these may vary from post to post. Usually in order to request an expedited appointment the applicant must first schedule an appointment for the first available slot and pay the machine readable visa (MRV) fee before a request to expedite can be considered. The MRV fee is a nonrefundable processing fee that must be paid by all visa applicants whether or not the visa is approved.

COMPLETE THE ONLINE DS-160 VISA APPLICATION

The State Department no longer accepts the paper DS-156, 157, or 158 visa applications and now requires all visa applicants to submit the DS-160 online electronic visa application form, which can be accessed on the State Department's website.[28] After a rough launch, the DS-160 system now operates reasonably well. The form must be submitted along with an upload of the applicant's photograph, and can only be electronically signed and submitted by the applicant himself or herself. The DS-160 can be submitted at any point prior to the applicant's scheduled appointment

---

26. E trader investor visas allow the holders to work in the United States but do not require prior approval of an I-129 petition; journalists may work in the United States only when in possession of an I visa, which also does not require an approved I-129; TN treaty nationals from Mexico and Canada may work in the United States in certain specified fields with a TN visa and do not require an approved I-129 petition.
27. http://travel.state.gov/visa/temp/wait/wait_4638.html.
28. https://ceac.state.gov/genniv/. Note, however, that most posts are still requiring applicants for E1/E2 treaty trader investor visas to submit the old paper supplemental form DS 156E when applying for E visas.

and does not have to be submitted at the same time that the visa appointment is made.

DETERMINE THE DOCUMENTARY REQUIREMENTS FOR THE VISA

In many instances the only *required* documentation that a visa applicant need present at his or her visa interview is a valid travel document/ passport and a copy of the confirmation sheet confirming submission of the electronic visa application and payment of the MRV fee. There is no requirement, for instance, that someone traveling to the United States on business present a letter from companies or business colleagues in the United States, nor does someone seeking to travel on tourism need to present a confirmed hotel reservation or itinerary. For such applicants, the primary reason for providing supplementary documentation is to satisfy the concerns that the consul may have about their individual ties to a residence abroad, but it bears repeating: there is *no* required list of such evidence that must be presented in order for the applicant to qualify for visa issuance.

That said, there are other non-immigrant visa categories that do have additional documentary requirements.[29] Some of these have been previously noted. Persons applying for petition-based work-authorizing non-immigrant visas will need to present a copy of the I-797 approval notice for the petition as evidence that USCIS has evaluated them and their qualifications and confirmed their eligibility for visa issuance, even though confirmation of petition issuance should normally be available to the consul through the PIMS system.[30] These applicants should also present a copy of the approved petition submission itself in case the consul has any questions about their employment and credentials. Although both issues should have been fully evaluated by USCIS in adjudicating the petition,

---

29. The best place to find information on documentary requirements for visa categories is the website of the embassy or consulate where the applicant will be applying. Most websites contain a link to the visa section, which will list the requirements for specific visa categories.
30. PIMS stands for "Petition Information Management Service." USCIS is required to send confirmation of petition approvals to the State Department's Kentucky Service Center, which then enters the approval in PIMS. Consuls conduct PIMS checks on all petition-based non-immigrant visa applicants to confirm that their petitions have been approved. Despite PIMS, as noted, many consular sections still ask for the applicant to present a copy of the I-797 petition approval notice.

consuls have the right to question the applicant further and will do so if they have any concerns that the petition may have been approved in error or that the applicant is not qualified for the position being offered to them.

F-1 student visa applicants must present evidence that they have been accepted by a degree-granting institution authorized to accept foreign students in the form of an I-20 issued and signed by the school. The I-20 will confirm that the student has been accepted and can pay his or her anticipated expenses. The applicant must also present a SEVIS (Student and Exchange Visitor Information System) receipt showing payment of this fee, which must be paid by all prospective foreign students and exchange visitors to cover the costs of the system that tracks foreign students and exchange visitors in the United States. Students are not required to present evidence that they can pay for their education, but should be prepared to do so, as consuls will want to know if the applicant and his or her family are capable of paying for his or her education without being at risk of having to work without authorization.

In addition to confirmation of payment of the SEVIS fee, J exchange visitor applicants must present a signed form DS 2019 from their program sponsor, which confirms that the program in which they wish to participate has been approved by the Department of State. The DS 2019 will also indicate whether the applicant will be subject to the INA section 212(e) two-year residency requirement that mandates their return to their country of residence for at least two years before they can apply to be admitted to the United States permanently.

WHAT HAPPENS ON THE DAY OF THE INTERVIEW ITSELF?

Once a visa applicant has made an appointment and has received a confirmed time to come to the embassy, they should appear at the appointed time at the entrance to the embassy or consulate (usually there will be a separate entrance for visa applicants) with their passport, appointment confirmation printout, and any required or optional supporting documents. Most visa sections will admit applicants in half-hour intervals, which allow time for in-processing through security and prevents the visa waiting room from becoming overcrowded. Although each embassy and consular section will be differently configured (some will house the consular section in a separate facility from the main chancery), the process of being admitted will be approximately the same. Applicants will be asked to produce their passports and appointment confirmation, then will be processed through security, which involves their going through a metal detector. Items that may not be brought into the building, such as mobile phones, laptops, large pieces of luggage or backpacks, and liquids, will be identified at this point. Because most embassies do not provide adequate storage for personal items, these should not be brought to the interview. If an applicant has an item that they cannot bring with them to the interview they will usually be given an opportunity to leave it off site and return without having to lose their appointment slot. Once the applicant has passed successfully through security, they will follow the signs directing them to the visa waiting room.

INSIDE THE CONSULAR SECTION

No consular section is exactly like another, although they all share certain features in common, and while the physical setup may vary, the process the applicant follows in each consular section is pretty much the same. If the consular section is busy enough to require electronic crowd control measures, the applicant, upon entering the section, will be given a number by a local member of the staff that will follow them through the application process. This number, for example, will be displayed on a Queuematic or other electronic numbering system to identify the service window that the applicant should approach, and when.

The document intake process is the first step that the applicant encounters after being admitted and obtaining a number. When the applicant's number is first called, it directs him to a designated window where he or she will be instructed to hand in their documents and passport. The document intake process is usually handled by a locally engaged staff employee, who will confirm the visa category for which the applicant is applying and examine the documents briefly to confirm that the applicant has brought with him or her the items that the consul will require to adjudicate the visa. The appointment can be terminated at this point if the applicant has not brought a required document, or has an expired or damaged passport, or has not properly completed and submitted the DS 160. Assuming all is in order with the documents; the applicant will then be guided to submit their biometric fingerprints, will be photographed, and will be asked to have a seat in the waiting area. Some time thereafter, the applicant's number will be displayed a second time, directing them to a different window, at which a consular officer will conduct the actual visa interview.

WHAT TAKES PLACE AT THE NON-IMMIGRANT VISA INTERVIEW?

There are many misconceptions about what takes place at a non-immigrant visa interview. Many of these stem from a fundamental misunderstanding of the purpose of the visa interview itself. Contrary to popular belief, the interview is not an inquisition nor is it necessarily an adversarial process. Rather, it is a two-step process whereby a consular officer first determines the intended purpose for which an alien seeks to enter the United States and then further determines if the alien has satisfied the requirements under the law to be authorized to seek admission with the appropriate visa.[31] The consul's questions are designed to gather information as to the purpose of travel and then determine the eligibility of the applicant to accomplish that purpose with the visa for which the applicant applies.

Occasionally an applicant will apply for a visa that does *not* allow them to perform the activity that they wish to undertake in the United States, but most of the time the consular officer will not need to challenge the purpose for which the applicant seeks entry to the United States, as this will be self-evident by virtue of the visa category for which they are applying. In practice this means that for most visa interviews the majority of the consul's questions are designed to determine whether the applicant is documentarily and legally eligible to be issued the visa.

WHAT KIND OF QUESTIONS DOES THE CONSUL ASK?

Usually the first question that the consul poses to the visa applicant will be something like "What is your purpose for entering the United States" or "Why do you want to go to the United States?" This gives the applicant the opportunity to explain why he or she has made the visa appointment and what they want to do in the United States. The consul will already know from the electronic visa application why the applicant is standing before him—so the purpose of the question is as much to enable the consul to evaluate the demeanor of the applicant as it is to get a specific

---

31. See INA § 222(h), which sets forth the requirement that most persons between the age of 14 and 79 be interviewed in person by a consular officer before a visa may be issued to them. There are limited exceptions to this requirement where consular officers can waive personal appearance by visa applicants, such as by applicants for diplomatic or official visas. Consular authority to waive personal appearance was significantly restricted after the terrorist attacks on September 11, 2001.

answer. After the initial questions, the consul will focus more intently on determining eligibility by confirming whether the documentary requirements have been met.

Once it is clear that the applicant is applying for the right visa and has satisfied the documentary requirements (which can occur very early in the interview), the consul's inquiry will usually turn to the question of the applicant's ties to a residence abroad—which most non-immigrant visa applicants must demonstrate before a visa can be issued to them.[32] If immigrant intent is an issue for the consul, the questions will focus on finding out what kind of personal, professional, and economic ties the applicant has to their overseas residence. The consul can also ask the applicant how long he or she intends to be in the United States and what they will do once their visit has ended. In each of these instances, the way in which the applicant answers the questions and addresses the consul's concerns about immigrant intent can be just as important as the actual evidence they present of their "home ties."

If the applicant has acknowledged any past problems with law enforcement, or any prior extended or unauthorized stays in the United States, the consul will seek to determine what took place and whether the applicant's circumstances involve any potential grounds of inadmissibility under U.S. law. If the consul uncovers any information at the interview that casts the applicant's assertions about the purpose of his travel or his ties to a residence abroad into doubt, the consul can pursue this by further questioning the applicant and evaluating the credibility of his explanation.

WHAT DECISIONS WILL THE CONSUL MAKE?

Most visa interviews last three to four minutes or less, and at the end of the interview, the consul will advise the applicant of his or her decision. A consul can do several things at the end of the interview. If the applicant has applied for the appropriate visa, has met the requirements, has overcome immigrant intent, and is not otherwise inadmissible under U.S. law, the consul will electronically approve the visa and will determine the period of validity and the number of entries that the visa will allow. If applicant has not met the documentary requirements but has overcome the statutory presumption of being an intending immigrant, the consul can refuse him under INA § 221(g) and ask him to send in the missing documents at a later date. If the consul finds the applicant has met the

---

32. INA § 214B, which creates the statutory presumption of being an intending immigrant, is discussed in more detail below.

requirements for the visa being applied for but has not overcome the statutory presumption of being an intending immigrant, he or she will deny the applicant under INA § 214(b). And if the consul finds the applicant has satisfied the documentary requirements and has overcome § 214(b) but is inadmissible under some other provision of U.S. law, the consul will deny the visa under that provision of the law. In each of these instances, the consul is required to provide the applicant with written notification that the visa has been denied and the statutory basis for the decision.[33] If the applicant is found inadmissible under a provision of the INA for which there is waiver relief available, the consul will advise the applicant of this and explain how the applicant can request the waiver.

All non-immigrant visa applicants are subject to mandatory security name checks through the consular data base before a visa can be issued to them. If an applicant's name check results in a possible "hit," the applicant will be told at the completion of his or her visa interview that visa issuance has been delayed pending further "administrative processing." If this happens, the consul will return the applicant's passport and advise him to wait until he has been instructed to send it back in for visa issuance. In most instances, administrative processing results in an additional delay in visa issuance of anywhere from a few days to several weeks. Administrative processing does not mean the applicant has not qualified for visa issuance or will be denied, but that the consul cannot approve any visa application until all required clearances have been received.

If the visa has been approved, the applicant will be instructed to pay the courier return fee and leave his passport with the consular section for the visa foil to be placed in it. If there are any additional issuance fees that approved applicants must pay, they will be collected by the cashier at this time. Usually it takes from three to five days for the consular section to print and place the visa foils in the successful applicant's passport and return them by courier to the applicant.

Section 214(b) Denials

It is impossible to make sense of many consular visa adjudications without an understanding of the operation of § 214(b) of the INA. Section 214 of the INA is one of the longer sections of the act and deals with the admission of non-immigrants; it establishes the premise that aliens seeking admission as non-immigrants (with a few exceptions) are presumed

---

33. 9 Foreign Affairs Manual, *supra* note 3, § 40.6 Exhibits II, III, and IV provide examples of refusal letters consular officers must fill out, sign, and submit to persons who have been denied visas.

to actually be immigrants unless they can establish *"to the satisfaction of a consular officer"* that they are entitled to a non-immigrant visa under one of the categories set forth in INA section 101(a)(15).[34] Section 214(b) is the source of the consular officer's powerful authority to deny a non-immigrant visa to any applicant whom has not been able to persuade him of his non-immigrant status.

Section 214(b) is a troublesome provision, both because of what it is and what it is not. In the first place, § 214(b) is *not* an independent statutory requirement for visa issuance; satisfying § 214B by demonstrating lack of immigrant intent will not serve to qualify a non-immigrant visa applicant for visa issuance if the applicant has not otherwise demonstrated visa eligibility under INA § 101(a)(15). Section 214(b) also does *not* impose a general statutory requirement to demonstrate lack of immigrant intent—as is evidenced by the fact that for several categories of non-immigrant visas it is not applicable.[35] What § 214(b) actually does is to create a basis for the refusal of a visa application when the applicant is required to demonstrate a residence abroad he or she does not intend to abandon, but has not been able to do so. Because it is not a statutory grounds of inadmissibility, § 214(b) is not a bar to future visa issuance and can be overcome at a subsequent visa interview.

Consular officers have come up with a variety of ways to describe the application of § 214(b) to a specific visa case. Among the more common of these are "failure to demonstrate a residence abroad you do not intend to abandon," "failure to demonstrate strong ties to a residence abroad," and "failure to overcome the presumption that you are an intending immigrant." What these have in common is their emphasis on the applicant's inability to show strong connections to an overseas residence as being the best measure of whether the applicant has immigrant intent and, therefore, is subject to § 214(b). Of necessity, the evaluation of an applicant's ties to a residence abroad—and the underlying intentions that the applicant has in applying for a visa in the first place—is subjective on the part of the consular officer. Thus, an applicant who may have well-demonstrated

---

34. Because of its central role in consular decision making, it is worth quoting the relevant portions of INA § 214(b): "Every alien (other than a non-immigrant described in subparagraph (L) or (V) or section 101 (a)(15), and other than a non-immigrant described in any provision of section 101 (a)(15)(H)(i) except sub-clause (b1) of such section) shall be presumed to be an immigrant until he establishes to the satisfaction of the consular officer, at the time of application for a visa, and the immigration officers, at the time of application for admission, that he is entitled to a non-immigrant status under section 101 (a)(15)."

35. Only B, F, H (except H-1) J, M, O-2, P, and Q visas have a requirement that the applicant demonstrate a residence abroad that he or she does not intend to abandon. *See* 9 Foreign Affairs Manual, *supra* note 3, § 41.11 N.2.1.

and tangible ties to their country of residence—employment, family members, property ownership, money in the bank—may nonetheless still fail to qualify for visa issuance if the consul is not persuaded that he intends to depart the United States after a temporary visit. The contrary is also true—an individual applicant may not appear to have strong reasons to return to a residence abroad, and still be able to persuade the consul that he or she has no immigrant intent. The subjective nature of visa adjudications when it comes to the question of § 214(b) is a constant irritation for immigration practitioners. What is not always recognized is that it is equally troubling for many consular officers and managers.

Overcoming § 214(b) involves no "bright line" standards. In general, applicants who are married, well grounded professionally, have traveled before outside their home country or to the United States, and have credible reasons for travel will have an easier time of overcoming § 214(b) than someone who is single, unemployed or only recently employed, has never traveled abroad, and has difficulty articulating the reasons for their travel to the United States Other factors that consuls will consider include the presence or lack of family ties in the United States and circumstances in the applicant's country of residence. Thus, even a well-employed and well-grounded applicant from a country undergoing significant political or economic turmoil will have a harder time overcoming § 214(b) than someone from a stable country which is economically thriving or growing.

Many visa applicants make the mistake of concluding that documentary evidence of their ties to a residence abroad will carry the day in rebutting immigrant intent. This is misleading, in that ultimately consuls evaluate the *applicant*, not his or her documents. However, to the extent that documentary evidence of ties to a residence abroad can reinforce an applicant's statements, it is a good idea to have these available at the visa interview. When visa applicants are not able to present such evidence at their interviews, either because they forgot to bring it or because it was not available at that time, returning for a new interview with new or additional evidence of ties that were not available at the first interview can help them to overcome § 214(b) and lead to visa issuance. Consuls will not hold earlier visa denials against an applicant with such new evidence. However, when an applicant returns with nothing new to present, just to "try again," this will rarely succeed and creates an impression of desperation that makes it even harder for the applicant to show lack of immigrant intent.

Statutory Grounds of Inadmissibility

As previously noted, persons can overcome § 214(b) and yet still be denied a non-immigrant visa. The most common basis for visa denial for someone who has overcome § 214(b) is INA § 221(g).[36] Section 221(g) denials result when the applicant fails to demonstrate they meet the requirement for the visa they seek, either by lack of documentation or by failure to show that they have satisfied one of more of the requisites for visa issuance. For example, someone applying for a student visa whose I-20 has expired will be refused under section 221(g) and advised to return with a new, valid I-20. Similarly, an applicant who has applied for an L visa but whom the consul discovers has not worked for the transferring company outside the United States for more than one year will also be denied under this section. In both instances, the refusal can be overcome relatively easily, but the consul's decision is still a refusal and must be acknowledged as such by the applicant in future visa applications.

The principle statutory bases for visa denial are found in subsection (a) of INA § 212, Excludable Aliens.[37] Under § 212(a), a visa applicant can be deemed inadmissible on health-related grounds (§ 212(a)(1)), criminal and related grounds (§ 212(a)(2)), security and related grounds (§ 212(a)(3)), for being likely to become a public charge (§ 212(a)(4)), for seeking entry to work without authorization from the Department of Labor (§ 212(a)(5)), for having entered the United States illegally or violated U.S. immigration laws in doing so (§ 212(a)(6)), for lacking proper documentation (§ 212(a)(7)), for being ineligible for citizenship (§ 212)(a)(8)), for having been previously removed or unlawfully present in the United States. (§ 212(a)(9)), or for certain "miscellaneous" grounds (§ 212(a)(10)), including being a practicing polygamist, an unlawful voter, or someone who renounced U.S. citizenship to avoid taxation.

Many of the grounds of inadmissibility in § 212(a) are rarely encountered. The most commonly imposed § 212(a) findings of inadmissibility are those based on criminal, health, and security grounds, those based on

---

36. INA § 221 deals with the issuance of visas; § 221(g) sets forth the circumstances when a visa may not be issued. As written it covers all instances when the consul believes or has reason to believe that the alien is not eligible for visa issuance including under § 212(a), but a § 221(g) finding where it appears to the consul that the applicant is ineligible for visa issuance under § 212(a) is not the same thing as a finding of ineligibility under that section. Consuls will sometimes deny an applicant under § 221(g) rather than pursue a § 212(a) finding because they lack sufficient evidence to confirm ineligibility at the time of the visa interview.

37. There are a few other statutory bases for findings of inadmissibility in INA § 212. Section 212(f) concerns individuals who are inadmissible under the president's authority to declare certain classes of individuals inadmissible when their admission would be detrimental to the U.S. Section 212(e) prevents certain exchange visitor visa recipients from receiving H or L non-immigrant visas or immigrant status until they have satisfied the two-year residency requirement in their home country after the completion of their exchange visit.

misrepresentations or immigration violations, and those based on previous removal from or unlawful presence in the United States. It is beyond the scope of this chapter to address in detail the various circumstances whereby a finding of § 212(a) inadmissibility can be imposed. Suffice it to say that determining inadmissibility is one of the more challenging aspects of consular work, and cases where a consular determination of inadmissibility has been made warrant careful examination to ensure that the finding is based on an accurate interpretation of the laws and regulations.

Waiver Relief

The INA makes provision for waiver relief of inadmissibility for both non-immigrant and immigrant visa applicants. This is a highly complex area and made even more challenging by the fact that certain statutory grounds of inadmissibility can be waived for non-immigrants but not for immigrants, while others apply only to immigrants and not non-immigrants. The statutory basis for the temporary admission of most inadmissible *non-immigrants* is INA § 212(d)(3)(A).[38] Statutory authority for waiver relief for inadmissible *immigrant* visa applicants can be found in INA § 212(g) (health related inadmissibility), § 212(h) (certain criminal and related grounds), § 212(a)(3)(D)(iv) (certain members of totalitarian parties), § 212(i) (certain aliens inadmissible for fraud or misrepresentation), and § 212(d)(11) (for certain aliens inadmissible for alien smuggling).

Waiver relief can be requested by an individual only after it has been determined by a consular officer that he or she is inadmissible under a provision of the INA for which waiver relief is available for non-immigrant or immigrant aliens. For most persons, this will take place following the conclusion of their non-immigrant or immigrant visa interview before a consular official, but there are circumstances when someone can request waiver relief from CBP upon arrival at a U.S. port of entry upon arrival or from USCIS when the individual has been admitted to the United States and subsequently found to be inadmissible. Persons seeking to adjust

---

38. INA § 212(d)(3)(A) authorizes waiver relief for non-immigrant aliens inadmissible under most but not all grounds of INA § 212(a); see footnote 9, *infra*. Additional authorization for waiver relief for non-immigrants inadmissible under § 212(a)(7)(B) for not having a passport valid for at least six months from the initial period of admission or proposed stay or a valid border-crossing card is found in § 212(d)(4). Aliens seeking L or H non-immigrant visas who are inadmissible because they are subject to the two-year foreign residence requirement as former exchange visitor can request waiver relief under § 212(e).

status to refugee or asylum status can also request waiver relief for most statutory grounds of inadmissibility.[39]

The consular officer's role in waiver cases is widely misunderstood. Waiver relief is granted upon request by the Secretary of the Department of Homeland Security, not the Secretary of State, and consuls have no authority to approve or deny a waiver request or to refuse to submit it to DHS for consideration. However, the consul does have discretion whether or not to submit the waiver request to DHS with a favorable recommendation that the waiver be approved. In practice, DHS is highly unlikely to approve a waiver request that the adjudicating consular officer does *not* recommend be approved. In determining whether to approve a request for waiver relief, DHS follows a three-step inquiry, initially set forth in the 1978 Board of Immigration Appeals case *Matter of Hranka*,[40] that considers the risk of harm to society if the applicant is admitted, the seriousness of the applicant's violation of the INA, and his or her reasons for seeking entry to the United States. Consular officers will also consider the *Hranka* standards in determining whether or not to recommend approval of an individual waiver request.

If the waiver request is granted, the non-immigrant visa that the applicant receives will contain an annotation confirming that the appropriate statutory waiver has been authorized. The fact that a waiver has been granted is no guarantee that a subsequent waiver request will be approved, but in most instances, applicants granted waiver relief who have honored the terms of their visas and not engaged in further activities that would render them inadmissible will be able to obtain subsequent waivers. Most initial waivers are approved for one entry. In some instances, applicants who request further waivers will be able to obtain authorization to make multiple entries with the waiver.

One commonly overlooked aspect of waiver cases is the fact that only non-immigrant visa applicants who have successfully overcome § 214(b) are eligible for waiver relief. A consular officer does not need to determine if an applicant is inadmissible if he believes that the applicant has failed to overcome the presumption of being an intending immigrant.

---

39. A particularly helpful guide for practitioners working on consular processing waiver cases can be found in 9 Foreign Affairs Manual, *supra* note 3, § 40.6 Exhibit 1, which contains a 23-page chart listing the classes of inadmissibility under INA § 212, identifies whether waiver relief is available under each for non-immigrants and immigrants, provides the statutory basis for both NIV and IV waiver relief, and further describes the factors that must be considered by consular officers in processing specific waiver requests.
40. 16 I. & N. Dec. 491 (B.I.A. 1978).

WHAT HAPPENS AFTER THE VISA IS APPROVED?

The adjudicating consul will advise the non-immigrant visa applicant at the completion of the visa interview whether his or her application has been approved. If the visa is approved, the consul will advise the applicant whether or not there are any additional fees that must be collected. If so, the applicant will be instructed to pay the additional fees at the cashier's window and obtain a receipt. What happens after that will vary from post to post, depending on how busy the consular section is and the reliability of the host country's postal system.

Printing and inserting the visa foils in the passports of persons whose applications have been approved is labor-intensive, and consular sections are simply unable to take care of this while the officers and staff are still interviewing visa applicants. In the past, successful applicants were told to leave their passports and to return in the afternoon to receive them back with their visas. This proved impractical at high-volume visa posts, where visa interviewing would drag on well into the afternoon, making it impossible to free up enough personnel to print and insert that day's approved visa foils by the end of the day. These posts were the first to adopt what has now become standard for most consular sections—the use of private courier or government postal delivery services to return passports and visas to applicants. In some consular sections, the service will be co-located within the consular section; in others, applicants are instructed to bring with them pre-authorized and paid postal delivery envelopes, and turn them into the section along with their passports. In both instances, this builds in additional processing time that must be taken into account by applicants in making their travel plans. Posts in countries which have unreliable mail delivery services or where there are no dependable courier services will still allow applicants to return to the consular section after a specific period of time to collect their passports and visas.

Consular sections rarely make mistakes in printing visas, but it does happen, so applicants should be careful to examine their visa foils when they receive back their passports to make certain their names have been correctly spelled, the other data on the visa foil is correct, and they have been issued the correct visa.

COMMON MISCONCEPTIONS ABOUT APPROVED VISAS

Certain aspects of visa processing and issuance are particularly confusing for visa applicants. One of the more common sources of confusion concerns the period of the visa foil's validity. An applicant who requests a visa valid for multiple entries and five years and whose application is approved can be surprised to receive back a visa valid for only one entry, three months. Rarely is this a mistake on the part of the consular officer. Many applicants fail to recognize that visa issuance in many countries is subject to reciprocity restrictions—that is, U.S. regulations restrict the period of validity and numbers of entries that can be granted to an applicant to those that would be granted to a U.S. citizen applying for the same kind of visa to enter the applicant's country of citizenship. Reciprocity also applies to fees: citizens of countries that levy additional fees on U.S. citizens for specific visa categories will have to pay additional visa fees when they apply for comparable U.S. visas.[41]

Many applicants also mistakenly assume that having a valid visa means they will be admitted to the United States. A valid U.S. visa is not an admissions stamp—it simply indicates that a consular officer has evaluated the applicant and has concluded that they are eligible to apply to be admitted. However, only DHS has the authority to admit or deny admission to an alien at the port of entry, and CBP officers can and do deny entry to persons holding valid visas if they determine that the alien is not admissible, either for having the incorrect visa, or for any other reason under the INA, including § 214(b).

A final area of confusion involves the period of authorized stay granted to the alien when he or she is admitted by CBP. The length of the validity of the visa has no relationship to the period of authorized stay. Someone with an E visa, for example, that will expire six months after they apply to enter can be admitted by CBP for longer than that six-month period—in some instances, up to two years. Similarly, a student visa holder whose visa expires after one year can be admitted by CBP for "duration of status," which means for as long as he or she remains in valid student status. In both instances, the fact that the visa used to gain admission expires has *no* impact on the alien's status in the United States if they are still within the period of authorized stay granted to them by CBP and stamped on their I-94 when they are admitted.[42] The corollary is true—someone in the United States whose period of authorized stay

---

41. The State Department maintains the Visa Reciprocity Schedule. Country-specific information about the period of validity and number of entries for visas issued to nationals of those countries as well as the additional fees, if any, that they must pay, can be found on the department's website, www.travel.state.gov.

42. CBP officials no longer provide paper I-94 forms to admitted aliens arriving by air and sea. The information previously included on the I-94 is now available to aliens on CBP's website (www.cbp.gov). Persons entering the United States across a land border will still receive a paper I-94 from CBP upon their admission.

expires *before* their visa does is no longer legally present in the United States once that happens, regardless of when their visa foil expires.

IMMIGRANT VISA PROCESSING

Immigrant visa processing is significantly different from non-immigrant visa processing and in most consular sections is handled by a separate "IV unit."[43] Any discussion about current immigrant visa processing must take place with the understanding that long-standing procedures followed by IV units in handling IV cases are rapidly changing because of two recent and significant policy and procedural shifts. The first of these concerns overseas filing of the I-130 immigrant visa petition. USCIS has the statutory authority to adjudicate immigrant visa petitions, but for many years, U.S. citizens residing abroad in countries without USCIS field offices were able to present family-based I-130 immigrant visa petitions to consular officers for adjudication based on a delegation of authority to consular officers by USCIS. Since August 15, 2011, overseas petitioners must now file family-based I-130 petitions directly with the USCIS lockbox facility in Chicago, unless there is a USCIS field office in their country of residence, in which case they have the option of filing the petition directly with that office. The second concerns the advent of the new DS-260 electronic immigrant visa application, which will replace the DS-230 paper immigrant visa application currently in use by most IV units. The DS-260 is being phased in worldwide. These new procedures and forms are changing the way that IV units perform their work.

STEPS FOR APPLYING FOR AN IMMIGRANT VISA

There are a few important facts to keep in mind in examining the consular processing of an immigrant visa application. Firstly, the Department of State's role in immigrant visa processing is more limited than in non-immigrant visa processing because of the requirement that applicants for immigrant visas must be the beneficiary of an approved petition filed on their behalf with USCIS before they can apply for immigrant visas. Secondly, that role is not mandatory or inevitable, because a significant percentage of persons who apply for immigrant status can

---

43. IV work has changed considerably over the years. While IV cases remain document-heavy and labor-intensive—individual cases take more time to prepare and process than non-immigrant cases—the increasing role of the National Visa Center in preparing visa cases means that most of the preliminary document checking that used to be handled by IV units has been completed by the time the file arrives in the consular section from NVC.

do so by applying to legally adjust status in the United States from non-immigrant to immigrant rather than by applying for a visa abroad via consular processing. And finally, the actual immigrant visa application and interview as conducted by a consular officer is but the final step of a lengthy process that began when the petition on behalf of the visa applicant was filed. This chapter focuses on what takes place inside the consular section, and so will only touch briefly on what happens before the scheduled immigrant visa interview.

Filing the Petition

There are two broad categories of immigrant visas—employment-related and family-based.[44] Both require a petitioner, either a qualified family member or a prospective employer, who seeks to bring an alien beneficiary to the United States in immigrant status. The petitioner in a family-based case files Form I-130 while a prospective employer files Form I-140. Petitions and supporting documents for I-130s are filed with USCIS, either by submission to the USCIS Chicago lockbox in Chicago,[45] or by submission to a USCIS field office abroad.[46] I-140 petitions are filed with the USCIS Lockbox in Dallas, Texas.[47]

After Petition Approval

Once USCIS has approved an immigrant visa petition, it will send it directly to the National Visa Center (NVC) in Portsmouth.[48] NVC notifies the petitioner and beneficiary when they have received the approved petition and communicates with them directly concerning the next steps, including the collection and submission of the documents that are required before the case can be submitted to a consular officer for adjudication.

---

44. A third category of immigrant visa, the Diversity (lottery Visa), will be discussed separately below.
45. USCIS P.O. Box 804625, Chicago, IL 60680-4017; for express mail and courier deliveries, USCIS, attn: I-130, 131 South.
46. USCIS has international offices co-located with U.S. Embassies and consulates in the following 25 countries: Austria, China (Beijing and Guangzhou), Cuba, Dominican Republic, El Salvador, Germany, Ghana, Greece, Guatemala, Haiti, Honduras, India, Italy, Jamaica, Jordan, Kenya, Mexico (Cuidad Juarez, Mexico City, Monterrey), Panama, Peru, Philippines, Russia, South Africa, South Korea, Thailand, and the United Kingdom.
47. USCIS P.O. Box 660867, Dallas, TX 75266; for express mail and courier delivery, USCIS attn: AOS, 2501 S. State Highway 121, Business, Suite 4500, Lewisville, TX 75067.
48. Before the NVC came on line, approved petitions were sent directly to the consular section in the U.S. embassy in the country where the beneficiary resided.

WHAT IS THE "PRIORITY DATE"?

The "priority date" is the date on which a preference-based immigrant petition is filed with USCIS or the date the labor certification application was accepted for processing by the Department of Labor (when a labor certification is required). Immigrant visa regulations are notoriously complex, as is evidenced by the fact that the two broad categories of immigrant visas—family-sponsored and employment-based (a third category, the Diversity Visa, will be discussed below)—are further subdivided into immediate relative and preference categories. Immediate relative family visas are not subject to any annual limits on the numbers of immigrant visas that can be issued to persons who qualify as immediate relatives, but family preference categories are subject to such limits.[49] For some years, worldwide demand for visas in these categories has exceeded the numbers of visas that can be issued each year. The resulting backlog—which is further complicated by the existence of individual country limits on the numbers of immigrant visas that can be issued to citizens of those countries in these categories—is managed by the Visa Office of the Department of State, which monitors the numbers of visas being processed worldwide in the preference categories and issues monthly Visa Bulletins listing the current priority dates for each preference category. Additional visa numbers become available each month depending on world wide demand. Employment-based immigrant visa categories are also subject to numerical limits and have separate priority dates published by the State Department in the Visa Bulletin.[50] Because the current priority dates can advance—and regress—on a monthly basis, and in no predictable patterns, it is very important to monitor the Visa Bulletins regularly.

HOW DOES NVC HANDLE APPROVED PETITIONS?

Understanding the role of the National Visa Center makes it easier to understand what takes place at the embassy at the time of the immigrant

---

49. Immediate relatives include the spouses, unmarried children under the age of 21, and parents of U.S. citizens. The preference categories include unmarried adult sons and daughters of U.S. citizens, spouses, children, and unmarried sons and daughters of legal permanent residents, married sons and daughters of U.S. citizens, and the brothers and sisters of adult U.S. citizens.

50. The Visa Bulletin is released by the department a few weeks before the start of each month and is available on the Visas page of the department's website, http://www.state .gov/.

visa interview. Basically NVC handles all of the preprocessing for immigrant visa interviews that used to be done by the individual immigrant visa units at U.S. embassies and consulates around the world. It also notifies embassies when files are complete and priority dates are current and schedules the immigrant visa interview for the applicant. NVC sends lists of required documents to the beneficiary, collects and reviews those original documents when they are received, and obtains and reviews the I-864 Affidavit of Support and supporting documentation from the petitioner. NVC does not adjudicate visas, and while the NVC will notify the beneficiary if there are documents that are missing or about which there are problems, if they are not forthcoming after a follow-up inquiry, NVC will send the file as it is to the embassy where it will be processed.

Once the beneficiary's immigrant visa appointment has been scheduled, NVC forwards his or her file and supporting documents directly to the immigrant visa unit where the interview will take place and notifies the beneficiary of the date and time of the interview.[51] The IV unit, after receiving the immigrant file from the NVC, will notify the beneficiary of receipt and reconfirm the scheduled appointment date and time. They will also provide the beneficiary with a list of approved panel physicians who can conduct the medical exam as well as the forms that the beneficiary must fill out and submit to the physician. It then becomes the applicant's responsibility to make certain they (and their dependents if they are applying as a family) receive their medical exams in a timely manner so that the results of all required lab tests can be completed and the file sent directly to the consular section prior to their visa interviews. Beneficiaries are no longer required to bring the results of their medical exams in a sealed envelope with them to the IV interview.

WHAT TAKES PLACE AT THE IMMIGRANT VISA INTERVIEW?

Each immigrant visa application requires the consular officer to carefully review the beneficiary's file and the numerous documents it contains,

---

51. Most immigrant visas interviews will take place in the beneficiary's country of last residence abroad, defined as the principle place of residence. 9 FOREIGN AFFAIRS MANUAL, *supra* note 3, § 42.61 N.1.1. Consular sections do have discretionary authority to accept nonresident immigrant visa applicants if the applicant is coming from the United States, would experience hardship if required to return to their place of last residence abroad, and their workloads permit them to take additional non-resident applicants.

so in practice each IV interview takes considerably longer than a non-immigrant visa interview. Most IV units will schedule a specific number of IV interviews each day to accommodate their staffing and workloads.

IV applicants must bring with them to their interviews their passports, three color photographs, appointment receipts, and any additional documentation that they were notified by NVC will be required at their interview. Prior to the interview, the applicant will be instructed to pay the immigrant visa application fee at the cashier's window and will thereafter be called to a specific interviewing window to be interviewed by the immigrant visa officer. The actual interview itself, unlike the non-immigrant visa interview, is conducted under oath, which each applicant over the age of 14 is required to take before signing the immigrant visa application itself. All original documents that were sent by the applicants to the NVC will be returned to them by the consul at the time of the visa interview.

The consul's principal role in adjudicating the immigrant visa application is to determine that all the required documents have been submitted and whether there is evidence of any statutory grounds of inadmissibility. For example, if the applicant's police clearances reveal that he or she was arrested or convicted in the past, the consul will examine these, determine if there is a basis for statutory inadmissibility, and advise the applicant of his or her findings. Similarly, the consul will discuss with the applicant any questions concerning the credibility of the evidence submitted along with the Form I-864 Affidavit of Support. If the panel physician reports a possible medical ground of inadmissibility, the consul will advise the applicant of this at the interview. Finally, the consul will examine the bona fides of the family relationship on which the immigrant visa application is based. Once the consul has determined that the relationship is valid and there are no statutory grounds of inadmissibility or missing documentation, he or she will approve the visa, and then the applicant will be instructed to leave his or her passport behind for visa processing.

The immigrant visa stamp itself resembles a non-immigrant visa foil and is placed directly in the applicant's passport. The immigrant visa is valid for one entry and will expire if not utilized within six months of issuance. When the passport is returned, the IV unit will also return the sealed package containing the medical examination report, which should not be opened by the applicant and must be presented as received to the officer at the port of entry who will admit the beneficiary as a legal immigrant. Once the beneficiary has been admitted as a legal permanent resident, CBP will provide a temporary "green card" stamp in their passport confirming their LPR status. The actual green card itself will arrive at the new immigrant's U.S. address within six weeks.

IV DENIAL AND WAIVER RELIEF

An immigrant visa applicant is subject to the same statutory grounds of inadmissibility as a non-immigrant under INA section 212(a). However, as previously noted, there is no general statutory basis for immigrant visa waivers as is the case with § 212(d)(3)(A) for non-immigrant visas. Moreover, waiver relief for inadmissible immigrant visa applicants is considerably more restricted than is the case for non-immigrant visa applicants and is subject to stricter criteria for eligibility. A person who is inadmissible under § 212(a)(2)(C) for having been a controlled substance trafficker, for instance, can obtain waiver relief for non-immigrant travel to the United States, but waiver of this grounds of inadmissibility is not available for immigrant visa applicants. Similarly, and perhaps surprisingly, waiver relief is available to a non-immigrant visa applicant who is inadmissible under § 212(a)(3)(B) for participation in terrorist activities but *not* for the same person who subsequently applies for an immigrant visa, nor is it available to immigrant visa applicants who have committed a single offense of simple possession of more than 30 grams of marijuana.[52] The restricted availability of waiver relief for immigrant visa applicants reflects the considerably higher stakes when someone who is inadmissible for criminal or other serious grounds of inadmissibility requests permanent rather than temporary admission to the United States. While there is consideration given to the extreme hardship that would result to a U.S. citizen or LPR if a spouse, parent, son, or daughter were denied waiver relief, this will not serve to authorize such relief where the statute does not make it available.

THE DIVERSITY VISA LOTTERY

The third kind of immigrant visa in addition to family-based and employment visas is the Diversity Visa, or DV. Fifty-five thousand DV "diversity immigrant" visas are made available each year to citizens of certain countries designated as "low admission" countries based on immigration visa issuances since 1965.[53] Persons who seek to obtain Diversity Visas must

---

52. INA § 212(h).

53. The Immigration and Nationality Act of 1965, Pub. L. No. 89-236, 79 Stat. 911, eliminated the "national origins" formula for admitting alien immigrants into the United States that had been in use since 1924 and adopted the preference-based family-based and employment-related system currently in use today. One of the practical results of this change was to reduce considerably the number of immigrant visas available to citizens of countries that had been sizeable sources of immigrant flow into the United States before

participate in an annual "lottery" conducted by the State Department by submitting an electronic request for a DV number to the department during a designated period. If selected, the lottery "winners" are notified by the department and, thereafter, administratively processed by the National Visa Center in the same manner as preference and immediate relative immigrant visa applicants. To be eligible to participate in the DV lottery, applicants must have at least a high school diploma or its equivalent, or in the alternative two years of work experience within the last five years in an occupation that requires at least two years of training.[54]

Diversity Visa winners do not have to have qualifying relatives in the United States, nor do they have to have an offer of employment. However, they are required to demonstrate that they have sufficient financial resources to support themselves in the United States upon their arrival, and they must also obtain police clearance, undergo medical examinations, and be determined in all other respects to be admissible under the law before their visas can be issued to them. Lottery winners must apply for and receive their Diversity Visas by the end of the fiscal year for which the lottery they enter is designated.

There are no significant differences between Diversity Visa applicants and immediate relative and preference immigrant visa applicants when it comes to consular processing. Although some consular sections that have processed sizeable numbers of DV cases in the past may have a separate unit and staff to handle these cases, the fact that country eligibility for participation in the lottery can change from year to year militates against such units becoming a permanent fixture of most consular sections. Because Diversity Visas offer a way to immigrate that would not otherwise be available for millions of people, they are highly sought after. Nearly 15 million people entered the 2012 DV lottery for a chance to receive one of the 55,000 Diversity Visas that can be issued during that fiscal year—a remarkable figure given the current economic difficulties in the United States. This high level of demand also gives rise to a greater risk of fraudulent relationship claims by individuals and families, as well

---

that time—mostly European—and to increase considerably the inflow from others. The Diversity Visa was authorized by Congress to attempt to redress this imbalance by giving an alternative means of qualifying for immigrant status outside the preference system for citizens of certain countries determined to be underrepresented in preference admissions since 1965.

54. The formulas used to determine DV eligibility are highly complicated, and the lottery itself is subject to a fair amount of controversy both within and without the government. More detail about the DV Lottery and Diversity Visas can be found in both 22 C.F.R. § 42.33 and INA § 203(c).

as attempts to evade the "one lottery application per person" restrictions on entering the lottery. Consular officers can uncover evidence that a person is not eligible for a Diversity Visa at the time of interview, either because they submitted more than one lottery entry or because of evidence challenging the credibility of the alleged family relationships of the applicant. Because a Diversity Visa must be issued within the fiscal year for which the applicant entered and won the lottery, if an applicant waits until the last minute to schedule his or her IV appointment and at the interview the consul has concerns that warrant further investigation or document review, the applicant can run out of time and lose the ability to obtain the visa if they are unable to demonstrate eligibility by the end of the fiscal year. For this reason, successful DV lottery entrants should move quickly to gather the required documents and schedule their IV interviews well in advance of the end of the fiscal year.

7

AN OVERVIEW OF U.S. NON-IMMIGRANT VISA CLASSIFICATIONS

Jim Alexander and Alix Mattingly[1]

The Immigration and Nationality Act (INA) places the burden on foreign travelers to establish that they are eligible for admission to the United States in one of the thirty-plus non-immigrant visa categories.[2] The fact that there are more than thirty non-immigrant visa categories is both a blessing and a curse. Foreign nationals could be eligible for classification in multiple non-immigrant visa categories, but choosing the wrong category could result in travel delays, unnecessary government filing fees, visa application denials, and even summary removal from the United States. Identifying the right non-immigrant visa category for a client requires in-depth knowledge of immigration case law, as well as an understanding of trends within the various government agencies involved in administering U.S. law, and the client's overall goals and objectives. This chapter provides a brief overview of the process to obtain a non-immigrant visa and to apply for admission as a non-immigrant before discussing all non-immigrant visa categories set forth in Section 101(a)(15) of the INA.[3]

APPLYING FOR A NON-IMMIGRANT VISA AND FOR ADMISSION TO THE UNITED STATES

INA Section 214(b) states that every applicant for admission to the United States is presumed to be an immigrant until he or she establishes to the satisfaction of the consular *and* immigration officer that he or she is eligible for admission in a non-immigrant classification, except for H-1B and

---

1. Jim Alexander is a managing shareholder at Maggio + Kattar PC and Alix Mattingly is counsel to the firm. Each practices exclusively in the area of immigration and nationality law, with a particular focus on business immigration and corporate compliance matters.
2. INA §§ 101(a)(15), 214(b).
3. A chart of all non-immigrant visa categories is appended to this article to serve as a quick reference.

L-1 visa holders and their dependent family members.[4] In other words, in most cases, the government has at least two opportunities to consider whether a foreign national traveler is eligible to enter the United States.[5] First, most travelers to the United States must apply for and obtain a non-immigrant visa in the appropriate non-immigrant category at a U.S. consulate.[6]

The evidentiary requirements to obtain a non-immigrant visa vary, depending on the non-immigrant visa category and the consular jurisdiction.[7] Before applying for a non-immigrant visa, an applicant should review the documentary requirements described on the relevant consular section's website.[8] Some non-immigrant classifications that allow for U.S. work authorization require that the Department of Labor (DOL) and/or United States Citizenship and Immigration Services (USCIS) approve an application or petition before a visa application to the local consulate can be made.[9] In fact, the Department of State (DOS) online system prevents many non-immigrant visa applicants from scheduling a visa interview until DOL or USCIS has issued a tracking or receipt number.[10]

Upon issuance of a non-immigrant visa, the foreign national traveler must apply for "admission" to the United States at a port of entry where an agent from United States Customs and Border Protection (CBP) determines whether the applicant is admissible to the United States in the non-immigrant category.[11] Assuming the CBP officer admits the non-immigrant to the United States, an I-94 entry card is generally issued and placed in the traveler's passport as evidence of the foreign national's visa classification and period of admission. The information contained on the I-94 card is critically important to determine the duration of authorized stay and the types of activities in which the foreign national may engage while in the United States.[12]

---

4. INA § 214(b).

5. Canadian citizens traveling to the United States are usually not required to apply for and obtain a non-immigrant visa before applying for admission to the United States at a port of entry. 8 C.F.R. § 212.1(a). This exemption does not apply to Canadian citizens seeking admission to the United States in E, K, S and V non-immigrant status. *Id.* Also, business travelers and tourists from certain countries are not required to obtain visas before seeking admission to the United States. *See* Section II, *infra*.

6. 8 C.F.R. § 211.1(a).

7. 22 C.F.R. § 41.105.

8. *See* www.travel.state.gov/visa/embassy.

9. *See generally* 8 C.F.R. § 214.2.

10. *See* https://ceac.state.gov/genniv/.

11. INA § 214(b). For a complete list of grounds of inadmissibility, refer to *id.* § 212.

12. Donald Neufeld, Lori Scialabba, Pearl Chang, Interoffice Memorandum, Consolidation

Under the INA, a non-immigrant who stays in the United States longer than the period of admission stated on the I-94 card accrues unlawful presence, unless an application or petition to extend or change non-immigrant status was submitted to USCIS prior to the I-94 card expiration date.[13] Generally, a period of unlawful presence since a foreign traveler's most recent admission to the United States renders the individual ineligible to apply for a change or extension of status. Moreover, a non-immigrant who has been unlawfully present for more than 180 days is barred from returning to the United Statesfor three years from their date of departure and a period of unlawful presence of one year or more will result in a ten-year bar from reentry.[14] In light of the severe consequences that arise due to visa status violations, counsel must be diligent to ensure clients comply with the terms and conditions of their non-immigrant status.

As explained above, most foreign nationals are admitted for a specific period of time. The period of authorized stay for each of the non-immigrant categories is set forth in USCIS regulations.[15] In order to remain lawfully in the United States beyond the initial period of admission on the I-94 card, a non-immigrant must file a request to change[16] or extend[17] non-immigrant status prior to the expiration of the individual's current status. Foreign nationals in specific non-immigrant categories are ineligible to extend and change status.[18] Moreover, USCIS regulations require specific forms and documentary evidence when requesting changes and extensions of status.[19] It is critical for practitioners to submit the correct forms and supporting documents when requesting changes or extensions of status as USCIS will reject incorrectly filed applications.[20]

PRACTICE POINTER:
Require potential clients to present their passports, I-94 cards, and all documents submitted to the USCIS, DOL, Department

---

of Guidance Concerning Unlawful Presence for Purposes of Sections 212(a)(9)(B)(i) and 212(a)(9)(C)(I) of the Act, *in* Revision to and Re-designation of Adjudicator's Field Manual (AFM) Chapter 30.1.(d) as Chapter 40.9 (AFM Update AD 08-03) (U.S. Citizenship and Immigration Services, May 6, 2009) [hereinafter Unlawful Presence Guidance].

13. INA § 212(a)(9)(B).

14. There are limited exceptions to the three- and ten-year bar. *See* INA § 212(a)(9)(B)(iii); *see also* Unlawful Presence Guidance, *supra* note 12.

15. 8 C.F.R. § 214.2.

16. *See id.* § 248.2. *But see id.* § 248.1(b).

17. *See id.* § 214.1(a)(3). *But see id.* § 214.1(c)(4).

18. *Id.* § 214.1(c)(3); *id.* § 248.2(a).

19. *Id.* § 214.1(c); *id.* § 248.3.

20. Forms are available on the USCIS website at www.uscis.gov.

of State, or other U.S. government agency at the first meeting to facilitate case analysis.

NON-IMMIGRANT VISA CATEGORIES

U.S. immigration law is extremely complex and this fact is underscored by the myriad non-immigrant visa categories and the requirements that pertain to each category. The categories presented below are in the order of appearance under INA § 101(a)(15).

Visas for Diplomats, Embassy Staff, Household Staff, and Immediate Family Members

A-1 visas are issued to a foreign government's diplomatic delegation[21] and A-2 visas are for other Embassy officials and employees. These individuals may bring immediate family to the United States in the same visa category accorded to the principal family member. The definition of family is broader for A-1 and A-2 visas than other non-immigrant visa categories.[22] The State Department recently announced that same-sex partners of A-1 and A-2 visa holders are eligible for A visas as well.[23] Moreover, in certain circumstances, A-1 and A-2 family members are eligible to apply for employment authorization.[24]

Both A-1 and A-2 visa holders are entitled to bring household staff to the United States. These workers are issued A-3 visas. A-3 workers may also bring their immediate family members to the United States. Unlike family members who are in A-1 and A-2 status, a family member in A-3 status is not authorized to work.[25]

The A visa category holds a special status within the non-immigrant visa system, as most grounds of inadmissibility, with the exception of security-related grounds, do not apply to certain accredited government officials, their families, attendants, servants, and personal employees.[26]

---

21. A-1 visas are specifically for the following members of a foreign government's delegation to the United States: ambassador; public minister; career diplomatic or consular officer. Additionally, immediate family members of the delegation are also eligible to apply for A-1 visas.
22. 8 C.F.R. § 214.2(a)(2).
23. *Id.* § 214.2(a)(2)(vi), 22 C.F.R. § 41.21(a)(3)(i).
24. 8 C.F.R. § 214.2(a)(5).
25. *Id.* § 214.2(a)(9).
26. INA § 212(d)(8). The inapplicability of certain grounds of inadmissibility apply to A visa holders who represent a country that provides reciprocal treatment to accredited officials

Under the 14th Amendment of the Constitution, children of foreign diplomatic officers do not acquire citizenship when they are born in the United States.[27] Rather, they are considered lawful permanent residents of the United States upon birth and should apply to register their status as permanent residents by filing an Application to Adjust or Register Status to Lawful Permanent Resident (Form I-485).[28]

Visas for Business Visitors and Tourists

The most frequently used temporary visa to travel to the United States is a B visa, which is issued for business (B-1) or tourism (B-2).[29] Some individuals may travel to the United States without first obtaining a B-1/B-2 visa under the visa waiver program (VWP).[30] However, there are exceptions to the ability to travel to the United States under the VWP.[31] Additionally, pre-clearance through the CBP Electronic System for Travel Authorization (ESTA) is now required for all VWP travelers to the United States.[32]

> ### PRACTICE POINTER:
> There are some cases in which a visitor should be eligible to enter the United States on the VWP. However, due to the nature of the visitor's activities in the United States, the applicant may need to apply for and obtain a visitor visa before seeking admission.

There are evidentiary requirements that apply to both business visitors and tourists.[33] Those requirements will be addressed in this section

---

from the United States, their families, attendants, servants and personal employees. *Id.*

27. U.S. Const. Amend. XIV. *See also* 8 C.F.R. § 101.3(a).

28. Not all A-1 and A-2 visa holders are foreign diplomatic officers. USCIS regulations state that a foreign diplomatic officer is a "person listed in the State Department List, also known as the Blue List."

29. INA § 101(a)(15)(B).

30. Visitors for business and/or pleasure may travel to the United States for a period of ninety (90) days or less, provided they have a valid passport from one of the following countries: Andorra, Australia, Austria, Belgium, Brunei, Chile, Czech Republic, Denmark, Estonia, Finland, France, Germany, Greece, Hungary, Iceland, Ireland, Italy, Japan, Latvia, Liechtenstein, Lithuania, Luxembourg, Malta, Monaco, Netherlands, New Zealand, Norway, Portugal, San Marino, Singapore, Slovak Republic, Slovenia, South Korea, Spain, Sweden, Switzerland, and the United Kingdom. 8 C.F.R. § 217.2(a). As noted above in Section I, "Designated Country," Canadian business visitors and tourists are also visa exempt. *Id.* § 212.1(a).

31. *Id.* §§ 217.2(b), 217.4.

32. *Id.* § 217.5; *see also* http://www.cbp.gov/xp/cgov/travel/id_visa/esta/.

33. 9 U.S. Dep't of State, Foreign Affairs Manual § 41.31 N1 [hereinafter Foreign Affairs Manual].

before addressing the specific requirements for B-1 and B-2 classification. Business travelers and tourists who are ineligible to enter the United States under the VWP must apply for a visa at a U.S. consulate.[34] B visa applicants must provide documentation on the purpose of their trip, their intention to return home, and their finances.[35] Specifically, visitors applying for a business or tourism visa must have a residence in a foreign country which they have no intention of abandoning.[36] Consular officers are required by law to presume that all B visa applicants have "immigrant intent" unless demonstrated otherwise; thus, B visa applicants must affirmatively demonstrate that they have "non-immigrant intent." Consular officers are more likely to deny B-1 and B-2 visa applications when the applicant is from a financially and/or politically unstable country. Thus, all B-1 and B-2 visa applicants, particularly from developing countries, should be prepared to present evidence of their strong ties to the country where they are applying for a visa.

PRACTICE POINTER:

Applicants for B visas should have evidence of their ties abroad, which may include permanent employment, business or financial connections, family ties, and social or cultural associations, that will assist in demonstrating their intent to return to a foreign country.

In addition to establishing the intention to depart from the United States, a B visa applicant should provide evidence that his or her visit to the United States is for a limited duration.[37] To establish a visit will be of a limited duration, applicants should be prepared to present specific and realistic plans, not just vague and uncertain intentions, for the entire period of their contemplated visit.[38]

The maximum period of admission on a B visa generally is six months.[39] However, CBP agents must be satisfied that applicants will depart the United States upon completion of the visit. The CBP officer has discretion to admit a visitor for a shorter period of time than six months. An extension of visitor status may be requested by submitting an Appli-

---

34. 8 C.F.R. § 211.1.
35. 9 FOREIGN AFFAIRS MANUAL, *supra* note 33, § 41.31 N1(b).
36. INA § 214(b).
37. *Id.* § 101(a)(15)(B).
38. 9 FOREIGN AFFAIRS MANUAL, *supra* note 33, § 41.31 N3.2.
39. 8 C.F.R. § 214.2(b).

cation to Change or Extend Non-immigrant Status (Form I-539) to the USCIS.

PRACTICE POINTER:

An applicant's proposed length of stay as a visitor in the United States will necessarily be defined by the maximum period allowable under U.S. law. The amount of time requested should be consistent with the time-frame limitations offered by business contacts, relatives, or friends and with other information provided to the consular officer.

Applicants for B visitor visa status must demonstrate that adequate financial arrangements have been made to enable them to fulfill the purpose of their visit to the United States, without unlawful employment, and to ensure their departure from the United States.[40] Evidence of an applicant's financial resources is generally essential for B-1/B-2 visa applications.

B-1 Business Visitor Visas

B-1 business visitors are admitted to the United States for a limited period of time for the purpose of engaging in commercial or professional activity, but not for employment or "local labor for hire."[41] Generally, a B-1 business visitor may not be compensated from a U.S. source. However, a U.S. source may provide an expense allowance that does not amount to actual compensation. For those who desire to enter the United States to conduct business and not for local employment, the B-1 visa offers expedited processing and simpler requirements than virtually all employment authorized non-immigrant visas. However, B-1 status requires non-immigrant intent and strong ties to one's home country, while other non-immigrant categories, such as H-1B and L-1 categories, do not have that requirement.[42]

A B-1 visa is automatically invalidated if the visa holder overstays or otherwise violates the terms of his or her non-immigrant visa status.[43] Such persons must apply for new visa stamps in their home countries,

---

40. 9 Foreign Affairs Manual, *supra* note 33, § 41.31 N4.
41. *Id.* § 41.31 N 7. *See also* Matter of Hira, 11 I. & N. Dec. 824 (A.G. 1966) (holding that a tailor's meetings in the United States, which involved taking body measurements, were permissible business visits that facilitate international commerce).
42. INA § 214(b).
43. *Id.* § 222(g).

barring extraordinary circumstances.[44] Persons who overstay their admission under the VWP cannot enter without a visa in the future.[45]

B-1 visitors must seek admission only to engage in business-related activities.[46] Examples of permissible B-1 business activities include:

- engaging in commercial transactions that do not involve employment in the United States, such as negotiating contracts and consulting with business associates;
- litigation;
- attending conventions, conferences, or seminars;
- undertaking independent research;
- participation in volunteer internships, or observing the conduct of business, professional, or vocational activities, such as temporary "elective clerkships" for foreign medical students;
- participation in volunteer programs, such as the service programs of recognized nonprofit and religious organizations;
- investigation of the possibility of establishing a U.S. company or investment that may qualify the B-1 visitor for L-1 intracompany transfer or E treaty investor or treaty trader status in the future;
- participation as a professional entertainer in certain cultural programs sponsored by a foreign country;
- utilization of U.S. music recording facilities for the distribution and sale of recordings outside the United States;
- taking photographs; or
- creating art for regular sale outside the United States.[47]

In many cases, a detailed letter from the applicant's overseas employer is helpful to prove the applicant has adequate financial resources and intent to depart the United States upon the conclusion of the visit.[48] This letter should state the purpose of their business travel to the United States, their salary, position, how long they have been employed, and the purpose and expected duration of their U.S. visit.

In limited circumstances, foreign nationals who will perform actual labor for compensation in the United States may be admitted as B-1 visitors.[49]

---

44. *Id.*
45. 8 C.F.R. § 217.1.
46. 8 C.F.R. § 214.2(b)(4).
47. 9 FOREIGN AFFAIRS MANUAL, *supra* note 33, § 41.31.
48. *Id.* § 41.31 N4.2.
49. *See id.* § 41.31 N8–12.

B-1 visa applicants may be authorized to work in the United States in the following limited situations:

- members of boards of directors of U.S. corporations coming to the United States to attend a board meeting or to perform other functions of board membership;
- members of religious or charitable organizations participating in a volunteer service program;
- certain foreign nationals who would be eligible for H-1B specialty worker or H-3 trainee or J-1 exchange visitor status;
- certain commercial or industrial workers servicing equipment purchased outside the United States; workers training U.S. workers to perform such services; supervisors or trainers of building or construction workers; and employees of foreign exhibitors at international expositions;
- personal or domestic servants of U.S. citizens residing abroad visiting the United States temporarily; servants of some U.S. citizens temporarily assigned to the United States; and the servants of some foreign nationals in non-immigrant status;
- certain professional athletes who compete for prize money only; under the North American Free Trade Agreement (NAFTA), citizens of Canada or Mexico as agents, buyers and manufacturers, production, marketing, sales, distribution, and service personnel;
- certain artists, other than photographers, who do not regularly sell their artwork in the United States;
- individuals coming to institutions of higher education and research provided they are engaged in traditional academic activities such as lecturing, demonstrating, etc., and the duration of the activity is for nine days or less.[50]

Consular officers adjudicating these applications are likely to scrutinize them closely. Moreover, upon arrival in the United States, the CBP could question whether the applicant for admission should be admitted as a B-1 visitor.[51] In certain cases, it is possible that a foreign traveler will be issued a B-1 visa in order to perform work on behalf of a foreign employer.[52] However, after several trips to the United States on the B-1 visa, the CBP agent at the port of entry could deny admission on the basis that the individual has been in the United States too long. Long-term

---

50. *Id.*
51. INA § 214(b).
52. 9 Foreign Affairs Manual, *supra* note 33, § 41.31 N9.1–9.9, N10.1–10.4, & N11.

assignments in B-1 status for foreign personnel should be considered carefully as the foreign worker's minor children who are admitted in B status would not be authorized to attend school in the United States.[53]

B-2: Visitors for Pleasure/Tourism

Visitors for pleasure are admitted to the United States for a limited period of time for the purpose of family visits, tourism, and/or medical treatment. Examples of permissible activities include:

- recreational activities;
- tourism and amusement;
- visiting friends and/or relatives;
- resting or obtaining medical treatment;
- accompanying a B-1 parent or spouse;
- attending social engagements.[54]

As explained above, B-2 visa applicants have the burden of proving eligibility for admission to the consular officer and the CBP agent. Thus, applicants must be prepared to present evidence that establishes nonimmigrant intent, ability to financially support themselves, and the limited duration of their visit.

Visas for Travelers in Transit

The C visa is an obscure visa category that serves limited purposes. Specifically, C visas are for the following individuals:

- Passengers en route to a final destination outside the United States on board a vessel temporarily at a U.S. port with no intention of landing, provided the ship originally embarked from a foreign port;[55]
- Certain travelers on their way immediately to the United Nations headquarters;[56] and
- Alien diplomats in transit through the United States.

Travelers in C status are not eligible to extend or change status while in the United States.[57] Additionally, the maximum period of admission for individuals in C status is 29 days.[58]

---

53. 8 C.F.R. § 214.2(b)(7). *But see* 9 FOREIGN AFFAIRS MANUAL, *supra* note 33, § 41.31 N10.4-1.
54. 9 FOREIGN AFFAIRS MANUAL, *supra* note 33, § 41.31 N13.
55. 8 C.F.R. § 214.1(a)(ii).
56. *Id.* § 214.1(a)(ii).
57. *Id.* §§ 214.1, 248.2.
58. *Id.* § 214.2(c)(3).

Visas for Crewmen

The D visa category is limited to individuals who are serving in a capacity required for the normal operations and service of a vessel or aircraft.[59] Applicants for D visas must establish that they intend to land temporarily in the United States solely for the purpose of fulfilling their role as a crewmember.[60] Under the INA, crewmen are precluded from applying to adjust status to lawful permanent residence.[61] It is important for counsel to determine whether individuals on board a ship or aircraft are crew persons, as defined under the INA, or serve in a supernumerary capacity that is beyond the normal operations and service of the vessel.[62]

Visas for Treaty Traders, Treaty Investors, and Australian Specialty Workers

The E visa category was established to give effect to treaties between the United States and foreign countries that provide for reciprocal benefits to nationals of each country who invest in the other country, or who conduct trade between the two countries. Some of the special benefits available to treaty traders and investors (E-1 and E-2 visa holders) not available to other non-immigrants are the following:

- Some E-1 and E-2 visas can be issued for up to five years and upon each admission to the United States, the E visa holder and their dependents will be admitted for two years from the date of entry.[63] This period can be extended almost indefinitely, usually in five-year increments, if the business can continue to show that it is a real and operating enterprise.[64]
- The application for E status can be made directly to a U.S. consulate and no separate or additional application must be made to the United States Citizenship and Immigration Services (USCIS).
- E visa holders are not required to maintain a foreign residence to which they intend to return, as long as it is their intention to leave

---

59. INA § 101(a)(15)(D).

60. *Id.*

61. INA § 245(c)(7).

62. Dree Collopy, Esq., *The Plight of the Crewman: The Need for an Immediate Relative Exception to the Prohibition on Adjustment of Status and Strategies for Representing Alleged Crewmen Under the Current Law*, Immigration Briefings (June 2010).

63. 8 C.F.R. § 214.2(e)(19)–(20).

64. 9 FOREIGN AFFAIRS MANUAL, *supra* note 33, § 41.51 N1.1, N1.2.

the United States at some time in the future when their period of stay expires.[65]

- E visa applicant's spouse and unmarried children under age also qualify for E status. Moreover, spouses are eligible to apply for work authorization once they enter the United States in E status.[66]

A key issue in the context of E visa applications is the citizenship of both the foreign traveler and the employer.[67] To apply for an E-1 or E-2 visa, an applicant must hold citizenship in a country that has entered into treaty of trade and navigation with the United States and the company must have the same citizenship.[68] Notably, the spouse and children of an E visa holder are not required to have the same nationality as the E visa principal.[69]

The DOS should be consulted for an updated list of treaty countries that have treaties with the United States that give effect to E-1 and E-2 classification.[70] In most cases, the foreign national's passport will be sufficient to establish citizenship for E visa purposes. However, for citizens of the United Kingdom, the treaty extends only to citizens who are inhabitants of British territory in Europe.[71] The citizenship of a company will be determined by the nationality of its owners.[72] Determining corporate citizenship becomes especially challenging when there are multiple corporate layers and the company is publicly traded.[73]

E-1 Treaty Trader
For E-1 visas, an applicant must establish the company is carrying on "substantial" trade "principally" between the United States and the treaty country.[74] Trade is defined in the E-1 regulations as "the existing international exchange of items of trade for consideration between the United

---

65. Michael Aytes, Interoffice Memorandum, Processing Guidelines for E-3 Australian Specialty Occupation Workers and Employment Authorization for E-3 Dependent Spouses, *in* Revisions to Adjudicator's Field Manual (AFM) Chapters 34.1 and 34.6 (AFM Update AD05-24) (U.S. Citizenship and Immigration Services, Dec. 15, 2005).

66. INA § 214(e)(6).

67. 9 Foreign Affairs Manual, *supra* note 33, § 41.51 N1.1(1)–(2), N1.2(1)–(2).

68. *Id.*

69. 22 C.F.R. § 41.51.

70. http://travel.state.gov/visa/fees/fees_3726.html.

71. United Kingdom Commerce and Navigation Treaty, *entered into force* July 3, 1815.

72. 9 Foreign Affairs Manual, *supra* note 33, § 41.51 N3.

73. *Id.* § 41.51 N3.1–3.3.

74. 8 C.F.R. § 214.2(e)(11).

States and the treaty country."[75] Title to the items of trade must pass from one country to the other in a commercial, traceable, and identifiable manner.

Under the E-1 visa regulations, there is no minimum in terms of number or dollar amount of transactions required to meet the definition of "substantial."[76] However, to be considered substantial, the trading enterprise must be of a sufficient size to ensure a continuous flow of numerous items of trade over time from one country to another.[77] E-1 guidance states that income from trading activities that is sufficient to support the trader and his or her family will be considered favorably in meeting this requirement.[78] Furthermore, the number of transactions is more significant than the total dollar amount of these transactions, although a large number of high-dollar-value transactions obviously will be looked upon positively by the embassy.[79]

It is important to note that "substantial" trade must be "existing" at the time one applies for E-1 status.[80] Intent to engage in trade, even if documented, will not in itself qualify an individual for E-1 status. However, successfully negotiated contracts binding upon the parties that call for the immediate exchange of items of trade may meet this requirement. To show that the trade activity is "principally" between the United States and the treaty country, one must demonstrate that more than 50 percent of the total volume of trade takes place between the United States and the treaty trading company's country of citizenship.[81]

E-2 Treaty Investor
The E-2 visa is useful for individuals who will live in the United States for extended periods of time to oversee an enterprise that represents a major investment in the United States.[82] Multiple investors of the same nationality can qualify for E-2 status based upon investments in the same enterprise.[83] Treaty nationals must own at least 50 percent of the ultimate enterprise.[84]

---

75. *Id.* § 214.2(e)(10).
76. *Id.*
77. 9 Foreign Affairs Manual, *supra* note 33, § 41.51 N4.1.
78. *Id.* § 41.51 N6(b).
79. *Id.* § 41.51 N6(a).
80. *Id.* § 41.51 N4.4.
81. *Id.* § 41.51 N7.
82. *Id.* § 41.51 N8.
83. *Id.* § 41.51 N12.3.
84. 8 C.F.R. § 214.2(e)(7).

To meet the requirements for E-2 visa classification, the investor must make a commitment of funds that represents an actual, active investment. Moreover, the investor's money must be "at risk," and not merely available.[85] To establish that funds are at risk, it is critical for investors to show that the investment has been irrevocably committed.[86] This requirement of an irrevocable commitment generally means that an investor will stand to lose money or personal assets if he or she walks away from the investment.[87] The source of the qualifying investments may include loans secured by the investor's personal assets; unsecured loans granted on the basis of the investor's signature; cash reserves placed in a business account at the disposal of the business; and the value of purchased equipment and property.[88] Nonqualifying investments include mortgage debt; loans for which a lending institution has recourse against a guarantor; cash not held in reserve by the corporation; and rental payments, inventory purchases, and other recurring costs beyond the start-up of the enterprise as such costs are assumed to be paid out of income generated by the enterprise and are not part of the investment attributable to the investor.[89]

Uncommitted funds in a bank account, even a business account, never represent an "active" investment, unless enough other evidence of business activities exists to show the funds are used in the routine operation of the business (e.g., payment of bills and payroll, purchase of inventories or equipment, etc.).[90] Passive or speculative investments held for potential appreciation in value are not considered active investments.[91] In limited circumstances, an investor may be able to hedge his or her risk by placing investment funds in escrow, to be released upon the issuance of the E visa.[92]

In addition, although there is no finite amount of investment required to qualify for E-2 status, to satisfy the "substantial" requirement, the DOS uses a "relative-proportionality" test.[93] The test is: (i) the amount invested weighted against the total cost of purchasing or creating the enterprise; (ii) the amount normally considered sufficient to ensure successful oper-

---

85. 9 FOREIGN AFFAIRS MANUAL, *supra* note 33, § 41.51 N8.1-2.
86. *Id.* § 41.51 N8.1-3(a).
87. *Id.*
88. *Id.* § 41.51 N8.1-2.
89. *Id.*
90. *Id.* § 41.51 N8.2-1.
91. *Id.* § 41.51 N9.
92. *Id.*
93. *Id.* § 41.51.

ation of the enterprise; and (iii) the magnitude of the investment.[94] The lower the cost of the enterprise, the higher, proportionally, the investment must be to be considered substantial. At the same time, a million-dollar investment may be insufficient, for example, if the enterprise is extremely large, such as a steel mill.

Further, the E-2 investment cannot simply be "marginal" in nature.[95] In other words, the applicant must be able to prove the investment will yield more than simply enough income to support the investor and his or her family.[96] The investment either must create job opportunities for U.S. workers, or the investor must have funds beyond those needed to operate his or her investment.[97]

The treaty investor must fulfill a key role in the company, either as a person who has developed and will direct the day-to-day investment, as a qualified manager, or as a specially trained and highly qualified employee necessary for the development of the investment.[98] Also, the treaty investor must "control" the company, i.e., he or she must own at least 50 percent of the company, and in many instances, even more.

E-3 Australian Special Occupation

The E-3 non-immigrant visa category provides Australian citizen professionals a simple, convenient option for productive employment in the United States. The E-3 category allows up to 10,500 Australian citizens to be admitted annually in this classification.[99]

Australian citizens (either by birth or naturalization) are eligible to work temporarily in the United States in E-3 status for an employer who agrees to pay the employee the prevailing wage for the position offered, provided that the job is a specialty occupation—that is, one requiring at least a bachelor's degree or its equivalent.[100] Additionally, the E-3 sponsoring employer must meet prevailing and actual wage requirements for the job opportunity, based on the approval of a labor condition application by the Department of Labor.[101] As discussed further in "H-1B Visas for Specialty Workers" below, an employer must keep certain supporting documentation on file and available for public inspection when filing a labor condition application.

---

94. *Id.* § 41.51 N10.2.
95. *Id.* § 41.51.
96. *Id.* § 41.51 N11.
97. *Id.*
98. *Id.* § 41.51 N14.2, N14.3.
99. *Id.* § 41.51 N16.8(e).
100. 22 C.F.R. § 41.51(c).
101. 9 FOREIGN AFFAIRS MANUAL, *supra* note 33, § 41.51 N16.8(b).

A significant benefit of this category is that the prospective employee presents the E-3 paperwork at a U.S. consulate abroad and does not require approval through USCIS prior to traveling to the United States in this work authorized capacity.[102] When the E-3 visa is presented to a U.S. immigration officer upon arrival in the United States, the E-3 visa entitles the holder to two (2) years of authorized employment with the sponsoring employer. The employer may seek extensions of the E-3's status indefinitely, so long as the services continue to be required by the business and the employee can demonstrate the intent to return abroad after the temporary employment in the United States concludes.[103]

Importantly, unlike the E-1, E-2, L-1, and H-1B non-immigrant visa categories, expedited review (premium processing) of E-3 petitions through USCIS is not presently available.[104] Moreover, E-3 workers are ineligible for automatic extensions of employment authorization based upon a timely filed application to extend E-3 status.[105] Finally, unlike H-1B workers, the INA does not authorize temporary employment upon the submission of a change of E-3 employers.[106] The easiest way to ensure an E-3 worker's employment eligibility is to have the employee apply for an E-3 visa at a U.S. consulate.

Immediate relatives (spouses and children under age) of E-3 visa holders need not be Australian citizens or nationals and E-3 spouses are eligible for U.S. work authorization.[107]

Visas for Academic Studies

Individuals coming to study in the United States for the "sole purpose" of pursuing an academic course of study at a designated institution should apply for an F-1 visa.[108] A database of information entitled the Student Exchange Visitor Information System (SEVIS) maintains the information on all students in the United States and monitors their continued attendance at the requisite educational institutions. Any changes to a student's program of study such as a transfer of academic institution, the change of academic program or field of study, dramatic change in course load, or the authorization for part time employment is all done through the SEVIS database.[109]

102. *Id.* § 41.51 N16.8(c).
103. *Id.* § 41.51 N16.1(c)(4).
104. www.uscis.gov (How Do I Use the Premium Processing Service?).
105. 8 C.F.R. § 274a.12(b)(20).
106. INA § 214(n).
107. 22 C.F.R. § 41.51(c)(2); INA § 214(e)(6).
108. 8 C.F.R. § 214.2(f).
109. *Id.* § 214.2(f)(1)(i)(A).

Most students pursuing a degree program in the United States take advantage of the opportunity to obtain employment during their courses of study. This can include Curricular Practical Training (CPT) or Optional Practical Training (OPT).[110] Based on the student's particular degree program, these can be authorized by the school's Designated Student Official (DSO).[111]

To qualify for a student visa, the prospective student must demonstrate to a consular officer that he or she is a "bona fide student," that he or she will attend the designated institution; that he or she has sufficient funds for the program and he or she does not intend to permanently reside in the United States.[112] Additionally, the spouse and under-21-year-old children of F-1 students are eligible for F-2 visas.[113]

Once an individual is issued a student visa, the student may enter the United States for their entire period of study and should be admitted for the "duration of their status" noted as "D/S" on the I-94 card.[114] While maintaining student status, the individual is authorized to remain in the United States. This can include breaks between semesters and also periods of authorized employment pursuant to CPT or OPT. Following the completion of their courses of study and any authorized periods of training, students may remain in the United States for up to sixty days.[115]

Visas for International Organizations' Representatives, Officers and Employees and Their Household Staff

G visas are available to the high-ranking members of a country's delegation to an international organization; the international organization's officers and employees; and the household staff for both the representatives and organization's officers and employees. Significantly, unlike most non-immigrant visa categories, the determination by the consular officer and the recognition by the Secretary of State is evidence of the proper classification under the Immigration and Nationality Act for an individual granted a G-1, G-2, G-3, or G-4 visa.[116] The deference given to consular officers and the Secretary of State is significant, as it results in individuals in these categories being admitted for an unspecified period of time. Thus, these individuals do not have an expiration date on their I-94 cards.

---

110. *Id.* § 214.2(f)(10)(i-ii).
111. *Id.*
112 INA § 101(a)(15)(F).
113. 8 C.F.R. § 214.2(f)(3).
114. *Id.* § 214.2(f)(5)(i).
115. *Id.*
116. *Id.* § 214.2(g)(1).

The fact that G-1, G-2, G-3, and G-4 individuals are admitted "duration of status" has significant implications in determining if and when these individuals begin to accrue unlawful presence.[117] The special status of international organization representatives, officers, and employees is further underscored by the fact that adult children are sometimes eligible to continue to hold G status after they turn 21 years old.[118] Interestingly, the State Department requires derivative family members to hold G status if the principal family member holds G status.[119] This policy can result in inconveniences to derivative family members who have an offer of employment but are experiencing delays in obtaining the employment authorization document.

G-1 Visas for Permanent Representatives, Immediate Family Members, and Household Staff

The G-1 visa is for the principal representative of a permanent mission to an international organization. Similar to the A-1 category for diplomats, the G-1 visa is available to the representative of an international organization and immediate family members. Additionally, the G-1 representative's household staff members are issued G-1 visas, with the exception of domestic employees.[120] G-1 visa holders should be on the State Department Blue List and, therefore, their children who are born in the United States are not U.S. citizens.[121] Furthermore, the spouse and certain children of G-1 representatives may be eligible for employment authorization.[122] The G-1 visa category, like the A visa category, holds a special status within the non-immigrant visa system as most grounds of inadmissibility do not apply.[123]

G-2 Visas for Other Representatives and Their Immediate Family Members

G-2 visas are for representatives of recognized governments who are traveling to the United States to attend meetings of an international organization. Spouses and children who are under the age of 21 are also eligible for G-2 visas. However, they are not eligible to apply for employment

---

117. *Id.* § 214.2(g). *See also* Unlawful Presence Guidance, *supra* note 12.
118. 8 C.F.R. § 214.2(g)(2)(iii)–(v).
119. http://travel.state.gov/visa/temp/types/types_2638.html#7.
120. 9 FOREIGN AFFAIRS MANUAL, *supra* note 33, § 41.24 N1.
121. 8 C.F.R. § 101.3(a)(2); *id.* § 101.3(b).
122. *Id.* § 214.2(g)(5)(i)–(ii).
123. INA § 212(d).

authorization and the broader definition of immediate family members applicable to G-1 does not apply to them.[124]

G-3 Visas for Representatives from Nonmember Countries and Others

A representative of a country that does not have membership in the international organization is eligible for a G-3 visa. Likewise, representatives from foreign governments to international organizations are issued G-3 visas when the government does not have de jure recognition by the United States.[125] It is noteworthy that the G-3 spouse and children are eligible to apply for employment authorization and children over 21 years old may be entitled to G-3 status.[126]

G-4 Visas for International Organization Officers and Employees and Their Families

The largest contingent of G visa holders seems to fall in the G-4 visa category. This visa category is available to the international organization's officers and employees. Officers and staff are able to bring spouses and children to the United States in G-4 status and these family members are often eligible to apply for employment authorization.[127] Furthermore, adult children are sometimes eligible to live with their parents in G-4 status.[128] As children who are born in the United States to G-4 parents do not enjoy privileges and immunities from U.S. law, they are citizens at birth.[129] Moreover, in light of the fact that many children with G-4 parents are more familiar with U.S. social and cultural norms, there are special provisions under the INA to facilitate G-4 derivative family members to obtain permanent resident status upon the death or retirement of a parent from an international organization.[130]

G-5 Visas for Household Staff of International Organization Representatives, Officers, and Employees

The G-5 visa is available to the household staff of G-1 through G-4 principal. The G-5 visa category applies to domestic employees as well as other individuals in the personal employment of a G visa holder (e.g.,

---

124. 8 C.F.R. § 214.2(g)(2), (5).
125. 9 Foreign Affairs Manual, *supra* note 33, § 41.24 N1.3.
126. 8 C.F.R. § 214.2(g)(2), (5).
127. *Id.* § 214.2(a)(2)(i)–(v).
128. *Id.*
129. U.S. Const. Amend. XIV.
130. INA § 101(a)(27).

attendants, servants, personal assistants, etc.). In order to apply for a G-5 visa, the applicant must present a contract between the household worker and the G visa holder. This agreement must include a description of job duties, compensation, and payment of transportation cost to the United States and onward.[131]

Significantly, unlike other G visa holders, an applicant for admission in G-5 status is limited to a period of admission of three years from the date of entry.[132] This means that a G-5 may accrue unlawful presence if he or she remains in the United States without timely filing an application to change or extend non-immigrant status.

Visas for Specialty Workers; Nurses; Short-Term and Seasonal Workers; and Trainees

The H visa category includes numerous, distinct sub-classifications: H-1B, H-1B1, H-1C, H-2B, and H-3 categories.[133] While each category has specific and unique attributes, the H-1B and H-2B are the most common.

H-1B Visas for Specialty Workers

A U.S. employer can file an H-1B specialty worker petition with USCIS on behalf of a foreign employee, provided that the job requires at least a bachelor's degree in a relevant discipline.[134] Eligible fields of endeavor include, but are not limited to, most computer science jobs, architecture, engineering, mathematics, physical sciences, social sciences, medicine and health, education, business specialties, accounting, law, or theology.[135] The potential H-1B worker must either have a university degree or a combination of education and experience equal to a degree in a field related to the offered job.[136] Three years of progressive experience in an occupational specialty is deemed equivalent to one year of university studies.[137]

Significantly, there are a limited number of H-1B visas available each fiscal year (65,000 new H-1B visa petitions as well as 20,000 for advanced degree holders from U.S. institutions).[138] Every fiscal year begins on Octo-

---

131. http://travel.state.gov/visa/temp/types/types_2638.html.
132. 8 C.F.R. § 214.2(g)(1).
133. *Id.* § 214.2(h).
134. *Id.* § 214.2(h)(4)(iii); H-1B classification is also available for fashion models pursuant to *id.* § 214.2 (h)(4)(ii).
135. *Id.* § 214.2(h)(4)(ii) (definition of specialty occupation).
136. *Id.* § 214.2(h)(4)(iii)(C).
137. *Id.* § 214.2 (h)(4)(iii)(D)(5).
138. The United States has entered into a free-trade agreement with Chile and Singapore that requires that 1,400 H-1B1 and 5,400 H-1B1be reserved out of the 65,000 total for Chilean

ber 1st; the earliest that a new H-1B visa petition may be filed for the following fiscal year is April 1st.[139] Fortunately, there are several types of employers and individuals that are not subject to the annual cap. For example, employees of colleges and universities—and their related or affiliated nonprofit entities—nonprofit research organizations, and government research organizations are exempt from this cap.[140] Importantly, individuals presently in H-1B status, who previously held H-1B status within the past six years and have not left the United States for more than one year after attaining such status, and physicians who held J-1 status and received a waiver of the two-year home residence requirement pursuant to the Conrad Waiver Program are not subject to the annual H-1B cap.[141]

H-1B status may be granted for an initial period of up to three years; however, extensions can be obtained for up to a total of six years and sometimes more.[142] Specifically, an H-1B may extend his or her stay in H-1B status beyond six years, in one-year increments, if a labor certification application or an I-140 employment-based adjustment application was filed at least 365 days prior to the expiration of his or her current H-1B status.[143] In addition, an extension beyond six years may be granted in three-year increments if the H-1B is the beneficiary of an approved immigrant visa petition in the first, second, or third employment-based category and, but for the per country quotas, would be eligible to complete the legal permanent residency process.[144] USCIS allows for the H-1B to "recapture" or add back time spent outside the United States during the original six-year period.[145] The extension can be for the same employer or a new employer.[146]

An H-1B authorizes a foreign worker to be employed only by the petitioning employer under the terms of the H-1B petition, and a foreign worker maintains lawful status in the United States by employment pursuant to the terms of the H-1B petition.[147] An H-1B worker may work for

---

and Singaporean citizens respectively. INA § 214 (g)(1)(A).

139. 8 C.F.R. § 214.2(h)(9)(i)(B).

140. INA § 214(g)(5)(A)–(B).

141. *Id.* § 214 (l)(2)(A).

142. 8 C.F.R. § 214.2(h)(9), (13), (15).

143. *See* American Competitiveness in the Twenty-First Century Act, Pub. L. No. 106-313, § 106(a), 114 Stat. 1251, 1253–54 (2000).

144. *See id.* § 104(c), 114 Stat. at 1253.

145. Michael Aytes, Policy Memorandum, Procedures for Calculating Maximum Period of Stay Regarding the Limitations on Admission for H-1B and L-1 Non-immigrants (AFM Update AD 05-21) (U.S. Citizenship and Immigration Services, Oct. 21, 2005).

146. *Id.*

147. 8 C.F.R. § 214.2(h)(2)(i)(C).

multiple employers simultaneously, provided that each employer files a separate H-1B petition.[148]

H-1B visa holders may bring their dependents (spouse and children under the age of 21) to the United States in H-4 status.[149] H-4s may attend school in the United States, but are not eligible for U.S. work authorization.[150]

Important Compliance Aspects: Labor Condition Applications and Record Keeping

Before an employer may submit an H-1B petition to the USCIS, it must obtain an approved LCA from the Department of Labor.[151] The LCA requirement associated with the filing of an H-1B visa petition involves, inter alia, the employer's determination of the actual wage paid to similarly employed workers in the relevant occupation, obtaining prevailing wage information from the Department of Labor (DOL) or another "authoritative source," and the filing of the LCA with the DOL regional office.[152]

The employer must pay the H-1B employee at least 100 percent of the prevailing wage or the actual wage, whichever is higher.[153] The *prevailing wage* is defined by the Department of Labor (DOL) as being the wage paid to workers in a specific job category within a specific geographic region based upon a DOL determination or another "authoritative source" (e.g., a geographic specific salary survey published within the past two years).[154] The *actual wage* is the salary paid by the employer to other employees "with similar experience and qualifications for the specific employment in question."[155] Once the employer defines the "specific employment in question" in terms of job duties and requirements, it must then differentiate among these individuals to determine which employees are "similarly employed" based upon the following factors: experience (length, type, etc.); qualifications (particular skills, etc.); education (what level is required); job responsibility and function; specialized knowledge; and other legitimate business factors.[156]

---

148. *Id.*
149. *Id.* § 214.2(h)(9)(iv).
150. *Id.*
151. *Id.* § 214.2(h)(4)(i)(B).
152. *Id.* § 214.2(h)(4)(i)(B)(1).
153. 20 C.F.R. § 655.731(c)(10); INA § 212(p)(3); INA § 212 (n)(1)(A)(i)(II).
154. 20 C.F.R. § 655.731(a).
155. *Id.*
156. *Id.*

DOL requires that the employer complete and retain an actual wage memorandum in a public inspection file, along with other LCA materials.[157] This memorandum must include the occupational title, education, experience level, and an explanation of other relevant factors that affect the wage rate of similarly employed workers.[158]

PRACTICE POINTER:

Payment of USCIS Filing Fees and Attorney's Fees

The Department of Labor takes the position that fees associated with obtaining an H-1B visa are an employer's business expense and should not be borne by the foreign national.[159] Therefore care must be taken if the payment of these fees by the foreign employee may bring his or her pay below the required rate of pay. Kindly remember the employer is required to pay the higher of the actual or the prevailing rate of pay.[160]

All employers must also determine if the company is an "H-1B dependent employer." H-1B dependent employers are those whose workforce is comprised of a significant number of H-1B workers.[161] Employers who are H-1B dependent, or those who have willfully violated the terms and conditions of a previously filed Labor Condition Application, face additional attestation requirements.[162] Ultimately, they can also expect a greater level of scrutiny on the petitions and applications they file. Penalties, including back pay, may be imposed in the event an employer makes a misrepresentation of fact on an LCA.[163]

As part of the LCA process, employers are required to document that they have complied with the attestations listed on the LCA.[164] Although none of this documentation needs to be submitted to the DOL with the LCA, some of it must be available for public inspection while the rest must be maintained for review in the event of a DOL investigation.[165]

---

157. *Id.* § 655.760(a).
158. *Id.*
159. *Id.*
160. *Id.*
161. *Id.* § 655.736–.739.
162. *Id.*
163. *Id.* § 655.810.
164. *Id.* § 655.760(a).
165. *Id.*

Separation of these records will avoid a confidentiality breach and an unnecessary disclosure of compensation data.

Finally, it is important to note that if an H-1B is dismissed by the employer prior to the end of their proposed period of stay, the employer is required to pay return transportation for the H-1B back to their home country or country of last residence.[166] In addition, it is important for the employer to notify the relevant agencies—the Department of Labor and USCIS—of the termination of employment to limit their continued liability for paying the stated wage on the Labor Condition Application (LCA).[167]

H-1C Visas for Professional Nurses Working in a Health Professional Shortage Area

The H-1C visa category is for foreign trained nurses who seek to work temporarily in U.S. hospitals located in a Health Professional Shortage Area (HPSA).[168] Extensions of stay for a period of up to three years are available to H-1C visa holders.[169] Please note that some other visa categories such as H-1B, H-2B, and TN are presently available to nurses engaged in particular positions and specialties within the nursing field.

H-2 Visas for Seasonal and Temporary Workers
H-2 Temporary Visas for Agricultural Workers

H-2A visas for temporary agricultural workers cover limited duration positions in farming, raising livestock, and practices related to family as well as the preparing of food for market, delivery, storage and the like.[170] The nature of the employment must be seasonal and temporary in nature and intended to support an employer who has a peak season during which more employees are required for a limited period (such as harvesting crops).[171] The temporary nature of the need is not intended to exceed one year.[172]

In order to successfully obtain an H-2A, the employer must show that there are insufficient workers in the United States that are willing,

---

166. 8 C.F.R. § 214.2(h)(4)(iii)(E).

167. Office of Foreign Labor Certification, U.S. Department of Labor Employment and Training Administration, *Frequently Asked Questions H-1B, H-1B1, and E-3 Programs: Round 1*, February 17, 2011.

168. *See generally* 8 C.F.R. § 214.2(h).

169. *Id.* § 214.2(h)(15)(ii)(A).

170. 20 C.F.R. § 655.103(c).

171. *Id.* § 655.103(b) (definition of H-2A worker).

172. *Id.* § 655.103(d).

qualified, and able to perform the work and that the employment of the seasonal worker will not negatively impact the wages and working conditions of similarly employed U.S. workers.[173]

The H-2A is a multistep application including recruiting, DOL review, a USCIS filing as well as the individual obtaining the appropriate visa at a U.S. consulate overseas and then being admitted to the United States.[174] The process is both time consuming and costly, and employers use this option as a last resort to local hires.

H-2B Seasonal and Temporary Visas for Nonagricultural Workers

H-2B visa holders fall within four categories:

- one-time occurrence—covering true one-time usages not likely to recur or one-time events of short durations;[175]
- seasonal need—usages tied to a season of the year by a recurring event;[176]
- peak load need—usages tied to supplanting a permanent staff with nonpermanent additions during busy periods;[177] or
- intermittent need—usages for short, occasional periods of time for positions the employer has never staffed with permanent workers.[178]

In fact, an employer may use a single H-2B petition to hire multiple temporary workers (even unnamed ones) for the same service, time, period, and location.[179] However, using the H-2B program requires extensive planning on the part of an employer, given both the extensive bureaucratic process in obtaining approval as well as the business realities of needing such workers in a very small window of time.

Obtaining H-2B visa classification is a three-step process. Initially, the employer must apply for a temporary labor certification from the DOL.[180] This application requires placing recruitment for the position, screening candidates to ensure no U.S. workers are available, and demonstrating that the employment of H-2B meets prevailing wage standards.[181] The

---

173. *Id.* § 655.100.
174. *Id.* § 655.100; 8 C.F.R. § 214.2(h)(5).
175. 8 C.F.R. § 214.2(h)(6)(ii)(B)(1).
176. *Id.* § 214.2(h)(6)(ii)(B)(2).
177. *Id.* § 214.2(h)(6)(ii)(B)(3).
178. *Id.* § 214.2(h))(6)(ii)(B)(4).
179. *Id.* § 214.2(h)(2)(G)(ii).
180. *Id.* § 214.2(h)(6)(iii).
181. 20 C.F.R. § 655.5–.23.

DOL can (and frequently does) make inquiries to ensure the employer is strictly following the temporary labor certification program's attestation and documentation requirements.[182]

Following temporary labor certification approval, the employer must file Form I-129 to secure approval of a non-immigrant petition on behalf of the temporary workers with USCIS. USCIS restricts the amount of H-2B workers to 66,000 per year and further limits usage of this cap to 33,000 for each of two separate six-month portions of the fiscal year.[183] In addition, an employer may not file the H-2B petition more than four months in advance of the need for the H-2B temporary worker.[184] Once the H-2B is approved by USCIS, the worker then presents the approved H-2B petition at a U.S. consulate abroad to apply for an H-2B visa.[185]

H-2B status, when initially approved, gives the individual one (1) year of authorized employment with the sponsoring employer.[186] The H-2B category also entitles spouses and children of the employee to accompany him or her in H-4 dependent status. The H-2B worker may receive one-year extensions up to three years total; however, the DOL requires a new temporary labor certification for each extension, and USCIS intensely scrutinizes such cases.[187] Also, the H-2B visa category does not recognize "dual intent," so an H-2B worker and any H-4 dependents must intend to return abroad at the end of the temporary employment.[188]

Finally, if the employer terminates an H-2B employee's services prior to H-2B status expiration, it must provide or pay the reasonable cost of transportation back to the employee's home country or last country of residence outside the United States.[189]

H-3 Visas for Trainees

H-3 visas are available for foreign nationals who will receive training in the United States in any field other than graduate medical education or training. To obtain H-3 status, an employer must establish that the proposed training is not available in the foreign national's home country, confirm that the foreign national will not be placed in a position regularly held by a U.S. worker, and state how the training will benefit the indi-

---

182. *Id.* § 655.50.
183. INA § 214(g)(9).
184. 8 C.F.R. § 214.2.(h)(9)(i)(B).
185. *Id.* § 214.2.(h).
186. *Id.* § 214.2.(h)(150(ii)(C).
187. *Id.*
188. INA § 214(b).
189. 8 C.F.R. § 214.2(h)(6)(iv)(E).

vidual in his or her career abroad.[190] H-3 petitions must include a detailed training time line that explains precisely how the trainee will accumulate the knowledge (e.g., observation, classroom instruction, on-the-job training). Productive employment is not permitted unless such employment is incidental and necessary to the training.[191]

H-3 status may not be granted to individuals who already possess substantial training and expertise in the proposed field of training.[192] Therefore, if the foreign national already possesses experience and/or expertise, the petitioning organization must explain precisely what new information the trainee will learn.[193]

An individual may hold H-3 trainee status for up to two years. Also, H-3 trainees generally are required to remain outside of the United States for at least six months following the completion of their training before they may be admitted in H or L visa status.[194]

Representatives of Information Media

Employees of foreign information media and their family members are eligible for I visas, provided the visa applicant's activities in the United States will be related to press, film, radio, or other information media and his or her home country provides reciprocal treatment to the United States information media.[195]

The purpose of the I visa category is to promote the exchange of news and information. The availability of I visas extends beyond foreign journalists and applies to some employees of independent production companies, film and video crews entering the United States for work related to educational and informational documentaries, and duly accredited foreign bureau representatives.[196] Additionally, it is possible for freelance journalists to obtain I visas for purposes of obtaining information for a foreign media that will not be used for commercial or entertainment

---

190. *Id.* § 214.2(h)(7)(i).

191. *Id.* § 214.2(h)(7)(ii)(A).

192. *Id.*

193. *Id.* § 214.2(h)(7)(iii).

194. *Id.* § 214.2(h)(9)(iii)(C)(1); *id.* § 214.2(h)(13)(v).

195. An information media organization is considered "foreign" if its home office is in a foreign country, the "government of which grants reciprocity for similar privileges to representatives of such a medium having home offices in the United States." 9 FOREIGN AFFAIRS MANUAL, *supra* note 33, § 41.52 N1.

196. *Id.* § 41.52 N2.1, N2.2, N3.

purposes. In such cases, the consular officer should require a contract between the journalist and the foreign media outlet.[197]

Visas for Exchange Visitors

The J-1 exchange visitor visa classification is intended to increase mutual understanding between the people of the United States and the people of other countries by means of educational and cultural exchanges. The U.S. Department of State (DOS) oversees and approves Exchange Visitor Programs to administer J-1 exchange visas for au pairs; camp counselors; college, university, or secondary students; government or "international" visitors; physicians; professors; research or short-term scholars; specialists; summer work or travel visitors; teachers; and trainees/interns.[198]

Foreign nationals coming to the United States in J-1 status must prove that they have sufficient "home ties" which will compel them to return to their home country upon completion of their J-1 program.[199] J-1 visa holders may be subject to a requirement that they return to and reside in their home country for two years before they may be granted an H or L visa status or permanent residence, unless they first obtain a *waiver* of this requirement from the U.S. government.[200]

Duration of a J-1 program may be a few weeks to several years, dependent on the category. Those employers who wish to sponsor a J-1 should keep in mind that federal regulations require that each J-1 exchange visitor, and his or her dependent spouse and children, have insurance in effect which covers them for sickness and/or accident throughout the duration of their stay.[201]

Spouses, and children under the age of 21, of a J-1 are eligible for a J-2 visa. J-2 spouses may apply to USCIS for an open-market work permit upon their arrival in the United States.[202]

J-1 Interns and Trainees
Within the J-1 visa category, interns and trainees are among the most frequently used for a variety of businesses. For purposes of this article, we will focus on these two types in further detail.

---

197. *Id.* § 41.52 N5.

198. *Id.* § 41.62 N.1.

199. *See generally* 22 C.F.R. Part 62.

200. J-2 spouses are also subject to the J-1 home residency requirement if their spouse is determined to be subject.

201. 22 C.F.R. § 62.14.

202. 8 C.F.R. § 214.2(j)(1)(v).

A J-1 *intern* is defined as a foreign national who either: (1) is currently enrolled in and pursuing studies at a degree or certificate granting post-secondary academic institution *outside* the United States; *or*, (2) has graduated from such an institution no more than 12 months prior to his or her exchange visitor program begin date, and who enters the United States to participate in a structured and guided work-based internship program in his or her specific academic field.[203]

Interns will have a program duration limit of 12 months. However, interns may participate in an unlimited number of additional internship programs as long as they maintain student status or begin a new internship program within 12 months of graduation. If an individual no longer meets these conditions, he or she may participate as a trainee after two years of residence outside the United States following the last internship program.[204]

Conversely, a J-1 *trainee* is appropriate for a foreign national who either has: (1) a degree or professional certificate from a foreign post-secondary academic institution and at least one year of prior related work experience in the occupational field acquired *outside* the United States, *or* (2) five years of work experience *outside* the United States in the occupational field, and who enters the United States to participate in a structured and guided work-based training program in the specific occupational field.[205]

Most trainees have a program duration limit of 18 months; *however, those in the hospitality field are limited to programs of 12 months' duration.* The trainees would be eligible for additional training programs after a period of no less than two years residence outside the United States following their initial training program.[206]

Applications for J-1 Program Sponsorship

Applications seeking J sponsor designation are voluminous and must cover all aspects of eligibility. Preparation time may be up to several months. After submission to the DOS, review time at the agency may take six months or more, and it is not at all uncommon for the DOS to request additional information and/or documentation before making a decision. For many organizations, key considerations in deciding whether to pursue designation include the costs involved in preparation and obtaining initial approval, to the ongoing costs and responsibilities involved in

---

203. 22 C.F.R. § 62.22.
204. *Id.*
205. *Id.*
206. *Id.*

administering a successful program, including the necessary oversight, reporting requirements, redesignation process, etc. Given these unavoidable costs and responsibilities, many companies, especially those which are bringing in a modest number of J-1s each year, opt to rely upon the services of an already approved J-1 program sponsor and consolidate all of their J-1 processing with an established J-1 sponsor.

Visas for Spouses, Fiancées, and Children

The K visa category was created in response to the difficulties that U.S. citizens often face when they marry or intend to marry a foreign national, especially when the foreign national is living outside the United States. Unfortunately, the process to apply for a K visa has become increasingly bureaucratic since its creation. As a result, there is virtually no difference in the processing time to obtain a K visa versus a family-based immigrant visa. In short, despite legislative efforts to bring relief to U.S. families, the agencies responsible for administering the process have rendered this option obsolete for most cases.

K visas always require at least three steps. First, the U.S. citizen must file an I-129F petition with USCIS on behalf of the foreign national spouse or fiancée.[207] If the petition is approved, the case will be forwarded to the Department of State's National Visa Center (NVC) and additional documentation is requested. Upon the National Visa Center's receipt of all necessary original documentation, the file will be transferred to the consulate that has jurisdiction over the applicant's place of residence and an interview will be scheduled. The requirements for both the K-1 and K-3 visas are discussed below.

K-1 Visas for U.S. Citizens' Fiancées and Their Children

A K-1 fiancé visa is a special type of temporary visa, which allows a U.S. citizen to bring his or her fiancé(e) to the United States for the purpose of marrying.[208] This option requires the United States citizen to file an I-129F petition with USCIS prior to marriage.[209] The purpose of this petition is to prove to USCIS that there is a bona fide fiancé relationship. Along with the petition, a petitioner submits evidence of U.S. citizenship, sworn statements from both the foreign national and U.S. citizen describing the development of their relationship/regular communication/intention to marry,

---

207. 8 C.F.R. § 214.2(k)(1).

208. *See generally* INA § 101(a)(15)(k); 8 C.F.R. § 214.2(k).

209. The children of a K-1 fiancée may be included on the I-129F and is authorized to accompany the K-1 parent to the United States in K-2 status. INA § 101(a)(15)(K)(iii).

photographs of the couple together, evidence of communication such as phone statements/plane tickets/correspondence, etc. Generally, the couple must have met prior to the U.S. citizen-sponsor's filing the K-1 petition. However, there are exceptions to the requirement that a couple must have previously met when such a meeting would violate long-established cultural practices or would result in extreme hardship.[210]

The time line, at the writing of this article, to obtain a K-1 visa is approximately 10–12 months, but the process could be shorter or longer, as government processing times fluctuate. USCIS regulations state that a K-1 fiancé(e) is authorized to work "for the period of admission in that status, as evidenced by an employment authorization document issued by the Service."[211] Unfortunately, only rarely does CBP issue I-94 cards for K-1 fiancé(e)s that specifically note "employment authorized." Otherwise, a K-1 fiancé(e) is eligible to apply for an employment authorization upon admission to the United States in K-1 status.[212]

After the fiancée enters the United States on the K-1 visa, the couple must marry within 90 days. After the marriage, the K-1 must apply to adjust status to permanent resident ("green card") based on marriage. This is a separate application submitted to USCIS, and usually involves an in-person interview with a USCIS officer.

K-3 Visas for the Spouses of U.S. Citizens and Their Children

A foreign national fiancé of a U.S. citizen is not eligible to apply for a family-based immigrant visa until lawfully married to a U.S. citizen.[213] K-3 visas are temporary visas available for foreign nationals who have valid marriages to United States citizens, who have an I-130 Immigrant Petition for Alien Relative pending on their behalf, and who seek to enter the United States for purposes of awaiting the approval of the petition. Thus, prior to the creation of the K-3 visa category, U.S. citizens suffered hardship due to separation from their loved ones while the USCIS and the State Department processed the immigrant petition and visa applications. Alternatively, the U.S. citizen was forced to live abroad while waiting for the government to schedule the immigrant visa interview.

The beginning of this process involves filing the I-130 with USCIS. Once the receipt notice is received (usually about two weeks after filing), an I-129F petition for K-3 classification must be filed, along with a

---

210. 8 C.F.R. § 214.2(k)(2).
211. *Id.* § 274a.12(a)(6).
212. *Id.*
213. INA §§ 101(a)(15), 214(b).

copy of the I-130 receipt notice. The process that follows is similar to that explained above for the K-1 visa.

PRACTICE POINTER:

Although the USCIS instructions for the I-129F are unclear as to whether it is only necessary to file the I-130 for the foreign spouse beneficiary before submitting the K-3 petition, the U.S. citizen petitioner should file I-130s for each immediate relative[214] who intends to immigrate to the United States. It is possible that the I-130 could be approved before the I-129F, which would result in USCIS denying the K-3 petition. If a U.S. citizen fails to file the I-130 for all immediate relative family members, there can be a significant delay in obtaining immigrant visas for the children.

A post-marriage temporary spouse visa (K-3 visa) generally takes the same amount of time to process as a K-1 visa. Additionally, like the K-1 visa holder, after arriving in the United States, the K-3 foreign national spouse needs to apply to adjust status to that of a legal permanent resident.

Intracompany Transferee

L-1 intra-company transferee status is available to qualified international executives, managers, and specialized knowledge employees transferred from an overseas organization to work for the same organization in the United States or for its related American entity.[215] An intracompany transferee may obtain L-1 status for an initial period of up to three years.[216] Extensions are available for a total of five years in the case of specialized knowledge employees and up to seven years for managerial or executive employees.[217]

To qualify for intracompany transferee status, it must be demonstrated that within the three years preceding the time of application the employee has been employed continuously abroad for one year by a firm, corporation or other legal entity, or a branch, affiliate or subsidiary

---

214. This now includes same-sex couples following the Supreme Court's decision finding DOMA unconstitutional. President Obama directed federal departments to ensure the decision and its implication for federal benefits for same-sex legally married couples are implemented swiftly and smoothly. To that end, USCIS now reviews immigration visa petitions filed on behalf of a same-sex spouse in the same manner as those filed on behalf of an opposite-sex spouse. *See* http://www.uscis.gov/family/same-sex-marriages.

215. 8 C.F.R. § 214.2(l)(1)(i).

216. *Id.* § 214.2(l)(7)(A)(2).

217. *Id.* § 214.2(l)(12)(i); *id.* § 214.2(l)(15)(ii).

thereof, and that the employee seeks to enter the United States temporarily to continue rendering services for the same employer, or a branch, subsidiary or affiliate thereof in a capacity that is managerial, executive, or involves specialized knowledge.[218]

For purposes of L-1 classification:

- "branch" means an operating division or office of the same organization housed in a different location.[219]
- "subsidiary" means (1) a firm, corporation, or other legal entity of which a parent owns, directly or indirectly, more than half of the entity and controls the entity; or (2) owns, directly or indirectly, half of the entity and controls the entity; or (3) owns, directly or indirectly, less than half of the entity, but in fact controls the entity.[220]
- "affiliate" means (1) one of two subsidiaries both of which are owned and controlled by the same parent corporation or individual, or (2) one of two legal entities owned and controlled by the same group of individuals, each individual owning and controlling approximately the same share or proportion of each entity.[221]

The L-1 beneficiary's spouse and unmarried children under 21 years of age are eligible for L-2 status. L-2 spouses are eligible to apply for employment authorization.[222]

L-1A Visas for Managers or Executives

"Managerial capacity" means an assignment within an organization in which the employee personally:

- manages the organization, department, subdivision, function, or component;
- supervises and controls the work of other supervisory, professional, or managerial employees, or manages an essential function within the organization or department or subdivision of the organization;
- has authority to hire and fire or recommend personnel actions (if another directly supervises employees), or if no direct supervision, functions at a senior level; and

---

218. *Id.* § 214.2(l)(1)(ii).
219. 9 FOREIGN AFFAIRS MANUAL, *supra* note 33, § 41.54 N.7.3.
220. *Id.*
221. *Id.*
222. INA § 214(c)(2)(E).

- exercises discretionary authority over day-to-day operations of the activity or function.[223]

"Executive capacity" means an assignment in an organization in which the employee primarily

- directs the management of an organization or a major component or function;
- establishes goals and policies;
- exercises wide latitude in discretionary decision making; and
- receives only general supervision or direction from higher level executives, the Board of Directors, or stockholders of the business.[224]

L-1B: Specialized Knowledge Professionals
"Specialized knowledge" is defined to include persons who have "special knowledge of the company product and its application in international markets" or who have "an advanced level of knowledge of processes and procedures of the company."[225] Characteristics of a specialized knowledge employee include the possession of knowledge that is valuable to the employer's competitiveness in the marketplace; unique qualifications that contribute to the U.S. employer's knowledge of foreign operating conditions; possession of knowledge which can be gained only through extensive prior experience with that employer; and employees abroad who have been given significant assignments which have enhanced the employer's productivity, competitiveness, image, or financial position.[226] Significantly, a specialized knowledge employee is *not* simply a highly skilled or professional worker. This visa classification has been a particularly scrutinized area both at USCIS and at consular posts worldwide at the time of writing to this article.

Blanket L-1 Visa Applications for Multinational Employers
A blanket L-1 approval notice allows an employer to transfer employees routinely by using the approval notices in support of numerous L-1 applications at a U.S. embassy or consulate abroad.[227] In order to qualify for a blanket L, an employer must meet specific criteria including doing

---

223. 8 C.F.R. § 214.2(l)(1)(ii)(B).
224. *Id.* § 214.2(l)(1)(ii)(C).
225. *Id.* § 214.2(l)(1)(ii)(D).
226. *Id.*
227. *See id.* § 214.2(l)(4).

business in the United States for at least one year, having three or more domestic and foreign branches, affiliates, or subsidiaries as well as annual sales and employee numbers.[228]

Visas for Vocational and Other Nonacademic Students

The M visa category is available to students (M-1) and their family members (M-2).[229] An M-1 student is required to present a duly executed Form I-20 upon submission of an application for M-1 visa at a U.S. consulate. The I-20 is obtained from the vocational or other nonacademic institution and must confirm the foreign national will be pursuing a full course of study.[230] The student's period of authorized admission to the United States is for a fixed period of time that shall not exceed a period of one year.[231]

Students must be careful to comply with the terms and conditions of M-1 status. Failure to maintain status could arise, inter alia, by transferring schools without obtaining USCIS approval,[232] unauthorized employment,[233] and a change in educational objective.[234]

Parents and Children of Special Immigrants

The N visa category is for parents (M-1) and children (M-2) whose immediate family members obtained permanent resident status under INA § 101(a)(27)(I)(i), (ii) and (L).[235] This provision of law ensures family unity for G-4 households when there has been a death or retirement of an international organization employee. The N visa holder is authorized to work in the United States incident to status.[236] Therefore, it is unnecessary to obtain an employment authorization document before working while in N status. An individual in N status should be admitted for three years and is eligible for extensions in increments of three years.[237] N status

---

228. *Id.*
229. *Id.* § 214.2(m)(1), (3).
230. *Id.* § 214.2(m)(9).
231. *Id.* § 214.2(m)(5). The exact period of stay shall include the period necessary to complete the course of study, plus practical training, plus 30 days. *Id.*
232. *Id.* § 214.2(m)(11)(ii).
233. *Id.* § 214.2(m)(13).
234. *Id.* § 214.2(m)(12).
235. INA § 101(a)(15)(N).
236. 8 C.F.R. § 214.2(n)(4).
237. *Id.* § 214.2(m)(17).

terminates once the child no longer qualifies as a child under the Immigration and Nationality Act.[238]

Temporary Visas for Individuals with Extraordinary Ability

O-1 classification allows foreign nationals who demonstrate extraordinary ability in the sciences, arts, education, business, or athletics through sustained national or international acclaim to come temporarily to the United States to continue work in the area of their extraordinary ability.[239] This visa type is also available to individuals who have a record of extraordinary achievement in motion picture and/or television productions.[240] Extraordinary ability in science, education, business, or athletics is defined as a level of expertise indicating that the person is one of the small percentage who have risen to the very top of the field of endeavor; in arts (including culinary arts and essential technical or creative personnel), it is defined as distinction, or a degree of skill or recognition substantially above that ordinarily encountered.[241]

O visas require a written advisory opinion from an appropriate institution describing the beneficiary's ability and achievements in the field and duties to be performed, or simply not objecting to the petition. The O classification is often a helpful alternative to other non-immigrant visas such as H-1Bs because this status can be extended nearly indefinitely and there is no "cap" (or October 1 start date for for-profit petitioners) or "prevailing wage" requirement, and those subject to the two-year foreign residence requirement are eligible for O-1 status.

O-2 classification applies to an individual who is coming temporarily to the United States solely to assist in the artistic or athletic performance by an O-1, and who has critical skills and experience with the O-1 visa applicant.[242] Several O-2s may be included on one application if they are all coming in support of the same principal.[243]

The authorized period of stay for an O is up to three years, but is discretionary and may be more limited based on the nature of the petition. O-1 extensions are granted in one-year increments for the same "event." However, a change of employer or a new position can qualify as a new event, and the O-1 may be granted a new period of stay for three years.[244]

---

238. *Id.* § 214.2(m)(3). *See also* INA § 101(b)(1).
239. 8 C.F.R. § 214.2(o)(1).
240. *Id.* § 214.2(o)(3)(v).
241. *Id.* § 214.2(o)(3)(ii).
242. *Id.* § 214.2(o)(1)(ii)(B).
243. *Id.* § 214.2(o)(2)(ii)(F).
244. *Id.* § 214.2(o)(3).

Petitions may also be filed by employers or agents, but may not be filed by an individual on their own behalf.[245]

Visas for International Athletes, Performers, Artists

The P visa category includes P-1 internationally known athletes (either individuals or members of a group or team) or entertainment group; P-2 individual and group performing artists participating in a reciprocal exchange program; P-3 culturally unique artists; and support personnel for primary P visa holders.[246] P-1 athlete applicants must have received international recognition, either individually if the applicant is applying individually, or as a team if the applicant is applying with a team, which means a high level of achievement in the field evidenced by a degree of skill and recognition substantially above that ordinarily encountered [247]

P-1 entertainer applicants must belong to an entertainment group that has received sustained international recognition for a substantial period of time, and each member must have had a relationship with the group for more than a year, with some exceptions.[248]

For P-2s, a labor union must be involved in establishing (or acknowledging the validity of) the exchange program between the United States and foreign country in which the applicant participates.[249]

P-3s are for applicants coming to the United States to develop, interpret, represent, coach, or teach an art or discipline that can be classified as a culturally unique style of artistic expression, methodology, or medium that is unique to a particular country, nation, society, class, ethnicity, religion, tribe, or other group.[250] Essential support personnel do not perform and cannot work apart from principal Ps, but provide highly skilled essential services that are integral to a performance and cannot readily be provided by a U.S. worker. Consultation with an appropriate labor union/ peer group is required in all cases.[251]

Visas for International Cultural Exchange Visa

The Q-1 visa is a temporary work visa intended for those foreign nationals who are coming to the United States for training, work, and

---

245. *Id.* § 214.2(o)(2)(i).
246. *Id.* § 214.2(p).
247. *Id.* § 214.2(p)(3).
248. INA § 214(c)(4)(B)(11).
249. 8 C.F.R. § 214.2(p)(5).
250. *Id.* § 214.2(p)(6).
251. *Id.* § 214.2(7)(1)(A).

most importantly, to share the history, culture, and traditions of their country(ies) or nationality.[252] A U.S. employer may file a petition with the USCIS seeking approval of such *an international cultural exchange program,* for a period of up to 15 months.[253] The employer must demonstrate that it has employees and that it provides goods and/or services on a regular, continuous, systematic basis.[254]

A Q-1 international cultural exchange program must satisfy the following requirements:

- *Accessible to the public:* The program must take place in a school, museum, business, or other establishment where the public, or a segment of the public sharing a common interest, is exposed to aspects of the foreign culture as part of a structured program.[255]
- *Cultural component:* The program's cultural component must be essential and integral to the Q-1 non-immigrant's training and/or work. This cultural aspect must be designed to exhibit or explain the attitude, customs, history, heritage, philosophy, or traditions of the Q-1 visa holder's country of nationality.[256]
- *Work component:* The Q-1's employment and/or training must be connected to the cultural component of the program and may not be independent of it. In essence, the work must serve as a means of achieving the goal of cultural exchange.[257]
- In addition, the employer must offer the individuals "wages and working conditions comparable to those [given] local domestic workers," and otherwise demonstrate an ability to pay the offered wages.[258]

In order to be eligible for Q-1 status, the foreign national would need to meet the following criteria:

- be at least 18 years old at the time the petition is filed;
- be qualified to perform the service/labor or receive the indicated training;
- have the ability to communicate effectively about the cultural attributes of his/her country to the public or a segment of it; and

---

252. *Id.* § 214.2(q).
253. *Id.*
254. *Id.*
255. *Id.* § 214.2(q)(3)(iii)(A).
256. *Id.* § 214.2(q)(3)(iii)(B).
257. *Id.* § 214.2(q)(3)(iii)(C).
258. *Id.* § 214.2(q)(4)(i).

- have resided or been physically present outside the United States for the immediate prior year, if he or she previously entered in Q-1 status.[259]

Q-1 petitions may include multiple participants, or beneficiaries; moreover, the sponsor is able to substitute or replace a named beneficiary on an approved petition (if for some reason an earlier-named beneficiary could no longer come to the United States). While an extension of stay is possible, the individual Q-1 beneficiary may not exceed a total of 15 months in Q-1 status.[260]

Upon approval of the Q-1 by USCIS, the named individuals would need to make appointments to appear at a U.S. consulate abroad to apply for Q-1 visa stamps in their passports. Like many other non-immigrant classifications, those seeking Q-1 status must be able to demonstrate ongoing and strong ties to the home country or, stated differently, that they have residences abroad to which they intend to return.[261]

Non-immigrant Visas for Religious Workers

Religious organizations that are recognized under the Internal Revenue Code as a 501(c)(3) tax-exempt institution may sponsor some ministers for R-1 status to perform certain functions in the United States.[262] Individuals who qualify for R-1 status are initially granted a 30-month period of stay by USCIS.[263] The maximum amount of time an individual may stay in the United States in R-1 status is five years.[264] USCIS regulations instruct that an extension of R-1 status may be granted for a period of up to 30 months, depending on the amount of time the religious worker has spent in R-1 status.[265]

The sponsoring religious organization must submit a Petition for Non-immigrant Worker and R Supplement to the USCIS,[266] along with a significant amount of documentation, including evidence confirming the following: the organization's tax exempt status,[267] job title and description of duties the beneficiary will perform,[268] ministerial qualifications of

---

259. *Id.* § 214.2(q)(3)(iv).
260. *Id.* § 214.2(q)(2)(ii).
261. *Id.*
262. INA § 101(a)(15)(R); 8 C.F.R. § 214.2(r).
263. 8 C.F.R. § 214.2(r)(4).
264. *Id.* § 214.2(r)(5).
265. *Id.* § 214.2(r)(6).
266. *Id.* § 214.2(r)(8).
267. *Id.* § 214.2(r)(9).
268. *Id.* § 214.2(r)(vii).

the beneficiary,[269] and the religious organization's denominational affiliation.[270] The religious worker category departs significantly from other temporary work visa categories in the area of compensation. Unlike many non-immigrant categories, such as the H-1B, H-2B and E-3, the R-1 non-immigrant category does not require employers to pay the actual or prevailing wage.[271] In fact, in certain circumstances, the employer may sponsor a foreign national who will support himself or herself during the period of employment.[272]

Importantly, religious organizations that sponsor R-1 workers are subject to investigations by the Department of Homeland Security. Revocation of an R-1 petition is authorized when an investigation reveals the R-1 worker is no longer employed by the organization; when the employer stated facts that were not true and correct; when the employer violated the terms and conditions of the approved petition; when the petitioner violated the terms and conditions of 101(a)(15)(R); and when the USCIS approval was in gross error.[273]

Visas for Individuals Who Assist Law Enforcement ("Snitch" Visa)

Individuals in possession of critical, credible information concerning a criminal organization or enterprise who is willing to supply the information to the relevant federal or state law enforcement agencies and who are physically present in the United States may be eligible for an S-1 visa.[274] There are 250 S visas available annually with 200 being in the S-1 category and 50 in the S-2 category. The S-2 category is for individuals who the Secretary of State and Attorney General jointly determine are in possession of credible information related to a terrorist organization. These visas are valid for a maximum duration of three years and do not allow for a change of status.[275] Family members (spouse and children under age) may accompany or follow to join an S visa holder in the discretion of the Attorney General and in the case of the S-2, the Secretary of State and are admitted as S-7.[276]

---

269. *Id.* § 214.2(r)(10).
270. *Id.* § 214.2(r)(9)(iii).
271. *Id.* § 214.2(r)(11).
272. *Id.* § 214.2(r)(11)(A).
273. *Id.* § 214.2(r)(18).
274. INA § 101(A)(15)(S)(i).
275. 8 C.F.R. § 214.2(t)(12)(i).
276. 8 C.F.R. § 214.2(t)(4).

T Visa for Victims of Trafficking

Each year 5,000 T visas are available for victims of severe forms of human trafficking. Severe trafficking includes a wide range of abusive situations, generally involving victims who are tricked or coerced into living or working in terribly inhumane conditions in the United States.[277] A T visa allows trafficking victims to remain in the United States and to assist in the investigation and prosecution of trafficking violations.[278] Individuals granted T visas can apply for permanent residence after three years of being in T visa status or once the relevant trafficking investigation or prosecution is complete for a period of up to four years. An individual granted T status is also eligible for employment authorization incident to their status.[279] Finally, certain family members of an individual with T visa status may also be eligible for permanent residency.[280]

TN or Trade NAFTA Visas

The TN non-immigrant visa category, created by the North American Free Trade Agreement (NAFTA), allows for the expedited visa processing of Canadian and Mexican professionals seeking short-term productive employment in the United States.[281] The TN category has no annual quota limitation and, like the H-1B and L-1, is available for a period of up to three years. Importantly, however, to qualify for TN status, the applicant must show that they do not have immigrant intent.[282]

Canadian or Mexican citizens are eligible to work temporarily in the United States. in TN status for an employer who offers a bona fide position for temporary employment included on NAFTA's specifically designated list of occupations.[283] The employee also must demonstrate their academic and professional credentials for the specific occupation and an intention to depart the United States after the completion of the temporary employment.[284]

---

277. INA § 101(a)(15)(T)(i); 8 C.F.R. § 214.11(a)–(b).

278. INA § 101(a)(15)(T)(i).

279. 8 C.F.R. § 214.11(t).

280. *Id.* § 245.23(23)(a).

281. *Id.* § 214.6.

282. *Id.*

283. The NAFTA treaty includes a listing of the various professions eligible for TN classification as well as the minimum degree or credentials for demonstrating status as a professional. *See* 8 C.F.R. § 214.6 Appendix 1603.D.1 of Annex 1603 of the NAFTA (annotated).

284. INA § 214(b); 9 Foreign Affairs Manual, *supra* note 33, § 41.59 N5.

Canadian citizens simply need to present their materials at a designated port of entry or preflight inspection to seek TN status. Mexican citizens must present their materials at a U.S. consulate to acquire TN visas prior to entering the United States. In both cases, TN employees may receive up to three (3) years of authorized employment and stay in the United States.[285]

The employer sponsoring the TN employee may seek extensions in increments of up to three years, based on business need and continuing proof that the TN employee still intends to return abroad after the temporary employment concludes.[286]

Spouses and children under age of the TN visa holder may travel to the United States in TD status. They are not, however, entitled to work authorization based on this status.[287]

Visas for Victims of Certain Crimes

Victims of certain designated crimes who have consequently suffered physical or mental harm may be eligible for one of 10,000 available U visas.[288] In order to qualify for a U visa, the individual must be willing to assist law enforcement officials in the investigation or prosecution of the underlying crime.[289] U visas are available for non-citizens who have suffered physical or mental abuse as a victim of certain crimes which are set forth by statute.[290] In order to establish eligibility, a non-citizen:

- must demonstrate that she has suffered substantial physical or mental abuse as a victim of qualifying criminal activity;
- must establish that the crime violated the laws of the United States or occurred in the United States or its territories and possession;
- must have information related to the crime;
- must have been (or is being or is likely to be) helpful to the investigation or prosecution of the crime; and
- be otherwise admissible.[291]

The non-citizen must obtain a certification from federal, state, or local law enforcement authorities, a judge, or a federal agency, including the

---

285. 8 C.F.R. § 214.6(d)(1).
286. *Id.* § 214.g(i)(3).
287. 9 FOREIGN AFFAIRS MANUAL, *supra* note 33, § 41.59 N14.3.
288. 8 C.F.R. § 214.14(b).
289. *Id.* § 214.14(a)(9).
290. INA § 214(p); *id.* § 101(a)(15)(U); 8 C.F.R. § 214.14(a)(9).
291. 8 C.F.R. § 214.14(b).

Department of Homeland Security, or other agencies with criminal investigative jurisdiction over their areas of expertise.[292]

CONCLUDING THOUGHTS

A wide variety of visa categories allow for foreign nationals to temporarily enter the United States to visit, to conduct business, to study, to live, and to work. The most important consideration in determining the appropriate visa category comes down to key factors about their personal background, their plans for the future, and their personal situation. Some threshold inquiries should include:

- What is the purpose of the travel to the United States?
- What is the duration of the visit to the United States?
- Will any remuneration be involved and, if so, what is the source?
- Is there any possibility that the individual's stay may be extended?
- Does the foreign national have a criminal background?
- Has the individual ever over-stayed a prior U.S. visa?
- Has the individual ever been denied a U.S. visa?
- What will the individual be doing during their stay in the United States?
- Will their spouse and children be joining them?
- Do they wish to consider legal permanent residency?

All of these factors should be reviewed closely with immigration counsel as plans are made for a foreign national to travel to the United States. Advance planning is key, as it will allow for any concerning issues to be reviewed and assessed. Ultimately, arriving in the United States in the right visa category and actively maintaining valid non-immigrant status facilitates future travel in the United States and the ability to consider other types of visa status.

---

292. *Id.* § 214.14(b).

8

WHAT EVERY IMMIGRATION LAWYER NEEDS TO KNOW ABOUT THE H-1B VISA

Adam Rosen[1]

One of the most commonly used work visas in the United States is the H-1B visa.[2] The first question that every employer will want to ask and to which every immigration lawyer must know the answer is how to get a particular foreign national to work at the particular employer. Oddly enough, the Immigration and Nationality Act (INA) refers to the act of bringing a foreign national to work in the United States as "importing"[3] the alien.[4] The actual process will remain largely the same whether the particular foreign national is starting out in the United States at the time this theoretical employer has expressed interest or outside the United States. Yet there are two different agencies that are primarily involved in the H-1B petition process; the U.S. Citizenship and Immigration Services (USCIS or Service), and the Office of Foreign Labor Certification (OFLC) at the U.S. Department of Labor (DOL). As a result, an immigration lawyer must be ready to represent his client before agencies enforcing different rules.

---

1. Adam J. Rosen is a Member of the Murthy Law Firm and a supervising attorney in the Special Projects Department. He represents companies and individuals before U.S. Citizenship and Immigration Services (USCIS), the Department of Labor (DOL), the Department of State (DOS), and various other government agencies with regard to both immigrant and non-immigrant employment-related and family-based applications and petitions. More specifically, Mr. Rosen handles administrative motions and appeals to USCIS and the Administrative Appeals Office of decisions in complex employment, and family-based petitions and applications.
2. The number of non-immigrant admissions to the United States in H-1B status was 473,015. However, this figure is actually less than the 733,692 admissions in TN status and than 498,899 admissions in L-1 status. *See* Table 25, Non-immigrant Admissions by Class of Admission: Fiscal Years 2003 to 2012—Continued, p. 63, UNITED STATES DEPARTMENT OF HOMELAND SECURITY, YEARBOOK OF IMMIGRATION STATISTICS: 2012. Washington, D.C.: U.S. Department of Homeland Security, Office of Immigration Statistics, 2013.
3. INA § 214(c).
4. *Id.* § 101(a)(3) defines an alien as "any person not a citizen or national of the United States."

So where does an employer begin when it decides to "import"[5] a foreign national to work in the United States in H-1B status? The H-1B visa is not available to interested employers and foreign nationals without limits. The law restricts who is eligible for the H-1B based on specific criteria laid out in the implementing regulations[6] as well as in the guidance[7] issued by USCIS to its adjudications officers. Established by INA § 101(a)(15)(h)(i)(b), the law requires there be a sponsoring employer seeking to hire someone to fill a "specialty occupation" position.[8]

> (H) an alien (i)(b) subject to section 212(j)(2) , who is coming temporarily to the United States to perform services . . . in a specialty occupation described in section 214(i)(1) or as a fashion model, who meets the requirements for the occupation specified in section 214(i)(2) or, in the case of a fashion model, is of distinguished merit and ability, and with respect to whom the Secretary of Labor determines and certifies to the Attorney General that the intending employer has filed with the Secretary an application under section 212(n)(1).[9]

The first question posed by many foreign nationals is often "how do I get an H-1B visa to work?" or by employers is "how can I hire an H-1B worker for my business?" It is important to keep in mind while going through the process of sponsoring a foreign national for H-1B status that the law is designed with several competing goals in mind: to protect the wages of U.S. workers, to ensure the fair treatment of foreign workers, and to facilitate U.S. employers hiring skilled foreign workers.

The H-1B is only available for employment of individuals with at least a U.S. bachelor's degree or the foreign equivalent in a specialty occupation position.[10] A specialty occupation position is one that generally requires the "theoretical and practical application" of specific knowledge and the "attainment" of a bachelor's degree to perform.[11] The job offered

---

5. *Id.* § 214(c).
6. *See* 8 C.F.R. § 214.2(h)(1)(i) (2014); INA § 214(g).
7. Although there is a range of guidance that has come from USCIS on multiple issues, one of the more controversial memoranda was the January 8, 2010 Memorandum from Donald Neufeld, Associate Director, Service Center Operations, Determining Employer-Employee Relationship for Adjudication of H-1B Petitions, Including Third-Party Site Placements, HQ 70/6.2.8, AD 10-24.
8. *See* 8 C.F.R. § 214.2(h)(ii) (2014); INA § 214(i).
9. INA § 101(a)(15)(h)(i)(b).
10. *See* 8 C.F.R. § 214.2(h)(iii) (2014); *id.* § 214.2(h)(iii)(D).
11. INA § 214(i)(1).

in an H-1B petition will be scrutinized by the USCIS adjudicator because there are many people who wish to be issued the H-1B, but do not qualify. It does consequently occur that an attorney will be compelled to advise his or her client that a particular person or job does not qualify for H-1B classification. This problem often arises because the specialty occupation requirement cannot be met.

In the regulations governing H-1B, there are four possible ways to qualify a petition as a specialty occupation.[12] One way is if the job "normally" requires a bachelor's degree for admission to employment.[13] A second way is if the bachelor's degree requirement is "common to the industry" or if the employer can show that its particular job, though similar to an industry not requiring this degree, is sufficiently complex to warrant a degree requirement.[14] Third, an employer could show that it normally requires that candidates in a particular job must present a bachelor's degree.[15] Finally, the job for a foreign worker may qualify for specialty occupation status if the duties are "so specialized and complex" that a bachelor's degree is required to perform properly.[16] This does often limit the types of jobs that the H-1B can be used for.[17] This is often the reason people will turn to other visa categories. However, as a work visa affording status in the United States, the H-1B extends a considerable number of benefits, including extensions beyond the six-year limit with a green card case pending,[18] the absence of any non-immigrant intent requirement,[19] and the ability to start new employment after the H-1B petition is filed with USCIS when one has already been in H-1B status.[20]

---

12. *See* 8 C.F.R. § 214.2(h)(4)(iii)(A) (2014).

13. *Id.* § 214.2(h)(4)(iii)(A)(1).

14. *See id.* § 214.2(h)(4)(iii)(A)(2).

15. *See id.* § 214.2(h)(4)(iii)(A)(3).

16. *See id.* § 214.2(h)(4)(iii)(A)(4).

17. There are numerous cases qualifying as Precedent Decisions binding on USCIS holding that the status of a particular occupation is professional by nature. Examples include an accountant, in *Matter of Arjani*, 12 I. & N. Dec. 649 (R.C. 1967), electronics specialist, in *Matter of Sea, Inc.*, 19 I. & N. Dec. 817 (Comm. 1988), a journalist, in *Matter of Perez*, 12 I. & N. Dec. 701 (DD 1968). Other sources of positions qualifying as professional are ones listed in INA § 101(a)(32), which defines a professional.

18. *See* American Competitiveness in the Twenty-First Century Act, Pub. L. No. 106-313, § 104(c), 114 Stat. 1251, 1253 (2000). *See also* Section II and Section III of the December 27, 2005, Memorandum from Michael Aytes, Acting Director of Domestic Operations, Interim guidance for processing I-140 employment-based immigrant petitions and I-485 and H-1B petitions affected by the American Competitiveness in the Twenty-First Century Act of 2000 (AC21) (Public Law 106-313), HQPRD 70/6.2.8-P.

19. *See* 8 C.F.R. § 214.2(h)(16) (2014).

20. *See* American Competitiveness in the Twenty-First Century Act, § 105, 114 Stat. at 1253.

The H-1B petition is prepared primarily using Form I-129, available on USCIS's website,[21] but it is not all that must be filed with the Service. There is also a labor condition application (LCA) requirement.[22] It is a certification by the U.S. Department of Labor (DOL) that must be submitted with the H-1B petition to USCIS.[23] The LCA is a critical component of every H-1B petition that can become the source of considerable liability for an employer. The LCA establishes a baseline for both the location and the wage; each wage set on the LCA is associated with a particular level.[24] An employer can become subject to fines, penalties, and back wages if an inappropriate level is selected.[25] The DOL can (and is advised to) request a prevailing wage determination in order to determine what the correct wage level is.[26] This is the primary reason that an attorney might consider requesting a PWD for an H-1B petition even though it is not required; the occupation, wage and level assigned by the DOL in the PWD provides a safe harbor[27] against charges of selection of an improper wage level.

The LCA is a certification by the U.S. Department of Labor that the employer is offering the foreign worker the higher of the required or prevailing wage and it will provide the same work conditions as other employed workers.[28] The role played by the U.S. Department of Labor has become one of critical importance. Delegated authority by Congress, the Secretary of Labor assigns his or her own responsibility under the Immigration and Nationality Act to the Office of Foreign Labor Certifica-

21. A copy of the Form I-129 and the instructions are available online at http://www.uscis.gov/i-129, and the ETA Form 9035E is available at http://www.foreignlaborcert.doleta.gov/form.cfm.

22. *See* 20 C.F.R. § 655.700(b)(2) (2013). While 8 C.F.R. § 214.2(h)(4)(i)(B)(1) (2014) (requiring "certification from the Department of Labor that it [petitioner] has filed a labor condition application") (emphasis added), indicates filing is sufficient, USCIS does require an approved LCA. USCIS provided a temporary exception to this requirement when the DOL experienced processing problems. *See* Response to Recommendation 43, Temporary Acceptance of Filed Labor Condition Applications for Certain H-1B Filings, Alejandro N. Mayorkas, Director, USCIS (January 28, 2010), noting that the agency would only provide a limited exception to its requirement of an approved labor condition application.

23. 20 C.F.R. § 655.700 (2013).

24. See the attestations on the labor condition application on ETA Form 9035E.

25. *See* H-1B Level or Degree of Wrongdoing Chart, p. 71e00-4, Chapter 71L Enforcement of H-1B Labor Condition Application (LCA), DOL Field Operations Handbook (April 17, 2006).

26. *See* Prevailing Wage Rate Request to ETA during an Investigation (20 C.F.R. § 655.731(d)), 71d06, Chapter 71L Enforcement of H-1B Labor Condition Application (LCA), DOL Field Operations Handbook (April 17, 2006).

27. *See* 20 C.F.R. § 655.731(a)(2)(ii)(A)(3) (2013).

28. INA § 212(n).

tion (OFLC).[29] OFLC is responsible for both the labor condition application and the labor certification[30] application. Often confused by people, they are critically different. The LCA, filed and certified on ETA Form 9035E, is a requirement for the approval by USCIS of an H-1B petition. The labor certification application, however, is filed on ETA Form 9089 and is a component of an application for lawful permanent resident status; it is neither required nor helpful for the process of winning approval of an H-1B petition.

The regulations issued by USCIS[31] and OFLC[32] impose a mandate to obtain a certified LCA for each H-1B petition that will be filed; such a requirement is absent from the specific language of INA § 212(n) enacting the requirement for the LCA. So the logical question becomes whether it is possible to file an H-1B petition without an approved LCA. The simple answer to that question is no. One should not be filing an H-1B petition without an LCA given that USCIS and the DOL interpret the existing statutory and regulatory provisions to require an approved LCA to be eligible for approval of an H1B petition.[33]

The purpose of the LCA is to protect the wages of U.S. workers and their continued employment.[34] The government seeks to accomplish this goal by requiring notice be given to U.S. workers employed at the work site of the fact that there will be a foreign worker hired and placed at their location. Each labor condition application that an employer wishes to file must be accompanied by notice to other workers in the same occupation at the work site intended for the foreign national. The notice must be posted in two conspicuous locations at the work site within the 30-day period prior to filing the LCA, with the last possible day to post being

---

29. See more information about OFLC at its online home page, http://www.foreignlabor cert.doleta.gov/.

30. INA § 212(a)(5)(A).

31. *See* 8 C.F.R. § 214.2(h)(4)(i)(B)(1) (2014).

32. *See* 20 C.F.R. § 655.700(b)(2) (2013).

33. While it might be possible to question the extent of the Secretary of Labor's authority to promulgate these rules, such a challenge is most likely to fail. *See* Durable Manufacturing Co. v. Department of Labor, 578 F.3d 497 (7th Cir. 2011) (holding that the Secretary of Labor has at least some legal authority to issue regulations).

34. *See* Matter of Mao v. George Nasser d/b/a Nasser Engineering & Computing Services, 2005-LCA-36 (May 26, 2006) (holding the LCA controls the employer's obligations to the foreign worker regarding the payment of wages).

the day of filing.[35] If there is a union, then the notice must be given to the union representative prior to filing the LCA.[36]

Each notice must identify that the employer is petitioning for an H-1B, the number of H-1B workers being sought, the occupational classification—not the title—the wages offered, the period of employment, the work site location, and that the LCA is available for the public to examine.[37] While the law does provide for electronic notice, the electronic notice must be accessible to other workers in the same occupation at the work site and these workers must be aware that this information is available for viewing.[38] As a practical matter, this may pose some problems for an employer filing an H-1B petition if the work site is a third-party location because the sponsor may not be able to obtain permission to post the notice electronically.

As part of an employer's responsibility under the LCA regulations, a public access file (PAF) must be maintained. This is a file that can be requested and viewed by any person and includes a series of documents that demonstrate the employer satisfied all of the requirements of the LCA program and regulations. The Department of Labor's regulations for an employer to comply with the attestations being made on the LCA are formulated as questions being posed by the agency and answered for the filer's benefit. Ultimately, this set of rules is critical because they are distilled into the PAF.[39] The PAF is a set of documents that serve as evidence that a company has in fact satisfied the law's requirements in filing an LCA. The PAF can be requested by anybody and agents of the DOL's Wage and Hour Division can and do request these documents.[40] While the law governing enforcement of these rules does not specify a time period, it is possible for WHD agents to provide some time to an employer when it is requested and reasonable.

The public access file is what its name states, a file for members of the public to access and inspect. The full list of documents is laid out in 20 C.F.R. § 655.760(a) (2013). Simply put though, the aim of the documents that are collected is to demonstrate to the public that the foreign worker is not being paid wages that will depress the wages of similarly employed U.S. workers. The retention requirement is connected to whether or not someone was employed using the LCA and the period of the LCA's validity.

---

35. *See* 20 C.F.R. § 655.734(a)(1)(ii) (2013).
36. *See id.* § 655.734(a)(1)(i).
37. *See id.* § 655.734(a)(1)(ii).
38. *See id.* § 655.734(a)(1)(ii)(B).
39. *See id.* § 655.760.
40. *See id.*

Either at the employer's principal place of business in the U.S. or at the place of employment, the employer shall retain copies of the records required by this subpart for a period of one year beyond the last date on which any H-1B nonimmigrant is employed under the labor condition application or, if no nonimmigrants were employed under the labor condition application, one year from the date the labor condition application expired or was withdrawn.[41]

The employer is also responsible for maintaining payroll records for workers in the same occupation as the non-immigrant employed with any particular LCA for three years from when the record was created.[42] If there is a government investigation initiated of the employer, none of these records that might generally be disposable can be discarded.

It is important for an attorney to advise the employer he or she represents that generally even a disgruntled employee can inspect these files maintained to comply with the Department of Labor's LCA regulations. However, the maintenance of these documents is required not only because the public can approach your client to produce these documents, but Wage and Hour Division agents will request them.

In the absence of the requested documents, the employer will be risking fines and penalties. Consequently, it is advisable that an employer periodically audit its PAFs to establish whether all of the required documents are where they ought to be. It will be important for an attorney to carefully evaluate the contents of each PAF to determine the full extent of liability.

The proffer of temporary employment by a company to a foreign national implicates a considerable role for the lawyer in the preparation of the LCA. It is important for the immigration lawyer to carefully advise an employer about the categorization of a job within a particular occupational classification as well as at a particular wage level. At first glance, these two steps may seem rather innocuous. However, a closer consideration will reflect that the advice given to a client at this stage of preparing an H-1B petition can be critical to what happens in the event of an investigation by the U.S. Department of Labor.

The law requires that an employer seeking to employ an alien in H-1B status pay the higher of the actual or prevailing wage.[43] The selection of a

---

41. *Id.* § 655.760(c).

42. *Id.*

43. *See id.* § 655.731(a). *See also* Administrator v. Integrated Informatics Inc., 2007-LCA-00026, slip op. at 12 (Jan. 31, 2011).

prevailing wage can be undertaken by a review of the OES Wage Library and an analysis of the job requirements with the Standard Vocational Preparation code.[44] On the other hand, you can also request a prevailing wage determination (PWD) from the DOL.[45] However, the speed at which such a request will arrive will vary. In the summer of 2011, the speed in question slowed to a halt upon the OFLC's decision to focus all its time on issuing PWDs for H-2A and H-2B petitions. While this might be a one-time event, it does highlight the dangers of relying on the DOL. Yet the prevailing wage issued by the DOL will provide a safe harbor in the event of an investigation by the Wage and Hour Division.

The PWD giving you a prevailing wage will do so with an occupational classification. The reason for this, of course, is that all wages are tied to specific occupations. For the immigration lawyer advising his clients about wages and classifications, it becomes critical to look at the occupations in the OES Wage Library to establish what the jobs are, what they typically require pursuant to the SVP, and what they pay. The OFLC has issued guidance that addresses how to select a particular wage level, which should be used by an attorney advising a client especially when a PWD is not being obtained from the DOL.[46] In 2010, the Bureau of Labor Statistics of the U.S. Department of Labor published a revised Standard Occupational Classification System, which changed the manner in which jobs are categorized.[47] OFLC is slowly going through the process of converting the O*Net OnLine discussed below and the OES Wage Library to reflect these new occupational titles.

A major goal of the LCA is to protect the wages of U.S. workers. So, investigations conducted by the Wage and Hour Division to determine whether LCA obligations have been correctly satisfied includes the agent looking at the extent of an employer's proper payment of wages. Now it is important to note, before proceeding further in this discussion, that "proper" will sometimes be a disputable concept and at times the impropriety of a particular wage will be fairly evident to an experienced attorney. This is another reason why it is critical in advising a client regarding

44. *See* 20 C.F.R. § 655.731(a)(2)(ii)(A)(2) (2013); *see also* Online Wage Library at the Foreign Labor Certification Data Center, http://www.flcdatacenter.com/.

45. *See* 20 C.F.R. § 655.731(a)(2)(ii)(A)(2) (2013).

46. *See* Prevailing Wage Determination Policy Guidance, Nonagricultural Immigration Programs (Revised November 2009), Employment and Training Administration, *available at* http://www.foreignlaborcert.doleta.gov/pdf/NPWHC_Guidance_Revised_11_2009.pdf.

47. The new Standard Occupational Classification System (SOC) finalized by the Bureau of Labor Statistics is available at http://www.bls.gov/SOC/. The SOC periodically undergoes revisions by the Bureau of Labor Statistics, which may result in changes to occupational codes.

the employment of H-1B workers and preparing the LCA that the duty to pay wages cannot be assumed lightly.

The obligation to pay the wage begins with the approval of the H-1B petition and the sponsored worker's presence in the United States.[48] Practical considerations that might strike an employer as a reasonable basis for declining to pay wages will generally be regarded as unacceptable under the terms and conditions of the LCA. In one case, the failure of an employer to pay the full LCA wage while the worker was studying to take a state licensing exam contributed to the fines and penalties found against the employer.[49] The law generally requires that an employer begin paying the required wage as soon as "the nonimmigrant 'enters into employment' with the employer."[50] It is important to remind an employer that it generally must pay the wages agreed to in the LCA unless the worker falls into the category of "nonproductive" as that term is defined in 20 C.F.R. § 655.731(c)(7) (2013). In 20 C.F.R. § 655.731(c)(7)(ii) (2013), DOL has strictly limited the circumstances when nonpayment of wages is permissible, to for example, when the non-immigrant voluntarily requests time off from work. The result can be severe penalties should the DOL investigate the employer and find a back-wages obligation.[51] In *Administrator v. Greater Missouri Medical Care Pro-Providers, Inc.*,[52] the complaining worker, Ms. Alena Gray Arat, had entered the United States on February 21, 2005, but she only started work as a therapist, the job for which she was sponsored in H-1B status, on May 6, 2005, when she obtained her therapist license.[53] The ALJ ruled that "I found that GMMPCPI violated the Act when it failed to pay required wages to its H-1B employees during nonproductive periods of employment from the date each employee arrived in Joplin, Missouri, to the date each obtained a state license

---

48. *See* Administrator v. Integrated Informatics, Inc., 2007-LCA-00026, slip op. at 12-14 (Jan. 31, 2011).

49. See *Administrator v. Itek Consulting Co.*, 2008-LCA-00046 (May 6, 2009), and *Administrator v. Greater Missouri Medical Care Pro-Providers, Inc.*, 2008-LCA-00026 (Oct. 18, 2011), both holding wages cannot be withheld while worker is obtaining a license.

50. 20 C.F.R. § 655.731(c)(6) (2013).

51. *See* Matter of Mao v. George Nasser d/b/a Nasser Engineering & Computing Services, 2005-LCA-36 (May 26, 2006) (explaining that the LCA imposes wage obligations on the employer). Penalties for the early termination of employment by the H-1B worker are prohibited by INA § 212(n)(2)(C)(I), and 20 C.F.R. § 655.731(c)(10)(i) (2013), but a bona fide liquidated damages clause is permissible. *See* Administrator v. Greater Missouri Medical Pro-Care Providers, Inc., 2008-LCA-00026, slip op. at 75-91 (Oct. 18, 2011).

52. 2008-LCA-00026 (Oct. 18, 2011).

53. *Id.* at 2.

(commonly referred to as 'benching').”[54] The problem faced by GMMPCPI as with Itek Consulting[55] is that the DOL regulations not only state what the employer is prohibited from doing, i.e., benching, but also provides illustrative examples of what would and would not qualify as a valid basis for not paying wages.[56] 20 C.F.R. § 656.731(c)(6)(i) states that studying for a licensing exam is not a valid basis to refuse to pay wages. In this case, the ALJ ultimately ruled that back wages were owed by the employer to the workers.

One of the most valuable lessons that an immigration lawyer can take from reading decisions of the Department of Labor's administrative law judges on LCA compliance—or lack thereof—is the threat of back wages. The Wage and Hour Division has taken its share of drubbings from the Inspector General's office.[57] The focus on back wages can produce tangible results that can be announced to the public, which undoubtedly helps people understand what this agency does as well as to reassure the public that the laws are being enforced. It is important to consider an employer's wage-payment practices to be able to fully assess the extent of violations of DOL regulations. The consequence of an employer's failure is severe because potentially large sums have to be paid out, this fact will be publicly announced by the DOL, and it is a typical area of focus for a WHD investigation.

The location of an H-1B job is also a factor in what wages are owed and will be often treated as a material issue. The job site is stated in two different places, the I-129 form and the LCA.[58] Historically, an employer would certify the labor condition application for a particular geographic area and state the specific address on the I-129; the LCA would only provide space for the city and state where the alien would work. With the introduction of the revised ETA Form 9035E and the iCert filing system, DOL invited employers to state the specific address.[59] However, in a DOL information session held in Baltimore, Maryland before iCert began operations, attended by the author, DOL officials explained that an employer

---

54. *Id.* at 4.
55. *See Administrator v. Itek Consulting Inc.,* 2008-LCA-00046 (May 6, 2009).
56. *Id.* at 6.
57. *See* Case Studies from Ongoing Work Show Examples in Which Wage and Hour Division Did Not Adequately Pursue Labor Violations, Statement of Gregory D. Kutz, Managing Director, Forensic Audits and Special Investigations, Testimony before the Committee on Education and Labor, House of Representatives, July 15, 2008 (GAO-08-973T).
58. A copy of the Form I-129 and the Instructions are available online at http://www.uscis.gov/i-129, and the ETA Form 9035E is available at http://www.foreignlaborcert.doleta.gov/form.cfm. *See* 8 C.F.R. § 100.3 (2014) and 8 C.F.R. § 103.2(a) (2014).
59. *See* ETA Form 9035E and instructions at http://www.foreignlaborcert.doleta.gov/form.cfm.

could continue to provide a geographic location without a specific street address. This would be necessary in the case of a roving employee, someone who is regularly moving from one location to another.[60] USCIS will require, pursuant to 8 C.F.R. § 214.2(h)(2)(i)(B), that an itinerary be included in the H-1B petition that is supported by an approved LCA. It is generally a good idea to caution a client regarding making changes to an H-1B employee's work location consistent with the law and with what is actually being sought by FDNS officials.

The location of a job is a material element of a job offer.[61] With the establishment of the Office of Fraud Detection and National Security within USCIS and site visits to H-1B petitioners, where an H-1B worker is performing his work has become an even more critical issue. The mission of FDNS as stated in Homeland Security Delegation No. 0150.1 is "to investigate alleged civil and criminal violations of the immigration laws, including but not limited to alleged fraud with respect to applications or determinations."[62] It was the practice for many years to merely file a new LCA when there was a change in job location.[63] The need to file another H-1B petition to USCIS for each location change was likely perceived as onerous, given the time to prepare the petition as well as because of the expense. So, when the immigration bar received a letter from Mr. Efren Hernandez, Director, Business and Trade Services Branch, Bureau of Citizenship and Immigration Services, on October 23, 2003, explaining that properly certifying a new LCA was sufficient when the place of employment changed, it proceeded on the understanding that this was an expression of policy that could be relied upon. In fact, the *Adjudicator's Field Manual* (hereafter AFM) incorporates this letter in Section 31.2(e), stating that "mere[ly] transfer[ing] . . . the beneficiary to another work site . . . does not require the filing of an amended petition." Yet the *AFM* also states that this assumes the "supporting" LCA "remains valid."[64] Historically, attorneys and employers understood this to allow employment

---

60. *See* 20 C.F.R. § 655.715 (2013) (defining place of employment as excluding locations away from home office where worker is briefly visiting). *See also id.* § 655.735 (governing short-term placement of H-1B workers at different sites than that which is on an LCA).

61. *See id.* § 655.715.

62. Homeland Security Delegation No. 0150.1, quoted in Privacy Impact Assessment for the Fraud Detection and National Security Data System (FDNS-DS), July 29, 2008, available at http://www.dhs.gov/xlibrary/assets/privacy/privacy_pia_cis_fdns.pdf.

63. Question 6 and Attachment C, Questions and Answers, USCIS American Immigration Lawyers Association (AILA) meeting, October 5, 2011. This reviews the policy memos and letters from the government on this question of whether an amended H-1B petition is required for a change to work site location.

64. *Id.*

162 What Every Lawyer Needs to Know about Immigration Law

at a new location even when a new LCA was certified. However, based on recent developments, if this language of the *AFM* has any remaining effect, it would be limited to those work site changes that remain within normal commuting distance of the location on the labor condition application.

In a meeting between the American Immigration Lawyers Association and USCIS on October 5, 2011, this question was posed to the Service. However, they responded that "We will take AILA's views into consideration when finalizing the policy on what circumstances would require an amended H-1B petition."[65] This does leave an open question until USCIS issues definitive guidance regarding the appropriate steps to take when a client has advised that the H-1B worker has been moved. While historical practice and a review of past guidance[66] seems to indicate that an amended H-1B petition is not required when the only change in employment is the location, actual practice is that agents of FDNS are alleging improprieties when it is discovered that the worker is at a new site and the employer merely obtained a new certified LCA.

The second major issue that any attorney preparing and filing an H-1B Petition must know about, and be prepared to advise clients about is the January 8, 2010, Memorandum from Donald Neufeld, Associate Director, Service Center Operations, Determining Employer-Employee Relationship for Adjudication of H-1B petitions, Including Third-Party Site Placements, HQ 70/6.2.8, AD 10-24 (hereinafter 2010 Neufeld memo).[67] Although USCIS claimed this issue to have been a long-standing requirement of any H-1B petition, it triggered fierce opposition including a lawsuit.[68] The 2010 Neufeld memo directs officers to consider the question of whether an H-1B petitioner has demonstrated that it has the right and ability to exercise control over the performance of work by the foreign national being sponsored. The memorandum lists out a series of questions and evidence that an officer might consider and that attorneys should be advising their clients to gather for submission for an H-1B petition.

---

65. *Id.*

66. *Id.*

67. This memorandum is available from USCIS at http://www.uscis.gov/USCIS/Laws /Memoranda/2010/H1B%20Employer-Employee%20Memo010810.pdf.

68. *See* Broadgate v. U.S. Citizenship and Immigration Services, 730 F. Supp. 2d 240 (D.D.C. 2010) (holding that USCIS did not violate the APA with issuance of the challenged 2010 Neufeld memorandum). *But see* Matter of Allan Gee, 17 I. & N. Dec. 296 (Acting Reg. Comm. 1979) (holding that the common-law control test is inapplicable).

1. Does the petitioner supervise the beneficiary and is such super-
    vision off-site or on-site?
2. If the supervision is off-site, how does the petitioner maintain
    such supervision, *i.e.*, weekly calls, reporting back to main office
    routinely, or site visits by the petitioner?
3. Does the petitioner have the right to control the work of the ben-
    eficiary on a day-to-day basis if such control is required?

    . . . .
5. Does the petitioner hire, pay, and have the ability to fire the
    beneficiary?
6. Does the beneficiary use proprietary information of the peti-
    tioner in order to perform the duties of employment?

    . . . .
11. Does the petitioner have the ability to control the manner
    and means in which the work product of the beneficiary is
    accomplished?[69]

Part of the list in the 2010 Neufeld memo is excerpted here to provide the reader a flavor of what USCIS is seeking. An attorney engaged
in the matter of preparing an H-1B petition should recognize that when
faced with a situation when the employer does not have evidence on this
list, advice and counseling should be extended to the clients. The government's official position being that this list is recommended and not
required,[70] one would think that an employer reporting that it does not
have these items is not a problem. The practical reality, though, is that an
employer will encounter a significant hurdle in the absence of this evidence. However, the law does account for situations when primary evidence is not available.[71]

8 C.F.R. § 103.2(b)(2) (2014) states that, for all applications and petitions,
when primary evidence is missing or cannot be obtained, secondary evidence can be submitted in its stead. The caveat is that the weight USCIS
will give such secondary evidence will depend on its probative value. The
governing standard in an H-1B petition, and most requests for immigration benefits, is the preponderance of the evidence standard.[72] The Service

---

69. Neufeld memorandum, at 3–4, http://www.uscis.gov/USCIS/Laws/Memoranda/2010
/H1B%20Employer-Employee%20Memo010810.pdf.
70. The idea that the list of evidence to demonstrate common law control is merely suggestive comes from the 2010 Neufeld memo itself, which claimed to lack any binding effect on
the public.
71. *See* 8 C.F.R. § 103.2(b)(2) (2014).
72. *See* Matter of E-M-, 20 I. & N. Dec. 77 (Comm'r 1989); Matter of Chawathe, 25 I. & N. Dec.

is required to weigh each piece of evidence to determine its reliability as part of the analysis required for probativeness. In many instances, a petitioner may therefore also want to include affidavits.[73] These are also identified in the law as an acceptable form of evidence.[74] Affidavits may not, by themselves, be enough to establish eligibility, but they can either bolster other evidence given to USCIS or address gaps in the record to help an adjudications officer draw conclusions. For example, in *Matter of Brantigan*,[75] the Board of Immigration Appeals remanded an I-130 petition for determination of a parent-child relationship after reviewing affidavits. The Board explained that the affidavits submitted in support of the existence of the required relationship raised the possibility that the petitioner and beneficiary were related.

It is important though to remember that evidence is something that exists independently of the attorney. It is very easy for an attorney to make his own statement in support of the client. However, as the Service will remind the lawyer who does so, "the representations of counsel do not constitute evidence."[76] Always be mindful of whether evidence submitted in support of the H-1B petition has actually been considered. The success or failure of a case will some times turn on the law, but evidence to buttress legal arguments should be gathered together as best as possible.

The third major question arising in H-1B petitions is whether the job a petitioner has for the foreign worker qualifies as a specialty occupation. There are four kinds of specialty occupation positions. USCIS commonly asks for an employer to establish that there is sufficient specialty occupation work to warrant approval of the H-1B petition.[77] It is always wisest for an attorney to consider all four definitions of a specialty occupation position in advance of filing the H-1B petition; if changes are required then they will have to be executed prior to filing the case with USCIS. Any change to a pending petition that may be regarded as a "material" change will be subject to the terms of *Matter of Michelin Tire*,[78] and a denial by USCIS. By considering 8 C.F.R. § 214.2(h)(4)(iii)(A)(1)–(4), an attorney will be able to both gather information and evidence before a case is filed

369 (AAO 2010).

73. *See* 8 C.F.R. § 103.2(b)(2) (2014).

74. *See id.*; Matter of Brantigan, 11 I. & N. Dec. 493 (B.I.A. 1966); Matter of Bourne, 16 I. & N. Dec. 367 (B.I.A. 1977).

75. 11 I. & N. Dec. 493 (B.I.A. 1966).

76. Matter of Obaigbena, 19 I. & N. Dec. 533 (B.I.A. 1988).

77. 8 C.F.R. § 214.2(h)(4)(iii)(A) (2014).

78. 17 I. & N. Dec. 248 (R.C. 1978).

and advise his or her client when there is a problem and how to fix it so that USCIS is presented with an H-1B petition that is highly approvable.

The supporting evidence that an attorney would use to consider and address specialty occupation status should start with a conversation with the H-1B petitioner. An employer should be able to provide some evidence or at least an explanation about its own employment and hiring practices. However, this does not conclude the work on this subject. An attorney should be turning to any trade or industry associations for information that might be useful and many private companies offer their services to provide opinion letters to explain why a job is a specialty occupation, i.e., a professional position. Yet this too does not end the research. The next place to turn to is the DOL. The DOL operates O*Net OnLine, which has multiple features including detailed information about occupations, such as tasks performed, tools and technologies used, knowledge required, and skills needed as well as the requirements of the position.[79] The Bureau of Labor Statistics has additional information ranging from the Occupational Outlook Quarterly,[80] an online publication that has articles on different types of jobs, to the Occupational Outlook Handbook (OOH),[81] which has a detailed profile on the different jobs that the BLS conducts research on. The OOH will typically be the place that an attorney will want to turn to because of the information it has regarding entry requirements to an occupation including whether a degree is required, and if so what kind. These resources are not meant to be comprehensive, but suggestive. It is important for an attorney to examine each case to comprehend what resources might best facilitate establishing the specialty occupation requirement.

A conflict may arise between the basis for the alien's qualification for H-1B status and lawful permanent resident ("green card") status. The basis for someone to qualify for a job offered under Part 204 of 8 CFR differs from the requirements of Part 214 of 8 C.F.R. for non-immigrants. The primary difference between the two is that the USCIS's regulations require a single degree, or as 8 C.F.R. § 204.5(k)(2) states a "foreign equivalent degree." It is important to be mindful of the fact that when a person is sponsored for one job in H-1B status, she may not be eligible for employment in that same job as a lawful permanent resident.

---

79. O*Net OnLine is available at http://www.onetonline.org/.

80. Current and past issues of the *Occupational Outlook Quarterly Online* are available at http://www.bls.gov/ooq/.

81. The 2014–2015 edition of the Occupational Outlook Handbook is available online at http://www.bls.gov/ooh/.

The arrival of a bad economy warranting a reduction in force is not the only instance when an immigration lawyer will be compelled to advise her clients regarding the treatment of H-1B workers. It is important to remind an employer that it is obligated to comply with all state and federal labor and employment laws. The end of an H-1B worker's employment can be the ultimate or penultimate event in a company's history. It will depend on what happens at that final stage. The law requires a bona fide termination to end any back-wage obligation.[82] This requires withdrawal of the H-1B petition, notification of termination in writing, and offer of return home transportation.[83]

In the absence of all three elements, an employer will risk a finding of back wages owed by the employer. One of the more striking instances of this was in *Limanseto v. Ganze Co.*, when the alien was abroad for virtually all of the three-year period that an H-1B was valid for. However, because the petitioner did not withdraw the H-1B petition from USCIS, the DOL concluded there was a back-wage obligation.[84]

Immigration lawyers should note that in the event of an economic downturn, there may be an option short of termination. It may be sufficient (and necessary) to file an amended H-1B petition to reduce the number of hours that the person is working. An employer might want to consider that strategy with either part-time employment or a range of hours. While this is permissible, it is important to advise your employer-client that when a range of hours is used, if there is a period when there is no productive labor required, the beneficiary must be paid wages based on average of the hours normally worked. The hourly basis for payment of wages cannot be any less than the minimum on the I-129 form.

In the final analysis, it is important to also ask your employer-client about whether there are any labor condition applications that have not been used to employ anybody. DOL reports that if such an LCA exists, the PAF must be maintained for one year after the LCA expires. However, that one-year period can be run sooner if the employer withdraws the labor condition application.

If there is going to be a change in the ownership of the company you represent, it is important to consider the consequences for this employer under U.S. immigration laws. In many aspects of U.S. immigration law, the ability of a business organization to continue employing an alien will

---

82. *See* 20 C.F.R. § 655.731(c)(7)(ii) (2013).
83. *See* Amtel Group of Florida v. Yongmahapakorn, ARB Case No. 04-087, 2004-LCA-00006, slip op. 8-13 (Sept. 29, 2006) (discussing the standard for bona fide termination).
84. *See* Limanseto v. Ganze Co., 2011-LCA-00005 (June 30, 2011) (holding wages owed because the company did not withdraw the H-1B petition).

be impacted by corporate changes. The ability to continue the employment of aliens in H-1B status, without interruption, when there is a corporate change was eased by the Visa Waiver Permanent Program Act, which added INA § 214(c)(10). This law requires that for a successor business to employ the predecessor's H-1B workers without filing new H-1B petitions, the new entity must have a list of the H-1B workers transferred to the new company, and have in each affected public access file a document with the affected LCA numbers and their certification dates, a description of the new company's wage system, the new company's FEIN, and an affidavit by an authorized representative accepting responsibility for all liabilities associated with these LCAs.[85] This does, at first glance, seem to be a rather beneficial provision to any new company seeking to save both on the expense of filing H-1B petitions as well as the problems posed by requests for evidence and possible denials. However, execution of this affidavit and assumption of the liabilities of the labor condition application will make the successor entity a fair target of the Wage and Hour Division for violations committed by the predecessor. It is possible that an investigation may arise regarding back wages or other violations, such as the failure to post the required notice under 20 C.F.R. § 655.733 (2013). With the usage of this relatively easy means of continuing the employment of H-1B workers, the new company may suffer severe consequences. Consequently, it is very important to consider the wisdom and value of taking advantage of INA § 214(c)(10) or filing new H-1B petitions.

Ultimately, any attorney advising any H-1B petitioning employer should be careful to advise his or her client of the law and obligations thereunder. While the applicable body of law has generally not changed, the manner in which it is being enforced has changed the law's effect in some instances. It thus becomes very important to advise clients cautiously and provide them with all options needed to add to your workforce.

---

85. *See* 20 C.F.R. § 655.630(e).

9

AUDITS IN THE EMPLOYMENT-BASED NON-IMMIGRANT CONTEXT: THE LABOR CONDITION APPLICATION

Brenda Oliver[1] *and Sonal Verma*[2]

The U.S. Department of Labor (DOL) plays a significant role in the H-1B visa process. The agency's job is to administer the Labor Condition Application (LCA) program, an essential component to the specialty occupation visa process.[3] The information below is written to provide an overview of what may trigger a DOL audit and issues of which employers should be aware.

---

1. Brenda Oliver is an associate at Fragomen, Del Rey, Bernsen & Loewy LLP. Brenda provides advice and counsel to U.S. and foreign employers to facilitate transfers of high level and special skilled employees to the United States. She has been assisting clients in obtaining non-immigrant visas, as well as immigrant visas and permanent residency based on employment and/or family sponsorship. She assists clients with preparation of and guidance in the process of non-immigrant visa petitions, employment-based permanent residency petitions and labor certification applications. She provides advice on I-9 compliance and assisting with company audits to ensure compliance with U.S. employment authorization practices. Additional representations have included assisting clients with outbound visa matters, citizenship and naturalization issues; obtaining OCS exemptions; preparation for consular processing; and general advice and counsel regarding immigration law.
2. Sonal J. Mehta Verma is an associate at Fragomen, Del Rey, Bernsen & Loewy LLP. Focusing her practice on corporate immigration matters, Sonal provides corporations and individuals with guidance and advice on all immigrant and non-immigrant visas. Sonal also provides advice and counsel for family matters, asylum cases, and removal issues. She is a past chapter chair of the Washington, DC Chapter of the American Immigration Lawyers Association (AILA). Sonal is a frequent guest speaker on a variety of immigration topics for community organizations and HR professionals, and has appeared as a guest on C-SPAN to discuss current trends in immigration law. Sonal has been included in the International Who's Who of Business Immigration Lawyers.
3. 20 C.F.R. § 655.700(a)(3).

LCA

When filing an LCA, an employer is attesting to the government certain facts regarding the wages, duties, and working conditions offered to the foreign national.[4] These attestations are:

- It will pay the higher of the prevailing wage or the actual wage paid to U.S. workers.
- The working conditions offered to the foreign national will not adversely affect similarly situated U.S. workers.
- There is no strike, lockout or work stoppage at the worksite involving the same or similar occupational classification offered to the foreign national.
- The employer has provided notice of filing of an LCA.

The employer also is obligated to post the LCA, or notice of filing an LCA, at the worksite for ten business days at two conspicuous locations, and must maintain a public access file concerning the LCA and the attestations. As part of the posting notice, the employer notifies the public that any interested or aggrieved party can make a complaint to the DOL regarding misrepresentation in the LCA or failure to comply with statements made in the LCA. An aggrieved party is defined as an employee, bargaining representative, competitor, or government agency. Should an interested or aggrieved party make a complaint, the DOL may initiate an investigation. While the DOL's Employment and Training Administration (ETA) administers the LCA process, the Employment Standards Administration (ESA) enforces compliance of the program through the Wage and Hour Division (WHD).

DOL Audits

If the DOL receives a complaint from an interested or aggrieved party, an investigation into whether a violation regarding compliance with LCA requirements occurred may be initiated and could possibly lead to an administrative hearing. The complaint must be filed no later than twelve months from the time the violation(s) occurred, and the WHD will investigate the allegations to determine if there is reasonable cause to believe a violation occurred. This must be done within ten days after the complaint is filed. If the WHD determines that an investigation should take place,

---

4. LCA instructions can be found at the Department of Labor, Employment and Training Administration, Foreign Labor Certification website: http://www.foreignlaborcert.doleta .gov/pdf/ETA_Form_9035CP_2009_Revised.pdf.

the complaint will be accepted for filing within 30 days, and an investigation will be conducted with a written determination issued thereafter.[5]

The WHD can initiate an investigation based on receiving credible evidence from a non-aggrieved party that violations of the LCA attestations occurred, that an H-1B dependent employer displaced U.S. workers, an H-1B dependent employer failed to appropriately inquire about the displacement of U.S. workers at a third-party work site, or an H-1B dependent employer failed to undergo good faith recruitment. While the non-aggrieved party must provide his identity and a detailed description of the possible violation when making a complaint, the WHD has the discretion to interview the non-aggrieved party and decide whether to disclose the person's identity. Nonetheless, the WHD will notify the employer that a complaint was made and allow the employer to submit a response in ten days. After reviewing the response, the WHD can refer the matter to the Secretary of Labor,[6] who can certify that reasonable cause exists to believe a violation has occurred. This will prompt an investigation into the allegations with a written determination provided within 30 days. There is no appeal regarding the determination on whether or not to investigate.

The WHD can conduct random investigations of an employer at any time during the five-year period after an employer has been found to be a willful violator of the LCA attestation, found to have willfully misrepresented material facts, or is an H-1B dependent employer determined by the DOL to have failed to offer employment to a U.S. worker who is equally or better qualified than the foreign national. An employer is considered to be H-1B dependent if they employ:

- 25 or less employees, and 8 or more are H-1B employees
- 26–50 employees, and 13 or more are H-1B employees
- 51 or more employees, and 15 percent of the workforce are H-1B employees

The 1998 American Competitiveness and Workforce Improvement Act of 1998 (ACWIA)[7] legislation, and the 2004 H-1B Visa Reform Act,[8] both enumerate the investigative authority of the DOL's WHD. While both pieces of law explain the process of the investigation, the 2004 act enhances the 1998 legislation in many instances. Below are some of the

---

5. 8 C.F.R. § 655.806.
6. This responsibility cannot be delegated to anyone other than the Secretary of Labor.
7. Pub. L. No. 105-277, 112 Stat. 2681-641 (1998).
8. Pub. L. No. 108-447, 118 Stat. 3353 (2004) (included in the Fiscal Omnibus Appropriations bill (H.R. 4818)).

similarities and differences between the 1998 ACWIA regulations and the 2004 H-1B Visa Reform Act.

1998 ACWIA

- Random investigation for a five-year period after having been found to be a willful violator.
- Investigation if credible evidence received from known source likely to have information of an employer's practice or conditions.
- Information must be received within 12 months after alleged violations/failures for the DOL to investigate.
- Enhanced civil penalties for violations.

2004 H-1B Visa Reform Act

- Investigation initiated if reasonable cause exists to believe that violation occurred.
- Investigation if credible evidence received from known source likely to have information of an employer's practice or conditions.
- Information must be received within 12 months after alleged violations/failures for the DOL to investigate.
- The DOL to create procedures for information to be provided regarding the allegations for the investigation.
- The DOL to notify employer before beginning an investigation.
- Investigation to last for 60 days; if evidence of violation found, the DOL provides notice of determination and opportunity for hearing.
- Good faith compliance defense established for employers.

PUBLIC ACCESS FILE

As part of the H-1B program and LCA requirements, an employer is required to maintain a public access file at its principal place of business or the place of employment.[9] The public access file must include the following documentation demonstrating the employer's compliance with attestations in the LCA:

- Signed LCA
- Prevailing wage documentation
- Confirmation of posting the LCA for the requisite time
- Actual wage memorandum

---

9. 8 C.F.R. § 655.705(c)(2).

- Declaration regarding strike, lockout or work stoppage
- Statement regarding the wages, benefits and working conditions

The public access file should be available to any member of the public requesting review of such file. It should be maintained in a separate location from where the employer maintains its I-9 files and other human resource/personnel files. Ensuring that the public access file is well maintained and documented should assist the employer in the event of a WHD audit.

While the LCA may be the mechanism that starts the audit, the DOL can review more than just the public access file. The DOL also can request to review the employer's payroll records, among others, to determine whether it is complying with the wages and statements in the LCA. Penalties for violating the LCA include civil penalties such as payment of back wages, or civil fines up to $35,000 per violation, possible debarment from the LCA program for up to three years, and other administrative remedies agreed upon by the parties.

Oftentimes, an individual on an H-1B visa will eventually seek permanent residency based on a permanent offer of employment by their H-1B employer. In order for an employer to sponsor an employee for permanent residence, it must engage in the Labor Certification process.

AUDITS IN EMPLOYMENT-BASED PERMANENT RESIDENCY: THE LABOR CERTIFICATION APPLICATION

The Labor Certification process, also called the Program Electronic Review Management (PERM) process, is often the first in a series of steps towards attaining lawful permanent residency based on employment in the United States. The Department of Labor administers the Labor Certification process, and is responsible for reviewing and adjudicating applications that have been filed by U.S. employers on behalf of their foreign workers.

TEST OF THE LABOR MARKET—RECRUITMENT EFFORTS

The Labor Certification process requires a test of the domestic labor market, as the Department of Labor's primary mandate throughout the process is to ensure that the jobs of U.S. workers are protected. In order for a Labor Certification (LC) application to be "certified," or approved, an employer must prove that there are no U.S. applicants ready, willing, qualified, and able to perform the position for which the LC application is filed, and that the employment of a foreign worker will not "adversely affect the wages and working conditions of workers in the United States similarly employed."[10] This is accomplished by complying with mandatory recruitment efforts and engaging in the good faith recruitment and consideration of U.S. applicants.

The mandatory recruitment efforts must be undertaken prior to the submission of the LC application.[11] Evidence of engaging in recruitment activities is not filed at the time of submitting the application with the Department of Labor, but the evidence must be retained in the event of an audit by the Department of Labor.[12] Mandatory recruitment efforts for all positions include a 30-day job order with the State Workforce Agency in the jurisdiction at which the employment will occur, together with two print advertisements in the Sunday classified section of a newspaper of general circulation in the area of intended employment.[13] Applications for professional positions, as listed in Appendix A to the preamble of the regulations, must also use three supplemental forms of recruitment, chosen from the following list:[14]

- Job fairs,
- Employer's website,
- Job search website other that the employer's,
- On-campus recruiting,
- Advertising with trade or professional organizations,
- Engaging private employment firms for recruitment services,
- Employee referral program with articulated incentives,
- Job postings with campus placement offices,
- Advertising in local and ethnic newspapers, and
- Advertising on radio and television.

It is not sufficient to simply retain receipts of placing advertisements in various media, actual copies of the advertisements placed, with dates clear and venue apparent must be retained in the event that the DOL requests review of recruitment activities through an audit.

---

10. INA § 212(a)(5)(A)(i); 20 C.F.R. § 656.1(a).
11. 73 Fed. Reg. 78020 (Dec. 19, 2008).
12. *Id.*
13. 20 C.F.R. § 656.17(e)(1)(i); *id.* § 656.10(d); 67 Fed. Reg. 30466, 30471 (May 6, 2001).
14. 20 C.F.R. § 656.17(e)(1)(ii)(A)–(J).

NOTICE OF FILING THE LC APPLICATION

In addition to recruitment activities, the employer is required to inform bargaining representatives (if a Collective Bargaining Agreement is in place for the position) of the job opportunity, or provide a ten-day notice of filing the LC to its employees, informing them of the job opportunity.[15] Notice must be posted regardless of whether or not the position is professional in nature. The vast majority of cases do not involve positions covered by a Collective Bargaining Agreement, and therefore, most cases will require a posting notice. The posting notice must be placed in a conspicuous location at the place of employment, and must be published in all in-house media, whether electronic or printed, in accordance with the employer's normal recruitment practices.[16] Common posting locations include bulletin boards by the Human Resources department, cafeteria, an employee break room, and a copy room. The posting notice must contain specific information about the job opportunity, including information pertaining to the position, such as the salary, job duties, and job title, and must also provide the address of the DOL Certifying Officer, so that any person providing "documentary evidence bearing on the application" may do so with the appropriate authority.[17] The actual notice must comply with the regulations at 20 C.F.R. §656.10, and should be kept with the recruitment documentation in an audit file (discussed below). Failure to post notice in accordance with the regulations will result in a denial of the LC because the notice requirement is "not a regulation to be lightly dismissed."[18]

POTENTIAL DOL AUDIT TRIGGERS AND THE AUDIT FILE

After submitting an LC application to the DOL, it may be selected for an audit. The DOL will select an application for a targeted audit based on predetermined "selection criteria," or at random in order to ensure quality control.[19] It is highly recommended that an Audit File be maintained

---

15. *Id.* § 656.10(d).
16. *Id.* § 656.10(d)(1)(ii).
17. *Id.* § 656.10(d)(3)(ii)–(iii).
18. Matter of Aramark Corporation, 2008-PER-00181 (BALCA Jan. 8, 2009) (citing Matter of Voodoo Contracting Corp., 2007-PER-1 (BALCA May 21, 2007)); Matter of Stone Tech Fabrication, 2008-PER-00187 (BALCA Jan. 5, 2009). *See also* Matter of Dunkin Donuts, 2008-PER-00135 (BALCA Jan. 5, 2009); Matter of Tekkote, a division of Jen-Coat, Inc., 2008-PER-00218 (BALCA Jan. 5, 2009).
19. 20 C.F.R. § 656.17(b)(3). *See also* 72 Fed. Reg. 27904 (May 17, 2007).

by the attorney or employer which contains all evidence of recruitment, as well as documentation of any unusual circumstances that are considered a business necessity. To establish business necessity, the employer must document that the "job duties and requirements bear a reasonable relationship to the occupation in the context of the employer's business and are essential to perform the job in a reasonable manner."[20]

Although the DOL has declined to share its "triggers" for non-random audits, anecdotal evidence suggests that there are several scenarios that will likely result in a triggered audit. This is based upon the DOL's mandate to protect the jobs of U.S. workers, and to ensure that the position in which an LC application is filed is not narrowly tailored to the experience and education held by the sponsored foreign national. Anecdotal information from the experience of practitioners suggests that some common audit triggers include, but are not limited to:

- *Foreign language requirement*: The employer must be able to articulate why a foreign language is required in order to perform the job duties and have ready a business necessity letter that explains the manner in which a foreign language is used to conduct regular business.
- *Experience gained with the employer*: Generally, experience gained with the employer cannot be utilized to qualify for the position in which a Labor Certification application is being filed if the experience is "substantially comparable." If a foreign national qualifies for the position in which an LC application is filed by virtue of experience that was gained with the sponsoring employer, the employer must be able to document that the experience gained is at least 51 percent different from the position for which the foreign national was originally hired. Position descriptions, percentage of time spent on various duties, organizational charts, and changes to salary may be used as evidence to demonstrate that the positions are not substantially comparable.
- *Combination of occupations*: If the position offered is a combination of two separate job classifications, as categorized by the DOL's Occupational Outlook Handbook, the employer must be prepared to explain why such a combination is a minimum requirement to perform the duties of the position. The employer must explain and prove that it normally employs workers in the combination of occupations, or that it is customary in the industry, or there is a business necessity for the combination.

---

20. 20 C.F.R. § 656.17(h)(1); 69 Fed. Reg. at 77351-52 (Dec. 27, 2004). Note that DOL has adopted the standard established by BALCA in Informatics Industries, Inc., 88-INA-82 (BALCA 1989) (en banc).

- *Job requirements that are beyond what is "normal" for the position*: When the employer indicates that the minimum requirements for the offered position exceed what is considered normal by the DOL, it must anticipate an audit and draft a business necessity letter to be kept in the audit file. The business necessity letter must explain how the employer determined the minimum requirements for the offered position, and why they are necessary to their enterprise.
- *Layoffs in the same or related occupation*: If the employer had layoffs within the 6-month period prior to filing the LC application, it must notify and consider all potentially qualified laid off U.S. workers and document the results for the audit file.[21]

In the event that an audit is conducted, and there is not sufficient documentation to establish appropriate recruitment for eligibility for the LC, the DOL Certifying Officer may choose to deny certification of the case.

SUPERVISED RECRUITMENT

Supervised recruitment is the mechanism by which the DOL manages and monitors recruitment activities after reviewing the employer's audit file and determining that the recruitment efforts originally conducted were insufficient for LC purposes, that the file did not contain adequate documentation, or that a material misrepresentation was made either in filing or during an audit.[22] The DOL will issue a Notification of Supervised Recruitment (NSR) after performing the audit, and the employer will be required to provide the DOL with a draft advertisement within 30 days of receipt of the NSR, in the format required by the DOL.[23]

If the draft ad is approved by the DOL, the Certifying Officer will issue a recruitment instructions letter, providing the employer with information on when and where to recruit.[24] The employer must direct applicants to send resumes to the Office of Foreign Labor Certification or the Atlanta Processing Center, and the resumes will be sent by DOL to the employer's counsel or agent, if represented. A request for recruitment report letter will then be sent to the employer, advising the employer of what must be contained in the report and instructing the employer to

---

21. 20 C.F.R. § 656.17(k).
22. *See generally* FAQs on Supervised Recruitment, *available at* http://www.foreignlabor cert.doleta.gov/faqsanswers.cfm.
23. 20 C.F.R. § 656.21(b)(1)–(2).
24. *Id.* § 656.21(c)(1).

respond to the request within 30 days of the date on the request.[25] The DOL will then review the reasons for rejecting U.S. workers, if there are any, and will issue a decision on the LC application.

If the DOL determines that an employer has engaged in a pattern or practice of failing to comply with supervised recruitment, or withdraws cases in supervised recruitment on a continual basis, the DOL could debar the employer from filing future LC applications.[26]

ENFORCEMENT ACTIONS IN THE LC CONTEXT

The LC process is electronic and attestation-based, and multiple enforcement actions can arise from filing non-meritorious or fraudulent applications. In 2008, a Fraud Detection and Prevention Unit was established by the DOL, which uses "data mining techniques to identify patterns that could lead to investigations."[27] In order to encourage proper use of the LC program, and create a sufficient deterrent to the filing of fraudulent applications, the DOL may utilize three enforcement tools: (1) investigation by the DOL, Department of Justice, or other government entity; (2) suspension of processing of all applications "involving such employer, attorney, or agent until completion of any investigation and/or judicial proceedings"; and (3) debarment of "an employer, attorney, agent, or any combination thereof."[28]

Investigation

An investigation is generally the first action by the DOL to determine whether there has been a possible violation of the LC regulations, rising to the level of fraud or willful misrepresentation in connection with the LC program.[29] The DOL will refer the matter to the governmental entity deemed appropriate, and in order for the issue investigated to be actionable, the employer must be determined to have willfully provided false

---

25. *Id.* § 656.21(e).

26. FAQs on Supervised Recruitment, *supra* note 22, at ¶¶ 5, 12.

27. DOL Stakeholders Meeting Report, July 15, 2008, *published on* AILA InfoNet as Doc. No. 08073066 (posted July 30, 2008).

28. 20 C.F.R. § 656.31.

29. *Id.* § 656.31(b)(1). *See also* R. Wasem, Immigration of Foreign Workers: Labor Market Tests and Protections, CRS Report for Congress (March 20, 2009).

or inaccurate information to the DOL.[30] The term "willful" is defined as "intentionally and knowingly [meant] to make a misrepresentation."[31]

The DOL has stated that "inadvertent errors and omissions . . . may not rise to the level of fraud" and "[t]he provision is not designed to impose penalties for innocent errors not in the control of the submitter, but is applicable to any material inaccuracy."[32] However, it is expected that both the employer and the attorney or agent will make themselves aware of the facts of the case, and will take steps to ensure the proper presentation of those facts in the LC application and related materials.[33]

Suspension

During the course of an investigation, the DOL may decide to "suspend processing of any permanent labor certification application involving such employer, attorney, or agent until completion of any investigation or judicial proceedings."[34] If an application is suspended, the employer will receive written notification, unless the investigative or prosecutorial agency has requested that such notification be withheld if it would "impede the effectiveness and outcome of investigations that are initiated or ongoing."[35] An initial period of suspension can be up to 180 days, but can be extended if needed to conclude an inquiry.[36] If there is no finding of fraud or willful misrepresentation, then the DOL will issue a decision on the LC application based on its merits.[37]

If the investigating authority determines that the employer knowingly and willfully provided false information in the LC or supporting documentation, it is deemed a federal offense "punishable by fine or imprisonment up to five years, or both, under 18 USC [§§] 2 and 1001."[38] The same penalties may be imposed on persons or entities that knowingly aid, abet, or counsel another to commit the offenses.[39]

---

30. 72 Fed. Reg. 27904 (May 17, 2009).
31. *Id.*
32. *Id.*
33. *Id.*
34. 20 C.F.R. § 656.31(b)(1).
35. 72 Fed. Reg. 27904 (May 17, 2009).
36. 20 C.F.R. § 656.31(b)(2).
37. *Id.* § 656.31(d).
38. *Id.* § 656.31(g).
39. *Id.*

Debarment

Debarment is the process by which an attorney or agent may not be issued any labor certifications, and the DOL may not issue labor certifications to the employer represented by a debarred attorney or agent.[40] Debarment is imposed if the employer, attorney, or agent is determined to have engaged in:

- The sale, barter, or purchase of labor certification applications;[41]
- Willfully assisting with the provision of false or inaccurate information when applying for the labor certification;[42]
- Any activity which results in a determination by a court, the Department of Homeland Security, or the Department of State of fraud or willful misrepresentation involving a permanent labor certification application;[43] or
- The pattern or practice of failure to comply with the terms of the labor certification application, the audit process, or with the requirements of supervised recruitment.[44]

It must be underscored that the DOL may debar an employer, attorney, and/or agent without prior notice, and if the party requests review of debarment, it is stayed during the period of review.[45] A notice of debarment can be issued by the DOL for up to six years after the date of filing the LC. The notice of debarment must be written and state the reason for debarment, date it will begin, the debarment period, and an explanation of opportunities to appeal the debarment.[46]

The permanent Labor Certification process is not to be entered into lightly. The DOL continues to make changes to processing guidelines, and has increased its investigations over the past few years. Their primary obligation is to protect the jobs of U.S. workers, and the DOL will continue to work hard to ensure that no entity misuses or abuses the program. It is worth consulting with a seasoned practitioner when preparing and filing an LC application so that inadvertent errors are avoided, and costly recruitment actions are properly managed.

---

40. 73 Fed. Reg. 78020 (Dec. 19, 2008).
41. 20 C.F.R. § 656.31(f)(1)(i).
42. *Id.* § 656.31(f)(1)(ii).
43. *Id.* § 656.31(f)(1)(iv).
44. *Id.* § 656.31(f)(1)(iii), (g), (f)(1)(iv).
45. DOL Stakeholders Meeting Report, July 15, 2008, *published on* AILA InfoNet as Doc. No. 08073066 (posted July 30, 2008).
46. 20 C.F.R. § 656.31(f)(2).

CONCLUSION

Employers' compliance with both the LCA program and the Labor Certification process set by the DOL is important to ensuring that they are able to continue hiring necessary employees for their workforce. Should the DOL audit an employer's LCA files or its labor certification case, having well maintained and properly documented files will help in response to the DOL.

10

IMMIGRATION CONSEQUENCES OF CORPORATE CHANGES: MERGERS, ACQUISITIONS, AND LAYOFFS

Michelle Funk[1]

In the corporate world, change is constant. Any kind of restructuring, merger, or layoff can have an impact in a variety of legal areas, including corporate law, employment law, and tax law. The extent of the impact on immigration matters varies widely based on the size of the foreign national population employed by the company or companies in question, as well as the types of visas they hold. Unfortunately, immigration counsel is often not consulted until late in the game, often after the changes have occurred. Whenever possible, it is advisable for the immigration consequences to be reviewed so that careful planning can take place in advance to ensure that the foreign national workforce is not disrupted.

CORPORATE RESTRUCTURING

A merger, acquisition, or other type of corporate restructuring can have a significant impact on a foreign national's immigration status. In some instances, it may mean that a foreign national is no longer eligible to hold a particular non-immigrant status. In others, a foreign national may become eligible for a new visa classification. Although U.S. Citizenship and Immigration Services (USCIS) has offered measures that ease the impact of such corporate changes, it remains critical to carefully analyze changes to determine whether any action is required to preserve both the foreign national's ability to remain in the United States, and the company's ability to continue employment.

---

1. Michelle Funk is a Senior Associate in the Northern Virginia Office of Berry Appleman & Leiden LLP. She concentrates her practice in the area of immigration law representing clients, including health care providers, business professionals, and technology firms, regarding a variety of business immigration matters. She advises clients on all aspects of the immigration process, from non-immigrant visas to permanent residence, with a focus on H-1B visas, PERM applications, and J-1 interested government agency waivers. She has represented clients at United States embassies abroad and before United States Citizenship and Immigration Services.

Because the impact of a corporate change varies depending on the particular non-immigrant or immigrant visa classification, it is important to carefully identify each foreign national who may be affected, determine his immigration status, and determine where he is in the permanent residence process, to properly evaluate options.

The H-1B visa classification is used for temporary professional workers, and is commonly utilized in the corporate world. Because the H-1B visa is tied to a particular employer, work location, and position, any material change in the terms and conditions of employment can impact an H-1B foreign national's status.[2]

Generally, a corporate restructuring does not require the filing of an amended H-1B petition as long as the other terms and conditions of employment remain the same. The law is clear in stating that "an amended H-1B petition shall not be required where the petitioning employer is involved in a corporate restructuring, including but not limited to a merger, acquisition or consolidation, where a new corporate entity succeeds to the interest and obligations of the original petitioning employer and where the terms and conditions of employment remain the same but for the identity of the petitioner."[3] USCIS guidance provides that "changes in the ownership structure of the petitioning entity do not require the filing of a new or amended petition. It is understood that the new owner(s) of the firm assumes the previous owner's liabilities which would include the assertions the prior owner made on the labor condition application."[4] Further guidance provides that where a second company assumes substantially all of the assets and liabilities of the first company, amended petitions are not required.[5] The assumption of liabilities is deemed by USCIS as narrow in focus, referring only to immigration-related liabilities, such as labor condition application (LCA) obligations, rather than non-immigration–related obligations and liabilities such as environmental or tort obligations.[6]

Although USCIS may not require an amended petition, the underlying LCA may be impacted, and DOL regulations should be carefully followed to ensure compliance. Corporate mergers and acquisitions may impact the labor condition application, the underlying prerequisite to the

---

2. 8 C.F.R. § 214.2(h)(2)(i)(E).

3. INA § 214(c)(10).

4. INS Memorandum, J. Hogan, Guidelines for the Filing of Amended H and L Petitions (Oct. 22, 1992), *reprinted in* 69 INTERPRETER RELEASES 1448–50, App. II (Nov. 9, 1992).

5. Letter from E. Hernandez, Director, Business and Trade Branch, USCIS, to L. Shotwell (Oct. 23, 2003).

6. *Id.*

H-1B petition filing. Before an H-1B petition can be filed by USCIS, the employer must obtain a certified LCA from the Department of Labor, whereby the employer attests that it will pay the H-1B the required wage rate;[7] that the employment of H-1B non-immigrants will not adversely affect the working conditions of workers similarly employed in the area of intended employment;[8] that there is not a strike or lockout in the course of a labor dispute at the place of employment;[9] and that the employer has provided notice of the filing of the labor condition application either to the bargaining representative of its employees, or by posting a notice at the work location.[10] For each labor condition application filed, the employer must maintain a public access file which includes a copy of the labor condition application with an original signature, along with supporting documents.[11] When the employer undergoes a corporate restructuring, whether through merger, acquisition, or other change, and does not file an amended H-1B petition pursuant to the memos outlined above, the surviving entity is required to provide a sworn statement by a responsible official of the new employing entity confirming that it accepts all obligations, liabilities, and undertakings under the LCAs filed by the prior employing entity, together with a list of each affected LCA and its date of certification, a description of the actual wage system, and the federal employer identification number (FEIN) of the new employing entity.[12] As a practical matter, before the new employing entity can offer a sworn statement, it is important to ensure that the prior company maintained appropriate labor condition application records and public access files. If those files are not available, or if they are not in compliance with Department of Labor regulations, it may be advisable to obtain new labor condition applications, create new public access files, and file amended H-1B petitions. Further, if the proper steps are not taken to assume the LCA obligations before the change becomes final, it is advisable to proceed with obtaining new LCAs and amended H-1B petitions for affected foreign nationals.

Although an amended H-1B petition may not be required, the foreign national may have issues when appearing at a consular post abroad to apply for a new visa with an H-1B in the name of the prior employing entity. It is advisable to provide the foreign national with a letter and/ or documentation confirming the corporate change as evidence that the

---

7. 20 C.F.R. § 655.731.
8. *Id.* § 655.732.
9. *Id.* § 655.733.
10. *Id.* § 655.734.
11. *Id.* § 655.760.
12. *Id.* § 656.760(a)(7).

H-1B petition remains valid. Of course, if the foreign national already has a valid visa stamp in his passport, it remains valid for travel even if it is determined that an amended petition must be filed.[13] The American Competitiveness in the Twenty-First Century Act of 2000 (AC21)[14] provided ameliorative guidance regarding H-1B foreign nationals seeking admission to the United States subsequent to a corporate restructuring, providing that such an employee may be admitted by presenting a letter from the new corporate entity stating that the new corporate entity has succeeded to the interests and obligations of the original H-1B petitioning employer, and the terms and conditions of employment remain the same.[15]

A corporate change can be particularly relevant in the L-1 context. The L-1 visa is permitted for foreign nationals who are entering the United States as an intracompany transferee, in either a managerial, executive,[16] or specialized knowledge[17] capacity. To qualify, the employer must show that the foreign national was, within the three years preceding the time of admission to the United States, employed abroad continuously for one year by a firm or corporation which is the branch, affiliate, parent, or subsidiary of the U.S. employer.

If there is a change in ownership that results in a change in the relationship between the entity in the United States and the entity abroad, such that the qualifying relationship no longer exists, the foreign national will no longer be eligible for L-1 status. The reverse may also hold true—if an entity abroad, through a merger, acquisition, or other similar change is able to demonstrate that it has entered into a qualifying relationship with a U.S. entity, the employees of the entity abroad may suddenly become qualified for L-1 status (assuming the other requirements for L-1 classification can be met). On the other hand, if both the U.S. entity, and one or more of its affiliates abroad are all acquired by a new owner, the qualifying relationship may still exist, and L-1 status can be preserved by filing an amended petition.

---

13. Letter from H. Odom, Chief, Advisory Opinions Division, Directorate for Visa Services, DOS, to M. Rothstein (Feb. 12, 1997), *reprinted in* 74 Interpreter Releases 592–93 (April 7, 1997).

14. Pub. L. No. 106-313, 114 Stat. 1251 (2000).

15. M. Pearson, Memorandum, Initial Guidance for Processing H-1B Petitions as Affected by the 'American Competitiveness in the Twenty-First Century Act' (Pub. L. No. 106-313) and Related Legislation (Pub. L. No. 106-311) and (Pub. L. No. 106-396) (INS, June 19, 2011).

16. 8 C.F.R. § 214.2(l)(1).

17. *Id.*

Qualifying employers may be eligible for an L-1 "blanket" approval, which allows intracompany managers or specialized knowledge employees to apply for the L-1 visa directly at the U.S. consulate, without prior approval of the individual petition from USCIS.[18] If a company is the beneficiary of an L-1 blanket approval, it is always helpful to update the blanket approval periodically to include newly acquired companies. Doing so is advantageous because a foreign national admitted under an approved blanket petition may be reassigned to any other organization listed in the approved petition without prior authorization from USCIS, as long as the foreign national will be performing virtually the same job duties.[19] This is strikingly different from an L-1 individual petition, which requires that an amended petition be filed when a foreign national is transferred from one company to another in the same organization, and becomes the employee of a new organization.[20]

An E visa is utilized for foreign nationals who enter the United States pursuant to the provisions of a treaty of commerce and navigation between the United States and a foreign nation.[21] It is available to those foreign nationals who will be carrying on substantial trade in services technology[22] as well as investors who will be developing and directing an investment enterprise.[23]

A fundamental requirement of the E visa is that it is only available to those nationals of a country with a treaty of freedom, commerce, and navigation in effect with the United States. For purposes of the E visa, the nationality of a business is determined by the nationality of the individual owners of that business.[24] Nationals of the qualifying treaty country must own at least 50 percent of the E visa enterprise.[25] In the corporate

---

18. *Id.* § 214.2(l)(4). The blanket approval requires that an employer and the affiliated entities abroad are engaged in commercial services; that the employer has an office in the United States that has been doing business for one year or more; that the employer has three or more domestic and foreign branches, subsidiaries, or affiliates; and that the employer and affiliated entities abroad have obtained approval for at least ten L-1 managers, executives, or specialized knowledge professionals during the preceding 12 months *or* that the employer has U.S. subsidiaries and affiliates with combined annual sales of at least $25 million *or* that the employer has a U.S. workforce of at least 1,000 employees.

19. *Id.* § 214.2(l)(5)(ii)(G).

20. J. Hogan, Memorandum, Guidelines for the Filing of Amended H and L Petitions (INS, Oct. 22, 1992), *reprinted in* 69 INTERPRETER RELEASES 1448–50, App. II, Nov. 9, 1992.

21. INA § 101(a)(15)(E).

22. *Id.* § 101(a)(15)(E)(i); 8 C.F.R. § 214.2(e)(1).

23. INA § 101(a)(15)(E)(ii); 8 C.F.R. § 214.2(e)(2).

24. 9 U.S. DEP'T OF STATE, FOREIGN AFFAIRS MANUAL § 41.51 N2 [hereinafter FOREIGN AFFAIRS MANUAL].

25. *Id.* § 41.51 N3.1; 22 C.F.R. § 41.51(c)(2).

context, ownership, and thereby nationality, is determined by the nationality of the owners of the stock.[26] The owner and all E visa employees of the company must possess the nationality of the qualifying treaty country, and hold themselves as nationals of that country.[27]

As such, any change in the ownership of the company can thereby change the nationality of the company, making a foreign national ineligible to continue to hold E visa classification. For example, if a qualifying investment enterprise is purchased and subsequently owned by a U.S. individual or company, the entity may no longer qualify to sponsor individuals for E visas, and those individuals holding E visas are no longer entitled to hold that status.

Further, by regulation, USCIS must be notified and must approve any substantial change in the terms and conditions of E status.[28] A change in the employing entity's basic characteristics, such as a merger, acquisition, or sale of the division where the foreign national is employed, is deemed to be a substantial change which would require the filing of either a new E petition with USCIS, or a new visa application with a consular post abroad.[29] Note that nonsubstantive changes do not require prior approval from USCIS or a consular post.[30] When in doubt, USCIS indicates it is always possible to file a new E petition (with the filing fee of course), with a complete description of the change, to request the appropriate advice to ascertain whether a change is substantive such that an amended petition or visa application is required.[31]

If there is not a change in corporate structure, but the employee is merely being transferred among subsidiaries of a common treaty enterprise, a new petition is not required as long as both the parent organization and its subsidiaries were listed in the original filing.[32] This would benefit a foreign national who is working for a subsidiary that is sold, allowing him to transfer to work for either the parent company, or another qualifying subsidiary.

Corporate changes can also have a significant impact on the foreign national's permanent residence process. Given that the processing and waiting times for permanent residence can be lengthy, it is important to

---

26. 22 C.F.R. § 41.51(a)(6).

27. 9 Foreign Affairs Manual, *supra* note 24, § 41.51 N3.3.

28. 8 C.F.R. § 214.2(e)(8)(iii).

29. *Id.*

30. *Id.* § 214.2(e)(8)(iv).

31. *Id.* § 214.2(e)(8)(v).

32. *Id.* § 214.2(e)(8)(ii).

try to ensure that the proper steps are taken to minimize the impact of those changes.

The Department of Labor (DOL) has contemplated changes in corporate structure, and has provided useful guidance for when those changes occur during the labor certification process, also known as the Program Electronic Review Management (PERM) labor certification process. The regulations require that the employer conduct PERM recruitment using its legal name at the time of recruitment,[33] and also require that the PERM Form ETA 9089 be filed in the employer's legal name at the time of filing.[34] However, given that 180 days can lapse between the time the first recruitment step is taken and the time of filing,[35] it is quite possible that during that intervening period the employer entity may change as the result of a corporate change. In that case, the DOL FAQ advise that if a merger, acquisition, or any other corporate change in ownership occurs between the time of recruitment and the time of submission, resulting in a difference between the employer's name shown on the advertising used to recruit for a job and the employer's name on the submitted Form 9089, the employer must be prepared to provide documentation proving that it is the successor in interest.[36] The DOL will make this determination based on a totality of the circumstances, including whether the current employer has assumed the assets and liabilities of the former entity with respect to the job opportunity.[37] In addition, if there is a change in corporate structure, the recruitment must be otherwise valid, so each position should be analyzed to ensure that there aren't changes in the terms and conditions of employment that would necessitate new recruitment.

The impact of a corporate restructure is more burdensome at the I-140 employment-based adjustment application stage, where employers are not given such broad latitude. When a corporate restructuring occurs any time after a PERM labor certification is certified, such that a new employing entity exists, the new employing entity is required to show that it qualifies as a "successor in interest" not just as to the particular job offer, but regarding all of the rights, duties, obligations, and assets of the original employer.[38]

---

33. 20 C.F.R. § 656.17(f)(1).

34. *Id.* § 656.17(a)(1).

35. *Id.* § 656.17(e)(1)(i).

36. "DOL Round 10 PERM FAQ" (May 9, 2007).

37. *Id.*

38. J. Puleo, Memorandum, Amendment to Labor Certifications in I-140 Petitions (Dec. 10, 1993), *reprinted in* 70 INTERPRETER RELEASES 1692–93, App. II (Dec. 20, 1993).

The American Competitiveness in the Twenty-First Century Act provided an extremely beneficial provision easing the impact of changes in employment that occur further along in the permanent residence process: adjustment of status portability. The law, and subsequent guidance, provides that USCIS will not deny an adjustment of status (AOS) application solely because a foreign national has changed employers, as long as the foreign national moves to a position which is in the same, or a similar occupation; the underlying I-140 petition has been approved; and the AOS application has been pending for more than 180 days.[39] A fuller discussion of adjustment of status portability is included below in discussion options for foreign nationals who have been terminated or laid off, but for corporate restructuring purposes, it is important to be aware that if the prerequisites to adjustment of status portability are met, the impact of such changes on immigration status can be mitigated.

The impact of an economic downturn is felt in the immigration context by both employers and foreign nationals. From the employer's perspective, a slowdown in the economy may necessitate small- or large-scale layoffs or reductions in force, and may impact the ability to sponsor their foreign national workforce for permanent residence through the PERM labor certification process. For the individual foreign national, visa status and the ability to pursue permanent residence is often tied to a particular offer of employment, and losing that employment can affect the ability to continue to work, and remain in the United States.

Because non-immigrant status is often tied to a particular employer, if a foreign national is laid off or otherwise terminated, it may mean that he is no longer in status, and is no longer entitled to continue employment. Failure to maintain non-immigrant status can also cause a foreign national to become removable from the United States.[40]

In the H-1B context, a foreign national remains in status as long as an employer/employee relationship exists. Once that relationship ends, the foreign national is no longer considered to be in status.[41] It is important to note there that there is a difference between a foreign national who is not maintaining status, and a foreign national who is unlawfully present. Unlawful presence occurs when a foreign national remains beyond a period of stay authorized by the attorney general, and can carry significant penalties. For example, a foreign national who is unlawfully present for more than 180 days can be barred from entering the United States for

---

39. INA § 204(j).
40. *Id.* § 237(a)(1)(C)(i).
41. *Id.*

a period of three years,[42] and a foreign national who is unlawfully present for more than 365 days can be barred from entering the United States for a period of ten years.[43] In addition, a foreign national who has been unlawfully present for even just one day may no longer avail himself or herself of the convenience of applying for visa renewals at the consular posts in Canada or Mexico, but must apply for any future visas at the consular post in their home country.[44] By contrast, while a foreign national who is out of status may not be eligible to extend or change his status in the United States, he is not barred from departing and applying for a new visa, and is not barred from future entries to the United States.

Typically, once employment ends, a foreign national holding H-1B status has the option of finding new H-1B employment, changing to another non-immigrant status, or returning home. Because status is tied to employment, important consideration should be given as to whether it is more advantageous to provide considerable layoff notice, as opposed to a shorter layoff period with a severance package. Payment of a severance package, without continuing active employment, does not allow the foreign national to maintain status,[45] and thus a longer period of layoff notice permitting the foreign national to find new employment or file a petition to change status may be preferable.

If the foreign national elects to seek new employment, his best course of action is for the new employer's H-1B petition to be filed before the current employment period ends. When the new petition is filed, it is advisable to include recent paystubs, or a letter from the terminating employer confirming dates of employment, to demonstrate that the foreign national continues to be employed and remains in status. Note that the regulations do not provide for a grace period for a foreign national whose employment has ended. As mentioned previously, once the employment is terminated, the foreign national is out of status. Because the regulations do not allow someone who is not maintaining status to extend or change their status, the extension of stay based on the new employer H-1B petition filed subsequent to termination may not be approved. Historically, although there is not a formal grace period included in the regulations, USCIS appears to informally allow a foreign national a period of a few weeks to find new employment, and for the new employer to prepare and file an H-1B petition.

---

42. *Id.* § 212(a)(9)(B)(i)(I).
43. *Id.* § 212(a)(9)(B)(i)(II).
44. *Id.* § 222(g).
45. Letter from T. Simmons, Chief, INS Business and Trade Service Branch to H. Joe, *reprinted in 76* Interpreter Releases 387 (March 8, 1999).

Note that under the H-1B portability provisions pursuant to the American Competitiveness in the 21st Century Act (AC21),[46] a foreign national who previously held H-1B status is eligible to begin working with the new employer as soon as the petition is received by USCIS, as long as the foreign national was lawfully admitted to the United States; subsequent to such admission has not worked without permission; and on whose behalf an employer has filed a new H-1B petition prior to the foreign national's period of authorized stay.[47]

Finally, the H-1B worker may elect to return to his home country. At a later date, he may be able to return, assuming that he is able to locate new employment for the filing of an H-1B petition, or becomes eligible for another status.

In all of the scenarios above, it is important for the employer to take the necessary steps to ensure that the employment relationship has ended. The regulations provide that an employer is liable for the reasonable costs of return transportation of the foreign national abroad if he is dismissed from employment before the end of the period of authorized admission.[48] Note that if the foreign national voluntarily terminates his employment, payment of return transportation costs is not required.[49] In addition, the regulations do not include a requirement to pay for the return transportation costs of dependent family members.

In addition to offering the foreign national return transportation, the employer should also take steps to withdraw the H-1B petition. Employers are required to immediately notify USCIS of any changes in the terms and conditions of employment which may affect status eligibility, and if the employer no longer employs the foreign national, the employer is required to send a letter explaining the change to the USCIS service center that approved the petition.[50]

It is also advisable to withdraw the underlying labor condition application. As outlined above, before an H-1B petition can be filed by USCIS, the employer must obtain a certified LCA from the Department of Labor, whereby the employer attests that it will pay the H-1B worker the required wage rate;[51] that the employment of H-1B non-immigrants

---

46. Pub. L. No. 106-313, 114 Stat. 1251 (2000).

47. *Id.*

48. 8 C.F.R. § 214.2(h)(4)(iii)(E). "Abroad" is defined in the regulation as the foreign national's "last place of foreign residence."

49. *Id.*

50. *Id.* § 214.2(h)(11)(i)(A).

51. 20 C.F.R. § 655.731.

will not adversely affect the working conditions of workers similarly employed in the area of intended employment;[52] that there is not a strike or lockout in the course of a labor dispute at the place of employment;[53] and that the employer has provided notice of the filing of the labor condition application either to the bargaining representative of its employees, or by posting a notice at the work location.[54] The obligation to pay the required wage rate continues until such time as there is a bona fide termination of the employment relationship.[55]

Indeed, a decision from a Department of Labor Administrative Law Judge[56] opined that an employer was required to pay wages for the entire duration of the LCA period, plus interest, where an employer did not effectuate a bona fide termination. According to the opinion, a bona fide termination can only occur when an employer is able to demonstrate that the following three steps have occurred:

- Notice was given to the foreign national employee,
- Notice was given to USCIS by requesting that the H-1B petition be withdrawn,[57]
- Payment was provided for the foreign national's return transportation home.

The decision was particularly draconian, given that the employee in question began working in F-1 status, and was terminated before the H-1B change of status took effect. In essence, the employee was terminated before the LCA wage obligations came into effect, and before the H-1B return transportation provision came into effect. Interestingly, the decision also advises in a footnote that "an employer with an approved labor condition application should withdraw it at the Department of Labor to end its obligation to pay the required wage rate," citing 20 C.F.R. § 655.750(b), which in turn only says that an employer "may" withdraw a labor condition application.

The L and E visas do not carry a requirement to provide return transportation to laid-off foreign nationals, or a requirement to withdraw the

---

52. *Id.* § 655.732.
53. *Id.* § 655.733.
54. *Id.* § 655.734.
55. *Id.* § 655.731(c)(7)(ii).
56. Limanseto v. Ganze & Co., OALJ Case No. 2011-LCA-00005 (June 30, 2011).
57. The decision actually indicates that notice must be given to Immigration and Customs Enforcement.

petition by notifying USCIS. In the L and E visa context it is important to note that because those visas are tied to a very particular relationship with the company, it is often not as simple to find new employment in the same classification. In that case, the foreign national may need to consider changing to H-1B status if he is otherwise qualified.[58] In contemplating a change to H-1B status, however, it is also important to be mindful of the H-1B cap,[59] as that can impact a foreign national's ability to change to H-1B status in a timely fashion.

Termination may also impact the foreign national's spouse, as dependent spouses of L and E visas are permitted to seek employment authorization.[60] However, once the foreign national's L or E visa status is terminated, the dependent spouse is no longer permitted to utilize that employment authorization.

From the company perspective, either a single layoff, or company-wide layoffs can impact the future ability to sponsor foreign nationals for permanent residence based on a PERM labor certification. The PERM labor certification process is predicated on a finding by the Secretary of Labor that there are not sufficient U.S. workers who are able, willing, qualified and available for the position offered to the foreign national in the area of intended employment.[61] When a company has initiated the layoffs of its U.S. workers, special consideration is required to ensure that those workers are not being displaced by permanent residence sponsorship of the foreign national.

Department of Labor regulations provide that, if there has been a layoff by the employer in the occupation, or related occupation in the area of intended employment within six months of filing a PERM labor certification, the employer must document that it has notified and considered all potentially qualified laid-off U.S. workers of the job opportunity involved in the application.[62] Within a particular company, the immigration pro-

---

58. The H-1B requires the foreign national to hold a bachelor's degree or equivalent, which is not always a requirement for L and E visas.

59. The "H-1B cap" limits the number of H-1B petition approvals to 65,000 per year, with limited exceptions to institutions of higher education and related or affiliated nonprofit organizations, nonprofit research organizations, and governmental research organizations. The H-1B is based on the fiscal year, with new H-1B cap numbers becoming available on October 1 of each year. Typically, the cap is reached well before the end of the fiscal year, leaving several months where it is not possible to file new H-1B petitions for cap subject employment.

60. INA § 214(c)(2)(E), (e)(6).

61. 20 C.F.R. § 656.1(a)(1).

62. *Id.* § 656.17(k). DOL defines a layoff as any involuntary separation of one or more

cess and human resource functions may be managed by different people. It is important to have a system which either alerts the relevant immigration team routinely of layoffs within the company, or allows the immigration team to access information regarding layoffs as each PERM labor certification is contemplated, and then filed.

In the I-140 arena, the timing of the layoff is a critical factor in determining the impact. Because an I-140 petition is employer specific, if the foreign national is laid off between the time the PERM is approved and the I-140 is filed, and if the employer does not have the intention to rehire the foreign national in the future, the I-140 filing is not viable. If the layoff occurs after the I-140 has been approved, but before the adjustment of status has been filed, then the I-140 can no longer be used as the basis of the adjustment of status filing. However, the approved I-140 does bestow the foreign national the ability to maintain the priority date granted by the approved I-140 petition,[63] as well as the ability to utilize the approved I-140 as the basis for a three-year H-1B extension going forward, notwithstanding the fact that he is now working for a new employer.[64]

There are some immigrant visa classifications that permit a foreign national to pursue either self-sponsorship or employment sponsorship, including the employment-based first preference extraordinary ability petition, and the employment-based second preference national interest waiver. For example, an I-140 based on extraordinary ability can be filed by either the employer or the foreign national. USCIS guidance provides that if the I-140 is filed by the employer, it remains valid, as long as the foreign national can demonstrate how he or she plans to continue to work in the United States.[65] As such, if the beneficiary of a pending or approved extraordinary ability I-140 petition is laid off, he or she should be prepared to present, at the time of a request for evidence or at the adjustment of status interview, documentation evidencing continued employment.

---

employees without cause or prejudice, and defines a related occupation as any occupation that requires workers to perform a majority of the essential duties involved in the occupation for which certification is sought.

63. INA § 204.5(e).

64. Letter from E. Hernandez, Director, Business and Trade Services, INS, to N. Schorr (Apr. 24, 2002). Under 8 C.F.R. § 314.2(h)(13)(iii), an H-1B worker's period of stay is limited to six years. However, under limited circumstances, such an employee may be permitted to extend his stay beyond the six-year limitation, including where an I-140 has been approved on his behalf, but his priority date is not current.

65. Letter from E. Skerrett, Chief, Immigration Branch for Adjudication (INS) to M. Nerenberg (Jan. 25, 1993).

Similarly, in the I-140 national interest waiver context, the I-140 can also be filed either by the employer or the foreign national. USCIS has advised that:

> When a service center approves a petition based on a national interest waiver, the job offer requirement is waived, regardless of whether an employer signed the I-140 petition. In determining the validity of an approved petition filed under the national interest provision, the primary issue is whether the alien still intends to be performing the activity or work which was the basis for the national interest waiver. If the national interest waiver was based on the alien's work with a particular employer, a petition filed by the employer would no longer be valid if the employer will not hire the alien. If, however, the basis for the national interest waiver was the alien's contributions to an industry which can be utilized by another employer, the petition may remain valid.[66]

The validity of each national interest waiver will be determined on a case by case basis. Interestingly, to qualify for a national interest waiver, a showing must be made that the work supporting the I-140 petition is in an area of substantial intrinsic merit, and that it will provide a benefit which is national in scope.[67] Given the high standard required to qualify for a national interest waiver, assuming the foreign national is able to find similar employment, it would seem that the I-140 is transferrable even if submitted by a prior employer.

As mentioned above, the American Competitiveness in the Twenty-First Century Act provided an extremely beneficial provision easing the burdens of terminated foreign nationals: adjustment of status portability. The law, and subsequent guidance, provides that USCIS will not deny an AOS application solely because a foreign national has changed employers, as long as the foreign national moves to a position which is in the same, or a similar occupation, the underlying I-140 petition has been approved, and the AOS application has been pending for more than 180 days.[68] Note that to comply with the adjustment of status portability provisions of AC21, the foreign national must notify USCIS by letter of his intent to work for a new employer, and if USCIS has reason to believe that the for-

---

66. Letter from E. Skerrett, Chief, Immigration Branch for Adjudication (INS) to W. Reich (Aug. 10, 1995).
67. Matter of New York State Department of Transportation, 22 I. & N. Dec. 215 (Acting Assoc. Comm. 1998).
68. INA § 204(j).

eign national's intent with regard to employment has changed, a request for evidence (RFE) may be issued to seek clarification.[69] In addition, the new employer must submit a letter verifying the offer of employment, job title, job description, and salary.[70] USCIS considers this information necessary to determine whether the new job is in the same or similar occupation, and to determine whether the foreign national continues to be admissible.

Foreign nationals can thus use adjustment of status portability as a protection should they be terminated or laid off. The advisable course of action is for the new company to file a letter with the appropriate USCIS service center confirming that the employee is now an employee of that company, and that he will be fulfilling the same, or similar, job duties as included in the labor certification supporting the approved I-140 petition.

It is important to remember, however, that key conditions must exist in order for portability to take effect:

- The new job must be the same as, or similar to, the prior job. To determine whether the new employment is the same or similar, USCIS will look at the job duties in the underlying labor certification and I-140 as compared with the new employment, the Standard Occupational Classification codes for both positions, and the wages of both positions.[71] They will not look at the geographic location for the position in making the determination.[72]

- The I-140 must be approved. Consider a foreign national who is terminated before the I-140 is approved. If the I-140 remains pending at the time the foreign national is laid off and seeks to change employment, USCIS guidance provides that the pending I-140 petition should be reviewed, and if it is approvable but for an ability to pay issue, based on a preponderance of the evidence it should be approved on its merits.[73] If additional evidence is necessary to make a proper adjudication, such as ability to pay, USCIS may send a request for evidence

---

69. M. Pearson, Memorandum, Initial Guidance for Processing H-1B Petitions as Affected by the 'American Competitiveness in the Twenty-First Century Act' (Pub. L. No. 106-313) and Related Legislation (Pub. L. No. 106-311) and (Pub. L. No. 106-396) (INS, June 19, 2011).

70. *Id.*

71. M. Aytes, Memorandum, Interim Guidance for Processing I-140 Employment-Based Immigrant Petitions and I-485 and H-1B Petitions Affected by the American Competitiveness in the Twenty First Century Act of 2000 (AC 21) (Public Law 106-313) (USCIS, Dec. 27, 2005). Note that the difference in wage is only a factor if it is "substantially" different.

72. *Id.*

73. *Id.*

to resolve the issue, so that a final decision can be made.[74] If an RFE has been issued, and a response is received that does not adequately address USCIS concerns, or the response is that the foreign national no longer works for the sponsoring employer, USCIS may deny both the I-140 petition on its merits, and the adjustment of status and portability request as if there was never an approved I-140 petition from which to port. Given the uncertainty in this scenario, the best course of action for a foreign national is to wait for the I-140 to be approved prior to taking advantage of the portability provisions where possible.

- If the I-140 is denied or revoked at any time (except when it is withdrawn by the employer after the AOS has been pending for more than 180 days) then it is no longer valid for adjustment of status portability.[75] In addition, if the I-140 is withdrawn by the employer before the foreign national's adjustment of status application has been pending for more than 180 days, it is no longer valid for portability purposes.[76]

- The adjustment of status application must be pending for more than 180 days. However, even in this area USCIS has provided leeway. Service centers and district offices are advised not to deny portability cases on the sole basis that a foreign national has left employment before the adjustment of status application has been pending for more than 180 days. The test used is whether, at the time the I-140 was filed and at the time of filing the Application to Adjust or Register Status to Lawful Permanent Resident (Form I-485) (if not filed concurrently), the I-140 employer had the intent to employ the foreign national and the foreign national intended to undertake employment upon adjustment. USCIS officers are advised to seek additional evidence where needed to determine both the employer and foreign national intent.[77]

The other parameters for adjustment of status portability are generous, allowing multinational managers and executives to port to a new job as a manager or executive even for an unrelated company.[78] It allows foreign nationals to port to self-employment, as long as the employment is the same or similar, and as long as the underlying I-140 represented the bona fide intention of the sponsoring petitioner to employ the beneficiary.[79] However, the foreign national cannot be searching for employment at the

---

74. *Id.*
75. *Id.*
76. *Id.*
77. *Id.*
78. *Id.*
79. *Id.*

time the I-485 is adjudicated; he must be able to demonstrate that he has a new and valid offer of employment. [80]

Corporate changes can have a significant impact on both the employer and its foreign national worker. Companies that plan in advance can take steps to minimize this impact. It is critical to evaluate the extent of the change—whether it is a merger, acquisition, or layoff—to determine which foreign national worker may be impacted, and what his options are going forward. In some cases, corporate changes may prevent a company from continuing to employ a particular worker. In other cases, it may mean that amended filings are required with the appropriate government agency to preserve the employee's role with the company. The consequences of any corporate change must be discovered and mitigated as soon as possible.

---

80. *Id.*

11

TEMPORARY AND PERMANENT IMMIGRATION OPTIONS FOR INTERNATIONAL MEDICAL GRADUATES

Khorzad Mehta[1]

INTRODUCTION

The landscape for the provision of health care in the United States has irreversibly changed in the last two years, chiefly through the enactment of, litigation regarding, and eventual Supreme Court validation of the Patient Protection and Affordable Care Act.[2] In fact, the ground continues to shift and settle.

What hasn't changed, however, is the fact that our nation suffers an alarming shortage of health care workers in general, and physicians in particular. Every year, the numbers of doctors coming out of our United States medical schools' graduating classes are less than the amount we need, as a nation, to serve our public health interest. Long-term solutions to this include establishing more medical schools and accrediting more residency programs for enhanced graduate medical training. In the short run, however, a key tool to combat our nation's health professional

---

1. Khorzad Mehta is an attorney at The Murthy Law Firm. After earning his Bachelor of Arts degree in Political Science from The Ohio State University, Khorzad earned his law degree from Case Western Reserve University School of Law. Khorzad represents individuals, families and U.S. employers with employment- and family-based immigrant and non-immigrant visa matters. He has a special interest in the representation of international physicians and their employers with J-1 waivers to improve access to health care for the rural, semi-rural, and low income populations of the United States; H and O non-immigrant petitions; labor certifications; and National Interest Waivers and Extraordinary Ability based immigrant petitions. Khorzad is an active member of the American Immigration Lawyers Association (AILA). He has been invited to speak at immigration lawyers' conferences nationwide and has served on government liaison committees at both the local and national levels.
2. Pub. L. No. 111-149, 124 Stat. 119 (2010), *amended* Health Care and Education Reconciliation Act of 2010, Pub. L. No. 111-152, 124 Stat. 1029.

shortage is by utilizing our existing immigration laws to welcome international medical graduates to the United States. Effective use of the immigration laws, as they pertain to international medical graduates, can address physician shortages, primary care crises, and generally improve access to affordable, quality health care for United States citizens.

Irrespective of what the provision of health care looks like in the United States in the years to come, the necessity for a qualified, talented force of health care workers is expected to continue to increase. This article will briefly summarize the temporary and permanent immigration options for international medical graduates.

TEMPORARY NON-IMMIGRANT OPTIONS FOR INTERNATIONAL MEDICAL GRADUATES

A non-immigrant visa is for an individual seeking to come to the United States temporarily for a specific purpose, such as work, tourism, or training.[3] With few exceptions, individuals applying for non-immigrant visas for admission to the United States must maintain an intent to return to their unabandoned residence in their home country at the completion of their activities in the United States. International medical graduates seeking to enter the United States to engage in training or take professional exams will utilize available non-immigrant visa options.

Visitor Visas (B-1) for International Medical Graduates

The B-1 temporary business visitor classification permits individuals with an unabandoned foreign residence to gain admission to the United States for temporary business activities.[4] The initial admission is permitted to be no greater than one year, though customarily the U.S. Customs and Border Protection Officer at a U.S. port of entry admits individuals seeking B-1 visitor classification for the minimum six month period as described in the regulations.[5]

An international medical graduate can utilize the B-1 temporary business visitor classification to seek admission to the United States. Many international medical graduates seek admission to the United States in B-1 category to 1) participate in an "elective clerkship,"[6] 2) observe U.S.

---

3. INA § 101(a)(15).

4. *Id.* § 101(a)(15)(B).

5. 8 C.F.R. § 214.2(b)(1), (b)(2).

6. 9 U.S. DEP'T OF STATE, FOREIGN AFFAIRS MANUAL § 41.31 N10.4-1 [hereinafter FOREIGN AFFAIRS MANUAL].

medical practices and consult with medical doctor colleagues,[7] 3) conduct independent research, and 4) lecture or speak at sponsored events.[8]

Elective Clerkship

Prospective international medical graduates routinely utilize the B-1 category to engage in "elective clerkships" in the United States. Oftentimes referred to as "rotations," elective clerkships permit prospective international medical graduates to receive practical experience and learn various subject in medicine under the supervision and direction of faculty physicians at a hospital operating under the auspices of a U.S. medical school. The prospective international medical graduate typically receives credit and evaluation towards medical school graduation as an approved part of their medical school curriculum through completion of the elective clerkship.

It is important to note that to qualify for admission as a B-1 temporary business visitor for this purpose, the prospective international medical graduate must be enrolled and not yet graduated from the foreign medical school. Moreover, the Foreign Affairs Manual clearly requires the elective clerkship to be completed at a hospital of a U.S. medical school.[9] Rotations or elective clerkships planned at unaffiliated stand-alone non-profit hospitals would likely not suffice based on a strict reading of the regulation. Prospective international medical graduates, like all visa applicants and/or applicants for admission, must be prepared to establish eligibility for the visa status and maintain records and documentation supporting their enrollment in a foreign medical school and their elective clerkship plan, rotation and program itinerary schedule.

Medical Doctors (Observers)

Qualified international medical graduates, otherwise qualified as H-1 non-immigrants, coming temporarily to the United States to observe medical practice or techniques and/or confer with medical colleagues, may utilize the B-1 category for admission. The regulation mandates that activities under this category are limited to observation and consultation only—patient care is strictly prohibited, as is remuneration.[10]

---

7. *Id.* § 41.31 N11.8.
8. *Id.* § 41.31 N8.
9. *Id.* § 41.31 N10.4-1.
10. *Id.* § 41.31 N11.8.

Independent Research

An international medical graduate coming to the United States to conduct independent research may utilize the B-1 category so long as they receive no salary or income from a U.S. source or institution for the research, or benefit a U.S. institution or entity directly by the research.

Lecturing/Guest Speaking

The B-1 category is appropriately used by international medical graduates when they seek to come to the United States in order to speak or lecture.[11] The international medical graduate may even receive an honorarium payment for the lecturing or speaking, provided that the activities are sufficiently short term (no more than nine days at any single institution); the honorarium is for the benefit of the organization providing the honorarium, and the honorarium is provided by an institution of higher education or an affiliated or related non-profit organization, or a governmental or nonprofit research institution; and the international medical graduate has not accepted honorarium payments from more than five institutions or organizations over the previous six months.[12]

J-1 Exchange Visitor Classification for Clinical and Research Programs

The J-1 exchange visitor category's purpose is to further the foreign policy interest of the United States by increasing the mutual understanding between the people of the United States and the people of other countries by means of mutual educational and cultural exchanges.[13] It is used by a number of different types of temporary visitors to the United States, including international medical graduates.

The hallmark of the J-1 exchange visitor classification is that INA § 212(e) imposes a home residency requirement on certain non-immigrants admitted to the United States in J-1 classification. The home residency requirement requires the non-citizen to depart the United States at the completion of their J-1 program and return to live in their home country for two years before they can qualify to be in H or L temporary status or permanent resident classification.

The home residency requirement, according to INA § 212(e), attaches to those non-citizens who entered the United States in J classification to engage in graduate medical education, to work in a field of endeavor that

---

11. *Id.* § 41.31 N8.
12. *Id.* § 41.31 N11.2.
13. *Id.* § 41.62 N 2.1.

is listed on their home country's skills list with the U.S. Department of State or received funding from the United States or other government for their program.

The home residency requirement may be waived if the non-citizen's home country issues a letter citing no objection to the non-citizen's not returning to their home country for two years. However, please note that international medical graduates who entered the United States in J-1 classification for a clinical J-1 graduate medical education program are ineligible to waive their home residency requirement via a no-objection letter from their home country.[14]

Non-citizens may also seek to waive their home residency requirement through sponsorship from a U.S. interested government agency, demonstrating extreme hardship to a qualifying U.S. citizen or lawful permanent resident spouse or child or establishing a likelihood of persecution if the non-citizen had to return to their home country to fulfill the home residency requirement.[15]

J-1—Clinical

The J-1 exchange visitor classification for clinical graduate medical education training (accredited residencies and fellowships) are utilized by international medical graduates and sponsored by the Educational Commission for Foreign Medical Graduates (ECFMG). ECFMG is the only program sponsor authorized to use this category.[16]

To qualify under this program, the international medical graduate must successfully receive ECFMG certification. Certification requires the international medical graduate to successfully pass Step 1 and Step 2 (Clinical Skills and Clinical Knowledge) of the United States Medical Licensing Examination.[17]

After certification by the ECFMG, the international medical graduate must secure a contract for graduate medical education after successfully entering a residency or fellowship program, administered by the National Resident Matching Program and the Electronic Residency Application Service or through the "Scramble."[18]

The ECFMG will issue SEVIS Form DS-2019, Certificate of Eligibility for Exchange Visitor (J-1) Status to the international medical graduate to present to the U.S. Embassy or Consulate at the time of J-1 visa application. In

---

14. INA § 212(e).
15. *Id.*
16. 9 Foreign Affairs Manual, *supra* note 6, § 41.62 N4.1.
17. www.ecfmg.org/evsp/index.html.
18. www.nrmp.org/res_match/index.html.

combination with the DS-2019, the international medical graduate will be required to provide proof of adequate education and training (in the form of an ECFMG certificate, and degrees and transcripts from medical schools), a statement of need from the Ministry of Health of the international medical graduate's home country, and the valid official contract or letter of agreement to enter the graduate medical education training program.[19]

Upon arrival in the United States, the international medical graduate must report to the ECFMG. Every year thereafter, as the international medical graduate progresses through their training program, the international medical graduate must reapply for a new DS-2019 for the next year of training.[20]

Transfers from graduate medical education institutions, and change of specialty are permitted under limited circumstances. Transfers of training program may be permitted, but require seamless transfer, so as to avoid gaps in training dates.[21] A change in specialty may be approved only once and only in the first two years after the date the international medical graduate enters the United States for graduate medical education in J-1 classification.[22]

The maximum period of stay in J-1 classification for graduate medical education is seven years.[23] Extensions beyond seven years may be authorized, provided the international medical graduate's home country provides a letter of support confirming an "exceptional need" for the international medical graduate's further training in the field sought. The Department of State weighs an exceptional need extension heavily against a future consideration of a waiver of an international medical graduate's home residency requirement.[24]

Extensions for American Board of Medical Specialties Board Examinations are also permitted, but are limited to expiration on the last day of the month the Board Exam is given and are for no longer than six months from the end date of the graduate medical education program. Work is not permitted during a status extension for Board Examination. Upon completion of the graduate medical education, the international medical graduate in J-1 classification is afforded a 30-day departure period for the purpose of making final plans prior to leaving the United States. As

---

19. 22 C.F.R. § 62.27(b).
20. www.ecfmg.org.
21. www.ecfmg.org.
22. 22 C.F.R. § 62.27(f).
23. 9 Foreign Affairs Manual, *supra* note 6, § 41.62 N4.1(d).
24. 22 C.F.R. §§ 62.27(e)(2), 62.43(c).

with extensions to sit for Board Examinations, no work authorization is granted during the departure period.

Also, please note that international medical graduates admitted to the United States in J-1 classification to engage in graduate medical education are subject to the home residency requirement. This requirement mandates that the international medical graduate return to their home country for an aggregate of two years prior to becoming eligible for H or L visa classification or permanent residence in the United States.[25]

J-1—Research (Short Term or Long Term)

International medical graduates oftentimes utilize the J-1 Research Scholar or Short-Term Research Scholar category to complete activities in the United States.[26] Oftentimes, this is done prior to seeking a clinical residency or fellowship training position in the United States as a way to bolster the international medical graduate's résumé and qualifications and set themselves apart from other candidates.

The J-1 Research Scholar category permits international medical graduates to conduct research, teach, observe, or consult in connection with a research project in a temporary position. Only those international medical graduates who have not been physically present in the United States greater than six months as a professor or research scholar in the preceding 12 months from their admission to the United States may be admitted as a research scholar.[27] The duration may not exceed five years in research scholar cases and six months in short-term research scholar cases.[28] Oftentimes, international medical graduates seeking admission in the J-1 Research Scholar category are subject to the home residency requirement if their field of study appears on their country's skills list. An international medical graduate subject to the home residency requirement, who has only sought admission in J-1 classification as a research scholar or short-term research scholar, may seek a waiver of their home residency requirement based on a no-objection-to-return statement issued by their home country; however, an international medical graduate is ineligible to seek a waiver of their home residency requirement if they entered the United States in J-1 classification to engage in a clinical graduate medical education residency program.

---

25. INA § 212(e).
26. 9 Foreign Affairs Manual, *supra* note 6, § 41.62 N4.8, N4.9.
27. *Id.* § 41.62 N4.8.
28. *Id.* § 41.62 N4.8, N4.9.

J-1 Waivers for International Medical Graduates

As stated above, international medical graduates are not permitted to waive their home residency requirement by receiving a no-objection-to-return statement from their home country. Although international medical graduates who qualify can utilize the hardship or persecution avenues to waive their home residency requirements, the vast majority are successful waiving their home residency requirements by receiving a sponsorship from a state department of health, or federal interested government agency.

The common thread running throughout these waiver sponsors is that their programs are designed to address critical health care shortages in federally designated underserved communities where demand for medical services outstrips supply.

State Department of Health Waivers (Conrad 30)

Every state in the United States is permitted to administer a program which may sponsor up to 30 waivers of the home residency requirement for international medical graduates who agree to practice medicine full time, 40 hours a week for three years in H-1B classification in federally designated shortage areas. Up to ten of the 30 waivers can be granted to international medical graduates who are not practicing in federally designated shortage areas but are servicing individuals primarily residing in federally designated shortage areas, also known as Flex 10.[29] These programs are known as the "Conrad 30" after the legislator who sponsored the law in Congress.[30]

As there are 50 state programs, and the law permits states wide latitude in their administration of their individual programs, there are considerable differences in the approach, requirements and process for each state program. Despite these variables, there are clear commonalities:[31]

- Each state program requires sponsored physicians to begin employment within 90 days of receiving the waiver.
- Each state requires the physician to work for no less than three years in H-1B classification.
- Each state requires the physician to serve patients in a federally designated shortage area or patients residing in federally designated shortage area.
- Each state requires the physician to engage in full-time employment.

---

29. INA § 214(l)(1)(D)(ii).
30. Act of Oct. 25, 1994, Pub. L. No. 103-416, 108 Stat. 4305.
31. INA § 214(l).

- Each state requires evidence or a statement describing the recruitment completed by an employer for the position for which the waiver is sought.
- Each state has the option to accept specialist trained physicians.
- Each state can sponsor up to ten waivers out of the 30 available per fiscal year for international medical graduates who are not practicing in a federally designated shortage area but are treating a population residing in federally designated shortage areas.

Appalachian Regional Commission Waiver Program
The Appalachian Regional Commission waiver program is the oldest operating clinical waiver program for international medical graduates. It places only primary care physicians in federally designated Health Professional Shortage Areas (HPSA) in the Appalachian region of the United States. Specialists and clinical practice in other federally designated shortage areas (Medically Underserved Areas (MUA) or Medically Underserved Populations (MUP)) are not permitted.[32]

Delta Regional Authority
The Delta Regional Authority waiver program places primary care and specialist physicians in 252 counties and parishes in the Mississippi Delta region in Alabama, Arkansas, Illinois, Kentucky, Louisiana, Mississippi, Missouri and Tennessee.

Unlike the Appalachian Regional Commission, the Delta Regional Authority will accept applications on behalf of primary care physicians or specialists practicing in HPSAs or MUA/Ps. Applications for specialists, however, must show the exceptional need for the specialty in the area of intended employment.[33]

Department of Health and Human Services Clinical Waiver
The U.S. Department of Health and Human Services Clinical Waiver is limited to primary care physicians and general psychiatrists who have completed their primary care training within 12 months of the start date of employment. Solely those facilities which are defined as a federally qualified health center (or look alike), rural health clinic or tribal medical facility operating in a health professional shortage area with a score of 7.0 or higher are permitted to apply.[34]

---

32. http://www.arc.gov/j1visawaiver.
33. http://www.dra.gov/delta-doctors/.
34. http://www.globalhealth.gov/global-programs-and-initiatives/exchange-visitor-program/requirements-waiver-clinical-care.html.

Veterans Health Administration Waiver

The Department of Veterans Affairs Veterans Health Administration is permitted to act as an interested government agency and recommend J-1 waivers for international medical graduates to practice medicine at Veterans Health Administration facilities. There is no limitation to sponsorship— the Veterans Health Administration may sponsor primary care physicians or specialists at facilities located within or outside of federally designated health professional shortage areas.[35]

O-1 Visas for International Medical Graduates

O-1 visa classification is sometimes utilized by international medical graduates as an alternative to another temporary non-immigrant classification, such as H-1B, when an international medical graduate is not eligible for additional H-1B time beyond the six-year maximum or is still subject to the home residency requirement. The O-1 petition is employer specific—it is filed by an employer on behalf of the international medical graduate.

The crux of eligibility of the O-1 category requires the international medical graduate to demonstrate that he or she is of extraordinary ability. The regulations permit an international medical graduate to show eligibility by providing evidence of having won a major international award, such as a Nobel Prize, or demonstrating sustained national or international acclaim and recognition for achievement in their field of expertise by showing evidence of three out of the following criteria: 1) receipt of nationally or internationally recognized prizes/awards for excellence in the field; 2) membership in associations in the field that require outstanding achievement of their members; 3) articles in major professional publications or other media about the international medical graduate and their work; 4) participation as the judge of the work of others, either individually or on a panel; 5) original scientific, scholarly, or business-related contributions of major significance to the field; 6) authorship of scholarly articles in professional or major trade publication or in other major media; 7) performance in a leading or critical role for organizations or establishments that have a distinguished reputation; or 8) command a significant salary or other remuneration in relation to others in the field.[36]

---

35. VHA Handbook 5005.1—www1.va.gov/vhapublications/ViewPublication.asp?pub_ID
+1219.
36. 8 C.F.R. § 214.2(o).

H-1B Visa Classification for International Medical Graduates

The H-1B visa is utilized by professionals seeking to come to the United States to engage in a specialty occupation as an employee of a U.S. employer.[37] International medical graduates routinely utilize the H-1B visa classification to engage in clinical graduate medical education residency and fellowship programs, or to conduct research as the professional employee of a U.S. employer. The H-1B visa classification benefits from the doctrine of dual intent, which permits non-immigrants in H-1B classification to simultaneously hold the intent to temporarily work in H-1B classification for an employer and permanently immigrate to the United States.[38]

As discussed elsewhere in this book, the H-1B visa is limited to 65,000 visas per government fiscal year.[39] Certain employers who can be classified as institutions of higher education, nonprofits affiliated or related to institutions of higher education, and nonprofit or governmental research organizations are exempt from the quota limitation.[40] Any employer who seeks to employ an individual in H-1B classification (whether an international medical graduate or other professional) must apply for and receive a certified labor condition application and pay a salary no less than the higher of the actual or prevailing wage for the position in the area of intended employment.[41] The H-1B visa classification is permitted for six years for a non-immigrant and can be extended beyond the sixth year if the non-immigrant is the beneficiary of a U.S. Department of Labor Program Electronic Review Management (PERM) Labor Certification filed one year before the expiration of the sixth year of H-1B classification or is the beneficiary of an approved immigrant petition for alien worker subject to immigrant visa backlogs in the preference category within which it was filed.[42]

Eligibility
Physicians seeking employment in a clinical capacity, i.e., seeing and treating patients, must have a license to practice medicine in the state of intended employment; be a graduate of a medical school either in the United States or abroad; have successfully completed Steps 1, 2, and 3 of

---

37. INA § 101(a)(15)(h).
38. 8 C.F.R. § 214.2(h)(16).
39. INA § 214(g)(1)(A).
40. *Id.* § 214(g)(5)(A)–(B).
41. *Id.* § 212(n)(1).
42. American Competitiveness in the Twenty-First Century Act, Pub. L. No. 106-313, 114 Stat. 1251 (2000).

the United States Medical Licensing Exam; and have been certified by the ECFMG.[43]

Special Issues
Six-Year Limit

The six-year limit[44] to H-1B classification can be a significant challenge for those physicians completing graduate medical education residencies and fellowships. Oftentimes, resident and fellowship training programs may exceed the six-year time limit. This can present a significant obstacle at the conclusion of the training, if the physician seeks to continue working in the United States. The physician and their employer would have to seek alternative options based on their individual posture.

Fiscal Year Cap on H-1B

As stated above, H-1B visas are limited to 65,000 per government fiscal year. Only H-1B petitions filed by employers as listed above, as well as extensions and H-1B petitions filed on behalf of former J-1 physicians who have received a waiver of their home residency requirement pursuant to INA § 214(l), are exempted from the government fiscal year limitation.

This presents an issue for physicians who have completed their residency or fellowship at institutions of higher education or nonprofit affiliated or related entities. They have never been counted against the fiscal year H-1B limitation. As such, when they complete their training and seek employment with other employers who may be cap subject, they can face a potential challenge. The numerical limitation on H-1B visas makes them subject to very high demand. Employers routinely commence applying for H-1B visas for new employees in April, six months before their earliest availability at the commencement of the government fiscal year in October. Oftentimes, the entire allotment of H-1B visas for a fiscal year is exhausted before the fiscal year starts. This presents an issue for physicians completing training, as the completion of their training (typically in July) leaves them with a gap until October (the first month that H-1B visas are available in a fiscal year) to commence work. Strategies to fill this gap may exist on a case by case basis with each physician.

J-1 Visa Waiver Fulfillment

The Immigration and Nationality Technical Correction Act of 1994 amended INA § 212(e)[45] by expanding the waiver authority of interested

---

43. 8 C.F.R. § 214.2(h)(4)(viii).
44. *Id.* § 214.2(h)(13)(iii).
45. Immigration and Nationality Technical Corrections Act of 1994, Pub. L. No. 103-416, 108 Stat. 4305, codified as amended at 8 U.S.C. § 1182(e).

government agencies to include state public health agencies and added INA § 214(l), which mandated physicians granted a waiver of their home residency requirement pursuant to a state public health agency of federal interested government agency sponsorship for clinical practice agree to work and practice medicine for a total of not less than three years in a designated shortage area or area serving a designated shortage area ("Flex Spots") in H-1B classification. Thus, any physician seeking waiver of their home residency requirement pursuant to section 214(l) must practice medicine in H-1B classification.

Alternative Non-Immigrant Visa Options for International Medical Graduates

E-3—For International Medical Graduates Holding Australian Citizenship

In 2005, the E-3 visa classification was created and permits citizens of Australia to work in the United States in a specialty occupation for up to 24 months initially.[46] Extension can be requested indefinitely.

International medical graduates may utilize the E-3, and evidentiary criteria are the same as those for H-1B classification. However, there are certain limitations to E-3 classification. Principally, the E-3 classification does not benefit from a grace period of work authorization while a timely filed extension is pending. As such, if an extension is not granted prior to the expiration of E-3 status, an international medical graduate would have to cease working until the extension is granted. Additionally, unlike the H-1B, an E-3 non-immigrant is not afforded portability when a new E-3 petition is filed on a non-immigrant's behalf. A non-immigrant changing employers would have to have an approved petition prior to starting work with a new employer. Finally, the E-3 visa classification does not benefit from the doctrine of dual intent, like the H-1B visa classification does; E-3 visa non-immigrants are expected to maintain an intent to return to their home country upon completion of their activities in E-3 classification inside the United States.

TN—For International Medical Graduates Holding Canadian or Mexican Citizenship

TN visa classification can be an avenue for international medical graduates from Canada or Mexico who aim to engage in academic occupations. Their duties must be primarily to teach or research. Engaging in direct patient care principally is prohibited in TN classification.[47]

---

46. INA § 101(a)(15)(E)(iii).
47. 8 C.F.R. § 214.6(c).

This visa option is very advantageous for academic physicians. However, those who intend to engage in clinical pursuits need not apply. Furthermore, although the TN status can be renewed indefinitely in three-year increments after an initial three-year period, it does not benefit from the doctrine of dual intent. Thus, TN status may present some obstacles to permanent residence in the United States.

E-2—Treaty Investor

International medical graduates who are nationals of a treaty country may utilize the E-2 Treaty Investor visa to enter the United States. To be eligible, the international medical graduate national of the treaty county must provide substantial capital investment in a proposed enterprise in the United States, ostensibly a medical practice. The enterprise has to be real and functioning and provide a service of commodity for profit. The income generated by the enterprise must also be more than that which would simply provide the investor with a comfortable living. All invested funds must be in the control of the international medical graduate and he or she must be able to develop and direct the enterprise. Additionally, if the international medical graduate intends to practice clinical medicine, he or she must be able to be licensed to practice medicine in the state of their intended investment enterprise.[48]

PERMANENT IMMIGRANT OPTIONS FOR INTERNATIONAL MEDICAL GRADUATES

An employer who seeks to have an international medical graduate work for an indefinite period in the United States may sponsor him or her for lawful permanent resident or green card status. Generally, a lawful permanent resident process initiated by an employer isspecific to job opportunity and the employer.[49]

PERM Labor Certification

In most cases, the first step involved in obtaining permanent residence is the filing of a labor certification application with the U.S. Department of Labor (DOL), through the PERM process. Unless the international medical graduate qualifies under one of the labor certification exempt permanent immigrant classifications, the PERM application must be approved before the case can move to the second step of the process. Generally,

---

48. INA § 101(a)(15)(e)(ii).
49. 20 C.F.R. § 656.17.

an employer must conduct extensive recruiting and advertising for the position and evaluate the qualifications of applicants for the position, to demonstrate to the DOL that there are no U.S. citizens or U.S. permanent residents ready, willing, and qualified to perform the particular job. A PERM application is specific to the employer, the position, the position duties, and the geographic location.

All PERM cases require the following: an application to the National Prevailing Wage Center to confirm the minimum salary required (prevailing wage), a job order for 30 days with the State Workforce Agency in the area of intended employment, evidence of an on-site job posting posted for ten consecutive business days, and evidence of advertising in two Sunday editions in the newspaper of general circulation in the area of intended employment.[50]

Additionally, applications for professional positions, such as international medical graduates, require at least three additional methods of advertising which can be chosen from the following: job fairs, employer's website, job search website other than the employer's (e.g., Monster. com), on-campus recruitment, trade or professional organizations, private employment search firms, employee referral programs, notice of job opening at a campus placement office, local and ethnic newspapers, and radio and television advertisements.[51]

Immigrant Petition for Alien Worker

This process is required of *all* employment-based green card cases. It is the second stage of the process for employees who have an approved PERM application from the DOL, as the U.S. Citizenship and Immigration Services (USCIS) must confirm the PERM approval and that the international medical graduate has the qualifications for the job offered in the PERM application.[52]

National Interest Waivers for Physicians

This classification is available to physicians who can demonstrate that they have made a commitment to work full-time in a clinical practice for a period of five years. The employment must take place in a health professional shortage area, medically underserved area, mental health professional area (for psychiatrists only), or at a Veterans Affair medical center. It also requires the physician to obtain confirmation from a state department of health or a federal agency which has knowledge of the

---

50. *Id.* § 656.17(e)(1)(i).
51. *Id.* § 656.17(e)(1)(ii).
52. 8 C.F.R. § 204.5(k).

physician's qualifications that confirms that the physician's work is in the public interest.[53]

Outstanding Researchers/Professors
This classification is available to an international medical graduate who is recognized internationally for his or her pioneering achievements in the sciences or other academic areas, demonstrated by extensive evidence of international preeminence and original scholarly contributions including publications in peer-reviewed journals, patents, the individual's serving in a role requiring judgment or critical review of others' work, citation of the individual's work by other authors, significant awards or prizes, and reference letters by preeminent members of the field supporting the individual's international acclaim and achievements. This category requires the sponsorship of the employer for whom the international medical graduate will prospectively work.[54]

Extraordinary Ability Professionals
This classification is available to a foreign national who holds sustained national or international recognition in the sciences, arts, education, business or athletics, demonstrated by extensive evidence including: prominent publications regarding the individual and/or the individual's work, publications written by the individual, significant awards or certificates, public recognition of the individual's accomplishments, the individual's serving in a role requiring judgment or critical review of others' work, the individual's serving in a prominent role in an organization, and evidence the individual is receiving a high salary. An international medical graduate who qualifies under this classification may sponsor himself or herself, or may be sponsored by an employer.[55]

Immigrant Visa or Adjustment of Status Application
This is the final stage in the employment-based green card process where the international medical graduate, along with his or her immediate family, applies to become a U.S. Lawful permanent resident. Applicants may select either adjustment of status or consular processing as the mechanism to complete the process. This third stage cannot be filed until the priority date is current.[56]

---

53. *Id.* § 204.12.
54. *Id.* § 204.5(i).
55. *Id.* § 204.5(h).
56. *Id.* § 245.1(a).

An application for adjustment of status (AOS) is available only to international medical graduates (and their family members) who are currently residing and physically present in the United States, and in legal status. The AOS application is filed at the appropriate USCIS regional service center, and can be filed concurrently with the Immigrant Petition for Alien Worker, listed above. Concurrent filings allow for work and international travel authorization while they are pending, and help reduce processing times.[57] If the priority date was current when the adjustment of status was filed, but then falls back while it is pending, the adjustment can remain pending, but cannot be approved until the priority is again current.[58]

Consular processing is an alternate way to complete the green card process. A personal interview at the appropriate U.S. consulate outside the United States is required of the foreign national and any dependent family members. No interim work or travel authorization is permitted, independent of the employee's temporary work status, through consular processing.

CONCLUSION

As baby boomers continue to age into advanced years, they are expected to live longer than their parents or any generation that preceded them. Our nation, and our citizens, will not thrive if our current health professional shortages continue. The existing immigration laws provide many specific options for international medical graduates and impose special requirements and limitations as well. When the different options fit together harmoniously, our nation as a whole benefits with the addition of a skilled physician to address our growing health needs.

---

57. *Id.* § 245.2(a)(2)(B).
58. *Id.* § 245.

12

WHAT IS SOCIAL SECURITY NO-MATCH AND WHAT DOES IT MEAN?

John Nahajzer[1] and Mark Yelich[2]

INTRODUCTION

At a time when the federal government continues to increase workplace enforcement activities, employers should implement, review, and consistently maintain and execute compliance programs in order to minimize potential risks and liability exposure. One compliance mechanism the federal government has used intermittently over the past few years is the Social Security Administration's (SSA) issuance of Social Security Number (SSN) no-match letters. No-match letters are issued to an employer where SSA finds that an employee's provided SSN is not consistent with information located in the SSA's records. An employer's rights and responsibilities continue to exist within a realm of uncertainty due to the absence of comprehensive guidance.

Over the past decade, the SSA regularly issued no-match letters to employers around the country and, after a hiatus from late 2007, announced that it would resume issuance in April 2011.[3] On October 26, 2011, the SSA informed the American Immigration Lawyers Association (AILA) that it had again suspended the issuance of employer letters as

---

1. John Nahajzer is a managing shareholder at Maggio + Kattar, PC. He focuses his practice on corporate business immigration. He regularly lectures in the area of corporate compliance, such as immigration implications of mergers and acquisitions, corporate best practices, I-9 compliance and audits, and no-match letters.

2. Mark Yelich is senior attorney at Maggio + Kattar, PC. He focuses his practice on employment-based immigration and advises clients on employer compliance requirements, such as H-1B postapproval maintenance issues, E-Verify procedures, and I-9 employment eligibility verification.

3. SSA POMS [Program Operations Manual System], RM 01105.027 Handling Inquiries about Letters from SSA Concerning Names and SSNs That Do Not Match Our Records (July 18, 2011), *available at* https://secure.ssa.gov/apps10/poms.nsf/lnx/0101105027; POMS NL 00901.050. Decentralized Correspondence (Decor) Notice (Mar. 22, 2011), *available at* https://secure.ssa.gov/apps10/poms.nsf/lnx/0900901050.

of August 29, 2011, due to budget constraints.[4] Although not always the case, no-matches are often caused by employees who are not authorized to work in the United States, and are using either a false SSN or an SSN assigned to someone else. Even though there is a temporary hold on the issuance of new no-match letters, many employers remain concerned given the Administration's focus on combating the employment of unauthorized workers. Against the backdrop of employers committed to compliance and the federal government undertaking workplace audits and investigations at unprecedented levels, no-match letters place employers in a dilemma. On the one hand, acute labor market shortages in certain industries and geographic locations around the United States may make employers reluctant to take adverse employment actions based upon the mere suspicion that an employee may not be employment authorized. On the other hand, these same employers may also face discrimination complaints after acting overzealously out of concern about potential immigration civil and, possibly, criminal liabilities.

This article aims to first provide an overview of the content and meaning of no-match letters. Next, this article will place no-match letters within the context of an employer's obligations under the Immigration and Nationality Act's (INA) twin provisions prohibiting the hiring of unauthorized workers and discriminating against individuals based on their immigration or citizenship status. A historical outline of the Department of Homeland Security's (DHS) proposed rulemaking will then be discussed, which also includes federal district court action. Finally, the article will provide practical advice to employers and suggest best practices that may help limit liability exposure.

WHAT IS A NO-MATCH LETTER?

The SSA issues no-match letters to employers or employees when there is a discrepancy between an employer's wage report and the information contained in the SSA's master database. The letter informs the recipient that the name or SSN does not match the name or SSN found in the SSA's database, thus the name "no-match" for this particular form of correspondence. To resolve discrepancies that arise during the SSA's annual wage-reporting process, the SSA sends two different types of correspondence: Decentralized Correspondence (DECOR) letters (since 1979) and

---

4. AILA/SSA Liaison Conference Call Minutes (November 8, 2011), p. 1, Exhibit, *available on* AILA InfoNet Doc. No. 11120761 (posted December 7, 2011).

Employer Correct Request or Educational Correspondence (EDCOR) letters (since 1994). The letters inform the recipient that, due to a discrepancy in the information provided, the SSA cannot post earnings for a particular employee, and requests that either the employer or employee (depending on the type of letter issued) provide corrected information where requested on the form and return it or the form to the SSA.

There are several government agencies and various federal laws that are potentially of concern when employers receive no-match letters. First, of course, is the SSA, the agency that issues no-match letters. Under current law, employers are not obliged to respond to SSA requests to provide clarification concerning SSNs that do not match the SSA's records. Moreover, the SSA has no enforcement authority and cannot assess penalties for an employer's failure to respond to an SSA no-match letter.

Second, employers may face Internal Revenue Service (IRS) liabilities regarding employer wage-reporting requirements. Although, arguably, employers are not mandated by the IRS to respond or take any action with respect to SSA no-match letters, best practices suggest that employers should, at minimum, notify their finance/tax advisors of the no-match letters to ensure that this is indeed the case. However, should employers receive no-match letters directly from the IRS, they could face significant penalties and should thus seek the immediate assistance of tax counsel. Immigration counsel should also be contacted immediately if IRS rules compel employers to take corrective action that may involve completion of new or reverification/correction of existing employment eligibility (I-9) forms.

Significantly, numerous SSA no-match letters received over time by an employer could bear substantial immigration consequences and legal liabilities, despite efforts made by employers to correct the problem. Employers may thus face liabilities if they do nothing and if they do too much.

Current guidance from U.S. Immigration and Customs Enforcement (ICE), the DHS sanctions/enforcement agency, makes it clear that ICE will make a subjective analysis (review of the totality of circumstances on a case-by-case basis) of an employer's actions upon receipt of SSA no-match letters to determine whether an employer should be subject to penalties concerning the employment of unauthorized workers. Such penalties would be based upon a finding or determination by ICE that an employer possessed either actual or constructive knowledge or notice of unauthorized employment. This finding would be based on circumstances surrounding the receipt of and actions taken in response to the no-match letters. ICE could become aware of an employer's SSN no-match situation in a number of ways, including an I-9 audit or notification from the SSA.

Various government entities, including ICE, SSA, and the Department of Justice's (DOJ) Office of Special Counsel (OSC), have noted that the receipt of a no-match letter does not, in and of itself, put an employer on notice that it is employing unauthorized workers. However, there are situations in which the SSA no-match letters would cause ICE to believe that an employer has been put on notice regarding its employment of unauthorized workers. Unfortunately, ICE guidance to employers (vis-à-vis examples of no-match situations) only includes scenarios and examples in which it is clear that an employee is unauthorized, and involves some action taken by an employer to try to correct an SSN discrepancy which is then ultimately resolved. In other words, there is always a positive outcome for employers in the ICE scenarios.

What the ICE examples do not address is the scenario that many employers have to deal with: receipt of numerous no-match letters over time listing the SSNs of dozens or perhaps hundreds of current and former employees covering prior tax years. This scenario becomes even more complicated when employers either make no attempt to contact affected employees and resolve the SSN discrepancies or contact the employees but do not reach any final resolution. In other words, the government does not say precisely how far employers must go in correcting no-matches to absolve themselves from immigration liabilities.

The government makes this problem more incomprehensible by also cautioning employers not to take too much corrective action if a no-match letter is received because such acts could expose employers to potential discrimination lawsuits and liabilities. Indeed, the SSN no-match letters caution employers not to assume that employees listed on such letters are not employment authorized. The end result is a situation in which employers have to deal with responding to potentially hundreds of government inquiries, thereby placing them, proverbially, "between a rock and a hard place."

At first glance, from an immigration and employment law perspective, the content of a no-match letter can seem quite innocent. Even the SSA acknowledges that such no-matches can be the result of typographical errors, incomplete or blank names reported, incomplete or blank SSNs reported, or name changes. Other possible reasons include mismatches for hyphenated surnames, dual surnames, or married names. The SSA's letter to employers contains a straightforward disclaimer:

> This letter does not imply that you or your employee intentionally provided incorrect information about the employee's name or SSN. It is not a basis, in and of itself, for you to take any adverse

action against the employee, such as laying off, suspending, firing, or discriminating against the individual.[5]

The letter then warns an employer of the following:

Any employer that uses the information in this letter to justify taking adverse action against an employee may violate state or Federal law and be subject to legal consequences. Moreover, this letter makes no statement about your employee's immigration status.[6]

While no-match letters issued to employers contain an explicit disclaimer that employers should not rely solely on these letters to take adverse employment action, no-match letters issued to employees stress that recipients have certain rights and further instructs employees how to protect these rights. The letter requesting employee information advises:

The fact that you have received this letter does not, in and of itself, allow your employer to change your job, lay you off, fire you or take other action against you. If you think your employer is discriminating against you because your name and Social Security Number do not match our records, see the attached information on important protections of your rights.[7]

Depending on the nature of the employment relationship and an employee's possible cause of action, the letter further instructs that employees should contact the National Labor Relations Board, Equal Employment Opportunity Commission, or the Office of Special Counsel for Immigration-Related Unfair Employment Practices.

It becomes obvious how an employer can find itself in a difficult position. On the one hand, the no-match letter makes no statement about an employee's immigration status or employment authorization and cautions an employer that it should not rely solely on the letter in taking adverse action. On the other hand, U.S. immigration enforcement authorities, the legacy Immigration and Naturalization Service (INS), and now ICE, have historically advised employers that the liability standard is one of the totality of circumstances, and that constructive knowledge could be imputed to

---

5. SSA, Decentralized Correspondence (Decor) Notice (March 22, 2011), Request for Employer Information, *available at* http://policy.ssa.gov/poms.nsf/lnx/0900901050. *See* Exhibit 1.
6. *Id.*
7. *Id.* Request for Employee Information. *See* Exhibit 2.

employers if, for example, no action is taken in response to such letters or if a large number of letters is received. Since one of the causes for a mismatch between an employer's earnings report submitted to the SSA could be an unauthorized worker who is using a false SSN or an SSN that belongs to someone else, an employer should not simply ignore no-match letters since they could indicate an individual's unauthorized status.

In response to a stakeholder's questions and concerns regarding an employer's responsibilities under the INA with respect to SSNs, the former General Counsel of legacy INS highlighted the fine, and sometimes blurry, line between actual and constructive knowledge. In his letter, then General Counsel Paul Virtue wrote:

> We emphasize that although it is incorrect to assume that an SSA discrepancy necessarily indicates unauthorized status, it would be equally incorrect for an employer to assume that in all cases it may safely ignore any possible INA relevance or consequences of SSA discrepancies. . . . In considering whether the totality of the circumstances rises to actual or constructive knowledge, the SSA notice is a relevant fact that would support a conclusion that it does.[8]

According to this statement, an SSN no-match letter, standing on its own is not sufficient to rise to the level of constructive knowledge and would not place any affirmative obligation on an employer to investigate whether or not an employee holds authorized status. If, as a result of receiving a no-match letter, an employer has no affirmative obligation to further inquire about one's immigration status, then what actions, if any, must the employer undertake? Can the employer simply ignore the notice and decide not to follow up with its employee? This is where legacy INS was careful to hedge and not entirely dismiss the SSA's notice. The abovementioned General Counsel's letter discussed how an employer's action in response to a no-match letter could bring it under the INA's provisions:

> [A]n employer should not ignore the consequences of the follow-up activity it *should* perform in response to an SSA notice in order to reconcile its records for SSA purposes, such as verifying names and SSNs by examining Social Security cards. While this activity is not required by the INA (nor is it prohibited by it), the knowledge obtained by an employer through this process may have INA implications . . . if an employee has been given the oppor-

---

8. Letter, Virtue, General Counsel, INS HQCOU 90/10.15-C (April 12, 1999), p. 2, *available on* AILA InfoNet Doc. No. 01061431 (posted June 14, 2001).

tunity for wage reporting purposes to explain and reconcile a reported discrepancy with SSA records, and has failed to do so satisfactorily, that is an entirely different situation from an initial SSA notice standing alone. The INS would be much more likely at that point to consider that employer to have violated section 274A, if it continues the employment without taking appropriate steps to reverify work authorization, and the employee is in fact unauthorized.[9]

It is the INA anti-discrimination provisions that further complicate the employer's position. So what do these sections of the statute say?

THE INA'S PROHIBITION OF UNLAWFUL EMPLOYMENT AND UNFAIR IMMIGRATION-RELATED EMPLOYMENT PRACTICES

The practical result is a sort of tug and pull between SSN no-match letters and the INA's statutory provisions governing unlawful employment and anti-discrimination. As discussed above, the no-match letter is both a notice and a disclaimer: it informs an employer or employee of some discrepancy, but also warns that it does not make any determination with respect to an employee's immigration status.

Section 274A of the INA (8 U.S.C. § 1324a) makes it unlawful for employers to hire for employment an alien, knowing the alien is unauthorized. The implementing regulation at 8 C.F.R. § 274a.1(*l*)(1) define "knowing" as including "not only actual knowledge but also knowledge which may fairly be inferred through notice of certain facts and circumstances which would lead a person, through exercise of reasonable care, to know about a certain condition." The regulation lists three nonexclusive examples of constructive knowledge:

Where an employer:

Fails to complete or improperly completes the Employment Eligibility Verification Form, I-9;

Has information available to it that would indicate that the alien is not authorized to work, such as Labor Certification and/or Application for Prospective Employment; or,

---

9. *Id.* (emphasis added).

Acts with reckless disregard for the legal consequences of permitting another individual to introduce an unauthorized alien into its work force or to act on its behalf.[10]

The accompanying provision, INA § 274B (8 U.S.C. § 1324b), prohibits employers from discriminating against an individual with respect to the hiring, recruitment, or referral of the individual for employment, or discharging the individual, based on national origin or citizenship status. These two provisions provide the statutory framework for the no-match context. In an attempt to fill in the law in this area, DHS proposed amendments to the regulations in 2007, but ultimately rescinded these amendments in 2009.

DEPARTMENT OF HOMELAND SECURITY RULEMAKING

On August 15, 2007, ICE published a final rule with new regulations describing an employer's legal obligations when the employer receives an SSA no-match letter. This rule outlined "safe-harbor" provisions that would shield an employer from claims that it violated immigration law by employing an unauthorized worker, but the rule limited this protective carve-out to instances of the employer's constructive knowledge only.[11] The August 2007 final rule expanded the definition of "knowing" in 8 C.F.R. § 274a.1(*l*)(1) to include two additional events: an employer's receipt of an SSA no-match letter and the employer's receipt of written notice from DHS (currently called a "Notice of Suspect Documents") that the immigration status or employment authorization document used to complete the Form I-9 is actually assigned to another person, or that the particular document does not exist in DHS records.

The August 2007 final rule also described procedures and steps that an employer could take to secure a safe harbor against claims that the employer had constructive knowledge. A reasonable employer may take the following steps:[12]

- Employer checks its records in an attempt to try to determine the cause of the no-match and, if corrected, notifies the relevant agency

---

10. 8 C.F.R. § 274a.1(*l*)(1)(i)-(iii) (2013).

11. Safe Harbor Procedures for Employers Who Receive a No-Match Letter, 72 Fed. Reg. 45611-24 (Aug. 15, 2007).

12. The following discussion closely tracks the language of the August 2007 final rule, 72 Fed. Reg. 45613-14.

of the updated corrections. ICE would regard an employer's actions under this step as prompt if taken within 30 days of receipt of the no-match letter.

- Employer contacts the employee to verify the employer's records and, if the records are correct yet there is still a mismatch, the employer requests the employee to resolve the matter with the relevant agency. ICE would regard an employer's actions under this step as prompt if taken within 30 days of receipt of the no-match letter.
- If the discrepancy is not resolved within 90 days, the employer and employee must complete a new employment eligibility verification form I-9 within 93 days of receipt of the no-match letter. When completing the new I-9, an employee cannot present a document containing the SSN in question (located in the no-match letter) or a document with a photograph.

It is important to reiterate that the safe-harbor provisions only apply to scenarios of constructive knowledge and provide no coverage where an employer has actual knowledge that an employee is unauthorized. Following the steps above would not permit an employer to circumvent its obligations under INA § 274A and 274B. The government would have the burden of proving the employer's actual knowledge in these cases. Moreover, in its comment section to the August 2007 rule, ICE noted that employers will not be able to avail themselves of the safe harbor if other evidence exists—independent from written SSA or DHS notices—that an employer did indeed have constructive knowledge of unauthorized employment.[13]

Under the August 2007 rule, if an employer is required to complete a new Form I-9 under the safe-harbor provisions, it must use a procedure that is somewhat different than that used for newly hired employees. Specifically, under this rule, the employee is required to complete Section 1, and the employer Section 2, within 90 days of the employer's receipt of the relevant written notice from the SSA or DHS. In doing so, the employer must not accept from the employee any of the documents referenced in any of the written government correspondence, any document that contains a disputed SSN, an alien number referenced in any written notice, or any receipt for an application for a replacement of such documents. Finally, the employee is required to present a document that contains a photograph in order to establish identity (List B) or both identity and employment authorization (List A). Employers must retain previous I-9s

---

13. Safe Harbor Procedures for Employers Who Receive a No-Match Letter, 72 Fed. Reg. 45614 (Aug. 15, 2007).

along with the new I-9, assuming it can be successfully completed by the employee.

If an employee is unable to complete the new I-9 successfully within the required time period, employers must terminate employment immediately or risk the imposition of fines and/or penalties by ICE. If an employee resigns during the reverification process, the employer is not obligated to complete the prescribed no-match procedures.

The no-match procedures prescribed time frames from the August 2007 rule can be illustrated in the following table:

Action	Time
Employer receives SSA or DHS notice indicating mismatch	Day 1
Employer checks own records, makes any necessary corrections, and verifies corrections with SSA or DHS	1–30 days
If necessary, employer notifies employee and asks employee to assist in correction	1–90 days
If necessary, employer corrects own records and verifies correction with SSA or DHS	1–90 days
If necessary, employer performs special I-9 procedure	91–93 days

In response to the August 2007 rule, the United States District Court for the Northern District of California, in *AFL-CIO v. Chertoff,* first granted a temporary restraining order against implementation of the regulation and then later granted the plaintiffs' motion for preliminary injunction.[14] The district court questioned DHS's analysis leading to a change in the Department's position, namely, that receipt of a no-match letter would impart constructive knowledge to an employer. In addition, the court was concerned that DHS had exceeded its authority by interpreting the INA's anti-discrimination provisions and had failed to conduct a regulatory flexibility analysis. In response to *AFL-CIO v. Chertoff,* DHS published a supplemental proposed rule on March 26, 2008[15] and a supplemental final rule on October 28, 2008,[16] responding to the district court's concerns. Neither changed the safe-harbor procedures contained in the August 2007 rule.

Then, in October 2009, after the new Administration completed a comprehensive review of existing programs and regulations, DHS rescinded

---

14. AFL-CIO v. Chertoff, 552 F. Supp. 2d. 999 (N.D. Cal. 2007).

15. Safe-Harbor Procedures for Employers Who Receive a No-Match Letter: Clarification; Initial Regulatory Flexibility Analysis, 73 Fed. Reg. 15944-55 (Mar. 26, 2008).

16. Safe-Harbor Procedures for Employers Who Receive a No-Match Letter: Clarification; Initial Regulatory Flexibility Analysis, 73 Fed. Reg. 63843-67 (Oct. 28, 2008).

the no-match amendments promulgated on August 15, 2007 and October 28, 2008.[17] In rescinding the no-match and safe-harbor regulations, DHS determined that it would realign its enforcement resources and efforts to refocus on the U.S. Citizenship and Immigration Services (USCIS) electronic employment verification system known as E-Verify and the ICE Mutual Agreement between Government and Employers program known by its acronym, IMAGE.[18] In addition, despite rescinding its no-match guidelines, DHS remains committed to the merits of the 2007 and 2008 rules and, based on its comments in the rescission notice, is likely to hold employers to the standard summarized in the October 2009 notice:

> Receipt of a no-match letter, when considered with other probative evidence, is a factor that may be considered in the totality of the circumstances and may in certain situations support a finding of "constructive knowledge." A reasonable employer would be prudent, upon receipt of a no-match letter, to check their own records for errors, inform the employee of the no-match letter, and ask the employee to review the information. Employers would be prudent also to allow employees a reasonable period of time to resolve the no-match with SSA.[19]

Notwithstanding the rescission of the no-match regulations and elimination of explicit safe-harbor procedures, employers are still at significant risk of I-9 liability where they fail to attempt to resolve large numbers of SSN discrepancies noted by the SSA through no-match letters. Moreover, as noted above, ICE generally views employers who try to take corrective action as good corporate citizens, and as such may view them in a favorable light during I-9 audits.

BEST PRACTICES—WHAT SHOULD EMPLOYERS DO?

In the current environment, where DHS has focused on employer compliance programs such as E-Verify and IMAGE to identify and prevent

---

17. Safe Harbor Procedures for Employers Who Receive a No-Match Letter: Rescission, 74 Fed. Reg. 51447-52 (Oct. 7, 2009).

18. See Proposed Rule, Safe Harbor Procedures for Employers Who Receive a No-Match Letter: Rescission, 74 Fed. Reg. 41801-05 (Aug. 19, 2009). Information about E-Verify can be accessed at http://www.dhs.gov/e-verify. Information about the IMAGE program can be accessed at http://www.ice.gov/image.

19. Safe Harbor Procedures for Employers Who Receive a No-Match Letter: Rescission, 74 Fed. Reg. 51449 (Oct. 7, 2009).

unauthorized employment, employers cannot turn a blind eye and remain idle as this would irresponsibly expose them to civil and, possibly, criminal penalties. But, with the patchwork of guidance to fill the vacuum left behind by the rescinded no-match rule, employers must carefully tread through this confusing intersection of immigration, employment, and tax law. What options do employers have?

Notwithstanding the temporary freeze on the issuance of new no-match letters, employers should take corrective action in the face of numerous no-match letters even without a clear requirement to do so. If employers take too little action, or no action at all, there is a risk that ICE would find, should it ever discover the existence of the no-match letters and that the employees listed in these letters were not in fact employment authorized, that such employers had constructive knowledge of the unauthorized employment based upon the sheer volume of the no-matches. Whenever attempting to resolve SSN no-matches, employers should consult with immigration counsel to devise a strategy that will minimize the disruption of employment services, worker anxiety, as well as the risk of exposure to potential immigration law liabilities.

Current civil penalties for first-time offenders who knowingly employ unauthorized workers range from $275 to $2,200 for each unauthorized individual if the offense occurred before March 27, 2008, and from $375 to $3,200 if the offense occurred after March 27, 2008.[20] Criminal penalties also may be imposed for any person or entity that engages in a pattern or practice of such violations. Pattern or practice means "regular, repeated, and intentional activities, but does not include isolated, sporadic, or accidental acts."[21] Such penalties may comprise a fine of not more than $3,000 for each unauthorized individual, imprisonment for not more than six months for the entire pattern or practice, or both.[22]

As the pendulum of an employer's possible responses to the receipt of no-match letters swings in the other direction, employers who take an overly aggressive approach in an effort to resolve SSN no-matches risk discrimination complaints from employees who were terminated due to a SSN no-match letter. As discussed above, the SSA added specific text to its SSN no-match letters cautioning employers not to assume that employees referenced in no-match letters are not employment authorized after thousands of workers were terminated by frightened employers who received SSN no-match letters.

---

20. 8 C.F.R. § 274a.10(b)(1)(ii)(A) (2013).
21. *Id.* § 274a.1(k).
22. *Id.* § 274a.10(a).

So, it seems that doing nothing or too little in the face of numerous SSN no-match letters exposes employers to potential sanctions, and that doing too much is not ideal either. How much is just right? What actions should employers take?

Gleaning from the proposed no-match amendments, employers concerned about no-match letters can take a number of steps, and they should do so with the assistance of immigration and/or employment counsel. Employers should first attempt to resolve no-matches by confirming via internal records whether an administrative error occurred in recording SSN information. If the discrepancy is a result of this type of error, payroll records and the information on the affected employee's Form I-9 may, of course, be corrected and communicated to the SSA.

If a typographical error did not occur, employers should assess whether the SSN information provided by employees is not valid. The no-match letters themselves offer guidance regarding invalid SSNs: (1) numbers that are listed with more or less than nine digits; (2) numbers whose first three digits are "000" or are in the "800" or "900" series; (3) numbers whose middle two digits are listed as "00"; and, (4) numbers whose last four digits are "0000." If an employee provided an invalid SSN, employers must then reverify the employee's work authorization by taking an entirely new Form I-9. An employee will need to provide the necessary documentation to demonstrate valid employment authorization, but an employer cannot specify any particular documents from the lists of available forms of identification or employment authorization located on the back of Form I-9.

In both of the above scenarios, employers should contact the SSA to relay the correct SSN information. In addition, affected I-9 forms will require correction or updating. Incorrectly altering information already listed on I-9 forms completed at the time of hire could lead to additional liabilities and fines for employers. Should I-9 forms require correction or reverification, immigration counsel should be consulted in order to ensure that any corrections to the forms are carried out in compliance with the law and guidance from current ICE I-9 audit practices and procedures.

If these steps fail to resolve the problem, and many times they do, employers are left with making a judgment call regarding what to do next. Current immigration law, despite the legacy INS General Counsel letter cited above, does not require that employers conduct any follow-up activities should the above steps not resolve the issue, although, as noted above, employers may incur liabilities under IRS regulations.

How else can employers establish a sound defense to the allegation that they possess actual or constructive knowledge of employing unauthorized workers through receipt of SSN no-match letters? Employers should establish and put in writing an SSN no-match policy and procedures, whereby employees who are caught up in SSN no-match situations are treated in a consistent and uniform manner in order to avoid any possible discrimination claims, and to demonstrate the employer's good-faith effort to undertake appropriate action in this respect.

The policy should require that employers contact relevant employees in writing, via certified mail, when a no-match letter is received, explaining the issue and asking the employees to rectify discrepancies directly with the SSA. If such follow-up activity results in an employee "coming clean" and admitting to having provided false SSN information when hired, employers should immediately consult internal policy and employment counsel to determine what personnel actions, if any, are to be taken. Usually, however, such a "Perry Mason moment" does not occur. Instead, many no-matches go unresolved. Under those circumstances, employers must act with extreme care and avoid sweeping these cases under the rug. A case-by-case strategy may be needed to formulate a strategy that best suits the situation at hand. For example, for some employers, a viable solution may be to resend the no-match notifications to employees, while for others, completing new I-9s or reverifying existing ones may be the best approach.

Of course, employers must also deal with the potential negative impact on their employees stemming from the need to resolve large numbers of SSN no-matches, including time off the clock, the loss of a significant number of or key employees, and strained employee relations. In addition, employers must be conscious of having to coordinate efforts to resolve SSN no-matches with any relevant labor unions. Finally, employers should be aware of any conflicts of interest that could arise if the same attorney represents both the employer and employee in immigration sponsorship petitions or applications.

In formulating a written policy on no-match letters, the DOJ's guidance regarding no-match letters can be instructive for employers. The OSC within DOJ has published Frequently Asked Questions[23] and several "Dos and Don'ts"[24] to assist employers. The DOJ advises employers of the following key points:

---

23. DOJ Office of Special Counsel for Immigration-Related Unfair Employment Practices, Frequently Asked Questions About Name/Social Security number "No-Matches" (date unknown), *available at* http://www.justice.gov/crt/about/osc/pdf/publications/SSA/FAQs.pdf.

24. DOJ Office of Special Counsel for Immigration-Related Unfair Employment Practices, Name and Social Security Number (SSN) "No-Matches" Information for Employers (Dos and Don'ts) (date unknown), *available at* http://www.justice.gov/crt/about/osc/pdf/publications/SSA/Employers.pdf.

DO:

1. Recognize that name/SSN no-matches can result because of simple administrative errors.
2. Check the reported no-match information against your personnel records.
3. Inform the employee of the no-match notice.
4. Ask the employee to confirm his/her name/SSN reflected in your personnel records.
5. Advise the employee to contact the Social Security Administration (SSA) to correct and/or update his or her SSA records.
6. Give the employee a reasonable period of time to address a reported no-match with the local SSA office.
7. Follow the same procedures for all employees regardless of citizenship status or national origin.
8. Periodically meet with or otherwise contact the employee to learn and document the status of the employee's efforts to address and resolve the no-match.
9. Review any document the employee chooses to offer showing resolution of the no-match.
10. Submit any employer or employee corrections to the SSA.

DON'T:

1. Assume the no-match conveys information regarding the employee's immigration status or actual work authority.
2. Use the receipt of a no-match notice alone as a basis to terminate, suspend or take other adverse action against the employee.
3. Attempt to immediately reverify the employee's employment eligibility by requesting the completion of a new Form I-9 based solely on the no-match notice.
4. Follow different procedures for different classes of employees based on national origin or citizenship status.
5. Require the employee to produce specific I-9 documents to address the no-match.
6. Require the employee to provide a written report of SSA verification (as it may not always be obtainable).

CONCLUSION

Most employers today maintain multiple compliance practices to eliminate or at least mitigate possible liability and financial exposure. An integral component of most compliance policies for businesses, depending on size, industry, workforce, etc., is an immigration compliance program. A business immigration compliance program itself contains many components, one of which should be an employer's no-match letter policy. The INA provides a dual-aim statutory scheme whereby employers are prohibited from employing unauthorized individuals, but employees are also afforded protections so that employers cannot discriminate against them based on national origin or citizenship status. Companies must take a reasonable and objective approach with respect to affected employees so as not to trigger potential discrimination claims. In light of this, a major incentive for business compliance is the fact that employers have, in effect, been deputized by the federal government to verify the employment eligibility of every new hire or else face potentially severe monetary or, in egregious cases, criminal sanctions.

In the absence of formal no-match rulemaking, employers who desire to be proactive and good corporate citizens must incorporate available guidance from different federal agencies into a written policy. Even the rescinded ICE rules should not be completely ignored. Consistent internal procedures and policies should be developed and refined over time and with the assistance of immigration and/or employment counsel. Establishment of an SSN no-match policy should provide guidance to employers to ensure that affected employees are treated in a consistent manner to avoid any possible discrimination claims. Therefore, it is key for employers not to immediately assume that an employee listed in a no-match letter is unauthorized to work in the United States and company personnel should, instead, follow the policy put in place to deal with these situations.

Finally, it is important to keep in mind that, although DHS abandoned no-match regulations in 2009 in favor of more robust and proactive workplace enforcement mechanisms such as E-Verify and IMAGE, no-match letters received by an employer, especially if there are a large number of them over a period of time, will still be treated as an important factor in the case of ICE work site inspection activities, such as through an I-9 audit and issuance of a Notice of Suspect Documents. If there are factors beyond mere receipt of no-match letters, such as substantive violations on a Form I-9 or failure to complete the E-verify process by enrolled employers, then an employer's treatment of no-match letters will come under additional scrutiny and certainly be taken into account when evaluating whether the employer has engaged in prohibited employment or employment-related activity. Employers should periodically perform internal I-9 audits to identify incorrect or incomplete I-9 records for their workforce, and then make the necessary corrections in conjunction with their employees. Internal audits are a useful compliance tool because companies have the advantage of performing them without the time restrictions and pressure that inherently accompany an ICE audit of I-9 records. Immigration counsel can provide the expertise needed to carry out a friendly audit as well as to develop and implement policies to maintain I-9 records moving forward.

Exhibit 1—Sample SSA no-match letter to employer

4002-10
DO NOT COPY

Form Approved
OMB No. 0960-0508

Social Security Administration
Retirement, Survivors, and Disability Insurance
Request for Employer Information

Social Security Administration
Data Operations Center
P.O. Box 39
Wilkes-Barre, PA 18767-0039

Date:

Sequence Number:

Employer Number:

We are writing to you about your Wage and Tax Statement (W-2) or Corrected Wage and Tax Statement (W-2c) for the employee shown below. Please complete the information on the back of this letter and return it to us promptly. We cannot put these earnings on the employee's Social Security record until the name and Social Security number you reported agree with our records.

Employee's Name:
Social Security Number:
Reported Earnings:
Tax Year:

The reasons the reported information does not agree with our records may include, but are not limited to:

- Typographical errors
- Incomplete or blank name reported
- Incomplete or blank Social Security number (SSN) reported
- Name changes

This letter does not imply that you or your employee intentionally provided incorrect information about the employee's name or SSN. It is not a basis, in and of itself, for you to take any adverse action against the employee, such as laying off, suspending, firing, or discriminating against the individual. Any employer that uses the information in this letter to justify taking adverse action against an employee may violate state or Federal law and be subject to legal consequences. Moreover, this letter makes no statement about your employee's immigration status.

For Spanish-speaking individuals: Esta carta no implica que usted ni su empleado intencionalmente proveyeron información incorrecta sobre el nombre o número de Seguro Social del empleado. El hecho de que haya recibido esta carta no constituye una razón, de por sí, para que tome alguna acción adversa contra el empleado, tal como suspenderlo, despedirlo o discriminar contra el individuo. Cualquier empleador que use la información en esta carta para justificar una acción adversa contra un empleado puede encontrarse en violación de la ley estatal o federal, y estar sujeto a enfrentar consecuencias legales. Además, esta carta no hace ninguna declaración sobre el estado inmigratorio de su empleado. Esta carta pide información sobre las ganancias que usted informó para su empleado. Si usted necesita una traducción de esta carta, por favor llámenos gratis al, 1-800-772-1213, de lunes a viernes, desde las 7 a.m. hasta las 7 p.m.

Please See Reverse

Form SSA-L4002-C1 (01/2011)

Exhibit 1—Sample SSA no-match letter to employer, *continued*

```
4002-10
DO NOT COPY
```

THIS IS WHAT YOU NEED TO DO

1. Compare the information shown on the front of this letter to your employment records.

2. If the records match, ask the employee to give you the name and Social Security number exactly as it appears on the employee's Social Security card. (While the employee must furnish the SSN to you, the employee is not required to show you the Social Security card. But, seeing the card will help ensure that all records are correct.)

3. If the employee's Social Security card does not show the employee's correct name or Social Security number, or if the employee needs to report a name change or replace a lost Social Security card, have the employee contact any Social Security office.

4. If you or the employee has been using an incorrect name or Social Security number, you must correct it.

5. Fill in the requested information below and return this letter in the enclosed envelope. (Do not attach a Form W-2c to this letter.)

REQUEST FOR EMPLOYER INFORMATION (Please Print--Use Black Ink or #2 Pencil)

1. Name shown on the employee's Social Security card:

   First   M.I.   Last

2. Social Security number on the employee's card: ☐☐☐ - ☐☐ - ☐☐☐☐

3. Do the earnings reported belong to this employee? ☐ Yes ☐ No (Explain)

4. Has the employee ever used another name? ☐ No ☐ Yes (Give other names used)

   First   M.I.   Last

5. Does the employee still work for you? ☐ Yes ☐ No (Give full last known address)

   ADDRESS

   CITY   STATE   ZIP

6. Daytime phone number where you can be reached __ __ __ - __ __ __ - __ __ __ __

If you have any questions, you may call us toll-free at 1-800-772-6270 from 7 a.m. to 7 p.m., Monday through Friday, Eastern time. If you call an office, please have this letter with you. It will help us to answer your questions.

Terry Stradtman
Associate Commissioner for
Central Operations

Enclosure:
Envelope

See Next Page

4002-10
DO NOT COPY

DO NOT RETURN THIS PAGE

POINTERS FOR CORRECT REPORTING

1) The Internal Revenue Code requires an employer to include each employee's Social Security number when filing returns, such as the W-2 Wage and Tax Statements. The employer identification number must also appear on such returns.
2) Ask for the employee's Social Security number and explain that the law requires the employee to give the number although (s)he may be ineligible for benefits.
3) Include the middle initial if shown on the employee's Social Security card. Format: John C. Smith

THE PRIVACY ACT

Section 205(a) of the Social Security Act allows us to ask for the information on this letter. The information you give us will be used to give the employee credit for the correct amount of wages. You do not have to complete this letter. However, if you do not, we cannot give the employee credit for the correct amount of wages. We may give this information to the Internal Revenue Service for tax administration purposes or to the Department of Justice for investigating and prosecuting violations of the Social Security Act.

We may also use the information you give us when we match records by computer. Matching programs compare our records with those of other Federal, State or local government agencies. Many agencies may use matching programs to find or prove that a person qualifies for benefits paid by the Federal government. The law allows us to do this even if you do not agree to it. Explanations about these and other reasons why information you provide us may be used or given out are available in Social Security offices. If you want to learn more about this, contact any Social Security office.

PAPERWORK REDUCTION ACT STATEMENT

This information collection meets the requirements of 44 U.S.C. § 3507, as amended by section 2 of the Paperwork Reduction Act of 1995. You do not need to answer these questions unless we display a valid Office of Management and Budget control number. We estimate that it will take about 10 minutes to read the instructions, gather the facts, and answer the questions. *You may send comments on our time estimate above to: SSA, 6401 Security Blvd., Baltimore, MD 21235-6401. Send only comments relating to our time estimate to this address, not the completed form.*

Exhibit 2—Sample no-match letter to employee

3365-10
DO NOT COPY

Form Approved
OMB No. 0960-0508

Social Security Administration
Retirement, Survivors, and Disability Insurance
Request for Employee Information

Social Security Administration
Data Operations Center
P.O. Box 39
Wilkes-Barre, PA 18767-0039

Date:

Sequence Number:

Employer Number:

We need more information so that we can give you credit for your earnings from the company and for the year shown below. We cannot put these earnings on your Social Security record until the name and Social Security number reported to us match our records. Unless this problem is corrected, you may not get retirement, disability, survivors or other benefits that you are due.

Company Name:
Employee's Name:
Social Security Number:
Reported Earnings:
Tax Year:

THIS IS WHAT YOU NEED TO DO

1. If your Social Security card does not show your correct name or Social Security number, or if you have lost your Social Security card, please call our toll-free number, 1-800-772-1213, or contact your local Social Security office.

2. Compare the information shown above to your Form W-2(s) and your Social Security card.
   - If the name and number shown on the Social Security card **agree exactly** with the information shown above, contact your local Social Security office so that we can find out why our records do not match what was reported for you by your employer. Do not mail this letter back to us.
   - If the name and number shown on the Social Security card **do not agree** with the information shown above, fill in the requested information on the reverse side of this letter, and mail it to us in the enclosed envelope. If you have been using an incorrect name or Social Security number, or your employer has been reporting earnings for you under an incorrect name or Social Security number, you must also correct this information with your employer.

IMPORTANT: THE FACT THAT YOU HAVE RECEIVED THIS LETTER DOES NOT, IN AND OF ITSELF, ALLOW YOUR EMPLOYER TO CHANGE YOUR JOB, LAY YOU OFF, FIRE YOU OR TAKE OTHER ACTION AGAINST YOU. IF YOU THINK YOUR EMPLOYER IS DISCRIMINATING AGAINST YOU BECAUSE YOUR NAME AND SOCIAL SECURITY NUMBER DO NOT MATCH OUR RECORDS, SEE THE ATTACHED INFORMATION ON IMPORTANT PROTECTIONS OF YOUR RIGHTS.

For Spanish-speaking individuals: Esta carta contiene información importante. Vea la página 3 para los detalles.

Please See Reverse

Form SSA-L3365-C1 (01/2011)

3365-10
DO NOT COPY

Most problems with names and Social Security numbers that do not match our records are the result of mistakes and do not involve intentional fraud. We want to work with you and your employer to correct your earnings record and to make sure that you receive credit for all of your work under the Social Security program.

Please fill out the following form if the name and number shown on your Social Security card do not agree with the information on page one of this letter. Please take this action now to make sure you receive any retirement, disability, survivors or other benefits owed to you.

For Spanish-speaking individuals: Esta carta pide información sobre las ganancias que su empleador informó. Si usted necesita una traducción de esta carta, por favor llámenos gratis al, 1-800-772-1213, de lunes a viernes, desde las 7 a.m. hasta las 7 p.m.

REQUEST FOR EMPLOYEE INFORMATION

1. Name shown on your Social Security card: (Please Print--Use Black Ink or #2 Pencil)

First   M.I.   Last

2. Social Security number on your card:

3. Does the **amount** of reported earnings on the front of this letter match any Form W-2 you received for the tax year shown?   ☐ Yes   ☐ No (Explain)

4. Have you ever used another name?   ☐ No   ☐ Yes (Give other names used)

First   M.I.   Last

5. Daytime phone number where you can be reached _ _ _ — _ _ _ — _ _ _ _

NOTE: Do NOT send a copy, or original, of a Form W-2c with this letter.

See Next Page

Exhibit 2—Sample no-match letter to employee, *continued*

3365-10
DO NOT COPY

KEEP THIS PAGE--IT INCLUDES IMPORTANT INFORMATION

Your employer may not take action against you based on this letter.

- If you think that any action against you is related to labor union activities or union organizing activities, you may contact the National Labor Relations Board (NLRB), an agency of the U.S. government (www.nlrb.gov). Check your local directory for the nearest NLRB office in your area.

- If you think that any action against you is related to your race, color, sex, religion, national origin, age or disability, you may call the Equal Employment Opportunity Commission (EEOC) toll-free at 1-800-669-4000, or 1-800-669-6820 (TDD for the deaf or hard of hearing), or visit the website at www.eeoc.gov.

- If you have questions or concerns about unfair practices by your employer that may be related to your national origin or citizenship status, you may call the Office of Special Counsel for Immigration-Related Unfair Employment Practices toll-free at 1-800-255-7688, or 1-800-237-2515 (TDD for the deaf or hard of hearing). Within the Washington, D.C., metropolitan area, call 202-616-5594.

Please See Reverse

For Spanish-speaking individuals:
GUARDE ESTA CARTA - CONTIENE INFORMACIÓN IMPORTANTE

Su empleador no puede tomar acción en su contra basándose en esta carta.

- Si usted piensa que cualquier acción en su contra está relacionada con las actividades del sindicato de trabajadores o actividades organizadas por el sindicato, usted se puede comunicar con la Junta Nacional de Relaciones del Trabajo (NLRB, siglas en inglés), agencia del gobierno de los Estados Unidos (www.nlrb.gov). Busque en su directorio local la oficina de la Junta Nacional de Relaciones del Trabajo más cercana.
- Si usted cree que cualquier acción en su contra está relacionada con su raza, color, sexo, religión, origen nacional, edad o incapacidad, puede llamar gratis a la Comisión de Igualdad de Oportunidades de Empleo (EEOC, siglas en inglés) al 1-800-669-4000 ó 1-800-669-6820 (TDD para las personas sordas o con problemas de audición), o puede visitar www.eeoc.gov/es/index.html en el Internet.
- Si usted tiene preguntas o dudas sobre prácticas injustas por parte de su empleador, que pueden estar relacionadas con su origen nacional o estado legal, puede llamar gratis a la Oficina del Consejero Especial para Prácticas de Empleo Injustas Relacionadas a la Condición de Inmigrante al 1-800-255-7688 ó 1-800-237-2515 (TDD para las personas sordas o con problemas de audición). Dentro del área metropolitana de Washington, D.C., llame al (202) 616-5594.

El hecho de que usted haya recibido esta carta no constituye una razón, de por sí, para que su empleador lo cambie de trabajo, suspenda, despida o tome alguna acción adversa en su contra.

Vea al dorso

13

WHAT EVERY LAWYER NEEDS TO KNOW ABOUT PERM (PROGRAM ELECTRONIC REVIEW MANAGEMENT LABOR CERTIFICATION)

Monique van Stiphout[1]

A BRIEF HISTORY OF PERM

The "Program Electronic Review Management" (PERM) Labor Certification was implemented by the U.S. Department of Labor on March 28, 2005, and all applications for Labor Certification filed on or after that date have been required to use the PERM system.[2] PERM was developed by the U.S. Department of Labor to streamline and standardize the Labor Certification process and, ideally, to reduce often extremely lengthy processing times.[3]

Prior to the implementation of PERM, employers had two options with respect to how to file an application for employment certification— through the filing of a "standard" application for employment certification or through a process known as "reduction in recruitment"(RIR).[4]

---

1. Monique van Stiphout is a senior attorney at Maggio + Kattar in Washington, D.C. She represents numerous national and international clients in the area of business immigration, which includes establishing corporate visa programs, accomplishing the transfer of executive, managerial and professional personnel to the United States employment-authorized non-immigrant status, as well as securing U.S. permanent residence and citizenship status. Monique also assists individuals with personal immigration filings including marriage-based visas. Monique holds a Juris Doctor from the Georgetown University Law Center and a Bachelor of Science in Foreign Service degree from Georgetown University. While at the Georgetown University Law Center, Monique was managing editor of the Georgetown Immigration Law Journal. Monique is a member of the Bar of the Court of Appeals of the District of Columbia, the Bar of the Court of Appeals of Maryland and the American Immigration Lawyers Association (AILA).
2. 69 Fed. Reg. 77,325 (Dec. 27, 2004).
3. *Id.*
4. U.S. Department of Labor, GAL 1-97, October 1, 1996.

Regardless of which process an employer chose, the legal requirements for certification were the same—the employer was required to demonstrate, through a test of the labor market, that there were no qualified *and* available U.S. workers for the position.[5] The difference between the two processes was primarily twofold: (1) a difference in how the employer conducted the required test of the labor market; and (2) a difference in processing at the State Workforce Agency (SWA) (formerly known as State Employment Security Agencies or SESAs), which gave preferential treatment to RIR applications.[6] In general, given the fact that employers were much more able to control costs using the RIR method, and the fact that these applications were given preferential processing by the SWAs, the RIR became the preferred method through which to process an application for employment certification.

The fact that applications had to be filed with the SWAs, which then were responsible for the preliminary adjudication of the application prior to forwarding to the U.S. Department of Labor, led to inconsistent standards and processing times. States with high unemployment tended to require much stricter pre-recruitment, and high-volume states such as New York and California had extremely lengthy backlogs, while applications in lower volume states were processed much more quickly. In order to standardize the process and streamline processing times, the Department of Labor developed the PERM system, which went into effect on March 28, 2005, and all applications filed on or after that date have been required to use the PERM system.[7]

Some of the major differences between the old RIR application and the new PERM application are the following:

1. The PERM application may be submitted electronically directly to the U.S. Department of Labor National Processing Center. (Previously, cases were submitted in hard copy to the local SWAs. Under PERM, the SWAs are no longer part of the adjudication process);[8]

2. Employers are not required to submit supporting documentation at the time of filing (although they must maintain all supporting documentation in the event of a DOL audit);[9]

---

5. 8 U.S.C. § 1153(b)(3).
6. U.S. Department of Labor, GAL 1-97, October 1, 1996.
7. 69 Fed. Reg. 77,325 (Dec. 27, 2004).
8. *OFLC Frequently Asked Questions and Answers—Standards/Major Differences*, U.S. DEPARTMENT OF LABOR (January 15, 2009), http://www.foreignlaborcert.doleta.gov/faqsanswers.cfm#stands2.
9. *Id.*

3. The employer must offer 100 percent of the prevailing wage (under the previous system, a five-percent variance from the prevailing wage was allowed);[10]
4. The required "Notice of Filing" must be posted for ten consecutive *business* days (as opposed to simply ten consecutive days);[11] and
5. The employer is *required* to conduct recruitment prior to filing and such recruitment must occur not less than 30 days and not more than 180 days prior to filing.[12]

As promised by the DOL, the PERM process has, for the most part, greatly reduced processing times (for cases not selected for audit). However, while faster, the overall process is fraught with potential pitfalls for the uninitiated.

JOB DESCRIPTION AND MINIMUM REQUIREMENTS OF THE POSITION

When assisting an employer through the PERM process, there are several issues that must be reviewed with the client and the employee *prior to beginning the process*. The most important part of the PERM process (and the employment-based green card process in general) is developing a job description upon which such sponsorship will be based.

The primary question that employers and counsel will receive from sponsored employees in the PERM context is, "Will my application be in the EB2 (Employment-Based, Second Preference) or EB3 (Employment-Based, Third Preference) category?" This is important to the employee because there are often significant processing time advantages to falling in the EB2 over the EB3 category (especially for employees from countries such as India and China, from which a large number of individuals wish to immigrate to the United States). Current U.S. law limits the overall number of individuals who may obtain Permanent Resident status in any given fiscal year to 480,000, divided between family-based and employment-based immigrants.[13] The law also contains limitations on the number of individuals that may immigrate from any one country in any given year.[14] In the

---

10. *Id.*
11. *Id.*
12. *Id.*
13. 8 U.S.C. § 1151.
14. *Id.* § 1152.

PERM context, employment-based immigration is further broken down into the following preferences:

A.   Second-preference (EB2), which category is reserved for individuals who are "members of the professions" holding an advanced degree, or its equivalent; or individuals of exceptional ability.[15] CIS regulations define a bachelor's degree plus five years of progressive, post-baccalaureate experience to be the equivalent of an "advanced" degree.[16] (In general, to qualify for sponsorship in the EB2 category, we must be able to demonstrate *both* that the position requires an advanced degree or its equivalent for entry into the position, *and* that the employee possessed an advanced degree or its equivalent at the time he or she was hired.)

B.   Third-preference (EB3), which is for professionals (individuals in positions which normally require a bachelor's or higher degree, but which do not rise to the level of "advanced" degree professionals); skilled workers (individuals in positions requiring at least two years of experience); and other workers (for all other permanent positions. Immigration in this category is limited to not more than 10,000 individuals per year).[17]

In general, there are a greater number of immigrant visas available for individuals who fall within the "second preference" category, and fewer individuals who qualify for the second preference, such that the wait times to actually obtain a green card are years shorter for individuals who fall within the second preference category.[18]

Keeping in mind the EB2 vs. EB3 differential, there are a number of factors to be taken into consideration when crafting a job description and minimum requirements for the position in the PERM context:

A.   The minimum requirements for the position must be the employer's objective minimum requirements for the job.[19] The employer must be able to demonstrate that it has not hired workers (including the employee being sponsored) with less training or experience for jobs similar to the one offered.[20]

B.   In most instances, the employer must be able to demonstrate that the sponsored employee met the minimum requirements for the position *at the time she or he was initially hired.*[21] Generally, the U.S. Department

---

15. *Id.* § 1153(b)(2).

16. 8 C.F.R. § 204.5(k)(2).

17. 8 U.S.C. § 1153(b)(3).

18. *Visa Bulletin,* U.S. Department of State, http://travel.state.gov/content/visas/english/law-and-policy/bulletin.html (last visited June 20, 2014).

19. 20 C.F.R. § 656.17(i)(1).

20. *Id.* § 656.17(i)(2). *See also* Texas State Technical Institute, 89-INA-207 (Apr. 17, 1990).

21. 20 C.F.R. § 656.17(i)(3).

of Labor takes the stance that experience gained with the sponsoring employer provides an unfair advantage to the sponsored employee over potentially qualified U.S. workers and therefore cannot be used to "qualify" the sponsored employee for the position.[22]

There are limited exceptions which allow an employer to take experience gained by the sponsored employee with the employer into consideration in the PERM context. These are:

1. The employee gained the experience in question while working for the employer in a position "sufficiently dissimilar" to the position for which she or he is being sponsored.[23] In determining whether a position is "sufficiently dissimilar," and therefore may be used to qualify an employee for the position for which she or he is being sponsored, the U.S. Department of Labor will consider the following factors:

    • the job duties (including the percentage of time spent performing each job duty in each job), supervisory responsibilities (if any), and minimum entry requirements for each position;
    • where the jobs fall within the employer's hierarchy/organizational chart;
    • prior employment practices (i.e., has the employer always required experience in one position for promotion/transfer into the other);
    • whether the new position is newly created, or if it has been previously filled (and, if so, by whom); and
    • the respective salaries or wages of each position.[24]

2. The employer can demonstrate that it is no longer feasible to train a worker to qualify for the position.[25] Historically, this has been a very difficult exception to prove;[26] however, a recent BALCA decision may indicate a shift in the DOL's approach to this exception.[27]

---

22. Central Harlem Group, Inc., 89-INA-284 (May 14, 1991); Apartment Management Co., 88-INA-215 (Feb. 2, 1989).

23. 20 C.F.R. § 656.17(i)(3(i).

24. Delitizer Corp. of Newton, 88-INA-482 (May 9, 1990) (en banc). *See also* Houston Graduate School of Theology, 90-INA-491 (Dec. 6, 1991).

25. 20 C.F.R. § 656.17(i)(3)(ii).

26. 58th Street Restaurant Corp., 90-INA-58 (Feb. 21, 1991); Fingers, Faces, and Toes, 90-INA-56 (Feb. 8, 1991).

27. *See* Kentiox, Inc., 2012-PER-0038 (May 22, 2014).

C. The job requirements must not exceed those established by the U.S. Department of Labor as the "normal" minimum requirements for the position; or, if they do exceed such requirements, the employer must establish the business necessity for such requirements in excess of the "normal" minimum requirements.[28]

To determine what the Department of Labor considers to be the "normal" minimum requirements for the position, employers should consult the "O*Net" online database (http://www.onetonline.org). When consulting the database, employers should select the occupation which most closely matches the position description. The Department of Labor categorizes each position into one of five "Job Zones." For each "Job Zone," the DOL has established standard minimum educational and professional experience requirements. To further complicate the evaluation, the Department of Labor also assigns a "Specific Vocational Preparation" or SVP range to each Job Zone, which outlines the specific amount of experience deemed "normal" for the occupation. The SVP range is inclusive of education required for the position (for example, a bachelor's degree is considered to be the equivalent of two years of Specific Vocational Preparation—so for an occupation for which the DOL considers the SVP to be two up to four years, if a bachelor's degree is required, the maximum amount of experience an employer could require and remain within the "normal" minimum requirements would be two years). A summary of the Job Zones, and the corresponding SVP ranges, is as follows:

Job Zone One: little or no preparation needed. According to the Department of Labor, occupations within this Job Zone *may* require a high school diploma or GED degree and little or no previous work experience. SVP Range—below 4.0 (three months or less).

Job Zone Two: some preparation needed. According to the Department of Labor, occupations within this Job Zone usually require a high school diploma and some previous work experience. SVP range—4.0 to less than 6.0 (experience of over three months up to and including one year).

Job Zone Three: medium preparation needed. According to the Department of Labor, occupations within this Job Zone require training in vocational schools, on-the-job experience, or an associate's degree plus previous work related experience. SVP range—6.0 to less than 7.0 (Experience of over one year and up to and including two years).

Job Zone Four: considerable preparation needed. According to the Department of Labor, most occupations within this Job Zone require a bachelor's degree, but some do not. In addition, these occupations gener-

---

28. 20 C.F.R. § 656.17(h)(1).

ally require a "considerable amount" of previous work related experience or knowledge. SVP range—7.0 to less than 8.0 (Over two years up to and including four years of experience).

Job Zone Five: extensive preparation needed. According to the Department of Labor, most occupations within this Job Zone require graduate school and many require more than five years of experience. SVP range—8.0 and above (over four years of experience).[29]

If an employer's minimum requirements fall outside the Department of Labor "normal" minimum requirements for the occupation, the employer must be able to demonstrate the business necessity of its requirements to the Department of Labor.[30]

Finally, an employer cannot include a foreign language as a minimum requirement for the position unless it is a documented business necessity for the position.[31] Such business necessity can be demonstrated if (1) the nature of the position is such that a foreign language requirement is intrinsic to the position (such as a language teacher or translator); or (2) the employer can demonstrate that the employee will need to communicate with a majority of the employer's clients, contractors or employees who cannot communicate in English.[32]

D. Finally, employers and counsel should review the sponsored employee's credentials to ensure that he or she met the objective minimum requirements described at the time he or she was hired by the company,[33] (note that if the employee did not meet the minimum requirements, then the requirements are not, in fact, the objective minimum requirements for the position, since the company has hired at least one individual with less than the stated requirements).

In addition, even for positions for which an advanced degree, or its equivalent, is typically required for entry into the position (such that it appears the position qualifies for the more preferential EB2 category), it is possible that even though the employee is qualified for the position, the employee's academic and/or professional credentials are such that he or she does not rise to the level of qualifying for the EB2 category. In reviewing an employee's credentials under these circumstances, employers and their counsel should be aware of the following:

---

29. *Job Zones,* O*NET ONLINE, http://www.onetonline.org/help/online/zones (last visited June 20, 2014); *Specific Vocational Preparation (SVP),* O*NET ONLINE, http://www.onetonline.org/help/online/svp (last visited June 20, 2014).

30. 20 C.F.R. § 656.17(h)(1).

31. *Id.* § 656.17(h)(2).

32. *Id.*

33. *Id.* § 656.17(i)(3).

1. If the individual possesses a master's or higher degree from an university outside of the United States, U.S. Citizenship and Immigration Services will review the *EDGE* (Electronic Database for Global Education) created by the American Association of Collegiate Registrars and Admissions Officers (AACRAO) to determine whether such degree rises to the level of equivalent to a master's degree awarded by a U.S. university.[34]

2. If the employee qualifies on the basis of possessing the equivalent of an advanced degree (i.e., a bachelor's degree plus five years of progressively responsible post-baccalaureate experience), the employer and counsel must review the employee's academic and professional credentials to ensure that:

    a. If the bachelor's degree is from a foreign university, it rises to the level of being equivalent to a bachelor's degree awarded by a U.S. university (based on academics only, not on education and experience).[35] In general, USCIS has held that a three-year bachelor's degree program (which is common in some countries such as India) does not rise to the level of being the academic equivalent of a four-year U.S. bachelor's degree.[36]

    b. USCIS has been known to require a "single-source" degree equivalency (i.e., a three-year bachelor's degree plus a one-year post-graduate degree has been rejected for purposes of rising to the level of being equivalent to a four-year U.S. bachelor's degree).[37]

    c. The five years of work experience is both (1) post-degree experience; and (2) progressively responsible (defined by USCIS as "employment experience that reveals progress, moves forward, and advances toward increasingly complex or responsible duties").[38]

---

34. Matter of Name-not-Provided., TSC, SRC-08-198-51124 (AAO Jan. 9, 2000).
35. Letter from Efren Hernandez III, Director, Business and Trade Services, INS, to Aron Finkelstein, Esq. (Jan. 7, 2003) (on file with American Immigration Lawyers Association (AILA), AILA Infonet Doc. No. 03041544).
36. Matter of Shah, 17 I. & N. Dec. 244 (Regional Comm'r 1977).
37. Snapnames.com v. Chertoff, 2006 WL 3491005 (D. Or. 2006). *But see* Letter, Hernandez, Director, Business and Trade Services, USCIS, HQ 70/6.2.8 (Jan. 7, 2003).
38. Memorandum from Cronin on Educational and Experience Requirements for Employment-Based Second Preference (EB-2) Immigrants to All Service Center Directors; all Regional Directors (Mar. 20, 2000) (on file with American Immigration Lawyers Association (AILA), AILA InfoNet Doc. No. 00032703 (posted Mar. 27, 2000)).

If the sponsored employee's academic and professional credentials do not meet these requirements, the application will fall within the EB3 category, regardless of the fact that the position requires an advanced degree or its equivalent.

PREVAILING WAGE REQUEST

Once the position description and minimum requirements have been established, the first required step in the PERM process is to request a prevailing wage determination from the U.S. Department of Labor's National Processing Center (NPC).[39] In determining the prevailing wage, the NPC will look to the following sources:

A. If there is a collective bargaining agreement in place which covers the position in question, the NPC will accept the wage set forth in the agreement as the "prevailing wage."[40]

B. If there is no collective bargaining agreement, the NPC will use the wages provided on the U.S. Department of Labor's Occupational Employment Statistics (OES) survey to determine the prevailing wage.[41] In general, for each occupation, the OES provides four wage levels, ranging from entry level (Level 1) to extremely experienced (Level 4). To determine which of the four wage levels to assign to the position in question, the NPC will review the occupational classification for the position to determine into which Job Zone and SVP (discussed at pp. 246–247) falls. The NPC will then determine if the employer's requirements for the position fall within the "normal" requirements for the position. While there are several factors taken into account by the NPC, the following is a simplified description of how the determinations are made:

1. If the employer's requirements are less than the minimum requirements for the position, it will generally issue a Level 1 wage for the prevailing wage;[42]
2. If the requirements fall within the lower half of the "normal" range, the prevailing wage will generally be issued at Level 2;[43]

---

39. 20 C.F.R. § 656.40(a).
40. *Id.* § 656.40(b)(1).
41. *Id.* § 656.40(b)(2).
42. ETA, Prevailing Wage Determination Policy Guidance, Nonagricultrual Immigration Programs (Nov. 2009, revised).
43. *Id.*

3. If the requirements fall within the higher part of the "normal" range, the prevailing wage will generally be issued at Level 3;[44] and
4. Finally, if the requirements exceed the "normal" range, the prevailing wage will generally be issued at Level 4.[45]

If the employer disagrees with the skill level assigned to the prevailing wage determination, it may submit a request for reconsideration and supplemental information to the NPC.[46] If the NPC does not accept the supplemental information, the employer has the option of (1) submitting a new prevailing wage application which includes a request to use an alternate survey (*see* discussion below on page 251; or, (2) appealing the decision of the NPC (*see* discussion below on page 251).[47]

C. Prior to submitting a prevailing wage request, an employer and counsel may review the OES wage levels online at http://www.flcdata center.com/. If the employer and counsel determines that an OES-based wage determination may not be the best objective measure of the actual prevailing wage for the position in question, it has the option of submitting the prevailing wage determination application with a request that the NPC consider an alternate, employer-provided wage survey.[48] When doing so, the employer must provide a description of the methodology of the survey so that the NPC can determine if it is an acceptable survey for prevailing wage purposes.[49] To be acceptable, the alternate wage survey must:

1. have been published within 24 months of the date of submission to the NPC;
2. be the most current edition of the survey; and
3. the data upon which the survey is based must have been collected within 24 months of the publication date of the survey.[50]

If the NPC finds the survey acceptable, it will issue the prevailing wage determination based upon the employer-provided survey. If it finds the survey unacceptable, it will inform the employer in writing of the rea-

---

44. *Id.*

45. *Id.*

46. 20 C.F.R. § 656.40(h).

47. *Id.* § 656.40(g)(5).

48. *Id.* § 656.40(g).

49. *Id.*

50. *Id.* § 656.40(g)(3).

sons the survey was found to be unacceptable.[51] Should this occur, the employer may (1) submit a request for reconsideration and supplemental information; (2) submit a new prevailing wage determination application; or (3) appeal the decision of the NPC.[52]

D.   Within 30 days of receiving an unfavorable determination from the NPC, an employer may send a request for a review of the decision to the Director of the NPC.[53] Such request must contain all documentation previously submitted to the NPC in connection with the prevailing wage determination application.[54] The Director will review the determination based solely upon the information in the record and either affirm or modify the prevailing wage determination.[55] If the employer receives an adverse decision on its request for review, it may request a review by the Board of Alien Labor Certification Appeals (BALCA) within 30 days of receiving the Director's decision.[56]

While it is important to know the process for appealing a prevailing wage determination, in practice, as most PERM applications are at least somewhat time sensitive, and as the Redetermination and Appeals process can take months (if not years) to resolve, most employers will opt to submit a new prevailing wage determination request rather than engage in the lengthy, and often ineffective, appeals process.

TEST OF THE LABOR MARKET/ REQUIRED RECRUITMENT EFFORT

With the exception of a handful of occupations which have been designated for "pre-certification" (known as "Schedule A" occupations, which include nurses, physical therapists, and persons of exceptional ability in the sciences, arts, or performing arts),[57] college and university professors (for which there is an alternate "optional" recruitment process),[58] and professional athletes, once the employer has received an acceptable prevailing wage determination, it is time to move forward with the required test of the labor market, which must be completed before a PERM application

---

51. *Id.* § 656.40(g)(4).
52. *Id.* § 656.40(g)(5).
53. *Id.* § 656.41(a).
54. *Id.*
55. *Id.* § 656.41(c).
56. *Id.* § 656.41(d).
57. *Id.* § 656.15.
58. *Id.* § 656.18.

can be submitted to the U.S. Department of Labor.[59] At a minimum, all advertisements placed in the context of the required recruitment effort must contain (1) the name of the employer and the general geographic area of employment; (2) direction on how to reply to the advertisement, including instructions on where applications and/or resumes should be sent or submitted; (3) a description of the job duties of the position that are specific enough to "apprise U.S. workers" of the position; (4) a wage which is not lower than either the prevailing wage or the wage offered to the sponsored employee; and (5) not contain any job duties or requirements that are greater than those contained in the prevailing wage request and to be included in the PERM application.[60] In general, it is good practice to avoid indicating the salary or salary range in any advertisements except for those where it is specifically required (such as the internal posting).

For every application to be filed under the PERM process, current Department of Labor regulations require an employer to undertake the following mandatory recruitment steps:

A. The employer is required to give "Notice" of the filing of the application. Where the occupation is covered by a collective bargaining agreement, such notice must be given to the bargaining representative of the union in question.[61] If there is no bargaining representative, the employer is required to post notice at the location of employment in a conspicuous and clearly visible manner for a minimum of ten consecutive business days.[62] In addition, if applicable, the employer must publish the notice in "any and all" in-house media in accordance with its normal procedures for recruitment for similar positions.[63] In addition to the information required for all recruitment undertaken in the PERM context, the internal posting notice must:

1. state that it is being posted in connection with the filing of a PERM Application for employment certification;
2. state that any person may provide information with respect to the application for employment certification to the certifying officer at the U.S. Department of Labor, and provide the address to which such information should be submitted;
3. contain the proffered salary or salary range; and

---

59. *Id.* § 656.17(e).
60. *Id.* § 656.17(f).
61. *Id.* § 656.10(d)(1)(i).
62. *Id.* § 656.10(d)(1)(ii).
63. *Id.*

4. be posted within 30 to 180 days prior to the filing of the PERM application.[64]

It is critical that the internal posting notice be consistent with the position description and minimum requirements contained on the prevailing wage determination application (and to be contained on the PERM application for employment certification); that the salary or salary range offered in the notice be both at or above the required prevailing wage and equal to or above the salary offered to the sponsored employer; and that the requirement regarding the timing of the posting be strictly adhered to.[65] Failure to meet any of these requirements is grounds for the potential denial of the employer's PERM application.[66]

B. The employer is required to place two print advertisements on two different Sundays in a newspaper of "general circulation" within the area of intended employment.[67] A newspaper of "general circulation" has been defined by the U.S. Department of Labor to be that newspaper which is most appropriate to the proffered position and the area of intended employment which is most likely to bring responses from qualified, able and available U.S. workers.[68] While the employer has discretion to choose the newspaper in which such advertisements will be placed, if the certifying officer does not agree with the employer's choice, the PERM application may be denied.[69] In order to avoid any potential questions regarding the employer's choice of newspaper, many practitioners advise employers to place the advertisements in the major newspaper covering the area of intended employment (for example, for jobs in the New York metropolitan area, placing the advertisements in The New York Times is the path that is least likely to draw questions from the Department of Labor).

C. The employer is required to place a job order with the State Workforce Agency (SWA) covering the area of intended employment, which Job Order must be posted for a minimum of 30 days.[70]

---

64. *Id.* § 656.10(d)(3).

65. *Id.* § 656.17(f).

66. *Id.* § 656.10(c).

67. *Id.* § 656.17(e)(1)(B)(i), (e)(2)(ii).

68. *OFLC Frequently Asked Questions and Answers—Acceptable Publications*, U.S. DEPARTMENT OF LABOR (Jan. 15, 2009), http://www.foreignlaborcert.doleta.gov/faqsanswers .cfm#stands2.

69. Peking Gourmet, 88-INA-323 (May 11, 1989) (en banc).

70. 20 C.F.R. § 656.17(e)(1)(i)(A), (e)(2)(i).

For "professional positions," defined as an occupation for which a bachelor's degree or higher is a usual educational requirement,[71] employers must also complete additional recruitment steps.[72] For this additional required recruitment, Department of Labor regulations delineate ten (10) acceptable methods of recruitment, of which employers are required to choose three (3).[73] The options for the additional recruitment steps are:

A. participation in job fairs for the occupation listed in the application;
B. employer website;
C. other job search websites;
D. on-campus recruiting;
E. trade or professional organizations;
F. private employment firms;
G. employee referral program with incentives;
H. campus placement offices;
I. local and ethnic newspapers; and
J. radio and television advertisements.[74]

In general, the employer should pick the recruitment methods which are appropriate to the position and which are most likely to reach qualified and available U.S. workers.[75]

EVALUATION OF APPLICANTS

All applications and/or resumes received by an employer in response to the required recruitment must be reviewed by the employer upon receipt.[76] DOL regulations require that the individual who would normally review resumes and interview applicants for recruitment efforts not undertaken in the immigration context should also be the individual who reviews resumes and, if necessary, interviews applicants within the context of the required test of the labor market for PERM.[77] Neither the employee who is the beneficiary of the PERM application, nor his or her

---

71. *Id.* § 656.3.
72. *Id.* § 656.17(e)(1)(ii).
73. *Id.*
74. *Id.*
75. *Id.* § 656.17(e)(2)(i). *See also* Iglesia Evangelica Emmanuel Church, 08-PER-161 (BALCA Mar. 17, 2009).
76. 20 C.F.R. § 656.10(b)(2).
77. *Id.* § 656.10(b)(2)(ii).

attorney may participate in reviewing the applications and/or resumes or in interviewing applicants in the PERM context.[78]

In reviewing applications and/or resumes received in response to the required recruitment effort, employers must determine whether the applicant appears to possess the minimum qualifications to be able to perform the duties as listed on the PERM application.[79] If, following an initial review of the applications and/or resumes, the employer determines that an applicant clearly does not possess the minimum requirements for the position as described on the PERM application, the employer may lawfully reject that applicant without having first contacted him or her.[80] If the applicant appears to be qualified for the position based upon the preliminary review of the resume and/or application, *or* where it is not clear whether an applicant possesses the minimum qualifications required, an employer should contact that applicant.[81] All required contact with an applicant must be completed "as soon as possible."[82] The "as soon as possible" standard hinges on the following factors: (a) whether the position requires extensive or minimal credentials; (b) whether recruitment is local; and (c) whether many or only a few persons applied for the position.[83] The DOL may view any delay in contacting potentially qualified applicants as a contributing factor to their unavailability, which may lead to a determination that the recruitment was not conducted in good faith as required.[84] The employer may attempt to justify untimely contact based on factors outside the normal recruitment process, which are outside of the employer's control, so long as the employer can demonstrate that it handled the outside interference in a reasonable fashion.[85] An unjustified delay in contacting potentially qualified applicants may be a basis for denial of the application.[86]

As indicated on p. 252, at no point during the required test of the labor market (either within the recruitment materials, or in speaking with applicants who have responded to the recruitment efforts) may an

---

78. *Id.* § 656.10(b)(2)(i).

79. United Parcel Service, 90-INA-90 (Mar. 28, 1991); Mancil-las International Ltd., 88-INA-321 (Feb. 7, 1990); Microbilt Corp., 87-INA-635 (Jan. 12, 1988).

80. ENY Textiles, Inc., 87-INA-641 (Jan. 22, 1988).

81. Nancy, Ltd., 88-INA-358 (Apr. 27, 1989) (en banc), *rev'd*, Nancy Ltd. v. Dole, Case No. 89-2257-CIV-Scott. (S.D. Fla. Aug. 8, 1990) (adopting magistrate's recommendation).

82. Loma Linda Foods, Inc., 89-INA-289 (Nov. 26, 1991) (en banc).

83. *Id.*

84. Creative Cabinet and Store Fixture, 89-INA-181 (Jan. 24, 1990) (en banc).

85. *Loma Linda Foods, Inc.*, 89-INA-289 (Nov. 26, 1991) (en banc).

86. Naegle Associates, Inc., 88-INA-504 (May 23, 1990).

employer offer wages or terms and conditions of employment which are less favorable than what is being offered to the sponsored employee.[87]

ASSEMBLING THE AUDIT FILE

While employers are not required to submit evidence of the required recruitment at the time the PERM application is submitted to DOL, regulations require that a copy of the PERM application and all supporting documentation be maintained for a period of five years from the date of filing.[88] It is critical that the employer gather all of the supporting documentation at the time the recruitment is done. The Board of Alien Labor Certification Appeals has held that failure to do so, where it results in an employer's inability to respond to an audit request, is grounds for denial.[89]

PERM applications submitted to the Department of Labor may be randomly selected for audit, or may be selected for audit following the Department of Labor's initial review of the application.[90] It is important to note that while an employer is required to maintain the required supporting documentation for five years following the filing of a PERM application, the Department of Labor can audit/review an application at any time while in process or after certification[91] (although logistically such review becomes much more difficult if it occurs more than five years following the filing of the application and the supporting documentation is therefore no longer available).

In preparation for a potential audit, the best practice is to prepare and maintain an "audit file," which includes the following materials:

A. A copy of the PERM application submitted to the U.S. Department of Labor;[92]

B. An original tear sheet from the two Sunday print advertisements;[93]

C. The original notices posted at the employer's work site, and certification regarding the posting of these documents;[94]

---

87. 20 C.F.R. § 656.17(f). *See also* ERF Inc., d/b/a Bayside Motor Inn, 89-INA-105 (Feb. 14, 1990).

88. 20 C.F.R. § 656.10(f).

89. Natural Nature, Inc., 2009-PER-00337 (Mar. 30, 2010).

90. 20 C.F.R. § 656.20(a).

91. *Id.*

92. *Id.* § 656.17(d)(3).

93. *Id.* § 656.17(e)(1)(i)(3).

94. *Id.* § 656.10(d).

    D. A screen shot of the posting with the state Job Bank on both the first and last day of the posting (as proof that the posting was placed for the required minimum 30-day period) and/or certification from the state Job Bank that the required posting was made, including the verbiage of the posting;[95]

    E. If the filing is for a professional position, evidence of the three additional recruitment steps:

       1. Job fairs—brochures or other advertisements for the fair listing the employer as a participant in the job fair;[96]

       2. Employer's website—dated screen shots of the job listing on site on the first and last day of the posting;[97]

       3. Other websites—dated screen shots of the job listing on the site on the first and last day of the posting;[98]

       4. On-campus recruitment—copies of the notification posting by the college's placement office naming the employer and the date it conducted interviews;[99]

       5. Trade or professional organizations—copies of the newsletters or trade journals containing the advertisements for the position;[100]

       6. Private employment firms—documentation which proves such recruitment occurred, such as contracts between the employer and the recruitment agency and copies of the advertisements placed for the position;[101]

       7. Employee referral program with incentives—dated copies of the employer notices or memorandum advertising the position and a copy of the incentive referral program;[102]

       8. Campus placement offices—a copy of the recruitment notice provided to the campus placement office;[103]

       9. Local and ethnic newspapers—the original newspaper containing the recruitment advertisement;[104]

      10. Radio and television advertisements—a copy of the text of the advertisement along with written confirmation from the

95. *Id.* § 656.17(e)(1)(A).
96. *Id.* § 656.17(a)(ii)(A).
97. *Id.* § 656.17(a)(ii)(B).
98. *Id.* § 656.17(a)(ii)(C).
99. *Id.* § 656.17(a)(ii)(D).
100. *Id.* § 656.17(a)(ii)(E).
101. *Id.* § 656.17(a)(ii)(F).
102. *Id.* § 656.17(a)(ii)(G).
103. *Id.* § 656.17(a)(ii)(H).
104. *Id.* § 656.17(a)(ii)(I).

       radio or television station stating when the advertisement
       was aired.[105]

F. A copy of the prevailing wage determination issued by the Department of Labor;[106]

G. A copy of all resumes and/or employment applications received in response to the required recruitment;[107]

H. A "recruitment report" which specifies the recruitment steps that were taken, the number of applications received in response to the recruitment effort, the number of hires (if any) made based upon the required recruitment effort and, if applicable, the number of U.S. workers rejected, categorized by reason for rejection.[108]

I. If the employer's minimum requirements for the position are greater than the Department of Labor's standard minimum requirements; or if the employer is requiring a foreign language for entry into the position; or if the job offered contains a combination of duties, the audit file should also include a statement of business necessity which describes why the higher standards are required to successfully fill the position.[109]

The Department of Labor is required to notify an employer that its PERM application has been selected for audit by a letter which advises the employer of the documentation sought by the Department of Labor, and provides a period of 30 days in which the employer may respond.[110] Regardless of whether the audit is "triggered" or "random," it is general practice for the Department of Labor to request all required supporting documentation in an audit request, as well as any additional information or materials it may require in order to fully evaluate the application.

An employer who receives an audit letter from the Department of Labor may request one extension of 30 days in order to prepare the response.[111] If an employer either fails to respond to the audit request, or responds but does not provide all of the requested materials, the Department of Labor may deny the application.[112] Alternatively, the Department of Labor may require that the employer undergo "supervised recruit-

---

105. *Id.* § 656.17(a)(ii)(J).
106. *Id.* § 656.10(e)(1)(i), (ii).
107. *Id.*
108. *Id.* § 656.17(g).
109. *Id.* § 656.17(h).
110. *Id.* § 656.20.
111. *Id.* § 656.20(c).
112. *Id.* § 656.20(b).

ment" (discussed below) for any PERM applications filed within two years following such denial.[113]

Following its review of the audit response, the Department of Labor may (1) certify the application; (2) deny the application; (3) request additional information or documentation; or (4) require the employer to engage in "supervised recruitment" for the position.[114]

SUPERVISED RECRUITMENT

As discussed above, the Department of Labor has discretionary authority to require an employer to undertake "supervised recruitment" either postfiling for an application already under review or, in some cases, for future applications following a failure to comply with a previous audit and/or supervised recruitment effort.[115]

When an employer is ordered to undertake supervised recruitment, the employer will be required to submit a draft of the advertisement to the Department of Labor for approval within 30 days of receiving notification of supervised recruitment.[116] The draft text of the advertisement must contain a description of the job duties and requirements which is consistent with and does not exceed those duties and requirements listed on the PERM application.[117] The advertisement must also direct applicants to respond to an address specified by the Department of Labor.[118] Once the Department of Labor approves the advertisement, the employer must place the advertisement as directed by the Department of Labor (the Department of Labor will determine both the publication in which the advertisement should be run, and the timing of the required recruitment).[119] In addition to, or as a replacement for, the print advertisement approved through this process, the Department of Labor has discretionary authority to require additional or different recruitment methods.[120] Once placed, the employer must notify the Department of Labor that it has completed the placement of the advertisement(s) as instructed.[121]

---

113. *Id.*
114. *Id.* § 656.20(d).
115. *Id.* § 656.21(a).
116. *Id.* § 656.21(b).
117. *Id.*
118. *Id.*
119. *Id.* § 656.21(c)(1).
120. *Id.* § 656.21(d).
121. *Id.* § 656.21(c)(2).

Individuals responding to the supervised recruitment are supposed to send their resumes/applications directly to the Department of Labor, which then forwards them to the employer.[122] However, the employer is also required to consider applications and/or resumes that it receives directly, and to provide these documents to the U.S. Department of Labor.[123]

Following its receipt of the notification from the employer that the required recruitment advertisement(s) have been placed, the Department of Labor will issue a request for a "Report of Recruitment."[124] The employer is required to provide the requested report within 30 days.[125] The report must:

A. identify and provide documentation of each recruitment source;[126]
B. state the number of U.S. workers that responded to the recruitment effort (inclusive of those applications forwarded to the employer by the Department of Labor, as well as any applications or resumes the employer may have received directly);[127]
C. state the names and addresses of the U.S. applicants;[128] and
D. provide specific and lawful job-related reasons that each U.S. applicant was rejected.[129] A U.S. applicant may not be rejected for lacking skills necessary to perform the duties of the position where those skills can be imparted within a reasonable period of on-the-job training.[130]

At each stage of the supervised recruitment process, failure by the employer to provide the requested documentation within the required 30-day time period will result in denial of the application.[131]

---

122. *Id.* § 656.21(b)(2)(i), (e)(3).
123. *Id.* § 656.21(e)(3).
124. *Id.* § 656.21(e).
125. *Id.* § 656.21(f).
126. *Id.* § 656.21(e)(4).
127. *Id.*
128. *Id.*
129. *Id.*
130. *Id.*
131. *Id.* § 656.21(f).

LABOR CERTIFICATION DETERMINATION AND VALIDITY

Following review of the PERM application for employment certification, the certifying officer may certify the application or deny the application.[132] The decision as to whether to certify or deny the application is based on the following factors:

A. The employer has met all of the requirements for PERM certification;[133]
B. The certifying officer is satisfied that there are no qualified, willing and available U.S. workers for the position;[134] and
C. The certifying officer is satisfied that the employment of the sponsored employee will not have an adverse affect on the wages and/or working conditions of similarly employed U.S. workers.[135]

If the PERM application is certified, the certifying officer will notify the employer in writing (either electronically or by mail), and will mail a complete copy of the certified application to the employer or its representative.[136] Once certified, the PERM application is valid for a period of 180 days, during which time the employer must file the subsequent Immigrant Petition (Form I-140) with U.S. Citizenship and Immigration Services.[137] The Immigrant Petition cannot be submitted beyond the validity period of the PERM application.[138] If the PERM application is denied, the certifying officer will notify the employer or its representative in writing of the reasons for denial, and provide information regarding procedures for review of the decision.[139] The employer must file any request for review within 30 days of the decision, or the denial becomes final.[140]

---

132. *Id.* § 656.24(a)(1).
133. *Id.* § 656.24(b)(1).
134. *Id.* § 656.24(b)(2).
135. *Id.* § 656.24(b)(3).
136. *Id.* § 656.24(c)–(d).
137. *Id.* § 656.30(b)(1).
138. *Id.*
139. *Id.* § 656.24(e).
140. *Id.*

14

IMMIGRATION OPTIONS FOR THE BEST AND BRIGHTEST

Alexander Dgebuadze and Rita Sostrin[1]

INTRODUCTION

Under U.S. immigration laws, all foreign-born individuals, or non-citizens, are admitted to the United States mainly as non-immigrants or immigrants. Non-immigrants[2] are non-citizens who seek entry to the United States for a specific, usually occupation-related purpose and for a specific, "temporary" duration of time. Most non-immigrant visa categories provide for multi-year stays in the country. The Visa Office of the Department of State has developed letter-number symbols for the various non-immigrant visa categories that generally correspond with the alphabetical subparagraphs

---

1. Alexander Dgebuadze (adgebuadze@sostrinimmigration.com) is a founding partner at Sostrin Immigration Lawyers, LLP in Los Angeles, CA. He focuses on business immigration law; represents clients in healthcare, academic, automotive, R&D, legal services, and high-technology sectors; and manages the firm's labor certification, investor, and international corporate transfer practice areas. Mr. Dgebuadze has served on various regional and national committees of AILA, has presented and written extensively on advanced immigration law topics, and, most recently, served as a contributing editor for *AILA's Guide to Labor Certification* (2011) and labor certification chapter editor for *Kuzban's Immigration Law Sourcebook* since 2012. Mr. Dgebuadze is listed in *The International Who's Who of Corporate Immigration Lawyers*.

   Rita Sostrin (rsostrin@sostrinimmigration.com) is a founding partner at Sostrin Immigration Lawyers, LLP in Los Angeles, California, a law firm dedicated to practicing exclusively U.S. immigration and nationality law. Ms. Sostrin focuses her practice on immigration of international professionals. She frequently receives invitations to speak at professional conferences and to write for legal publications. Ms. Sostrin is included in *The International Who's Who of Corporate Immigration Lawyers* and *Chambers USA*, and was honored by *Presidential Award* of the American Immigration Lawyers Association (AILA) for her outstanding contributions. She currently serves as chair of the AILA—USCIS California Service Center Liaison Committee, senior editor of the *Immigration & Nationality Law Handbook* and member of AILA's periodicals review board.

2. *See* Immigration and Nationality Act (INA), 8 U.S.C.A. § 101(a)(15).

of INA § 101(a)(15).[3] Immigrants are non-citizens admitted for permanent residence, i.e., to work and reside in the United States permanently.[4] Unlike non-immigrants, immigrants, popularly known as green card holders, may apply for naturalization to become citizens of the United States, but they may choose to remain in permanent resident status indefinitely. INA § 203 describes the categories and allocation of employment-based immigrant visa numbers, including "priority workers,"[5] advanced-degree professionals and "aliens of exceptional ability,"[6] professionals and skilled workers,[7] and major investors.[8]

By virtue of their talents, skills, abilities and knowledge, the "best and brightest"[9] born in other countries qualify for admission to the United States in select non-immigrant visa categories. These include O-1 aliens of extraordinary ability and achievement,[10] E-1 treaty traders,[11] E-2 treaty investors,[12] L-1A intracompany managers and executives,[13] L-1B "specialized knowledge" non-citizens,[14] and H-1B "specialty occupation" workers.[15]

The immigrant categories for which the best and brightest most commonly qualify include EB-1-1 aliens or extraordinary ability,[16] EB-1-2 outstanding professors and researchers,[17] EB-1-3 multinational executives

---

3. Thomas Alexander Aleinikoff, David A. Martin & Hiroshi Motomura, Immigration and Citizenship: Process and Policy, 392 (5th ed. 2003) [hereinafter Aleinikoff].

4. There are four distinct categories of immigrants admitted to the United States for permanent residence: these are (a) family-sponsored immigrants—INA, 8 U.S.C.A. § 1153(a); (b) employment-sponsored immigrants—INA, 8 U.S.C.A. § 1153(b); (c) diversity immigrants—INA, 8 U.S.C.A. § 1153(c); and (d) refugees—INA, 8 U.S.C.A. § 1157—and asylees—INA, 8 U.S.C.A. § 1158. This article will review immigrant classifications that are part of the larger "employment-based" category described in INA, 8 U.S.C.A. § 203(b).

5. *Id.* § 1153(b)(1).

6. *Id.* § 1153(b)(2).

7. *Id.* § 1153(b)(3).

8. *Id.* § 1153(b)(5).

9. For purposes of this article, the "best and brightest" are those individuals who have unique talents, skills, abilities, or knowledge, or a combination thereof. For instance, a foreign-born individual with a STEM (science, technology, engineering, or mathematics) degree at the beginning of his or her career would be considered among the best and brightest.

10. INA, 8 U.S.C.A. § 1101(a)(15)(O).

11. *Id.* § 1101(a)(15)(E)(i).

12. *Id.* § 1101(a)(15)(E)(ii).

13. *Id.* § 1101(a)(15)(L).

14. *Id.*

15. *Id.* § 1101(a)(15)(H).

16. *Id.* § 1153(b)(1)(A).

17. *Id.* § 1153(b)(1)(B).

and managers,[18] EB-2 advanced-degree professionals or aliens of exceptional ability,[19] and EB-5 investors.[20]

This chapter aims to provide an overview and a roadmap for analyzing immigration options for the best and brightest non-citizens attracted by the employment, investment and related business opportunities available in the United States.

NON-IMMIGRANT VISA OPTIONS

O Non-immigrants

The O visa category[21] was created by Congress by the Immigration Act of 1990[22] to cover "aliens" of "extraordinary ability in the sciences, arts, education, business, or athletics,"[23] and "aliens" of "extraordinary achievement in motion picture and/or television productions."[24]

An "alien of extraordinary ability" is a non-citizen who is able to demonstrate "sustained national or international acclaim and who is coming temporarily to the United States to continue to work in the area of extraordinary ability."[25] Those applying in the area of *science, education, business* or *athletics* must additionally prove that they have achieved "a level of expertise" indicating that they are "one of the small percentage who have risen to the very top of the field of endeavor."[26]

Sustained acclaim can be demonstrated through either evidence of a one-time achievement (a major, internationally recognized award such as the Nobel Prize),[27] or through evidence of at least three (3) of the following eight (8) evidentiary criteria:[28]

- Receipt of nationally or internationally recognized prizes or awards for excellence in the field of endeavor.

---

18. *Id.* § 1153(b)(1)(C).
19. *Id.* § 1153(b)(2).
20. *Id.* § 1153(b)(5).
21. *Id.* § 1101(a)(15)(O).
22. Immigration Act of 1990, Pub. L. No. 101-649, 104 Stat. 4978 (1990).
23. 8 C.F.R. § 214.2(o)(1)(ii)(A)(1).
24. *Id.* § 214.2(o)(1)(ii)(A)(2).
25. INA, 8 U.S.C.A. § 101(a)(15)(O)(i); 8 C.F.R. § 214.2(o)(1)(ii)(A)(i).
26. 8 C.F.R. § 214.2(o)(3)(ii).
27. *Id.* § 214.2(o)(3)(iii)(A).
28. *Id.* § 214.2(o)(3)(iii)(B)(1)–(8).

- Membership in associations in the field that require outstanding achievements of their members, as judged by recognized national or international experts.
- Published material in professional or major trade publications or major media about you, relating to your work in the field.
- Participation on a panel, or individually, as a judge of the work of others in the same or allied field.
- Original scientific or scholarly contributions of major significance.
- Authorship of scholarly articles in the field, in professional journals, or other major media.
- Evidence that you have been employed in a critical or essential capacity for organizations or establishments that have a distinguished reputation.
- Evidence that you have either commanded a high salary or will command a high salary or other remuneration for services.

Non-citizens qualifying as aliens of extraordinary ability in the arts, including the performing arts, fine arts, visual arts, and culinary arts, must be able to demonstrate "distinction" defined as "a high level of achievement evidenced by a degree of skill and recognition substantially above that ordinarily encountered," such that he or she would be considered "prominent, renowned, leading, or well-known" in his or her field of arts.[29]

An O-1 non-immigrant *in motion picture or television productions* is a non-citizen who is able to adduce a "record of extraordinary achievement" in his or her field.[30] Extraordinary achievement is defined as "a very high level of accomplishment in motion picture or television production evidenced by a degree of skill and recognition significantly above that ordinarily encountered" such that the candidate would be considered "outstanding, notable, or leading in the motion picture or television field."[31]

The evidentiary criteria for determining O-1 non-immigrant visa category eligibility of aliens of extraordinary ability in the *arts* and aliens of extraordinary achievement in the *motion picture and television* industries include a one-time achievement (a major, internationally recognized

---

29. *Id.* § 214.2(o)(3)(ii).
30. *Id.* § 214.2(o)(1)(ii)(A)(2).
31. *Id.* § 214.2(o)(3)(ii).

award such as an Academy Award, a Grammy, an Emmy, or a Director's Guild Award),[32] or evidence of at least three of the six following criteria:[33]

- Performing services as a leading or starring participant in productions or events with distinguished reputations as shown by critical reviews, ads, publicity releases, publications, contracts or endorsements.
- Receipt of national or international recognition for achievements through critical reviews or other published material by or about you in major papers, trade journals, or other professional publications.
- Performing in a lead, starring, or critical role for organizations and establishments that have a distinguished reputation evidenced by media articles, testimonials, and the like.
- Record of major commercial or critically acclaimed successes.
- Significant recognition from organizations, critics, government agencies, or recognized experts.
- Evidence that you have either commanded or will command a high salary or other remuneration in relation to others in the field.

The law also mandates that a *peer group advisory opinion* from an appropriate consulting entity, union or management group be submitted.[34] If no such unions exist in the alien's field, he or she may obtain a letter from a professional organization in the field confirming the O-1 candidate's sustained national or international acclaim.[35]

O-1 visas can be granted for an initial period of up to *three (3) years*,[36] and can be extended indefinitely in one-year increments.[37] There is no limit on how many extensions an O-1 visa holder may receive, as long as the beneficiary continues to have a sponsoring employer. The O-1 is an "employer-specific" visa, which allows non-citizen beneficiaries to work only for their sponsoring employers. Spouses and children of O-1 visa holders are classified as O-3 "dependents."[38] Holders of O-3 status are not entitled to work in the United States.

As with virtually every other non-immigrant category, the O-1 visa category is subject to the statutory presumption of immigrant intent.

---

32. *Id.* § 214.2(o)(3)(iv)(A), (o)(3)(v)(A).
33. *Id.* § 214.2(o)(3)(iv)(B)(1)–(6), (o)(3)(v)(B)(1)–(6).
34. *Id.* § 214.2(o)(5).
35. *Id.*
36. INA, 8 U.S.C.A. § 1184(c)(3)(a); 8 C.F.R. § 214.2(o)(6)(iii).
37. 8 C.F.R. § 214.2(o)(12)(ii).
38. *Id.* § 214.2(o)(1)(i).

Under INA § 214(b), an O-1 non-immigrant is "presumed to be an immigrant until he establishes to the satisfaction of the consular officer . . . and the immigration officers . . . that he is entitled to a non-immigrant status under section 101(a)(15)." However, USCIS regulations provide that approval of a permanent labor certification or filing of an immigrant visa petition for an alien "shall not" be the basis for denying his or her admission in O-1 non-immigrant status or extension of stay.[39] The regulations further provide that an alien may legitimately come to the United States as an O-1 non-immigrant "for a temporary period" and simultaneously "lawfully seek to become a permanent resident of the United States."[40]

E Non-immigrants

The best and brightest foreign-born entrepreneurs seeking business and investment opportunities in the United States ordinarily apply for E visas.[41] According to Secretary of Homeland Security Janet Napolitano, "[t]he United States must continue to attract the best and brightest from around the world to invest their talents, skills, and ideas to grow our economy and create American jobs."[42] The government hopes that its renewed focus on start-up businesses and entrepreneurship will "fuel the nation's economy and stimulate investment by attracting foreign entrepreneurial talent of exceptional ability or who otherwise can create jobs, form startup companies, and invest capital in areas of high unemployment."[43]

Increasing globalization of the world economy and growth in international trade and investment opportunities in the United States have made the E visa category "a prominent vehicle for non-immigrant admissions."[44] INA § 101(a)(15)(E) provides for two distinct entrepreneurial classifications.[45] The E-1 "treaty trader" is a non-immigrant who is

---

39. *Id.* § 214.2(o)(13).
40. *Id.*
41. INA, 8 U.S.C.A. § 1101(a)(15)(E).
42. Department of Homeland Security Press Release, Secretary Napolitano Announces Initiatives to Promote Startup Enterprises and Spur Job Creation, Aug. 3, 2011, *available at* http://www.dhs.gov/ynews/releases/20110802-napolitano-startup-job-creation-initiatives .shtmhttp://www.dhs.gov/ynews/releases/20110802-napolitano-startup-job-creation -initiatives.shtm.
43. *Id.*
44. ALEINIKOFF, *supra* note 3, at 407.
45. INA, 8 U.S.C.A. § 1101(a)(15)(E), subsection (iii), also provides for a "specialty occupation" visa which requires U.S. employer sponsorship and is specific to Australian nationals only. This so-called "E-3" visa is similar in key respects to the "H-1B" "specialty occupation" category discussed later in this article.

admitted pursuant to a treaty of commerce and navigation between the United States and the candidate's country of citizenship, "solely to carry on substantial trade, including trade in services or trade in technology, principally between the United States and the foreign state of which he is a national.[46] The E-2 "investor" is a non-immigrant who is admitted pursuant to the relevant treaty of commerce and navigation "solely to develop and direct the operations of an enterprise in which he is actively in the process of investing, a substantial amount of capital."[47]

USCIS regulations provide definitions of key terms for attaining E-1 "treaty trader" status. Trade is defined as "the existing international exchange of items of trade for consideration between the United States and the treaty country."[48] Additionally, "[d]omestic trade or the development of domestic markets without international exchange does not constitute trade for purpose of section 101(a)(15)(E) of the Act."[49] Further, substantial trade is defined as "an amount of trade sufficient to ensure a continuous flow of international trade between the United States and the treaty country," involving "numerous transactions over time."[50] Trade is "principal" if "over 50 percent of the volume of international trade . . . is conducted between the United States and the treaty country of the treaty trader's nationality."[51]

As with E-1 treaty traders, USCIS regulations define key statutory terms applicable to the E-2 treaty investor classification. Investment "is the treaty investor's placing of capital, including fund and other assets . . . at risk in the commercial sense with objective of generating profit."[52] The capital "must be subject to partial or total loss if investment fortunes reverse."[53] The enterprise "must be a real, active and operating commercial or entrepreneurial undertaking which provides services or goods for profit."[54] Further, a substantial amount of capital is defined as:

> (i) Substantial in relationship to the total cost of either purchasing an established enterprise or creating the type of enterprise under consideration;

---

46. *Id.* § 1101(a)(15)(E)(i); 8 C.F.R. § 214.2(e)(1)(i).
47. INA, 8 U.S.C.A. § 1101(a)(15)(E)(ii); 8 C.F.R. § 214.2(e)(2)(i).
48. 8 C.F.R. § 214.2(e)(9).
49. *Id.*
50. *Id.* § 214.2(e)(10).
51. *Id.* § 214.2(e)(11).
52. *Id.* § 214.2(e)(12).
53. *Id.*
54. *Id.* § 214.2(e)(13).

(ii) Sufficient to ensure the treaty investor's financial commitment to the successful operation of the enterprise; and

(iii) Of a magnitude to support the likelihood that the treaty investor will successfully develop and direct the enterprise.[55]

The enterprise may not be marginal. A "marginal" enterprise is one that "does not have the present or future capacity to generate more than enough income to provide a minimal living for the treaty investor and his family."[56]

In addition to "principal" E-1 treaty traders and E-2 treaty investors, the E visa category contemplates admission of employees of treaty traders and treaty investors who "engage in duties of an executive or managerial character" or who possess "special qualifications that make the alien's services essential to the efficient operation of the enterprise."[57]

Although non-citizens admitted in E status pursuant to INA § 101(a)(15)(E) must "maintain an intent to depart the United States upon the termination or expiration of E-1 or E-2 status," USCIS may not deny E status "solely on the basis of an approved request for permanent labor certification or a filed or approved immigrant visa preference petition."[58]

E visas can be granted for a period of up to five (5) years,[59] with each admission in E status being for up to two (2) years.[60] In other words, while the E visa holder may be eligible to apply for admission to the United States (i.e., cross the border) for a period of up to five years, each time he or she actually enters the United States, the validity of the E status will be for two years. There is no limit on how many extensions the beneficiary may receive,[61] as long as he or she continues to meet all classification requirements. The E visas are "employer-specific," allowing for work only for the sponsoring business. Spouses and children of E visa holders receive the same classification as the principal treaty trader or treaty investor[62] and are admitted for the same period of time as the principal.[63] A spouse of an E non-immigrant is eligible to work in the United States

---

55. *Id.* § 214.2(e)(14).
56. *Id.* § 214.2(e)(15).
57. *Id.* § 214.2(e)(3), (e)(17)–(18).
58. *Id.* § 214.2(e)(1)(ii), (e)(2)(iii), (e)(5).
59. *Reciprocity by Country,* U.S. DEPARTMENT OF STATE, http://travel.state.gov/visa/fees /fees_3272.html/list_of_treaty_countries.htm (last visited Nov. 5, 2011).
60. 8 C.F.R. § 214.2(e)(20)(i).
61. *Id.* § 214.2(e)(20).
62. *Id.* § 214.2(e)(4).
63. *Id.* § 214.2(e)(19)(ii).

and may be issued an employment authorized endorsement or work permit.[64] Conversely, children of E visa holders are not eligible for work.[65]

L Non-immigrants

United States Congress created the L visa category[66] in 1970 in response to the growing need of U.S. and foreign multinational corporations to move key personnel from their overseas locations to their U.S. operations.[67] The L classification is specifically used by international companies to transfer managers, executives and individuals with specialized knowledge between the corporation's global offices. Thus, USCIS regulations refer to L-1 visa holders as "intracompany transferees."[68]

One of the main requirements of the category is that a sponsoring U.S. employer and the related company abroad must have a "qualifying" relationship, which means that each of these entities must be related to the other as a "branch," "parent," "subsidiary," or "affiliate."[69] Further, the candidate must have been employed by a qualifying entity abroad as a manager, executive, or in a capacity requiring specialized knowledge for at least one (1) continuous year of the three (3) years preceding his or her application for admission to the United States. Additionally, the candidate must be coming to the United States to serve in a capacity that is managerial, executive or requires specialized knowledge.[70] Managers and executives are eligible for the L-1A classification, and persons with specialized knowledge apply as L-1B non-immigrants.

USCIS regulations define "managerial capacity" as an assignment where an employee primarily:

(1) Manages the organization, or a department, subdivision, function, or component of the organization;

(2) Supervises and controls the work of other supervisory, professional, or managerial employees, or manages an essential function within the organization, or a department or subdivision of the organization;

---

64. INA, 8 U.S.C.A. § 1184(e)(6).
65. *Id.*
66. *Id.* § 101(a)(15)(L).
67. ALEINIKOFF, *supra* note 3, at 406.
68. 8 C.F.R. § 214.2(l)(1)(i).
69. *Id.* § 214.2(l)(1)(ii)(G).
70. *Id.* § 214.2(l)(1)(i).

(3) Has the authority to hire and fire or recommend those as well as other personnel actions (such as promotion and leave authorization) if another employee or other employees are directly supervised; if no other employee is directly supervised, functions at a senior level within the organizational hierarchy or with respect to the function managed; and

(4) Exercises discretion over the day-to-day operations of the activity or function for which the employee has authority. A first-line supervisor is not considered to be acting in a managerial capacity merely by virtue of the supervisor's supervisory duties unless the employees supervised are professional.[71]

"Executive capacity" means an assignment in which the employee primarily:

(1) directs the management of the organization or a major component or function of the organization;

(2) establishes the goals and policies of the organization, component, or function;

(3) exercises wide latitude in discretionary decision-making; and

(4) receives only general supervision or direction from higher level executives, the board of directors, or stockholders of the organization.[72]

Lastly, "specialized knowledge" means "special knowledge possessed by an individual of the petitioning organization's product, service, research, equipment, techniques, management, or other interests and its application in international markets, or an advanced level of knowledge or expertise in the organization's processes and procedures."[73]

L-1 visas can be granted for an initial period of up to three (3) years,[74] and may be extended in increments of two (2) years.[75] L-1A visa hold-

---

71. *Id.* § 214.2(l)(1)(ii)(B).
72. *Id.* § 214.2(l)(1)(ii)(C).
73. *Id.* § 214.2(l)(1)(ii)(D).
74. *Id.* § 214.2(l)(7)(i)(A)(2)–(3).
75. *Id.* § 214.2(l)(15)(ii).

ers may receive a total of seven (7) years in L-1A status,[76]and L-1B visa holders may receive a total of five (5) years in L-1B status.[77] Thus, unlike the O and E-1/E-2 holders, L-1 non-immigrants are not allowed indefinite extensions of stay. The L-1 is an "employer-specific" visa, which allows the beneficiary to work for the sponsoring employer only.

Spouses and children of L-1 visa holders are classified as L-2 dependents. An L-2 spouse is entitled to work in the United States and may apply for an employment authorization endorsement or another form of work permit.[78]

An L-1 visa holder is not required to maintain foreign residence and "may legitimately come to the United States for a temporary period as an L-1 non-immigrant and, at the same time, lawfully seek to become a permanent resident of the United States."[79]

The statute does not limit L-1 eligibility to large corporations, and thus, this visa classification may be utilized by sole proprietorships and partnerships. However, USCIS is on record stating that the L classification "was not created for self-employed persons to enter the United States to continue self-employment, unless they are otherwise qualified" for L-1 status.[80] In order to prevent foreign-born individuals from buying a small or start-up firm in the United States, which would then file an L-1 petition on behalf of its sole stakeholder, in 1987, USCIS issued a new regulation imposing special requirements on "new office" L-1 petitions.[81] This is in sharp contrast with the Obama Administration's recent efforts to attract more investors and entrepreneurs to the United States to create American jobs and reinvigorate the sagging economy.[82]

H-1B Non-immigrants

The H-1B visa classification extends work authorization to non-citizens who wish to come to the United States "to perform services . . . in a specialty occupation."[83] INA § 214(i)(1) defines specialty occupation as an occupation requiring

---

76. INA, 8 U.S.C.A. § 1184(c)(2)(D)(i); 8 C.F.R. § 2142.2(l)(15)(ii).

77. INA, 8 U.S.C.A. § 1184(c)(2)(D)(ii); 8 C.F.R. § 2142.2(l)(15)(ii).

78. INA, 8 U.S.C.A. § 1184(c)(2)(E).

79. 8 C.F.R. § 214.2(l)(16).

80. Temporary Alien Workers Seeking Classification under the Immigration and Nationality Act, 52 Fed. Reg. 5738, 5739 (1987).

81. ALEINIKOFF, *supra* note 3, at 407; 8 C.F.R. § 214.2(l)(1)(ii)(F), (l)(3)(v)–(vi).

82. Department of Homeland Security Press Release, *supra* note 42.

83. INA, 8 U.S.C.A. § 1101(a)(15)(H)(i)(b).

    A. theoretical and practical application of a body of highly special-
ized knowledge, and

    B. attainment of bachelor's degree or higher degree in the specific
specialty (or its equivalent) as a minimum for entry into the
occupation.

As an alternative to the attainment of a degree, a non-citizen may
qualify for H-1B status through "experience in the specialty equivalent
to the completion of such degree, and . . . recognition of expertise in the
specialty through progressively responsible positions relating to the
specialty."[84]

USCIS regulations provide four (4) alternative criteria for determining whether a particular occupation is a "specialty occupation":

1. A baccalaureate or higher degree or its equivalent is normally the
   minimum requirement for entry into the particular position;
2. The degree requirement is common to the industry in parallel positions among similar organizations or, in the alternative,
   an employer may show that its particular position is so complex
   or unique that it can be performed only by an individual with a
   degree;
3. The employer normally requires a degree or its equivalent for the
   position; or
4. The nature of the specific duties [is] so specialized and complex
   that knowledge required to perform the duties is usually associated with the attainment of a baccalaureate or higher degree.[85]

Thus, to qualify for H-1B status, a non-citizen must be offered a position which requires a "degree in . . . the specific specialty . . . or its equivalent" (e.g., a bachelor degree in biology, computer science, engineering,
etc.), and the non-citizen must have the requisite degree or equivalent.

Additionally, a United States employer seeking approval of an H-1B
petition must file a "labor condition application" with the U.S. Department of Labor "agreeing to various attestation requirements"[86] regarding the sponsored position's wages,[87] working conditions,[88] strikes and

---

84. *Id.* § 214(i)(2)(C)(i)–(ii).
85. 8 C.F.R. § 214.2(h)(4)(iii)(A).
86. INA, 8 U.S.C.A. § 1182(n); 20 C.F.R. § 655.700.
87. 20 C.F.R. § 655.731.
88. *Id.* § 655.732.

lockouts,[89] and notice.[90] Among other requirements, the law requires that an H-1B candidate be paid the greater of "the actual wage paid by the employer to all other individuals with similar experience and qualifications . . . or . . . the prevailing wage level for the occupational classification in the area of employment."[91] These requirements do not apply to the previously discussed non-immigrant visa classifications.

The total number of H-1B visas that may be granted each year is 65,000,[92] plus there is an additional pool of 20,000 H-1B visas for individuals with a master's or higher degree from a United States institution.[93] The 65,000 annual limit does not apply to institutions of higher education, nonprofit research organizations affiliated with institutions of higher education, and governmental research organizations.[94]

H-1B visas can be granted for an initial period of up to three (3) years,[95] and can be extended for an additional period of three (3) years for a total stay of six (6) years.[96] The H-1B is an "employer-specific" visa, which allows the beneficiary to work only for the sponsoring employer.[97] The beneficiary may change employers by having a new employer file an H-1B transfer petition.[98] Additionally, any changes to the beneficiary's original employment due to a corporate reorganization, merger, promotion or assignment to a new company location may require an amended petition.[99]

Spouses and Children of H-1B Workers Are Not Entitled to Work in the United States[100]

Lastly, INA § 214(b) specifically exempts H-1B non-immigrants from non-immigrant intent. USCIS regulations provide that a non-immigrant "may legitimately come to the United States for a temporary period as an . . .

89. *Id.* § 655.733.
90. *Id.* § 655.734.
91. INA, 8 U.S.C.A. § 1182(n)(1)(A).
92. *Id.* § 1184(g)(1)(A)(vii).
93. *Id.* § 1184(g)(5)(C).
94. *Id.* § 1184(g)(5)(A)–(B).
95. 8 C.F.R. § 214.2(h)(9)(viii)(A)(1).
96. INA, 8 U.S.C.A. § 1184(g)(4).
97. 8 C.F.R. § 214.2(h)(2)(i)(D).
98. *Id.*
99. *Id.* § 214.2(h)(2)(i)(E).
100. *Id.* § 214.2(h)(9)(iv).

H-1B non-immigrant and, at the same time, lawfully seek to become a permanent resident of the United States."[101]

IMMIGRANT VISA OPTIONS

EB-1 Aliens of Extraordinary Ability, Outstanding Professors and Researchers, and Multinational Managers and Executives

INA § 203(b) groups EB-1-1 aliens of extraordinary ability,[102] EB-1-2 outstanding professors and researchers,[103] and EB-1-3 multinational executives and managers,[104] are "priority workers" eligible for up to 28.6 percent of the worldwide level of employment-based immigrant visas,[105] or roughly 40,000 annually. These immigrants possess such talents and skills that they are accorded "priority" admission status which does not contemplate the test of the labor market to locate qualified domestic workers for employment in the United States.[106] In other words, these immigrants are desirable whether or not they compete with U.S. workers.[107]

An *alien of extraordinary ability* is a non-citizen who is able to demonstrate "sustained national or international acclaim" in "the sciences, arts, education, business, or athletics," "whose achievements have been recognized in the field through extensive documentation," and whose admission "will substantially benefit prospectively the United States."[108]

As with O-1 visas, a candidate may demonstrate sustained acclaim through either evidence of a one-time achievement (a major, internationally recognized award such as the Nobel Prize or an Academy Award),[109] or through evidence of at least three (3) of the following ten (10) regulatory criteria:[110]

* Receipt of lesser nationally or internationally recognized prizes or awards for excellence in the field of endeavor.

---

101. *Id.* § 214.2(h)(16)(ii).
102. INA, 8 U.S.C.A. § 1153(b)(1)(A).
103. *Id.* § 1153(b)(1)(B).
104. *Id.* § 1153(b)(1)(C).
105. *Id.* § 201(d).
106. *Id.* § 1182(a)(5)(A); *id.* § 204(b).
107. ALEINIKOFF, *supra* note 3, at 282, 332.
108. INA, 8 U.S.C.A. § 1153(b)(1)(A)(1)(i)–(iii).
109. 8 C.F.R. § 204.5(h)(3).
110. *Id.* § 204.5(h)(i)–(x).

- Membership in associations in the field that require outstanding achievements of their members, as judged by recognized national or international experts.
- Published material in professional or major trade publications or major media about you, relating to your work in the field.
- Participation on a panel, or individually, as a judge of the work of others in the same or allied field.
- Original scientific or scholarly contributions of major significance.
- Authorship of scholarly articles in the field, in professional journals, major trade publications, or other major media.
- Evidence that you have performed in a critical or leading role for organizations or establishments that have a distinguished reputation.
- Evidence that you have commanded a high salary or other remuneration for services.
- Display of your work at artistic exhibitions or showcases.
- Evidence of commercial successes in the performing arts, as shown by box office receipts or record, cassette, compact disk, or video sales.

The law permits EB-1-1 aliens to self-petition, as formal employer sponsorship in the United States is not required.[111]

An *outstanding professor* or *researcher* is a non-citizen who is "recognized internationally as outstanding in a specific academic area."[112] Unlike EB-1-1 aliens of extraordinary ability, EB-1-2 outstanding researchers and professors require employment sponsorship.[113] Thus, a university or institution of higher education, or a private company which "employs at least 3 persons full-time in research activities and has documented accomplishments in an academic field" may serve as the sponsoring employer.[114]

International recognition can be demonstrated through evidence of at least two (2) of the following six (6) regulatory criteria:[115]

- Receipt of major prizes or awards for outstanding achievement in the field.
- Membership in professional associations that require outstanding achievements of their members.
- Published material about your work in professional publications.

---

111. INA, 8 U.S.C.A. § 1154(a)(E); 8 C.F.R. § 204.5(h)(5).
112. INA, 8 U.S.C.A. § 1153(b)(1)(B).
113. *Id.* § 1154(a)(F); 8 C.F.R. § 204.5(i); 8 C.F.R. § 204.5(i)(3)(iii).
114. INA, 8 U.S.C.A. § 1153(b)(1)(B)(iii).
115. 8 C.F.R. § 204.5(i)(3)(i)(A)–(E).

- Participation, either individually or on a panel, as a judge of the work of others in the field.
- Original scientific or scholarly contributions to the field.
- Authorship of scholarly books or articles in the field in scholarly journals with international circulation.

In addition to meeting the requisite criteria, the non-citizen must also possess "at least three years of experience in teaching and/or research in the academic field."[116] USCIS regulations define "academic field" as "a body of specialized knowledge offered for study at an accredited United States university or institution of higher education."[117] Lastly, a "permanent" research position is defined as either a "tenure-track, research" position, or one "for a term of indefinite or unlimited duration, and one in which an employee will ordinarily have an expectation of continued employment unless there is good cause for termination."[118]

A *multinational executive or manager* is a non-citizen who

in the 3 years preceding the time of the alien's application for classification and admission into the United States . . . , has been employed for at least 1 year by a firm or corporation or other legal entity or an affiliate or subsidiary thereof and the alien seeks to enter the United States in order to continue to render services to the same employer or to subsidiary or affiliate thereof in a capacity that is managerial or executive.[119]

INA § 101(a)(44) defines "managerial capacity" as an assignment within an organization in which the employee primarily

(i) manages the organization, or a department, subdivision, function, or component of the organization;

(ii) supervises and controls the work of other supervisory, professional, or managerial employees, or manages an essential function within the organization, or a department or subdivision of the organization;

---

116. *Id.* § 204.5(i)(3)(ii).
117. *Id.* § 204.5(i)(2).
118. *Id.*
119. INA, 8 U.S.C.A. § 1153(b)(1)(C).

(iii) if another employee or other employees are directly supervised, has the authority to hire and fire or recommend those as well as other personnel actions (such as promotion and leave authorization) or, if no other employee is directly supervised, functions at a senior level within the organizational hierarchy or with respect to the function managed; and

(iv) exercises discretion over the day-to-day operations of the activity or function for which the employee has authority. A first-line supervisor is not considered to be acting in a managerial capacity merely by virtue of the supervisor's supervisory duties unless the employees supervised are professional.[120]

The term "executive capacity" is defined as an assignment within an organization in which the employee primarily

(i)   directs the management of the organization or a major component or function of the organization;

(ii) establishes the goals and policies of the organization, component, or function;

(iii) exercises wide latitude in discretionary decision-making; and

(iv) receives only general supervision or direction from higher level executives, the board of directors, or stockholders of the organization.[121]

Like the EB-1-2 category for outstanding professors and researchers, the EB-1-3 category for multinational managers and executives requires employer sponsorship.[122] The category is also similar to the L-1 nonimmigrant visa category in that a sponsoring U.S. employer and the related company abroad must have a qualifying corporate relationship, which means that each of these entities must be related to the other as a "parent," "subsidiary" or "affiliate."[123] The U.S. employer must have been

---

120. *See also* 8 C.F.R. § 204.5(j)(2).
121. INA, 8 U.S.C.A. § 1101(a)(44)(B); 8 C.F.R. § 204.5(j)(2).
122. INA, 8 U.S.C.A. § 1154(a)(F).
123. 8 C.F.R. § 204.5(j)(2).

doing business in the United States for at least one year.[124] Regulations define "doing business" as "the regular, systematic, and continuous provision of goods and/or services by a firm, corporation, or other entity and does not include the mere presence of an agent or office."[125] The qualifying entity must be "multinational" in nature, i.e., conduct business in two or more international locations, including one in the United States.[126] Lastly, the EB-1-3 category requires an offer of employment from a U.S. employer in the form of a statement, which must indicate that the noncitizen will be employed in a qualifying managerial or executive capacity, and "clearly describe the duties to be performed by the alien."[127]

EB-2 Advanced Degree Professionals and National Interest Waivers

Not all talented and skilled non-citizens will qualify as EB-1 "priority workers" since EB-1 subcategories have narrowly defined qualification standards. For those who do not meet them, the INA provides a separate employment-based classification for "aliens who are members of the professions and holding advanced degrees or aliens of exceptional ability."[128]

Although immigration attorneys think of advanced degree professionals as more than merely "skilled" workers, INA § 212(a)(5)(A) categorizes them as "skilled labor." Indeed, INA § 212(a)(5)(A) provides that aliens seeking to enter the United States to perform "skilled or unskilled labor" are inadmissible unless the DOL has determined and certified that

> there are not sufficient workers who are able, wiling, qualified (or equally qualified in the case of alien described in subclause (ii)) and available at the time of application for a visa and admission to the United States and at the place where the alien is to perform such skilled or un skilled labor, and the employment of such aliens will not adversely affect the wages and working conditions of workers in the United States.[129]

Thus, unlike the individuals applying in the EB-1 category, non-citizens seeking admission to the United States as EB-2 advanced degree professionals must first obtain an individual "labor certification" from the Department

---

124. *Id.* § 204.5(j)(3)(D).
125. *Id.* § 204.5(j)(2).
126. *Id.*
127. *Id.* § 204.5(j)(5).
128. INA, 8 U.S.C.A. § 1153(b)(2).
129. *Id.* § 212(a)(5)(A)(i).

of Labor (DOL).[130] The "labor certification" requires that the sponsoring U.S. employer test the local labor market for qualified and available domestic workers at locally competitive wages before seeking permanent employment certification from DOL on behalf of the selected candidate. Although highly desirable in the United States, U.S. immigration laws subject these individuals to labor market tests because they compete with U.S. workers for jobs in the United States. The labor certification requirement, including an exemption from it, is a statutory prerequisite that must be satisfied by every entering immigrant in the employment-based second and third preference categories.[131]

Once the U.S. employer obtains a DOL certification for the sponsored position, the non-immigrant may apply for immigrant benefits under INA § 203(b)(2) and 8 C.F.R § 204.5(k).

USCIS regulations define "advanced degree" as meaning:

> Any United States academic or professional degree or a foreign equivalent above that of baccalaureate. A United States baccalaureate degree or a foreign equivalent degree followed by at least five years of progressive experience in the specialty shall be considered the equivalent of a master's degree. If a doctoral degree is customarily required by the specialty, the alien must have United States doctorate or a foreign equivalent degree.[132]

In other words, to claim employment-based second preference status, non-citizens must satisfy the advanced degree requirement either by possessing a U.S. or foreign master's degree, or a bachelor's degree or a foreign degree equivalent, plus five years of post-baccalaureate experience.

Additionally, USCIS regulations reference INA § 101(a)(32) for the definition of "profession" as "any occupation for which a United States baccalaureate degree or its foreign equivalent is the minimum requirement for entry."[133]

Lastly, for EB-2 advanced degree professions, employer sponsorship and the labor certification requirement go hand in hand. USCIS regulations provide that "[e]very petition under this classification must be accompanied by an individual labor certification from the Department of Labor,"[134] unless specifically exempted by statute or regulation. Further,

---

130. *Id.* §§ 204(b), 212(a)(5)(A).
131. ALEINIKOFF, *supra* note 3, at 334.
132. 8 C.F.R. § 204.5(k)(2).
133. *Id.*
134. *Id.* § 204.5(k)(4)(i).

INA § 203(b)(2)(A) requires that the services of an alien be "sought by an employer in the United States."

On the other hand, INA § 203(b)(2)(B) specifically permits the Secretary of Homeland Security to waive the requirement that the alien's "services in the sciences, arts, professions, or business be sought by an employer in the United States," if such a waiver is deemed in "national interest." Similarly, the regulations provide that the Director may exempt the requirement of a job offer, and thus of a labor certification, for aliens of exceptional ability in the sciences, arts, or business if exemption would be in the national interest.[135]

These exemptions from the labor certification requirement and a job offer from a U.S. employer are commonly known as *national interest waivers.* Applicants for national interest waivers must either qualify as advanced degree professionals, or as individuals of exceptional ability in the sciences, arts, professions or business whose admission "will substantially benefit prospectively the national economy, cultural or educational interest, or welfare of the United States."[136]

"Exceptional ability" is defined as "a degree of expertise significantly above that ordinarily encountered in the sciences, arts, or business."[137] To prove exceptional ability, three (3) of the following evidentiary criteria must be demonstrated:

A. An official academic record showing that the beneficiary has a degree, diploma, certificate, or similar award from a college, university, school, or other institution of learning relating to the area of exceptional ability;

B. Evidence in the form of letter(s) from current or former employer(s) showing that the beneficiary has at least ten years of full-time experience in the occupation for which he or she is being sought;

C. A license to practice the profession or certification for a particular profession or occupation;

D. Evidence that the beneficiary has commanded a salary, or other remuneration for services, which demonstrates exceptional ability;

E. Evidence of membership in professional associations; or

---

135. *Id.* § 204.5(k)(4)(ii).
136. INA, 8 U.S.C.A. § 1153(b)(2)(A)–(B).
137. 8 C.F.R. § 204.5(k)(2).

F. Evidence of recognition for achievements and significant contributions to the industry or field by peers, governmental entities, or professional or business organizations.[138]

The INA and regulations do not otherwise elaborate on the *national interest waiver* standards, and these are instead derived from administrative decisions. USCIS's internal appellate body, called Administrative Appeals Office, recommended the following factors in determining whether to grant or deny a national interest waiver: (1) improving national economy; (2) improving wages and working conditions of U.S. workers; (3) improving educational and training programs for U.S. children and underqualified workers; (4) improving health care; (5) providing more affordable housing for young, aged, or poor U.S. residents; (6) improving the U.S. environment and leading to more productive uses of national resources; and (7) a request by an interested U.S. government agency.[139]

USCIS later tightened its requirements and in the precedent decision of *Matter of New York State Dept. of Transportation (NYSDOT)*,[140] developed a three-prong test for determining national interest waiver eligibility, including whether (1) the non-citizen seeks employment in the area of substantial intrinsic merit; (2) the benefit will be national in scope; and (3) the national interest would be adversely affected if a labor certification were required of the alien.

EB-5 Investors

Of the worldwide level of employment-based immigrant visas,[141] INA § 203(b)(5)(A) allocates up to 7.1 percent, or approximately 10,000 visas annually, to "employment creation" non-citizens. Applicants for the fifth-preference (EB-5) immigrant visa status must invest, or be in the process of investing, $1,000,000[142] in a "new commercial enterprise," and create at least ten full-time jobs for United States citizens, permanent residents and other authorized individuals.[143] USCIS regulations define "commercial enterprise" as "any for-profit activity formed for the ongoing conduct

---

138. *Id.* § 204.5(k)(3)(ii).

139. Matter of [name not provided], Case No. EAC-92-091-50126 (AAU July 12, 1992) (the Mississippi Phosphate case), *reported in* 69 No. 41 INTERPRETER RELEASES 1364–65 (Oct. 26, 1992).

140. *EB-5 Immigrant Investor Pilot Program*, USCIS, http://www.uscis.gov/USCIS/Resources /Resources%20for%20Congress/Congressional%20Reports/EB-5%20Investor%20Pilot%20 Program.pdf (last visited Dec. 8, 2011).

141. INA, 8 U.S.C.A. § 1154(d).

142. *Id.* § 1153(b)(5)(A)(i), (C).

143. *Id.* § 1153(b)(5)(A)(ii).

of lawful business," excluding "a noncommercial activity such as owning and operating a personal business,"[144] and list additional standards for determining a "new" commercial enterprise in 8 C.F.R. § 204.6(h).

The baseline amount of $1,000,000 is lowered for qualified immigrants investing in a "targeted employment area,"[145] to $500,000.[146] At least 3,000 visa numbers are available to non-citizens investing in targeted employment areas out of the 10,000 visas for the entire classification.[147] The statute also contemplates an increase in the amount of the required investment if the new enterprise is established in the "high employment area,"[148] although the regulations state that this amount is $1,000,000.[149]

The law defines the term "targeted employment area" as an area, which, "at the time of the investment, [is] a rural area or an area . . . with unemployment [] of at least 150 percent of the national average rate[]."[150] A "rural" area is one "within a metropolitan statistical area or within the boundary of any city or town having a population of 20,000 or more."[151] Employment is "full-time" if it "requires at least 35 hours of service per week."[152]

In 1993, Congress supplemented the basic EB-5 procedure described in INA § 203(b)(5) by creating the "Immigrant Investor Pilot Program,"[153] which currently runs through September 30, 2012.[154] Only 300 visas are available annually to non-citizens applying under the Immigrant Investor Pilot Program.[155] The Immigrant Investor Pilot Program provides for investments that are affiliated with an economic unit called a "regional center,"[156] and contain less restrictive job creation requirements.[157] A current list of approved EB-5 regional centers is available online at http://www.uscis.gov/eb-5centers. The job creation requirement may be met by

---

144. 8 C.F.R. § 204.6(e).

145. INA, 8 U.S.C.A. § 1153(b)(5)(B)(ii).

146. *Id.* § 1153(b)(5)(C)(ii).

147. *Id.* § 1153(b)(5)(B)(i).

148. *Id.* § 1153(b)(5)(C)(iii).

149. 8 C.F.R. § 204.6(f)(3).

150. INA, 8 U.S.C.A. § 1153(b)(5)(B)(ii); 8 C.F.R. § 204.6(e).

151. INA, 8 U.S.C.A. § 1153(b)(5)(B)(ii); 8 C.F.R. § 204.6(e).

152. INA, 8 U.S.C.A. § 1153(b)(5)(D); 8 C.F.R. § 204.6(e).

153. *See* Departments of Commerce, Justice, and State, the Judiciary, and Related Agencies Appropriation Act of 1993, Pub. L. No. 102-395, § 610, 106 Stat. 1828, 1874 (1992).

154. *See* USCIS, EB-5 Immigrant Investor Pilot Program, at http://www.uscis.gov/USCIS/Resources/Resources%20for%20Congress/Congressional%20Reports/EB-5%20Investor%20Pilot%20Program.pdf (last accessed Dec. 8, 2011).

155. 8 C.F.R. § 204.6(m)(2).

156. *Id.* § 204.6(e).

157. *Id.* § 204.6(m)(7)(ii).

showing that the investment will create the requisite jobs either directly or indirectly as "demonstrated by reasonable methodologies."[158]

Unlike any other immigrant visa category, EB-5 applicants must first obtain conditional resident status and later petition to remove conditions to become full-fledged permanent residents.[159] This two-tier process was mandated by Congress which was concerned about possible fraud in the category.[160]

CONCLUSION

The aim of this chapter is to help non-immigration attorneys navigate U.S. immigration options for the best and brightest non-citizens who wish to come to the United States. Foreign-born professionals are an important force in advancing America's science, education, economy, and culture.[161] As the U.S. economy continues to struggle, they offer new hope for job creation[162] and are, generally, good for the economy.[163] But as this overview demonstrates, U.S. immigration laws and policies are complex and highly technical, which often leads to bad decisions by immigration officials.[164]

Thus, a simpler, modernized system of immigration laws geared towards attracting the world's top talent would most benefit this country's interests. The reform might also include creating new visa classifications for science and technology professionals, particularly those educated at U.S. graduate schools, as well as for international entrepreneurs.

---

158. *Id.* § 204.6(j)(4)(iii), (m)(3).

159. INA, 8 U.S.C.A. § 1186; 8 C.F.R. § 216.

160. ALEINIKOFF, *supra* note 3, at 281–82.

161. *See* S. Anderson, *The Multiplier Effect*, INT'L EDUCATOR 14–21 (Summer 2004).

162. Madeline Zavodny, *Immigration and American Jobs*, AMERICAN ENTERPRISE INSTITUTE FOR PUBLIC POLICY RESEARCH (2011), http://www.renewoureconomy.org/sites/all/themes/pnae/img/NAE_Im-AmerJobs.pdf.

163. *Let Them Come*, THE ECONOMIST (2011), http://www.economist.com/node/21526893.

164. Ben Forer and Christine Brouwer, *Immigrant Entrepreneur Gets Visa after 'World News' Story*, ABC NEWS (2011), http://abcnews.go.com/WN/Economy/immigrant-entrepreneur-visa-world-news-story/story?id=14867513#.TvJx4jWJeTw.

15

MAINTAINING LAWFUL PERMANENT RESIDENT STATUS

Margaret B. Hobbins[1]

INTRODUCTION

Maintaining permanent residency with employment, family, and academic obligations abroad can be a challenge. As so many have learned the hard way, lawful permanent residency is not permanent. It is an important privilege whose rules must be well understood by attorneys and clients alike to avoid the pitfalls of being refused admission or placed in removal proceedings. This chapter will discuss:

- When a client is at risk of abandonment
- Defending against a charge of abandonment
- How to prevent abandonment in the first place
- What options exist once the client has been abroad for over one year
- How departures abroad affect eligibility for naturalization

Advising a client about abandonment of permanent resident status requires a thorough understanding of the client's current situation, immigration history, and future plans. With this information, the attorney can help create a plan of action to either protect or defend the client's permanent residency.

---

1. Margaret Hobbins is an attorney at Maggio + Kattar, PC in Washington, D.C., where she focuses her practice on humanitarian and family-based immigration matters before the U.S. immigration courts, the Board of Immigration Appeals, U.S. Citizenship and Immigration Services (USCIS), and U.S. consulates overseas. Prior to joining Maggio + Kattar, Ms. Hobbins worked as a staff attorney for the Pennsylvania Immigration Resource Center and was a judicial law clerk in the Attorney General's Honors Program at the Baltimore and York Immigration Courts. She is a member of the American Immigration Lawyers Association (AILA) and serves on the AILA National Family Immigration Committee.

288 What Every Lawyer Needs to Know about Immigration Law

DEPARTURES FROM THE UNITED STATES AFTER OBTAINING PERMANENT RESIDENT STATUS

A lawful permanent resident (LPR) returning to the United States after a temporary visit abroad is categorized as a "special immigrant," and is generally not considered to be seeking admission to the United States.[2] However, certain circumstances affect this privilege. A permanent resident card will cease to be valid after an absence of one year or more from the United States.[3] Additionally, an LPR will be found to be "seeking admission" to the United States if (1) they have been absent from the United States for a continuous period over 180 days or (2) they have abandoned or relinquished their permanent resident status.[4] These conditions set forth in INA § 101(a)(13)(C) show that the ability to reenter the United States is not just a question of the duration of the departure. Regardless of the validity of a green card, or of the time spent abroad, Customs and Border Protection (or a consular officer or immigration judge) can find that an LPR is seeking admission for having abandoned their permanent residency. Determining whether an LPR has abandoned their permanent residence is a fact-specific question of intent. The critical point here: *returning to the United States for brief periods of time, always before 180 days have elapsed, is not sufficient to maintain lawful permanent residency.*

So what exactly happens when an LPR who has spent a significant amount of time abroad arrives at a port of entry? The Customs and Border Protection (CBP) officer may refer the LPR to secondary inspection to investigate whether or not the traveler is seeking admission under section 101(a)(13)(C)—i.e., whether they have abandoned their residency. The officer may then question the LPR about the purpose of their trip, their ties to the United States, and their conduct during their stay abroad. CBP can also parole the LPR into the United States for deferred inspection at a later date, where the LPR can come prepared with evidence and representation. The CBP officers commonly take written statements from the traveler at secondary inspection or deferred inspection that will later be used as evidence if removal proceedings are initiated. If the investigation is not resolved in favor of the LPR, CBP will issue a Notice to Appear (NTA) and parole the LPR in for removal proceedings at the local immigration court. The NTA will charge the LPR as being inadmissible pursuant to INA § 212(a)(7)(A)(i)(I), as an immigrant who at the time of application for admission "is not in possession of a valid unexpired immigrant visa,

---

2. INA § 101(a)(27)(C).
3. 8 C.F.R. § 211.1(a)(2).
4. INA § 101(a)(13)(C).

reentry permit, border crossing identification card, or other valid entry document."[5]

DEFENDING AGAINST A CHARGE OF ABANDONMENT

Burden of Proof

Once an LPR presents a "colorable claim" to returning resident status, then the burden is on the Department of Homeland Security (DHS) to establish by "clear, unequivocal, and convincing evidence" that the LPR has in fact abandoned their residency.[6] Practically speaking, the CBP officer in secondary inspection is unlikely to be persuaded by an LPR explaining the government's high burden to establish abandonment. Regardless, CBP officers, DHS trial attorneys, and immigration judges should all be reminded that it is not the LPR that needs to be making the case—it is the government. Particularly in the context of prosecutorial discretion, when DHS's stated goals are to decrease the number of non-priority respondents in removal proceedings, it is important to point out the weakness of DHS's case against your client and their poor chances of meeting such a significant burden of proof.

What Constitutes a Temporary Visit Abroad?

An LPR is considered a returning resident when they are returning from a temporary visit abroad.[7] Thus, abandonment of residency hinges on the definition of the term "temporary."[8] When does an LPR's absence from the United States go beyond temporary, such that they have lost their privileged status? As the Board of Immigration Appeals sets forth in *Matter of Kane*, temporary cannot be defined exclusively in terms of time.[9] Instead, the subjective intent of the LPR will control the analysis, which invites a fact-specific inquiry. It is important to note what kind of intent is relevant here. A simple intent to return to the United States sometime in the future is insufficient. The LPR must show a continuous, uninterrupted intent to return to the United States within a "relatively short period of time."[10] *Matter of Kane* sets forth three elements to determine subjective intent: (1) purpose for departing; (2) termination date; and (3) intent to return to

---

5. *Id.* § 212(a)(7)(A)(i)(I).

6. *See* Singh v. Reno, 113 F.3d 1512, 1514 (9th Cir. 1997).

7. 8 C.F.R. § 211.1(b)(1).

8. *See* Matter of Kane, 15 I. & N. Dec. 258, 262 (B.I.A. 1975).

9. *Id.*

10. *See Singh*, 113 F.3d at 1514.

the United States as a place of employment, business, or actual home.[11] The Board also emphasizes that the location of the LPR's ties, such as family, job, or property ties, are indicative of their intent.

The Ninth Circuit, in *Chavez-Ramirez v. INS*, provides a similar definition of temporary:

> We hold that a permanent resident returns from a "temporary visit abroad" only when (a) the permanent resident's visit is for "a period relatively short, fixed by some early event," or (b) the permanent resident's visit will terminate upon the occurrence of an event having a reasonable possibility of occurring within a relatively short period of time. If as in (b), the length of the visit is contingent upon the occurrence of an event and is not fixed in time and if the event does not occur within a relatively short period of time, the visit will be considered a "temporary visit abroad" only if the alien has a continuous, uninterrupted intention to return to the United States during the entirety of his visit.[12]

The Court specifies that the factors relevant in determining the LPR's intent to return include both ties to the United States and conduct in the foreign country. The abandonment analysis therefore is not a precise formula, but requires that the adjudicator take into account the totality of the LPR's circumstances.

Purpose for Departing

The Board states in *Matter of Kane*, that the LPR should have a "definite" purpose for departing the United States, such as education, professional training, or liquidation of assets. In the Ninth Circuit case, *Khodagholian v. Ashcroft*, the respondent traveled to Iran to sell his family's home.[13] This trip had a definite purpose, which the respondent potentially could have satisfied within a relatively short period of time. The respondent's plans changed due to circumstances outside of his control, specifically the Iranian government prohibiting his departure until an old tax bill was settled. But the original purpose of the trip still indicated that the respondent was cutting ties with Iran in order to further establish his life in the United States. Evidence to demonstrate the intended purpose of a trip can include the following:

---

11. *See Kane*, 15 I. & N. at 262–63.
12. *See* Chavez-Ramirez v. INS, 792 F.2d 932 (9th Cir. 1985).
13. *See* Khodagholian v. Ashcroft, 335 F.3d 1003, 1005 (9th Cir. 2003).

- affidavits from the individual and others explaining the purpose of the trip abroad;
- legal records showing liquidation of assets in the foreign country;
- academic records indicating a study abroad program with a defined end date;
- medical records of an ailing relative; and
- employment letter if employed by a U.S. company abroad.

Termination Date

Matter of Kane also emphasizes that the trip abroad should be expected to terminate within a relatively short period, "fixed by some early event." Without a target termination date, it is difficult to prove an intention to return within a relatively short time period. Again, an intention to return eventually is unlikely to satisfy an adjudicator. In *Matter of Huang*, the respondent argued that she was abroad for a definite purpose—her husband's doctoral studies—that had a fixed end date. However, the respondent's husband's five-year program was extended, and the Board noted "the record has not shown a clear demarcation as to when the husband's relationship with the university would end and she and her family could return to the United States."[14] Interestingly, in *Hana v. Gonzales*, the Sixth Circuit noted that the respondent, Hana, went abroad to assist her family members with their emigration to the United States, which she (erroneously) believed would take three years. In spite of the fact that Hana was abroad for far longer, the court found her intended termination date of three years to be convincing, and consistent with her stated goal of bringing her family to the United States on a permanent basis.

Ties to the United States

When the original purpose of the trip expands—or when the termination date does not come about as quickly as hoped—case law turns to examining ties to the United States to ascertain whether or not the applicant maintained a continuous, uninterrupted intention to return within a relatively short period of time.[15] Evidence of family, property, and employment ties may be the best evidence available to the client to demonstrate their intent to return to the United States. The Foreign Affairs Manual lists the following factors as evidence of an individual's intent to maintain their residency:

---

14. *See* Matter of Huang, 19 I. & N. Dec. 749, 756 (B.I.A. 1988).
15. *See* Matter of Kane, 15 I. & N. Dec. 258, 263 (B.I.A. 1975).

- Possession of a driver's license
- U.S. employer and evidence of salary
- Evidence of children's enrollment in schools
- Evidence of filing U.S. tax returns
- Evidence of property ownership[16]

Additional factors to consider include the following:

- Location of family members
- Pension accounts
- Membership in professional associations
- Procurement of business or professional licenses

In the Ninth Circuit case, *Matter of Singh*, the respondent's failure to establish a home and career in the United States ultimately persuaded the court that he had abandoned his residency.[17] Mr. Singh worked sporadically at a restaurant, but had no permanent employment. He also stayed in housing provided by his employer while in the United States, never purchasing or even renting a home of his own. With his family members in the United Kingdom, Mr. Singh had very few ties to support his intent to return to the United States as his place of residence. In contrast, in *Khodagholian*, the respondent's wife and children were in the United States while he was abroad. His son was attending college and his daughter was in high school. While Mr. Khodagholian only worked intermittently in the United States, his wife had been consistently employed until shortly before their hearing. These ties proved persuasive to the court, in spite of Mr. Khodagholian's failure to file U.S. tax returns and his 15-month trip to Iran.

Conduct and Ties Abroad

Conduct while abroad and ties to another country are of critical importance in proving a continuous, uninterrupted intent to return to the United States. The Foreign Affairs Manual includes the following five factors as evidence of abandonment of residency:

- Extended or frequent absences
- Disposition of property or business affiliations in the United States
- Family, property, or business ties abroad

---

16. 9 U.S. Dep't of State, Foreign Affairs Manual § 42.22 N13 [hereinafter Foreign Affairs Manual].
17. *See* Matter of Singh, 113 F.3d 1512 (9th Cir. 1997).

- Conduct while outside the United States such as, employment by a foreign employer, voting in foreign elections, running for political office in a foreign country
- Failure to file U.S. income tax returns

While failure to file U.S. income tax returns can be overcome with other positive factors, it is extremely difficult to overcome filing U.S. tax returns as a "nonresident." Filing as a nonresident raises a rebuttable presumption that the LPR has abandoned their permanent residence.[18] Aside from providing evidence showing that the LPR filed the nonresident tax return fraudulently, it is extremely difficult to rebut the presumption of abandonment in this situation.

Another factor cited by the Ninth Circuit in *Chavez-Ramirez* was the respondent's failure to inquire about her permanent resident status or attempt to take actions to preserve it while living abroad.[19] In *Chavez-Ramirez*, the respondent was a nun who left her order in the United States in 1973 to return to Mexico to care for her sick mother. The mother did not recuperate as hoped, and Chavez remained to provide the care she needed. After two years, the respondent's sister took over this role, and the respondent married and had a child. Chavez claimed that she always intended to return to the United States, but that she and her husband were working to accumulate enough money to support themselves in the United States while they sought employment. She did not make any inquiries regarding her immigration status until she applied for a visa in 1978. The fact that Ms. Chavez established a residence, married, gave birth in Mexico, and made no previous effort to inquire about her permanent resident status indicated that she did not have a continuous, uninterrupted intention to return to the United States.

Applying for a visitor visa also generally supports a finding of abandonment of residency.[20] The respondent in *Singh* traveled to the United States on a visitor visa four times, and indicated on his last trip that he was in the United States for "pleasure" and was only remaining for three weeks.[21] The court found this to be evidence of abandonment, especially in light of the fact that the respondent was a "seasoned world traveler." There are, however, exceptions to the general rule that applying for a

---

18. *See* Legacy Immigration and Naturalization Service (INS) Memorandum, D. Martin (May 7, 1996), *reprinted in* 73 INTERPRETER RELEASES 929, 948–50 (Jul. 15, 1996); 8 C.F.R. § 316.5(c)(2).
19. *See* Chavez-Ramirez v. INS, 792 F.2d 932, 938 (9th Cir. 1985).
20. *See Singh*, 113 F.3d at 1515; *Chavez-Ramirez*, 792 F.2d 932.
21. *See Singh*, 113 F.3d at 1515.

visitor visa as a permanent resident is highly inadvisable. The Foreign Affairs Manual states that a permanent resident did not necessarily abandon their residency if they were issued a visitor visa "as a matter of convenience when time did not permit the alien to obtain a returning resident visa." (Returning resident visas are discussed below.) The following example is provided:

> For example, a permanent resident alien is temporarily assigned abroad but employed by a U.S. corporation. The alien has been outside the United States for more than one year and thus may not return to the United States using the Form I-551, Permanent Resident Card. The alien has never relinquished permanent residence in the United States; has continued to pay U.S. income taxes; and perhaps even maintains a home in the United States. The fact that the alien was issued a non-immigrant visa (NIV) for the purpose of making an urgent business trip would not reflect negatively on the retention of resident status.[22]

In sum, a past application for a visitor or other non-immigrant visa is not necessarily the end of the abandonment analysis, but is certainly not advisable.

Imputing a Parent's Abandonment of Residency to a Minor Child

Abandonment of permanent residency of a parent will be imputed to a minor child in the parent's custody and control.[23] The Ninth Circuit, in *Khoshfahm v. Holder,* clarified that the intent of the parent will be imputed to the child until the age of eighteen.[24] Once the minor reaches age eighteen, the adjudicator must look to the intent of the young adult. Interestingly, the Foreign Affairs Manual notes that this rule of imputed intent is to be followed "unless [the consular officer] conclude[s] that the parents have a separate intention for the child to return to the United States for residence."[25] If a client who has abandoned their residency attests to having a different intention for a minor child, this should be documented

---

22. 9 FOREIGN AFFAIRS MANUAL, *supra* note 16, § 42.22 N10.
23. *See* Matter of Huang, 19 I. & N. Dec. 749, 750 n.1 (B.I.A. 1988); Matter of Zamora, 17 I. & N. Dec. 395, 396 (B.I.A. 1980).
24. *See* Khoshfahm v. Holder, Case No. 10-71066 (August 25, 2011).
25. 9 FOREIGN AFFAIRS MANUAL, *supra* note 16, § 42.22 N5.

through affidavits and any other available evidence and presented to the adjudicator.

Tips on How to Present Your Client's Case

- Develop the story.
- Get to the bottom of the original purpose behind your client's departure and their mindset at the time regarding their return date.
- Determine what factors kept your client abroad for longer than they intended.
- Brainstorm with your client regarding their ties to the United States—including less conventional ties.
- Discuss with your client the life they were leading while abroad.
- Prepare your clients.
- Your client should be ready to tell their complete story to the consulate, if applying for a returning resident visa, or to Customs and Border Protection, if attempting to reenter on their green card.
- The more supporting evidence that your client has, the better. Their ties and their conduct abroad, as appropriate, should be thoroughly documented.

Maintaining and Restoring Permanent Residency While Living Abroad

The duration of an LPR's absence abroad is clearly only one factor among several when analyzing abandonment of residency. It is therefore not possible to maintain residency simply by returning to the United States for short visits every so often, always within 180 days. Protecting residency against abandonment requires a comprehensive approach in which the LPR plans out the duration of their trip abroad, thinks ahead about their conduct abroad, and works to maintain all possible ties to the United States. There is no magic formula, but thorough planning and documentation will go a long way to maintaining permanent resident status.

Reentry Permits

A reentry permit serves as evidence of a permanent resident's intent to return to the United States and can facilitate an LPR's reentry after a departure abroad of over 180 days. It is a common myth that reentry permits protect permanent residency during the permit's validity without exception. Unfortunately, this is not the case. In *Moin v. Ashcroft*, the Fifth Circuit held that a reentry permit "merely serves as evidence of an alien's intent to return, which the Government may refuse by clear, unequivocal, and convincing evidence."[26] Reentry permits should therefore be part of a comprehensive strategy to maintain residency, not relied on exclusively.

Reentry permits are initially granted for a two-year period. The permits will generally be granted in one-year increments after the applicant has been abroad for more than four of the last five years since becoming a permanent resident. However, USCIS can continue to issue two-year permits to the following LPRs:

- Those traveling on order of the U.S. government;
- Those employed by a public international organization of which the United States is a member; and
- Professional athletes who regularly compete in the United States and worldwide.[27]

The applicant must be present in the United States: (1) at the time of filing the application; and (2) for the biometrics appointment that will be scheduled approximately one month from filing. According to the Form I-131 instructions, the departure of the applicant after the biometrics appointment "usually" does not affect the application. However, departure prior to the biometrics appointment can cause the application to be denied. Practitioners should be able to get a sense of the risk of a denial in this situation by talking to other practitioners in the locality.

It is important to note that a reentry permit does not protect continuous residence for naturalization purposes! The reentry permit only assists with establishing your client's intent to return to the United States in the abandonment context.

Returning Resident (SB-1) Visas

If a client has already been abroad for over one year without a valid reentry permit, the returning resident visa (or SB-1) may be the best option for restoring the client's permanent resident status and facilitating their return to the United States. The Foreign Affairs Manual explains that the returning resident visa is available to permanent residents who can prove to a consular officer that:

1.   The alien departed the United States with the intention to return to an unrelinquished domicile; and

---

26. *See* Moin v. Ashcroft, 335 F.3d 415, 419 (5th Cir. 2003).
27. 8 C.F.R. § 223.2(c)(2).

2. The alien's stay was for reasons beyond the alien's control and for which the alien was not responsible.[28]

The SB-1 visa is applied for at the consulate, and requires the submission of Form DS-117 as well as an application fee. The DS-117 requests information about the reasons for the individual's trip abroad, the justification for the trip's long duration, ties to the United States, and an explanation of the efforts the applicant has made to retain their permanent resident status.

The same *Matter of Kane* abandonment analysis discussed above applies in determining the applicant's eligibility for the returning resident visa. The applicant should therefore submit evidence of their lawful permanent resident status and extensive documentation of their family, property, and employment ties to the United States. It is also important to include any evidence that the prolonged nature of the trip was beyond the applicant's control, a factor that the Foreign Affairs Manual stresses as key to eligibility.[29] Once a returning resident visa application is approved, the applicant must go through the standard immigrant visa consular processing steps of obtaining a medical examination and the necessary police clearances.[30] Even with an approved SB-1 visa, clients should be prepared for questioning by CBP upon entry.[31] The client should therefore arrive with their supporting evidence accessible and be ready to explain the circumstances of their prolonged absence abroad.

MAINTAINING RESIDENCE FOR NATURALIZATION PURPOSES

Clients departing abroad should be advised not only about the pitfalls of abandonment of residency, but also how their departure will affect their ability to apply for U.S. citizenship in the future. Maintaining residency to avoid abandonment unfortunately does little for two key requirements for naturalization: continuous residence and physical presence.

---

28. 9 FOREIGN AFFAIRS MANUAL, *supra* note 16, § 42.22 N1.1.
29. *Id.* § 42.22 N1.1.
30. *Id.* § 42.22 N1.
31. *See* Custom and Border Protection Inspector's Field Manual, Chapter 13, 13.5 Returning Residents with SB-1 Visas.

Continuous Residence

In order to be eligible for naturalization, among other requirements, applicants must have been continuously residing in the United States for the five-year period immediately preceding their application.[32] For applicants married to U.S. citizens, the required period is three years.[33] The statute allows applicants to file naturalization applications up to three months prior to meeting the continuous residence requirement.[34] Residence for naturalization purposes is a distinct concept from residence for abandonment purposes. The definition of residence, as it pertains to naturalization, is defined as the applicant's "domicile, or principal actual dwelling place, without regard to the alien's intent."[35] Continuous residence is presumed to be broken by an absence from the United States lasting over six months but less than one year.[36] This presumption can be rebutted with evidence that the applicant did not disrupt the continuity of their residence. The analysis has some similarity with the abandonment analysis, and includes the following factors: place of employment during the absence, location of immediate family members, and retention of full access to the applicant's U.S. abode.[37] An absence from the United States for one year or more will automatically break the continuity of the applicant's residence. It is imperative to again note that a reentry permit does not protect the continuity of residence for naturalization.[38] For those who have been absent for over one year, but maintained their residency through a reentry permit or obtained an SB-1 visa, they must wait four years and one day to apply for naturalization (or two years and one day for those married to U.S. citizens).

The only possibility for preserving continuous residence while residing abroad is through the N-470, Application to Preserve Residence for Naturalization Purposes. This benefit is available to the very few who can meet its strict requirements:

1. The applicant is going or has gone abroad for employment by:
    - The U.S. government or an American institution of research recognized as such by the Attorney General; or

---

32. INA § 316(a).
33. *Id.* § 319(a).
34. *Id.* § 334(a).
35. 8 C.F.R. § 316.5(a).
36. INA § 316(b).
37. 8 C.F.R. § 316.5(c)(1)(i).
38. *Id.* § 316.5(a).

- An American firm or corporation engaged in whole or in part in the development of foreign trade and commerce of the United States; or
- A public international organization of which the United States is a member by treaty or statute and by which the alien was not employed until after being lawfully admitted for permanent residence.

2. Since becoming a permanent resident, the applicant has resided in the United States for an uninterrupted period of 1 year (with no absences whatsoever).[39]

The N-470 can be filed from abroad, but must be submitted prior to one year of continuous absence from the United States. An approved N-470 will only preserve the continuity of the applicant's residency; it will not replace a reentry permit for purposes of returning to the United States. Importantly, the N-470 will not affect the physical presence requirement for naturalization, with two exceptions discussed below. The N-470 therefore has a rather limited application, and will only assist the minority of applicants who can meet its requirements.

Physical Presence

Applicants for naturalization must also meet the separate but related requirement of physical presence in the United States: each applicant must have been physically present in the United States for half of the statutory period of residence (five years or three years for applicants married to U.S. citizens). This requirement is strictly applied, with some exceptions carved out in the INA. Firstly, lawful permanent residents abroad with an approved N-470 who are employed by or under contract with the U.S. government will not be subject to the physical presence requirements for naturalization.[40] Additionally, residents with a "religious vocation" who go abroad in connection with their religious functions for a religious denomination organized in the United States may be considered to have constructive physical presence during their absence if they spent one uninterrupted year in the United States after obtaining permanent residency. Members of the U.S. military and their spouses also qualify for certain exceptions to the physical presence requirements.[41]

---

39. INA § 316(b).
40. *Id.* § 316(b)–(c).
41. *Id.* § 328(d); *id.* § 319(e).

Expedited naturalization under INA § 319(b) waives both the physical presence and continuous residence requirements with respect to certain LPRs whose U.S. citizen spouses are employed abroad. In order to qualify, the applicant's spouse must be employed by:

1. The United States Government;
2. An American institution of research recognized as such by the Attorney General; or
3. An American firm or corporation engaged in whole or in part in the development of foreign trade and commerce of the United States, or a subsidiary thereof; or
4. A public international organization in which the United States participates by treaty or statute.

Section 319(b) requires that the applicant's spouse be "regularly stationed abroad," which is defined in the regulations as employment abroad for at least one year.[42] The applicant must also declare a "good faith intention" to reside abroad with their spouse and to return to the United States at the end of the spouse's employment contract.[43] Because no period of physical presence or continuous residence is required by INA § 319(b), an applicant for adjustment of status can become a resident and U.S. citizen in a single day by filing both the adjustment and naturalization applications with the proper evidence of eligibility.

CONCLUSION

With regard to maintaining residency while abroad, an ounce of prevention can save the client from the traumatic ordeal of being refused admission or paroled in for removal proceedings. While not every client will come to an attorney prior to their departure, the ones that do should be armed with the information they need to create their own plan to maintain their residency. Attorneys can also develop language to be included in each file closing letter for clients who have just obtained their residency, warning of the fact that permanent residency is not in fact permanent. And of course, each client departing the United States who comes in for advice should be evaluated for eligibility for expedited naturalization or preserving the continuity of their residency through an N-470. After all, citizenship is the ultimate cure for LPRs with international obligations.

---

42. 8 C.F.R. § 319.2(a)(1).
43. *Id.* § 319.2(a)(4).

16

FAMILY-BASED IMMIGRATION LAW

Stephanie DiPietro[1]

> *"Break up the institution of the family, deny the inviolability of its relations, and in a little while there would not be any humanity."*
>
> —E.H. Chapin in *Living Words*[2]

During the late 1800s through the early 1900s, Congress enacted numerous immigration laws which were discriminatory in nature. However, federal courts helped to create exceptions to these laws for the sake of family unity. For example, while the Chinese Exclusion Act of 1882 suspended immigration to the United States for Chinese individuals, federal courts created an exception to permit wives and children of Chinese merchants and United States citizens to still immigrate to the United States.[3]

The United States Court of Appeals for the Second Circuit held in *Lau v. Kiley* that the Immigration and Nationality Act has a "humane purpose . . . to reunite families" and that family reunification is the "foremost policy underlying the granting of preference visas under our immigration laws."[4] Due to the enormous societal value of strong family units, United States immigration laws have strived towards keeping families together

---

1. Stephanie DiPietro is the principal attorney with the Law Office of Stephanie DiPietro, P.C., in New York City. Her practice is focused on family- and employment-based immigration, waivers, and naturalization. She is a graduate of Syracuse University (2001) and Roger Williams University School of Law (2004). She is a frequent speaker at American Immigration Lawyers Assocation's National Conference, the New York Chapter's Annual Symposium, CLE classes sponsored by AILA's New York Chapter and the Practicing Law Institute. Ms. DiPietro is the current treasurer of the New York Chapter of AILA and the former co-chair of the New York Chapter's District Director Committee.

2. Edwin Hubbell Chapin, Living Words 59 (Boston, A. Tompkins 1861).

3. Erika Lee, At America's Gates: Chinese Immigration during the Exclusion Era, 1882–1943 (2003).

4. Kalishi v. Dist. Dir of INS, 620 F.2d 214, 217 (9th Cir. 1990); Delgaod v. INS, 473 F. Supp. 1343, 1348 (S.D.N.Y. 1979) (quoting Lau v. Kiley, 563 F.2d 543, 547 (2d Cir. 1977)).

and reuniting family members who are apart. Family immigration in the United States has been restricted to a North American definition of family (e.g., "The strongest rights to family reunification exist between spouses, and between minor, unmarried, and dependant children and their parents.").[5]

Within this chapter, I will explain the types of familial relationships that qualify for immigrant visas, how to apply for these visas, visa wait times, how to remove conditional resident status and how to obtain a K non-immigrant visa.

WHAT TYPES OF FAMILIAL RELATIONSHIPS QUALIFY FOR AN IMMIGRANT VISA?

Permanent resident status or a "green card" allows a foreign national to permanently remain in the United States. Green cards based upon familial relationships fall under one of the following two categories: immediate relative and family preference.

Section 101(b)(1) of the Immigration and Nationality Act (INA) defines an "immediate relative" as a United States citizen's spouse,[6] parents, or unmarried children under the age of 21.[7] Immigrant visa issuance to immediate relatives is unlimited. Therefore, unlike the family preference category, there is no wait list for permanent resident status as an immediate relative.

REQUIREMENTS FOR IMMEDIATE RELATIVES

For a United States citizen to file a petition for his or her foreign national spouse, the marriage must be:

- valid under the laws of the country in which the wedding took place;
- not contrary to public policy; and

---

5. Nora V. Demleitier, *How Much Do Western Democracies Value Family and Marriage?: Immigration Law's Conflicted Answers*, 24 Immigr. & Nat'lity L. Rev. 351, 355 (2003).
6. Following the U.S. Supreme Court's decision in *United States v. Windsor*, 570 U.S. ___, ___ S.Ct. ___, 2013 WL, President Obama directed federal departments to ensure the decision and its implication for federal benefits for same-sex legally married couples are implemented swiftly and smoothly. To that end, USCIS now reviews immigration visa petitions filed on behalf of a same-sex spouse in the same manner as those filed on behalf of an opposite-sex spouse. *See* http://www.uscis.gov/family/same-sex-marriages.
7. INA § 201(b)(1).

- not fraudulent or sham attempt to circumvent United States immigration law.[8]

For a United States citizen to file a petition for his or her parent, the petition must be filed by a United States citizen son or daughter 21 years of age or older.[9]

For a United States citizen to file a petition for his or her unmarried child under the age of 21, the foreign national will be considered a child if he or she is:

- a legitimate child;
- stepchild if the qualifying relationship was created prior to the child's 18th birthday;
- legitimized child either under the law of the place of the child's residence or under the law of the father's residence or domicile if it occurs before the child's 18th birthday;
- adopted child if the qualifying relationship was created prior to the child's 16th birthday and the child has been in the legal custody of and resided with the adopting parent for a minimum of two years; or
- orphan under the age of 16 due to death, abandonment, disappearance, or desertion of parent or where the sole surviving parent is incapable of caring for the child.[10]

OTHER FAMILY-BASED PETITIONS

Under the Immigration Act of 1990, 480,000 immigrant visas are allotted annually to family based immigration for those family members that are not "immediate relatives" as defined in the INA. There are a limited number of immigrant visas allocated by Congress to family petitions which fall under one of the four following preference categories:

- Family 1st Preference: unmarried sons and daughters of United States citizens over the age of 21 years (23,400 visas)[11]

---

8. U.S. Citizenship and Immigration Services, Adjudicator's Field Manual § 21.3.
9. INA § 201(b)(2)(A)(i), 8 U.S.C. § 1101(b)(2).
10. INA § 101(b)(1).
11. *Id.* § 203(a)(1), 8 U.S.C. § 1153(a)(1).

- Family 2nd Preference: spouses and unmarried sons and daughters (irrespective of age) of a lawful permanent resident of the United States (114,000 visas)[12]
- Family 3rd Preference: married sons and daughters (irrespective of age) of United States citizen (23,400 visas)[13]
- Family 4th Preference: brothers and sister of United States citizen (United States citizen must be age 21 or older) (65,000 visas)[14]

How does a foreign national know when an immigrant visa under a family preference category becomes available?

Under the family preference categories as opposed to immediate relatives, a green card may not be immediately available since the amount of green cards available each government fiscal year are limited. When the number of qualified foreign nationals in a family preference category exceeds the available number of green cards, a wait period occurs. This wait period may be 20 years or longer in some categories. The allotment of immigrant visas for each family preference category is refreshed at the start of the government's fiscal year (October 1st) and available green cards are chronologically issued based upon the foreign national's priority date (i.e., the date in which the I-130 Immigrant Petition was filed) and the foreign national's country of chargeability, which is defined as the country of birth, not necessarily citizenship.

Immigrant visa availability can be tracked monthly by checking the Visa Bulletin located on the United States Department of State website (http://www.travel.state.gov). If the foreign national's priority date is on or before the "current" priority date, an immigrant visa is available to the foreign national if he or she is located outside the United States or the Form I-485, Adjustment of Status Application, can be approved if the foreign national is inside the United States If the foreign national's priority date is after the current priority date, an immigrant visa is unavailable to the foreign national.

If instead of listing a date for a particular family preference category a "C" is listed for "current," then green cards are available for this category because the number of qualified foreign nationals in this family preference category is less than the available number of immigrant visas. If instead of listing a date for a particular family preference category a "U" is listed, then visas are unavailable in this family preference category until the start of the next governmental fiscal year.

---

12. *Id.* § 203(a)(2); 8 U.S.C. § 1153(a)(2).
13. *Id.* § 203(a)(3); 8 U.S.C. § 1153(a)(3).
14. *Id.* § 203(a)(4); 8 U.S.C. § 1153(a)(4).

Can a foreign national move between family preference categories or convert to an immediate relative?

Certain actions may terminate an approved I-130 petition or may permit a foreign national to move between family preference categories while maintaining his or her original priority date. The U.S. Department of State's Foreign Affairs Manual (FAM)[15] outlines priority date retention after conversion from one family preference category to another family preference category.

An immediate relative may move between family preference categories as follows:

- With the exception of a marriage terminated due to domestic violence, an immediate relative loses his or her ability to obtain an immigrant visa if he or she divorces the United States citizen before he or she is granted permanent resident status.[16]
- If a minor child of a United States citizen marries before being granted permanent resident status, the petition of the foreign national automatically converts to family third preference.[17] The foreign national retains the priority date from the original filed petition. However, he or she may need to wait for an immigrant visa depending on the foreign national's priority date and country of chargeability.
- If an unmarried immediate relative turns 21 after the immigrant visa petition has been filed with United States Citizenship and Immigration Services (hereinafter referred to as "USCIS"), he or she may remain an immediate relative because the Child Status Protection Act (CSPA) may prevent the foreign national from "aging out" of his or her category.[18]

A foreign national eligible for an immigrant visa based upon an approved family first preference category may be eligible to convert family-based categories as follows:

- If the unmarried son or daughter of a United States citizen who has an approved family first preference petition marries, his or her approved petition automatically converts to third preference.[19] The

---

15. 9 U.S. DEP'T OF STATE, FOREIGN AFFAIRS MANUAL § 42.53 N2.4. [hereinafter FOREIGN AFFAIRS MANUAL].

16. 8 C.F.R. § 205.1(a)(3)(i)(D).

17. 9 FOREIGN AFFAIRS MANUAL, *supra* note 15, § 42.53 N2.4-1(a).

18. Child Status Protection Act, Pub. L. No. 107-208, 116 Stat. 927 (2002); INA § 201(f)(1).

19. 8 C.F.R. § 204.2(i).

foreign national retains the priority date of the original first prefer-ence petition despite obtaining an immigrant visa or adjusting status under family third preference.[20]

A foreign national eligible for an immigrant visa based upon an approved family second preference petition may move between family preference categories as follows:

- Upon the lawful permanent resident spouse or parent's naturaliza-tion, the spouse or unmarried child under the age of 21 who has an approved second preference petition automatically converts to imme-diate relative.[21]
- Upon the lawful permanent resident parent's naturalization, the approved family second preference subcategory B petition for the unmarried son or daughter 21 years of age or older automatically converts to family first preference category.[22] The unmarried son or daughter 21 years or older retains the priority date from the time of the filing of the family second preference petition.[23]
- If a child of a lawful permanent resident marries, he or she completely loses immigrant visa eligibility under this petition.[24] However, if the child becomes widowed or divorced, then he or she regains family second preference and he or she retains the priority date from the original filed petition.[25]
- If a child with an approved petition under family second preference subcategory A reaches the age of 21, he or she is no longer entitled to an immigrant visa under this category. Rather, he or she automati-cally converts to family second preference subcategory B.[26]
- If a child with an approved petition under family second preference subcategory A turns age 21 after his or her priority date is current and files his or her adjustment of status application within one year of the priority date becoming current, then according to Child Status Protection Act, a child can subtract from her age the number of days it took United States Citizenship and Immigration Services to issue a

20. 9 FOREIGN AFFAIRS MANUAL, *supra* note 15, § 42.53 N2.4-1(a).
21. *Id.* § 42.53 N2.4-3(a)–(b); 8 C.F.R. § 204.2(i)(3).
22. 9 FOREIGN AFFAIRS MANUAL, *supra* note 15, § 42.53 N2.4-3(c).
23. *Id.*
24. 8 C.F.R. § 205.1(a).
25. 9 FOREIGN AFFAIRS MANUAL, *supra* note 15, § 42.53 N2.4-1(c).
26. *Id.* § 42.53 N2.4-2(b).

decision on the initial visa.[27] If the child's age in days adds to be less than 21 years, the child is prevented from "aging out."[28]

A foreign national eligible for an immigrant visa based upon an approved family third preference petition may move between family preference categories as follows:

- If the married son or daughter of a United States citizen becomes widowed or divorced, his or her approved family third preference petition converts to family first preference.[29] The son or daughter of the United States citizen retains the original priority date from the family third preference petition.[30]

Lastly, if a foreign national's family preference petition is revoked under INA § 203(g) (8 U.S.C. § 1153(g)) or 8 C.F.R. § 205 or if a new petition is filed on his or her behalf by a different lawful permanent resident or United States citizen, the priority date from the initial petition is nontransferable to the new petition.[31]

FAMILY IMMIGRANT VISA PROCESS

All family-based immigrant visa cases begin with filing of Form I-130, Petition for Alien Relative with USCIS. This petition establishes the foreign national's eligibility to immigrate to the United States based upon a familial relationship to a qualifying relative. Once the petition is approved, the foreign national will either process for a green card in the United States through "adjustment of status" or process for an immigrant visa abroad through "consular processing."

Adjustment of Status is a process involving the filing of Form I-485, Application to Register Permanent Residence or Adjust Status, by a foreign national residing inside the United States with USCIS. The foreign national is fingerprinted, interviewed, and undergoes a medical exam within the United States. Consular processing is a process involving an application for an immigrant visa at the United States embassy or consulate of the foreign national's country of last residence or country of birth. The foreign national

---

27. Child Status Protection Act, Pub. L. No. 107-208, § 3, 116 Stat. 927, 928 (2002), INA § 203(h)(i).
28. *Id.*
29. 9 FOREIGN AFFAIRS MANUAL, *supra* note 15, § 42.53 N2.4-1(c).
30. *Id.*
31. *Id.* § 42.53 N2.5.

is interviewed and undergoes a medical exam abroad and he or she must obtain police certificates from every country where he or she lived for one year or more since the age of 16. A foreign national may not pursue both Adjustment of Status and consular processing at the same time.

Some immediate relatives who are present in the United States (with some exceptions which will be discussed below) may file Form I-485, Application to Register Permanent Residence or Adjust Status simultaneously with Form I-130. Family preference petition applicants need both an approved I-130 petition and a current priority date before pursuing either adjustment of status or consular processing.

FORM I-485 ADJUSTMENT OF STATUS APPLICATION

In order to be eligible for adjustment of status in the United States, a foreign national must satisfy the requirements under INA section 245(a). According to INA section 245(a), an individual must have been inspected and admitted or paroled into the United States and

1. the alien makes an application for such adjustment,
2. the alien is eligible to receive an immigrant visa and is admissible to the United States for permanent residence, and
3. an immigrant visa is immediately available to him at the time his application is filed.[32]

An individual can be inspected and admitted by the U.S. Customs and Border Protection (CBP) at a port of entry (i.e., land entry, airport, or seaport). According to INA section 245(c), an individual who enters the United States without being inspected and admitted by CBP, overstays his or her non-immigrant status or works without authorization is ineligible for filing for adjustment of status.[33] Immediate relatives are eligible to adjust status despite overstaying his or her non-immigrant status or working without authorization. Otherwise, in order to be eligible for adjustment of status despite committing the above-referenced actions, the foreign national must be eligible for INA section 245(i).

In order to be eligible for adjustment of status under section 245(i) in addition to satisfying the above-referenced requirements of section 245(a), the individual must have:

---

32. INA § 245(a).
33. *Id.* § 245(c).

1. Filed on or before April 30, 2001, a visa petition or application for labor certification; and
2. If the petition or application was filed between January 14, 1998, and April 30, 2001, then the principal applicant must show he or she was present in the United States on December 21, 2000.

Examples of foreign nationals who are permitted to apply for adjustment of status through section 245(i) includes those individuals who:

- entered without inspection or illegally;
- failed to maintain non-immigrant status or otherwise committed visa violations;
- worked without authorization;
- are admitted as an individual "in transit without a visa";
- are admitted upon a D visa (as a crew member);
- are admitted upon an S visa (as a witnesses for a criminal or terrorism case).

However, section 245(i) waives only disqualifying factors for adjustment of status under section 245(a). Therefore, if the bar to adjustment is under another section (e.g., section 212) then the foreign national is still ineligible to adjust status despite being eligible for section 245(i). These individuals include:

- Stowaways;
- Terrorists or those who engage in terrorist activities;
- K visa entrant who failed to marry the United States citizen-petitioning spouse within 90 days of being admitted into the United States;
- J-1 visa entrant who failed to obtain a waiver of the two-year home residency requirement under INA section 212(e);
- A, E, or G entrants who failed to obtain a waiver through I-508 and I-566;
- S visa informants who lack permission from the Attorney General to seek adjustment of status;
- Individuals with final orders of removal, deportation, or exclusion or person granted voluntary departure;
- Those with grounds of inadmissibility under INA section 212 including:
  - INA § 212(a)(6)(C) committed fraud or misrepresentation in order to obtain an immigration benefit (e.g., entry into the United States on a fraudulent passport);

- INA § 212(a)(9)(B) acquired unlawful presence and incurred the 3- or 10-year bar to re-entry into the United States;[34]
- INA § 212(a)(9)(C)(i)(I) individuals who re-entered or attempted to re-enter the United States after having been unlawfully present in the United States for more than one year or after issuance of a final order.[35]

The Adjustment of Status process provides the foreign national with the ability to obtain an employment authorization document (EAD) and advance parole (AP)[36] and there is no prolonged separation from family in the United States during visa adjudication. Additionally benefits from the Adjustment of Status process include a right to bring immigration counsel to the interview, and if the USCIS adjudications officer denied the application, the decision can be reopened or reconsidered. Lastly, Adjustment of Status involves only one governmental office (USCIS) versus three governmental offices (USCIS, DOS, and CBP) with consular processing.

CONSULAR PROCESSING

Consular processing is the only immigrant visa-processing option for foreign nationals residing outside the United States. The disadvantages for a foreign national in pursuing consular processing include being ineligible for an employment authorization document (EAD) and advance parole (AP), absence from family members in the United States, no Section 245(i) amnesty to forgive overstay or entry without inspection, no right to counsel at the immigrant visa appointment, and no appeal of the consular officer's decision.

If the foreign national did not originally select consular processing on his or her I-130 petition but selects consular processing at a later date, he or she will need to file Form I-824, Application for Action on an Approved Application or Petition to have the file sent to the NVC. Transfer of the petition from USCIS to the NVC can take approximately three months, according to the USCIS website at the time of the writing of this chapter.[37] However, based upon this practitioner's personal experience with filing Form I-824, the transfer typically takes closer to six months to a year. This

---

34. Matter of Lemus-Losa, 24 I. & N. Dec. 373 (B.I.A. 2007).
35. Matter of Diaz, 25 I. & N. Dec. 188 (B.I.A. 2010).
36. 8 C.F.R. §§ 274a.12(c)(9), 1274a.12(c)(9).
37. www.uscis.gov.

is a significant delay for a foreign national wishing to pursue an immigrant visa in a prompt and efficient manner.

Once the I-130 petition has been approved, his or her file is transferred to the National Visa Center. The NVC will collect the visa fees and do an initial case processing of the application. Upon certifying the case, the National Visa Center will forward the foreign national's file to the United States embassy in their country of nationality or last residence and schedule the foreign national for an immigrant visa appointment. Upon conclusion of the appointment, the consular officer will issue a decision or request additional documentation if necessary. The foreign national will submit his or her passport for an immigrant visa to be placed into same and depending upon the United States embassy, the passport will either be returned to them in person at a future appointment or mailed to his or her attention. By entering the United States on the immigrant visa, the foreign national is admitted as a permanent resident.

REMOVAL OF CONDITIONAL RESIDENT STATUS

A conditional resident is an individual who gains status based upon marriage to a United States citizen when the marriage occurred less than two years prior to the granted residency.[38] An individual is a conditional resident for a two-year period. A conditional resident has the same responsibilities and rights as a permanent resident (i.e., ability to work in the United States, travel outside the United States, live in the United States, file petitions on behalf of certain relatives, etc.). However, unlike a permanent resident, a conditional resident must file Form I-751, petition to Remove Conditional Resident Status within the 90-day period before the expiration of their conditional resident card.[39] The I-751 Petition must demonstrate the ongoing marital union.[40]

If the conditional resident's spouse is unwilling to file an I-751 petition jointly, then the conditional resident may file a waiver application to waive the joint filing requirement. To request a waiver of the joint filing requirement, the conditional resident must also file Form I-751 based upon one of the following circumstances:

---

38. 8 C.F.R. § 216.4(a)(1).
39. *Id.*
40. *Id.* § 216.4(a)(5).

- Good-faith marriage which ended by annulment or divorce;[41]
- Good faith marriage wherein the United States citizen spouse subjected the conditional resident to battery or extreme cruelty;[42] or
- Termination of conditional resident status would result in extreme hardship to the conditional resident.[43]

If the U.S. citizen-spouse dies during the period of conditional permanent residence, according to *Matter of Rose*, the conditional resident must still file Form I-751; however no separate waiver is required if the petition spouse passed away within the two-year conditional resident period.[44]

Failure to file a timely I-751 petition will result in the automatic loss of the individual's lawful status in the United States and the individual will be placed in removal proceedings. USCIS may accept an untimely I-751 petition if the individual can establish there was a good reason for failure to file the petition within the required time and that circumstances were outside of the individual's control.[45] A conditional resident who is outside the United States during the 90-day period leading up to the expiration of his or her status may file an I-751 petition while he or she is outside the United States.[46] However, the conditional resident should be prepared to return to the United States for biometrics and if required to appear for an interview with USCIS. A conditional resident may travel abroad while their I-751 petition is being adjudicated by using his or her I-751 receipt notice (which serves as proof of the extension of the individual's conditional resident status) and the expired conditional resident card to reenter the United States.[47]

ARE CHILDREN OF CONDITIONAL RESIDENTS REQUIRED TO FILE A SEPARATED I-751 PETITION?

A child is considered a conditional resident when he or she obtained status based upon a parent's marriage to a United States citizen which occurred less than two years before admission or adjustment to status. If a child acquires their conditional status at the same time or within

41. INA § 216(c)(4)(B).
42. *Id.* § 216(c)(4)(C).
43. *Id.* § 216(c)(4)(A).
44. Matter of Rose, 25 I. & N. Dec. 181 (B.I.A. 2010).
45. D. Neufield, Memorandum, Adjudication of Form I-751, Petition to Remove Conditions on Residence Where CPR Has a Final Order of Removal, Is in Removal Proceedings, or Has Filed an Unexcused Untimely Petition or Multiple Petitions (USCIS, October 9, 2009).
46. 8 C.F.R. § 216.4(a)(4).
47. *Id.* § 216.4(a)(1).

90 days of the conditional resident parent, the children will be included on the I-751 petition or waiver application submitted by the parent.[48] However, if the child acquires conditional resident status more than 90 days after the conditional resident parent, then he or she must file their own Form I-751 petition or waiver application.[49]

K VISA

What Is a K Visa?

In order to provide United States citizens with more opportunities to petition for a foreign-born fiancé or spouse, two categories of K visas were created under the Immigration and Nationality Act of 1952.[50]

A K-1 visa is a dual intent non-immigrant visa which allows the fiancé of a United States citizen to enter the United States for the purpose of marrying his or her United States citizen spouse within 90 days of arrival. If the foreign-born fiancé fails to marry his or her United States citizen-fiancé, he or she must depart the United States within 30 days or else he or she will be removed in accordance with sections 1229a and 1231.[51]

A K-3 visa is a dual intent non-immigrant visa which allows the spouse of a United States citizen to enter the United States for the purpose of adjusting status within the United States.[52] To qualify for a K-3 visa, the qualifying marriage must have already occurred and the non-immigrant visa must be issued in the country where the marriage took place. The purpose of the K-3 visa is to shorten the period of time the married couple is apart by providing an option of obtaining a non-immigrant visa abroad.

How Does a United States Citizen File a K-1 Visa for His or Her Fiancé?

First, the United States citizen must file Form I-129F, Petition for Alien Fiancé with the USCIS office with jurisdiction over the petitioner.[53] Second, the petitioner must demonstrate that he or she has met the foreign-born

---

48. *Id.* § 216.4(a)(2).
49. *Id.*
50. Immigration and Nationality Act of 1952, Pub. L. No. 82-144, 66 Stat. 163 (enacted June 27, 1952).
51. 8 U.S.C. § 1184(d).
52. INA § 101(a)(15)(K)(ii); 8 U.S.C. § 1101(a)(15)(K)(ii); 22 C.F.R. § 41.81; 9 FOREIGN AFFAIRS MANUAL, *supra* note 15, § 41.81; 8 C.F.R. § 214.2(k); 66 Fed. Reg. 42587–95 (August 14, 2001).
53. INA § 214(d); 8 U.S.C. § 1184(d); 9 FOREIGN AFFAIRS MANUAL, *supra* note 15, § 41.81 N.2; O.I. 214.2(k); 8 C.F.R. § 214.2(k).

fiancée within the past two years. However, this requirement can be waived if for cultural or traditional reasons the bride and groom cannot meet before their wedding date.[54] Third, the petitioner must demonstrate that he or she intends to marry within 90 days of the admission of the foreign born spouse, and that both are legally free to marry. Fourth, if the petitioner has a criminal history, he or she must provide certified dispositions and police records disclosing criminal convictions involving domestic violence, sexual assault, child abuse and neglect, dating violence, elder abuse, stalking, certain violent crimes, and crimes related to a controlled substance or alcohol where the petitioner has been convicted on at least three occasions not arising out of a single act.[55]

Within 90 days of entry into the United States, the marriage must occur and Form I-485, Application to Register Permanent Residence or Adjust Status filed on behalf of the foreign born individual with USCIS. A K-1 entrant can not change status.[56] A K-1 entrant can not adjust status based upon any other ground than marriage to the United States citizen who sponsored his or her K-1 visa.[57] An adjustment of status interview will scheduled and if the application is approved, a conditional resident card will be issued because the marriage is less than two years old. In a year and nine months, the United States citizen-spouse and foreign-born spouse must file a petition to remove the condition of their marriage.

Children of a K-1 visa holder can accompany their parent to the United States If the child is unmarried and under the age of 21 years, then he or she is a derivative applicant of his or her parent's K visa.[58] However, to be eligible for a K-2 visa, the petitioner must list each child's name on Form I-129F, Petition for Alien Fiancé. However, a separate visa application must be filed for each child. The child may enter the United States with his or her parent or follow to join the parent within one year of the issuance of the parent's visa. An K-2 visa holder may not enter the United States prior to the K-1 visa parent.

---

54. 8 C.F.R. § 214.2(k)(2); 50 Fed. Reg. 30011, 30013 (August 10, 1988).

55. Memo, Aytes, Assoc. Dir. Domestic Operations, USCIS HQOPRD 70/6.2.11 (July 21, 2006).

56. INA § 248; 8 U.S.C. § 1158.

57. INA § 245(d).

58. 8 C.F.R. § 214.2(k)(6)(ii); Memo, Aytes, Assoc. Dir. Domestic Operations, HQOPRD AD07-04 (March 15, 2007).

How Does a United States Citizen File a K-3 Visa for His or Her Spouse?

First, the United States citizen must file Form I-130, Petition for Alien Relative with USCIS office with jurisdiction over the petitioner. Upon obtaining the I-130 receipt, the United States citizen must file Form I-129F, Petition for Alien Fiancé with the USCIS office with jurisdiction over the petitioner. The petitioner must establish his or her United States citizenship, his or her legal marriage to the foreign born spouse and both of their abilities to legally enter into said marriage (e.g., divorce decrees or death certificate for spouses from previous marriages of petitioner or beneficiary).

As of February 1st, 2010, when USCIS approves both petitions at the same time or when USCIS approves the I-130 before the I-129F petition, the K-3 visa petition will be administratively closed and the U.S. citizen-spouse and foreign-citizen spouse will only be permitted to proceed with the immigrant visa petition (IR-1 or CR-1). If the NVC receives the approved I-129F petition before it receives the approved I-130 petition, then the NVC will process the K-3 visa. The approved I-129 F petition is valid for four months.[59] If the foreign born spouse entered the United States using a K-3 visa, he or she can not change to another status.[60] Also, the K-3 entrant may only adjust status based upon marriage to the individual who petitioned their K-3 visa.[61]

The children of a K-3 visa holder may obtain a K-4 visa. A separate Form I-129F, Petition for Alien Fiancé, is not required per child so long as the petitioner lists each child's name on the Form I-129F, Petition for Alien Fiancé being submitted on the spouse's behalf.[62] A separate I-130 petition does not need to be filed on each child's behalf in order to add his or her name to the I-129F petition. However, a separated visa application must be filed for each child to obtain a K-4 visa. Like the K-3 visa application, if the foreign-born spouse's I-130 petition arrives at the NVC at the same time or before the approval of the I-129F petition, and he or she must pursue immigrant visa processing, then a separate Form I-130 petition must be filed for each child with USCIS.

---

59. 9 FOREIGN AFFAIRS MANUAL, *supra* note 15, § 41.81 N5.2, N6.1 N6.2; Cable DOS O2-State-79357 8 C.F.R. § 214.2(k)(5); 9 FOREIGN AFFAIRS MANUAL § 41.81, Note 3.1.
60. 8 C.F.R. § 248.1(a).
61. *Id.* §§ 245.1(c)(6)(i), 1245(c)(6)(i).
62. Cable DOS 00-state-242292 at paragraph 11 (January 30, 2001).

17

AN INTRODUCTION TO ASYLUM LAW AND PROCEDURE

Dree K. Collopy, Esq.[1]

INTRODUCTION

At the beginning of 2013, some 35.8 million people worldwide had been forcibly displaced due to conflict and persecution.[2] Unable to turn to their own governments for protection, refugees depend upon the compassion and humanity of foreign governments in seeking safety and freedom. Accordingly, implicit in the core humanitarian purpose of U.S. asylum law is the requirement that it be as effective as possible in offering reliable protection to bona fide refugees. Although this may seem like a simple concept, the human rights considerations involved in refugee and asylum law often collide with national self-interests, the challenges involved in maintaining the integrity of the application process, and the economic

---

1. Dree K. Collopy is a partner of Benach Ragland LLP. As an experienced advocate, she provides zealous and ethical representation to individuals before the U.S. Immigration Courts, U.S. District Courts, U.S. Circuit Courts of Appeals, U.S. Citizenship and Immigration Services, Immigration and Customs Enforcement, Customs and Border Protection, and the U.S. consulates abroad. Dree devotes her practice to defending and representing individuals in removal proceedings, asylum matters, federal court litigation, VAWA and U visa petitions, waivers of inadmissibility, and complex adjustment of status and naturalization applications. A recognized immigration law expert, Dree frequently lectures on cutting-edge immigration issues. She has authored several articles and is currently writing the seventh edition of AILA's Asylum Primer. As Chair of the AILA National Asylum and Refugee Liaison Committee, Dree builds relationships and works cooperatively with government officials to maintain the integrity of our asylum system and ensure that our laws are implemented with accuracy and fairness. She teaches the Immigration Litigation Clinic at the Catholic University of America Columbus School of Law, where Dree earned her J.D. and Certificate in Law and Public Policy. She earned her Bachelor of Arts in Political Science and Spanish at Grinnell College.

2. This figure included 10.4 million refugees, 23.8 million internally displaced and stateless persons, and more than 928,230 individuals with pending asylum applications. *See* United Nations High Commissioner for Refugees, Populations of Concern to UNHCR, *available at* http://www.unhcr.org/528a0a0fe.html.

and political realities of the sheer scale of the world refugee crisis.[3] This collision has generated one of the most compelling, but also one of the most complex, areas of immigration law. This chapter is meant to provide a brief introduction to this complicated area of the law.

SOURCES OF LAW

A generous, open-door immigration policy characterized the first 100 years of the United States' existence. Yet, even in the beginning of federal immigration regulation, the United States offered protection to the persecuted.[4] As inscribed on the icon of freedom in the United States, the Statue of Liberty, "Give me your tired, your poor, Your huddled masses yearning to breathe free, The wretched refuse of your teeming shore, Send these, the homeless, tempest-tossed to me, I lift my lamp beside the golden door!"[5] This spirit of offering protection to individuals fleeing persecution is the core concept and the origin of U.S. asylum law, which has evolved significantly since the dedication of the Statue of Liberty in 1886.

In the wake of World War II, the United Nations was confronted with massive displacement of people around the world. In response, it created the Office of the United Nations High Commissioner for Refugees ("UNHCR") on December 14, 1950, to help the approximately one million Europeans who were still displaced by the war. Its mandate was to coordinate international action to provide necessary protections for refugees to safeguard their rights and well-being, while also addressing various related social and humanitarian concerns.[6] Originally, UNHCR was meant to complete its work and disband within three years. However, the following year, in 1951, the United Nations Convention Relating to the Status of Refugees ("Refugee Convention")[7] was adopted, setting forth the legal foundation for refugee law and policy. After several historical conflicts led to an outpouring of additional refugees[8] and reiter-

---

3. *See generally* Stephen H. Legomsky, Immigration and Refugee Law and Policy ch. 11 (2005).

4. *See* D. Martin, Asylum Case Law Sourcebook, at xvii (1998).

5. Emma Lazarus, The New Colossus (1883).

6. UNHCR History, http://www.unhcr.org/pages/49c3646cbc.html (last visited Oct. 28, 2011).

7. Convention Relating to the Status of Refugees, July 28, 1951, 189 U.N.T.S. 150 [hereinafter Refugee Convention].

8. Some of these historical conflicts were the decolonization of Africa in the 1960s, the Cold War, and related regional and internal conflicts around the world. UNHCR History, http://www.unhcr.org/pages/49c3646cbc.html (last visited Oct. 28, 2011).

ated the importance of the legal foundation that UNHCR had created for their protection, the United Nations implemented its 1967 United Nations Protocol Relating to the Status of Refugees ("Refugee Protocol"), which adopted Articles 2–34 of the Refugee Convention.[9]

The United States acceded to the Refugee Protocol in 1968, and the Refugee Convention and Refugee Protocol have been the principal international agreements governing U.S. obligations toward refugees ever since. In fact, many of the Refugee Convention and Refugee Protocol's provisions have been incorporated into domestic law, most significantly the definition of "refugee"[10] and the principle of nonrefoulement, which is the prohibition of the return of refugees to countries where their lives or freedom would be threatened.[11] The United States is also a signatory to the related UN Convention Against Torture and Other Cruel, Inhuman or Degrading Treatment or Punishment ("Convention Against Torture"), which was enacted into United States law in 1998.[12] These international agreements, along with other treaties that the United States has ratified, as well as customary international law, lay the foundation of U.S. asylum law.

U.S. asylum law has continued to build upon this foundation through laws[13] contained within and amending the Immigration and Nationality Act (INA);[14] federal agency regulations; operations instructions and field manuals; policy directives, memoranda, and statements; administrative interpretation of the statute and regulations by the Department of Justice, Department of Homeland Security, Department of State, and the Attorney General; and judicial interpretation of the statute and regulations by

---

9. Protocol Relating to the Status of Refugees, Oct. 4, 1967, 606 U.N.T.S. 267 [hereinafter Refugee Protocol].

10. Refugee Convention, *supra* note 7, art. 1, *incorporated by reference*, Refugee Protocol, *supra* note 9, at art. I, sec. 2; Immigration and Nationality Act of 1952, Pub. L. No. 82-414, § 101(a)(42), 66 Stat. 163 (codified as amended at 8 U.S.C. § 1101 *et seq.*).

11. Refugee Convention, *supra* note 7, art. 33, *incorporated by reference*, Refugee Protocol, *supra* note 9, art. I(1).

12. Convention Against Torture and Other Cruel, Inhuman or Degrading Treatment or Punishment, Dec. 10, 1984, 1465 U.N.T.S. 85 (June 26, 1987) (enacted into U.S. law on October 21, 1998 by Fiscal Year 1999 Omnibus Consolidated and Emergency Supplemental Appropriations Act, Pub. L. No. 104-277, Div. G, Sub. B, Title XXI § 2242 of the Foreign Affairs Reform and Restructuring Act of 1998, 112 Stat. 2681-822) [hereinafter Convention Against Torture].

13. The most significant of these acts include the Refugee Act of 1980, Pub. L. No. 96-212, 94 Stat. 102; Illegal Immigration Reform and Immigrant Responsibility Act of 1996, Pub. L. No. 104-208, div. C, 110 Stat. 3009; Uniting and Strengthening America by Providing Appropriate Tools Required to Intercept and Obstruct Terrorism Act, Pub. L. No. 107-56, 115 Stat. 272 (2001); REAL ID Act of 2005, Pub. L. No. 109-13, 119 Stat. 302.

14. *See generally* INA.

the federal courts. As Congress considers changes to the INA, the Department of Homeland Security contemplates issuing new regulations and policy memoranda, and asylum applicants and their advocates strive for fairer applications of the current law, asylum law in the United States continues to evolve.

THE TWO THEATERS OF U.S. ASYLUM LAW

In U.S. asylum law, the search for protection occurs in two different theaters—outside U.S. territory and within the United States. Outside U.S. territory, refugees seek legal admission to the United States, much like family members and employees seek legal admission when applying for visas. These individuals are often referred to as "overseas refugees." In order to be granted U.S. refugee status, overseas refugees must be interviewed by U.S. Department of State officers throughout the world, and must demonstrate that they meet the definition of "refugee" under the INA.[15] If they meet the definition of "refugee," they are then categorized into three groups: Priority 1, persons with emergency needs; Priority 2, special groups of interest in the United States; and Priority 3, family members of persons already resettled in the United States. The President, in consultation with Congress, has the authority to designate the number of refugees permitted per year, as well as which groups of refugees are to be designated as "emergency flow refugees" versus "normal flow refugees."[16]

On the domestic side, refugees already within the United States seek permission to remain in the United States, much like those seeking relief from removal before the immigration courts. These individuals are often referred to as "asylum-seekers." In order to be granted asylum in the United States, asylum-seekers must also demonstrate that they meet the definition of "refugee" under the INA.[17] There are two main ways to claim asylum in the United States:[18] affirmatively, by submitting an

---

15. *See* INA § 207(a) (providing for the admission of refugees who apply for admission from outside the United States); *id.* § 101(a)(42)(A) (delineating the contours of refugee classification).

16. *Id.* § 207(a)(1); *id.* § 207(b) (articulating that certain refugees may be designated as emergency flow refugees if their admission is justified by "grave humanitarian concerns" or if their admission is "otherwise in the national interest").

17. *Id.* § 101(a)(42)(A).

18. There are different procedures for individuals who seek asylum and withholding of removal at the border or from detention, involving credible and reasonable fear interviews by asylum officers in order to avoid expedited removal from the United States. If the asylum officer finds that these individuals have a credible or reasonable fear, they are permitted to present their claims in asylum or withholding of removal only proceedings before an immigration judge. This chapter does not discuss these procedures.

application to the Department of Homeland Security, U.S. Citizenship and Immigration Services, or defensively, by submitting or renewing an application before the U.S. Department of Justice, Executive Office for Immigration Review, United States Immigration Courts while subject to removal proceedings.

Accordingly, while these two separate groups of individuals must meet very similar legal requirements derived from the same sources of law, different procedures are required. This chapter will focus on the domestic side of asylum law involving asylum-seekers, or individuals who are seeking protection from persecution while already in U.S. territory.

ASYLUM UNDER INA § 208(A)

The Attorney General may, in his or her discretion, grant asylum to an individual who qualifies as a "refugee" within the meaning of section 101(a)(42) of the INA.[19] This discretion extends to Department of Homeland Security officials.[20] Under the INA, a refugee is defined as any person outside his or her country of nationality, or if stateless, outside his or her country of habitual residence, who, because of a "well-founded fear of persecution on account of race, religion, nationality, membership in a particular social group or political opinion," is unable or unwilling to return to or avail him or herself of the protection of that country.[21] This definition incorporates the refugee standard developed in the Refugee Protocol.[22] An asylee is an individual who meets this definition of "refugee" and is physically present in the United States at the time he or she seeks protection.[23]

Country of Nationality or Habitual Residence

Since an individual must first show that he or she is outside his or her country of nationality and that his or her claim of persecution originates in that country,[24] a threshold question in determining eligibility

---

19. INA § 208(b).

20. *See generally* Homeland Security Act of 2002, Pub. L. No. 107-296, 116 Stat. 2135, 2200, 2310, 2311 (2000).

21. INA § 101(a)(42)(A).

22. Refugee Protocol, *supra* note 9.

23. INA § 208(a).

24. United Nations High Commissioner for Refugees, Handbook on Procedures and Criteria for Determining Refugee Status ¶ 90 (1992), *available at* http://www.unhcr.org/3d58e13b4.html [hereinafter UNHCR Handbook].

for asylum is the individual's nationality, or if the individual is stateless, the individual's country of last habitual residence.[25] "Nationality" refers to the individual's citizenship or state of permanent allegiance,[26] while "last habitual residence" is defined as a "place of general abode" or the individual's "principal, actual dwelling place in fact, without regard to intent."[27]

Once the country of nationality is established, the asylum applicant must demonstrate that he or she is unable or unwilling to return to, or unable or unwilling to avail himself or herself of, the protection of that country because of persecution or a well-founded fear of persecution.[28] An applicant's fear of return and refusal of their own government's protection is what makes him or her "unwilling" to return to the country in question, while circumstances beyond the will of the applicant or a refusal of protection by the government in question are what make him or her "unable" to avail him or herself of the protection of that country.[29]

Persecution

The applicant's inability or refusal to return to his or her country of nationality or habitual residence must stem from a "well-founded fear of persecution."[30] To meet the requirements of this standard, the applicant must first show that the harm experienced or feared amounts to "persecution."[31] "Persecution" is a broad term that is not defined in the INA; however, case law has defined persecution as "a threat to the life or freedom of, or the infliction of suffering or harm upon, those who differ in a way regarded as offensive."[32] Persecution may encompass more

---

25. Wangchuck v. DHS, 448 F.3d 524, 528 (2d Cir. 2006); Dhoumo v. BIA, 416 F.3d 172, 173 (2d Cir. 2005). *See also* Asylum Officer Basic Training Course, *Lesson: Asylum Eligibility Part I*, at 13 (Mar. 6, 2009), *available at* http://www.uscis.gov/USCIS/Humanitarian/Refugees%20 &%20Asylum/Asylum/AOBTC%20Lesson%20Plans/Definition-Refugee-Persecution-Eligi blity-31aug10.pdf [hereinafter AOBTC].
26. INA § 101(a)(22).
27. *Id.* § 101(a)(33).
28. *Id.* § 101(a)(42).
29. UNHCR HANDBOOK, *supra* note 24, ¶ 98-100.
30. INA § 101(a)(42)(a).
31. AOBTC, *supra* note 25, at 16.
32. Matter of Acosta, 19 I. & N. Dec. 211, 222 (B.I.A. 1985). *See also* Li v. Att'y Gen. of the U.S., 400 F.3d 157, 164–68 (3d Cir. 2005); Matter of Kasinga, 21 I. & N. Dec. 357, 365 (B.I.A. 1996) (holding that persecution is the infliction of harm or suffering by a government, or by persons a government is unwilling and unable to control, to overcome a characteristic of the victim).

than threats to life or freedom.[33] Some examples of persecution include human rights violations, such as genocide; slavery; torture and other cruel, inhuman, or degrading treatment; prolonged detention without notice of and an opportunity to contest the grounds for detention; and rape and other severe forms of sexual violence.[34] There is no requirement that the individual have suffered serious injuries, and in fact, persecution does not have to be physical.[35] In some circumstances, serious threats made against the applicant,[36] cumulative instances of harassment or discrimination considered in totality,[37] or even the violation of an applicant's fundamental beliefs may constitute persecution.[38] Nonphysical harm that amounts to persecution may also include psychological harm,[39] harm to family members or other third parties,[40] or "the deliberate imposition of severe economic disadvantage or the deprivation of liberty, food, housing, employment or other essentials of life."[41] However, the harm suffered must be more than mere harassment or discrimination in order to amount to persecution.[42] Moreover, generalized conditions of hardship that affect entire populations,[43] as well as treatment that society regards as unfair, unjust, or unlawful[44] generally does not constitute persecution.

---

33. INS v. Stevic, 467 U.S. 407 (1984).

34. AOBTC, *supra* note 25, at 22.

35. *See* Matter of T-Z-, 24 I. & N. Dec. 163, 169–71 (B.I.A. 2007). *See also* Singh v. INS, 134 F.3d 962, 967 (9th Cir. 1998); Borca v. INS, 77 F.3d 210, 215–17 (7th Cir. 1996).

36. Salazar-Paucar v. INS, 281 F.3d 1069, 1074 (9th Cir. 2002), *amended by* 290 F.3d 264 (9th Cir. 2002).

37. Chand v. INS, 222 F.3d 1066, 1073 (9th Cir. 2000); Korablina v. INS, 158 F.3d 1038, 1045 (9th Cir. 1998); Singh v. INS, 94 F.3d 1353, 1360 (9th Cir. 1996); Matter of O-Z- & I-Z-, 22 I. & N. Dec. 23 (B.I.A. 1998).

38. Fatin v. INS, 12 F.3d 1233, 1242 (3d Cir. 1993).

39. Matter of A-K-, 24 I. & N. Dec. 275 (B.I.A. 2007). *See also* Mashiri v. Ashcroft, 383 F.3d 1112 (9th Cir. 2004); Khup v. Ashcroft, 376 F.3d 898, 904 (9th Cir. 2004). *But see* Shoaira v. Ashcroft, 377 F.3d 837, 844 (8th Cir. 2004).

40. A-K-, 24 I. & N. Dec. at 278 (recognizing that harm to a third party may constitute persecution of the applicant where the harm is serious enough to amount to persecution and the persecutor's motive in harming the third party was to cause harm to the applicant).

41. Matter of Laipenieks, 18 I. & N. Dec. 433, 456–57 (B.I.A. 1983), *rev'd on other grounds*, 750 F.2d 1427 (9th Cir. 1985).

42. Matter of A-E-M-, 21 I. & N. Dec. 1157, 1159 (B.I.A. 1998). *See also* Ivanishvili v. Gonzales, 433 F.3d 332, 340 (2d Cir. 2006); Sahi v. Gonzales, 416 F.3d 587, 589 (7th Cir. 2005); Mikhailevitch v. INS, 146 F.3d 384, 390 (6th Cir. 1998); Balazoski v. INS, 932 F.2d 638, 642 (7th Cir. 1991).

43. Capric v. Ashcroft, 355 F.3d 1075, 1084 (7th Cir. 2004).

44. Fatin v. INS, 12 F.3d 1233, 1240 (3d Cir. 1993).

Past Persecution

If the harm suffered or feared amounts to persecution, the applicant must then present evidence of either past persecution that he or she has already suffered, or evidence that his or her fear of future persecution is "well-founded."[45] Past persecution is sufficient in and of itself to establish eligibility for asylum.[46] When an individual shows that he or she has suffered past persecution, there is a rebuttable presumption that he or she also has a well-founded fear of future persecution.[47] This presumption may be rebutted if a "preponderance of the evidence establishes that since the time the persecution occurred conditions in the applicant's country of nationality have changed to such an extent that the applicant no longer has a well-founded fear of being persecuted if she were to return,"[48] or if it is shown that the applicant could reasonably be expected to relocate safely to another part of the country.[49]

However, for cases involving certain forms of past persecution, where the harm is "permanent and continuing," the presumption of well-founded fear of future persecution cannot be rebutted.[50] Likewise, even if there has been a fundamental change in the country conditions, and even if internal relocation is an option for the applicant, the adjudicator may still grant asylum to the applicant if "the applicant has demonstrated compelling reasons for being unwilling or unable to return to the country arising out of the severity of the past persecution" or if "the applicant has established that there is a reasonable possibility that he or she may suffer other serious harm upon removal to that country."[51] In other words, a favorable exercise of the adjudicator's discretion may be warranted for humanitarian reasons, even if future persecution is unlikely.[52] A grant of asylum under these circumstances is often referred to as "humanitarian asylum."

---

45. *See, e.g.,* Matter of Chen, 20 I. & N. Dec. 16, 18 (B.I.A. 1989).
46. 8 C.F.R. § 208.13(b)(1)(i). *See also* Matter of H-, 21 I. & N. Dec. 337, 345–46 (B.I.A. 1996); Matter of D-V-, 21 I. & N. Dec. 77, 79–80 (B.I.A. 1995); *Chen,* 20 I. & N. Dec. at 18–19.
47. 8 C.F.R. § 208.13(b)(1)(i).
48. *Id. See also* Matter of H-, Int. Dec. 3276 at 15, 24 (B.I.A. 1995).
49. Balliu v. Gonzales, 467 F.3d 609, 612 (7th Cir. 2006); Un v. Gonzales, 415 F.3d 205, 209 (1st Cir. 2005).
50. Matter of Y-T-L-, 23 I. & N. Dec. 601 (B.I.A. 2003). *See* Mohammad v. Gonzales, 400 F.3d 785, 799–800 (9th Cir. 2005). *But see* Matter of A-T-, 24 I. & N. Dec. 296, 299–301 (B.I.A. 2007).
51. 8 C.F.R. § 208.13(b)(1)(iii).
52. Matter of Chen, 20 I. & N. Dec. 16, 19 (B.I.A. 1989).

Well-Founded Fear of Future Persecution

An applicant need not have suffered past persecution in order to qualify for asylum, as long as he or she is able to show a well-founded fear of future persecution.[53] To demonstrate a well-founded fear, the applicant must show that there is a "reasonable possibility" of persecution,[54] which the U.S. Supreme Court has quantified in its decision in *INS v. Cardoza-Fonseca*.[55] The Court stated, "One can certainly have a well-founded fear of an event happening when there is less than a 50% chance of the occurrence taking place," and suggested that even a 10 percent chance of persecution may amount to a "reasonable possibility" of persecution.[56] In order to prevail on a fear of future persecution claim, the applicant must show that a reasonable person in his or her circumstances would fear persecution if removed to his or her home country.[57] Thus, the determination of whether a fear is well-founded does not rest on probability of persecution, but rather, on whether the fear is based on facts that would lead a reasonable person in similar circumstances to fear persecution.[58]

In order to be "well-founded," an asylum-seeker's fear must be both "subjectively genuine" and "objectively reasonable" given the conditions in his or her home country.[59] An applicant's "candid, credible and sincere testimony demonstrating a genuine fear of persecution satisfies the subjective component,"[60] while the objective component requires "credible, direct and specific evidence in the record, of facts that would support *reasonable* fear that the applicant faces persecution."[61] "[S]o long as an objective situation is established by the evidence, it need not be shown that the situation will probably result in persecution, but it is enough that persecution is a reasonable possibility."[62]

The Board of Immigration Appeals (BIA) in *Matter of Mogharrabi* set forth its test for determining whether an applicant for asylum has

---

53. INA § 101(a)(42).

54. 8 C.F.R. § 208.13(b)(2)(i)(B).

55. INS v. Cardoza-Fonseca, 480 U.S. 421, 431 (1987).

56. *Id.* at 440. *See also* Diallo v. INS, 232 F.3d 279, 284 (2d Cir. 2000) (finding that a fear may be well-founded "even if there is only a slight, though discernible, chance of persecution").

57. Matter of Mogharrabi, 19 I. & N. Dec. 439, 445 (B.I.A. 1987).

58. *Id.*

59. *Id.*; 8 C.F.R. § 208.13(b)(2).

60. Berroteran-Melendez v. INS, 955 F.2d 1251, 1256 (9th Cir. 1992) (citation omitted). *See also* Matter of Acosta, 19 I. & N. Dec. 211 (B.I.A. 1985); UNHCR Handbook, *supra* note 24, ¶ 39.

61. Berroteran-Melendez v. INS, 955 F.2d 1251, 1256 (9th Cir. 1992) (emphasis in original).

62. INS v. Stevic, 467 U.S. 407, 424–25 (1984). *See* 8 C.F.R. § 208.13(b)(2)(i)(B).

a well-founded fear of future persecution.[63] To establish a well-founded fear of persecution, the applicant must demonstrate: (1) that he or she possesses a belief or characteristic that the persecutor seeks to overcome; (2) that the persecutor is already aware, or could become aware, that the applicant possesses this belief or characteristic; (3) that the persecutor has the capability of punishing the applicant;[64] and (4) that the persecutor has the inclination to punish the applicant.[65]

Some important considerations that can significantly impact the well-founded fear analysis include whether the applicant could avoid persecution by relocating to another part of the country "if under all circumstances it would be reasonable to expect the applicant to do so,"[66] the amount of time that the applicant spent in the country following persecution,[67] whether the applicant ever returned to the country of persecution following the harm suffered,[68] and whether there is a pattern or practice of persecution.[69] An applicant need not show that he or she will be singled out individually for persecution if the applicant shows that (1) there is a pattern or practice of persecution on account of any of the protected grounds against a group or category of persons similarly situated to the applicant;[70] and (2) the applicant belongs to or is identified with the persecuted group, so that a reasonable person in the applicant's position would fear persecution.[71]

---

63. Matter of Mogharrabi, 19 I. & N. Dec. 439, 446 (B.I.A. 1987).

64. Some factors to be considered in evaluating capability are whether the persecutor is the government; if nongovernmental, whether the government is unwilling or unable to control the persecutor; and the extent to which the government has the ability to enforce its will throughout the country. *See* AOBTC, *Lesson: Asylum Eligibility Part II*, at 7 (Mar. 13, 2009).

65. Some factors to be considered in evaluating inclination are any previous threats or harm from the persecutor and the persecutor's treatment of individuals similarly situated to the applicant. *See* AOBTC, *Lesson: Asylum Eligibility Part II*, at 7 (Mar. 13, 2009).

66. 8 C.F.R. § 208.13(b)(2)(ii); Matter of C-A-L-, 21 I. & N. Dec. 754 (B.I.A. 1997); Matter of Acosta, 19 I. & N. Dec. 211 (B.I.A. 1985); UNHCR HANDBOOK, *supra* note 24, ¶ 91.

67. Castillo v. INS, 951 F.2d 1117 (9th Cir. 1991). *See also* Li v. Ashcroft, 396 F.3d 530 (3d Cir. 2005).

68. Rodriguez v. INS, 841 F.2d 865 (9th Cir. 1987). *See also* Damaize-Job v. INS, 787 F.2d 1332 (9th Cir. 1986).

69. 8 C.F.R. § 208.13(b)(2)(iii).

70. *Id.* § 208.13(b)(2)(iii)(A).

71. *Id.* § 208.13(b)(2)(iii)(B).

Nexus: Persecution on Account of a Protected Ground

In addition to establishing a well-founded fear of persecution, the applicant must show that the persecution suffered or feared is "on account of," or motivated by, one of the enumerated statutory grounds: race, religion, nationality, membership in a particular social group, or political opinion.[72] This element is often referred to as the "nexus" requirement, which necessitates that the applicant provide at least some evidence of the persecutor's motive, "either direct or circumstantial."[73] This requires an examination of the persecutor's views of the applicant.[74] However, ultimately, it is not the persecutor's subjective intent that is relevant, but rather, the objective persecution.[75] If an asylum applicant is unable to prove that his or her persecutor was or would be motivated by one of the five enumerated grounds, the application will be denied.

However, the applicant is not expected to prove the exact motivation of his or her persecutor, and courts have recognized that a persecutor may have mixed motive.[76] In mixed motive cases, the applicant must "establish that race, religion, nationality, membership in a particular social group, or political opinion was or will be *at least one central reason* for persecuting the applicant."[77] This standard was enacted as part of the REAL ID Act of 2005 and applies to all asylum applications filed on or after May 11, 2005.[78] In *Matter of J-B-N- & S-M-*, the BIA provided clarification of the "one central reason" standard, holding that Congress "purposely did not require that the protected ground be *the* central reason for the actions of the persecutors," but rather, that there be a nexus between the persecutor's motives and one of the enumerated grounds.[79] In *Matter of S-P-*, the Board of Immigration Appeals listed five factors to consider in determining the motive of the persecutor: (1) indications that the abuse was directed toward modifying a perceived political view or punishing a criminal act; (2) treatment of others in similar circumstances; (3) conformity to procedures for criminal prosecutions or military law; (4) the extent to which antiterrorism laws are defined and apply to suppress

---

72. INS v. Elias-Zacarias, 502 U.S. 478 (1992).

73. *Id.* at 483. *See also* Matter of J-B-N- & S-M-, 24 I. & N. Dec. 208, 214 (B.I.A. 2007) (finding that the burden of proof for the persecutor's motive may be met by testimonial evidence).

74. *Elias-Zacarias*, 502 U.S. 478.

75. Pitcherskaia v. INS, 118 F.3d 641 (9th Cir. 1997).

76. Matter of Fuentes, 19 I. & N. Dec. 658, 662 (B.I.A. 1988).

77. INA § 208(b)(1)(B)(i) (emphasis added).

78. REAL ID Act of 2005, Pub. L. No. 109-13, 119 Stat. 302 (May 11, 2005) [hereinafter REAL ID Act].

79. Matter of J-B-N- & S-M-, 24 I. & N. Dec. 208, 212–13 (B.I.A. 2007).

political opinion as well as illegal conduct; and (5) the extent to which suspected political opponents are subjected to arbitrary arrest, detention, and abuse.[80] Mixed motive can be established by "direct or circumstantial evidence"; however, the protected ground cannot be "incidental, tangential, superficial, or subordinate to another reason for harm."[81]

Race, Religion, and Nationality

The first statutory enumerated ground for persecution, race, is interpreted in its widest sense to include "all kinds of ethnic groups that are referred to as 'races' in common usage."[82] According to UNHCR, "Discrimination for reasons of race has found world-wide condemnation as one of the most striking violations of human rights" and "will frequently amount to persecution in the sense of the 1951 Convention."[83] Persecution on account of religion, the second statutory enumerated ground, may assume various forms, including the prohibition of membership in a religious community, of worship or observance in private or in public, of religious instruction, of religious conversion, or serious measures of discrimination imposed on persons because they practice their religion or belong to a particular religious community.[84] Nationality, the third enumerated ground, refers to an individual's citizenship, but also, to membership in an ethnic or linguistic group. Occasionally, it may overlap with the grounds of "race"[85] or even political opinion.[86] As the UNHCR Handbook notes, "The co-existence within the boundaries of a State of two or more national (ethnic, linguistic) groups may create situations of conflict and also situations of persecution or danger of persecution."[87]

Membership in a Particular Social Group

Perhaps the most complicated ground for asylum is the fourth ground, "membership in a particular social group."[88] According to the UNHCR, "A 'particular social group' normally comprises persons of similar background,

---

80. Matter of S-P-, 21 I. & N. Dec. 486, 494 (B.I.A. 1996).

81. J-B-N- & S-M-, 24 I. & N. Dec. at 214.

82. UNHCR Handbook, *supra* note 24, ¶ 68; AOBTC, *Lesson: Asylum Eligibility Part III*, at 15 (Mar. 12, 2009).

83. UNHCR Handbook, *supra* note 24, ¶¶ 68–69.

84. *Id.* ¶¶ 71–72.

85. *Id.* ¶ 74.

86. *Id.* ¶ 75 (noting that "nationality" frequently intersects with persecution on account of "political opinion," especially when a particular nationality, ethnic, or linguistic group in a country shares the same political position).

87. *Id.*

88. INA § 101(a)(42)(A).

habits or social status."[89] Social group asylum claims typically involve persecution of a group because the government has no confidence in the group's loyalty to the regime, or the group is held to be an obstacle to the government's policies in some way.[90] In presenting evidence of persecution based on membership in a particular social group, the asylum-seeker must identify the group, prove membership in that group, and then establish persecution or well-founded fear of persecution based on that membership.

"Particular social group" is not defined in the INA or the federal regulations. Rather, it has been defined by case law. In the seminal case of *Matter of Acosta*, the BIA defined particular social group to be "persons all of whom share a common, immutable characteristic," and clarified that particular social group is to be determined on a case-by-case basis.[91] However, the characteristic that defines the group "must be one that the members of the group either cannot change, or should not be required to change because it is fundamental to their individual identities or consciences."[92] The BIA further explained that the shared characteristic "might be innate, like sex, color, or kinship ties, or it might be a shared past experience such as former military leadership or land ownership."[93] Some examples of accepted social groups defined by immutable or fundamental characteristics include sexual orientation or sexual identity;[94] family;[95] clan membership;[96] land ownership and education;[97] and former status, occupation, or experience.[98]

In recent years, the BIA has added further requirements to the particular social group analysis, including "social distinction" and "particularity."[99] Social distinction is generally understood to require that the group be

---

89. UNHCR Handbook, *supra* note 24, ¶ 77.

90. *Id.* ¶ 78.

91. Matter of Acosta, 19 I. & N. Dec. 211, 233 (B.I.A. 1985).

92. *Id.*

93. *Id.*

94. Matter of Toboso-Alfonso, 20 I. & N. Dec. 819 (A.G. 1994). *See also* Karouni v. Gonzales, 399 F.3d 1163 (9th Cir. 2005); Amfani v. Ashcroft, 328 F.3d 719 (3d Cir. 2003); Hernandez-Montiel v. INS, 225 F.3d 1084 (9th Cir. 2000).

95. Lwin v. INS, 144 F.3d 505 (7th Cir. 1998); Gebremichael v. INS, 10 F.3d 28 (1st Cir. 1993).

96. Matter of H-, 21 I. & N. Dec. 337 (B.I.A. 1996).

97. Tapiero de Orjuela v. Gonzales, 423 F.3d 666 (7th Cir. 2005).

98. Benitez-Ramos v. Holder, 589 F.3d 426 (7th Cir. 2009); Sepulveda v. Gonzales, 464 F.3d 770 (7th Cir. 2006); Lukwago v. Ashcroft, 329 F.3d 157 (3d Cir. 2003).

99. Matter of M-E-V-G-, 26 I. & N. Dec. 227 (B.I.A. 2014), and Matter of W-G-R-, 26 I. & N. Dec. 208 (B.I.A. 2014), clarifying Matter of E-A-G-, 24 I. & N. Dec. 591 (B.I.A. 2008), Matter of S-E-G-, 24 I. & N. Dec. 579 (B.I.A. 2008), Matter of A-M-E- & J-G-U-, 24 I. & N. Dec. 69 (B.I.A. 2007), and Matter of C-A-, 23 I. & N. Dec. 951 (B.I.A. 2006).

perceived and recognized as a group by society.[100] It does not mean "ocular" visibility.[101] Particularity refers to the group being sufficiently distinct that it would constitute a discrete class of persons with definable boundaries.[102] Groups that are perceived as being too overbroad, too diffuse, too amorphous, or too subjective have been rejected as particular social groups.[103] Social distinction and particularity must be analyzed in the "context of the country of concern and the persecution feared."[104] Most circuits adopted the BIA's previous social visibility (now social distinction) and particularity requirements;[105] however, the Seventh Circuit rejected both, pointing out that members of many targeted groups "take pains to avoid being socially visible."[106] Now that the BIA has renamed social visibility as "social distinction" and clarified this and its "particularity" requirements, it is yet to be seen how the circuit courts will respond in review.

Perhaps because of these added requirements to the particular social group analysis, there are several lines of unsettled particular social group jurisprudence which have yielded a significant amount of case law in recent years. Two of the most debated are gender-based claims, involving victims of female genital cutting, domestic violence, and forced marriage,[107] and gang-based claims, involving victims of forced recruit-

---

100. *M-E-V-G-*, 26 I. & N. Dec. at 240–43; *W-G-R-*, 26 I. & N. Dec. at 215–18. *See also* Matter of C-A-, 23 I. & N. Dec. 951 (B.I.A. 2006).

101. *M-E-V-G-*, 26 I. & N. Dec. at 227; *W-G-R-*, 26 I. & N. Dec. at 208.

102. *M-E-V-G-*, 26 I. & N. Dec. at 239–40; *W- G- R-*, 26 I. & N. Dec. at 213–15.

103. *Id. See also* C-A-, 23 I. & N. Dec. 951, S-E-G-, 24 I. & N. Dec. 579; A-M-E- & J-G-U-, 24 I. & N. Dec. 69.

104. A-M-E- & J-G-U-, 24 I. & N. Dec. 69.

105. Umana-Ramos v. Holder, 724 F.3d 667, 671 (6th Cir. 2013); Orellana-Monson v. Holder, 685 F.3d 511, 521 (5th Cir. 2012); Gaitan v. Holder, 671 F.3d 678, 681 (8th Cir. 2012); Rivera-Barrientos v. Holder, 666 F.3d 641, 649–53 (10th Cir. 2012); Scatambuli v. Holder, 558 F.3d 53 (1st Cir. 2009); Ramos Lopez v. Holder, 563 F.3d 855 (9th Cir. 2009); Davila-Mejia v. Mukasey, 531 F.3d 624 (8th Cir. 2008); Koudriachova v. Gonzales, 490 F.3d 255 (2d Cir. 2007). *But see* Valdiviezo-Galdamez v. Att'y Gen. of U.S., 663 F.3d 582 (3d Cir. 2011); Perdomo v. Holder, 611 F.3d 662 (9th Cir. 2010) (describing social visibility and particularity as "factors to consider" rather than requirements); Gatimi v. Holder, 578 F.3d 611, 615–16 (7th Cir. 2009) (rejecting the social visibility requirement); Castillo-Arias v. U.S. Att'y Gen., 446 F.3d 1190 (11th Cir. 2006).

106. Gatimi v. Holder, 578 F.3d 611 (7th Cir. 2009); Benitez-Ramos v. Holder, 589 F.3d 426 (7th Cir. 2009).

107. Bah v. Gonzales, 462 F.3d 637, 643 (6th Cir. 2006); Abebe v. Gonzales, 432 F.3d 1037, 1043 (9th Cir. 2005); Mohammad v. Gonzales, 400 F.3d 785, 795–96 (9th Cir. 2005); Niang v. Gonzales, 422 F.3d 1187, 1189 (10th Cir. 2005); Abay v. Ashcroft, 368 F.3d 634, 641–42 (6th Cir. 2004); Kebede v. Ashcroft, 366 F.3d 808, 811 (9th Cir. 2004); Abankwah v. INS, 185 F.3d 18, 23–24 (2d Cir. 1999); Matter of A-K-, 24 I. & N. Dec. 275 (B.I.A. 2007); Matter of A-T-, 24 I. & N. Dec. 296, 299–301 (B.I.A. 2007); Matter of Kasinga, 21 I. & N. Dec. 357, 365 (B.I.A. 1996);

ment, extortion, and gang violence targeted at prosecution witnesses, family members, former gang members, and males of certain socioeconomic classes.[108] As applicants and their advocates continue to fight for the protection of these groups despite the challenges involved, the legal standards for establishing persecution on account of membership in a particular social group remain unsettled.

Political Opinion

Persecution on account of the fifth enumerated ground, political opinion, means "persecution on account of the *victim's* political opinion, not the persecutor's."[109] Political opinion encompasses more than just political ideology or action, as it requires adjudicators to consider the claim within the context of the country itself.[110] According to the UNHCR, political opinions are "opinions not tolerated by the authorities, which are critical of their policies or methods."[111] A person may express his or her political opinion or

---

Matter of D-V-, 21 I. & N. Dec. 77, 78–79 (B.I.A. 1993). *See also* Gao v. Gonzales, 440 F.3d 62, 70–71 (2d Cir. 2006); Yadegar-Sargis v. INS, 297 F.3d 596 (7th Cir. 2002); Fatin v. INS, 79 F.3d 955 (9th Cir. 1996); Sharif v. INS, 87 F.3d 932 (7th Cir. 1996); Safaie v. INS, 25 F.3d 636, 640 (8th Cir. 1994); Matter of R-A-, 24 I. & N. Dec. 629 (A.G. 2008); Matter of R-A-, 22 I. & N. Dec. 906 (A.G. 2001); Matter of S-A-, 22 I. & N. Dec. 1328, 1335 (B.I.A. 2000). The Center for Gender and Refugee Studies has legal expertise and many resources available to attorneys representing women fleeing gender-based violence. *See generally* Center for Gender and Refugee Studies, http://cgrs.uchastings.edu/ (last visited Oct. 28, 2011).

108. W-G-R-, 26 I. & N. Dec. 208; S-E-G-, 24 I. & N. Dec. 579; Matter of E-A-G-, 24 I. & N. Dec. 591 (B.I.A. 2008); *C-A-*, 23 I. & N. Dec. 951. *See also* Martinez v. Holder (4th Cir., Jan. 24, 2014 revised); Henriquez-Rivas v. Holder, 2013 WL 518048 (9th Cir. 2013); *Gaitan,* 671 F.3d 678; *Orellana-Monson,* 685 F.3d 511; Garcia-Callegas v. Holder, 666 F.3d 828 (1st Cir. 2012); *Valdiviezo-Galdamez,* 663 F.3d 582; Uzama v. Holder, 629 F.3d 440 (4th Cir. 2011); Rivera-Barrientos v. Holder, 658 F.3d 1222 (10th Cir. 2011); Escobar v. Holder, 657 F.3d 537 (7th Cir. 2011); Crespin v. Holder, 632 F.3d 117 (4th Cir. 2011); Martinez-Seren v. Holder, 2010 WL 3452840 (9th Cir. 2010); Bonilla-Morales v. Holder, 607 F.3d 1132 (6th Cir. 2010); Urbina-Mejia v. Holder, 597 F.3d 360 (6th Cir. 2010); Soriano v. Holder, 569 F.3d 1162 (9th Cir. 2009); *Benitez Ramos,* 589 F.3d 426; *Gatimi,* 578 F.3d 611; *Scatambuli,* 558 F.3d 53; Quinteros-Mendoza v. Holder, 556 F.3d 159 (4th Cir. 2009); Amilcar-Orellana v. Mukasey, 551 F.3d 86 (1st Cir. 2008); Arteaga v. Mukasey, 511 F.3d 940 (9th Cir. 2007); Shehu v. U.S. Att'n'y Gen., 482 F.3d 652 (3d Cir. 2007); Ucelo-Gomez v. Mukasey, 509 F.3d 70 (2d Cir. 2007).

109. INS v. Elias-Zacarias, 502 U.S. 478, 482 (1992) (emphasis in original).

110. Castro v. Holder, 597 F.3d 93, 102–06 (2d Cir. 2010) (stating that the immigration judge failed to consider the claim of a Guatemalan police officer who reported drug corruption within the police within the "context" and "backdrop of Guatemala's volatile political history"); Ahmed v. Keisler, 504 F.3d 1183, 1193–98 (9th Cir. 2007).

111. UNHCR HANDBOOK, *supra* note 24, ¶ 80. The U.S. government recognized a specific situation of intolerance of individuals for their critique of a government's policies, by amending the definition of refugee in 1996 to provide protection to individuals who have

beliefs through actions as well as words.[112] Unexpressed political opinions or beliefs may also be grounds for asylum if the persecutor could become aware of those opinions or beliefs.[113] Even neutrality may be a political opinion, particularly if it is shown that it was a conscious choice of the applicant and that the persecution was motivated by that neutrality.[114]

Political opinions can also be "imputed" to an applicant. Persecution based on a political opinion that the applicant is erroneously believed to hold can also warrant a grant of asylum.[115] In fact, U.S. Citizenship and Immigration Services (USCIS) has taken the position that any of the five protected grounds for asylum may be imputed to an asylum applicant, thus warranting a grant of asylum. When an individual is persecuted or fears persecution due to an imputed characteristic related to the five protected grounds, the persecution may be on account of that ground even if the applicant does not actually possess that characteristic.[116]

Persecution at the Hands of the Government or a Group That the Government Is Unable or Unwilling to Control

Once an asylum-seeker demonstrates past persecution or a well-founded fear of persecution on account of one of the enumerated statutory grounds, he or she must then show that the persecution suffered or feared is by

---

suffered or who fear persecution because of their resistance to coercive population control measures in their home countries. These individuals are deemed to have been persecuted or to fear persecution on account of their political opinion. *See* INA § 101(a)(42)(B). *See also* Matter of G-C-L-, 23 I. & N. Dec. 359, 361–62 (B.I.A. 2002); Matter of C-Y-Z-, 21 I. & N. Dec. 915, 919–20 (B.I.A. 1997); Matter of X-P-T-, 21 I. & N. Dec. 634, 638 (B.I.A. 1996). China's one-child policy, forced sterilization, and forced abortion have all been found to be coercive population control measures.

112. Chang v. INS, 119 F.3d 1055, 1063 (3d. Cir. 1997) (holding that the applicant had expressed his political opinion through his actions in defying the orders of the Chinese government). *See also* Fedunyak v. Gonzales, 477 F.3d 1126, 1129 (9th Cir. 2007). *But see* Pavlyk v. Gonzales, 469 F.3d 1082, 1089 (7th Cir. 2006).

113. Matter of Mogharrabi, 19 I. & N. Dec. 439, 446 (B.I.A. 1987). *But see* Sharif v. INS, 87 F.3d 932, 935 (7th Cir. 1996).

114. *See, e.g.*, Rivera-Moreno v. INS, 213 F.3d 481, 483–84 (9th Cir. 2000); Umanzor-Alvarado v. INS, 896 F.2d 14, 15–16 (1st Cir. 1990); Arteaga v. INS, 863 F.2d 1227, 1231–32 (9th Cir. 1988). *See also* Sagarminaga v. INS, 113 F.3d 1247 (10th Cir. 1997); Lopez-Zeron v. U.S. Dept. of Justice, 8 F.3d 636 (8th Cir. 1993); Matter of Vigil, 19 I. & N. Dec. 572, 576–77 (B.I.A. 1988).

115. INS v. Elias-Zacarias, 502 U.S. 478 (1992); Hamdan v. Mukasey, 528 F.3d 986, 992–93 (7th Cir. 2008); Ahmed v. Keisler, 504 F.3d 1183, 1194–95 (9th Cir. 2007); Singh v. Gonzales, 406 F.3d 191, 196–97 (3d Cir. 2005). *See also* Matter of S-P-, 21 I. & N. Dec. 486, 497 (B.I.A. 1996).

116. AOBTC, *Lesson: Asylum Eligibility Part III: Nexus and the Five Protected Characteristics*, at 15–16 (Mar. 12, 2009), *available at* http://www.uscis.gov/USCIS/Humanitarian/Refugees %20&%20Asylum/Asylum/AOBTC%20Lesson%20Plans/Nexus-the-Five-Protected-Character istics-31aug10.pdf.

the government or a group that the government is unable or unwilling to control.[117] Government actors may include political leaders, military and intelligence forces, and members of the police or law enforcement. If the persecutor is not a government actor, the applicant must show that the government was unable or unwilling to control the persecutor, or in other words, that the government has not taken reasonable steps to provide meaningful protection to the applicant.[118] Asylum-seekers are not required to show that the government's refusal to protect them was on account of one of the protected grounds, only that the government was unable or unwilling to prevent the persecution.[119] If seeking protection from or reporting persecution to government authorities would be futile or would result in further abuse, the applicant is not expected or required to report abuse to government authorities.[120] On the other hand, if the applicant does report persecution to government authorities, and they provide a prompt response, it may be strong evidence that the government is, in fact, willing to protect the applicant.[121]

BARS TO ASYLUM

Even if the asylum-seeker is able to demonstrate eligibility for asylum according to the legal standards discussed above, there are various statutory bars to asylum that may prevent the adjudicator from being able to grant the application.[122] These bars to asylum include: (1) if the applicant ordered, incited, assisted or otherwise participated in the persecution of others;[123] (2) if the applicant has been convicted by a final judgment of a particularly serious crime in the United States, and therefore, constitutes a danger to the community;[124] (3) if there are serious reasons for believing that the applicant has committed a serious, nonpolitical crime

---

117. INA § 208(b)(1). *See Elias-Zacarias*, 502 U.S. at 481–83.

118. Aliyev v. Mukasey, 549 F.3d 111, 118–19 (2d Cir. 2008); Ngengwe v. Mukasey, 543 F.3d 1029, 1035–36 (8th Cir. 2008); Nabulwala v. Gonzales, 481 F.3d 1115 (8th Cir. 2007).

119. *See, e.g.*, Valdiviezo-Galdamez v. Att'y Gen. of the U.S., 502 F.3d 285, 288–89 (3d Cir. 2007).

120. Matter of S-A-, 22 I. & N. Dec. 1327, 1333–35 (B.I.A. 2000). *See also, e.g.*, Lopez v. Att'y Gen. of the U.S., 504 F.3d 1341, 1345 (11th Cir. 2007); Ornelas-Chavez v. Gonzales, 458 F.3d 1052, 1057 (9th Cir. 2006).

121. Ortiz-Araniba v. Keisler, 505 F.3d 39, 42 (1st Cir. 2007).

122. INA § 208(a)(2), (b)(2); 8 C.F.R. §§ 208.13(c)(1), 1208.13(c)(1).

123. INA §§ 101(a)(42)(B), 208(b)(2)(A)(i). This bar to asylum also applies to withholding of removal. *Id.* § 241(b)(3)(B)(i).

124. *Id.* § 208(b)(2)(A)(ii). If a conviction is an aggravated felony for which there is an aggregate term of imprisonment for five years, it is a conviction for a particularly serious crime and automatically bars a grant of asylum. *See* Matter of B-, 20 I. & N. Dec. 427 (B.I.A. 1991).

outside of the United States prior to his or her arrival;[125] (4) if there are reasonable grounds for regarding the alien as a danger to the security of the United States; (5) if the applicant is described as a terrorist or has given material support to a terrorist organization;[126] (6) if the applicant has firmly resettled in another country prior to his or her arrival in the United States;[127] (7) if there is a safe third country available to the applicant in which the applicant's life or freedom would not be threatened and where he or she would have access to full and fair procedures for determining asylum eligibility;[128] (8) if the applicant previously applied for and was denied asylum, unless the applicant demonstrates the existence of changed circumstances which materially affect the applicant's eligibility for asylum;[129] and (9) if the applicant did not file his or her application for asylum within one year of his or her arrival in the United States.[130]

There are two exceptions to the one-year filing deadline: (1) if the applicant demonstrates the existence of "changed circumstances" that materially affect his or her eligibility for asylum,[131] and (2) if the applicant demonstrates "extraordinary circumstances" relating to the delay in filing his or her application.[132] Examples of "changed circumstances" may include changes in the applicant's country of nationality; changes in the applicant's circumstances, including changes in applicable U.S. law and activities that the applicant becomes involved in outside of the country of persecution that place the applicant at risk; and if the applicant ages out, divorces, or becomes widowed, necessitating that he or she now file his or her own application.[133] Examples of "extraordinary circumstances" may include serious illness or mental or physical disability; legal disability; ineffective

---

125. INA § 208(b)(2)(A)(iii).

126. INA §§ 212(a)(3)(B)(i)(I)–(IV), (VI), 237(a)(4)(B). This bar is waivable under certain circumstances, including for persons who provided material support to terrorist organizations under duress. *See id.* § 212(d)(3)(B)(i); Memo, Chertoff, Secy. of DHS, Exercise of Authority under Sec. 212(d)(3)(B)(i) (Apr. 27, 2007).

127. 8 C.F.R. §§ 208.13(c)(2)(i)(B), 208.15. An applicant is deemed firmly resettled if he or she entered the country with, or while in the country received, an offer of permanent resident status, citizenship, or other type of permanent status. *See id.* §§ 208.15, 1208.15. The government has the burden of proving firm resettlement, and the applicant may rebut firm resettlement by demonstrating an exception under *id.* § 208.15(a)–(b).

128. INA § 208(a)(2)(A).

129. *Id.* § 208(a)(2)(C)–(D). This bar only applies if the applicant for asylum was issued a final order of removal. It does not apply if the previous application was denied only by the Asylum Office.

130. *Id.* § 208(a)(2)(B), (d); 8 C.F.R. § 208.4(a)(4)–(5).

131. *See* 8 C.F.R. §§ 208.4(a)(4), 1208.4(a)(4).

132. *See id.* §§ 208.4(a)(5), 1208.4(a)(5).

133. *See id.* §§ 208.4(a)(4), 1208.4(a)(4).

assistance of counsel; maintaining lawful immigrant or non-immigrant status and then losing that status; filing within one year but having USCIS reject the application as incomplete; and the death or serious illness or incapacity of the applicant's legal representative or a member of the applicant's immediate family.[134] In addition to demonstrating the presence of changed or extraordinary circumstances, the applicant must also show that he or she filed an application within a reasonable time of those circumstances.[135]

Even if the applicant demonstrates eligibility for relief and that no bars to asylum apply, an asylum application may also be denied in the exercise of discretion.[136] However, discretionary denials of asylum are rare, and generally require "egregious negative activity by the applicant."[137] In making a discretionary determination, the asylum adjudicator must balance the positive and negative factors and consider the "totality of the circumstances."[138] Overall, "[t]he danger of persecution should generally outweigh all but the most egregious of adverse factors."[139]

If an individual's asylum application is denied due to failure to meet the legal standards discussed above, due to one of the bars to asylum, or due to a negative exercise of discretion, he or she may still be eligible for other related forms of relief, such as withholding of removal under INA § 241(b)(3) or protection under the Convention Against Torture. The legal standards for these two forms of relief are discussed briefly below.

WITHHOLDING OF REMOVAL UNDER INA § 241(B)(3)

An application for asylum is automatically considered to be an application for withholding of removal.[140] Withholding of removal is a similar, but

---

134. *See id.* §§ 208.4(a)(5), 1208.4(a)(5).

135. *Id.* §§ 208.4(a)(4)–(5), 1208.4(a)(4)–(5).

136. INA § 208(a), (b)(1); 8 C.F.R. § 1208.14(a). *See* INS v. Cardoza-Fonseca, 480 U.S. 421, 423 (1987); Matter of A-H-, 23 I. & N. Dec. 774, 780–83 (A.G. 2005); Matter of Mogharrabi, 19 I. & N. Dec. 439, 449 (B.I.A. 1987).

137. Zuh v. Mukasey, 547 F.3d 504, 507–14 (4th Cir. 2008).

138. *Id.* at 511. Positive factors may include family, business, community, and employment ties to the United States, as well as length of residence and property ownership; evidence of hardship if deported, particularly if it would yield a lack of family reunification; evidence of service to the community and rehabilitation; general humanitarian considerations such as age and health; and other relief granted. *Id.* Negative factors may include the circumstances of any negative factors; significant violations of the immigration laws; the existence of a criminal record and the severity and recency of the record, including recidivism; lack of candor with immigration officials; and other bad character evidence or undesirability of the individual to be a resident. *Id.*

139. Matter of Pula, 19 I. & N. Dec. 467, 474 (B.I.A. 1987).

140. 8 C.F.R. § 1208.3(b).

more limited, form of relief. Rather than a grant of permission to remain in the United States, withholding of removal under INA § 241(b)(3) involves avoiding removal to the country of persecution, but not necessarily other countries. In fact, in order to grant withholding of removal, an immigration judge must first enter an order of removal against the applicant.[141] Additionally, an individual who is granted withholding of removal may be removed to a third country if he or she would not face persecution there and if the third country is willing to accept the individual.[142]

INA § 241(b)(3) is based on Article 33 of the Refugee Protocol, which places a mandatory prohibition against returning an individual to a country where his or her "life or freedom would be threatened."[143] Under the INA, the Attorney General may not remove a person to a country where his or her life or freedom would be threatened because of his or her race, religion, nationality, membership in a particular social group, or political opinion.[144] There are many similarities between asylum and withholding of removal. For instance, a finding of past persecution gives rise to a presumption that the individual's life or freedom would also be threatened in the future.[145] However, if past persecution is not established, applicants for withholding of removal must demonstrate a "clear probability" of persecution, or in other words, that it is "more likely than not" that he or she would be persecuted if removed to his or her home country.[146] This is a higher legal standard than the "reasonable possibility" standard required to demonstrate eligibility for asylum.[147] Also, unlike asylum, withholding of removal is not discretionary; if an applicant's life or freedom would be threatened in his or her home country on account of one of the enumerated grounds, withholding that individual's removal to that particular country is mandatory.[148]

A grant of withholding of removal is a more limited form of relief than asylum, because it does not necessarily confer a right on the applicant to remain in the United States, become a permanent resident, obtain many federally funded benefits, or bring his or her spouse and children to the United States. Asylum provides more permanent protection than withholding of removal, because an individual who is granted asylum may

---

141. Matter of I-S- & C-S-, 24 I. & N. Dec. 432 (B.I.A. 2008).
142. 8 C.F.R. §§ 208.16(f), 1208.16(f); INS v. Cardoza-Fonseca, 480 U.S. 421, 428 (1987); Choeum v. INS, 129 F.3d 29, 40 n.9 (1st Cir. 1997).
143. Refugee Protocol, *supra* note 9, art. 33.
144. INA § 241(b)(3)(A). *See* Popova v. INS, 273 F.3d 1251 (9th Cir. 2001); Leiva-Montalvo v. INS, 173 F.3d 749 (9th Cir. 1999).
145. 8 C.F.R. §§ 208.16(b)(1)(i), 1208.16(b)(1)(i).
146. *Cardoza-Fonseca*, 480 U.S. at 423; INS v. Stevic, 467 U.S. 407, 429–30 (1984).
147. *Cardoza-Fonseca*, 480 U.S. at 431; Niang v. Gonzales, 492 F.3d 505 (4th Cir. 2007); Capric v. Ashcroft, 355 F.3d 1075, 1095 (7th Cir. 2004); Lim v. INS, 224 F.3d 929, 938 (9th Cir. 2000).
148. *Cardoza-Fonseca*, 408 U.S. at 429.

apply for permanent resident status after one year of physical presence in the United States in asylee status,[149] and may eventually become a U.S. citizen. An asylee is often eligible for federally funded benefits, and may also bring his or her spouse and children to the United States as accompanying or following-to-join asylees, whereas an individual granted withholding of removal may not.[150] The core purpose of withholding of removal under INA § 241(b)(3) is simply to not return an individual to a specific country if their life or freedom would be threatened there.

Like asylum, there are certain bars to a grant of withholding of removal.[151] The removal of an individual whose life or freedom would be threatened will not be withheld in the following situations: (1) if the applicant was a Nazi or engaged in genocide;[152] (2) if the applicant ordered, incited, assisted or otherwise participated in the persecution of any person on account of race, religion, nationality, membership in a particular social group or political opinion;[153] (3) if the applicant has been convicted by a final judgment of a particularly serious crime, and thus constitutes a danger to the community;[154] (4) if there are serious reasons for considering that the individual has committed a serious, nonpolitical crime before his or her arrival in the United States;[155] and (5) if there are reasonable grounds to believe that the applicant is a danger to the security of the United States, which includes any individual described in INA § 237(a)(4)(B).[156]

PROTECTION UNDER THE CONVENTION AGAINST TORTURE

Another form of relief similar to asylum and withholding of removal under INA § 241(b)(3) is protection under the Convention Against

---

149. INA § 209.

150. 8 C.F.R. § 1208.21.

151. *See* INA § 241(b)(3)(B); 8 C.F.R. §§ 208.16(d)(2), 1208.16(d)(2).

152. These bars to withholding of removal under INA § 241(b)(3) are bars to withholding only, not to asylum.

153. *Id.* § 241(b)(3)(B)(i); Matter of A-H-, 23 I. & N. Dec. 774, 783–85 (A.G. 2005).

154. INA § 241(b)(3)(B)(ii); 8 C.F.R. §§ 208.16(d)(2), 1208.16(d)(2); Matter of N-A-M-, 24 I. & N. Dec. 336, 342–43 (B.I.A. 2007). Particularly serious crimes include aggravated felonies for which the individual was sentenced to an aggregate term of imprisonment of five years. *See* INA § 241(b)(3)(B); Matter of L-S-, 22 I. & N. Dec. 645 (B.I.A. 1999); Matter of S-S-, 22 I. & N. Dec. 458 (B.I.A. 1999). *See also* Matter of Y-L-, 23 I. & N. Dec. 270 (A.G. 2002).

155. INA § 241(b)(3)(B)(iii); Matter of McMullen, 19 I. & N. Dec. 90 (B.I.A. 1984).

156. INA § 241(b)(3)(B)(iv); *A-H-*, 23 I. & N. Dec. at, 787–90. As for asylum, this bar is waivable under certain circumstances, including for persons who provided material support to terrorist organizations under duress. *See* INA § 212(d)(3)(B)(i); Memo, Chertoff, Secy. of DHS, Exercise of Authority under Sec. 212(d)(3)(B)(i) (Apr. 27, 2007).

338   *What Every Lawyer Needs to Know about Immigration Law*

Torture.[157] It is the policy of the United States "not to expel, extradite, or otherwise effect the involuntary return of any person to a country in which there are substantial grounds for believing the person would be in danger of being subjected to torture."[158] "Torture" is defined as:

> any act by which severe pain or suffering, whether physical or mental, is intentionally inflicted on a person for such purposes as obtaining from him or her or a third person information or a confession, punishing him or her for an act he or she or a third person has committed or is suspected of having committed, or intimidating or coercing him or her or a third person, or for any reason based on discrimination of any kind.[159]

The BIA has defined torture as an act causing severe physical or mental pain or suffering that must be "an extreme form of cruel and inhuman treatment" and not lesser forms.[160] The act must be "specifically intended" to inflict severe physical or mental pain or suffering, and an act that results in unanticipated or unintended severity of pain or suffering does not constitute torture.[161] Additionally, the act must have an "illicit purpose" such as "obtaining information or a confession, punishment for a victim's or another's act, intimidating or coercing a victim or another, or any discriminatory purpose."[162] The act must be an intentional governmental act directed against a person in the offender's custody or control and "negligent acts or acts by private individuals not acting on behalf of the government" are not included within the definition of torture.[163] Finally, the act "does not include pain or suffering arising only from, inherent in, or incidental to lawful sanctions" such as a judicially imposed death penalty.[164] However, although "lawful sanctions" cannot be torture, a government cannot exempt itself from its obligations under the Convention Against Torture by defining acts that would constitute torture as lawful forms of punishment.[165]

---

157. *See generally* Convention Against Torture, *supra* note 12.
158. Fiscal Year 1999 Omnibus Consolidated and Emergency Supplemental Appropriations Act, Pub. L. No. 104-277, Div. G, Sub. B, Title XXI § 2242 of the Foreign Affairs Reform and Restructuring Act of 1998, 112 Stat. 2681-822, at ¶ 1.
159. 8 C.F.R. §§ 208.18(a)(1), 1208.18(a)(1).
160. Matter of J-E-, 23 I. & N. Dec. 291, 297–99 (B.I.A. 2002).
161. *Id.*
162. *Id.*
163. *Id.*
164. *Id.*
165. 8 C.F.R. §§ 208.18(a)(3), 1208.18(a)(3); Ghebrehiwot v. Attn'y Gen. of the U.S., 467 F.3d 344, 358–59 (3d Cir. 2006); Nuru v. Gonzales, 404 F.3d 1207, 1218–23 (9th Cir. 2005).

In sum, the six basic elements of torture include: (1) an intentional act; (2) the infliction of severe pain or suffering; (3) an applicant under the custody or control of the offender; (4) an act for one of many wrongful purposes, including obtaining information or a confession, punishment, intimidation, coercion, or discrimination; (5) an act sanctioned by a public official; and (6) an act not arising out of lawful sanctions.[166] Rape, murder, female genital cutting, and severe forms of psychological or mental harm, including threatened harm and being forced to watch or listen to harm being inflicted on others,[167] have been found to constitute torture.[168]

The legal standard for protection under the Convention Against Torture is the same as for withholding of removal under INA § 241(b)(3)—an individual should be granted protection under the Convention Against Torture if he or she shows that it is "more likely than not" that he or she will be subject to torture upon removal.[169] Also like withholding of removal under INA § 241(b)(3), a final order of removal must be entered against the applicant prior to granting protection under the Convention Against Torture.[170]

Protection under the Convention Against Torture differs from asylum and withholding of removal under INA § 241(b)(3) in four significant ways: (1) the torture suffered does not have to be "on account of" any enumerated statutory ground; (2) the Convention Against Torture protects individuals from future torture only;[171] (3) there are no bars to protection under the Convention Against Torture;[172] and (4) the act of torture *must* be done "by or at the instigation of or with the consent or acquiescence of a public official or other person acting in an official capacity," not by

---

166. 8 C.F.R. §§ 208.18(a)(1), 1208.18(a)(1).

167. To be considered torture, acts which constitute mental pain or suffering must be caused by or result from intentional or threatened infliction of severe physical pain or suffering, administration or threat of mind altering substances or other procedures to disrupt profoundly an individual's senses or personality (either against the applicant or to another), threat of imminent death (either against the applicant or another). *See* 8 C.F.R. §§ 208.18(a)(4), 1208.18(a)(4); Ni v. BIA, 439 F.3d 177, 179–80 (2d Cir. 2006); Al-Saher v. INS, 268 F.3d 1143 (9th Cir. 2001).

168. Tunis v. Gonzales, 447 F.3d 547, 550 (7th Cir. 2006); Mohammed v. Gonzales, 400 F.3d 785, 802 (9th Cir. 2005); Comollari v. Ashcroft, 378 F.3d 694, 697 (7th Cir. 2004); Zubeda v. Ashcroft, 333 F.3d 463, 472–73 (3d Cir. 2003).

169. 8 C.F.R. §§ 208.16(c)(2), 1208.16(c)(2); 136 Cong. Rec. at S. 17492 (daily ed., Oct. 27, 1990); Matter of M-B-A-, 23 I. & N. Dec. 474 (B.I.A. 2002); *J-E-*, 23 I. & N. Dec. at 303.

170. Alali-Amin v. Mukasey, 523 F.3d 1039 (9th Cir. 2008).

171. *See, e.g.,* Niang v. Gonzales, 422 F.3d 1187, 1202 (10th Cir. 2005); El Himri v. Ashcroft, 378 F.3d 932, 938 (9th Cir. 2004). However, past torture is probative evidence of the likelihood that an individual will be tortured again in the future. *See* 8 C.F.R. §§ 208.16(c)(3)(i), 1208.16(c)(3)(i).

172. Convention Against Torture, *supra* note 12, art. 3(1).

private actors.[173] An official's "acquiescence" must include awareness of the torture and failure to intervene in breach of a legal responsibility to do so.[174]

Although there are no bars to protection under the Convention Against Torture, if an applicant is barred from withholding of removal under INA § 241(b)(3), he or she is also barred from withholding of removal under the Convention Against Torture. Rather than withholding of removal under the Convention Against Torture, these individuals are entitled only to "deferral of removal,"[175] which can be terminated more easily than withholding of removal.[176] Moreover, an individual who is granted deferral of removal may be held in detention and is not necessarily entitled to employment authorization.[177]

BURDEN OF PROOF

For asylum, withholding of removal, and protection under the Convention Against Torture, the burden of proof is on the applicant to establish that he or she is eligible for relief.[178] The "reasonable possibility" burden of proof to establish eligibility for asylum, however, is lower than the "clear probability" burden of proof that is required to establish eligibility for withholding of removal and protection under the Convention Against Torture.[179]

In determining whether an applicant has met his or her burden of proof for any of these three forms of relief, the fact-finder may weigh credible testimony along with other evidence of record.[180] The applicant's testimony may be sufficient, without corroboration, to sustain his or her burden of proof, but only if the applicant's testimony is credible, persuasive, and specific.[181] General and vague testimony is not sufficient, as an applicant must show "specific, detailed facts supporting the reasonableness of his or her fear."[182]

---

173. 8 C.F.R. §§ 208.18(a)(1), 1208.18(a)(1).
174. *Id.* §§ 208.18(a)(7), 1208.18(a)(7).
175. *Id.* §§ 208.17, 1208.17.
176. *Id.* §§ 208.17(d), 1208.17(d).
177. *Id.* §§ 208.17(c), 1208.17(c). *See also id.* §§ 241.3–241.5.
178. *Id.* §§ 208.13(a), 1208.13(a).
179. INS v. Cardoza-Fonseca, 480 U.S. 421 (1987).
180. INA § 208(b)(1)(B)(ii).
181. *Id.*
182. Matter of Y-B-, 21 I. & N. Dec. 1136 (B.I.A. 1998).

The enactment of the REAL ID Act of 2005 modified the basis for credibility determinations made by fact-finders in asylum and withholding of removal applications.[183] The fact-finder may now base a credibility determination on the following: (1) demeanor, candor, or responsiveness of the applicant or witness; (2) consistency between the applicant or witness's written and oral statements; (3) internal consistency of such statements; (4) consistency of such statements with other evidence on the record; (5) any inaccuracies or falsehoods in such statements, without regard to whether these inaccuracies or falsehoods go to the heart of the applicant's claim; and (6) any other relevant factor.[184] An applicant should be given the opportunity to respond to and explain any apparent inconsistencies,[185] and his or her testimony will generally be found credible when it is plausible, detailed, internally consistent, consistent with the application, and unembellished.[186] In finding an applicant not credible, the adjudicator must offer a specific, cogent reason for the finding.[187]

Although an applicant's credible and detailed testimony is enough to satisfy his or her burden of proof, corroborating evidence is essential to any asylum, withholding of removal, or Convention Against Torture claim. Such evidence may include the applicant's identity documents, expert testimony regarding country conditions, supporting affidavits from witnesses or individuals with personal knowledge of past events or current country conditions, human rights reports and newspaper articles, and documentation from the applicant's home country that corroborates specific aspects of his or her claim. Under the REAL ID Act of 2005, "Where the trier of fact determines that an applicant should provide evidence that corroborates otherwise credible testimony, such evidence must be provided unless the applicant does not have the evidence and cannot reasonably obtain the evidence."[188] An applicant should provide "supporting evidence, both of general conditions and of the specific facts sought to be relied on by the applicant, where such evidence is available" and where

---

183. *See generally* REAL ID Act *supra* note 78.

184. INA § 208(b)(1)(B)(iii). The provisions of the REAL ID Act apply only to applications filed on or after May 11, 2005. *See* REAL ID Act *supra* note 78. *See also* Matter of S-B-, 24 I. & N. Dec. 42 (B.I.A. 2006).

185. UNHCR HANDBOOK, *supra* note 24, ¶ 199.

186. Matter of B-, 21 I. & N. Dec. 66, 70–72 (B.I.A. 1995).

187. Tewabe v. Gonzales, 446 F.3d 533, 540 (4th Cir. 2006); *see also* Mulanga v. Ashcroft, 349 F.3d 123, 138 (3d Cir. 2003); Secaida-Rosales v. INS, 331 F.3d 297, 307 (2d Cir. 2003); Paramasamy v. Ashcroft, 295 F.3d 1047, 1054 (9th Cir. 2002); Daiga v. INS, 183 F.3d 797, 798 (8th Cir. 1999); Matter of O-D-, 21 I. & N. Dec. 1079, 1082 (B.I.A. 1998).

188. *B-*, 21 I. & N. Dec. at 70–72.

it is reasonable to expect such corroborating evidence.[189] Where such evidence is not available, the applicant must provide an explanation of why that evidence is unavailable.[190] However, the applicant should be given the "benefit of the doubt" where the testimony is generally credible and does not counter commonly known facts.[191] According to the UNHCR, the benefit of the doubt should only be given after "all available evidence has been obtained and checked and when the examiner is satisfied as to the applicant's general credibility."[192]

Although the burden of proof is generally on the applicant to establish eligibility for relief, the burden of proof shifts to the government in certain situations. For instance, if the applicant establishes past persecution on account of one of the protected grounds, there is a presumption that the applicant also has a well-founded fear of future persecution and the burden shifts to the government to rebut that presumption.[193] In such circumstances, the government must show by a preponderance of the evidence that the conditions in the applicant's country of nationality have fundamentally changed since he or she suffered persecution,[194] or that the applicant could avoid persecution by relocating to another part of the country and that it would be reasonable to expect him or her to do so.[195] It is also the government's burden of proof to demonstrate that any bars to asylum or withholding of removal apply. Upon such a showing, the burden then shifts to the applicant to prove by a preponderance of the evidence that the bar is not applicable.[196]

ASYLUM APPLICATION PROCEDURES

The two most common ways for the asylum application process to commence are by filing affirmatively with USCIS or by filing with a U.S.

---

189. Matter of S-M-J-, 21 I. & N. Dec. 722, 724–25 (B.I.A. 1997).

190. Matter of O-D-, 21 I. & N. Dec. 1079, 1081 (B.I.A. 1998); *S-M-J-*, 21 I. & N. Dec. at 724.

191. *S-M-J-*, 21 I. & N. Dec. at 725.

192. UNHCR HANDBOOK, *supra* note 24, ¶ 204. *See also* Matter of Y-B-, 21 I. & N. Dec. 1136, 1139 (B.I.A. 1998); *S-M-J-*, 21 I. & N. Dec. at 725; Matter of Pula, 19 I. & N. Dec. 467, 476 (B.I.A. 1987).

193. 8 C.F.R. § 208.13(b)(1)(i).

194. *Id. See also* Matter of H-, Int. Dec. 3276 at 15, 24 (B.I.A. 1995).

195. Balliu v. Gonzales, 467 F.3d 609, 612 (7th Cir. 2006); Un v. Gonzales, 415 F.3d 205, 209 (1st Cir. 2005).

196. 8 C.F.R. §§ 208.16(d)(2), 1208.16(d)(2).

Immigration Court in defense of removal.[197] There are separate procedures for affirmative and defensive asylum applications.

Affirmative Applications before USCIS

If filing affirmatively, the application is heard and decided by a corps of asylum officers who are under the jurisdiction of the Department of Homeland Security, Director of International Affairs, and who receive training on international law, human rights, and U.S. asylum law.[198] The applicant must prepare and file his or her application in triplicate,[199] plus one additional copy per derivative family member in the United States, with the regional USCIS Service Center having jurisdiction over his or her place of residence.[200] The application must include the completed and signed I-589 application form, passports and identification documents, photographs of the applicant and each derivative family member, proof of family relationships for any derivatives, and corroborating documentation in support of the asylum claim. The application must be specific and detailed.[201]

Upon receipt of the application, the USCIS Service Center will review the application and return any applications that are incomplete.[202] If the application is complete, the applicant will receive an official Receipt Notice from USCIS. Next, the applicant will receive a Biometrics Notice scheduling him or her for an appointment to have his or her fingerprints and photograph taken for background and security check purposes.[203] The applicant will then be scheduled for an interview before the nearest USCIS Asylum Office, and will receive an Interview Notice by mail. "In the absence of exceptional circumstances," the asylum interview "shall

---

197. There are separate procedures and standards for children who seek asylum in the United States. INA § 208(b)(3)(C); Q&A, USCIS Initiates Procedures for Unaccompanied Children Seeking Asylum (March 25, 2009); Memo, Langlois, Chief, USCIS Asylum Division, HQRAIO 120/12a, Implementation of Statutory Changes Providing USCIS with Initial Jurisdiction over Asylum Applications Filed by Unaccompanied Alien Children (March 25, 2009) at 2.

198. 8 C.F.R. §§ 208.1(B), 1208.1(b).

199. At the time this chapter was written, the regulations no longer require the application to be filed in triplicate; however, the instructions for the I-589 form still require the application to be filed in triplicate. *See* Form I-589 Instructions, at 7, www.uscis.gov/sites/default/files/files/form/i-589instr.pdf (last visited May 18, 2014).

200. *Id.* §§ 208.3(a), 208.4(b)(1)–(2), 1208.3(a), 1208.4(b)(1)–(2).

201. INS v. Elias-Zacarias, 502 U.S. 478 (1998).

202. 8 C.F.R. §§ 208.3(C)(3), 1208.3(c)(3). It is important that the applicant follow the instructions for the I-589 form carefully, as they have been incorporated into the regulations and have the force of law. *Id.* § 103.2(a)(1).

203. INA § 208(d)(5)(A)(i).

commence not later than 45 days after the date an application is filed," and the application shall be adjudicated within 180 days.[204] The asylum officer is required to notify the applicant of his or her right to counsel and to provide the applicant with a list of pro bono legal services.[205] Additionally, the asylum officer must notify the applicant of the consequences of filing a frivolous asylum application.[206]

On the day of his or her interview, the asylum seeker may choose to bring an attorney or representative, as well as affidavits of witnesses and other corroborating evidence.[207] The interview itself is considered to be nonadversarial, and takes place in private with an asylum officer, who may administer oaths and question the applicant and witnesses.[208] If the applicant does not speak English, he or she must bring an interpreter to the interview. The interpreter must be at least 18 years old and cannot also serve as a witness or the applicant's attorney. Failure to bring an interpreter, without good cause, may result in the application being deemed abandoned.[209] Failure of the applicant to appear for the interview may result in the application being dismissed, unless notice of the interview was not mailed to the applicant's current address or there are exceptional circumstances that caused the applicant's failure to appear.[210] At the end of the interview, the applicant or his or her attorney will have the

---

204. *Id.* § 208(d)(5)(A)(ii)–(iv). However, at the time this chapter was written, there were large backlogs of asylum applications in most of the asylum offices around the country. *See* Asylum Office Workload for October–December 2013, http://www.uscis.gov/sites /default/files/USCIS/Outreach/Notes%20from%20Previous%20Engagements/Asy-Affirm ativeAsylum-Oct-Nov-Dec13.pdf.

205. *Id.* § 208(d)(4).

206. *Id.* An applicant who knowingly files a frivolous asylum application "shall be permanently ineligible for any benefits" under the INA if he or she was given notice of the consequences of filing a frivolous application. *Id.* § 208(d)(6); 8 C.F.R. §§ 208.3(c)(5), 208.20, 1208.3(c)(5), 1208.20. In order to make a finding that an application is frivolous, the immigration judge must find that material aspects of the application were false and that such fabrications were made knowingly and deliberately. 8 C.F.R. §§ 208.20, 1208.20. A frivolous finding can only be made by the immigration judge or Board of Immigration Appeals in a final order if, during the course of proceedings, the adjudicator is satisfied that the applicant had sufficient opportunity to respond to alleged discrepancies. 8 C.F.R. §§ 208.20, 1208.20; Matter of Y-L-, 24 I. & N. Dec. 151, 155 (B.I.A. 2007) (clarifying the standard an immigration judge must follow in making a frivolous finding).

207. 8 C.F.R. §§ 208.9(b), 1208.9(b). However, please note that many asylum offices require that all supporting evidence be submitted in advance of the interview. Practitioners should be sure to research procedures at their local asylum office.

208. *Id.*

209. *Id.* §§ 208.9(g), 1208.9(g).

210. INA § 208(d)(5)(A)(v); 8 C.F.R. §§ 208.10, 1208.10. *See also* 8 C.F.R. § 103.2(B)(9), (13), (15).

opportunity to make a closing statement on the evidence.[211] The applicant may also be given a brief extension of time to supplement the record if additional documentation is needed or requested.[212]

Following the interview, "except as otherwise provided by the asylum officer," the applicant must appear in person at the Asylum Office to receive the officer's decision, which must be in writing and is not appealable.[213] The asylum officer may grant, deny, or refer the applicant to removal proceedings before a U.S. Immigration Court. The officer will approve the application if the applicant has met his or her burden of proof to demonstrate eligibility for asylum. If the officer does not approve the application, one of two situations may transpire: (1) if the applicant is not in valid immigration status, he or she may be referred to immigration court for removal proceedings, or (2) if the applicant is in valid immigration status, he or she may receive a Notice of Intent to Deny to which he or she may respond with rebuttal evidence.[214] If upon receipt of the rebuttal evidence, the asylum officer still denies the application, the applicant is restored to his or her valid status and removal proceedings are not commenced.[215] The written denial must state the basis for denial or referral to the immigration court and must include an assessment of the applicant's credibility.[216] Although there is no appeal of the asylum officer's decision, the applicant may file a motion to reopen or a motion to reconsider before USCIS.[217] The applicant may also challenge the asylum officer's denial of asylum in federal court.[218]

Defensive Applications before the Immigration Courts

If referred to the immigration court, the applicant will receive a Notice to Appear in Immigration Court for removal proceedings, and will be scheduled for a Master Calendar Hearing, which is an initial status hearing before an immigration judge.[219] At the Master Calendar Hearing, the applicant must plead to the factual allegations and charges of removability listed in the charging document, the Notice to Appear, and may then

---

211. 8 C.F.R. §§ 208.9(d), 1208.9(d).
212. *Id.* §§ 208.9(e), 1208.9(e).
213. *Id.* §§ 208.9(d), 208.19, 1208.9(d), 1208.19.
214. *Id.* §§ 208.23, 1208.23. *See also* AOBTC, *Lesson: Decision Writing Part I* (June 21, 2004).
215. 8 C.F.R. §§ 208.14(c)(2)–(3), 1208.14(c)(2)–(3). *See also* AOBTC, *Lesson: Decision Writing Part I* (June 21, 2004).
216. 8 C.F.R. §§ 208.19, 1208.19.
217. *Id.* § 103.5.
218. *See, e.g.,* Fleurinor v. INS, 585 F.2d 129, 135 (5th Cir. 1978).
219. 8 C.F.R. §§ 208.14(c)(1), 239.1(a)(20), 1208.14(c)(1), 1239.1(a)(20).

renew his or her asylum application before the immigration court.[220] The renewed application is automatically considered a request for withholding of removal under INA § 241(b)(3) and a request for protection under the Convention Against Torture.[221] Upon receipt of the renewed application, the immigration judge must advise the asylum applicant of the right to counsel and the consequences of filing a frivolous application.[222] The judge will then schedule the applicant, now the "respondent," for an Individual Hearing on the merits of his or her application. A copy of the I-589 application, along with a biometrics fee and Form EOIR-28 Notice of Entry of Appearance as Attorney, must also be filed with the USCIS Nebraska Service Center.[223]

Prior to the Individual Hearing and in accordance with the court's filing rules, the respondent may file a list of proposed witnesses and additional supporting documentation, such as evidence of the general conditions in his or her country of nationality or habitual residence and any reasonably available corroborating evidence.[224] The respondent must then present his or her credible testimony and the credible testimony of any witnesses at the Individual Hearing in order to demonstrate to the immigration court his or her eligibility for asylum, and in the alternative, withholding of removal under INA § 241(b)(3) or protection under the Convention Against Torture.[225]

As discussed above, it is generally the respondent's burden of proof to establish eligibility for asylum, withholding of removal, and Convention Against Torture relief. However, there are shifting burdens involved throughout the process, such as when the respondent demonstrates that he or she has suffered past persecution, or when the Department of Homeland Security shows evidence of a bar to relief.[226] If the respondent meets his or her burden of proof, he or she will be granted asylum by the immigration judge and will no longer be in removal proceedings.[227] On the other hand, if the immigration judge denies the respondent's application for asylum, the respondent will be ordered removed and either

---

220. *Id.* §§ 208.14(b)–(c), 1208.14(b)–(c).

221. *Id.* §§ 208.3(b), 208.16, 208.17, 1208.3(b), 1208.16, 1208.17.

222. INA § 208(d)(4)(A).

223. 8 C.F.R. § 1003.47.

224. Matter of O-D-, 21 I. & N. Dec. 1079, 1081 (B.I.A. 1998); Matter of Y-B-, 21 I. & N. Dec. 1136, 1139 (B.I.A. 1998); Matter of S-M-J-, 21 I. & N. Dec. 722, 724–25 (B.I.A. 1997); Matter of B-, 21 I. & N. Dec. 66, 70–72 (B.I.A. 1995).

225. INA § 208(b)(1)(B)(ii)–(iii); Matter of S-B-, 24 I. & N. Dec. 42 (B.I.A. 2006); *Y-B-*, 21 I. & N. Dec. 1136; *B-*, 21 I. & N. Dec. at 70–72.

226. *See supra* pages 340–42.

227. 8 C.F.R. §§ 208.13(a), 208.16(b)–(c), 1208.13(a), 1208.16(b)–(c), 1240.11(c)(3)(iii), 1240.33(c)(3), 1240.49(c)(4)(iii).

granted withholding of removal under INA § 241(b)(3), granted protection under the Convention Against Torture, or granted no relief.

Appeals to the Board of Immigration Appeals

If the asylum-seeker wants review of the immigration judge's decision, he or she may file a Notice of Appeal, Form EOIR-26, with the BIA, the appellate body that is authorized to review asylum and withholding of removal decisions made by immigration judges.[228] The BIA will then set a briefing schedule for the Respondent and the Department of Homeland Security to submit their briefs on appeal. Upon receipt of the briefs, the BIA will review the briefs and the record of proceedings. Oral argument may be requested but is rarely granted.

On appeal before the BIA, the standard of review for all questions of law, application of legal standards, discretion, and judgment is "de novo," while any questions of fact, including credibility determinations made by the immigration judge, are reviewed under a "clearly erroneous" standard.[229] Upon review, if the BIA raises its own concerns regarding an applicant's credibility, it must give the applicant the opportunity to respond or provide explanations for any inconsistencies.[230] Failure to do so is a violation of due process.[231] The BIA must interpret the INA and the federal regulations to achieve results that are consistent with constitutional protections, however, the BIA lacks jurisdiction to address constitutional challenges to the INA and the federal regulations.[232]

Motions to Reopen and Motions to Reconsider

Following the immigration court or BIA proceedings, an applicant ordered removed may move to reopen his or her case in certain circumstances. Usually, the applicant must show that there is material evidence that was unavailable at the time of the original hearing that could not have been discovered or presented at that hearing.[233] There are time and numerical limitations to motions to reopen; generally, only one motion to reopen will be permitted and it must be filed within 90 days of the final order.[234]

---

228. *Id.* § 1003.1.

229. *Id.* § 1003.1(d)(3); Matter of S-H-, 23 I. & N. Dec. 462, 464 (B.I.A. 2002).

230. Stoyanov v. INS, 172 F.3d 731, 735 (9th Cir. 1998).

231. *Id. See also* Campos-Sanchez v. INS, 164 F.3d 448, 450 (9th Cir. 1998).

232. *See, e.g.,* Matter of L-S-J-, 21 I. & N. Dec. 973, 974 (B.I.A. 1997).

233. 8 C.F.R. § 1003.2(c)(1); Kaur v. BIA, 413 F.3d 232, 234 (2d Cir. 2005); Gebremaria v. Ashcroft, 378 F.3d 734, 737–39 (8th Cir. 2004); Sinistaj v. Ashcroft, 376 F.3d 516, 519 (6th Cir. 2004).

234. 8 C.F.R. §§ 208.4(b)(3)(ii), 1003.2(c)(2), 1208.4(b)(3)(ii). There are exceptions to the time and numerical limitations, including where the order was entered *in absentia*, where the BIA reopens the case *sua sponte*, where the parties agree to reopening, where the Department

An applicant may also file a motion to reconsider with the immigration judge or BIA within 30 days of the decision.[235] A motion to reconsider is a "request that the Board reexamine its decision in light of additional legal arguments, a change of law, or perhaps an argument or aspect of the case which was overlooked."[236] Both motions to reopen and motions to reconsider should be accompanied by supporting documentation.[237]

Appeals to the U.S. Circuit Courts of Appeals

If the asylum applicant is in removal proceedings and the BIA issues a final order of removal, he or she may seek further review in the U.S. Circuit Courts of Appeals.[238] The circuit courts will consider only the BIA decision on review, unless the BIA adopted the decision of the immigration judge in lieu of conducting its own de novo review.[239] Review of certain issues on removal has been restricted by recent laws amending the INA.[240] However, these restrictions do not preclude review of constitutional claims or questions of law.[241] Questions of law include not only statutory interpretation, but also questions regarding the application of the INA and the regulations to undisputed facts.[242] The circuit courts review due process claims and purely legal questions de novo.[243] However, administrative findings of fact and discretionary determinations are conclusive unless "any reasonable adjudicator would be compelled to conclude to the contrary"[244] and unless "manifestly contrary to the law

---

of Homeland Security asks for reopening due to fraud in the original proceeding or where a crime supports termination of asylum, and where there are changed circumstances in the country of removal that could not have been discovered or presented in the previous proceedings. *See* INA § 240(c)(y)(C)(ii); 8 C.F.R. §§ 1003.2(a), (c)(3)(i)–(iv), 1003.23(b)(4)(i). All motions to reopen must comply with the regulations. *See* 8 C.F.R. §§ 208.4(b)(3)(ii), 1003.2, 1003.23, 1208.4(b)(3)(ii).

235. 8 C.F.R. § 1003.23(b)(1)–(2).

236. Matter of Ramos, 23 I. & N. Dec. 336, 338 (B.I.A. 2002).

237. 8 C.F.R. §§ 103.5(a)(2), 1003.2(c)(1).

238. INA § 242(a)(1).

239. *See, e.g.,* Lata v. INS, 204 F.3d 1241 (9th Cir. 2000); Ghaly v. INS, 58 F.3d 1425, 1430 (9th Cir. 1995).

240. *See generally* REAL ID Act, *supra* note 78.

241. *See* INA § 242(a)(2)(A)–(D).

242. *See, e.g.,* Ramadan v. Gonzales, 479 F.3d 646, 648 (9th Cir. 2007).

243. INS v. Cardoza-Fonseca, 580 U.S. 421, 446–48 (1987). *See also* Velazquez v. Ashcroft, 103 F. App'x 142 (9th Cir. 2004); Jahed v. INS, 356 F.3d 991, 997 (9th Cir. 2004); Kerciku v. INS, 314 F.3d 913, 917 (7th Cir. 2003); Shan Liao v. U.S. Dept. of Justice, 283 F.3d 61 (2d Cir. 2002); Girma v. INS, 283 F.3d 664, 666 (5th Cir. 2002); Morales v. INS, 208 F.3d 323, 327 (1st Cir. 2000); Bradvica v. INS, 128 F.3d 1009, 1012 (7th Cir. 1997).

244. INA § 242(b)(4)(B).

and an abuse of discretion."[245] The circuit courts may also review denials of motions to reopen or reconsider under the abuse of discretion standard.[246] There is generally no judicial review of the following: a finding that the applicant can go to a safe third country, a finding that the applicant was previously denied asylum, a finding that the applicant did not file his or her application within one year of entry, a finding that the applicant is a terrorist, and a finding that the applicant did not meet the changed or extraordinary circumstances exceptions to the one-year filing deadline.[247]

Grants of Asylum

When asylum is granted, it is granted for an indefinite period of time, as long as the individual meets the definition of refugee.[248] However, it does not convey a right to remain permanently.[249] The principal applicant and any derivative applicants included on the application are granted asylum together. Persons granted asylum, or "asylees," may also bring their spouse and children to the United States to "accompany" or "follow to join" them by filing a Form I-730 petition within two years of the grant of asylum.[250] This two-year period may be extended for humanitarian reasons.[251] The I-730 may benefit spouses and children who are outside of the United States, or those who are in the United States but were not included in the principal applicant's application.[252] After-acquired spouses and children of the principal are not eligible to accompany or follow to join the principal asylee. For spouses and children to accompany or follow to join the principal applicant, the spousal or parental relationship must have existed at the time that the principal applicant's asylum was approved, except for children born or adopted after approval.[253]

In addition to the ability to bring their family members to the United States, asylees are immediately authorized for employment upon a grant

---

245. *Id.* § 242(b)(4)(D); Huang v. INS, 436 F.3d 89, 96–102 (2d Cir. 2006).

246. *See* Nken v. Holder, 585 F.3d 818, 822–23 (4th Cir. 2009); Jiang v. Att'y Gen. of the U.S., 568 F.3d 1252, 1257–58 (11th Cir. 2009); Li v. Att'y Gen. of the U.S., 488 F.3d 1371, 1374–76 (11th Cir. 2007); Kebe v. Gonzales, 473 F.3d 855 (7th Cir. 2007); INS v. Abudu, 485 U.S. 94 (1988).

247. INA § 208(a)(3), (b)(2)(D).

248. 8 C.F.R. §§ 208.14(e), 1208.14(e).

249. INA § 208(c)(2).

250. *Id.* § 208(b)(3); 8 C.F.R. §§ 208.21(a), (d), 1208.21(a), (d).

251. 8 C.F.R. § 208.21(c).

252. *Id.* §§ 208.21(c)–(d), 1208.21(c)–(d).

253. *Id.* §§ 208.21(b), 1208.21(b).

of asylum.[254] They may also obtain refugee travel documents to travel abroad by filing I-131 applications.[255] However, asylees must not return to their country of persecution, because they may be considered to have "voluntarily re-availed [themselves] of the protection of [their] country of nationality."[256] This may result in a fact-specific investigation and subsequent revocation of their asylum status.[257]

REVOCATION AND TERMINATION OF ASYLUM

Asylum or withholding of removal may be revoked by an asylum officer or an immigration judge under other circumstances as well.[258] If there is fraud in the application, if the applicant falls under one of the categories of ineligibility specified in INA § 208(c)(2), if the applicant no longer fears persecution because there are changed conditions in the country of origin, or if the applicant has committed an act that would have initially barred asylum or been grounds for denial, the individual's grant of asylum or withholding of removal may be revoked.[259] An asylum officer may seek to terminate affirmative grants of asylum in the following circumstances: (1) where the asylee no longer meets the definition of refugee due to changed circumstances; (2) where grounds for denial, such as being a persecutor or firmly resettled, are now in existence; (3) where the asylee acquires a new nationality; and (4) where the asylee travels back to the country of persecution and avails himself of the country's protection.[260] If an asylee's grant of asylum is terminated, the asylee status of his or her spouse and children will also be terminated.[261]

---

254. INA § 208(c)(1)(B); 8 C.F.R. §§ 208.7, 1208.7.

255. INA § 208(c)(1)(C); 8 C.F.R. § 223.2.

256. Refugee Convention, *supra* note 7, art. 1(C)(1).

257. Memo, Cooper (HXCOU90/15-P) (c. Sept. 2000), *reprinted in* 77 No. 37 INTERPRETER RELEASES 1384, 1391–98 (Sept. 25, 2000); Fact Sheet, USCIS, Traveling Outside the United States as an Asylum Applicant, as Asylee, or a Lawful Permanent Resident Who Obtained Such Status Based on Asylum Status (Jan. 4, 2007).

258. 8 C.F.R. §§ 208.24(a)–(b), (f), 1208.24(a)–(b), (f).

259. *Id.* §§ 208.24, 1208.24.

260. U.S. CITIZENSHIP AND IMMIGRATION SERVICES, AFFIRMATIVE ASYLUM PROCEDURES MANUAL (Nov. 2013), *available at* www.uscis.gov/sites/default/files/files/nativedocuments/Asylum_Procedures_Manual_2013.pdf.

261. 8 C.F.R. §§ 208.24(d), 1208.24(d).

ADJUSTMENT OF STATUS OF ASYLEES TO PERMANENT RESIDENCE

A person granted asylum, either as a principal or a derivative, may apply to adjust his or her status to permanent residence after one year of physical presence in the United States.[262] The one-year period begins to accrue on the date of the asylum grant, or in the case of a spouse or child who has accompanied or followed to join the principal applicant, the date the I-730 was approved.[263] Asylees and derivative family members adjust under INA § 209 rather than INA § 245, and they may adjust status in the United States even if they initially entered without inspection.[264] For an asylee to adjust status to permanent residence, he or she must apply on Form I-485, be physically present in the United States for at least one year following the grant of asylum, continue to be a refugee within the meaning of INA § 101(a)(42), not be firmly resettled in another country, and be admissible to the United States as an immigrant under the INA.[265]

Certain grounds of inadmissibility are automatically waived for asylees,[266] while other grounds, including drug trafficking and security-related grounds, cannot be waived.[267] All other grounds of inadmissibility, including criminal grounds, may be waived under INA § 209(c) for "humanitarian purposes, to assure family unity, or when it is otherwise in the public interest."[268] However, waivers for violent or dangerous crimes are usually not granted.[269] An application for a 209(c) waiver is filed on Form I-602.[270]

If adjustment of status is denied, there is no appeal of the denial. However, the applicant may file a motion to reopen or reconsider with USCIS, or renew his or her adjustment of status application in removal proceedings.[271] If the application to adjust status is approved, the applicant's admission as a permanent resident is backdated one year.[272]

---

262. INA § 209(a)(1); 8 C.F.R. §§ 209.1, 1209.1.
263. Memo, Yates, Deputy Ex. Assoc. Comm. Office of Field Operations, HQ 70/20.11, 70/6.1.5, 70/6.1.6, 70/34.2 (May 15, 2000), *reprinted in* 77 No. 24 INTERPRETER RELEASES 832, 837–48 (June 26, 2000).
264. INA § 209.
265. *Id. See also* 8 C.F.R. §§ 209.2(b), 1209.2(b).
266. INA § 212(a)(4)–(5), (a)(7)(A).
267. *Id.* § 212(a)(2)(C), (a)(3)(A)–(C), (E).
268. *Id.* § 209(c). *See* 8 C.F.R. §§ 209.2, 1209.2; Matter of H-N-, 22 I. & N. Dec. 1039 (B.I.A. 1999).
269. *See* Matter of Jean, 23 I. & N. Dec. 373, 381–84 (AG 2002).
270. *See* Memo, Aytes, Acting Dir. Operations, USCIS, HQPRD 70/23.10 (Oct. 31, 2005).
271. 8 C.F.R. §§ 103.5, 209.2(c), 1209.2(c).
272. *Id.* § 209.2(f).

Becoming a permanent resident of the United States brings the asylee one step closer to permanent protection and one step farther from statelessness, as he or she may become eligible to apply for U.S. citizenship five years after the date of admission as a permanent resident.[273] For many asylees, obtaining U.S. citizenship is the much-welcomed end of a long and difficult road to safety and freedom.

CONCLUSION

As the law continues to evolve based on the collision of human rights considerations and national self-interests, offering reliable protection to bona fide refugees continues to be the core humanitarian purpose of U.S. asylum law. As refugees continue to depend upon the compassion and humanity of foreign governments in seeking protection, it is a fundamental responsibility of the U.S. government and refugees' advocates to work together to maintain the integrity of the U.S. asylum system and to secure the safety and freedom that these individuals fleeing persecution and torture deserve as members of the human race.

---

273. An asylee's date of admission as a permanent resident is recorded "as of the date one year before the date of the approval of the application." 8 C.F.R. § 209.2(f).

18

U.S. CITIZENSHIP AND NATURALIZATION

Jennifer Hermansky[1]

For most non-U.S. citizens, naturalization is the final and happy destination in a long journey through the immigration process. Many immigrants will spend between ten and twenty years in both non-immigrant and lawful permanent resident status before becoming eligible for U.S. citizenship through naturalization. Advising and guiding an immigrant through the process can be both rewarding and challenging. This chapter will discuss the different ways that individuals can acquire U.S. citizenship, including citizenship at birth, through parental relationships, and naturalization.

As a threshold matter, it is important to distinguish between derivation of citizenship and citizenship through naturalization. The former involves a client who can make a claim that he or she is a citizen; perhaps he or she is in need of assistance obtaining documentation of U.S. citizenship. The latter involves a process by which lawful permanent residents of the United States become citizens after making an application for naturalization, undergoing an examination by the Department of Homeland Security (DHS), and taking the oath of allegiance to the United States. This chapter primarily will discuss citizenship through naturalization. However, it also will touch upon the various ways an individual derives citizenship either at birth or at a later date through a parental relationship.

DERIVING U.S. CITIZENSHIP

Individuals can derive U.S. citizenship either through birth in the United States or one of its territories, or through a parental relationship. You may come into contact with a client who always believed he was a U.S. citizen, only to find out that he cannot prove that citizenship later in life. You

---

1. Jennifer Hermansky is an associate in the Philadelphia office of Greenberg Traurig, LLP. She focuses her practice on employment-based immigration, including non-immigrant and immigrant petitions, labor certification applications, immigrant investor petitions, and applications for permanent residence. She also represents clients in family-based immigration cases, as well as naturalization and citizenship issues.

353

also may come into contact with a client who was born outside the United States, but who now wishes to make a claim to citizenship because his parents or grandparents lived in the United States. Oftentimes, attorneys get involved when the client learns from another administrative agency, such as Social Security, that they do not have a record of citizenship for the individual. Or, the individual will have a difficult time obtaining or extending a driver's license, or completing and documenting a Form I-9 at a new job.

When representing a client who is exploring a claim to U.S. citizenship, it is important to understand the client's complete history, from where and when he was born, when and where his parents were born and where they resided, and even when and where his grandparents were born and where they resided. These facts can be the key to determining whether the client has a claim to U.S. citizenship.

Citizenship at Birth

The United States follows the principle of *jus soli:* citizenship is acquired through birth in the United States or certain territories. The Fourteenth Amendment to the Constitution states that "all persons born or naturalized in the United States . . . are citizens of the United States." While there has been some debate over the past few years of whether the United States should continue the principle of *jus soli* or move to the principle of *jus sanguinis*, that is, citizenship determined by parentage, we remain a "right of the soil" country for now.

Congress has expressly stated that "a person born in the United States, and subject to the jurisdiction thereof" is a citizen at birth.[2] The key to proving citizenship at birth is producing a birth certificate, although the absence of an official birth certificate is not entirely decisive.[3] The Immigration and Nationality Act (INA) outlines further the classes of persons who are citizens and nationals at birth. Persons born in the United States to a member of an Indian, Eskimo, Aleutian, or other aboriginal tribe are citizens at birth.[4] Persons born outside the United States and its outlying possessions of parents both of whom are citizens of the United States and one of whom has had a residence in the United States or one of its outlying possessions prior to the birth of such person also are citizens at birth.[5]

---

2. 8 U.S.C. § 1401(a).
3. United States v. Breyer, 841 F. Supp. 679, 684 (E.D.Pa. 1993) (citing Liacakos v. Kennedy, 195 F. Supp. 630 (D.D.C. 1961); 4 GORDON & MAILMAN, IMMIGRATION LAW AND PRACTICE § 99.02[1][b]).
4. 8 U.S.C. § 1401(b).
5. *Id.* at § 1401(c).

If a person is born outside the United States, he or she also is a citizen at birth if he or she has: (1) one U.S. citizen parent who has been physically present[6] in the United States or one of its outlying possessions for a continuous period of one year prior to the birth of such person, and (2) the other parent is a national,[7] but not a citizen of the United States.[8] An individual also is a citizen at birth if born in an outlying possession of the United States of parents, one of whom is a citizen of the United States who has been physically present in the United States or one of its outlying possessions for a continuous period of one year at any time prior to the birth of such person.[9]

An individual who is born outside of the United States and its outlying possessions who has one U.S. citizen-parent and one alien parent is a citizen at birth if the U.S. citizen parent, prior to the birth of such person, was physically present in the United States or its outlying possessions for a period or periods totaling not less than five years, at least two of which were after attaining the age of fourteen years.[10] Periods of honorable service in the armed forces of the United States, or periods of employment with the United States government or with certain international organizations, may be included in order to satisfy the physical-presence requirement.[11]

For many individuals, the key to proving citizenship at birth in these cases is documenting the U.S. citizen-parent's physical presence in the United States. There is a presumption of alienage for individuals who were born abroad, and consequently the burden of proof falls on the individual claiming citizenship by a preponderance of the evidence.[12] Submission of the applicant's birth certificate, parents' birth certificates, tax records, school records, real estate records, leases, and bank records can help to meet this burden.

---

6. Physical presence is discussed in detail below, Section II.b., page 359.

7. A "national" of the United States is a person born in an outlying possession of the United States. 8 U.S.C. § 1408. The outlying possessions are defined in *id.* § 1101(A)(29) as American Samoa and Swains Island. All U.S. citizens are U.S. nationals but only a relatively small number of persons acquire U.S. nationality without becoming U.S. citizens. They cannot vote or hold office, but they can work in the United States without restriction and they can apply for U.S. citizenship through naturalization.

8. *Id.* § 1401(d).

9. *Id.* at § 1401(e).

10. *Id.* at § 1401(g).

11. *Id.*

12. 8 C.F.R. § 341.2(c). *See also* Matter of Tijerina-Villarreal, 13 I. & N. Dec. 327, 330 (B.I.A. 1969).

If you are assisting a client in proving U.S. citizenship at birth, and the individual has a claim to citizenship under 8 U.S.C. § 1401, the individual can apply for a certificate of citizenship using Form N-600 and file it with U.S. Citizenship and Immigration Services ("USCIS").[13] USCIS will determine citizenship and issue a formal certificate of citizenship, which is used to obtain a U.S. passport. Alternatively, the individual can apply directly for a U.S. passport.[14] The certificate of citizenship and passport are primary evidence of U.S. citizenship.

The Transmission Rule

As you will notice, many of the laws governing citizenship require the applicant to prove that a parent has spent periods of time physically present in the United States These are requirements for the "transmission" of citizenship from parent to child. In these cases, the transmission law that was in effect *at the time of child's birth* controls.[15] This is important to remember, as the citizenship laws have changed greatly over time.

Derived Citizenship through Parent's Naturalization or Birth in the United States

An individual also can derive citizenship through a parent's naturalization or birth in the United States.[16] Under 8 U.S.C. § 1431, the Child Citizenship Act of 2000, a child derives citizenship if: (1) one parent is a citizen by birth or naturalization; (2) the child is under 18; (3) the child is residing in the United States as a lawful permanent resident; and (4) the child is residing in the United States in the legal and physical custody of the U.S. citizen parent.[17] A client may have a claim to U.S. citizenship through derivation under this section of the law even if the U.S. citizen-parent does not meet the physical presence requirements for the child to be a citizen at birth.

There is a presumption of legal custody by the U.S. citizen-parent if any one of the following are true: (1) the biological child resides with both parents who are married and not separated; (2) the biological child resides with a surviving natural parent and the other is deceased; or (3) the child is born out-of-wedlock but has been legitimated and resides

---

13. Visit www.uscis.gov/forms to download Form N-600 and its accompanying instructions.
14. 22 C.F.R. § 51.44(b)(2).
15. United States v. Flores-Villar, 536 F.3d 990, 994–98 (9th Cir. 2008), *cert. granted*, No. 09-581, 2010 WL 1005955 (Mar. 22, 2010).
16. The first inquiry always is whether the client may have a claim that he or she was a citizen *at birth*, as described above. If no such claim is possible, then the next inquiry is whether the client has derived citizenship through a parent at some time after birth.
17. Pub. L. No. 106-395, § 101, 114 Stat. 1631, 1631 (2000). *See also* 8 C.F.R. § 320.

with the natural parent.[18] Joint custody is sufficient for legal custody.[19] If the child is adopted, a formal adoption decree is required. Step-children of U.S. citizens do not count.[20] The applicant also uses Form N-600 and applies for the certificate of citizenship from USCIS, thereafter obtaining a U.S. passport as primary evidence of citizenship.

The Child Citizenship Act of 2000 went into effect on February 27, 2001. For children who turned age 18 prior to this law's enactment, there are heavier burdens on the applicant to prove U.S. citizenship.[21] Like the law on acquisition of citizenship at birth, the law on acquisition of citizenship through derivation from a U.S. citizen parent has changed many times, and a full discussion is outside the scope of this chapter.

Practice Tip: A complete and helpful guide to the laws for citizenship is available in the Department of State's Foreign Affairs Manual (FAM).[22] Because the transmission rule requires research into the citizenship law in effect at the time of the child's birth, the FAM is a helpful resource for the history of the citizenship laws and can assist in this research.

CITIZENSHIP THROUGH NATURALIZATION

Although you may occasionally have a client who has a claim to U.S. citizenship at birth or through derivation from a parent, the large majority of cases involving citizenship are applications for naturalization. This is an affirmative application to USCIS to become a citizen of the United States. It is the formal mechanism set in place by Congress under Article I, § 8, cl. 4 to the Constitution whereby lawful permanent residents of the United States acquire citizenship through a "uniform law of naturalization."

Basic Requirements

The basic criteria for naturalization are:

1. The applicant must be a lawful permanent resident (or a "green card" holder).[23] The only exception to this rule is if a person

---

18. 8 C.F.R. § 320.1.
19. *Id.*
20. Matter of Guzman-Gomez, 21 I. & N. Dec. 824 (B.I.A. 2009).
21. 8 U.S.C. § 1431, as amended by Pub. L. No. 95-417, repealed by Pub. L. No. 106-395, 114 Stat. 1631.
22. *See* 7 U.S. Dep't of State, Foreign Affairs Manual § 1100 *et seq., available at* http://www.state.gov/m/a/dir/regs/fam/ [hereinafter Foreign Affairs Manual].
23. 8 U.S.C. § 1429.

honorably served in the U.S. military in a time of war or declared hostilities during period designated by the president by executive order;[24]

2. The applicant must be 18 years or older;[25]
3. The applicant must meet the "continuous residence" and "physical presence" requirements;[26]
4. The applicant must meet the good moral character requirements prior to filing and up to the time of admission as a U.S. citizen;[27]
5. The applicant must be attached to the principles of the Constitution and well-disposed to the good order and happiness of the United States;[28]
6. The applicant must be willing to bear arms, perform noncombatant service or work of national importance;[29] and
7. The applicant must demonstrate knowledge of the English Language, U.S. history and government.[30]

When advising an applicant for naturalization, it is very important to understand the alien's immigration history, criminal history, work history, international travel history, and residence both in the United States and abroad to accurately assess whether the client should file an application for naturalization. Denial of a naturalization application on certain grounds can land a client in removal proceedings.[31]

Practice Tip: There are special naturalization rules for individuals who served in the U.S. military. If your client discloses that he or she has served in a branch of the U.S. military, or has a spouse that is serving or has served in a branch of the U.S. military, visit www.uscis.gov/military for information on the special military naturalization programs (which waive the residency and physical presence requirements for applicants).

---

24. *Id.* § 1440(a).
25. *Id.* § 1445(b).
26. *Id.* § 1427(a)(1).
27. *Id.* § 1427(a)(3).
28. *Id.*
29. *Id.* § 1448(a)(5)(A)–(C).
30. *Id.* § 1423(a)(1); 8 C.F.R. § 312.1-2.
31. For example, if an individual has committed certain crimes as a lawful permanent resident, he or she may lack the requisite good moral character for naturalization. The denial of a naturalization application may also draw attention to the Department of Homeland Security that the individual is also removable from the United States, triggering the issuance of a Notice to Appear before an immigration judge. Consequences can be severe, so preparation and thorough intake are key to preparing the application.

Examining the Residence Requirements

There are four main residence requirements in the naturalization application: (1) time spent as a lawful permanent resident; (2) time residing in the state where the application is being filed; (3) time spent physically present in the United States; and (4) time spent continuously residing in the United States from the time of filing the application until the time of admission to citizenship.

To be eligible for naturalization, the applicant must be a continuous resident for five years after lawful permanent resident status is achieved.[32] If the applicant is married to a U.S. citizen for three years and the parties have been living in marital union for three years and actually residing together during that time, then a person need only be a permanent resident for three years before applying for naturalization.[33]

Further, the applicant must have resided for at least three months in the state where the application has been filed.[34]

Practice Tip: This is sometimes overlooked by the attorney or the applicant. Thus, it is important to examine the past residences of the applicant for the entire five years preceding the application for naturalization.

The applicant also must be physically present in the United States for at least one-half of the five (or three) years immediately preceding the application for naturalization.[35] As a practical matter, the Form N-400, Application for Naturalization, requires the applicant to list all days spent outside of the United States over the previous five years; it requires a tally, to the best of the applicant's ability, of all days spent outside the United States during that period.

Practice Tip: Advise non-citizen clients to keep a list of all days spent outside the United States to ease the naturalization process, including trips by car to Canada and Mexico. This will avoid the necessity of recreating all international trips from passport stamps and plane tickets.

Finally, the applicant also must reside continuously in the United States from the date of filing the application to admission as a U.S. citizen.[36] Absences of over six months but less than one year raise a rebuttable

---

32. 8 U.S.C. § 1427(a)(1); 8 C.F.R. § 316.5.

33. 8 C.F.R. § 319.1(a)(3).

34. 8 U.S.C. §§ 1427(a)(1), 1430(a). Residence is defined as the place of general abode; the place of general abode of a person means his principal, actual dwelling place in fact, without regard to intent. *Id.* § 1101(a)(33).

35. *Id.* § 1427(a).

36. *Id.* § 1427(a)(2); 8 C.F.R. § 316.2(a)(6).

presumption that the continuity of residence has been interrupted.[37] Absences of one year or more disrupt the continuity of residence.[38]

There are several exceptions to the continuity of residence rule. Time spent abroad by a spouse or child or a member of the Armed Forces residing with the family member abroad is deemed to be time spent in the United States[39] Employees of the U.S. government, an American research institute,[40] a U.S. firm engaged in the development of foreign trade and commerce, or a public international organization of which the United States is a member can be exempted from the requirement if they first file Form N-470 to preserve their residence in the United States[41] The same exceptions apply to permanent resident spouses of U.S. citizens who work for the U.S. government, an American research institute, a U.S. firm engaged in the development of foreign trade and commerce, or a public international organization of which the United States is a member.[42]

A person with a disruption in continuous residence may reapply for naturalization four years and one day following the date of return to the United States[43] If the permanent resident is married to a U.S. citizen and living with them, thereby implicating the three-year period of residence for naturalization, the individual must meet two years and one day of residence following the return before filing for naturalization.[44]

The Good Moral Character Requirement

Naturalization requires the applicant to be a person of good moral character for five years (or three years in the case of marriage to a U.S. citizen) prior to filing the N-400, Application for Naturalization.[45] This requirement extends all the way up through when the applicant takes the oath of allegiance and is sworn in as a U.S. citizen. A determination of good moral character is governed both by the statute and as a matter of discretion.

Every good moral character determination is a two-part inquiry. First, USCIS will determine if there is a statutory bar under 8 U.S.C. § 1101(f) to finding good moral character ever (in the case of a convicted murderer or aggravated felon who can never naturalize) or within the requisite period

---

37. 8 U.S.C. § 1427(b); 8 C.F.R. § 316.5(c)(1)(i).
38. 8 C.F.R. § 316.5(c)(1)(ii).
39. 8 U.S.C. § 1439.
40. *See* 8 C.F.R. § 316.20.
41. 8 U.S.C. § 1427(b)–(c).
42. *Id.* § 1430(b).
43. 8 C.F.R. § 316.5(c)(1)(ii).
44. *Id.*
45. 8 U.S.C. § 1427(a)(3); 8 C.F.R. § 316(a)(3).

under the statute (either three or five years). If there is a statutory bar to finding good moral character, the application must be denied. If there is no statutory bar to finding good moral character, then USCIS determines if there is some discretionary reason for denial of the application on good moral character grounds. For example, is the applicant convicted of a crime outside the three- or five-year period? Has the applicant failed to pay court-ordered child support? Has the applicant failed to file income tax returns or pay U.S. taxes? USCIS will balance these negative character factors against the other equities in the application in deciding whether to approve or deny the naturalization application.

Statutory Grounds of Denial for Good Moral Character

Good moral character is defined in the Immigration and Nationality Act.[46] Specifically, the INA dictates that certain classes of individuals cannot be found to have good moral character *during the statutory period required*, including habitual drunkards, polygamists, prostitutes, smugglers, aliens convicted[47] of a crime involving moral turpitude (CIMT), aliens convicted of multiple crimes, aliens convicted of a drug crime, except for a single offense of simple possession of marijuana under 30 grams, and an alien who has been confined to a penal institution for an aggregate period of 180 days or more.[48] Additionally, an individual who *at any time* has been convicted of an aggravated felony and that conviction was entered on or after November 29, 1990, can never establish good moral character for purposes of naturalization.[49]

Most often, the issue of good moral character arises when a lawful permanent resident client has been convicted of a crime. Aliens convicted of aggravated felonies (and whose conviction was entered on or after November 29, 1990) can never establish good moral character, even if the conviction occurred outside of the statutory period of good moral character, and thus, they can never naturalize.[50] Aggravated felonies are defined in 8 U.S.C. § 1101(a)(43), and include murder, rape, trafficking of guns and drugs, crimes of violence, serious fraud convictions, alien smuggling, and theft offenses among other things. Such an alien is both removable from the United States and ineligible for naturalization, and

---

46. 8 U.S.C. § 1101(f).
47. Attorneys should take note that while a final record of conviction is primary evidence of the bar to good moral character, an admission of the crime will also bar a finding of good moral character. *See id.* § 1101(f)(3).
48. *Id.*
49. *Id.* § 1101(f)(8).
50. *Id.*

so filing the application serves only the detrimental purpose of alerting the Department of Homeland Security that the alien is removable. You should refer the client immediately to an experienced immigration attorney if he or she discloses an aggravated felony conviction.

Aliens convicted of CIMTs[51] and aliens convicted of multiple crimes[52] or a drug crime, except for a single offense of simple possession of marijuana under 30 grams,[53] are ineligible for naturalization if the conviction(s) occurred during the required period of good moral character (either three or five years). CIMTs are not defined in the INA; instead, a patchwork of immigration cases from the Board of Immigration Appeals (BIA) and the U.S. Circuit Courts of Appeals have determined which crimes are CIMTs. The most common elements involving moral turpitude include fraud, larceny, or intent to harm persons or things. A full discussion of which crimes are categorized as CIMTs is outside of the scope of this chapter. However, attorneys familiarizing themselves with the various CIMTs should visit the State Department's website[54] for an excellent list of common crimes involving moral turpitude, including crimes against property, crimes against persons, family or morality, crimes against the government, and attempts, accessories to crimes, and conspiracy. This list can be utilized as a research starting point for determining whether a crime is considered a CIMT.

Additionally, an alien cannot establish good moral character during the requisite period if the alien has been convicted for two or more offenses (other than purely political offenses), regardless of whether or not the convictions arose from a single trial or arose from a single scheme of conduct involving moral turpitude and whether or not the offenses involved moral turpitude, if the aggregate sentence of confinement actually imposed is five years or more.[55] Drug crimes also are a serious issue, unless the conviction is for a single offense of simple possession of 30 grams or less of marijuana.[56] Moreover, an alien who, during the good moral character period, has been confined as a result of conviction to a penal institution for an aggregate period of 180 days or more is ineligible for naturalization, regardless of whether the offense, or offenses, for which he has been confined were committed within or

---

51. *Id.* § 1101(f)(3).
52. *Id.*
53. *Id.*
54. *See* 9 Foreign Affairs Manual, *supra* note 22, § 40.21 (Notes), *available at* http://www .state.gov/documents/organization/86942.pdf.
55. 8 U.S.C. § 1101(f)(3). *See also id.* § 1182(a)(2)(B).
56. *Id.* § 1101(f)(3). *See also id.* § 1182(a)(2)(C).

outside the good moral character period.[57] If any of these statutory bars apply, the applicant cannot establish good moral character during the requisite period, and the application should not be filed until at least five years have passed and the applicant can demonstrate rehabilitation and good moral character.

Practice Tip: It is important to be absolutely certain of all law enforcement contact with the client. The Form N-400, Application for Naturalization,[58] asks not only about criminal convictions, but also about any arrests the client has had and any charges that have been filed against the alien. The form also asks if the alien has ever been arrested, cited, or detained by any law enforcement officer (including USCIS or former INS and military officers), or if the alien has ever been placed in an alternative sentencing or rehabilitation program.[59] With these questions, USCIS is determining whether there is a statutory ground of ineligibility based on moral character or whether, as a matter of discretion, the application should be denied.

Discretionary Denials for Good Moral Character

Failure to support dependents, adultery tending to destroy a marriage, and commission of unlawful acts that adversely reflect upon the applicant's moral character, regardless of whether they constitute CIMTs, have been used to deny naturalization applications as a matter of discretion.[60] Convictions outside of the statutory period of good moral character of either three or five years also are still influential on the application. Naturalization is a discretionary application; therefore, crimes committed outside of the good moral character period do not demand ineligibility, but they do have bearing on the application.[61] USCIS will balance the negative factors against the applicant's good moral character.

---

57. *Id.* § 1101(f)(7).

58. This form can be found on the USCIS website: www.uscis.gov/forms.

59. Such programs include diversion, deferred prosecution, withheld adjudication, or deferred adjudication. In many circumstances, these programs can be considered a "conviction" under the INA, even though they may no longer be considered a conviction under state law. Under INA § 101(a)(48), "conviction" is defined as a formal judgment of guilt of the alien entered by a court or, if adjudication of guilt has been withheld, where (i) a judge or jury has found the alien guilty or the alien has entered a plea of guilty or nolo contendere or has admitted sufficient facts to warrant a finding of guilt, and (ii) the judge has ordered some form of punishment, penalty, or restraint on the alien's liberty to be imposed.

60. 8 C.F.R. § 316.10(b)(3).

61. 8 U.S.C. § 1427(e); 8 C.F.R. § 316.10(a)(2).

Practice Tip: Rehabilitate your client. If a client is seeking naturalization and he or she has a CIMT conviction outside the statutory period of good moral character, or has a conviction of a crime that is not a CIMT but which occurred during the good moral character period, have the client prepare evidence of his or her "good moral character." Such evidence can include donations to charitable organizations, volunteer activities, participation in a church or other community-based organization, etc. The client should have this ready for presentation to the officer at the naturalization interview, should USCIS require evidence of good moral character and rehabilitation.

Other Common Pitfalls and Roadblocks to Naturalization

Other than the criminal convictions discussed above, USCIS examines additional elements of good moral character that could present issues for clients, including false claims to U.S. citizenship, failure to register for the selective service, a bad driving record or history of DUIs, and failure to file and pay federal, state and local taxes.

"But I Thought I Was a Citizen?"
False Claims to U.S. Citizenship

False claims to U.S. citizenship are very problematic for alien clients. In general under immigration law, making a false claim to U.S. citizenship is considered a serious fraud against the government and makes the alien permanently inadmissible to the United States, and removable from the United States[62] It is important to properly screen the client as an applicant for naturalization to determine whether the client has ever called himself a U.S. citizen on Form I-9 when he started a new job, on a Social Security application, on an application for benefits with another administrative agency, or in the course of registering to vote in a federal, state, or local election.

If the client was actually convicted under 18 U.S.C. § 1015(f) for making a false claim to U.S. citizenship to vote or to register to vote, or if the client is convicted under 18 U.S.C. § 611 for voting in a federal election as a non-citizen, he or she will have a conviction of a CIMT, as a fraud against the U.S. government.[63] If there is no conviction, USCIS will determine if there is a discretionary reason for denial of the naturalization application, including unlawful voting, unlawfully registering to vote, or a false claim to U.S. citizenship. There will be a balancing of the equities in the

---

62. 8 U.S.C. §§ 1182(a)(6)(C)(ii), 1227(a)(6).
63. *Id.* § 1101(f)(3).

application. If a client discloses a false claim to citizenship or unlawful voting, the alien should contact an experienced immigration attorney.

There is only one narrow exception to this rule: in the case of an alien who makes a false statement or claim of citizenship, or who registers to vote or votes in a federal, state, or local election (including an initiative, recall, or referendum) in violation of a lawful restriction of such registration or voting to citizens, if each natural parent of the alien (or, in the case of an adopted alien, each adoptive parent of the alien) is or was a citizen (whether by birth or naturalization), the alien permanently resided in the United States prior to attaining the age of 16, and the alien reasonably believed at the time of such statement, claim, or violation that he or she was a citizen, no finding that the alien is, or was, not of good moral character may be made based on it.[64]

As a practical matter, filing a naturalization application for a client who has made a false claim to U.S. citizenship within the requisite period of good moral character will result in a discretionary denial of the application, and could result in the initiation of removal proceedings. At a minimum, the client should be advised to wait until he or she meets the requisite period of good moral character after the false claim was made or the unlawful voting occurred. During that time, the applicant also can work on his or her good moral character by donating to charitable organizations, volunteering and being active in the community. The client also must be fully warned of the risks of filing the application, including the risk of a discretionary denial for the false claim to citizenship, even though it may be outside of the requisite period of good moral character.

Selective Service Registration? What's That?

Almost all male U.S. citizens, and male aliens living in the United States, who are 18 through 25, are required to register with Selective Service.[65] Non-citizens who are not required to register with Selective Service include men who are in the United States on student or visitor visas, and men who are part of a diplomatic or trade mission and their families.[66] Almost all other male non-citizens are required to register, including illegal aliens, legal permanent residents, and refugees.[67] The general rule is

---

64. *Id.* § 1101(f).
65. Visit http://www.sss.gov/FSwho.htm to determine who must register for the Selective Service Registration.
66. *Id.*
67. *Id.*

that if a male non-citizen takes up residency in the United States before his 26th birthday, he must register with Selective Service.[68]

Knowingly and willfully failing to register with the Selective Service Registration between 18 and 26 years of age during the statutory period of good moral character can result in the denial of a naturalization case. As a practical matter, USCIS can deny the application on the basis that the applicant refuses to bear arms pursuant to INA § 337(a)(5)(A).[69] Also in practice, an applicant is not permanently barred from establishing good moral character even if he knowingly and intentionally failed to register with the Selective Service. In general, males over 31 seeking to naturalize are outside the five-year statutory good moral character period and are ordinarily eligible for naturalization. Again, USCIS will balance the equities of the case, including failure to register with the Selective Service against other evidence of good moral character presented in the application.

When a Bad Driving Record Presents a Roadblock

Unfortunately, speeding, reckless driving and driving under the influence convictions are ever-increasing on the rap sheets of clients. The N-400 application asks for the applicant to disclose any arrests, charges, citations, or convictions received ever. This includes traffic infractions. As a practical matter, a pattern of disregard of the driving laws may result in a lack of good moral character finding at the USCIS level. However, courts have found that failure to pay parking fines and repeated parking tickets could not be used as a basis to find a lack of good moral character.[70] The attorney should weigh the gravity and frequency of traffic violations against the other positive factors in the application. Repeated DUIs, for example, could signify a disregard for the laws of the United States, and could demonstrate a lack of good moral character. In short, be prepared to rehabilitate the client to balance out these negative factors.

Failure to File Tax Returns or Pay Taxes

The N-400 application inquires whether the applicant has failed to file a required federal, state, or local tax return since becoming a permanent resident of the United States. The form also asks if the applicant filed as a

---

68. *Id.*

69. *See* Memo, Virtue, G.C. to Penca, Eastern Reg. Counsel (HQCOU 90/15-P, HQCOU 70/33-P) (April 27, 1998).

70. Yin-Shing Woo v. United States, 288 F.2d 434, 435 (2d Cir. 1961). *See also* Etape v. Napolitano, 664 F. Supp. 2d 498, 518 (D. Md. 2009).

"nonresident" or if the applicant owes any federal, state, or local taxes that are overdue. In practice, failing to file tax returns or to pay taxes owed are discretionary factors in the good moral character determination. Deliberate failure to file tax returns or pay taxes due can be used as a reason to deny the application on discretionary grounds.

Practice Tip: Determine the date on which the applicant became either a conditional permanent resident of the United States (if applicable) or the date on which the applicant became a lawful permanent resident of the United States Inquire about the tax history of the client in detail from that point forward, making sure that tax returns were filed each year as a "resident" and not a "nonresident." If there is a pattern of a failure to pay taxes owed within the statutory period of good moral character, advise of the possible risk of denial.

The Application Procedure

An Application for Naturalization is filed on Form N-400 with USCIS. Applicants can obtain the form instructions and download the current version of the form at the USCIS website: www.uscis.gov. The current USCIS filing fee for the N-400 application is $680. Instructions on where to file the application based on the applicant's residence also are found on the USCIS website.

An application should be fully completed, and should include a copy of the lawful permanent resident card of the applicant, along with two (2) passport-style photos of the applicant. If the applicant has been convicted of a crime, an original record of conviction should be attached showing the final disposition. Once completed, the application can be filed up to three months before the continuous residence requirements are met.[71]

Practice Tip: As discussed above, under 8 U.S.C. § 1431, the Child Citizenship Act of 2000, a child derives citizenship if (1) one parent is a citizen by birth *or naturalization*; (2) the child is under 18; (3) the child is residing in the United States as a lawful permanent resident; and (4) the child is residing in the United States in the legal and physical custody of the U.S. citizen-parent.[72] Including a lawful permanent resident child under 18 on the N-400 application of the parent will allow the child to derive citizenship from the parent when he or she naturalizes. The child does not file his or her own application for naturalization. After the parent's naturalization, the child can apply directly for a U.S. passport or can file Form N-600 with

---

71. 8 U.S.C. § 1445(a). *See also* 8 C.F.R. § 334.2(b).
72. Child Citizenship Act of 2000, Pub. L. No. 106-395, § 101, 114 Stat. 1631, 1631 (2000). *See also* 8 C.F.R. § 320.

USCIS to obtain his or her own certificate of citizenship, which is primary proof of U.S. citizenship and also can be used to obtain a U.S. passport.

Once the application is filed, USCIS will commence a background check on the applicant, including FBI background checks.[73] USCIS will schedule the applicant for a "biometrics" appointment, and at the appointment, USCIS will capture the electronic fingerprints and photo of the applicant. The fingerprints are run through several databases for both security clearance checks and criminal background checks. Also at the biometrics appointment, the naturalization applicant will receive a book from USCIS that contains a list of 100 questions that could be asked on U.S. history and government at the naturalization interview. The applicant should utilize this resource when studying for the naturalization test, further discussed below.

After completion of the background checks, the file will be forwarded from a USCIS service center to a USCIS district office for scheduling of the naturalization examination, a.k.a. the naturalization interview and tests.

The Naturalization Examination

USCIS immigration officers must conduct an examination of applicants for naturalization.[74] The naturalization examination is essentially a two-part interview: first, a determination regarding the applicant's naturalization eligibility, including the good moral character inquiry, and secondly, a test of the English language, and U.S. history and government.

During the naturalization interview, the USCIS officer must establish that the applicant continues to qualify for naturalization. This includes a complete review of the N-400 application form with the applicant during the interview. In most instances, many months can pass between the time the applicant completes and signs the Form N-400 and the naturalization examination. During that time, the applicant may have arrests or other issues that bear on good moral character.

Practice Tip: It is important to thoroughly prepare a client for the naturalization examination. This includes a review of the form with the client. Have the client confirm that he or she has not been arrested, cited, charged, detained, or convicted since filing the application. Confirm with the client that tax returns were filed and taxes paid if tax season has passed since the filing of the application.

---

73. 8 U.S.C. § 1446(a), Pub. L. No. 105-119, Title I, 111 Stat. 2440, 2448–49 (1997). *See also* 8 C.F.R. §§ 335.1, 335.2.

74. 8 U.S.C. § 1446(a). *See also* 8 C.F.R. §§ 335.2, 332.1.

After a thorough review of the application form with the applicant, the USCIS officer will move onto the test portion of the examination. Applicants for naturalization must demonstrate elementary-level reading, writing, and understanding of the English language,[75] and U.S. history and government.[76] During this second part of the naturalization examination, the applicant will answer ten questions on U.S. history and government, out of the 100 standard questions on the naturalization test. To pass the test, the applicant need only get six questions correct. If the questions are answered correctly, the USCIS officer will then administer an English test, which requires the applicant to read an elementary-level sentence and then write the answer (the answer is given by the USCIS officer).[77] If an applicant fails the English or civics test, he or she will be offered a second test within 90 days.[78]

The applicant also must demonstrate an attachment to the Constitution and take the oath of allegiance to the United States.[79] As part of the naturalization examination, the USCIS officer conducting the interview will inquire about the applicant's attachment to the Constitution and his or her willingness to take the oath of allegiance. Prepare the client that he or she likely will need to explain what the oath of allegiance means, and they should always review the oath again prior to the interview.

USCIS shall grant the application if the applicant has complied with all requirements for naturalization.[80] A decision to grant or deny the naturalization application must take place "at the time of the initial examination or within 120 days after the date of the initial examination."[81] The

---

75. 8 U.S.C. § 1423(a)(1). *See also* 8 C.F.R. § 312.1.

76. 8 U.S.C. § 1423(a). *See also* 8 C.F.R. § 312.2.

77. There is a limited exception to the English test. Applicants who are over 50 years of age and have lived in the United States for 20 years in lawful permanent resident status need not take the English test. 8 U.S.C. § 1423(b)(2). Applicants who are over 55 and who have lived in the United States for 15 years in lawful permanent resident status are also exempt from the English test. *Id.* Persons who are physically or developmentally disabled or who have a mental impairment are exempt from the English language and history and government requirements. *Id.* § 1423(b)(1). As a practical matter, however, the disability waiver is difficult to obtain and must be accompanied by credible, medical evidence of the disability.

78. 8 C.F.R. § 312.5.

79. 8 U.S.C. § 1427(a)(3). *See also* 8 C.F.R. § 316.11.

80. 8 C.F.R. § 335.3(a).

81. *Id.* In fact, if USCIS does not make a decision within 120 days following the naturalization examination, the applicant can file a civil lawsuit in the United States District Court under 8 U.S.C. § 1447(b) to seek judicial determination of the application or an order that USCIS complete adjudication of the application within a specific time frame.

process is not over at the naturalization examination, however. The applicant still must take the oath of allegiance to the United States.

Oath of Allegiance

If a naturalization application is granted, USCIS must schedule the applicant for a ceremony at which the applicant takes the "oath of renunciation and allegiance" and is sworn in as a citizen of the United States.[82] Usually, the oath ceremony is scheduled for another date and time after the naturalization examination, so the applicant can return with friends and family who would like to share in the ceremony. At the oath ceremony, the new citizen returns his or her lawful permanent resident or "green card."[83] In exchange, he or she receives a naturalization certificate, which is primary evidence of U.S. citizenship. The naturalization certificate is then used to obtain a U.S. passport for international travel.

Administrative and Judicial Review of Denials

Unfortunately, not all applications for naturalization are approved. If, after an examination under 8 U.S.C. § 1446, an application for naturalization is denied, the applicant may request a hearing before an immigration officer.[84] This is essentially an administrative appeal of the naturalization application. A person whose application for naturalization is denied, after a hearing before an immigration officer under 8 U.S.C. § 1447(a), may seek review of such denial before the United States District Court for the district in which such person resides.[85] The review is de novo, and the court makes its own findings of fact and conclusions of law and shall, at the request of the petitioner, conduct a hearing de novo on the application.[86] The appeal may involve an evidentiary hearing including the right to subpoena witnesses.[87]

THE END OF THE ROAD—THE U.S. PASSPORT

The culmination of the naturalization process is obtaining a U.S. passport for international travel. With certain limited exceptions, U.S. citizens must

---

82. 8 U.S.C. § 1448(a).
83. Under 8 C.F.R. § 338.14, no certificate of naturalization shall be delivered unless the applicant surrenders the green card.
84. 8 U.S.C. § 1447(a).
85. *Id.* § 1421(c).
86. *Id.*
87. *Id.* § 1447(c), (d). *See also* 8 C.F.R. § 336.2.

reenter the United States using a U.S. passport, and, in general, it is unlawful for any U.S. citizen to depart or enter the United States without a U.S. passport.[88] If a passport is granted, it is conclusive proof of U.S. citizenship.[89]

Practice Tip: Visit the U.S. State Department's website at http://travel .state.gov/ for a host of resources for obtaining passports by U.S. citizens.

HELPFUL RESOURCES FOR ATTORNEYS

USCIS has many helpful resources for both naturalization applicants and attorneys. On its website in the Citizenship Resource Center, http://www .uscis.gov/portal/site/uscis/citizenship, USCIS posts both videos and publications on the naturalization process. The videos include: "Becoming a U.S. Citizen: An Overview of the Naturalization Process" and "The USCIS Naturalization Interview and Test." USCIS also publishes reading vocabulary flash cards, writing vocabulary flash cards and a reading test vocabulary list. USCIS also posts practice naturalization tests on its website.

The USCIS publication, "A Guide to Naturalization," is also a helpful resource for naturalization applicants and attorneys.[90] The Guide describes the benefits and responsibilities of citizenship, FAQs, eligibility requirements, document checklists, and a naturalization eligibility worksheet.

Another helpful resource for attorneys is the USCIS Adjudicator's Field Manual. Found on the www.uscis.gov website under "Laws" and then "Immigration Handbooks, Manuals and Guidance," this field manual guides adjudicators in deciding naturalization and citizenship applications. Part VII specifically deals with nationality and naturalization, and contains citations to statute, regulations and case law governing the eligibility requirements for transmission and acquisition of citizenship as well as naturalization.

Attorneys who do not regularly practice immigration law should utilize the resources in this chapter to effectively represent non-citizen clients on their path to citizenship. I hope you will find that assisting a client through the naturalization process is both rewarding and challenging.

---

88. 8 U.S.C. § 1185(b); 8 C.F.R. § 235.1(b); 22 C.F.R. §§ 53.1, 53.2.
89. 22 U.S.C. § 2705.
90. This guide is also found in the Citizenship Resource Center.

19

IMMIGRATION CONSEQUENCES OF CRIMINAL CONVICTIONS: WHAT CRIMES AND CRIMINAL ACTIVITIES CAN GET YOUR CLIENT INTO TROUBLE

Anna Gallagher[1]

INTRODUCTION

This chapter will provide an overview of the types of crimes and criminal activities that can result in a non-citizen's removal from the United States. Because of the severe consequences which many non-citizens face as a result of certain criminal convictions and related activities, it is vital that criminal defense and immigration counsel work together prior to taking any decision on how to proceed in a criminal matter. In fact, after the Supreme Court's decision in *Padilla v. Kentucky*,[2] criminal defense counsel are now required to advise their clients of the immigration consequences of a plea and potential conviction. Thus, in order to protect themselves and their clients, criminal defense counsel must be at least conversant with the potential immigration consequences that their clients may face as a result of a criminal conviction, criminal activities, or admission to certain criminal acts.

---

1. Anna Marie Gallagher is a shareholder at Maggio + Kattar in Washington, D.C. and head of litigation within the firm. Anna has practiced in the field of immigration and refugee law for more than two decades, working in the United States, Central America, and Europe. Her experience includes private practice, advocacy in the nonprofit sector, and several years in academia. In addition to her practice and teaching experience, Anna has authored several articles and books on U.S. immigration and nationality issues. Anna is the board member of ASISTA, a nonprofit organization dedicated to advocating on behalf of immigrant victims of domestic violence and sexual assault (www.asistahelp.org). She is also a member of the Board of Trustees of the American Immigration Council (www.americanimmigration council.org). Anna remains active in international refugee and migrant issues and is the president of the International Detention Coalition, an international nongovernmental organization dedicated to the promotion of human rights for refugees and migrants around the world who are subject to administrative detention (www.idcoalition.org).
2. 130 S. Ct. 1473 (2010).

This chapter will equip counsel from both the criminal defense and the immigration bars with sufficient information to identify what crimes and/or criminal activity can get a client into trouble. Specifically, it will provide information on the following:

- Defense counsel's obligation to advise
- Inadmissibility vs. deportability
- Crimes that subject a non-citizen to removal
- Definition of conviction for immigration purposes
- Records to prove a criminal conviction
- Available resources

DEFENSE COUNSEL'S OBLIGATION TO ADVISE ON IMMIGRATION CONSEQUENCES AFTER *PADILLA*

Prior to the passage of the Antiterrorism and Effective Death Penalty Act of 1996 (AEDPA),[3] and the Illegal Immigration Reform and Immigrant Responsibility Act of 1996 (IIRAIRA),[4] few in the criminal defense bar were familiar with immigration law, much less with the immigration consequences of criminal convictions, activities or admissions to certain criminal acts. Provisions contained in both AEDPA and IIRAIRA changed the landscape of immigration law significantly. As a result of these changes, non-citizens convicted of a broad variety of crimes, even seemingly minor ones, now face deportation with no consideration given to the length of their residence in the United States family and community ties or history of good moral character post-conviction.

Despite the serious implications of certain convictions, many in the criminal defense bar rarely communicated with immigration practitioners to discuss prophylactic strategies on behalf of their clients. However, as more and more non-citizens were deported because of their crimes, the criminal bar began to recognize the importance of consulting with immigration counsel. Although often not familiar with the intricacies of immigration law, most defense attorneys now recognize that many actions taken in representing their clients in a criminal proceeding may result in immigration consequences. Thus, immigration collaboration between the defense and the immigration bars has grown significantly during the past several years. As a result of a decision issued in 2010, the Supreme Court has made this collaboration mandatory.

---

3. Antiterrorism and Effective Death Penalty Act of 1996, Pub. L. No. 104-132, 110 Stat. 1214 (1996).
4. Div. C of the Omnibus Appropriations Act of 1996, Pub. L. No. 104-208, 110 Stat. 3009.

Overview of the *Padilla* Decision

On March 31, 2010, the Supreme Court issued a landmark decision, finding that the failure to affirmatively advise a client of the immigration consequences of a guilty plea falls below the standard of a reasonable attorney.[5] In that decision, the Supreme Court reviewed the case of Jose Padilla, longtime lawful permanent resident, who had pled guilty to a drug trafficking offense in reliance on his attorney's statement that he would not face deportation. After realizing that his attorney had been wrong, Mr. Padilla attempted to vacate his conviction based upon his Sixth Amendment right to effective counsel.

The Supreme Court found that Mr. Padilla's counsel was "Constitutionally deficient" and held that a failure to affirmatively advise a client on the immigration consequences of a guilty plea falls below the standard of a reasonable attorney.[6] Thus, silence is not sufficient. While acknowledging the complexity of immigration law, the Court held that when immigration consequences are clear, a defense attorney must advise of the possible consequences. When consequences are unclear, an attorney must, at a minimum, warn a client of a risk of deportation.

There has been quite a bit of litigation concerning the retroactivity of *Padilla* and issues relating to prejudice as a result of ineffective assistance of counsel and its effect on a noncitizen's ultimate disposition. A detailed discussion of these issues is beyond the scope of this article. However, it is important to note that the Supreme Court has held that its decision in *Padilla v. Kentucky* does not apply retroactively to cases already final on direct review.[7] The Court has also held that the Sixth Amendment right to effective assistance of counsel applies to "all 'critical' states of the criminal proceedings."[8]

Why It Is Difficult to Advise of the Exact Consequences

It is often difficult to predict the exact immigration consequences of a criminal plea, involvement in, or admissions to certain criminal activities. Immigration law is unsettled. In order to determine immigration consequences, a practitioner must apply numerous generic definitions contained in the Immigration and Nationality Act (e.g., aggravated felony, crime of moral turpitude, burglary, theft, crime of violence, etc.) to the state or municipal statute under which his or her client has been charged. Federal

---

5. *Padilla*, 130 S. Ct. 1473.
6. *Id.*
7. Chaidez v. United States, 133 S. Ct. 1103 (2013).
8. Laffler v. Cooper, 132 S. Ct. 1376 (2012).

immigration definitions are terms of art, and it is not immediately obvious if a definition matches a particular federal, state, or municipal statute.

In addition, there are over 250 immigration judges across the country who decide these issues in removal proceedings. Often, there is no established case law to guide an immigration judge as to whether a particular offense constitutes a ground of removal. Because it is impossible to determine to which immigration judge a client's case will be assigned, it is equally difficult to advise a client as to the exact immigration consequences that he or she may face.

Finally, it is often challenging to advise of the precise consequences of a plea because of conflicting federal circuit court case law. After completion of criminal proceedings, non-citizens are often detained by Immigration and Customs Enforcement (ICE) and transferred to other jurisdictions. Federal circuit courts of appeal reach different decisions on criminal immigration issues. Defense counsel may advise a client to plead guilty to an offense with no immigration exposure in one federal circuit only to have the client transferred to another jurisdiction where he or she, in fact, faces immigration consequences as a result of the plea.

What Information Does Counsel Need in Order to Adequately Advise?

In order to adequately advise your client of the immigration consequences of his or her actions and, hopefully, consult with immigration counsel to seek assistance, you will need to ask the following questions:

* When did your client enter the United States? Some grounds of removal will be triggered depending on the date of entry. For example, a person who is convicted of a crime involving moral turpitude (CMT) within five years of legal admission to the United States is subject to removal.[9]
* How did your client enter? (e.g., without inspection, with an immigrant visa, with a green card, with a non-immigrant visa, parole) The manner of entry determines which set of immigration laws will apply to your client—grounds of inadmissibility versus grounds of deportation.[10]
* What is your client's current immigration status? Did he or she ever have a green card, a non-immigrant visa, or other permission to be in the United States? When and how did he or she obtain such? Even

---

9. INA § 237(a)(2)(A)(i), 8 U.S.C. § 1227 (2014).
10. *Id.* § 212, 8 U.S.C. § 1182 (grounds of inadmissibility); *id.* § 237, 8 U.S.C. § 1227 (grounds of deportation).

though a client may have entered illegally or overstayed, he may be eligible for certain relief from removal. Also, his current status determines which set of immigration laws governs.

- Has your client ever been deported or placed in removal proceedings? This is important to know in order to determine if your client may be barred from receiving certain legal status because of past immigration violations, such as deportation, illegal reentry after a deportation, or illegal reentry after having been in the United States more than a year. If your client is ineligible to receive legal status until well into the future because of past immigration violations, the immigration consequences may be of less importance to him or her as compared to facing a possible lengthy jail sentence.
- What is your client's criminal history? It is essential to know your client's past criminal history. If he or she has a prior conviction(s), which already makes him or her subject to removal, the immigration consequences of the current criminal proceeding may be irrelevant.

If you have difficulty in determining your client's status or the relevant law in the case, you should consult an immigration attorney.

IS YOUR CLIENT INADMISSIBLE OR DEPORTABLE?

In order to determine which set of immigration laws apply to your client, you must first determine if he or she is inadmissible or deportable. This depends on the client's current status and/or manner of entry to the United States.

It is important, first, to understand certain legal terms, which you may have heard in discussing immigration issues. The term "removal" is a term which can mean inadmissible or deportable. It refers to the process of removing a non-citizen from the United States for violations of U.S. immigration laws. Removal proceedings refer to administrative hearings held before an immigration judge.

A person who has been legally admitted to the United States but has violated the conditions of admission, either by overstaying a visa, having been convicted of a crime, or some other immigration violation, is deportable. The non-citizen must be physically inside the United States to be deportable.

A person who is seeking admission to the United States but is ineligible for certain reasons, including conviction of certain crimes, certain criminal conduct, or past immigration violations, is inadmissible. It is important to understand that a person subject to the grounds of inadmissibility under Immigration and Nationality Act (INA) § 212 can be physically inside or outside of the United States. For example, a person who enters the country without inspection and is here for ten years will still be inadmissible when he applies for legal status. At times, a person who has legal status may also be inadmissible. For example, a lawful permanent resident (LPR) who is convicted of a crime and then travels abroad can be found inadmissible for the conviction upon his or her return to the United States.

To conclude, the terms "deportable" and "inadmissible" are subsets of the term "removable." The following categories of non-citizens are considered inadmissible: (1) undocumented persons who enter the country illegally; (2) LPRs at a border or airport who have certain criminal convictions; and (3) persons paroled into the United States.[11] The following categories are examples of persons considered to be deportable: (1) non-citizens with Visa/Border Crossing cards; (2) LPRs inside the United States with certain criminal convictions; and (3) persons who entered with non-immigrant visas.

WHAT CRIMES SUBJECT A NON-CITIZEN TO REMOVAL?

As discussed above, persons seeking admission to the United States who are inadmissible or persons who have been admitted and who are deportable are placed in what is known as removal proceedings.[12] Non-citizens seeking entry to the United States, or non-citizens who are already in the United States, may be considered inadmissible under INA § 212 (inadmissible aliens) or deportable under INA § 237 (deportable aliens), and therefore may be placed in removal proceedings for the following crimes or criminal activity (state or federal):[13]

---

11. A non-citizen may be allowed to enter the United States temporarily for health issues, to face criminal prosecution, to act as a witness, or for other reasons. In such cases, the person is "paroled" into the United States but has not been officially admitted and, thus, is subject to the grounds of inadmissibility if he is placed in removal proceedings.
12. INA § 240, 8 U.S.C. § 1229A (2014).
13. For information on federal offenses, see D. Kesselbrenner and S. Lin, Selected Immigration Consequences of Certain Federal Offenses (2010), *available at* http://www.national immigrationproject.org/legalresources/fed_chart_2010%20update.pdf. For information on selected state offenses (Arizona, California, Connecticut, Florida, Illinois, Massachusetts, North Carolina, New Jersey, New Mexico, New York, Oregon, Texas, Vermont, Virginia) visit the website of the National Immigration Project at www.nationalimmigrationproject .org and click on Criminal & Deportation Defense. The website of the NYSDA Immigration Defense Project also contains reference charts for state offenses from NY, NJ, CT, and VT (www.immigrantdefenseproject.org/webPages/deportation.htm).

- Crimes of Moral Turpitude
  - *Inadmissibility Ground*—Conviction of, or admission to commission of a crime involving moral turpitude (other than a purely political offense) or an attempt or conspiracy to commit such crime.[14]
  - *Deportation Ground*—Conviction of a crime involving moral turpitude (other than a purely political offense) committed within five years of the date of admission and for which a sentence of one year or longer may be imposed.[15]
- Multiple Criminal Convictions
  - *Inadmissibility Ground*—Conviction of two or more offenses (other than purely political offenses) regardless of whether the conviction was in a single trial or whether the offenses arose from a single scheme of misconduct and regardless of whether the offenses involved moral turpitude, for which the aggregate sentences to confinement were five years or more.[16]
  - *Deportation Ground*—Conviction of two or more crimes involving moral turpitude, not arising out of a single scheme.
- *Aggravated Felony*—Persons convicted of an aggravated felony as defined under INA § 101(a)(43), including an attempt or conspiracy to commit an aggravated felony.[17]
- *High-Speed Flight*—Non-citizens convicted of a violation of 18 U.S.C. § 758 (relating to high speed flight from an immigration checkpoint).[18]
- *Failure to Register as a Sex Offender*—Conviction under 18 U.S.C. § 2250 for failure to register as a sex offender.[19]
- *Miscellaneous Crimes*—A conviction for a crime relating to espionage, treason and sedition, violation of the Military Selective Service Act, or the Trading with the Enemy Act.[20]
- *Controlled Substance Violation*—Violation of (or a conspiracy or attempt to violate) any law or regulation of a state, the United States, or a foreign country relating to a controlled substance as defined in 21 U.S.C. § 802.[21]
- *Controlled Substance Trafficker*—Involvement in illicit trafficking in any controlled substance or in any listed chemical or knowingly aiding, abetting, assisting, conspiring, or colluding with others in the

---

14. INA § 212(a)(2)(A)(i)(I), 8 U.S.C. § 1182 (2014).
15. *Id.* § 237(a)(2)(A)(i), 8 U.S.C. § 1227.
16. *Id.* §§ 212(a)(2)(B), 8 U.S.C. § 1182; 237(a)(2)(A)(ii), 8 U.S.C. § 1227.
17. *Id.* § 237(a)(2)(A)(iii); *id.* § 101(a)(43)(U), 8 U.S.C. § 1101.
18. *Id.* § 237(a)(2)(A)(iv), 8 U.S.C. § 1227.
19. *Id.* § 237(a)(2)(A)(v), 8 U.S.C. § 1227.
20. *Id.* § 237(a)(2)(D), 8 U.S.C. § 1227.
21. *Id.* §§ 212(a)(2)(A)(i)(II), 8 U.S.C. § 1182, 237(a)(2)(B)(i), 8 U.S.C. § 1227.

illicit trafficking of any controlled substance or listed substance or chemical.[22]

- *Certain Relatives Who Benefit from Drug Trafficking*—Non-citizen spouse and children of drug traffickers who knowingly benefit from drug trafficking.[23]
- *Drug Abusers and Addicts*—Non-citizens who are drug abusers or addicts.[24]
- *Prostitution and Commercialized Vice*—Persons coming to the United States to engage in prostitution, or who have engaged in prostitution within ten years of the date of application for admission; persons who procure or attempt to procure, or procured or attempted to procure or to import, prostitutes or persons for the purpose of prostitution, or receives or received proceeds of prostitution within ten years of application for admission, or who are coming to the United States to engage in any other unlawful commercialized vice, whether or not related to prostitution.[25]
- *Non-citizens Involved in Criminal Activity Who Have Asserted Immunity*—Certain non-citizens who have committed certain serious offenses for which they received immunity and departed from the United States.[26]
- *Certain Firearm Offenses*—Non-citizens convicted under any law of purchasing, selling, offering for sale, exchanging, using, owning, possessing, or carrying, or of attempting or conspiring to do so, any weapon, part, or accessory which is a firearm or destructive device (as defined in 18 U.S.C. § 921(a)).[27]
- *Smuggling*—Non-citizens who have knowingly encouraged, induced, assisted, abetted, or aided any other non-citizen to enter the United States in violation of law.[28]
- *Crimes of Domestic Violence, Stalking, Violation of Protection Order, Crimes Against Children*—Non-citizens convicted of a crime of domestic violence, stalking, child abuse, child abandonment or neglect. Non-citizens found to have violated a protection order by a court that involves protection against credible threats of violence, repeated

---

22. *Id.* § 212(a)(2)(C), 8 U.S.C. § 1182.
23. *Id.* § 212(a)(2)(C)(ii), 8 U.S.C. § 1182.
24. *Id.* § 237(a)(2)(B)(ii), 8 U.S.C. § 1227.
25. *Id.* § 212(a)(2)(D), 8 U.S.C. § 1182.
26. *Id.* § 212(a)(2)(E), 8 U.S.C. § 1182.
27. *Id.* § 237(a)(2)(C), 8 U.S.C. § 1227.
28. *Id.* §§ 212(a)(6)(E)(ii), 8 U.S.C. § 1182; 237(a)(1)(E), 8 U.S.C. § 1227.

harassment, or bodily injury to the non-citizen or non-citizens covered by the protection order.[29]

- *Foreign Government Officials Who Have Committed Serious Violations of Religious Freedom.*[30]
- *Significant Traffickers in Persons*—Non-citizens who have trafficked in persons.[31]
- *Money Laundering*—Non-citizens who have engaged, are engaging, or seek to enter the United States to engage in an offense relating to laundering of money or who are or have been knowing aiders, abettors, assisters, conspirators, or colluders with others in the offense.[32]
- Security and Related Grounds, Terrorist Activities
  - *Inadmissibility Ground*—Activities involving the violation of laws relating to espionage, sabotage, or laws prohibiting the export of goods, technology or sensitive information.[33]
  - *Deportation Ground*—Activities involving the violation of laws relating to espionage, sabotage, or laws prohibiting the export of goods, technology or sensitive information; criminal activity which endangers public safety or national security; activities relating to the overthrow of the U.S. government by force, violence or other unlawful means; terrorist activities.[34]
- *Participation in Persecution or Genocide*—Participation in Nazi persecution, genocide, or the commission of any act of torture or extrajudicial killing.[35]
- *Failure to Register Change of Address or Falsification of Documents*—A conviction under INA § 266(c) (fraudulent statements); a conviction for a violation or attempt or conspiracy to violate the Foreign Agents Registration Act of 1938, Registration Act of 1940 or 18 U.S.C. § 1546 (fraud and misuse of visas, permits and other documents).[36]

Crimes of Moral Turpitude

A non-citizen may be inadmissible and subject to removal based on a conviction of a crime involving moral turpitude, committed[37] within five

---

29. *Id.* § 237(a)(2)(E), 8 U.S.C. § 1227.
30. *Id.* §§ 212(a)(2)(G), 8 U.S.C. § 1182; 237(a)(4)(E), 8 U.S.C. § 1227.
31. *Id.* § 212(a)(2)(H), 8 U.S.C. § 1182.
32. *Id.* § 212(a)(2)(I), 8 U.S.C. § 1182.
33. *Id.* § 212(a)(3), 8 U.S.C. § 1182.
34. *Id.* § 237(a)(4)(A), (B), 8 U.S.C. § 1227.
35. *Id.* §§ 212(a)(3)(E), 8 U.S.C. § 1182; 237(a)(4)(D), 8 U.S.C. § 1227.
36. *Id.* § 237(a)(3)(B), 8 U.S.C. § 1227.
37. The operative date is the date the offense was committed, not the date of the convic-

years after admission,[38] and for which a sentence of one year or longer may be imposed.[39] A non-citizen may also be deportable and subject to removal based on convictions of more than one crime involving moral turpitude occurring at any time after admission, not arising out of a single scheme of misconduct,[40] regardless of whether the convictions resulted from a single trial.

A crime of moral turpitude "refers generally to conduct which is inherently base, vile, or depraved, and contrary to the accepted rules of morality."[41] Crimes of moral turpitude include crimes against individuals, crimes against the government, crimes against property, sexual offenses, fraud, and some weapons and drug offenses.[42] A non-citizen convicted for a petty offense involving moral turpitude is not subject to removal under the grounds of inadmissibility. A conviction is considered a petty offense when the maximum penalty possible for the crime could not exceed imprisonment for one year and the non-citizen was sentenced to a term of imprisonment of less than six months.[43] Although non-citizens convicted of crimes of moral turpitude may be subject to removal or prevented from entering the United States after a temporary departure, there are still remedies under immigration laws to obtain relief, including immigrant and non-immigrant waivers[44] and cancellation of removal.[45]

---

tion. *See* Matter of Sanchez, 17 I. & N. Dec. 218 (B.I.A. 1980); Matter of Yanez-Jacquez, 13 I. & N. Dec. 449 (B.I.A. 1970), *rev'd on other grounds*, Yanez-Jacquez v. INS, 440 F.2d 701 (5th Cir. 1971); Matter of M.S., 9 I. & N. Dec. 643 (B.I.A. 1962); Matter of C–P–, 8 I. & N. Dec. 504 (B.I.A. 1959).

38. Where a person enters without inspection and later adjusts status, the date of admission is the date of adjustment of status. Matter of Rosas, 22 I. & N. Dec. 616 (B.I.A. 1999).

39. INA § 212(a)(2)(A)(i)(I), 8 U.S.C. § 1182 (2014).

40. *Id.* § 237(a)(2)(A)(ii), 8 U.S.C. § 1227.

41. Matter of Franklin, 20 I. & N. Dec. 867, 868 (B.I.A. 1994), *aff'd*, Franklin v. INS, 72 F.3d 571 (8th Cir. 1995).

42. For a comprehensive review and description of what crimes constitute crimes of moral turpitude and the potential immigration consequences, see D. KESSELBRENNER, L. ROSENBERG & N. TOOBY, IMMIGRATION LAW AND CRIMES ch. 6 (2008). (hereinafter KESSELBRENNER ET AL.].

43. INA § 212(a)(2)(A)(ii)(II), 8 U.S.C. § 1182 (2014).

44. Non-citizens seeking admission on non-immigrant visas may be eligible for a waiver of certain criminal grounds of exclusion under INA § 212(d)(3). It does not waive the grounds of espionage, sabotage, genocide, and Nazi persecution. Non-citizens with certain criminal convictions seeking admission for immigrant status may be eligible for a waiver under INA § 212(h). However, the waiver is not available for controlled substance and trafficking offenses. For a detailed discussion of § 212(h) waivers, see KESSELBRENNER ET AL., *supra* note 40, §§ 10.4–10.20.

45. LPRs who have been lawfully admitted for permanent residence for not less than five years, who have resided in the United States continuously for seven years after having

Aggravated Felony

The Anti-Drug Abuse Act of 1988[46] created a new category of removable criminal offenses—murder, rape, and sexual abuse of a minor—known as aggravated felony. Subsequent provisions in the Immigration Act of 1990,[47] the Immigration and Nationality Technical Corrections Act of 1994,[48] AEDPA,[49] and IIRAIRA[50] have significantly broadened the scope of crimes in this category.

AEDPA expanded the offenses classified as "aggravated felonies" and the concurrent grounds of removal. Less than six months after the changes brought about by AEDPA, Congress reconfigured immigration law with the passage of IIRAIRA. As with AEDPA, IIRAIRA significantly expanded the definition of an aggravated felony in INA § 101(a)(43), which began as one paragraph in 1988 and now contains 21 paragraphs with many subparagraphs. With the expansion of the definition of an aggravated felony under IIRAIRA, some 50 general classes of crimes are specifically enumerated as aggravated felonies.

The term "aggravated felony" applies to offenses in violation of state or federal laws.[51] Classification of a conviction as a misdemeanor under state law does not automatically exclude it from consideration as an aggravated felony.[52] Foreign convictions are considered to be aggravated felonies if the term of imprisonment was completed within the previous 15 years.[53] The definition of certain aggravated felonies depends also

been admitted in any status, and who have not been convicted of an aggravated felony may be eligible for cancellation of removal. INA § 240A(a), 8 U.S.C. § 1229A (2014).

46. Pub. L. No. 100-690, subtitle J, 102 Stat. 4181, §§ 6001 *et seq.* (Nov. 18, 1988).

47. Immigration Act of 1990, Pub. L. No. 101-649, 104 Stat. 4978 (1990) (IMMACT90).

48. Immigration and Nationality Technical Corrections Act of 1994, Pub. L. No. 103-416, 108 Stat. 4305 (1994) (INTCA).

49. Antiterrorism and Effective Death Penalty Act of 1996, Pub. L. No. 104-132, 110 Stat. 1214 (1996).

50. Div. C. of the Omnibus AppropriationsAct of 1996, Pub. L. No. 104-208, 110 Stat. 3009–546.

51. Matterof Ponce de Leon, 21 I. & N. Dec. 154 (B.I.A. 1996).

52. Lopez v. Gonzales, 549 U.S. 47 (2006) (overruling Matter of Yanez-Garcia, 23 I. & N. Dec. 390 (B.I.A. 2002)) (certain state misdemeanors may be classified as aggrravated felonies under federal law if they are defined as such under federal law); Matter of Aruna, 24 I. & N. Dec. 452 (B.I.A. 2008) (state law misdemeanor for conspiracy to distribute marijuana constitutes aggravated felony where its elements are similar to those of federal felonyoffense); Wireko v. Reno, 211 F.3d 833 (4th Cir. 2000) (misdemeanor sexual battery with a 12-month suspended sentence held to be a crime of violence and, therefore, an aggravated felony); Francis v. Reno, 269 F.3d 162 (3d Cir. 2001) (misdemeanor crime of violence (COV) cannot be an aggravated felony if a COV is defined as a state misdemeanor under 18 U.S.C. § 16(b)).

53. INA § 101(a)(43), 8 U.S.C. § 1101 (2014). For a discussion of the issue of the characterization of misdemeanors as felonies under the immigration laws, see Johnson, *The AEDPA and*

upon the sentence and/or the dollar amount for certain criminal offenses, such as crimes of violence, theft, and fraud.

Prior to the passage of IIRAIRA, the definition of aggravated felony had several effective dates depending upon the provision. However, IIRAIRA eliminated the different effective dates and determined that the definition applies to convictions on, before, or after the effective date of September 30, 1996.[54]

The following crimes are considered to be aggravated felonies as defined under INA § 101(a)(43):

- Murder, rape, and sexual abuse of a minor, INA § 101(a)(43)(A);[55]
- Illicit trafficking in a controlled substance, INA § 101(a)(43)(B);
- Illicit trafficking in firearms or destructive devices or in explosive devices, INA § 101(a)(43)(C);
- Certain offenses relating to laundering of monetary instruments or engaging in monetary transactions in property derived from specific unlawful activity if the amount of the funds exceeded $10,000, INA § 101(a)(43)(D);[56]

---

the IIRIRA: Treating Misdemeanors as Felonies for Immigration Purposes, 27 J. Legis. 477 (2001).

54. IIRAIRA, Pub. L. No. 104-208, § 321, 110 Stat. 3009, amending INA § 101(a)(43), 8 U.S.C. § 1101 (2014). See also Seale v. INS, 323 F.3d 150 (1st Cir. 2003); Bell v. Reno, 218 F.3d 86 (2d Cir. 2000) (convictions preceding the 1988 Anti-Drug Abuse Act still trigger deportation); Flores-Leon v. INS, 272 F.3d 433 (7th Cir. 2001); Aragon-Ayon v. INS, 206 F.3d 847 (9th Cir. 2000) (deportation proper for conviction occurring before November 1988); Lettman v. Reno, 207 F.3d 1368 (11th Cir. 2000) (convictions before 1996 still trigger deportation). For an in-depth discussion of litigation regarding effective date arguments, see Kesselbrenner et al., supra note 40, § 7.23.

55. A victim of sexual abuse who is under 18 is a "minor" for purposes of determining whether a non-citizen has been convicted of sexual abuse of a minor. Matter of V–F–D–, 23 I. & N. Dec. 859 (B.I.A. 2006). Misdemeanor sexual abuse of a minor is an aggravated felony. Matter of Small, 23 I. & N. Dec. 448 (2002); United States v. Gonzales-Vela, 276 F.3d 763 (6th Cir. 2001); Guerrero-Perez v. INS, 256 F.3d 546 (7th Cir. 2001); United States v. Marin-Navarette, 244 F.3d 1284 (11th Cir. 2001), cert. denied, 122 S. Ct. 317 (2001). See also Hernandez-Alvarez v. Gonzales, 432 F.3d 763 (7th Cir. 2005) (indecent solicitation of a child considered sexual abuse of a minor and, therefore, an aggravated felony even where crime did not involve a minor but, rather, an adult undercover investigator). But see United States v. Pallares-Galan, 359 F.3d 1088 (9th Cir. 2004) (offense involving minor victim not necessarily "sexual abuse of a minor" if it covers conduct other than sexual abuse); Singh v. Ashcroft, 383 F.3d 144 (3d Cir. 2004) (Delaware criminal offense of unlawful sexual conduct in third degree does not constitute sexual abuse of a minor and, therefore, is not an aggravated felony where statute does not establish age of victim).

56. Where a respondent was convicted of an offense described in 18 U.S.C. § 1956 relating to laundering of a monetary instrument in the amount of $1,300 and ordered to pay restitution of over $900,000, the respondent was not convicted of an aggravated felony. Chowdhury v. INS, 249 F.3d 970 (9th Cir. 2001).

- Offenses relating to explosive materials and firearms, INA § 101(a)(43)(E);
- Crime of violence for which the term of imprisonment is at least one year, INA § 101(a)(43)(F);
- Theft offense, including receipt of stolen property, or burglary offense for which the term of imprisonment is at least one year, INA § 101(a)(43)(G);
- Certain offenses relating to the demand for or receipt of ransom, INA § 101(a)(43)(H);
- Certain offenses relating to child pornography, INA § 101(a)(43)(I);
- Certain offenses relating to RICO, or certain gambling offenses, for which a sentence of one year imprisonment or more may be imposed, INA § 101(a)(43)(J);
- Offenses relating to the owning, controlling, managing, or supervising of a prostitution business; or certain offenses relating to transportation for the purpose of prostitution; or certain offenses relating to peonage, slavery, and involuntary servitude, INA § 101(a)(43)(K);
- Certain offenses relating to gathering or transmitting national defense information or disclosure of classified information, sabotage, or treason, INA § 101(a)(43)(L);
- Offense involving fraud or deceit in which the loss to the victim or victims exceeds $10,000; or certain offenses relating to tax evasion where the revenue loss to the government exceeds $10,000, INA § 101(a)(43)(M);
- Certain offenses relating to alien smuggling, except in the case of a first offense for which the alien has affirmatively shown that the alien committed the offense for the purpose of assisting, abetting, or aiding only the alien's spouse, child, or parent, INA § 101(a)(43)(N);[57]
- Certain improper entry or illegal reentry offenses committed by an alien who was previously deported on the basis of an aggravated felony conviction, INA § 101(a)(43)(O);
- Offense of falsely making, forging, counterfeiting, mutilating, or altering a passport or instrument, or certain other offenses relating to document fraud, for which the term of imprisonment is at least 12 months, except in the case of a first offense for which the alien has affirmatively shown that the alien committed the offense for the purpose of assisting, abetting, or aiding only the alien's spouse, child, or parent, INA § 101(a)(43)(P);

---

57. Matter of Martinez-Serrano, 25 I. & N. Dec. 151 (B.I.A. 2009); Patel v. Ashcroft, 294 F.3d 465 (3d Cir. 2002) (conviction for harboring alien met definition of "aggravated felony" despite fact that non-citizen had no part in harbored alien's illegal admission or entry).

- Offense relating to the failure to appear by a defendant for service of sentence if the underlying offense is punishable by imprisonment for a term of five years or more, INA § 101(a)(43)(Q);
- Commercial bribery, counterfeiting, forgery, or trafficking in vehicles the identification numbers of which have been altered for which the term of imprisonment is at least one year, INA § 101(a)(43)(R);[58]
- Obstruction of justice, perjury or subornation of perjury, or bribery of a witness, for which the term of imprisonment is at least one year, INA § 101(a)(43)(S);[59]
- Offense relating to failure to appear before a court pursuant to a court order to answer to, or dispose of, a charge of a felony for which a sentence of two years' imprisonment or more may be imposed, INA § 101(a)(43)(T);
- Attempt or conspiracy to commit any of the above offenses, INA § 101(a)(43)(U).

Aggravated Felony—Crimes of Violence

One of the broadest categories of aggravated felonies is the provision defining crime of violence. In order for a crime of violence to be considered an aggravated felony, the sentence imposed must be at least one year. Under INA § 101(a)(43)(F), a crime of violence is defined by 18 U.S.C. § 16 as:

> (a) an offense that has as an element the use, attempted use, or threatened use of physical force against the person or property of another, or (b) any other offense that is a felony and that, by its nature, involves a *substantial risk* that physical force against the person or property of another may be used in the course of committing the offense.[60]

In representing persons facing potential "crime of violence" convictions, look closely at the criminal code or statutory definition of the charge. Determine whether it is, in fact, a crime of violence as defined under 18 U.S.C. § 16 under the categorical approach. Review the applicable circuit's case law on crimes of violence to distinguish the client's offense. Remember that there must be a finding that the offense contains

---

58. Matter of Gruenangerl, 25 I. & N. Dec. 351 (B.I.A. 2010) (briber of public official not "commercial").

59. Denis v. Attorney General, 633 F.3d 201 (3rd Cir. 2011) (evidence tampering is particularly serious crime rendering non-citizen ineligible for withholding of removal under INA § 241(b)(3)).

60. INA § 101(a)(43)(F), 8 U.S.C. § 1101 (2014).

an element of the use, attempted use, or threatened use of physical force or a finding that an offense involves a "substantial risk" that force may be used.

Addressing the issue of intent and crimes of violence, the Supreme Court in *Leocal v. Ashcroft*[61] held that convictions of driving under the influence (DUI) under statutes that require a mens rea of negligence or less are not crimes of violence as defined under 18 U.S.C. § 16 and, therefore, are not aggravated felonies. The Court in addressing the issue of intent and the use of physical force held that it requires a higher degree of intent than negligent or accidental conduct. However, the Court left open the issue of whether a conviction under a statute requiring a mens rea of recklessness would constitute a crime of violence. The Board of Immigration Appeals (BIA) has held that a DUI offense does constitute a crime of violence where it requires a mens rea of at least recklessness.[62]

Courts have held the following offenses to be crimes of violence under 18 U.S.C. § 16: kidnapping;[63] stalking;[64] attempted sexual child abuse;[65] sexual assault;[66] criminal sexual abuse;[67] attempted lewd assault;[68] statutory rape;[69] third degree assault;[70] simple assault and reckless endangerment;[71] and criminal contempt.[72] However, courts have held that the following crimes do not constitute crimes of violence under 18 U.S.C. § 16: misdemeanor vehicular homicide;[73] criminal mischief;[74]

---

61. Leocal v. Ashcroft, 543 U.S. 1 (2004).

62. Matter of Ramos, 23 I. & N. Dec. 336 (B.I.A. 2002).

63. Cheom v. INS, 129 F.3d 29 (1st Cir. 1997).

64. Matter of Malta, 23 I. & N. Dec. 656 (B.I.A. 2004).

65. United States v. Reyes-Castro, 13 F.3d 377 (10th Cir. 1993).

66. Chery v. Ashcroft, 347 F.3d 404 (2nd Cir. 2003).

67. Patel v. Ashcroft, 401 F.3d 400 (6th Cir. 2005).

68. Ramsey v. INS, 55 F.3d 580 (11th Cir. 1995).

69. Matter of B, 21 I. & N. Dec. 287 (B.I.A. 1996).

70. Matter of Martin, 23 I. & N. Dec. 491 (B.I.A. 2002). *But see* Persaud v. Edward J. McElroy, 225 F. Supp. 2d 420 (S.D.N.Y. 2002) (conviction for second degree assault under New York law not crime of violence).

71. Singh v. Gonzales, 432 F.3d 533 (3d Cir. 2005).

72. Matter of Aldabesheh, 21 I. & N. Dec. 983 (B.I.A. 1999). A conviction for first degree criminal contempt under New York law with a sentence to imprisonment of at least one year is a COV under 18 U.S.C. § 16(b).

73. Francis v. Reno, 269 F.3d 162 (3d Cir. 2001); Omar v. INS, 298 F.3d 710 (8th Cir. 2002) (Minnesota criminal vehicular homicide is a COV).

74. United States v. Landeros-Gonzales, 262 F.3d 424 (5th Cir. 2001) (criminal mischief conviction for spray painting graffiti on another's property did not support an aggravated felony enhancement for subsequent sentencing on a non-citizen's illegal reentry conviction).

battery;[75] assault;[76] manslaughter;[77] sexual assault;[78] second degree assault;[79] and felony endangerment.[80]

Aggravated Felony—Theft and Burglary Offenses

The BIA has held that taking of property constitutes a theft offense, for purposes of the aggravated felony definition, whenever there is criminal intent to deprive the owner of the rights and benefits of ownership of such property, even if the deprivation is less than total or permanent.[81] The BIA has also found that the "receipt of stolen property" parenthetical under INA § 101(a)(43)(G) includes the category of offenses involving knowing receipt, possession, or retention of property from its rightful owner.[82] Attempted possession of stolen property is considered a theft offense.[83] A misdemeanor state theft offense for which the term of imprisonment is one year has been found to be an aggravated felony.[84]

Vehicle theft has been found by the BIA to be a theft offense and, therefore, an aggravated felony under INA § 101(a)(43)(G).[85] However, the BIA has also held that burglary of a vehicle under Texas law is not an

---

75. Johnson v. United States, 130 S. Ct. 1265 (2010) (crime involving criminal force must also involve violent physical force to be a crime of violence); Larin-Ulloa v. Gonzales, 462 F.3d 456 (5th Cir. 2006) (aggravated battery under Kansas law not an aggravated felony); Flores v. Ashcroft, 350 F.3d 666 (7th Cir. 2003) (Indiana crime of battery not a COV because elements of offense do not require use of physical force).

76. Chrzanoski v. Ashcroft, 327 F.3d 188 (2d Cir. 2003) (although Connecticut assault provision requires proof that defendant intentionally caused physical injury, it is not a COV because it does not require proof that defendant used physical force to cause injury).

77. Jobson v. Ashcroft, 326 F.3d 367 (2d Cir. 2003) (statute in question covered passive conduct or omissions that do not require use of force).

78. Xiong v. INS, 173 F.3d 601 (7th Cir. 1999) (Wisconsin second degree sexual assault not a COV because it includes conduct not encompassed in federal definition).

79. United States v. Royal, 731 F.3d 333 (4th Cir. 2013).

80. United States v. Hernandez-Castellanos, 287 F.3d 876 (9th Cir. 2002) (Arizona felony endangerment not a COV where not all of the conduct punishable involves substantial risk that physical force may be used).

81. Matter of V–Z–S–, 22 I. & N. Dec. 1338 (B.I.A. 2000). *See also* United States v. Corona-Sanchez, 291 F.3d 1201 (9th Cir. 2002).

82. Matter of Bahta, 22 I. & N. Dec. 1381 (B.I.A. 2000).

83. *Id.*

84. United States v. Christopher, 252 F.3d 444 (11th Cir. 2001). *See also* United States v. Graham, 169 F.3d 787 (3d Cir. 1999).

85. *V–Z–S–*, 22 I. & N. Dec. 1338. *See also* Hernandez-Mancilla v. INS, 246 F.3d 1002 (7th Cir. 2001) (possession of stolen vehicle is an aggravated felony); United States v. Vazquez-Flores, 265 F.3d 1122 (10th Cir. 2001) (attempted receiving or transferring a stolen vehicle is an aggravated felony).

aggravated felony.[86] The BIA applied a federal standard to determine if the state offense fit within the definition of aggravated felony. Noting the absence of any definition of burglary in the INA, it turned to the generic definition of burglary as noted by the Supreme Court in *Taylor v. United States* and held that the state definition did not fit the federal definition. Therefore, the state offense did not constitute an aggravated felony.[87]

At least three federal courts of appeals have adopted the *Taylor* definition in interpreting the term "burglary offense" under INA § 101(a)(43)(G).[88] For example, the Fifth Circuit in *Lopez-Elias v. Reno*[89] found that although the petitioner had been charged with burglary of a vehicle with intent to commit theft, the statute itself did not require actual commission of theft. Therefore, the petitioner did not commit a theft offense under INA § 101(a)(43)(G). The court also found that the petitioner did not commit a burglary offense. However, it did hold that the petitioner had committed a crime of violence and therefore may have been deportable as an aggravated felon if legacy INS had so charged. Following the reasoning in *Lopez-Elias*, the court held in *Santos v. Reno*[90] that burglary of a vehicle did not constitute a theft or burglary offense under INA § 101(a)(43)(G), but concluded it did constitute a crime of violence.[91]

The Supreme Court has held that aiding and abetting theft is a crime which falls within the generic definition of theft as noted in *Taylor v. United States*. Therefore, a violation of the California Vehicle Code under which "any person who drives or takes a vehicle not his or her own, without the consent of the owner . . . or any person who is a party or an accessory to or an accomplice in the driving or unauthorized taking or stealing, is guilty of a public offense,"[92] is an aggravated felony.[93]

86. Matter of Perez, 22 I. & N. Dec. 1325 (B.I.A. 2000).

87. Taylor v. United States, 495 U.S. 575 (1990).

88. Sareang Ye v. INS, 214 F.3d 1128 (9th Cir. 2000); Lopez-Elias v. Reno, 209 F.3d 788 (5th Cir. 2000); Solorazano-Patlan v. INS, 207 F.3d 869 (7th Cir. 2000).

89. 209 F.3d 788 (5th Cir. 2000).

90. 228 F.3d 591 (5th Cir. 2000).

91. *See also* Matter of Brieva, 23 I. & N. Dec. 766 (B.I.A. 2005) (unauthorized use of motor vehicle is a COV); United States v. Galvan-Rodriguez, 169 F.3d 217 (5th Cir. 1999) (unauthorized use of motor vehicle is a crime of violence for sentence enhancement in illegal reentry case). *But see* Nguyen v. Holder, 571 F.3d 524 (6th Cir. 2009) (auto theft as defined under California Penal Code not a crime of violence).

92. CAL. VEH. CODE ANN. § 10851(a).

93. Gonzales v. Duenas-Alvarez, 127 U.S. 815 (2007).

Aggravated Felony—Fraud and Deceit Offenses

An offense is not considered to be "fraud or deceit" for the purposes of the definition of aggravated felony unless fraud or deceit is a necessary or proven element of the crime.[94] Even where a statute includes the element of intent to deceive, the crime may not constitute an aggravated felony. In *Sui v. INS*,[95] the Second Circuit held that possession of counterfeit securities with intent to deceive does not necessarily constitute an attempt to pass these securities and cause a loss. Legacy INS could not evade the monetary loss requirement by charging the offense under INA § 101(a)(43)(U) (attempt). Further, the court held that the respondent could not be deported under INA § 101(a)(43)(M)(i) because the loss to the victim did not exceed $10,000.[96] However, an offense may fall under § 101(a)(43)(U) as an attempt, even without actual loss, if the attempted loss to the victim(s) exceeded $10,000 and the record of conviction demonstrates a substantial step towards the commission of the offense.[97]

The amount of loss for which a non-citizen was convicted and not the amount of restitution, or other losses, determines whether the conviction is an aggravated felony.[98] INA § 101(a)(43)(M) requires an actual loss to the victim or victims in excess of $10,000.[99] The BIA has held that because the phrase "in which the loss to the victim or victims exceeds $10,000" is not tied to an element of the fraud or deceit offense, the loss determination is not subject to limitations imposed by the categorical approach, the modified categorical approach, or a divisibility analysis.[100] The United States Supreme Court agrees with this view and has held that the loss to the victim is a factual inquiry, the outcome of which can be determined during removal proceedings by clear and convincing evidence.[101] Evidence of loss, therefore, can be proven by evidence outside the record of conviction, such as restitution orders, presentence reports and admissions dur-

---

94. Valansi v. Ashcroft, 278 F.3d 203 (3d Cir. 2002).
95. 250 F.3d 105 (2d Cir. 2001).
96. *See also* Chang v. INS, 307 F.3d 1185 (9th Cir. 2002) (where petitioner convicted of cashing a counterfeit check in amount of $605.30 and sentenced to eight months incarceration and restitution in the amount of $30,000 for other alleged fraudulent transactions for which petitioner not convicted, court held not an aggravated felony).
97. Matter of Onyido, 22 I. & N. Dec. 552 (B.I.A. 1999).
98. Dulal-Whiteway v. DHS, 501 F.3d 116 (2d Cir. 2007); Obasohan v. U.S. Att'y Gen., 479 F.3d 785 (11th Cir. 2007); Alaka v. Att'y Gen. of the U.S., 456 F.3d 88 (3d Cir. 2006).
99. Pierre v. Holder, 588 F.3d 767 (2d Cir. 2009); Ming Lam Sui v. INS, 250 F.3d 105 (2d Cir. 2001).
100. Matter of Babaisakov, 24 I. & N. Dec. 306 (B.I.A. 2007).
101. Nijhawan v. Holder, 557 U.S. 29 (2009).

ing plea colloquies, as long as the loss relates to the conduct for which the person was convicted and, for removal purposes, is shown by clear and convincing evidence.[102] Several courts have rejected the notion that INA § 101(a)(43)(M)(i) applies only to individuals and corporations and that the government cannot be a victim.[103]

Controlled Substance Offenses

Persons convicted of a narcotics related offense or involved in narcotics activity, whether through trafficking or use, may be subject to removal under the following categories:

- Conviction for possession of a controlled substance or relating to a controlled substance;[104]
- Being a controlled substance trafficker;[105]
- A conviction for an aggravated felony;[106] or
- Being a drug abuser or addict.[107]

It is important to review the elements of the crime for which your client is charged or has been convicted and compare it to the relevant statutory provisions mentioned above to determine if it is in fact a controlled substance offense that may result in a finding of deportability or inadmissibility. Deportability for a controlled substance offense may be based on a misdemeanor or felony offense, regardless of sentence imposed. An exception to the ground of deportability exists where a non-citizen is convicted for possession of 30 grams or less of marijuana.[108] Possession of that amount of marijuana is a bar to admissibility (i.e., in seeking adjustment of status), but there is a waiver available.[109] Possession of cocaine is not considered an aggravated felony but possession of crack cocaine is considered an aggravated felony.[110]

---

102. *Id.*

103. Kawashima v. Gonzales, 503 F.3d 997 (9th Cir. 2007); Balogun v. U.S. Att'y Gen., 425 F.3d 1356 (11th Cir. 2005).

104. INA §§ 212(a)(2)(B)(i)–(ii), 8 U.S.C. § 1182 (2014), 237(a)(2)(B)(i), 8 U.S.C. § 1227 (2014).

105. *Id.* § 212(a)(2)(C), 8 U.S.C. § 1182.

106. *Id.* § 101(a)(43)(B), 8 U.S.C. § 1101.

107. *Id.* § 237(a)(2)(B)(ii), 8 U.S.C. § 1227.

108. *Id.* § 237(a)(2)(B)(i), 8 U.S.C. § 1227. The exception does not apply if the drug possession occurred within a correctional facility. Matter of Moncada-Servellon, 24 I. & N. Dec. 62 (B.I.A. 2007).

109. INA § 212(h), 8 U.S.C. § 1182 (2014).

110. Matter of L–G–, 20 I. & N. Dec. 905 (B.I.A. 1994).

If the controlled substance conviction constitutes a drug trafficking offense as defined in 18 U.S.C. § 924(c)(2), a non-citizen is subject to removal as an aggravated felon regardless of the date of conviction. Section 924(c)(2) defines a drug trafficking offense as follows:

> For purposes of this subsection, the term "drug trafficking crime" means any felony punishable under the Controlled Substances Act (21 U.S.C. § 801 *et seq.*), the Controlled Substances Import and Export Act (21 U.S.C. § 951 *et seq.*), or the Maritime Drug Law Enforcement Act (45 U.S.C. App. 1901 *et seq.*).

Drug offenses are often classified differently state by state. In some states, possession of cocaine may be a felony, while in others, possession offenses are considered misdemeanors.[111] Under the BIA's test as developed in *Matter of Barrett*[112] and *Matter of Davis*,[113] a conviction is a drug trafficking crime for purposes of INA § 101(a)(43)(B) if the conviction involves illicit trafficking in any controlled substance or if the conviction is defined as a drug trafficking crime under 18 U.S.C. § 924(c).

Under the first prong of the *Barrett/Davis* test, a conviction for "illicit trafficking in a controlled substance" occurs:

- If the offense is a felony under the law of the convicting state or federal body, and
- The offense contains a trafficking element which involves the unlawful trading or dealing of a controlled substance.[114] In order to determine if an offense is a drug trafficking crime, counsel must look beyond the title of the statute.[115]

Under the second prong of the *Barrett/Davis* test, a state drug conviction can be an aggravated felony if it is analogous to an offense punishable

---

111. For an interesting discussion relating to the federal analysis of drug crimes, see I. Greenstein, *Into the Rabbit's Hole: When a Misdemeanor Is a Felony—The* Davis/Barrett *Hypothetical Federal Felony Analysis of Drug Crimes, in* IMMIGRATION & NATIONALITY LAW HANDBOOK 137 (AILA 2006–2007).

112. Matter of Barrett, 20 I. & N. Dec. 171 (B.I.A. 1990).

113. Matter of Davis, 20 I. & N. Dec. 536 (B.I.A. 1992).

114. *Id.*

115. Gerbier v. Holmes, 280 F.3d 297 (3d Cir. 2002) (guilty plea to possession of cocaine under Delaware trafficking statute not a trafficking offense); Leyva-Licea v. INS, 187 F.3d 1147 (9th Cir. 1999) (solicitation to possess marijuana under Arizona law not a drug trafficking crime).

under one of the three federal statutes mentioned in 18 U.S.C. § 924(c)(2) (the Controlled Substance Act, the Controlled Substance Import and Export Act, or the Maritime Drug Law Enforcement Act). It is not necessary that a conviction under this approach contain a trafficking element.[116]

The Supreme Court in *Lopez v. Gonzales* held that a state felony conviction for possession of a controlled substance that would not qualify as a felony under federal law is not an aggravated felony under INA § 101(a)(43)(B).[117] Therefore, a state misdemeanor conviction may be a felony if it so qualifies under federal law.[118] Whether a controlled substance offense qualifies as a federal felony is determined by 21 U.S.C. § 844(a).

Following *Lopez*, the BIA addressed the issue of whether multiple possession offenses constitute an aggravated felony.[119] Acknowledging that it was bound by *Lopez* and the relevant circuit court decisions interpreting the federal recidivist offense at 21 U.S.C. § 844(a), the BIA held that a second or subsequent state conviction for simple possession of a controlled substance is not an aggravated felony under INA § 101(a)(43)(B), unless the non-citizen's status as a recidivist drug offender was either admitted by the non-citizen or determined by a judge and jury in connection with a criminal prosecution for that particular offense and could have resulted in a federal felony conviction regardless of whether the offender was actually charged as a recidivist.[120] The Fifth Circuit affirmed this decision. The United States Supreme Court reversed, holding that the defendant must also have actually been convicted of a crime that is itself punishable as a felony under federal law. The Court held that the "mere possibility that the defendant's conduct, coupled with facts outside of the record of conviction, could have authorized a felony conviction under federal law" was insufficient to deem such a conviction an aggravated felony.[121] The Court distanced itself from the "hypothetical federal conviction" approach that had gained support with several circuits.[122]

116. *Davis*, 20 I. & N. Dec. 536.

117. Lopez v. Gonzales, 549 U.S. 47 (2006) (overruling Matter of Yanez-Garcia, 23 I. & N. Dec. 390 (B.I.A. 2002)).

118. Matter of Aruna, 24 I. & N. Dec. 492 (B.I.A. 2008).

119. Matter of Carachuri-Rosendo, 24 I. & N. Dec. 382 (B.I.A. 2007).

120. *Id.*

121. Carachuri-Rosendo v. Holder, 560 U.S. —, 130 S. Ct. 2577 (2010).

122. See United States v. Pacheco-Diaz, 506 F.3d 545 (7th Cir. 2007); United States v. Palacios-Suarez, 418 F.3d 692 (6th Cir. 2005); United States v. Sanchez-Villalobos, 412 F.3d 572 (5th Cir. 2005), *cert. denied*, 546 U.S. 1137 (2006); United States v. Simpson, 319 F.3d 81 (2d Cir. 2002).

Although the issue of recidivism seems to have been settled in favor of defendants, it remains important to carefully research the status of the law in the applicable jurisdiction and to raise any legal issues before the immigration judge and the BIA in order to preserve them for appeal.[123]

As noted above, it is important to review the definition and elements of the crime with which the client is charged or has been convicted and compare them to the definitions contained in 18 U.S.C. § 924(c)(2) to determine if, in fact, the crime is a controlled substance conviction for immigration purposes. Carefully review the relevant federal and administrative case law and authorities, published and unpublished, to learn the relevant interpretations of controlled substance crimes for immigration purposes.

Drug sale convictions, including those without remuneration, are considered drug trafficking crimes where the elements of the state offense correspond to the elements of the federal felony offense.[124] In *Matter of Aruna*, the BIA held that the federal statute defining distribution of any amount of marijuana is a felony offense, regardless of amount or remuneration. However, it noted that its decision applies to cases arising in all circuits with the exception of the Third.[125] In *Steele v. Blackman*,[126] the Third Circuit held that three drug convictions—two misdemeanor criminal sale of marijuana (without remuneration) convictions and a misdemeanor criminal possession of marijuana conviction—did not constitute trafficking crimes, and therefore, were not aggravated felonies. However, even in the Third Circuit, a conviction for distribution of a controlled substance generally will result in the removal of a non-citizen as an aggravated felon. Counsel should not forget that possession of crack cocaine is also an aggravated felony.[127]

Any alien who has been a drug abuser or addict at any time after entry is deportable. Therefore, during criminal proceedings, it is particularly important to avoid admissions on the record relating to a client's use of or addiction to a controlled substance.

---

123. For more information on courts of appeals cases, contact the Legal Action Center of the American Immigration Council, the local chapter of AILA or the National Immigration Project.

124. Matter of Aruna, 24 I. & N. Dec. 452 (B.I.A. 2008).

125. *Id.*

126. 236 F.3d 130 (3d Cir. 2001).

127. Matter of L–G–, 20 I. & N. Dec. 905 (B.I.A. 1994).

Domestic Violence

If a client is convicted of a crime of domestic violence, he or she may be subject to removal on three separate grounds: (1) as a person convicted of a *crime of domestic violence;*[128] (2) as a person convicted of a *crime of moral turpitude;*[129] or (3) as a person convicted of a crime of violence, which is an *aggravated felony.*[130]

Under INA § 237(a)(2)(E), a non-citizen may be subject to removal for a conviction of a crime of domestic violence as follows:

> (i) Domestic violence, stalking, and child abuse: Any alien who at any time after entry is convicted of a crime of domestic violence, a crime of stalking, or a crime of child abuse, child neglect, or child abandonment is deportable. For purposes of this clause, the term "crime of domestic violence" means any crime of violence (as defined in 18 U.S.C. § 16) against a person, committed by a current or former spouse of the person, by an individual with whom the person shares a child in common, by an individual who is cohabiting with or has cohabited with the person as a spouse, by an individual similarly situated to a spouse of the person under the domestic or family violence laws of the jurisdiction where the offense occurs, or by any other individual against a person who is protected from that individual's acts under the domestic or family violence laws of the United States or any State, Indian tribal government, or unit of local government.

Carefully examine the statute or code under which a client has been charged or convicted to determine:

- Does it contain the same elements as the statutory definition of crime of violence in 18 U.S.C. § 16 as referred to in INA § 101(a)(43)(F)?
- Is it a crime of domestic violence as defined under INA § 237(a)(2)(E)?
- Can you arrange for a plea to a lesser, nondomestic violence-related offense, avoiding any mention of such in the record of proceedings?[131]

---

128. INA § 237(a)(2)(E), 8 U.S.C. § 1227 (2014).

129. Matter of Tran, 21 I. & N. Dec. 291 (B.I.A. 1996).

130. If the conviction results from a charge of assault and the sentence imposed is one year or more, the crime may be considered a COV and, therefore, an aggravated felony. INA § 101(a)(43)(F), 8 U.S.C. § 1101 (2014).

131. 8 CFR § 1003.41. The immigration judge will generally not look behind the conviction to determine additional possible grounds of removability. Matter of Short, 20 I. & N. Dec. 136 (B.I.A. 1989).

Not all crimes that appear to be crimes of domestic violence qualify as such for immigration purposes. The BIA has held that a conviction for domestic battery in violation of §§ 242 and 243(e)(1) of the California Penal Code does not categorically qualify within the Ninth Circuit as a "crime of domestic violence" under INA § 237(a)(2)(E)(i).[132] The BIA has also held that a misdemeanor offense of assault and battery against a family or household member in violation of the Virginia Code is not categorically a crime of violence and, thus, not categorically a crime of domestic violence under the Immigration and Nationality Act.[133]

Under INA § 237(a)(2)(A)(i), a non-citizen convicted of domestic violence may also be subject to deportation for conviction of a *crime of moral turpitude*. That provision states as follows:

> Any alien who—(I) is convicted of a crime involving moral turpitude committed within five years (or 10 years in the case of an alien provided lawful permanent resident status under section 245(j) of this title) after the date of admission, and (II) is convicted of a crime for which a sentence of one year or longer is deportable.[134]

Under INA § 101(a)(43)(F), a non-citizen may also be subject to removal if the domestic violence conviction is found to be a crime of violence and, therefore, an aggravated felony as defined by 18 U.S.C. § 16.[135]

In order to avoid a charge and conviction for an aggravated felony, attempt to obtain a sentence of less than one year. Criminal defense counsel and the prosecutor should work together to craft a sentence, including incarceration if necessary, that is less than one year. In many cases, courts want defendants accused of domestic violence crimes to understand the seriousness of the offense. Such concerns can be satisfied by fashioning a plea agreement that provides for a short period of incarceration followed by supervised release, the whole not to exceed 364 days.

---

132. Matter of Sanudo, 23 I. & N. Dec. 968 (B.I.A. 2006). *See also* Fernandez-Ruiz v. Gonzales, 466 F.3d 1121 (9th Cir. 2006) (Arizona conviction for domestic violence assault not a "crime of domestic violence" under the INA).
133. Matter of Velasquez, 25 I. & N. Dec. 278 (B.I.A. 2010).
134. Crimes of domestic violence are considered to be crimes of moral turpitude. *Tran*, 21 I. & N. Dec. 291.
135. Flores v. Ashcroft, 350 F.3d 666 (7th Cir. 2003) (Indiana battery offense not a COV and, therefore, not an aggravated felony for crime of domestic violence deportation purposes because elements of offense do not require use of physical force).

In representing a client faced with possible conviction(s) for domestic violence crimes, limit the record to avoid any references to the nature of the crime. On multiple charges of assault, try to avoid a conviction for more than one. If the attorney obtains only one simple assault conviction and avoids any mention of the domestic nature of the crime in the record, the client may avoid removal for domestic violence as well as for minor assault that does not constitute a crime of moral turpitude.[136]

Firearm Offenses

There are two types of firearm offenses that may expose clients to removal. One is for illicit trafficking in firearms under 19 U.S.C. § 921, which is considered an aggravated felony. The other is broader and defined under INA § 237(a)(2)(C) as follows:

> Any alien who at any time after admission is convicted under any law of purchasing, selling, offering for sale, exchanging, using, owning, possessing or carrying, or of attempting or conspiring to purchase, sell, offer for sale, exchange, use, own, possess, or carry, any weapon, part, or accessory which is a firearm or destructive device (as defined in section 921(a) of title 18, U.S. Code) in violation of any law is deportable.

Convictions for attempt or conspiracy to commit firearms offenses are grounds for removal.[137] Where use of a firearm is an essential element of the crime, (i.e., where use of a firearm elevates the charge to more serious penalties), the conviction is a firearms offense.[138] A sentence enhancement for using a firearm, however, is not a conviction for a firearms offense.[139] A conviction where the statute is divisible (e.g., possession of a dangerous weapon) is not considered a ground of removal unless the record of conviction establishes the crime involved was a firearm.[140]

Two categories of firearms offenses are considered aggravated felonies: (1) illicit trafficking in firearms or destructive materials (INA § 101(a)(43)(C)), and (2) miscellaneous federal firearms and explosive materials offenses (INA § 101(a)(43)(E)).[141] In order to determine if an offense involves illicit

---

136. Matter of Fualaau, 21 I. & N. Dec. 475 (B.I.A. 1996) (assault in the 3d degree is not a CMT).

137. Matter of St. John, 21 I. & N. Dec. 593 (B.I.A. 1997).

138. Matter of P–F–, 20 I. & N. Dec. 661 (B.I.A. 1993).

139. Matter of Rodriguez-Cortez, 20 I. & N. Dec. 587 (B.I.A. 1992).

140. Matter of Pichardo, 21 I. & N. Dec. 330 (B.I.A. 1996).

141. The B.I.A. in *Matter of Vasquez-Munoz*, 23 I. & N. Dec. 207 (B.I.A. 2001), held that possession of a firearm by a felon in violation of CAL. PENAL CODE § 12021(a)(1) is an aggravated

trafficking in firearms under § 101(a)(43)(C), review the definitions of firearms and destructive devices under 18 U.S.C. § 921(a)(3). This section does not include any mention of criminal offenses involving ammunition, other than "armor piercing ammunition." Illicit trafficking in explosives is also considered an aggravated felony under § 101(a)(43)(E).[142]

State firearm offenses, which can be analogous to federal offenses, may be considered aggravated felonies.[143] Therefore, in determining whether a client's state firearms conviction constitutes an aggravated felony, make sure to carefully compare the state statute with the relevant federal statutes cited in INA § 101(a)(43)(C) and (E). Distinguish where possible in order to present arguments that the client's conviction does not constitute an aggravated felony.

An LPR convicted of a non-trafficking firearm offense may be eligible for relief from removal.[144] Also, if the client has a U.S. citizen spouse or parent, he or she may be eligible to adjust status without needing a waiver.[145] If the firearms conviction is also an aggravated felony, one may need to seek a waiver under INA § 212(h).

HOW TO DETERMINE WHETHER A CONVICTION SUBJECTS YOUR CLIENT TO REMOVAL

In determining whether a conviction forms the basis for removal as an aggravated felony, a controlled substance violation, a firearms offense, or a crime involving domestic violence, courts look to the categorical and modified categorical approaches. The BIA in addition to using the categorical and modified categorical approaches also uses an additional

---

felony. The B.I.A. overruled its earlier decision in that case after the Ninth Circuit concluded that possession of a firearm by a felon under the Cal. Penal Code constituted an aggravated felony "as an offense described in 18 U.S.C. § 922(g)(1)." United States v. Castillo-Rivera, 244 F.3d 1020 (9th Cir. 2001).

142. The definition of explosive materials is contained in 18 U.S.C. § 841(d).

143. Vasquez-Muniz, 23 I. & N. Dec. 207. *But see* United States v. Sandoval-Barajas, 206 F.3d 853 (9th Cir. 2000) (Washington state offense of unlicensed possession of a firearm by a non-citizen is not "described in" the federal statute prohibiting possession of a firearm by an undocumented non-citizen and, therefore, is not an aggravated felony); United States v. Hernandez-Neave, 291 F.2d 296 (5th Cir. 2001) (defendant's conviction for unlawfully carrying firearm in place licensed to sell alcoholic beverages not a COV).

144. INA § 240A(a), 8 U.S.C. § 1229A (2014). Under this provision, if your client has been an LPR for not less than five years, has resided continuously in the United States for seven years after having been admitted in any status, and has not been convicted of an aggravated felony, he or she may be eligible for cancellation of removal.

145. Matter of Rainford, 20 I. & N. Dec. 598 (B.I.A. 1992).

standard to determine if a conviction subjects a non-citizen to removal; looking to the "non-elemental facts" of a conviction to decide if it can form the basis for removal.

Categorical Approach

The categorical approach describes the way that immigration judges, the BIA and reviewing federal courts generally decide if a state or federal offense constitutes a conviction under immigration law and, thus, triggers removal. Under the categorical approach, an immigration judge compares the "generic" ground of removal with the minimum conduct necessary to form a criminal conviction under the state or federal statute under which a non-citizen was convicted. The immigration judge can look only to the statutory definition of the state or local offense, compare it to the ground of removal charged, and may not consider other evidence concerning prior crimes, including facts underlying the conviction(s).[146] If every violation contained in the relevant criminal state or federal statute falls within the ground of removal under the INA, then the conviction triggers removal. Thus, an offense will only be considered a conviction for removal purposes (e.g., an aggravated felony) if the full range of conduct included in the criminal statute falls within the meaning of that term.[147] To apply the categorical approach to determine if the conviction forms the basis for removal, the following steps should be taken:

- Obtain a copy of the record of conviction.
- Obtain a copy of the criminal statute under which your client was convicted. As statutes change over time, be sure to obtain a copy of the statute that applied at the time of the conviction. Be sure to obtain a copy of the sentencing provisions that applied to your client's conviction to determine if it was a misdemeanor or felony.

Compare the elements of the ground of removal to the elements of the criminal statute under which your client was convicted.

If the full range of conduct covered by the criminal statute falls within the meaning of the provision of deportability or inadmissibility, your client is subject to removal.

---

146. Taylor v. United States, 495 U.S. 575 (1990). *See also* Shephard v. United States, 544 U.S. 13 (2005).

147. United States v. Baron-Medina, 187 F.3d 1144 (9th Cir. 1999) (lewd or lascivious act on a child under 14 constitutes "sexual abuse of a minor" and is therefore, an "aggravated felony") (relying on *Taylor*, 495 U.S. 575).

In *Nijhawan v. Holder*,[148] the Supreme Court issued a decision in a case where the petitioner challenged the government's abandonment of the categorical approach relating to the $10,000 monetary loss required to establish fraud as an aggravated felony under INA § 101(a)(43)(M). In this case, the Court permitted the adjudicator to consider and rely on factual admissions and findings made for sentencing purposes, once a conviction has already occurred.[149] The court applied a "circumstance-specific" approach instead of the categorical approach to determine the $10,000 loss requirement, but made clear that this approach only applies where the factor at issue is found to refer to a specific way in which the non-citizen offender committed a crime in the particular situation. It is important to note that the Court made it clear that the categorical approach applies to most aggravated felonies, which refer to generic crimes rather than particular factual circumstances relating to the commission of a crime on a particular occasion.[150]

Modified Categorical Approach

Most courts use a modified categorical approach. Under this approach, if the criminal statute covering your client's conviction is divisible, that is, if it includes conduct that would constitute a conviction for removal purposes and conduct that would not, the immigration judge will follow what is called the modified categorical approach and look to the record of conviction.[151]

In applying the modified categorical approach to determine if a conviction triggers removal, the immigration judge can look beyond the language of the state or federal statute of conviction to documents that constitute the record of conviction, including the charging document, the judgment of conviction, jury instructions, a signed guilty plea, the transcript of the plea proceedings, and any explicit factual findings by the trial court to which the non-citizen assented.[152] An immigration judge can also consider the contents of police reports as part of the record of convic-

---

148. Nijhawan v. Holder, 557 U.S. 29 (2009).
149. *Id.*
150. *Id.*
151. United States v. Corona-Sanchez, 291 F.3d 1201 (9th Cir. 2002).
152. Shepard v. United States, 544 U.S. 13 (2005); Sandoval-Lua v. Gonzales, 499 F.3d 1121 (9th Cir. 2007); Larin-Ulloa v. Gonzales, 462 F.3d 456 (5th Cir. 2006); Canada v. Gonzales, 448 F.3d 560 (2d Cir. 2006); Tokatly v. Ashcroft, 371 F.3d 613 (9th Cir. 2004).

tion if they were specifically incorporated into the guilty plea or were admitted by the non-citizen during the criminal proceedings.[153]

To apply the modified categorical approach, follow the steps mentioned above under the categorical approach and also do the following:

- If the criminal statute is divisible, review the criminal record, including the charging document, the plea agreement, the transcript of the colloquy and any specific factual findings that the criminal court judge made to which your client agreed.[154]

Non-elemental Facts

The BIA has abandoned the categorical approach in determining whether certain convictions constitute aggravated felonies. In 2007, the BIA issued a pair of decisions that limit the application of the categorical approach. In *Matter of Babaisakov*,[155] the BIA addressed the scope of evidence that an immigration judge may consider to determine whether a conviction for an offense involving fraud or deceit was one in which the loss to the victim was more than $10,000, as required by INA § 101(a)(43)(M)(i). The BIA held that the immigration judge may consider any evidence admissible in removal proceedings relating to the loss to the victim and is not restricted to the record of conviction. In making this finding, the BIA held that the loss requirement of the particular aggravated felony was not an element of the fraud or deceit offense in question. Therefore, facts relating to the loss can be determined from evidence beyond the record of conviction that may be considered in the categorical and modified categorical approaches.[156]

In *Matter of Gertsenshteyn*, the BIA distinguished between grounds of removal that require exclusive focus on the elements of the prior conviction, and thus require analysis under the categorical approach, and those grounds that include requirements not tied to the elements of the state or federal criminal statue—nonelement requirements for removal.[157] The

---

153. Matter of Milian-Dubon, 25 I. & N. Dec. 197 (B.I.A. 2010).

154. *Shephard*, 544 U.S. 13. *See also* Matter of Ajami, 22 I. & N. Dec. 949 (B.I.A. 1999) (IJ can look to indictment, plea, verdict and sentence).

155. Matter of Babaisakov, 24 I. & N. Dec. 306 (B.I.A. 2007).

156. The B.I.A. recognized that its decision represents a departure from principles involving aggravated felony charges based on fraud or deceit crimes but declined to address conflicting circuit court law. *Babaisakov*, 24 I. & N. Dec. at 322.

157. Matter of Gertsenshteyn, 24 I. & N. Dec. 111 (B.I.A. 2007), *rev'd*, 544 F.3d 137 (2d Cir. 2008).

402 *What Every Lawyer Needs to Know about Immigration Law*

BIA held that these do not describe a category of a state or federal offense, but rather act to limit or aggravate factors meant to distinguish between more or less serious violations of the statute in question. Such factors can be proven by evidence outside the record.[158]

In a subsequent decision, the BIA expanded its holding in *Babaisakov* and discussed the scope of evidence necessary to prove that an offense constitutes a particularly serious crime.[159] The BIA held that once the elements of an offense bring it within the ambit of a particularly serious crime, all reliable information may be considered to make that determination, including but not limited to the record of conviction and sentencing information.

However, the BIA refused to extend its finding in *Matter of Babaisakov* and *Matter of Gertsenshteyn* to the nonaggravated felony of child abuse under INA § 237(a)(2)(E)(i). In order to be removable under this ground, a criminal offense must include the minority of the complaining witness as an element of the crime.[160]

Crimes Involving Moral Turpitude

In a significant departure from previous practice, the attorney general in *Matter of Silva-Trevino*, held that the immigration judge may consider any additional evidence necessary or appropriate to resolve the issue of whether a crime is one involving moral turpitude.[161] In making this determination, immigration judges and the BIA should:

- Look to the statute of conviction under the categorical approach and determine whether there is a realistic probability that the state or federal criminal statute under which the non-citizen was convicted would be applied to reach conduct that does not involve moral turpitude;
- If the categorical approach does not resolve the issue, engage in a modified categorical approach and examine the record of conviction, including documents such as the indictment, the judgment of conviction, jury instructions, a signed guilty plea, and the plea transcript; and
- If the record of conviction is inconclusive, consider any additional evidence deemed necessary or appropriate to resolve whether the conviction is for a crime of moral turpitude.[162]

---

158. *Id.*
159. Matter of N-A-M-, 24 I. & N. Dec. 336 (B.I.A. 2007).
160. Matter of Velasquez-Herrera, 24 I. & N. Dec. 503 (B.I.A. 2008).
161. Matter of Silva-Trevino, 24 I. & N. Dec. 687 (AG 2008).
162. *Id.*

This decision represents a significant departure from the way in which immigration judges, the Board and courts of appeals have analyzed crimes to determine if they are crimes of moral turpitude and essentially discards the application of both the categorical and modified categorical approaches.[163] However, with the exception of the Seventh and Eighth Circuits,[164] all circuits have found that the categorical approach applies to the determination of whether a crime constitutes a crime of mortal turpitude for immigration purposes.[165] Therefore, the impact of this decision may, in fact, be minimal.[166]

The Board later clarified that the traditional categorical approach used by the Supreme Court in *Duenas-Alvarez*[167] applied to its categorical analysis in *Silva-Trevino* but affirmed its position that the modified categorical approach may be used if the categorical approach is inconclusive. Several federal circuits have thus far rejected the Board's analysis and limited the question whether the crime is one of moral turpitude to the traditional categorical or modified approach.[168]

IS THE CONVICTION A CONVICTION FOR IMMIGRATION PURPOSES?

In addition to examining the elements of an offense in order to determine if it constitutes a crime for which a client may be subject to removal, attorneys must also determine if the conviction itself constitutes a conviction for immigration purposes.[169] To do this, first look at the definition of conviction under INA § 101(a)(48)(A), which provides:

---

163. *Id.*

164. Ali v. Mukasey, 521 F.3d 737 (7th Cir. 2008); Bobadilla v. Holder, 679 F.3d 1052 (8th Cir. 2012).

165. Silva-Trevino v. Holder, 742 F.3d 197 (5th Cir. 2014); Olivas-Matla v. Holder, 716 F.3d 1199 (9th Cir. 2013); Prudencio v. Holder, 669 F.3d 472 (4th Cir. 2012); Lajardo v. U.S. Att'y Gen., 659 F.3d 1303 (11th Cir. 2011); Jean-Louis v. Att'y Gen. of U.S., 582 F.3d 462 (3rd Cir. 2009).

166. For a detailed discussion and analysis of *Silva-Trevino*, see Jennifer Lee Koh, *The Whole Better Than the Sum*, 26 Geo. Immigr. L.J. 257 (2012); Pooja R. Dadhania, Note, *The Categorical Approach for Crimes Involving Moral Turpitude after* Silva-Trevino, 111 Colum. L. Rev. 313 (2011).

167. 549 U.S. 183 (2007).

168. Fajardo v. U.S. Atty. Gen., 2011 WL 4808171 (11th Cir. 2011); Jean Louis v. Attorney General, 582 F.3d 462 (3d Cir. 2009).

169. For a concise overview of what constitutes a conviction for immigration purposes, see A. J. Greer and T. L. Donovan, *"Conviction" as Defined under the Immigration and Nationality Act: An Evolving Meaning*, 06–3 Immigration Briefings (Mar. 2006).

The term "conviction" means, with respect to an alien, a formal judgment of guilt of the alien entered by a court or, if adjudication of guilt has been withheld where:

1. a judge or jury has found the alien guilty or the alien has entered a plea of guilty or *nolo contendere* or has admitted sufficient facts to warrant a finding of guilt, and
2. the judge has ordered some form of punishment, penalty, or restraint on the alien's liberty to be imposed.

Prior to the passage of IIRAIRA, the INA did not contain a statutory definition of "conviction." Case law determined what dispositions were considered convictions for immigration purposes. This new statutory definition overrules the previous definition of conviction explained by the BIA in *Matter of Ozkok*.[170] In *Ozkok*, the BIA excluded from the definition certain dispositions where the adjudication of guilt had been withheld based on fulfillment of certain conditions.

The statutory definition of conviction includes nearly any conviction regardless of the type of sentence imposed. The prior requirement under *Ozkok* that the conviction be final, i.e., that appellate review be exhausted, may also be in doubt. In *Matter of Punu*,[171] the BIA held that a conviction exists under the Texas deferred adjudication statute even where further appellate review remains possible. However, practitioners should still argue that a conviction is not considered final until all avenues of appeal have been exhausted.

The phrase *term of imprisonment* often determines if a conviction is an aggravated felony for immigration purposes. For example, a crime of violence where the term of imprisonment is one year or more is considered an aggravated felony. Counsel should note that a client may be considered an aggravated felon, and thus deportable, without ever serving a day in jail. In order to avoid a potential finding that your client's conviction constitutes an aggravated felony (crime of violence, theft), counsel should urge criminal defense counsel to advocate for sentences of less than one year. Where the court is concerned about the seriousness of the offense and wants to sentence a defendant to a year, defense counsel should attempt to negotiate a period of incarceration for less than a year to satisfy the judge's concerns.

Where a *deferred adjudication* statute requires admission of sufficient facts to warrant a finding of guilt and some form of punishment is

---

170. Matter of Ozkok, 19 I. & N. Dec. 546 (B.I.A. 1988).
171. Matter of Punu, 22 I. & N. Dec. 224 (B.I.A. 1998).

ordered (i.e., the program itself), such adjudication is considered a conviction for immigration purposes.[172]

A non-citizen is not subject to deportation if the conviction was for
a *petty offense*. A conviction is considered a petty offense when the maximum penalty possible for the crime could not exceed imprisonment for
one year and the non-citizen was not sentenced to a term of imprisonment in excess of six months.[173] However, a non-citizen may still be subject to removal if he or she has been convicted of a petty offense within
five years of admission.[174]

A person found guilty of a *violation* does not have a conviction for
immigration purposes.[175] In *Matter of Eslamizar,* the BIA noted that the
Oregon Revised Statutes provide that violation proceedings are tried by a
court sitting without a jury, the defendant need not be provided counsel
at public expense, and the state need only prove the violation by a preponderance of the evidence—not beyond a reasonable doubt as required
in full criminal proceedings.[176] The BIA also addressed the applicability
of the decision to foreign convictions, holding that nothing in its decision should be taken as asserting that a foreign conviction must comply
with all requirements of the U.S. Constitution applicable to criminal tri-
als. Rather, the foreign proceeding must, at a minimum, be criminal in
nature under the governing laws of the prosecuting jurisdiction, whether
that may be in the United States or in the foreign country.[177]

Imposition of court costs and surcharges qualifies as a conviction for
immigration purposes under INA § 101(a)(48)(A)(ii). In *Matter of Arturo,* the
BIA addressed the issue of whether the imposition of costs and surcharges
following a plea in criminal proceedings constitutes a "penalty" or "punishment" and, therefore, a conviction under INA § 101(a)(48)(A)(ii).[178] In
that case, the respondent entered a plea of nolo contendere in Florida state
court to the charge of possession of a controlled substance. Adjudication
of guilt was withheld. Under Florida law, people who plead guilty or nolo
contendere, including in cases where adjudication of guilt is withheld, can
be assessed additional costs and surcharges. The respondent in this case

---

172. Matter of Salazar, 23 I. & N. Dec. 223 (B.I.A. 2002); *Punu,* 22 I. & N. Dec. 224.

173. INA § 212(a)(2)(A)(ii)(II), 8 U.S.C. § 1182 (2014).

174. *Id.* § 237(a)(2)(A)(i), 8 U.S.C. § 1227.

175. Matter of Eslamizar, 23 I. & N. Dec. 684 (B.I.A. 2004), *overruling* Matter of C–R–, 8 I. &
N. Dec. 59 (B.I.A. 1958) (police court adjudication of petty theft under municipal ordinance,
on a standard of preponderance of the evidence, constituted a conviction).

176. *Eslamizar,* 23 I. & N. Dec. at 687.

177. *Id.* at 688.

178. Matter of Arturo, 24 I. & N. Dec. 459 (B.I.A. 2008).

was assessed $458 as a result of his plea. The BIA, in reaching its decision, reviewed federal and state case law which found that costs, surcharges, and other assessments do in fact constitute a "penalty" or "punishment" within the criminal scheme. For these reasons, the BIA held that the respondent was subject to removal as a result of a conviction for violating a law relating to controlled substances.[179]

Convictions that have been *expunged* may be considered convictions for immigration purposes. In *Matter of Roldan*,[180] the BIA held that it will not recognize any "state action, whether it is called setting aside, annulling, vacating, cancellation, expungement, dismissal, discharge, etc., of the conviction . . . that purports to erase the record of guilt of an offense pursuant to a state rehabilitative statute." This means that even if an expungement has been granted because a client has been "rehabilitated" or complied with certain rehabilitative requirements under the state statute or code, the resulting expungement may not work to avoid removal. However, if a conviction has been expunged because of constitutional or procedural infirmities, such an expungement may avoid removal. The Ninth Circuit overruled *Roldan* and held that the statutory definition of conviction did not change its position that equal protection requires the benefits under the Federal First Offender Act (FFOA) to be extended to non-citizens whose offenses are expunged under state rehabilitative laws, as long as they would have been eligible for relief under FFOA had their offenses been prosecuted in federal court.[181] Other circuits, however, have upheld *Roldan*.[182]

Expungement of a foreign conviction pursuant to a foreign rehabilitation statute will not prevent a finding of inadmissibility for a controlled substance offense, even where the non-citizen would have been eligible for first offender treatment had he been prosecuted in the United States.[183] The Ninth Circuit also reversed the BIA in *Dillingham*, reaching a similar conclusion as it did in *Roldan*, and held that a non-citizen's equal rights protections were violated when the BIA refused to recognize the effects

---

179. *Id.*

180. 22 I. & N. Dec. 512 (B.I.A. 1999).

181. Lujan-Armendariz v. INS, 222 F.3d 728 (9th Cir. 2000).

182. Salazar-Regino v. Gonzales, 415 F.3d 436 (5th Cir. 2005); Ramos v. Gonzales, 414 F.3d 800 (7th Cir. 2005); Elkins v. Comfort, 393 F.3d 1159 (10th Cir. 2004); Resendez-Alcarez v. U.S. Att'y Gen., 383 F.3d 1262 (11th Cir. 2004); Madriz-Alvarado v. Ashcroft, 383 F.3d 321 (5th Cir. 2004); Acosta v. Ashcroft, 341 F.3d 218 (3rd Cir. 2003); Gill v. Ashcroft, 335 F.3d 574 (7th Cir. 2003).

183. Matter of Dillingham, 21 I. & N. Dec. 1001 (B.I.A. 1997).

of the British expungement statute that would have qualified for federal first offender treatment if it had occurred in the United States.[184]

A *postconviction sentence modification* may be given effect in immigration proceedings. In *Matter of Song*,[185] the BIA distinguished expunged convictions from sentence modifications. In that case, the respondent's conviction for a theft offense under INA § 101(a)(43)(G) and sentence to one year imprisonment constituted an aggravated felony. The criminal court later reduced the respondent's criminal sentence nunc pro tuncto 360 days. The BIA addressed the issue of whether the original criminal sentence or the reduced sentence determined whether the respondent had been convicted of an aggravated felony. It held that its decision in *Roldan* was not binding because that case addressed the issue of the definition of "conviction" under INA § 101(a)(48)(A). The issue before the BIA in *Song* involved § 101(a)(48)(B), which defines "term of imprisonment." The BIA gave effect to the reduced sentence and concluded that the respondent's conviction could not be considered an aggravated felony under INA § 101(a)(43)(G) because he was no longer sentenced to a one-year term of imprisonment.[186]

Vacatur of a judgment may eliminate a conviction for immigration purposes depending upon the reasons for vacatur. Where a conviction is vacated for rehabilitation reasons, it remains a conviction for immigration purposes.[187] However, where a conviction is vacated because of a defect in the underlying criminal proceedings, it is no longer valid for immigration purposes.[188]

Juvenile delinquency adjudications are not considered convictions for immigration purposes.[189] However, a juvenile adjudication may affect a client's eligibility for family unity benefits. The Family Unity Program[190] provides for an automatic stay of deportation and employment authorization for spouses and unmarried children of persons granted temporary

184. Dillingham v. INS, 267 F.3d 996 (9th Cir. 2001).

185. 23 I. & N. Dec. 173 (B.I.A. 2001).

186. *See also* Matter of Cota, 23 I. & N. Dec. 849 (B.I.A. 2005) (B.I.A. gave effect to sentence reduction even where the sole purpose was to avoid immigration consequences, holding that where a sentence was modified nunc pro tunc expressly to avoid deportation, the immigration court and the B.I.A. must recognize the modified sentence; Matter of Pickering, 23 I. & N. Dec. 621 (B.I.A. 2003), distinguished).

187. *Pickering*, 23 I. & N. Dec. 621; Matter of Rodriguez-Ruiz, 22 I. & N. Dec. 1378 (B.I.A. 2000).

188. Matter of Adamiak, 23 I. & N. Dec. 878 (B.I.A. 2006).

189. Matter of Ramirez-Rivero, 18 I. & N. Dec. 135 (B.I.A. 1981). *See also* 22 C.F.R. §§ 40.21(a)(2), 40.22(a).

190. 8 C.F.R. § 236.10.

or permanent residence status as special agricultural worker, amnesty, or as Cuban or Haitian entrants. However, a minor child can lose those benefits if he or she is convicted of an act of juvenile delinquency, which, if committed by an adult, would be considered a felony involving violence or an act of violence.[191]

Under some circumstances, sentences under youth act schemes may not constitute convictions for immigration purposes. The BIA has held that an adjudication of youthful offender status under New York law that corresponds to a determination of juvenile delinquency under the Federal Juvenile Delinquency Act does not constitute a judgment of conviction for immigration purposes.[192] If your client was adjudicated for a criminal offense under a special scheme for youthful offenders, carefully review the sentencing statute to determine if it is similar to the Federal Juvenile Delinquency Act.[193]

If a person receives a full and conditional *pardon* from the president of the United States or the governor of a state or constitutionally recognized executive body, he is not subject to removal for crimes of moral turpitude, multiple criminal convictions, aggravated felonies, and high-speed flight from immigration checkpoints.[194] However if he was convicted of an offense that falls under other grounds of deportability and is subsequently granted a pardon, then he will be deportable under the grounds that are not covered by the pardon.[195]

WHAT RECORDS ARE PERMISSIBLE TO PROVE A CRIMINAL CONVICTION?

In any proceeding before an immigration court, any of the following documents or records are admissible as evidence to prove a criminal conviction:

- A record of judgment and conviction;
- A record of plea, verdict, and sentence;

---

191. *Id.* § 236.18.
192. Matter of Devison, 22 I. & N. Dec. 1362 (B.I.A. 2000).
193. 18 U.S.C. §§ 5031–42.
194. INA § 237(a)(2)(A)(v), 8 U.S.C. § 1227 (2014). For more on pardons, see A. M. Gallagher, *Remedies of Last Resort: Private Bills and Pardons*, 06–2 IMMIGRATION BRIEFINGS (Feb. 2006); A. M. Gallagher, *AILA's Focus on Private Bills & Pardons in Immigration* (2008).
195. Matter of Suh, 23 I. & N. Dec. 626 (B.I.A. 2003) (a pardon for child abuse conviction did not pardon the domestic violence ground of deportability).

- A docket entry from court records that indicates the existence of a conviction;
- Minutes of a court proceeding or a transcript of a hearing that indicates the existence of a conviction;
- An abstract of a record of conviction prepared by the court in which the conviction was entered, or by a state official associated with the state's repository of criminal justice records, which indicates the charge or section of law violated, the disposition of the case, the existence and date of conviction, and the sentence;
- Any document or record prepared by, or under the direction of, the court in which the conviction was entered that indicates the existence of a conviction.

Additionally, any other evidence that reasonably indicates the existence of a criminal conviction may be admissible as evidence of a conviction.[196] However, a police report cannot be used to prove a conviction[197] unless the contents of such were specifically incorporated into a guilty plea or admitted by a non-citizen during criminal proceedings.[198] Immigration judges generally will not look behind the conviction to determine additional grounds of removability.[199] At least one federal court has held that admission under oath of a conviction is sufficient to establish removability based on that conviction.[200]

HAS THE CLIENT MADE AN ADMISSION TO THE COMMISSION OF CERTAIN CRIMES OR CRIMINAL ACTIVITY?

Non-citizens may also be subject to removal for criminal behavior that does not necessarily result in conviction. Under certain circumstances, adverse immigration consequences may be triggered if a non-citizen admits to certain criminal activity,[201] if a person is a drug abuser or addict,[202] if there is reason to believe that a person is a drug trafficker,[203] or

---

196. 8 C.F.R. § 1003.41.
197. Matter of Terixeira, 21 I. & N. Dec. 316 (B.I.A. 1996).
198. Matter of Milian-Dubon, 25 I. & N. Dec. 197 (B.I.A. 2010).
199. Matter of Short, 20 I. & N. Dec. 136 (B.I.A. 1989).
200. Fequierre v. INS, 279 F.3d 1325 (11th Cir. 2002).
201. INA § 212(a)(2)(A)(i)(II), 8 U.S.C. § 1182 (2014).
202. *Id.* § 237(a)(2)(B)(ii), 8 U.S.C. § 1227.
203. *Id.* § 212(a)(2)(C)(i), 8 U.S.C. § 1182.

if he or she is the spouse or child of a drug trafficker who has knowingly profited from drug trafficking.[204]

Non-citizens who admit to a crime relating to a controlled substance[205] or to a crime of moral turpitude[206] are subject to removal and are statutorily barred from establishing good moral character.[207] As such, they may be barred from various forms of discretionary relief and naturalization.

In order for an admission of wrongdoing to constitute grounds to deny admission or remove a non-citizen from the United States, four factors must be present.[208] First, the conduct in question must constitute a crime under the law of the place where committed.[209] Second, the non-citizen must admit to conduct that necessarily involves moral turpitude. It cannot be an admission to a broad criminal statute.[210] Third, the consular officer or inspecting/investigating officer should provide an applicant for admission with a definition of the crime before a non-citizen can make a valid admission to a crime of moral turpitude or a crime involving a controlled substance.[211] Fourth, any admission must be freely made and voluntary.[212]

RESOURCES TO ASSIST IN DETERMINING IMMIGRATION CONSEQUENCES

Many non-citizens facing criminal proceedings may not have the funds to hire private immigration counsel to prepare a detailed legal memo advising of the potential immigration consequences of a particular plea. Many are represented by public defenders who themselves face challenges in terms of high caseload and low resources. Given the Supreme Court's

---

204. *Id.* § 212(a)(2)(C)(ii), 8 U.S.C. § 1182.

205. *Id.* § 212(a)(2)(A)(i)(II), 8 U.S.C. § 1182.

206. *Id.* § 212(a)(2)(A)(i)(I), 8 U.S.C. § 1182.

207. *Id.* § 101(f)(3), 8 U.S.C. § 1101.

208. Matter of J–, 2 I. & N. Dec. 285 (B.I.A. 1957); Matter of G–M–, 7 I. & N. Dec. 40 (A.G. 1956).

209. Matter of M–, 1 I. & N. Dec. 229 (B.I.A. 1942); Matter of E–N–, 7 I. & N. Dec. 153 (B.I.A. 1956). *See also* 22 C.F.R. § 40.21(a)(1) (2003).

210. Matter of A–, 3 I. & N. Dec. 168 (B.I.A. 1948).

211. Matter of K–, 9 I. & N. Dec. 715 (B.I.A. 1962). The Department of State recognizes that a person is not ineligible for a visa based upon admission or conviction relating to simple possession of a controlled substance if the acts occurred prior to the applicant's 18th birthday. 9 U.S. Dep't of State, Foreign Affairs Manual § 40.21(b) N2.1–2.2; 22 C.F.R. § 40.21(b) (2003).

212. Matter of G–, 1 I. & N. Dec. 225 (B.I.A. 1942).

holding in *Padilla v. Kentucky*, defense counsel is now obliged to advise on immigration consequences or face allegations of ineffective assistance of counsel and bar complaints. Given the severe consequences of particular pleas and convictions, immigration counsel should collaborate closely with defense counsel in order to protect the non-citizen as much as possible from harsh immigration consequences. Public defenders and court appointed counsel should seek approval of vouchers for expert immigration services in order to assist them in determining the best course for their clients facing criminal proceedings.

In addition to speaking directly with immigration counsel and contracting his or her services, defense counsel should access as much helpful supporting materials as possible. The following organizations provide comprehensive materials on criminal immigration issues and serve as an invaluable resource to both the immigration and the criminal defense bars.

- National Immigration Project: The National Immigration Project website has a number of resources available to the criminal defense and immigration bar on criminal immigration issues, including analyses of immigration consequences of federal and state crimes. For more information, visit the Project's website at http://www.nationalimmigration project.org/legalresources.htm.
- Immigrant Defense Project: The Immigrant Defense Project is a group that educates immigrants, their criminal defenders, and other advocates on the immigration consequences of criminal convictions. The IDP website contains practical resources to assist counsel and their clients in determining the best options for moving forward in criminal proceedings. For more information, visit the IDP website at http://immigrantdefenseproject.org/.
- American Immigration Lawyers Association: AILA is the national association of over 11,000 attorneys and law professors who practice and teach immigration law. AILA has thirty-six chapters in the United States, Canada, and Europe. AILA attorneys represent non-citizens before the Department of Homeland Security, the Immigration Courts, the Board of Immigration Appeals, and the federal courts in matters relating to the immigration status of their clients. AILA attorneys regularly collaborate with defense counsel in obtaining the best option possible for clients facing criminal proceedings. Defense counsel are encouraged to reach out to local chapter members for individual matters and to invite AILA members to provide presentations on criminal immigration issues. For more information on AILA, visit its website at http://www.aila.org.

20

WHAT EVERY LAWYER NEEDS TO KNOW ABOUT NON-CITIZENS AND THE UNITED STATES MILITARY

Margaret D. Stock[1]

Rumors about non-citizens and the United States military abound on the Internet and sometimes in print and other media. Even members of Congress and senators have been known to put out misleading information on non-citizens and military service.[2] This brief primer will tell lawyers what they need to know to correct this misinformation and point clients in the right direction on issues relating to the military service of non-citizens.

UNAUTHORIZED IMMIGRANT MEN MUST REGISTER FOR THE DRAFT

One commonly-asked question is "Must unauthorized immigrants register for Selective Service?" Today, there is no military draft in effect, but draft registration is ongoing and is managed by the Selective Service Agency. And although there is no draft today, past draft laws can affect the admissibility to the United States of non-citizens who failed to comply with them.

Certain individuals—such as F-1 foreign students, J-1 exchange visitors, B-2 tourists, and others who maintain lawful non-immigrant status—are not required to register with Selective Service. All other eighteen- to twenty-six-year-old male residents of the United States, both citizen and

---

1. Attorney, Cascadia Cross Border Law Group LLC, Anchorage, Alaska. The author served for 28 years as a Military Police Officer in the U.S. Army Reserve before transferring to the Retired Reserve in 2010.
2. Senator Jeff Sessions, Ten Things You Need To Know About S.3827, The DREAM Act, *available at* http://cfif.org/v/index.php/commentary/58-immigration/821-ten-things-you-need-to-know-about-s3827-the-dream-act (stating that "There is ALREADY A Legal Process in Place For Illegal Aliens to Obtain U.S. Citizenship Through Military Service"). Continue to read this chapter to find out why Senator Sessions' statement is misleading.

non-citizen, are required to register unless they fall within one of the statutory exemptions.[3] The Selective Service System maintains a helpful chart explaining who must register and under what circumstances.[4] Unauthorized immigrant men are required to register.

Failure to register is not only a criminal offense[5] but can result in the loss of eligibility for federal jobs, federal financial aid, and other benefits, and—in the case of non-citizens who fail to register—denial of a naturalization application.

If there is a draft, non-citizens may claim exemption from serving on the grounds of "alienage"—but a claim of exemption from mandatory military service on the grounds of "alienage" (that is, not being a native of the United States) may result in a permanent bar to naturalization and may prevent someone from obtaining lawful permanent residence in the future.[6]

UNAUTHORIZED IMMIGRANTS CAN BE DRAFTED IF THERE IS A DRAFT, BUT THEY CANNOT ENLIST VOLUNTARILY

The unified military enlistment statute, 10 USC § 504(b)(1), enacted in 2006, provides that enlistment in the U.S. military is limited to:

A. A national of the United States, as defined in section 101(a)(22) of the Immigration and Nationality Act.[7]

B. An alien who is lawfully admitted for permanent residence, as defined in section 101(a)(20) of the Immigration and Nationality Act.[8]

---

3. 50 U.S.C.S. App. § 456(a) (listing registration exemption for commissioned officers, enlisted men, cadets, and other members of the U.S. Armed Forces, as well as certain diplomatic personnel).

4. The latest version of the chart can be found at www.sss.gov/PDFs/WhoMustRegister Chart_7-23-08.pdf.

5. 50 U.S.C. App. § 462(a).

6. *See* INA § 314 (8 U.S.C.A. § 1426); *see also* Daniel Levy, U.S. Citizenship and Naturalization Handbook §§ 7:77–:83 (2010–2011 ed.) (military-related bars to naturalization).

7. 8 U.S.C. § 1101(a)(22) (2014). Note that all U.S. citizens are also U.S. nationals, but not all U.S. nationals are U.S. citizens. U.S. nationals from American Samoa and Swain's Island are permitted to enlist in the U.S. Armed Forces under this statute, but they must naturalize as U.S. citizens to have all the rights and privileges of a U.S. citizen. INA § 325 (8 U.S.C. § 1436) (2014) permits them to naturalize under certain relaxed conditions.

8. 8 U.S.C. § 1101(a)(20) (2014).

C. A person described in section 341 of one of the following compacts:
   i. The Compact of Free Association between the Federated States of Micronesia and the United States . . . .[9]
   ii. The Compact of Free Association between the Republic of the Marshall Islands and the United States . . . .[10]
   iii. The Compact of Free Association between Palau and the United States . . . .[11]

The statute does contain an exception, however:

(2) Notwithstanding paragraph (1), the Secretary concerned may authorize the enlistment of a person not described in paragraph (1) if the Secretary determines that such enlistment is vital to the national interest.[12]

It is commonly believed that the U.S. military accepts enlistments from undocumented immigrants,[13] but this is a false belief. No branch of the military knowingly allows undocumented immigrants to enlist. Although unauthorized or undocumented immigrants are required to register for Selective Service, they cannot lawfully enlist in the military unless a Service Secretary determines that their enlistment is "vital to the national interest," as required in 10 USC § 504(b)(2). No Service Secretary has to date authorized any undocumented immigrant to enlist, and since at least 2004, the U.S. Armed Forces have checked every non-citizen recruit's immigration status by querying a U.S. government database,[14]

---

9. Pub. L. No. 108-188, 117 Stat. 2784 (2003); 48 U.S.C. § 1921 note.

10. Pub. L. No. 108-188, 117 Stat. 2823 (2003); 48 U.S.C. § 1921 note.

11. Pub. L. No. 99-658, 100 Stat. 3678 (1988); 48 U.S.C. § 1931 note.

12. 10 U.S.C. § 504(b) (2006).

13. Deborah Davis, *Illegal Immigrants: Uncle Sam Wants You* (July 25, 2007), *available at* www .inthesetimes.com/article/3271/illegal_immigrants_uncle_sam_wants_you. Note: This article by Ms. Davis contains many factual inaccuracies, including a statement that Immigration and Customs Enforcement (ICE) processes naturalization applications, that the U.S. military can obtain a green card for recruits, and that recruits can join the military without having a Social Security number. In fact, USCIS processes naturalization applications, not ICE; the U.S. military does not routinely sponsor its recruits for green cards; and everyone who enlists in the U.S. military must have a valid Social Security number.

14. USCIS operates a system called SAVE (Systematic Alien Verification for Entitlements), which is used to verify the documents submitted by potential enlistees. Military recruiting personnel use an automated system, or submit Form G-845 via fax to a special USCIS office, which verifies the person's status and replies back to the military, which then makes a determination whether the person is eligible for enlistment, based on the information provided by USCIS.

so that undocumented immigrants with false "green cards" or invalid Social Security numbers can no longer enlist as they once did.[15] News reports and anecdotal accounts indicate that undocumented immigrants who have attempted to enlist have been turned away, or, in some cases, arrested and deported.[16] Undocumented immigrants who enlist or attempt to enlist using fraudulent documents can face criminal charges and discharge from the military.[17] If an undocumented immigrant manages to enlist and serves honorably in wartime, however, wartime naturalization authority can allow the person to naturalize through his or her honorable military service.[18]

Because legal status is required of non-citizens who try to enlist, the vast majority of non-citizen enlistees are lawful permanent residents (including conditional lawful permanent residents (CPRs)) who have enlisted after having obtained their "green cards." A much smaller group of enlistees include legally present non-LPRs who have been specifically authorized to enlist by the Secretaries of the Services in which they are enlisted under the terms of a program—discussed in more detail below—known by the acronym "MAVNI" (Military Accessions Vital to the National Interest).

OVERSEAS ENLISTMENT PROGRAMS, EXCEPT FOR PACIFIC ISLANDERS, NO LONGER EXIST

In the past, the United States has occasionally had overseas enlistment programs. Thus, under the Lodge-Philbin Act[19] and the U.S.-Philippines

---

15. Margaret D. Stock, *Essential to the Fight: Immigrants in the Military Eight Years after 9/11*, IMMIGRATION POLICY CENTER (Nov. 2009) (discussing how a few undocumented immigrants enlisted in the military prior to the military creating a process for checking immigration status electronically with DHS).

16. Douglas Gillison, *Marines? Looking For a Few Good Aliens*, VILLAGE VOICE, Sept. 27, 2005.

17. *Id.*

18. Discharge from the military is not mandated but is up to the individual's commander. *See, e.g.*, Army Regulation 635-200 (Jun. 6, 2005, with Rapid Action Revision dated Dec. 17, 2009), ¶¶ 5-10, 7-17(b)(2), 7-21(a)(6).

19. The Lodge-Philbin Act allowed certain foreign nationals overseas to join the U.S. Armed Forces. *See* Act of June 30, 1950, Pub. L. No. 81-597, 64 Stat. 316. The act permitted initially up to 2,500 non-resident aliens (later expanded to allow up to 12,500) to enlist. If they successfully served for five years, they could apply for U.S. citizenship. Members of this force who died during active service or from injuries or illness during active service could obtain posthumous citizenship. Applications could be filed as recently as November 2004 (or within two years of their death).

Military Bases Agreement of 1947,[20] certain non-citizens living overseas were permitted to enlist in the United States military. Today, no such programs exist—with the exception of programs to recruit persons from Micronesia, Palau, and the Marshall Islands, as described above—and U.S. military recruiters are generally prohibited from recruiting persons who are outside the United States and its possessions.[21]

SOME LEGALLY PRESENT ALIENS WITHOUT GREEN CARDS MAY ENLIST UNDER THE MAVNI PROGRAM

Although no Service Secretary has approved the enlistment of any unauthorized immigrants, the Service Secretaries have authorized the enlistment of a small number of lawfully present persons who are not lawful permanent residents (LPRs) under the "vital to the national interest" prong of the enlistment statute. In November 2008, Secretary of Defense Robert Gates authorized the Services to conduct a new pilot enlistment program titled "Military Accessions Vital to the National Interest" (MAVNI), under which up to 1,000 legally present non-LPRs with critical skills were allowed to join the U.S. Armed Forces despite their lack of LPR status.[22] Under the MAVNI program, the Army, Navy, and Air Force began recruiting certain non-LPRs, but lawfully present, non-citizens who were U.S.-licensed health care professionals or fluent in one of more than thirty strategic languages. Because of the ongoing war, these new enlistees were permitted to naturalize almost immediately under INA § 329, which allows for naturalization of non-LPRs in wartime. At the time of this writing, the pilot program was judged to be highly successful.[23] The program is currently operating and enlists about 1,500 people each year.

---

20. In the U.S.-Philippines Military Bases Agreement of 1947, the parties agreed that the United States could recruit Filipinos for voluntary service in the U.S. military; this agreement was renegotiated in 1952 to provide that 1,000 Filipinos could be recruited for the U.S. Navy each year, and the number was revised upwards to 2,000 per year in 1954. The agreement was renewed periodically until the Military Bases Agreement was terminated n 1992, which ended overseas Filipino enlistment in the U.S. Armed Forces. Some Filipinos who enlisted under the terms of the agreement are still serving in the Navy today, however.

21. *See, e.g.*, Army Regulation 601-210 (Feb. 8, 2011), § 2-4(a)(6) ("Conducting recruiting activities in foreign countries, including Canada, is prohibited, however, unless such activities are specifically authorized").

22. *See* Department of Defense News, *Fact Sheet: Military Accessions Vital to the National Interest* (2012), *available at* www.defenselink.mil/news/mavni-fact-sheet.pdf.

23. Brian Mitchell, *Army in New Push for Skilled Immigrants*, MILITARY.COM, July 9, 2009.

MAVNI is not an overseas recruiting program, but only applies to certain non-citizens who are lawfully present in the United States but who do not yet have LPR status. Under the specialized MAVNI enlistment pilot program, non-LPRs may enlist if they have been legally present in the United States in E, F, H, I, J, K, L, M, O, P, Q, R, S, T, TC, TD, TN, U, or V status, or are in the United States in refugee, asylee, or temporary protected status (TPS) status.[24] The program requires that a potential enlistee must have been in one of these statuses for at least two years (changing between them does not disqualify the person). If a person is qualifying for enlistment under a non-immigrant category, the person cannot have been outside the United States for a continuous period of more than 90 days. The MAVNI pilot program also required that a potential enlistee speak one of many needed languages[25] or be a U.S.-licensed and educated medical professional.[26] The medical professionals recruited are primarily doctors, dentists, and nurses, though some other medical professionals also qualify.[27] The Army has also sought to extend any future MAVNI program to chaplains of the Roman Catholic faith.[28] The MAVNI pilot program was implemented by the Army, Navy, and Air Force; the program is also expected to be extended to the Marine Corps in future years.

The MAVNI program offers significant advantages to non-citizens who do not yet have LPR status but who qualify for the program and are willing to serve in the U.S. Armed Forces. Under MAVNI, for example, a non-immigrant J-1 doctor may elect to enlist for three years of active duty, or six years in the Selected Reserve. She will then contract to serve as an officer and doctor in the U.S. Armed Forces during her service. She

---

24. *See* Department of Defense News, *Fact Sheet: Military Accessions Vital to the National Interest* (2012), *available at* www.defenselink.mil/news/mavni-fact-sheet.pdf.

25. A list of qualifying languages can be found at www.defenselink.mil/news/mavni-fact-sheet.pdf, which is reproduced in the Appendix. An updated list of languages with additional qualifying languages is expected to be published if and when the MAVNI program is restarted in the future.

26. Doctors must be U.S.-licensed, and nurses must be U.S.-licensed and have obtained a bachelor's or master's degree in nursing from a U.S.-accredited school or college of nursing.

27. Health-care workers can get more information by writing to the Army at its website at https://www.goarmy.com/info/form/GetBrcFormRedirectByUrl.do?url=/info/mavni/healthcare. Others can inquire at www.goarmy.com/info/mavni.

28. U.S. Army Recruiting Command, *Recruiter Journal* (Dec. 2010), at 22, *available at* http://www.usarec.army.mil/hq/apa/download/dec10.pdf ("Another tactic awaiting implementation for chaplain recruiting is MAVNI (Military Accessions Vital to the National Interest); MAVNI will permit foreign born Roman Catholic priests in the United States on religious worker and student visas to make application to the Army Chaplain Candidate program or Army chaplaincy.").

is required to apply for U.S. citizenship as soon as she enlists,[29] and USCIS will expedite her application under a law that requires adjudication of military naturalization cases within six months.[30] Assuming that this J-1 doctor has good moral character and is able to pass the English and civics exam, she will be granted U.S. citizenship. This J-1 doctor need not have LPR status in order to naturalize under the wartime military naturalization statute, INA § 329. She need not comply with INA § 212(e) (8 U.S.C. § 1182), obtain a waiver, or fulfill a two-year home residency requirement. She must, however, serve honorably for at least five years—either on active duty or in the Reserves—or DHS can act to revoke her U.S. citizenship.[31]

THE DREAM ACT, IF PASSED, WOULD ALLOW CERTAIN UNAUTHORIZED IMMIGRANTS TO OBTAIN TEMPORARY STATUS AND ENLIST

As stated above, undocumented immigrants are not permitted to enlist in the U.S. Armed Forces, which today generally require a non-citizen to have obtained LPR status before enlisting (and always require a valid Social Security number, which unauthorized immigrants cannot obtain). One proposal that would have allowed more immigrants to serve in the U.S. military has made little headway despite bipartisan support. The Development, Relief, and Education for Alien Minors (DREAM) Act would conditionally legalize young undocumented immigrants who entered the United States before the age of 16, have at least five years' continuous presence in the United States, have graduated from a U.S. high school, and have stayed out of trouble with the law.[32] Upon applying for benefits under the original version of the DREAM Act, an undocumented immigrant would be granted six years of conditional lawful permanent resident status. During that time, the immigrant would have been

---

29. INA § 329, 8 U.S.C. § 1440 (2014) (no minimum period of residency or physical presence required; LPR status not required as a prerequisite for naturalization).

30. Military Personnel Citizenship Processing Act of 2008, Pub. L. No. 110-382, § 3, 122 Stat. 4087 (2008).

31. *See* INA § 329(c), 8 U.S.C. § 1440 (2014) ("Citizenship granted pursuant to this section may be revoked in accordance with section 340 if the person is separated from the Armed Forces under other than honorable conditions before the person has served honorably for a period or periods aggregating five years.").

32. Development, Relief, and Education for Alien Minors Act of 2009, S. 729, 111th Cong. (2009) (a bill that would provide temporary residence to certain unlawfully present young people, allowing them to obtain permanent status if they attend college or join the military).

required to (1) graduate from a two-year college, (2) complete at least two years towards a four-year college degree, or (3) serve honorably in the U.S. military for at least two years.[33] At the end of the six years, if the immigrant continued to show "good moral character," he or she would be granted LPR status without conditions. Because attending college is a very expensive proposition, the third option—joining the Armed Forces—would have been a likely choice for many of the young people who would be affected by the bill, hundreds of whom have already demonstrated an interest in joining the military.

Opponents of the DREAM Act have argued that it is a "sugar-coated amnesty" rewarding those who have violated U.S. immigration laws, but passage of the bill would be highly beneficial to the U.S. military. Passage of the DREAM Act could provide a new source of soldiers with foreign language qualifications and cultural skills in a time when fewer and fewer American citizens are able to meet military enlistment standards. While the Armed Forces have reported recently that they are meeting their recruiting goals,[34] they are still short recruits with foreign language and cultural skills. Over the coming years, as the U.S. population ages, it will become increasingly difficult for the Armed Forces to attract enough qualified recruits.[35]

The DREAM Act as originally written would require no change to military rules for enlisting recruits because it would grant conditional lawful permanent residence status to non-citizens, and Conditional LPRs are already permitted to enlist under existing enlistment law and regulations.[36] Under current immigration law, these young people have no means of legalizing their status. Despite having attracted more than 200 cosponsors from both sides of the political aisle in the past, DREAM Act bills have repeatedly failed in both the House and Senate since first being introduced in 2003. A revised version of the DREAM Act, which passed the House in the fall of 2010 but failed to pass in the Senate,[37]

---

33. While the conditions on a DREAM Act person's status could be lifted after two years of military service, the person would still be required to serve on active duty or in the Reserve Components for a total of eight years, pursuant to 10 U.S.C. § 651 (2010). All persons—U.S. citizens and others—who enlist in the U.S. military today incur an eight-year "statutory" obligation, regardless of the contractual term of active duty described in their enlistment contract.

34. Gerry J. Gilmore, *Army, Other Services Have Record Recruiting Year*, AMERICAN FORCES PRESS SERVICE, October 14, 2009.

35. Eric Schmitt, *Army Officials Voice Concern Over Shortfall in Recruitment*, NEW YORK TIMES, March 4, 2005.

36. *See* 10 U.S.C. § 504(b).

37. H.R. 5281, Development, Relief, & Education for Alien Minors Act of 2010.

would have amended the original language of the DREAM Act to make it harder for DREAM beneficiaries to serve in the U.S. military. This new version of DREAM would have created a new temporary non-LPR status for DREAM Act beneficiaries,[38] and would have required them to wait more than ten years to obtain LPR status and then U.S. citizenship.[39] This version of the bill, had it passed, would have allowed military service by DREAM Act beneficiaries, but would have severely limited their choice of jobs and career path. Those persons obtaining status under this version of DREAM would not be able to naturalize through military service in peacetime, and would thus have very limited career options in the U.S. Armed Forces. Unable to naturalize, they would be unable to become officers, obtain security clearances, or serve as military linguists until completing more than ten years of service.

Senator Richard Durbin (D-IL) reintroduced a new version of the DREAM Act as § 952 on May 11, 2011;[40] a companion bill was introduced in the House on the same day as H.R. 1842.[41] This latest version of DREAM would grant conditional lawful permanent residence to certain aliens who (1) have been continuously physically present in the United States for five years before the date of enactment, (2) were 15 years old or younger when they initially entered the United States, (3) have been of good moral character since they entered the United States, (4) have earned a high school diploma or GED or been admitted to college; and (5) are under age 35 on the date of enactment. They must register with Selective Service, if required to do so. After filing an application with DHS and completing certain background checks and a medical exam, they may be approved for conditional lawful resident status, which would allow them to join the U.S. Armed Forces; their conditional lawful permanent resident status would be granted for six years. They may remove the conditions on their status by serving in the Uniformed Services[42] for at least

---

38. 111th Cong., 2010.

39. H.R. 5281 at § 8(c) ("An alien shall file an application for adjustment of status during the period beginning 1 year before and ending on either the date that is 10 years after the date of the initial grant of conditional nonimmigrant status or any other expiration date of the conditional nonimmigrant status as extended by the Secretary of Homeland Security in accordance with this Act. The alien shall be deemed to be in conditional nonimmigrant status in the United States during the period in which such application is pending.").

40. S. 952, 112th Cong. (2011).

41. H.R. 1842, 112th Cong. (2011).

42. As a practical matter, DREAM Act beneficiaries who choose to serve in the Uniformed Services will be required to enlist in the Air Force, Army, Coast Guard, Marines, or Navy (or a Reserve Component of one of those Services) because the National Oceanic and Atmospheric Administration (NOAA) and the Public Health Service (PHS), which are the other two Uniformed Services, require U.S. citizenship for their members.

two years; if they have been discharged, they must receive an honorable discharge.[43] They are prohibited from applying for naturalization while they hold conditional lawful permanent residence status.[44] Accordingly, under this bill, DREAM Act beneficiaries would be able to join the U.S. Armed Forces just like any other LPR but would be unable to take advantage of the relaxed naturalization rules available to other LPR military personnel until they have served for more than six years and have had the conditions removed on their status.

NON-CITIZEN MILITARY PERSONNEL MAY ONLY ENLIST IN JOBS OPEN TO NON-CITIZENS, BUT ARE OTHERWISE SUBJECT TO THE SAME RULES AS OTHER ENLISTEES

Because today the U.S. military is an all-volunteer force, every person who enlists signs a contract, and incurs a specific contractual obligation, which is reflected in the enlistment contract. Typical enlistment contracts call for two, three, four, or more years of active duty service, depending on the job for which the person enlists.[45] In addition to the contractual obligation, all persons who join the U.S. military (including U.S. citizens) are subject to a six- to eight-year statutory military service obligation that requires them to remain on the military rolls for six to eight years total, even if they are no longer on active duty or in a Selected Reserve unit.[46] After completing their minimum contractual enlistment period, enlistees may serve any remaining statutory military service obligation in the Selected Reserve, Inactive National Guard, or Individual Ready Reserve.

---

43. S. 952, 112th Cong. § 4(c)(1)(B) ("The Secretary shall terminate the conditional permanent resident status of an alien, if the Secretary determines that the alien— . . . was discharged from the Uniformed Services and did not receive an honorable discharge."). It is unclear whether receiving a "general discharge under honorable conditions," see earlier discussion, would meet this requirement.

44. DREAM Act of 2011, S. 952, 112th Cong. § 5(c)(2) ("An alien may not apply for naturalization during the period that the alien is in permanent resident status on a conditional basis under this Act").

45. Contracts for two years of active duty service are relatively rare, as most jobs in the military require a considerable amount of training, and the Services often do not want to enlist a person, provide them with more than a year of training at government expense, and then have them leave the Service a short while later.

46. *See* 10 U.S.C. § 651 (2009). *See also, e.g.*, Army Regulation 135-91, Service Obligations, Methods of Fulfillment, Participation Requirements, and Enforcement Procedures (Feb. 1, 2005), ¶ 2-1 ("The statutory MSO [Military Service Obligation] is incurred on initial entry into the Armed Forces whether by induction, enlistment, or appointment . . . . On and after 1 June 1984, all soldiers incurred an 8-year statutory MSO.").

The six- to eight-year statutory obligation applies to every person who joins the U.S. military. Thus, if a non-citizen joins the Army today and signs a contract to serve on active duty for four years, she may be released from active duty when the four years are over—but she must then typically remain in a Reserve status for four additional years.

Non-citizens who enlist in the U.S. military have the same military service obligation as U.S. citizens, but their job options are not the same. Non-citizens may only fill military jobs that are legally open to non-citizens. Most jobs in the U.S. military require a security clearance, and except under very limited circumstances,[47] non-citizens are not eligible for a security clearance.[48] Persons who are not U.S. citizens or nationals also cannot attend the Service Academies (except as foreign exchange students),[49] obtain an ROTC scholarship,[50] or accept a Regular Army[51] or National Guard[52] commission as an officer or warrant officer.[53] In some

---

47. *See* Exec. Order No. 12,968, 60 Fed. Reg. 40,245, Access to Classified Information, Sec. 2.6 (Aug. 4, 1995) ("Where there are compelling reasons in furtherance of an agency mission, immigrant alien and foreign national employees who possess a special expertise may, in the discretion of the agency, be granted limited access to classified information only for specific programs, projects, contracts, licenses, certificates, or grants for which there is a need for access. Such individuals shall not be eligible for access to any greater level of classified information than the United States Government has determined may be releasable to the country of which the subject is currently a citizen, and such limited access may be approved only if the prior 10 years of the subject's life can be appropriately investigated. If there are any doubts concerning granting access, additional lawful investigative procedures shall be fully pursued.").

48. *See* Exec. Order No. 12,968, Sec. 3.1(b) ("[E]ligibility for access to classified information shall be granted only to employees who are United States citizens for whom an appropriate investigation has been completed . . . .").

49. *See, e.g.,* Army Regulation 210-26, United States Military Academy (Dec. 9, 2009), ¶ 3-5 ("On the date of admission a candidate, except one appointed as a foreign cadet under the provisions of 10 USC 4344 (2014), must be a citizen or national of the United States.").

50. *See, e.g.,* Army Regulation 145-1, Senior Reserve Officers' Training Corps Program: Organization, Administration, & Training (July 22, 1996), ¶ 3-8 ("Students must be citizens of the United States (except as provided in para 3–29)"). As an aside, this regulation contains errors regarding immigration and citizenship law and is substantially in need of revision.

51. 10 U.S.C. § 532 (2014) ("an original appointment as a commissioned officer (other than as a commissioned warrant officer) in the Regular Army, Regular Navy, Regular Air Force, or Regular Marine Corps may be given only to a person who—(1) is a citizen of the United States . . . .").

52. 32 U.S.C. § 313 (2014) ("To be eligible for appointment as an officer of the National Guard, a person must—(1) be a citizen of the United States").

53. Under 10 U.S.C. § 12201 (2014), the Army Reserve may commission persons who are U.S. citizens, LPRs, or persons who previously served in the armed forces.

cases, non-citizens must obtain U.S. citizenship if they want to re-enlist after their first term of service is completed.[54]

Because U.S. immigration and citizenship law is quite complicated, however, and because military recruiters and military officials are not expert at its intricacies, it is quite common for recruiters and military officials to make mistakes with regard to a person's immigration or citizenship status. In fact, many persons who are U.S. citizens are wrongly identified as non-citizens by recruiters, and denied military job opportunities to which they may be legally entitled.

MILITARY SERVICE CAN PROVIDE AN EXPEDITED ROUTE TO NATURALIZATION

A significant advantage of military service has been that non-citizens serving in the military have traditionally been permitted to obtain U.S. citizenship in an expedited fashion; statutes providing for such expedited citizenship date back to the Civil War era.[55] Expedited citizenship not only benefits them, but it benefits the U.S. military by reducing or eliminating legal problems relating to military service by non-citizens[56] and allowing them to be utilized fully in more jobs and duty assignments.[57]

---

54. The Army previously required immigrants to obtain U.S. citizenship if they wanted to serve longer than eight years, but that requirement was recently rescinded. *See* Army Regulation 601-210, Active and Reserve Components Enlistment Program (June 7, 2007), ¶¶ 2-4a(2) and 3-4.

55. Act of July 17, 1862 (sec. 2166, R.S., 1878) (making special naturalization benefits available to those with service in the "armies" of the United States).

56. Such legal problems can include claims by foreign countries that their citizens serving in the U.S. military are under the jurisdiction of the foreign government for various purposes. These problems are often lessened when non-citizen service members naturalize in the United States because the naturalization can sometimes work as a renunciation of the foreign citizenship. Once a non-citizen naturalizes through military service, the United States may also require that non-citizen to renounce his or her foreign citizenship as a condition of service; the United States cannot require such a renunciation when the person does not yet have U.S. citizenship.

57. A non-citizen serving in the U.S. military cannot normally obtain a security clearance or serve in any job that requires one, including the Army job of Military Linguist. *See* Exec. Order No. 12,968 (Aug. 2, 1995), 60 Fed. Reg. 40243-40254 (Aug. 7, 1995) ("Where there are compelling reasons in furtherance of an agency mission, immigrant alien and foreign national employees who possess a special expertise may, in the discretion of the agency, be granted limited access to classified information only for specific programs, projects, contracts, licenses, certificates, or grants for which there is a need for access. Such individuals shall not be eligible for access to any greater level of classified information than the United States Government has determined may be releasable to the country of which the subject is currently a citizen . . . .").

While most LPRs are required to wait three to five years before applying for U.S. citizenship, two special military-related immigration statutes provide that qualified members of the U.S. Armed Forces are permitted to apply for U.S. citizenship after one year of service (when no Presidential order regarding ongoing hostilities is in effect)[58] or immediately (when a Presidential executive order regarding wartime hostilities is in effect).[59]

President George Bush issued a military naturalization executive order on July 3, 2002, retroactive to September 11, 2001, and that order remains in effect as of this writing.[60] While that executive order remains in effect, LPR military members may be able to naturalize under more than one statute. In contrast, military personnel who are not LPRs or U.S. nationals may only naturalize under INA § 329.

A significant potential new disability also attaches to military naturalizations: Persons naturalized through military service after November 24, 2003, may face possible revocation of their U.S. citizenship based on postnaturalization misconduct or failure to serve honorably for a period or periods aggregating five years.[61] Thus, anyone applying for naturalization through military service today should be cautioned that while the process provides unique advantages, it also potentially has a major disadvantage as well.

Significantly, both INA § 328 and INA § 329 generally waive the normal age, "continuous residence," "physical presence," and state residence requirements of the "regular" naturalization statute. Thanks to changes made by the National Defense Authorization Act of 2004,[62] both military naturalization statutes also allow current service members and veterans to apply for naturalization without paying any application or biometrics fees.[63] The same law allows overseas naturalization of currently serving military personnel.[64] Both statutes further provide that

---

58. *See* INA § 328, 8 U.S.C. § 1439 (2014).

59. *See* INA § 329, 8 U.S.C. § 1440.

60. Exec. Order No. 13,269 of July 3, 2002, 67 Fed. Reg. 45,287 (July 8, 2002).

61. INA §§ 328(f), 329(c); 8 U.S.C. §§ 1439(f), 1440(c).

62. National Defense Authorization Act for Fiscal Year 2004, Pub. L. 108-136, 117 Stat. 1390 [hereinafter NDAA 2004].

63. *Id.* § 1701(b), 117 Stat. 1691.

64. *Id.* § 1701(d), 117 Stat. 1692. *See also* American Forces Press Service, *Troops Earn U.S. Citizenship in Iraq* (Mar. 4, 2009) *available at* www.defenselink.mil/news/newsarticle .aspx?id=53336 (describing how more than 250 American military members were sworn in as U.S. citizens in Baghdad, Iraq, during the thirteenth U.S. naturalization ceremony conducted overseas since USCIS began overseas military naturalization ceremonies). USCIS takes the position that overseas naturalization is not available unless the person is a currently serving member of the U.S. military. Veterans must therefore naturalize inside the United States, even if they claim eligibility for naturalization under INA § 328 or § 329.

military naturalization applicants may be naturalized notwithstanding the pendency of removal proceedings.[65] Finally, both statutes require an applicant to show good moral character,[66] but the period of good moral character has been reduced to one year for most applicants.[67] Under agency regulation, an applicant must establish that he "[h]as been, for at least one year prior to filing the application for naturalization, and continues to be, of good moral character."[68]

With regard to this last requirement, the courts have held that the usual statutory bars[69] to showing good moral character for purposes of naturalization do apply, so that—to give just one example—persons deemed to be aggravated felons[70] cannot naturalize under the military

---

65. INA § 328(a)(2), 8 U.S.C. § 1439(a)(2) ("notwithstanding section 318 insofar as it relates to deportability, such applicant may be naturalized immediately if the applicant be then actually in the Armed Forces of the United States, and if prior to the filing of the application, the applicant shall have appeared before and been examined by a representative of the Service"); INA § 329(b)(1), 8 U.S.C. § 1440(b)(1) ("he may be naturalized regardless of age, and notwithstanding the provisions of section 318 as they relate to deportability and the provisions of section 331").

66. INA § 328 has been interpreted by the Service to allow a presumption of good moral character if the person has served honorably as documented in military records by an honorable discharge; this presumption, however, can be overcome by contrary evidence. *See* Yuen Jung v. Barber, 184 F.2d 491 (9th Cir. 1950) (rejecting argument that honorable discharge is conclusive evidence of good moral character that prevents immigration authorities from inquiring further). The latter case involved an issue whether the applicant's behavior prior to his military service could be considered; it remains to be seen whether the presumption of good moral character based on an honorable discharge can be challenged by information about a lack of good moral character during the time an applicant was in the military.

67. The one-year good moral character requirement under INA § 329 is not statutory, but rests on a regulation and an agency interpretation that has been upheld by the courts. *See* 8 C.F.R. § 329.2(e); Lopez v. Henley, 416 F.3d 455, 457–58 (5th Cir. 2005) (upholding agency requirement that a person seeking citizenship through military service must establish good moral character); Nolan v. Holmes, 334 F.3d 189 (2d Cir. 2003) (although nothing in INA § 329 requires a showing of good moral character, *Chevron* deference will be applied to uphold regulation requiring one year of good moral character); *see also* Castiglia v. INS, 108 F.3d 1101, 1102 (9th Cir. 1997); Cacho v. Ashcroft, 403 F. Supp. 2d 991, 994 (D. Haw. 2004).

68. 8 C.F.R. § 329.2(d).

69. The statutory bars to showing good moral character are found at INA § 101(f), 8 U.S.C. § 1101 (2014).

70. INA § 101(f)(8), 8 U.S.C. § 1101 (2014), contains the aggravated felony bar to showing good moral character. This bar applies to prevent naturalization altogether of persons convicted of an aggravated felony on or after November 29, 1990, the effective date of IMMACT 90. *See* 8 C.F.R. § 316.10(b)(1) ("An applicant shall be found to lack good moral character, if the applicant has been: (i) Convicted of murder at any time; or (ii) Convicted of an aggravated felony as defined in section 101(a)(43) of the Act on or after November 29, 1990.").

naturalization statutes, even if they have served honorably in wartime.[71] If a military naturalization applicant is not barred statutorily from show-ing good moral character, he or she may still be denied naturalization if the totality of the circumstances show a lack of good moral character in the one-year period and continuing to the date of naturalization. Conduct prior to the one-year period may also be taken into account.

Although they contain common elements, the two military natural-ization statutes also diverge in significant ways. First, the "peacetime" military naturalization statute, INA § 328, applies at all times and requires no presidential executive order, but it does require an applicant for mili-tary naturalization to have LPR status and file during service or within six months of leaving the service if he or she seeks exemption from the usual continuous physical presence and residency requirements.[72] This statute applies to anyone on active duty or in any of the Reserve Compo-nents, including the Individual Ready Reserve or the inactive National Guard.[73] It does not require that the person have enlisted or reenlisted while in the United States.

During wartime, military personnel may also naturalize without obtaining LPR status first. Under INA § 329, immigrants who are in the U.S. Armed Forces can naturalize regardless of their length of time in service or their immigration status.[74] This statute applies during speci-fied statutory periods, or when a presidential executive order exists that has invoked the statute, as shown in the following Table. Presidents have long used this statute to bestow citizenship benefits on immigrants in the military. The Table lists the currently applicable periods of conflict in which Section 329 has been in effect by statute or Presidential Executive Order. Note that not every overseas deployment of U.S. forces into combat is covered by this statute or an executive order invoking this statute; for example, as of this writing, no president has issued an executive order to naturalize military personnel who served between 1991 and 2001, when

---

71. *See, e.g.*, Boatswain v. Gonzales, 414 F.3d 413 (2d Cir. 2005) (holding that the aggravated felony bar in INA § 101(f)(8) applies to applicants for naturalization under INA § 329).

72. A veteran may still file under INA § 328 more than six months after being discharged, but in those cases, the veteran must meet the usual requirements under naturalization laws for "continuous physical presence" and "residence." Thus, there is little advantage to filing under this section—other than saving filing fees—if a person has been discharged for more than six months.

73. United States v. Rosner, 249 F.2d 49 (1st Cir. 1957) (INA § 328 does not require an appli-cant to be in "active service" for the required period; inactive Reserve service also meets the statutory requirement).

74. INA § 329, 8 U.S.C. § 1440.

the U.S. military engaged in numerous combat operations in places like Bosnia, Haiti, Panama, and Somalia, among others.

Table: Application of INA § 329

Conflict	Dates	Source of Authority	Notes
World War I	No specific dates listed	INA § 329(a), 8 U.S.C. § 1440(a)	
World War II	September 1, 1939 through December 31, 1946	INA § 329(a), 8 U.S.C. § 1440(a)	
Korean War	June 25, 1950 through July 1, 1955	INA 329(a), 8 U.S.C. § 1440(a)	
Vietnam War	February 28, 1961 through October 15, 1978	Exec. Order No. 12,081, 43 Fed. Reg. 42237 (1978)	
Grenada Campaign (but see note)	October 25, 1983 through November 2, 1983	Exec. Order No. 12,582, 52 Fed. Reg. 3395 (1987) (but attempting to limit scope of INA § 329 geographically)	A Circuit Court has ruled that the Executive Order was invalid because it attempted to limit the scope of INA § 329, and therefore further Section 329 naturalizations during this period are not permitted. See Reyes v. INS, 910 F.2d 611 (9th Cir. 1990). Also, President Clinton revoked the Grenada designation by Executive Order in 1994. Exec. Order No. 12913, 59 Fed. Reg. 23115 (1994).
Persian Gulf Conflict	August 2, 1990 through April 11, 1991	Exec. Order No. 12,939, 59 Fed. Reg. 61231 (1994)	
Post September 11, 2001 Conflict	September 11, 2001 to present	Exec. Order No. 13,269, 67 Fed. Reg. 45287 (2002)	

INA § 329 differs in several respects from INA § 328. First, the statute requires service during certain designated periods of conflict. In the modern era, this means that the applicant must serve during a period in which an executive order specifically invokes INA § 329. Second, the statute requires enlistment or reenlistment while in the United States or other specified locations, unless the applicant has obtained LPR status.[75] Thirdly—and most importantly—the statute does not require a person to have LPR status unless the person has not enlisted or reenlisted in one of the areas specified above. Thus, persons having no immigration status at all may naturalize under this statute, if they meet its requirements. Accordingly, although undocumented immigrants are not permitted to enlist in the U.S. Armed Forces, those who have ended up in the military by accident[76] or through the use of false documentation[77] are sometimes— but not always—able to naturalize in wartime under INA § 329, despite their lack of LPR status. A representative example is the case of Juan Escalante, a Mexican citizen and undocumented immigrant who enlisted in the United States Army, inside the United States, using a false green card.[78] Mr. Escalante was naturalized while still in the Army after his case came to the attention of immigration and military authorities.[79] Although Mr. Escalante had enlisted using a false document, his military service was honorable, and he was permitted to naturalize under INA § 329.[80] Other undocumented immigrants have not been naturalized, however, typically because their status has been uncovered early in their military career and they have been given uncharacterized "entry level" discharges that do not meet the INA § 329 "honorable service" requirement.

Another notable difference between INA § 328 and INA § 329 is that INA § 328 does not require any specified type of service, while INA § 329

75. INA § 329(a), 8 U.S.C. §1440(a).

76. Some immigrants with an Employment Authorization Document (EAD) but not a green card mistakenly believe that they are eligible to enlist, and some military recruiters have been unaware of the difference between an EAD and a green card and have inadvertently allowed immigrants to enlist who are not actually eligible to do so under military regulations requiring a green card for enlistment.

77. *See* Douglas Gillison, *The Few, the Proud, the Guilty: Marines Recruiter Convicted of Providing Fake Documents to Enlist Illegal Aliens*, VILLAGE VOICE, October 11, 2005. This article notes that the Pentagon began verifying the alien registration numbers of recruits with the Department of Homeland Security in 2004 after learning that undocumented immigrants were enlisting with false green cards.

78. Florangela Davila, *Army Private Receives New Rank: U.S. Citizen*, SEATTLE TIMES, Feb. 12, 2004 (recounting story of Juan Escalante, an undocumented immigrant who received his U.S. citizenship through service in the Army).

79. *Id.*

80. *See also* In re Watson, 502 F. Supp. 145, 150 (D.D.C. 1980) ("improper induction or enlistment into the armed forces . . . does not bar naturalization under § 329(a)").

requires service in "active duty status"[81] or in the Selected Reserve of the Ready Reserve. The inclusion of the latter type of service is a recent change to the statute. Congress in 2003 passed the National Defense Authorization Act for Fiscal Year 2004 [NDAA 2004],[82] which amended the INA to extend the benefit of naturalization under INA § 329 to individuals who have served honorably as members of the Selected Reserve of the Ready Reserve of the U.S. Armed Forces during designated periods of hostilities.[83] Prior to passage of NDAA 2004, service members needed federal active duty service in order to qualify under INA § 329, but such service is no longer required. This amendment is effective as of September 11, 2001.[84]

Most members of the National Guard and Reserve who train regularly are members of the Selected Reserve.[85] When a National Guard member or Reservist is a member of the Selected Reserve, he or she may now naturalize under INA § 329 based on that service. The applicant is not required to have active duty service or be part of a National Guard or Reserve unit that has been ordered to active federal duty or mobilized.

For lawyers, yet another interesting aspect of INA § 329 is that it allows persons who are otherwise inadmissible or removable to naturalize. Thus, someone who is subject to the grounds of inadmissibility under INA § 212[86] may potentially naturalize under INA § 329, so long as he or she can show the requisite good moral character and meet the law's other requirements. For example, a J-1 visa holder who enlists in the military during wartime can naturalize under INA § 329 notwithstanding the

---

81. In 10 U.S.C. § 101(d) (2014), "active duty" is defined as "full-time duty in the active military service of the United States [including] full-time training duty, annual training duty, and attendance, while in the active military service, at a school designated as a service school by law or by the Secretary of the military department concerned. Such term does not include full-time National Guard duty."

82. Pub. L. No. 108-136, 117 Stat. 1392 (2003).

83. NDAA 2004, *supra* note 82, § 1702, 117 Stat. at 1693 ("Section 329(a) of the Immigration and Nationality Act (8 U.S.C. 1440(a)) is amended by inserting 'as a member of the Selected Reserve of the Ready Reserve or' after 'has served honorably'").

84. *See* INA § 329(a), 8 U.S.C. § 1440(a), 117 Stat. at 1693 (2014); *see also* NDAA 2004, *supra* note 82, § 1702 (effective as if enacted on Sept. 11, 2001).

85. 10 U.S.C. § 10143 (2014) ("Within the Ready Reserve of each of the reserve components there is a Selected Reserve. The Selected Reserve consists of units, and, as designated by the Secretary concerned, of Reserves, trained as prescribed in section 10147(a)(1) of this title [10 U.S.C.S. § 10147(a)(1)] or section 502(a) of title 32, as appropriate."). Title 32 units are National Guard units, and drilling National Guard members are part of the Selected Reserve, as are drilling Reservists.

86. INA § 212, 8 U.S.C. § 1182 (2014).

existence of a bar to admissibility under INA § 212(e). Likewise, someone who is inadmissible for having made a false claim to U.S. citizenship may be able to naturalize under INA § 329, because making a false claim to U.S. citizenship is a ground of inadmissibility[87] and a ground of deportability,[88] but not an absolute bar to naturalization.[89] While a false claim to U.S. citizenship may be taken into account in considering, under the totality of the circumstances, whether a military member has good moral character, USCIS may still naturalize the person under INA § 329.

The key to naturalization through military service is that the military service must have been "honorable," as determined by the branch of the U.S. Armed Forces in which the person served or is serving. If the person is still serving at the time that the naturalization application is filed, then the character of the person's service is determined by the statements on the Form N-426, Request for Certification of Military or Naval Service, which must be filed with the naturalization application package. A representative of the military branch will complete Form N-426 and certify the person's service as honorable or otherwise.[90] If the person has been discharged from the military, then USCIS will accept an uncertified Form N-426 as long as it is submitted with a copy of Defense Department Form DD-214, Certificate of Release or Discharge from Active Duty, or NGB (National Guard Bureau) Form 22, National Guard Report of Separation and Record of Service.[91] USCIS will review the DD-214 or NGB 22 to determine whether the person's service was honorable or otherwise[92] and will verify this information with military authorities.

---

87. INA § 212(a)(6)(C)(ii)(I), 8 U.S.C. § 1182 (2014) ("Any alien who falsely represents, or has falsely represented, himself or herself to be a citizen of the United States for any purpose or benefit under this Act . . . or any other Federal or State law is inadmissible.").

88. INA § 237(a)(3)(D)(i), 8 U.S.C. § 1227 (2014) ("Any alien who falsely represents, or has falsely represented, himself to be a citizen of the United States for any purpose or benefit under this Act . . . or any Federal or State law is deportable.").

89. The bars to showing good moral character, which also operate to bar a non-citizen from naturalizing during the period when good moral character is required, are found at 8 U.S.C. § 101(f). Two of these bars are permanent and cannot be overcome with the passage of time—the bar based on a conviction for murder and the bar based on an aggravated felony conviction on or after November 29, 1990.

90. The certification may be made by any military official who has access to the individual's military personnel file; military personnel files are now maintained online, so a military personnel official need not have a "paper file" to certify the form.

91. *See* Donald Neufeld, USCIS Memorandum, HQ 70/34.5, HQ 70/34.6, AD09-24, Acceptance of DD Form 214 as Certification of Military or Naval Service for Veterans of the U.S. Armed Forces, Apr. 29, 2009, *available on* AILA InfoNet.

92. *Id.*

Another unique aspect of the special military naturalization statutes is that they specifically allow military personnel to naturalize notwithstanding the pendency of removal proceedings. Because military naturalization offers this unique avenue of relief to potentially deportable aliens, Immigration and Customs Enforcement (ICE) will sometimes exercise its discretion favorably when determining whether to place a military member or veteran into removal proceedings or to reinstate a removal order against a non-citizen with prior military service.

In mid-2009, the Army and USCIS started a program whereby non-citizen Army recruits can file their naturalization applications when they report to Basic Combat Training (BCT) and have those applications adjudicated so that the soldiers graduate from BCT and become U.S. citizens at the same time.[93] USCIS will accept the applications at the Army's BCT sites, assist the soldiers with completing the applications, interview and test the soldiers while they are at BCT, and conduct a ceremony (in conjunction with Army authorities) for soldiers whose applications are approved. The Navy has implemented a similar process at its Great Lakes boot camp training site,[94] the Air Force has also begun naturalizing recruits during basic training graduation at Lackland Air Force Base in Texas,[95] and the Marine Corps began its boot camp naturalizations in 2013. A military member who wishes to file for naturalization at basic training should bring the completed Application for Naturalization (Form N-400) and an uncertified Request for Certification of Military or Naval Service (Form N-426) to basic training. Depending on the branch of service and unit, the person may have the opportunity to submit the application packet, have the naturalization interview, and take the Oath of Allegiance to become a U.S. citizen before graduating from basic training.

A veteran must have received an Honorable or General Under Honorable Conditions discharge in order to be eligible for naturalization under INA §§ 328 or 329. An LPR veteran with another type of discharge may

---

93. USCIS News Release, *52 Soldiers Become U.S. Citizens at Army Basic Training* (May 6, 2010), *available at* http://www.uscis.gov/portal/site/uscis/menuitem.5af9bb95919f35e66f61 4176543f6d1a/?vgnextoid=ead760657dd68210VgnVCM100000082ca60aRCRD&vgnextchan nel=a2dd6d26d17df110VgnVCM1000004718190aRCRD.

94. Susanne M. Schafer, *Army, Navy Add Citizenship Option to Boot Camp*, Associated Press, Apr. 21, 2011.

95. Mike Joseph, *Five AF Basic Trainees Become U.S. Citizens*, Air Force Print News (Sep. 8, 2011), *available at* http://www.aetc.af.mil/news/story.asp?id=123271143.

be able to naturalize through civilian naturalization procedures but not through INA §§ 328 or 329.

NON-CITIZEN MILITARY MEMBERS MAY SOMETIMES BE ELIGIBLE FOR POSTHUMOUS CITIZENSHIP

President Bush's 2002 Executive Order declaring that immigrants in the military were eligible for expedited naturalization after September 11, 2001 also triggered the application of INA § 329A, a statute that allows posthumous U.S. citizenship to be granted to non-citizens who are serving honorably on active duty during periods of conflict[96] when they die "as a result of injury or disease incurred in or aggravated by"[97] military service. A deceased immigrant may be granted posthumous citizenship under this statute regardless of his or her immigration status, and the grant of posthumous citizenship can confer immigration benefits on his or her parents, spouse, and children.[98] The next-of-kin or other approved representative of the deceased must file an application for posthumous citizenship within two years of the death, or by November 24, 2005— whichever is later.[99]

NON-CITIZENS WHO SERVE IN THE MILITARY ARE NOT PROTECTED FROM DEPORTATION AND MAY LOSE U.S. CITIZENSHIP IF THEY FAIL TO SERVE HONORABLY AFTER BEING NATURALIZED

Once a non-citizen enlists in the U.S. military, he or she must be careful to serve honorably for the required period of time, or the consequences can be more severe than for a U.S. citizen military member who misbehaves or obtains a less-than-honorable discharge. Under the unique military naturalization statutes, persons who naturalize through military service after November 24, 2003, can have their U.S. citizenship revoked if they

---

96. INA § 329A, 8 U.S.C. § 1440-1, added by Section 2 of the Posthumous Citizenship for Active Duty Service Act of 1989, Pub. L. No. 101-249, 104 Stat. 94 (Mar. 6, 1990).

97. INA § 329A(b)(2), 8 U.S.C. § 1440 (2014).

98. INA § 319(d), 8 U.S.C. § 1430 (2014); 8 C.F.R. § 319.3(a). See Pub. L. No. 108-136, §§ 1703(f)–(h), 1705, 117 Stat. 1695–6 (effective as if enacted on Sept. 11, 2001). Potential benefits to certain family members include retention of immediate relative status, the ability to self-petition for an immigrant visa, and the ability to naturalize immediately upon being granted LPR status.

99. *See* INA § 329A, 8 U.S.C. § 1440 (2014).

fail to serve honorably for a period or periods aggregating five years.[100] Misbehavior while in uniform—even if it does not result in a formal conviction by a court-martial—can result in the denial of immigration benefits and possible removal from the United States upon discharge. Military members can also be subject to administrative proceedings that can result in an unfavorable discharge or adverse personnel action. The type of discharge that a veteran receives, or the reason for a discharge, can affect his or her eligibility for naturalization or other immigration benefits. Counsel advising military members or veterans should be careful to review a military record fully to spot immigration issues related to military administrative punishment, non-judicial punishment, discharges, and court-martial convictions.

During their time in service, military members are subject not only to military administrative action, but also to the Uniform Code of Military Justice (UCMJ),[101] which contains both procedural and substantive criminal law provisions. Under the UCMJ military members who are accused of misconduct can be subject to both judicial and non-judicial punishment. Often, non-judicial punishment under Article 15[102] of the UCMJ will not result in the most serious immigration consequences because military non-judicial punishment is not a conviction.[103] But the acts committed that resulted in punishment under Article 15 can affect a good moral character determination in connection with a naturalization application[104] and may affect a non-citizen's inadmissibility or deportability in

---

100. Both INA § 328 and INA § 329 were amended in 2004 to add provisions allowing DHS to revoke U.S. citizenship granted under those sections if a person "is separated from the Armed Forces under other than honorable conditions before the person has served honorably for a period or periods aggregating five years." *Id.* § 328(f) (codified as amended at 8 U.S.C. § 1439(f)); INA § 329(c) (codified as amended at 8 U.S.C. § 1440(c)).

101. 10 U.S.C. §§ 801–946 (2014).

102. 10 U.S.C. § 815. Such punishment is commonly called an "Article 15" in the Army or Air Force, a "mast" or "Captain's Mast" in the Navy, and "office hours" in the Marine Corps.

103. *See, e.g.*, 18 U.S.C.S. Appx. § 4A1.2(g) (Federal Sentencing Guidelines Manual (2010 ed.)): "Sentences resulting from military offenses are counted if imposed by a general or special court-martial. Sentences imposed by a summary court-martial or Article 15 proceeding are not counted." *Id.*

104. These acts can affect a good moral character determination not because they are convictions, but because USCIS is permitted to use its discretion when deciding whether someone has good moral character. *See* INA § 101(f), 8 U.S.C. § 1101 (2014) ("The fact that any person is not within any of the foregoing classes shall not preclude a finding that for other reasons such person is or was not of good moral character.").

cases where a conviction is not required for the ground of inadmissibility or removability to apply.[105]

Another military-related bar to naturalization is the desertion bar. A person is barred from naturalizing if he or she, "at any time during which the United States has been or shall be at war, deserted or shall desert the military, air, or naval forces of the United States."[106] Desertion under the Uniform Code of Military Justice requires an intent to remain away permanently or an intent to avoid hazardous duty or shirk important service;[107] practitioners should note that the law does not bar the naturalization of persons who have been convicted of the lesser-included offense of "absent without leave."[108] For the desertion bar to apply, the person must have been convicted by a court-martial or other court of competent jurisdiction.[109]

Despite these bars, non-citizen LPRs who face potentially adverse immigration consequences as a result of an alienage or a nonhonorable discharge may be able to naturalize under the civilian naturalization statutes. For example, an LPR who is administratively discharged from the U.S. Armed Forces after being charged with desertion is not necessarily barred from naturalizing. Although the law bars the naturalization of anyone who "at any time during which the United States has been or shall be at war, deserted or shall desert the military, air, or naval forces of the United States,"[110] this bar to naturalization does not apply unless the person has been convicted by a court-martial or other court of competent jurisdiction. If a person was not convicted by a court-martial because he accepted an administrative discharge in lieu of court-martial, he or she may be able to naturalize, notwithstanding the desertion charge. A person's listing on official military records as a deserter does not in and

---

105. For example, a person can be deported for having made a false claim to U.S. citizenship after Sep. 30, 1996, even if the person has not been convicted of any such offense. *See id.* § 237(a)(1)(A); *id.* § 212(a)(6)(C)(ii).

106. *Id.* § 314.

107. Art. 86, UCMJ.

108. Art. 85, UCMJ. If a person has been away from duty for more than 30 days, the government in a court-martial is allowed to assume there was no intent to return, and the burden shifts to the defense to show that there was an intent to return.

109. INS Interpretation 314.1 ("While conviction of desertion by court martial was first required by the above 1940 statute, the courts imposed a similar requisite under the earlier law; and, neither an admission of desertion, a finding of desertion by a civil court, nor a listing of a person on official military records as a deserter precluded naturalization in the absence of the required conviction.").

110. INA § 314, 8 U.S.C. § 1425 (2014).

of itself bar him or her from naturalizing.[111] Again, however, the person must meet the "regular" requirements for naturalization, including showing that he or she is an LPR and has good moral character during the required statutory period.

On the other hand, the administrative discharge—even an honorable one—on account of alienage may be problematic because of INA § 315(a), which makes permanently ineligible for citizenship "any alien who applies or has applied for exemption or discharge from training or service in the Armed Forces . . . on the ground that he is an alien."[112] The wartime military naturalization statute specifically prohibits the naturalization of anyone who is discharged on account of alienage.[113]

Immigration lawyers are aware that immigration law is extraordinarily complex and changes almost daily, and is further subject to various administrative interpretations and circuit court of appeals opinion splits. Numerous books and other publications exist to provide expert advice on how to determine the immigration consequences of a particular criminal conviction, and those materials are not duplicated here.

It is a surprise to many people that a non-citizen who has served in the United States Armed Forces has no special immunity from being deported from the United States. Yet non-citizen military personnel and veterans are subject to the same removal laws as other non-citizens; by regulation, military correctional officials are required to report their incarceration to the Department of Homeland Security for potential deportation.[114] That said, it is also the case that non-citizen military personnel and veterans may be eligible for the exercise of prosecutorial discretion in meritorious cases. As discussed above, military personnel and veterans may also avoid deportation or removal by naturalizing through

---

111. INS Interpretation 314.1.

112. INA § 315(a), 8 U.S.C. § 1426 (2014).

113. *Id.* § 329(a), 8 C.F.R. § 329.1; as noted above, the peacetime military naturalization statute, INA § 328, contains no similar bar.

114. For example, Army Regulation 190-47, The Army Corrections System (June 2006), states in paragraph 10-3: "In all cases where non-U.S. citizens convicted of crimes are confined in an ACS facility, information on charge(s), final judicial action, and place of incarceration will be forwarded to the Bureau of Citizenship and Immigrations Services (BCIS), ATTN: Investigations Division, 4420 N Fairfax Drive, Arlington, VA 22203. Additionally, facilities will coordinate with the BCIS to review records for possible deportation of prisoners. Access to diplomatic representatives will be made available to foreign nationals." It is unclear why the Army Corrections System is coordinating with USCIS to arrange deportations, but presumably USCIS knows to pass the information along to ICE, which would appear to be the proper agency to act on the information.

their military service, if they qualify for naturalization, and may naturalize while in removal proceedings.

NEW USCIS POLICY MEMORANDUM FOR MILITARY FAMILY MEMBERS

All lawyers practicing in the area of immigration law should make themselves aware that on November 15, 2013, USCIS issued a Policy Memorandum formalizing a procedure whereby some parents, spouses, and children of certain military members may be "paroled in place" and allowed to adjust status before USCIS. The Policy Memorandum applies to parents, spouses, and children who have entered the United States without inspection but are present in the United States when they request the parole. They must be the immediate relatives of a current military member—including active duty members and Selected Reservists, such as National Guard members—or the immediate relatives of a military veteran who served on active duty or in the Selected Reserve of the Ready Reserve. A person who entered the United States without inspection, but who is "paroled in place," may adjust status in the United States by filing a one-step adjustment application with USCIS. This new Policy Memorandum benefits hundreds of military family members; those covered by the new Policy Memorandum are no longer required to leave the United States to seek immigrant visas overseas. Such family members also are now saved the difficulty and expense of filing provisional waivers (I-601As) for their unlawful presence.

DUAL CITIZENSHIP

Contrary to popular belief, the U.S. government as a general matter does recognize dual citizenship.[115] The government's recognition that many U.S. citizens are also citizens of other countries, however, does not mean that the U.S. government approves of dual citizenship for members of the U.S. Armed Forces. Dual citizenship can apparently prevent enlistment into certain jobs in the military, and can pose problems for U.S. military personnel, who may be asked whether they are willing to renounce their

---

115. *See, e.g.,* U.S. Office of Personnel Management, *Citizenship Laws of the World, available at* http://www.opm.gov/extra/investigate/is-01.pdf (stating that the U.S. government recognizes dual citizenship); *see also* Kennedy v. Mendoza-Martinez, 372 U.S. 144, 158 (1963) (discussing U.S. military obligations of dual citizen of Mexico and the United States).

citizenship in another country as a condition of obtaining a security clearance. Dual citizenship can also create significant legal problems for members of the U.S. Armed Forces; to give just one example, a U.S. Army soldier who is a dual citizen of Syria and the United States may be told by the Syrian government that he must perform mandatory Syrian military service because of his Syrian citizenship. Because the soldier is in the U.S. Army, however, his Syrian military obligation will conflict with his U.S. military obligation. The soldier may therefore need to avoid any travel to Syria, at least until he is no longer subject to arrest by the Syrian government for failure to perform his military duties to Syria.

The U.S. government may ask a U.S. military member to declare his or her willingness to renounce citizenship in another country as a condition of service in the U.S. military. The U.S. government, however, does not control whether another country recognizes a renunciation of citizenship as valid; some countries do not recognize the right of expatriation and will consider a person to be one of their citizens even if the person has renounced his or her citizenship. Military personnel with questions about dual citizenship are advised to consult an expert immigration attorney. In this author's experience, U.S. military personnel are often given erroneous information about dual citizenship issues by their chain of command, by U.S. government officials, and even by well-meaning members of the Judge Advocate General's Corps. Additionally, some countries use the renunciation process as a subterfuge to collect intelligence information on U.S. citizens and their families, so proceeding through a formal renunciation process with a foreign government can create a security vulnerability for the U.S. military member or lead to persecution of the military member's foreign family members.

21

PRACTICE BEFORE IMMIGRATION COURTS

Ofelia L. Calderón[1] and Xavier F. Racine[2]

Abbiate speranza, voi ch'entrate.
Have hope all ye who enter here.

INTRODUCTION

Representing foreign nationals in deportation, now called removal proceedings, is arguably one of the most challenging tasks in the legal field. Although accurately described as civil administrative proceedings, the stakes are high and the rules of the game are often inconsistent and dependent on whether the individual facing deportation has representation. Successful practice before the immigration courts can involve written and oral substantive legal argument, witness and evidence preparation, and finally the presentation of a full hearing on the merits of the foreign national's case.

A recent study conducted by the Katzmann Immigrant Representation Study Group and the Vera Institute of Justice in New York showed startling numbers.[3] The study showed that for those individuals not in detention, 74 percent of those with lawyers obtained favorable outcomes, whereas only 13 percent of those without lawyers had favorable outcomes. For detained foreign nationals, 18 percent of those represented by attorneys obtained favorable outcomes while only 3 percent of those without representation won their cases. The importance of legal representation in this context is clear.

---

1. Ofelia L. Calderón is a partner at Calderón Seguin PLC in Fairfax, Virginia. The firm handles immigration, criminal, and domestic matters.
2. Xavier F. Racine is a founding partner at Priale & Racine PLLC. The firm handles criminal and immigration matters with a focus on removal proceedings and litigation.
3. Katzmann Immigrant Representation Study Group and the Vera Institute of Justice, *The New York Immigrant Representation Study: Preliminary Findings* (May 3, 2011).

This article seeks to give a broad overview of the immigration court practice for those practitioners who are less familiar with immigration litigation. As the focus of the article is on practice and procedure, the article does not cover the possible applications for relief available to a non citizen.

WHO ARE THE PLAYERS?

There are over 260 immigration judges spread out over 59 immigration courts in the United States. Ostensibly, immigration judges are responsible for holding removal (deportation)[4] and bond proceedings for individuals who are charged with violating the Immigration and Nationality Act. Although they act independently in making decisions about who can stay and who cannot, immigration judges are in fact quite limited. They are attorney-employees of the U.S. Department of Justice. In practice, immigration judges are bound rigidly by the relevant statutes, regulations, and precedent cases handed down by the appellate body above. Immigration judges are generally unable to consider questions of Constitutional import. Immigration courts are the trial courts of the immigration system and they hear thousands of cases each year. Reviewing their decisions is the Board of Immigration Appeals (BIA). Both the immigration courts and the Board of Immigration Appeals are housed within the Executive Office for Immigration Review (EOIR), which is a part of the Department of Justice.

The Board of Immigration Appeals is the highest administrative body for interpreting and applying immigration laws. By regulation, the BIA is authorized to have up to 15 board members, including the Chairman and Vice Chairman who share responsibility for BIA management. The BIA is located at EOIR headquarters in Falls Church, Virginia. As noted above, BIA decisions are binding on the immigration courts unless overturned by the Attorney General or a federal court.

The U.S. government is represented by attorneys who are employed by the Department of Homeland Security, or DHS.[5] These attorneys are

---

4. Prior to April 1, 1997, an alien was either placed in exclusion or deportation proceedings, depending on whether the alien made an entry into the United States. After the enactment and passage of the Illegal Immigration Reform and Immigrant Responsibility Act of 1996 ("IIRAIRA"), Pub. L. No. 104-208, 110 Stat. 3009 (September 30, 1996), the deportation and exclusion proceedings were combined into one unified proceeding known as "Removal."

5. The Department of Homeland Security was created shortly after the terrorist attacks in September of 2001 through the passage of the Homeland Security Act of 2002. Previously, the organization charged with implementing immigration laws was the Immigration and

known as the trial attorney (TA) or the assistant chief counsel (ACC) or the government's attorney. On the other side is, of course, the non-citizen, or alien, who is being charged with violating the Immigration and Nationality Act. Discussed in more depth below is the fact that although the statute confirms that every non-citizen in removal proceedings has a right to counsel, that right to counsel is assured without expense to the government. Despite the complexity of immigration law, many respondents are simply unable to obtain counsel for financial reasons. In fact, according to the Executive Office for Immigration Review, 41% of all respondents who appeared before the immigration court in 2013 were without representation.[6]

WHAT KIND OF PROCEEDING AM I DOING?

If your client is before the immigration court, he or she is usually either in deportation proceedings or removal proceedings.[7] They are the same—but not. "Deportation" was the legal term used prior to April 1, 1997. When the U.S. Congress passed the Illegal Immigration Reform and Immigrant Responsibility Act of 1996 (IIRAIRA), deportation and its sister, exclusion, ceased to exist and everything became "removal." There are older cases that surface every now and then that remain deportation proceedings, and it is important to be aware of this because some of the rules are different. How does one know? By looking at the document that initiated proceedings for your client.

INITIATION OF PROCEEDINGS; AKA, HOW DID I GET HERE?

When proceedings are initiated, a document called a Notice to Appear (Form I-862), or NTA, is issued. Prior to April 1, 1997, that document was called an Order to Show Cause (Form I-221), or OSC. This is the charging document. It is similar to a warrant or an indictment. This document tells the recipient (usually the non-citizen) in written form the nature of proceedings, the factual allegations against the non-citizen, and the grounds under which DHS is charging that he or she is removable. The NTA also has language indicating the consequences for failing to appear

---

Naturalization Service (INS), which was housed within the Department of Justice (DOJ).

6. U.S. Department of Justice, FY 2013 Statistical Yearbook (April 2014), http://www.justice.gov/eoir/statspub/syb2000main.htm.

7. INA § 240.

at a proceeding and in some cases includes the date, location, and time when the non-citizen is scheduled to appear before the immigration court. Proceedings are initiated when the NTA is served on the non-citizen (once called the respondent in proceedings) and filed with the immigration court. On occasion, the respondent is served but the court isn't. This is called a failure to prosecute. Until the NTA is filed with the court, respondent is not required to appear.

WHO ISSUES THE NTA?

The regulations governing the issuance of this document and the initiation of removal proceedings are found at INA § 239, 8 C.F.R. §§ 239 and 1239. It is vital at this initial phase to conduct a detailed analysis of the NTA. A good practitioner should look over the NTA carefully for errors, which may be substantive or procedural. For example, within the regulations is a laundry list of special agents, supervisors, and officers of DHS who are permitted to issue the document. These agents and officers can be employed by the subagencies of DHS, such as U.S. Citizenship and Immigration Services (USCIS), Customs and Border Protection (CBP), or Immigration and Customs Enforcement (ICE). It is always worthwhile to review this list, If the NTA is not properly issued, it is defective and then termination is appropriate.

When CBP issues the NTA, it usually takes place during the apprehension of a non-citizen attempting to enter the United States without inspection or at a port of entry where CBP has determined there is a problem with the admission of a non-citizen. When ICE issues the NTA, it is normally because they have encountered the non-citizen through its enforcement or investigation operations. When USCIS issues the NTA, it normally follows the agency's denial of a benefit.

Another important issue related to the NTA is service. In immigration proceedings, the service of the NTA is governed by § 239 of the INA and the regulations are found at 8 C.F.R. § 1003.13. In removal proceedings, the NTA shall be served in person on the alien or, if personal service is not practicable, through service by mail to the alien or the alien's counsel of record. Of course, mailing and serving is not always the same as receiving.

Generally speaking, problems with notice and service arise from the manner in which the different agencies interact. As noted above, the NTA must be filed with the immigration court to generate an actual hearing date and time. An officer may issue an NTA that states "to be set" for date and time, or there may actually be a date and time, but that date and time is not certain until the NTA is filed with the immigration court. To avoid missing a hearing, the non-citizen (now the "respondent") and/or the attorney can confirm this information by calling EOIR at (1 800) 898-7180. Additionally, the respondent and/or the attorney should be sure to comply with the address obligation by filing Form EOIR-33 with the immigration court and DHS in the event of any change of address. Failure to attend a hearing in immigration court can and does result in the issuance of an order of removal *in absentia*.[8]

VENUE, OR WHERE SHOULD I BE IN PROCEEDINGS?

In immigration proceedings, venue is generally proper where the respondent resides or is physically located. Venue is initially determined by the filing of the NTA as venue lies with the immigration court where the NTA is filed.[9] The most common example of the need to change venue is a change in the physical location of the respondent. This may come about either through a residential relocation or in cases where a respondent is detained. Detained individuals are often released on bond and return to their normal residences in a place other than the original immigration court's jurisdiction.

In this circumstance, a motion to change venue is necessary. Pursuant to 8 C.F.R. § 1003.20, venue may be changed by the immigration court upon motion by either party. Such a motion must describe with specificity the reason for the change of venue, and in most cases, requires evidence such as proof of new residence for the respondent in the new location. A successful motion to change venue should comply with the Immigration Court Practice Manual[10] and include written pleadings to

---

8. Although dire, the consequences of failing to appear because of notice or service may be ameliorated. *See* Matter of Munoz-Santos, 20 I. & N. Dec. 205 (B.I.A. 1990) (finding that notice of hearing is properly served when the Notice to Appear or Order to Show Cause is sent by regular mail to the last known address provided by the unrepresented respondent.) *But see* Matter of G-Y-R, 23 I. & N. Dec. 181 (B.I.A. 2001); Matter of M-D-, 23 I. & N. Dec. 540 (B.I.A. 2002); Qumsieh v. Ashcroft, 2005 U.S. App. LEXIS 10390 (6th Cir. 2005); Sedha v. INS, 2004 U.S. App. LEXIS 26790 (9th Cir. 2004) (holding that in removal proceedings an in absentia order may only be entered where an alien has received, or can be charged with receiving, a Notice to Appear informing him of the consequences of failing to provide a current address under section 239(a)(1)(F) of the INA).

9. 8 C.F.R. § 1003.14.

10. Executive Office for Immigration Review, Immigration Court Practice Manual (February 2008), http://www.justice.gov/eoir/vll/OCIJPracManual/ocij_page1.htm.

the Notice to Appear, which identify the form of relief (if any) respondent intends to seek.

INADMISSIBILITY VS. REMOVABILITY; AKA, AM I IN OR OUT?

One of the most misunderstood concepts in immigration law is the difference between inadmissibility and removability. Truly, it confounds even seasoned practitioners. In a nutshell, inadmissibility generally refers to § 212 of the INA while removability generally refers to § 237 of the INA. In a smaller nutshell—inadmissibility refers to conditions that prevent a non-citizen from being admitted to the United States while removability refers to conditions that cause a non-citizen to be kicked out of the United States. Why is this important?

This is important because it determines at the outset who carries the burden of proof and what standard of proof must be shown. When a respondent is in § 212 proceedings initiated at a port of entry and is an applicant for admission, the burden is carried by the respondent to show he or she is *clearly and beyond a doubt* entitled to admission and is not inadmissible under § 12(a) of the INA.[11] When a respondent is in § 212 proceedings and DHS suspects unlawful entry, the burden is carried by the respondent to show by *clear and convincing* evidence that he or she has been admitted lawfully.[12] When a respondent is in § 237 proceedings after being lawfully admitted to the United States, the burden is on DHS to show by *clear and convincing* evidence that the respondent is subject to removal.[13]

This is not the end, however, because the burden can and does shift. For example, once removabilty is determined and a respondent applies for relief, the burden is carried by the respondent regardless of whether the proceedings are under § 212 or § 237.[14]

ANATOMY OF A REMOVAL HEARING

What Are the Rules?

The rules of practice in immigration court tend to be more relaxed than other federal courts. There is no adherence to the Federal Rules of Civil Procedure or the Federal Rules of Evidence. Previously, there were local

---

11. INA § 240(c)(2)(A).
12. *Id.* § 240(c)(2)(B).
13. *Id.* § 240(c)(3)(A).
14. *Id.* § 240(c)(4).

rules for each of the immigration courts but that has changed in recent years with the advent of the Immigration Court Practice Manual. This manual is found on the EOIR website at http://www.justice.gov/eoir/vll /OCIJPracManual/ocij_page1.htm and is an incredibly useful tool for procedural matters.[15]

Master Calendar

The first hearing before the immigration court is called the master calendar hearing. For non-immigration practitioners, this is like a preliminary hearing. Because of the lack of immigration courts and the zeal of ICE, there are usually many respondents present at this hearing. Unless there are special circumstances, these hearings are open. At the master calendar hearing, an attorney is expected to "plead" to the NTA. Pleading means that the attorney will concede or deny proper service of the NTA followed by admitting or denying the allegations and charges listed on the NTA.[16] Upon answering to these charges, the attorney will indicate what form, if any, of relief the respondent seeks from removal. If the attorney is prepared to go forward at that moment, the attorney may also ask for a final hearing on the merits of the case. If not, the attorney may ask for additional time to submit the applications.

Individual Merits

Once all of the procedural steps described are complete, the case is set for a final hearing to present the merits of a case. This is called the individual merits hearing. Consistent with its name, this is an individualized hearing for the respondent. Only parties necessary to his or her case are present. During this hearing, the attorney presents the evidence and witnesses that support whatever application for relief the respondent has filed. Like other trial courts, this is probably the best chance a respondent has to win his or her case, so it is vitally important that all available evidence and witnesses are presented during this hearing.

In some cases, the application for relief is termination, which means the attorney does not believe his or her client is deportable or inadmissible. In most cases, the respondent is subject to removal but may be able to apply for some sort of relief from removal such as asylum or cancellation of removal. There are many different types of relief and it would be

---

15. Notwithstanding the Immigration Court Practice Manual, practitioners should still consult with local attorneys, as there are immigration judges who maintain additional rules for their own courtroom.

16. Executive Office for Immigration Review, Immigration Court Practice Manual (February 2008), http://www.justice.gov/eoir/vll/OCIJPracManual/appendix_M.pdf.

impossible to cover them all in the scope of this practice and procedure primer.

It is important to note that although there is no court reporter, all removal proceedings are recorded. When a case is appealed to the BIA, a transcript is ordered and all parties receive a copy of that transcript. This transcript and the evidence submitted represent the only record of the case so preserving objections, arguments, and testimony is advised.

BOND PROCEEDINGS; AKA, DO I NEED TO STAY IN JAIL?

Briefly noted in the introduction is the fact that some respondents in immigration proceedings are detained. Detained respondents are held in two types of facilities. One type is an immigration-only facility where all of the inmates are held for immigration purposes. The other type consists of existing state, local, or federal jails that DHS contracts with to house immigration detainees. Neither of these types of facilities are necessarily convenient and create new obstacles for the practitioner to overcome.[17] Some ICE facilities have their own immigration courts inside them such as in York, Pennsylvania or Oakdale, Louisiana. Other ICE facilities do not and use video conferencing to conduct hearings. This means that the respondent is seen on a television from the jail while the immigration judge, ACC, and maybe the attorney are standing in a different location altogether. Detained cases present challenges in communication and preparation. Whenever possible, a bond hearing should be requested to attempt to secure release of the respondent.

When a non-citizen/respondent comes into ICE custody, a determination is made at the outset about whether to release or continue detention. ICE may hold a non-citizen arrested without a warrant for 48 hours, or longer "in the event of emergency or other extraordinary circumstances."[18] During this initial period, ICE must make a decision regarding custody and also whether to issue the NTA. Unless the person is subject to the mandatory detention provisions of the INA, ICE can release a non-citizen on bond or on his or her own recognizance.[19] There is also a newer program called Alternatives to Detention where the person may be released with an electronic monitoring device.

---

17. For more information, see National Immigration Forum, *Immigrants Behind Bars: How? Why? How Much?*, available at http://immigrationforum.org/images/uploads/2011/Immigrants_in_Local_Jails.pdf.
18. 8 C.F.R. § 287.3(d).
19. *Id.* § 236.1(d); *id.* § 126.1(d).

If a respondent is not lucky enough to obtain release directly from ICE at the time of his or her arrest, or if the bond set by ICE is too high, a request for custody or bond redetermination may be made to the immigration court.[20] Anyone can make this request, but not everyone is eligible to be heard. The immigration court does not have jurisdiction to hear bond requests from certain people.[21] Those unfortunate individuals are "arriving aliens"[22] (essentially non-citizens who arrive at the port of entry and are not "admitted" but not people who enter without inspection), non-citizens described in the terrorism and security related ground of deportability,[23] non-citizens in exclusion proceedings, non-citizens with final administrative orders under INA § 242(a)(2), and finally non-citizens subject to mandatory detention under INA § 236(c)(1), 8 U.S.C. § 1226(c)(1).[24]

Practitioners should note that while the immigration judge does not have jurisdiction to hear a bond case for these categories, the immigration judge does have jurisdiction to review whether a person belongs in those groups. These types of hearings are frequently called *Joseph* hearings.[25] This is challenging the ground of deportability itself—for example, my client is not subject to mandatory detention because DHS is "substantially unlikely to prevail" in showing my client is deportable under whatever section subjects him to mandatory detention. This is not the same as challenging the limitations of the statute, but it often requires a significant legal argument either orally or through a written brief.

A request for custody/bond redetermination to the immigration court may be made orally or through motion. Practitioners should note that bond proceedings are separate from removal or deportation proceedings. They are run parallel to the removal proceedings at times but are considered a separate and distinct proceeding. In fact, there is a *separate* bond file that is created by the court, and generally bond proceedings are not recorded as is the case with removal proceedings. Evidentiary rules tend to be looser (even than for normal removal proceedings) and the "burden" is always on the respondent to show he or she is eligible for bond.

---

20. *Id.* § 1003.19(a); *id.* §§ 236.1(d), 1236.1(d).
21. *Id.* §§ 236.1(c)(11), 1236.1(c)(11); *id.* § 1003.19(h)(2).
22. INA § 1.1(q).
23. *Id.* §§ 237(a)(4), 1227(a)(4).
24. It is possible to challenge detention under INA § 236(c) by arguing that case does not fit within the statute. *See, e.g.,* Waffi v. Loiselle, 527 F. Supp. 2d 480 (E.D. Va. 2007); Matter of West, 22 I. & N. Dec. 1405 (B.I.A. 2000).
25. Matter of Joseph, 22 I. & N. Dec. 799 (B.I.A. 1999).

The respondent must show that his or her release would not pose a danger to society and that he or she is not a flight risk.[26] The BIA has laid out common factors to consider, such as family ties, hardship to family members, previous criminal history, prior immigration history, community ties, length of residence, and financial ability.[27] A good practitioner documents as many of these factors as possible and presents this evidence to the court in support of his or her motion.

Bond issues in general are complicated. There are frequently complex legal issues and sometimes those issues even require litigation in federal courts.

Note that findings by the immigration court for bond proceedings do not necessarily mean the same finding for the removal proceedings. Example: an immigration judge may find that a criminal conviction is not a crime involving moral turpitude for bond purposes, but still find the conviction demonstrates a lack of good moral character for an application presented in removal proceedings. Remember the proceedings are separate.

This author frequently files a bond motion before proceedings are truly initiated because of the lag time between the issuance of the NTA, filing of the NTA with the immigration court, and scheduling of an initial master calendar hearing. As noted above, the bond proceeding is separate and may be conducted in the absence of the NTA pursuant to 8 C.F.R. § 1003.14(a).

ALTERNATIVE PROCEEDINGS; AKA, WHY CAN'T I APPLY FOR WHATEVER I WANT?

There are some non-citizens who are not entitled to a full removal hearing under INA § 240. "Arriving aliens," those not admitted or paroled into the United States who have not resided in the United States for at least two years, individuals interdicted at sea, and those paroled into the United States after April of 1997 whose parole has terminated, are subject to "administrative" or "expedited" removal without a hearing under INA § 235(b)(1). nonlawful permanent residents who have been convicted of an aggravated felony[28] are subject to "expedited" removal without a hearing under INA § 238(b). A non-citizen who has a prior order of removal that is being reinstated is subject to removal without a hearing under INA

---

26. *See, e.g.,* Matter of Patel, 15 I. & N. Dec. 666 (B.I.A. 1976); Matter of San Martin, 15 I. & N. Dec. 167 (B.I.A. 1974); Matter of Adenji, Int. Dec. No. 3417 (B.I.A. 1999); Matter of Guerra, 24 I. & N. Dec. 37 (B.I.A. 2006).
27. *Matter of Patel,* 15 I. & N. Dec. 666.
28. INA § 101(a)(43).

§ 241(a)(5). Non-citizens subject to this type of removal are not given an opportunity to present their case before an immigration judge except in the following circumstances:

- A person subject to § 235(b)(1) who expresses a fear of persecution will be placed in "credible fear proceedings." This means that a DHS officer will conduct an interview to determine if the person has the requisite credible fear.[29] If yes, most people are then placed in regular removal proceedings under INA § 240 and have the same rights applicable to everyone in such proceedings. Stowaways, visa waiver entrants, S visa applicants, and some individuals inadmissible on security grounds are not placed in removal proceedings. They are placed in *asylum only proceedings* and can only present a case for asylum or withholding of removal or Convention Against Torture relief. If no, the negative finding may be reviewed by the immigration court.[30] The immigration court review must take place within seven days of the negative finding by DHS. There is no appeal of the immigration court finding.
- A person subject to § 235(b)(1) who claims to be a U.S. citizen, lawful permanent resident, asylee, or refugee will be placed in "claimed status review." The person makes a statement under oath, and then the immigration court reviews the claim.[31] If the immigration judge verifies status, proceedings may be terminated (particularly in the case of a U.S. citizen) or, if nonetheless deportable, removal proceedings under INA § 240 may be initiated. If status is not verified, DHS continues with removal. There is no appeal to the "claimed status review."
- A person subject to § 238(b) who expresses a fear of persecution will be placed in "reasonable fear proceedings." Again, a DHS officer conducts an interview to determine whether the person has a "reasonable fear of persecution or torture," meaning a reasonable possibility that he or she would be persecuted on account of race, religion, nationality, membership in particular social group, or

---

29. "Credible fear of persecution" means that there is a significant possibility that the alien can establish eligibility for asylum under INA § 208 or withholding of removal under INA § 241(b)(3). 8 C.F.R. §§ 208.30(e)(2), 1003.42(d). "Credible fear of torture" means there is a significant possibility that the alien is eligible for withholding of removal ("restriction on removal") or deferral of removal under the Convention Against Torture pursuant to 8 C.F.R. § 208.16 or § 208.17. 8 C.F.R. §§ 208.30(e)(3), 1003.42(d).

30. 8 C.F.R. § 208.30(g).

31. *Id.* § 1235.3(b)(5).

political opinion if returned to his or home country.[32] If yes, the person is placed in "withholding only" proceedings where they can only apply for withholding of removal under INA § 241(b)(3) or Convention Against Torture relief. If no, the negative finding may be reviewed by the immigration court within ten days. There is no appeal of the immigration court finding.

- A person subject to § 241(a)(5) who expresses a fear of persecution will be placed in "reasonable fear proceedings" described directly above.

THE SHIELD AND THE SWORD: RIGHTS IN PROCEEDINGS

Right to Representation

Current statutes[33] guarantee that aliens shall have the privilege of being represented, at no expense to the government, by counsel of their choosing who is authorized to practice in removal proceedings. no court of appeals has mandated government-funded counsel for respondents in removal proceedings, despite that some have discussed the applicability of the Due Process Clause of the Fifth Amendment.[34] The Due Process argument for appointing counsel arises out of Supreme Court precedent[35] that holds that the right to counsel may extend beyond criminal proceedings especially when deprivation of liberty and risk of confinement are possible consequences facing the individuals at the center of those proceedings. Removal proceedings often involve detained aliens, some of which remain in custody for extended periods of time and in the case of

32. *Id.* § 1208.31(c).

33. INA § 240b2B(4)(A).

34. Aguilera-Enriquez v. INS, 516 F.2d 565, 568 n.3 (6th Cir. 1975) ("[w]here an unrepresented indigent alien would require counsel to present his position adequately to an immigration judge, he must be provided with a lawyer at the Government's expense. Otherwise, 'fundamental fairness' would be violated") (citing Murgia-Melendez v. INS, 407 F.2d 207 (9th Cir. 1969)). *See also* United States v. Campos-Asencio, 822 F.2d 506, 509 (5th Cir. 1987) ("[A]n alien has a right to counsel if the absence of counsel would violate due process under the [F]ifth [A]mendment.").

35. *See In Re* Gault, 387 U.S. 1 (1967) (establishing a per se rule that juveniles in delinquency proceedings at risk for confinement were entitled to court appointed counsel under the Due Process Clause even though they were not in criminal proceedings and therefore could not rely on Sixth Amendment protection). But see Lassiter v. Department of Social Services of Durham County, 452 U.S. 18 (1981), where the Court shifted to a "case by case" approach and moved from a per se rule to a "presumption that an indigent litigant has a right to appointed counsel only when, if he loses, he may be deprived of his physical liberty."

mentally incompetent and juvenile detained respondents, a strong case could be made for appointment of counsel to guarantee a fundamentally fair hearing.

Right to Examine Evidence

Often, a respondent's eligibility for relief and success in obtaining that relief will be wholly dependent on obtaining evidence that is not in his or her possession. For example, a respondent may be grandfathered under INA § 245(i) and eligible to pursue adjustment of status but not have any record of his previously submitted immigrant petition or alien labor certification. Similarly, a respondent may be eligible for NACARA relief and recall having obtained temporary protected status in 1991 but have no proof of the now 20-year-old filing. Pursuant to 8 U.S.C. § 1229a(c)(2)(B), Congress provided that an alien in removal proceedings "shall have access to any document not considered by the Attorney General to be confidential that pertains to the alien's admission or presence in the United States." This language is mirrored in INA § 240(b)(4)(B), which states that an alien shall have a reasonable opportunity to examine the evidence against the alien, to present evidence on the alien's own behalf, and to cross-examine witnesses presented by the government, but these rights shall not entitle the alien to examine such national security information as the government may proffer in opposition to the alien's admission to the United States or to an application by the alien for discretionary relief under this act. The INA also provides for a complete record to be kept of all testimony and evidence produced during the course of removal proceedings,[36] and numerous cases have been remanded from the BIA for defective or incomplete transcripts.

The best way to obtain a copy of a respondent's entire file is to file a Freedom of Information Act (FOIA)[37] request, which for USCIS involves filing a form G-639 and form G-28. FOIA requests are divided into three tracks according to their complexity. Track 1 is comprised of the more simple requests (i.e., requests for a limited number of documents), track 2 covers more complex requests (i.e., requests for an entire Alien file), and track 3 is reserved for respondents in removal proceedings. Track 3 requests must be identified as such and must be accompanied by some evidence of the pending removal proceedings.[38] Requests can also be expedited

---

36. INA § 240(b)(4)(C).
37. 5 U.S.C. § 552.
38. Form I-862, Notice to Appear, documenting the scheduled date of the subject's hearing before the immigration judge; or Form I-221, Order to Show Cause, documenting the

in certain circumstances.[39] The status of a FOIA request can be tracked online,[40] via telephone,[41] or by sending an e-mail to USCIS.[42] There is a mandated 20-day time limit for responses to FOIA requests,[43] but USCIS may take additional time upon serving notice and establishing the presence of "unusual circumstances."[44] In reality, FOIA responses are seldom if ever received in 20 days. Consequently, a FOIA request is far from a perfect resource given the tremendous backlogs currently in place and the fact that immigration judges may be unwilling to grant lengthy continuances based on pending FOIA requests. Accordingly, a respondent's right to have access to his file is sometimes restricted by FOIA shortcomings and any such restrictions should be objected to on the record.

The importance of this access was recently considered by the Ninth Circuit Court of Appeals[45] as it addressed the government's insistence on FOIA compliance. The Ninth Circuit recognized that due process considerations required a respondent to have access to his file irrespective of strict compliance with FOIA procedures.[46] Other courts have also recently

---

scheduled date of the subject's hearing before the immigration judge; or Form I-863, Notice of Referral to Immigration Judge; or a written notice of continuation of a scheduled hearing before the immigration judge.

39. USCIS may grant expedited processing on a case-by-case basis in accordance with established guidelines (6 C.F.R. § 5.5(d)) if the requester establishes either (1) circumstances in which the lack of expedited treatment could reasonably be expected to pose an imminent threat to the life or physical safety of an individual; or (2) an urgency to inform the public about an actual or alleged federal government activity, if made by a person primarily engaged in disseminating information. In addition, a request for expedited processing must include a statement, certified true and correct, explaining the basis for requesting expedited treatment.

40. http://www.uscis.gov/portal/site/uscis/menuitem.8d416137d08f80a2b1935610748191a0/?vgnextoid=f3a2ba87c7a29110VgnVCM1000004718190aRCRD&vgnextchannel=f3a2ba87c7a29110VgnVCM1000004718190aRCRD.

41. (816) 350-5570.

42. uscis.foia@dhs.gov.

43. 5 U.S.C. § 552(a)(6)(A).

44. *Id.* § 552(a)(6)(B).

45. Dent v. Holder, No. 09-71987, 2010 U.S. App. LEXIS 23255 (9th Cir. Nov. 9, 2010).

46. "The government relies on a regulation (not a statute) providing that an individual seeking access to records about himself 'must submit a written request' to the Freedom of Information Act (FOIA) office. The regulation does not purport to address removal hearings specifically. It is a general regulation governing records requests. If it applied to removal proceedings, a serious due process problem would arise, because FOIA requests often take a very long time, continuances in removal hearings are discretionary, and aliens in removal hearings might not get responses to their FOIA requests before they were removed. The doctrine of constitutional avoidance requires us to construe the statute and the regulation, if possible, to avoid a serious constitutional question. We construe the 'shall

assaulted the current FOIA processing times and multitrack system find-ing that "USCIS has engaged in a pattern and practice of violating FOIA's time limit provisions"[47] and "USCIS's Track 3 FOIA processing policy and regulation were promulgated in violation of the APA and FOIA."[48] Given this emerging case law and the possible grounds for federal appellate relief, it is important to note all objections and FOIA obstacles into the record of removal proceedings.

Right to Contact Consulate

The assistance of foreign consular staff working in the United States can be invaluable to both pro se respondents and aliens with counsel espe-cially when dealing with detained respondents. Certain consulates will visit detained aliens in prison, explain the general procedure of removal proceedings, contact their family members, help locate and obtain medi-cal, military, school or identity documents and in some cases even provide emergency financial assistance. The assistance they render to detained aliens with counsel should not be understated. For example, a detained alien who has been granted voluntary departure under safeguards may not have a passport or any other ID document in his possession and no means of obtaining one even with the assistance of counsel. Embassy representatives can dispatch a consular representative to the appropriate detention center and expeditiously provide Immigration and Customs Enforcement with a travel document to ensure a timely departure and avoid prolonged detention.

---

have access' statute to provide a rule for removal proceedings, and the regulation to apply generally in the absence of a more specific rule. It would indeed be unconstitutional if the law entitled an alien in removal proceedings to his A-file but denied him access to it until it was too late to use it. That would unreasonably impute to Congress and the agency a Kafkaesque sense of humor about aliens' rights." *Id.*

47. Hajro & Mayock v. USCIS, No. 08-1350-PSG (N.D. Cal., San Jose Div., Oct. 13, 2011).

48. *Id.*

The right to consular access[49] is guaranteed under the Vienna Convention on Consular Relations,[50] a multilateral treaty signed by 114 countries and 45 signatories, including the United States, and is also guaranteed under several bilateral treaties between the United States and other countries as well as by DHS Regulations.[51]

Right to an Interpreter

As the large majority of respondents in removal proceedings are not native English speakers, they should avail themselves of the interpreter services provided by the court and requests should be made by counsel (either orally at a master calendar hearing or in the form of a written request prior to the individual hearing) to guarantee the presence of an interpreter. Interpreters are provided at government expense to individuals in removal proceedings whose command of the English language is inadequate to fully understand and participate in removal hearings before immigration judges. The immigration court will arrange for an interpreter both during the individual calendar hearing and, if necessary, the master calendar hearing and use staff interpreters employed by the immigration court, contract interpreters, and telephonic interpretation services.

In cases involving rare dialects or uncommon languages, it is sometimes advisable to have an "independent" interpreter (i.e., one not provided

---

49. Article 36(1) of the Vienna Convention reads as follows: "(1) consular officers shall be free to communicate with nationals of the sending State and to have access to them. Nationals of the sending State shall have the same freedom with respect to communication with and access to consular officers of the sending State; (2) if he so requests, the competent authorities of the receiving State shall, without delay, inform the consular post of the sending State if, within its consular district, a national of that State is arrested or committed to prison or to custody pending trial or is detained in any other manner. Any communication addressed to the consular post by the person arrested, in prison, custody or detention shall also be forwarded by the said authorities without delay. The said authorities shall inform the person concerned without delay of his rights under this sub-paragraph; (3) consular officers shall have the right to visit a national of the sending State who is in prison, custody or detention, to converse and correspond with him and to arrange for his legal representation. They shall also have the right to visit any national of the sending State who is in prison, custody or detention in their district in pursuance of a judgment. Nevertheless, consular officers shall refrain from taking action on behalf of a national who is in prison, custody or detention if he expressly opposes such action." *See Bilateral Consular Conventions*, U.S. Dept. of State, Bureau of Consular Affairs, http://travel.state.gov/content /travel/english/legal-considerations/international-treaties-agreements/bilateral-consular -conventions.html.

50. Vienna Convention on Consular Relations, adopted Apr. 24, 1963, 21 U.S.T. 77, 596 U.N.T.S. 261 (entered into force with respect to the United States of America Dec. 14, 1967).

51. 8 C.F.R. § 236.1(e) (2009).

by the court but perhaps by the respondent) present during a hearing to ensure accurate translations. Most immigration judges will allow these interpreters to sit and observe the hearing with the consent of the respondent, and it is an important safeguard especially in asylum proceedings where credibility and a respondent's testimony is of particular import.

Additional considerations in dealing with interpreters are the cultural and personal issues surrounding the individual respondents in need of interpretation services. Some lesbian, gay, bisexual, transgender, and/or HIV-positive asylum seekers feel uncomfortable testifying about such personal issues in front of someone from their country, and this level of comfort should be addressed in advance. Certain cultures and nationalities also attach a stigma to speaking a dialect so, for example, a respondent will sometimes tell the court he or she speaks Mandarin when in fact he or she only speaks Fujian. Additional factors sometimes stigmatized include the presence of mental health issues or of sexual abuse. While no statutory right or guarantee exists, requests for same sex interpreters have at times been granted by some immigration judges in rape or sexual abuse cases.

Mental Competency Issues

The issue of dealing with mental competency in immigration court is an evolving one, especially as more attention is being focused on the dire repercussions of having an inadequate system in place. In 2008, Mark Lyttle, a U.S. citizen born in North Carolina, was deported after completing a misdemeanor sentence for inappropriately touching one of the orderlies at the psychiatric facility in which he had been receiving treatment for his bipolar disorder. Due to his numerous mental health issues, he was coerced into signing documents stating he was from Mexico and ordered deported by an immigration judge soon thereafter. Speaking no Spanish and with no ID and no funds, he alternated between homelessness and prison eventually being deported to Honduras and then Guatemala. After reaching out to the U.S. embassy in Guatemala, he was finally able to communicate with his brothers serving in the U.S. military and obtain a U.S. passport to return to the United States. Upon returning to the United States he was arrested by ICE again and detained for six days until DHS finally acknowledged he was a U.S. citizen and released him.[52]

New practitioners should familiarize themselves with recent BIA precedent[53] for incompetent respondents and determine from the outset whether service of the NTA is effective, whether the respondent

---

52. http://www.ajc.com/news/north-carolina-man-sues-681887.html.
53. Matter of M-A-M, 25 I. & N. Dec. 474 (B.I.A. 2011).

understands and can participate in the proceedings, and how to formulate a strategy in the client's best interest moving forward with the case. The first step in effective representation will involve making a determination about a client's competency level. The BIA addressed common indicators[54] in reaching a finding of incompetency in *Matter of M-A-M*,[55] but it is important for practitioners to communicate with DHS as they have an affirmative obligation under the regulations[56] to provide the court with relevant materials in their possession that would inform the court about a respondent's mental competency. Ultimately, Federal Regulations, BIA and Circuit Court law[57] precedent all provide for moving forward with removal proceedings even in cases of respondents with limited competency. As long as procedural safeguards are in place, a respondent understands the nature of the proceedings, and

---

54. These factors include observations about the respondent, "such as the inability to understand and respond to questions, the inability to stay on topic, or a high level of distraction." The record may contain evidence of mental illness or incompetency including direct assessments of the respondent's mental health, such as medical reports or assessments from past medical treatment or from criminal proceedings, as well as testimony from medical health professionals. It may also include evidence from other relevant sources, such as school records regarding special education classes or individualized education plans; reports or letters from teachers, counselors, or social workers; evidence of participation in programs for persons with mental illness; evidence of applications for disability benefits; and affidavits or testimony from friends or family members. *Id.*

55. *Id.*

56. 8 C.F.R. § 1240.2(a) (2010) ("[DHS] counsel shall present on behalf of the government evidence material to the issues of deportability or inadmissibility and any other issues that may require disposition by the immigration judge."). *See also* Matter of S-M-J-, 21 I. & N. Dec. 722, 726–27 (B.I.A. 1997) (discussing generally the DHS's role in introducing evidence), *disapproved of on other grounds*, Ladha v. INS, 215 F.3d 889 (9th Cir. 2000).

57. *See* Nee Hao Wong v. INS, 550 F.2d 521, 523 (9th Cir. 1977) (holding that the due process rights of an alien with a mental illness were not violated where he was represented by counsel and was accompanied by a state court-appointed conservator who testified fully on his behalf); Brue v. Gonzales, 464 F.3d 1227, 1232–34 (10th Cir. 2006) (concluding that procedural safeguards were in place and the alien had an opportunity to be heard at a meaningful time and in a meaningful manner where the alien was represented and was able to answer the questions posed to him and provide his version of the facts); Mohamed v. Gonzales, 477 F.3d 522, 526–27 (8th Cir. 2007) (immigration judge was not required to determine competency where the respondent answered the charges against him, testified in support of his claim for withholding of removal, arranged for two witnesses to appear on his behalf, was aware of the nature and object of the proceedings, and vigorously resisted removal); Munoz-Monsalve v. Mukasey, 551 F.3d 1 at 608 (1st Cir. 2008) (concluded that an alien's due process rights were not violated where he was represented, his attorney does not request an evaluation, and the record did not contain evidence of a lack of competency).

can fairly and fundamentally present his case for relief, a respondent's due process rights will be held not to have been violated.

The regulations carve out special procedural safeguards for respondents classified as "incompetent respondents" at 8 C.F.R. § 1240.4.[58] This regulation sets forth that "[w]hen it is impracticable for the respondent to be present at the hearing because of mental incompetency, the attorney, legal representative, legal guardian, near relative, or friend who was served with a copy of the notice to appear shall be permitted to appear on behalf of the respondent."[59] The regulation goes on to state that "[i]f such a person cannot reasonably be found or fails or refuses to appear, the custodian of the respondent shall be requested to appear on behalf of the respondent."[60] The regulations also prohibit an immigration judge from accepting "an admission of removability from an unrepresented respondent who is incompetent . . . and is not accompanied by an attorney or legal representative, a near relative, legal guardian, or friend."[61] When an immigration judge decides, pursuant to this regulation, not to accept an admission of removability, the court is required to "direct a hearing on the issues."[62]

Once a determination has been made that proceedings can move forward with or without specific procedural safeguards, practitioners should avail themselves of all possible options available to aid in representation of a respondent with competency issues. These include requesting that a respondent's presence be waived; requesting an immigration judge, a family member, or close friend to assist the respondent in providing information; requesting that venue be changed to facilitate the respondent's ability to obtain medical treatment and/or legal representation or to enable a respondent to be closer to family. A request can also be made for an immigration judge to continue proceedings to allow for further evaluation of competency or an assessment of changes in the respondent's condition.

Practitioners representing respondents with mental health and competency issues should also be mindful of humanitarian options present in these cases both as they relate to custody and relief. The most recent

---

58. *See also* INA § 240(b)(3), 8 U.S.C. § 1229a(b)(3) (directing the Attorney General to "prescribe safeguards to protect the rights and privileges" of aliens who are incompetent, where "it is impracticable by reason of an alien's mental incompetency for the alien to be present at the proceeding").

59. 8 C.F.R. § 1240.4.

60. *Id.*

61. *Id.* § 1240.10(c).

62. *Id.*

prosecutorial discretion memorandum[63] from ICE lists as one of the factors to consider "whether the person suffers from serious mental or physical illness," meaning the Office of Chief Counsel having jurisdiction in a particular case may be willing to join a request to the court for administrative closure. In the case of a detained respondent with mental competency or other medical issues, the Enforcement and Removal Operations Office having jurisdiction over the case can be contacted to request alternatives to detention (such as being placed on electronic ankle bracelets/call in supervision) and even release under humanitarian parole.[64]

RIGHTS TO DUE PROCESS

In immigration proceedings, the Fifth Amendment entitles aliens to due process of law.[65] Included in the rights that the Due Process Clause requires in removal proceedings is the right to a full and fair hearing.[66] A removal hearing must be conducted in a manner that satisfies principles of fundamental fairness.[67] For example, aliens "shall have the privilege of being represented" at no expense to the government.[68] In addition, the act requires that an alien have a "reasonable opportunity" to examine and present evidence and to cross-examine witnesses.[69] In very rare instances, an IJ may fail to act as a neutral fact finder and as a result the alien's due process rights may be violated.[70] The key duty of counsel in these cases is

63. *See* John Morton, Memorandum, Exercising Prosecutorial Discretion Consistent with the Civil Immigration Enforcement Priorities of the Agency for the Apprehension, Detention, and Removal of Aliens (June 17, 2011), http://www.ice.gov/doclib/secure-communities/pdf/prosecutorial-discretion-memo.pdf.
64. See INA Section 212(d)(5), Title 8, United States Code, Section 1182(d)(5), providing authority to the Attorney General to parole aliens into the United States; Sections 402 and 421 of the Homeland Security Act of 2002, Pub. L. No. 107-29; transferring authority for immigration matters, including parole, to the Secretary of DHS; Title 8, Code of Federal Regulations, Section 212.5: providing regulations for the parole of aliens into the United States with special emphasis on INA 212.5(b)(1) "(1) Aliens who have serious medical conditions in which continued detention would not be appropriate."
65. Reno v. Flores, 507 U.S. 292, 306 (1993).
66. Matter of M-D-, 23 I. & N. Dec. 540, 542 (B.I.A. 2002) (citing Landon v. Plasencia, 459 U.S. 21, 32–33 (1982)).
67. Matter of Beckford, 22 I. & N. Dec. 1216, 1225 (B.I.A. 2000). *See also* Shaughnessey v. United States *ex rel.* Mezei, 345 U.S. 206, 212 (1953) (stating that immigration proceedings must conform to traditional standards of fairness encompassed in due process).
68. INA §§ 240(b)(4)(A), 292; 8 U.S.C. §§ 1229a(b)(4)(A), 1362 (2006).
69. INA § 240(b)(4)(B); *see also* 8 C.F.R. § 1240.10(a)(4).
70. *See* Colmenar v. INS, 210 F.3d 967, 971 (9th Cir. 2000) (due process violation where "the IJ behaved not as a neutral fact-finder interested in hearing the petitioner's evidence, but as

to make objections on the record to preserve a respondent's federal appellate claims of due process violations. Whether it's a non-neutral comment by an IJ or denial of an opportunity to present a witness or denial of a continuance to obtain a copy of a file, it is vital that an objection be made on the record that due process safeguards are not being complied with.

Rights of Juveniles

Juveniles[71] benefit from specific rights above and beyond those afforded adult respondents in removal proceedings. These range in scope from being allowed to bring a toy or pillow to a court hearing[72] to qualifying for certain forms of relief.[73] Additionally, there are specific provisions[74] for proper service of charging documents on juveniles that can at time form the basis to terminate removal proceedings or reopen orders of removal for lack of notice/service. In addition to proper service of the Notice to Appear, the regulations[75] also provide for mandatory service on juveniles of Notice of Rights (I-770) to ensure due process obligations are met.

When DHS determines that a juvenile is unaccompanied and must be detained, he or she is transferred to the care of the Department of Health

---

a partisan adjudicator seeking to intimidate Colmenar and his counsel"); Reyes-Melendez v. INS, 342 F.3d at 1006–09 (9th Cir. 2003) (holding that due process required remand in suspension of deportation case where IJ was "aggressive," "snide," and accused applicant of moral impropriety and that IJ's moral bias against petitioner precluded full consideration of the relevant hardship factors); "Removing Judges: The Cases of Immigration Judges Jeffrey Chase and Noel Ferris," http://cdm16501.contentdm.oclc.org/cdm/ref/collection /judicial/id/310; "Some immigrants meet harsh face of justice," http://articles.latimes .com/2006/feb/12/nation/na-judges12.

71. In the context of removal proceedings, a juvenile is defined as an alien under 18 years of age. An unaccompanied juvenile is defined as an alien under 18 years of age who does not have a parent or legal guardian in the United States to provide care and physical custody.

72. *See* Immigration Court Practice Manual 88 (Chapter 4, Rule 4.22), *available at* http:// www.justice.gov/eoir/vll/OCIJPracManual/ocij_page1.htm (last visited June 10, 2014).

73. A special provision of the Immigration and Nationality Act allows certain qualifying minors to petition for immigrant status as a Special Immigrant Juvenile (SIJ). INA § 101(a)(27)(J), 8 U.S.C. § 1101(a)(27)(J). This provision is reserved for those aliens under 21 years of age who have been declared dependent on a juvenile court or placed under the custody of a government agency, who are eligible for long-term foster care and in whose best interest it is not to return to their home country.

74. The regulations state that if the alien is a minor under 14 years of age, "service shall be made upon the person with whom the . . . minor resides; whenever possible, service shall also be made on the near relative, guardian, committee, or friend." 8 C.F.R. § 103.5a(c)(2)(ii). *See also id.* § 236.2(a) (2010).

75. *See id.* § 1236.3(h).

and Human Services, Office of Refugee Resettlement (ORR), which provides for the care and placement, where possible, of the unaccompanied juvenile.[76] Unaccompanied minors can be released into the custody of a legal guardian or family member without requiring a bond determination either by ICE or an immigration judge but documentation is usually requested by ORR to establish legal custody (such as a power of attorney) of the designated adult and their financial viability (such as paycheck stubs or employment letter or tax return copies). Additional documentation such as police clearances/background checks can also be required of the individuals taking custody of the children.[77]

Post Proceedings

Appeals
A decision from the immigration court can be appealed by either or both parties[78] within 30 days[79] of the Judge's oral decision or date of mailing of the decision and must be filed with the Board of Immigration Appeals with service on the appropriate office of chief counsel. The BIA has an online practice manual[80] which includes rules, deadlines, when fees are required, and sample pleadings and forms. The online practice manual also delineates instances where a stay is automatic or discretionary and includes the accompanying procedures. The 30-day filing deadline for an appeal is strictly enforced by the BIA, the "mailbox rule" does not apply, and failure of courier services to meet the deadline has been held not to excuse late filing.[81] If the opportunity to appeal is knowingly and voluntarily waived, the decision of the immigration judge becomes final.[82] If a party waives appeal at the conclusion of proceedings before the immigration judge, that party generally may not file an appeal thereafter.[83] If a party wishes to challenge the validity of his or her waiver of appeal, the party may do so in one of two ways: either in a timely motion filed with the immigration judge that explains why the appeal waiver was not valid

---

76. *See* 6 U.S.C. § 279.

77. *Key Documents for the Unaccompanied Children's Services Program*, OFFICE OF REFUGEE RESETTLEMENT, http://www.acf.hhs.gov/programs/orr/resource/unaccompanied-childrens -services.

78. 8 C.F.R. § 1003.3.

79. *Id.* § 1003.38.

80. http://www.justice.gov/eoir/vll/qapracmanual/apptmtn4.htm.

81. Matter of Liadov, 23 I. & N. Dec. 990 (B.I.A. 2006).

82. 8 C.F.R. § 1003.39.

83. *See id.* § 1003.3(a)(1); Matter of Shih, 20 I. & N. Dec. 697 (B.I.A. 1993). *See also* 8 C.F.R. § 1003.1(d)(2)(i)(G).

or in an appeal filed directly with the BIA that explains why the appeal waiver was not valid.[84]

Evidence on Appeal and Standard of Review

The Board considers only evidence that was admitted in the proceedings below and will treat new evidence as a motion to remand proceedings to the immigration judge for consideration of that evidence. The Board may, at its discretion, take administrative notice of commonly known facts not appearing in the record. For example, the Board may take administrative notice of current events and contents of official documents, such as country condition reports prepared by the State Department; however the Board will not consider representations made by counsel in a brief or motion as constituting evidence.[85]

The BIA will generally defer to the factual findings of an immigration judge, unless clearly erroneous,[86] but retains independent judgment and discretion, subject to applicable governing standards, regarding pure questions of law and the application of a particular standard of law to those facts. Some issues on appeal involve closely intertwined questions of facts and law and the Board has held that to determine whether established facts are sufficient to meet a legal standard, such as a "well-founded fear," they are entitled to weigh the evidence in a manner different from that accorded by the immigration judge, or to conclude that the foundation for the immigration judge's legal conclusions was insufficient or otherwise not supported by the evidence of record.[87]

Summary Affirmance

Under certain circumstances, the Board may affirm the decision of an immigration judge without giving any rationale or opinion and summarily dismiss an appeal. It is important when filing an appeal to be specific and detailed in stating the grounds of the appeal, specifically identifying the findings of fact, the conclusions of law, or both, that are being challenged.[88] An appeal, or any portion of an appeal, may be summarily dismissed if the Notice of Appeal and any brief or attachment fails to adequately inform the Board of the specific reasons for the appeal.[89] There

---

84. Matter of Patino, 23 I. & N. Dec. 74 (B.I.A. 2001).
85. Matter of Fedorenko, 19 I. & N. Dec. 57 (B.I.A. 1984).
86. Matter of A-S-B-, 24 I. & N. Dec. 493 (B.I.A. 2008).
87. *Id.*
88. 8 C.F.R. § 1003.3(b).
89. *Id.* § 1003.1(d)(2)(i)(A).

are many reasons why an appeal may be summarily dismissed[90] but it is important to address these three main points in an appeal as they are the ones most commonly cited[91] and relied upon by the BIA to summarily dismiss an appeal:

1. the immigration judge or DHS decision reached the correct result
2. any errors in the decision were harmless or nonmaterial
3. either (a) the issues on appeal are squarely controlled by existing Board or federal court precedent and do not involve the application of a precedent to a novel factual situation, or (b) the factual and legal issues raised on appeal are not so substantial that the case warrants the issuance of a written opinion

Motions to Reopen/Reconsider

As a general rule, a motion to reopen must be filed within 90 days of an immigration judge's final order[92] and is numerically capped to permit only one such motion.[93] Some exceptions permit filing outside the time and number limits only in specific circumstances[94] and there are special

---

90. *See id.* § 1003.1(d)(2)(i) ("the appeal is based on a finding of fact or conclusion of law that has already been conceded by the appealing party; the appeal is from an order granting the relief requested; the appeal is filed for an improper purpose; the appeal does not fall within the Board's jurisdiction; the appeal is untimely; the appeal is barred by an affirmative waiver of the right of appeal; the appeal fails to meet essential statutory or regulatory requirements; the appeal is expressly prohibited by statute or regulation").

91. *See id.* § 1003.1(e)(4).

92. *Id.* § 1003.23(b)(1).

93. *Id.* § 1003.23(b)(1).

94. *See id.* § 1003.23(b)(4):

Exceptions to filing deadlines—

(i) *Asylum and withholding of removal.* The time and numerical limitations...shall not apply if the basis of the motion is to apply for asylum under section 208 of the Act or withholding of removal under section 241(b)(3) of the Act or withholding of removal under the Convention Against Torture, and is based on changed country conditions arising in the country of nationality or the country to which removal has been ordered, if such evidence is material and was not available and could not have been discovered or presented at the previous proceeding. The filing of a motion to reopen under this section shall not automatically stay the removal of the alien. However, the alien may request a stay and, if granted by the immigration judge, the alien shall not be removed pending disposition of the motion by the immigration judge. If the original asylum application was denied based upon a finding that it was frivolous, then the alien is ineligible to file either a motion to reopen or reconsider, or for a stay of removal.

(ii) *Order entered in absentia or removal proceedings.* An order of removal entered in absentia or in removal proceedings pursuant to section 240(b)(5) of the Act may be rescinded only rules for certain motions to reopen by battered spouses, children, and parents.[95] A motion to reopen may also be filed when a respondent has been the victim of ineffective assistance of counsel and prejudiced by that ineffective assistance.[96] Most circuit courts of appeal[97] have held that as

---

upon a motion to reopen filed within 180 days after the date of the order of removal, if the alien demonstrates that the failure to appear was because of exceptional circumstances as defined in section 240(e)(1) of the Act. An order entered in absentia pursuant to section 240(b)(5) may be rescinded upon a motion to reopen filed at any time if the alien demonstrates that he or she did not receive notice in accordance with sections 239(a)(1) or (2) of the Act, or the alien demonstrates that he or she was in federal or state custody and the failure to appear was through no fault of the alien. However, in accordance with section 240(b)(5)(B) of the Act, no written notice of a change in time or place of proceeding shall be required if the alien has failed to provide the address required under section 239(a)(1)(F) of the Act. The filing of a motion under this paragraph shall stay the removal of the alien pending disposition of the motion by the immigration judge. An alien may file only one motion pursuant to this paragraph.

(iii) *Order entered in absentia in deportation or exclusion proceedings.*

    (A) An order entered in absentia in deportation proceedings may be rescinded only upon a motion to reopen filed:

        (1) Within 180 days after the date of the order of deportation if the alien demonstrates that the failure to appear was because of exceptional circumstances beyond the control of the alien (e.g., serious illness of the alien or serious illness or death of an immediate relative of the alien, but not including less compelling circumstances); or

        (2) At any time if the alien demonstrates that he or she did not receive notice or if the alien demonstrates that he or she was in federal or state custody and the failure to appear was through no fault of the alien.

    (B) A motion to reopen exclusion hearings on the basis that the immigration judge improperly entered an order of exclusion in absentia must be supported by evidence that the alien had reasonable cause for his failure to appear.

    (C) The filing of a motion to reopen under paragraph (b)(4)(iii)(A) of this section shall stay the deportation of the alien pending decision on the motion and the adjudication of any properly filed administrative appeal.

    (D) The time and numerical limitations set forth in paragraph (b)(1) of this section shall not apply to a motion to reopen filed pursuant to the provisions of paragraph (b)(4)(iii)(A) of this section.

(iv) *Jointly filed motions.* The time and numerical limitations set forth in paragraph (b)(1) of this section shall not apply to a motion to reopen agreed upon by all parties and jointly filed.

95. INA § 240(c)(7)(C)(iv).

96. *See* Matter of Lozada, 19 I. & N. Dec. 637 (B.I.A. 1988); Matter of Assaad, 23 I. & N. Dec. 553 (B.I.A. 003); Matter of Compean, Bangaly & J-E-C-, 24 I. & N. Dec. 710 (A.G. 2009).

97. Rodriguez-Lariz, 282 F.3d 1218 (9th Cir. 2002); Socop-Gonzalez v. INS, 272 F.3d 1176 (9th Cir. 2001) (en banc); Iavorski v. INS, 232 F.3d 124 (2d Cir. 2000); Borges v. Gonzales, 402 F.3d 398, 406–07 (3d Cir. 2005); Tapia-Martinez v. Gonzalez, 482 F.3d 417 (6th Cir. 2007); Asere v.

long as the affected respondent acted diligently, the filing deadline for motions to reopen may be equitably tolled.

When faced with a scenario where a motion is numerically or time barred and the DHS will not join in the motion, counsel should consider filing a motion to reopen sua sponte requesting an immigration judge to reopen the case on his or her own motion.[98] A sua sponte motion is sparingly granted by courts and the limited guidance from the BIA directs it be used only in extraordinary circumstances,[99] but it can be a very powerful tool and last resort measure in compelling cases.

Depending on the nature of the motion to reopen, a filing fee or fee waiver request may be required.[100] If the motion is based on eligibility for relief, the motion must be accompanied by a copy of the application for that relief and all supporting documents, if an application is normally required. The motion to reopen must also state the new facts that will be proven at a reopened hearing if the motion is granted, and must be supported by affidavits or other evidentiary material.[101]

A motion to reconsider either identifies an error in law or fact in the immigration judge's prior decision or identifies a change in law that affects an immigration judge's prior decision and asks the immigration judge to reexamine his or her ruling. It is based on the existing record and does not seek to introduce new facts or evidence. A motion to reconsider must be filed within 30 days of the immigration judge's final administrative order[102] and, as a general rule, a respondent is limited to only one motion to reconsider.[103] Motions filed prior to July 31, 1996, do not count toward the one-motion limit. Although a party may file a motion to reconsider the denial of a motion to reopen, a party may not file a motion to reconsider the denial of a motion to reconsider.[104]

Gonzales, 439 F.3d 378, 381 (7th Cir. 2006); Hernandez-Moran v. Gonzales, 408 F.3d 496 (8th Cir. 2005). *See* Kanyi v. Gonzales, 406 F.3d 1087, 1091 (8th Cir. 2005); Mahamat v. Gonzales, 430 F.3d 1281, 1283 (10th Cir. 2005); Galvez Piñeda v. Gonzales, 427 F.3d 833, 838–39 (10th Cir. 2005).

98. *See* 8 C. F. R. § 1003.23(b)(1).

99. Matter of J-J-, 21 I. & N. Dec. 976 (B.I.A. 1997).

100. *See* IMMIGRATION PRACTICE MANUAL ch. 3.4 (Filing Fees) (last revised Dec. 3, 2013).

101. 8 C.F.R. § 1003.23(b)(3).

102. *Id.* § 1003.23(b)(1).

103. *Id.*

104. *Id.*

22

LITIGATING IMMIGRATION
MATTERS IN FEDERAL COURT

Thomas K. Ragland and Jennifer D. Cook[1]

WHY GO TO FEDERAL COURT?

For most immigration attorneys, bringing an action in federal court is the option of last resort, often following an unreasonable delay or an outright denial by an office within the Department of Homeland Security (DHS), or after receiving an adverse decision from the Board of Immigration Appeals (BIA). The former might be challenged by an action in a U.S. district court, whereas the latter might be challenged by filing a petition for review in a U.S. court of appeals. To many immigration practitioners, going into federal court is an intimidating prospect, requiring them to venture outside their comfort zone and become proficient in a very different, and unfamiliar, legal forum. When pursued skillfully, however, federal court litigation can be an extremely effective means of achieving a favorable result for a client, and one that may simply be unobtainable in the administrative realm.

There are a variety of reasons to consider litigating an immigration matter in federal court, not least of which is the opportunity for one more level of appeal. More significantly, though, when a case is brought before a federal district court judge or panel of circuit court judges, the matter is removed from the all-too-familiar DHS/Immigration Court/BIA administrative domain, which often can seem frustratingly biased against, or simply unmoved by, your client's plight. Federal court offers the invaluable prospect of presenting your case to judges who are usually exceptionally qualified and astute, who may preside over a capital murder trial one day and your mandamus action the next, and who typically will view the matter objectively on its merits rather than through an immigration

1. Thomas K. Ragland and Jennifer D. Cook are founding partners of Benach Ragland LLP, a boutique immigration law firm in Washington D.C., established in April 2012. The authors wish to acknowledge the American Immigration Council Legal Action Center's practice advisories as an invaluable resource in developing this chapter.

prism. Moreover, because many federal judges do not hear a great number of immigration cases, it is a complex area of law in which they may not be fully versed. As the petitioning attorney, you are in an advantageous position to educate the court and, thereby, to be an extremely effective advocate for your client.

Nonetheless, the decision to challenge agency action in federal court should be reached only after careful consideration. Each federal district court and circuit court of appeals has its own rules and procedures, in addition to the Federal Rules of Civil and Appellate Procedure, so a practitioner must become conversant and comfortable in the rules that govern the jurisdiction in which the action or appeal is brought. Before filing suit or submitting a petition for review, you must also be aware of the obstacles—jurisdictional, procedural, and precedential—to bringing a successful claim.

A number of jurisdictional bars in the Immigration and Nationality Act (INA) will foreclose certain challenges altogether.[2] The circuit in which the action or appeal is brought already may have issued a precedent opinion on the issue you seek to present, thereby resolving the matter. In addition, agency interpretations of such arguably ambiguous statutory terms as "extreme hardship" and "moral turpitude" are afforded broad deference by the courts, so long as those interpretations are reasonable. Under the deference doctrine articulated by the U.S. Supreme Court in *Chevron, U.S.A., Inc. v. Natural Resources Defense Council, Inc.,*[3] if Congress has not spoken on the precise question at issue, and has delegated to the agency the authority to resolve ambiguities, courts need only decide whether the agency's decision is based on a permissible construction of the statute.[4] Furthermore, the U.S. Supreme Court has held that prior judicial interpretation of an administrative agency statute is not necessarily binding on the agency in subsequent decision making because there is "a 'presumption that Congress, when it left ambiguity in a statute meant for implementation by an agency, understood that the ambiguity would be resolved, first and foremost, by the agency, and desired the agency (rather than the courts) to possess whatever degree of discretion the ambiguity allows.'"[5] The agencies comprehend and capitalize upon this deferential standard of review.[6] As an attorney hoping to use the federal courts to

---

2. *See* INA § 242(a)(2), 8 U.S.C. § 1252(a)(2) (2012).

3. 467 U.S. 837 (1984).

4. *Id.* at 843.

5. National Cable & Telecomms. Ass'n v. Brand X Internet Servs., 545 U.S. 967, 982 (2005) (quoting Smiley v. Citibank (South Dakota), N.A., 517 U.S. 735, 740–41 (1996)).

6. *See, e.g.,* Board of Immigration Appeals: Affirmance without Opinion, Referral for Panel

achieve favorable outcomes for your clients, you must take the time to learn when such actions are possible and make an informed determination of whether those actions have a chance to succeed.

Practical Considerations—Naming the Respondents and Service

Once you and your client have decided to file a complaint, appeal, or petition for review in federal court, you must decide whom to sue. Actions generally are brought against the officers or agencies responsible for the decision being challenged, and who are capable of providing the relief being sought. The responsible agency official (e.g., Secretary, Commissioner, Director, Attorney General) typically is listed by name in the complaint, and that individual is being sued in his or her official capacity. You may wish to name more than one official or entity (e.g., both the Secretary of Homeland Security and the Director of U.S. Citizenship and Immigration Services) because the court can proceed to the merits of the case as long as the court has subject matter and personal jurisdiction over at least one respondent.

Most immigration-based federal court actions are brought against one or more officers or components within the Department of Homeland Security (DHS) or the Department of Justice (DOJ), depending on which agency issued the decision being challenged. In the courts of appeals, the decision is straightforward. Because, in the vast majority of cases, you're seeking review of a decision issued by the BIA, and the BIA is a component of the Executive Office for Immigration Review (EOIR) within DOJ, the named defendant is the U.S. Attorney General. In the district courts, the possible respondents are more varied, and the choice of whom to sue depends on the specific entity responsible for the challenged decision. Within DHS, U.S. Immigration and Customs Enforcement (ICE) is responsible for the detention and removal of non-citizens; U.S. Citizenship and Immigration Services (USCIS) is responsible for adjudications of applications for immigration and citizenship benefits; and U.S. Customs and Border Protection (CBP) is responsible for immigration and customs inspections and border patrol. In addition, the Federal Bureau of Investigation (FBI) might be named in cases involving delayed background checks and the Federal Bureau of Prisons (BOP) might be a proper respondent

---

Review, and Publication of Decisions as Precedents, 73 Fed. Reg. 34,654, 34,661 (June 18, 2008) ("The Supreme Court's decision in *Brand X Internet* offers an important opportunity for the Attorney General and the Board to be able to reclaim *Chevron* deference with respect to the interpretation of ambiguous statutory provisions in the immigration laws, notwithstanding contrary judicial interpretations, as long as the agency interpretation is within the scope of *Chevron* step two deference.").

in a complaint concerning detention conditions. The Department of State (DOS) is responsible for foreign affairs, including visa issuance, and the appropriate agency officials and consular officers should be named in a suit challenging a visa denial by a U.S. consulate. Finally, petitions for writ of habeas corpus should name the warden of the facility in which the person is detained and should be filed in the district of confinement.[7] Other officials who are responsible for the individual's detention—and conditions of detention—also should be named, including the Director of ICE and the local ICE Field Office Director.

Once filed, Federal Rules of Civil Procedure (FRCP) 4(i)(1)(A) through (C) provide that in suits against the United States, counsel must serve the summons and complaint on the local U.S. Attorney's Office, the U.S. Attorney General, and, if the action is attacking the validity of an order of an officer or agency not named as a party to the action, that U.S. agency or officer. FRCP 4(i)(2) provides that counsel must serve the summons and complaint on the United States and on the U.S. agency or officer. To serve DHS, USCIS, ICE, or any DHS official in his or her official capacity, the summons and complaint must be sent to the appropriate agency's Office of the General Counsel. After the summons and complaint have been served, the original summons must be filed with the district court and constitutes proof of service.

In court of appeals cases, the petition for review must be served "on the Attorney General and on the officer or employee of the Service in charge of the Service district in which the final order of removal under section 240 was entered."[8] The petitioner simultaneously must file a certificate of service listing the names and addresses of those served and the manner of service. Federal Rules of Appellate Procedure (FRAP) 15(c). Respondents may be added or removed (FRAP 21) or substituted (FRAP 25) after a complaint has been filed.

PETITIONS FOR REVIEW IN U.S. COURTS OF APPEALS

Section 242 of the INA sets forth the jurisdictional basis for petitions for review as well as the rules and procedures governing such petitions. The courts of appeals have exclusive jurisdiction to review "a final order of removal,"[9] which has been interpreted to include a BIA decision to issue a

---

7. *See* Rumsfeld v. Padilla, 542 U.S. 426, 447 (2004).
8. INA § 242(b)(3)(A), 8 U.S.C. § 1252(b)(3)(A) (2012).
9. INA § 242, 8 U.S.C. § 1252 (2012) (except for an expedited removal order entered under INA § 235(b)(1)).

final removal order, deny a motion to reconsider or reopen, deny asylum in asylum-only proceedings, or issue a reinstated order of removal or an expedited order of removal.

"Final" Orders of Removal and Exhaustion

Generally speaking, a party must exhaust administrative remedies before seeking relief from a federal court. Exhaustion is required where it is mandated by Congress in the relevant statute,[10] or where a court requires that "non-mandatory" administrative appeals be exhausted.[11]

Because the INA reserves authority for the courts of appeals to review "final" orders of removal,[12] petitioning for review of an immigration judge's (IJ) decision generally is prohibited, and most circuit courts will dismiss a petition for review filed before the BIA has ruled on an appeal.[13] Remands add a layer of complexity to defining "finality." Circuit courts have exercised jurisdiction over a petition for review of an IJ decision issued following a remand from the BIA, where the BIA has already fully resolved the issues raised in the petition for review.[14] Some circuit courts have held that a BIA decision is final even if the BIA remands to the IJ to rule upon a request for voluntary departure,[15] but courts also

---

10. *See, e.g.,* INA § 242(d), 8 U.S.C. § 1252(d) (2012) ("A court may review a final order of removal only if . . . the alien has exhausted all administrative remedies available to the alien as of right[.]").

11. The Supreme Court has held that in federal court cases brought under the Administrative Procedure Act (APA), a plaintiff is not required to exhaust "non-mandatory" administrative remedies. Darby v. Cisneros, 509 U.S. 137, 146–47 (1993). For a case to be exempt from the exhaustion requirement under the Supreme Court's decision in *Darby v. Cisneros,* the suit must be brought under the APA, there must be no statute or regulation mandating an administrative appeal, and the agency decision being challenged must be final for purposes of the APA.

12. INA § 242(a)(1), 8 U.S.C. § 1252(a)(1) (2012). This provision provides that, with the exception of expedited removal orders, "[j]udicial review of a final order of removal" is governed by 28 U.S.C. § 158.

13. *See, e.g.,* Moreira v. Mukasey, 509 F.3d 709, 713 (5th Cir. 2007); Jaber v. Gonzales, 486 F.3d 223, 228 (6th Cir. 2007). *But see* Khan v. Att'y Gen. of the United States, 691 F.3d 488, 493 (3d Cir. 2012); Herrera-Molina v. Holder, 597 F.3d 128, 132 (2d Cir. 2010).

14. *See, e.g.,* Popal v. Gonzales, 416 F.3d 249, 253 (3d Cir. 2005). However, if the BIA remands a case for completion of identity, law enforcement, or security checks, 8 C.F.R. § 1003.47(h) requires the IJ to consider the results of the investigation. If new information is presented, the IJ may hold a further hearing, and a subsequent BIA appeal may be required. *Id.*

15. *See, e.g.,* Perafan Saldarriaga v. Gonzales, 402 F.3d 461 (4th Cir. 2005), *cert. denied,* 546 U.S. 1169 (2006); Perez-Vargas v. Gonzales, 478 F.3d 191, 194 n.4 (4th Cir. 2007); Del Pilar v. United States, 326 F.3d 1154, 1156–57 (11th Cir. 2003) (per curiam); Castrejon-Garcia v. INS, 60 F.3d 1359, 1361–62 (9th Cir. 1995). *But see* Voluntary Departure: Effect of a Motion to

have required completion of the remanded proceedings and a second BIA appeal before they will consider a petition for review, if the purpose of the remand could prevent deportation.[16]

The BIA orders removal in the first instance if it reverses an IJ's decision to grant relief from removal and also finds the applicant ineligible for any other relief. If the IJ already had found the person subject to removal, even in exercising discretion to cancel that removal, some courts have held that the BIA's order is final for purposes of judicial review.[17]

Finally, exhaustion is not required for a constitutional challenge (e.g., due process)[18] or for an appeal involving a citizenship claim.[19]

Jurisdiction

A federal court action challenging a BIA or DHS decision may assert a variety of legal claims: that the agency erroneously applied or interpreted the INA or its implementing regulations; that the agency violated a constitutionally protected right, such as due process or equal protection; that the agency made erroneous findings of fact or its conclusions are not supported by substantial evidence; or that the agency abused its discretion in the manner in which it reached its decision. A plaintiff must assert the legal authority for the court's jurisdiction and the court must conclude that such jurisdiction exists before it will proceed to a consideration of the merits.

Congress enacted a number of significant jurisdiction-stripping provisions during a broad-ranging revision of the INA in 1996, limiting the federal courts' authority to review certain types of agency decisions. INA § 242(a)(2)(B) generally prohibits review of discretionary decisions, including waivers of removal under INA §§ 212(h) and 212(i), cancella-

---

Reopen or Reconsider or a Petition for Review, 73 Fed. Reg. 76,927 (Dec. 18, 2008), *amending* 8 C.F.R. § 1240.26(i) to provide that a grant of voluntary departure on or after January 20, 2009, automatically terminates upon the filing of a petition for review. See *Hakim v. Holder,* 611 F.3d 73, 77 (1st Cir. 2010), and *Pinto v. Holder,* 648 F.3d 976 (9th Cir. 2011), for contrasting holdings on how to apply this 2009 final rule.

16. *See, e.g.,* Perkovic v. INS, 33 F.3d 615, 618 (6th Cir. 1994). *But see Hakim,* 611 F.3d at 77–78, citing *Perkovic* as comparable to voluntary departure precedent superseded by 2009 final rule.

17. *See, e.g.,* Giraldo v. Holder, 654 F.3d 609, 612–14 (6th Cir. 2011); Sosa-Valenzuela v. Gonzales, 483 F.3d 1140, 1146 (10th Cir. 2007); Solano-Chicas v. Gonzales, 440 F.3d 1050, 1053–54 (8th Cir. 2006); Delgado-Reynua v. Gonzales, 450 F.3d 596, 601 (5th Cir. 2006) ("[W]here the BIA reverses an IJ's grant of discretionary relief and gives effect to the IJ's original order of removability, the BIA has merely eliminated "'impediments to removal' and effected the original removal order."); Lazo v. Gonzales, 462 F.3d 53, 54–55 (2d Cir. 2006); *Del Pilar,* 326 F.3d at 1156.

18. *See, e.g.,* Bosede v. Mukasey, 512 F.3d 946, 952 (7th Cir. 2008).

19. *See, e.g.,* Minasyan v. Gonzales, 401 F.3d 1069, 1075 (9th Cir. 2005).

tion of removal, voluntary departure, adjustment of status, as well as "any other decision or action" specified to be in the discretion of the Attorney General or Secretary of Homeland Security. However, a number of courts have held that they retain authority to review non-discretionary aspects of discretionary forms of relief, including adjustment of status and cancellation of removal.[20]

INA § 242(a)(2)(C) prohibits review of removal orders arising from criminal offenses under INA § 212(a)(2) or certain sections of INA § 237(a)(2). However, courts retain jurisdiction over whether the crime qualifies as a removable offense (e.g., crime involving moral turpitude or aggravated felony). Courts also retain the authority to review whether the individual to be removed is, in fact, subject to removal as charged and is not a U.S. citizen. INA § 242(a)(2)(D) grants courts authority to review petitions raising constitutional claims or questions of law.

In addition, although asylum is a discretionary form of relief, INA § 242(a)(2)(B)(ii) explicitly preserves the courts' jurisdiction to review most aspects of an asylum determination. Review is limited only with respect to certain asylum-related determinations, such as whether an asylum-seeker established changed circumstances or extraordinary circumstances that excuse a delay in filing the asylum claim.[21]

Mechanics

Venue for a Petition for Review is restricted to the court of appeals for the judicial circuit in which the IJ completed the removal proceedings. INA § 242(b)(2). Attorneys of record must be admitted to the bar of the circuit court.

---

20. *See, e.g.,* Uddin v. USCIS, 437 F. App'x 196, 199 (3d Cir. 2011) ("Any other rule would allow the agency to insulate its non-discretionary statutory eligibility analysis from judicial review simply by labeling the decision discretionary."); Sharkey v. Quarantillo, 541 F.3d 75, 85 (2d Cir. 2008) ("8 U.S.C. § 1252(a)(2)(B) does not strip courts of jurisdiction to review nondiscretionary decisions regarding an alien's eligibility for relief specified in 8 U.S.C. § 1252(a)(2)(B)(i)."); Singh v. Gonzales, 413 F.3d 156, 160 n.4 (1st Cir. 2005) ("[8 U.S.C. § 1252(a)(2)(B)(i)] limits judicial review of discretionary denials of adjustment of status applications. In this case, the IJ denied Singh's application based on a finding that he did not meet the statutory prerequisite of admissibility. This is not a discretionary denial; it is mandated by statute. 8 U.S.C. § 1252 does not limit our review over these types of denials."); Sepulveda v. Gonzales, 407 F.3d 59, 62–63 (2d Cir. 2005); Pinho v. Gonzales, 432 F.3d 193, 204 (3d Cir. 2005) (stating that "[n]on-discretionary actions . . . and purely legal determinations made by the agency, remain subject to judicial review" and that the "[d]etermination of *eligibility* for adjustment of status—unlike the *granting* of adjustment itself—is a purely legal question and does not implicate agency discretion.") (emphasis in original).

21. INA § 208(a)(3), 8 U.S.C. § 1158(a)(3) (2012).

In addition to the rules set forth in INA § 242, petitioners should familiarize themselves with the Federal Rules of Appellate Procedure (FRAP) and the local rules of the circuit court in which the petition is brought. FRAP 15–20 specifically govern review or enforcement of orders of administrative agencies, boards, commissions, or officers; the general provisions for filing documents in the courts of appeals are found at FRAP 25–48. Be aware that separate petitions for review must be filed for each BIA decision being challenged. Each petition for review must "(A) name each party seeking review either in the caption or the body of the petition—using such terms as 'et al.,' 'petitioners,' or 'respondents' does not effectively name the parties;[22] (B) name the agency as a respondent (even though not named in the petition, the United States is a respondent if required by statute); and (C) specify the order or part thereof to be reviewed." FRAP 15(a)(2). The petition also must contain a Corporate Disclosure Statement (FRAP 26.1) and a Certificate of Service (FRAP 15(c) and 25). Finally, the petition must conform to the typeface and other requirements of FRAP 32. Form 3 in the Appendix of Forms to the FRAP provides a sample Petition for Review.

Petitions for review must be received by the appropriate court of appeals no later than 30 days after the date that the BIA or DHS issued the decision being challenged.[23] The 30-day deadline for filing a petition for review is not extended either by the filing of a motion to reopen or reconsider or by the grant or extension of voluntary departure. Filing a petition for review does not provide an automatic stay of removal, thus a separate motion for a stay must be filed with the court.[24] Absent a stay, ICE may execute an order of removal once the BIA issues its final decision in removal proceedings under INA § 240, or once DHS issues its final order in expedited removal proceedings under INA § 235(b)(1)(iii) or § 238(b), or in reinstated removal proceedings under INA § 241(a)(5). However, an

---

22. This rule applies even if the other petitioners are family members and the BIA decision was made under only one family member's name. Separate petitions for review need not be filed for each family member.

23. If the last day to file the petition is a Saturday, Sunday, or legal holiday, the filing period runs until the first business day after the Saturday, Sunday, or legal holiday. Fed. R. App. P. 26(a). The petition for review must be *received* by the court clerk's office on or before the thirtieth day; the date the petition is postmarked is not relevant.

24. *See* Nken v. Holder, 556 U.S. 418, 425–26 (2009) (courts of appeals should apply the "traditional" criteria governing stays when adjudicating a stay of removal: (1) whether the applicant has made a strong showing that he or she is likely to succeed on the merits; (2) whether the applicant will be irreparably injured absent a stay; (3) whether issuance of a stay will substantially injure the other parties interested in the proceeding; and (4) where the public interest lies).

individual may continue to litigate his or her petition for review even after having been physically removed from the United States.[25] Any period of voluntary departure is terminated by the filing of a petition for review.[26]

Once a petition for review is filed, the court generally issues an order that sets forth the schedule for the parties to submit the Certified Administrative Record of Proceedings, the Petitioner's Opening Brief, the Respondent's Answering Brief, and, if filed, the Petitioner's Reply Brief. Most courts issue a schedule of due dates rather than relying on the time frame that can be calculated by reference to the statute or federal rule, and either party may move to extend the briefing schedule or to hold briefing in abeyance. Contents of Briefs and requirements such as word count and format are governed by the appropriate FRAP and local circuit rule. Written motions are governed by FRAP 27 and the corresponding local circuit rules. Either party may file a statement explaining why oral argument should or should not be permitted. FRAP 34. If the court determines that oral argument is necessary, the court clerk will notify the parties of the date, time, place, and amount of time allotted for argument.

The court's judgment or decision is entered on the docket after the clerk receives the court's opinion or upon the court's instruction. FRAP 36. A petition for rehearing may be filed within 45 days after entry of judgment, unless otherwise specified by the court or local circuit rule. FRAP 35 and FRAP 40.

ACTIONS IN DISTRICT COURT

In district courts, claims are most often filed under the Mandamus Act,[27] to compel adjudication of a delayed application; the Administrative Procedure Act (APA),[28] to challenge a variety of nonremoval and nondetention decisions; and petitions for writ of habeas corpus under 28 U.S.C. § 2241, to challenge the legality, duration, or conditions of detention.

---

25. *See, e.g.,* Spina v. DHS, 470 F.3d 116, 124–25 (2d Cir. 2006); Alwan v. Ashcroft, 388 F.3d 507, 510–11 (5th Cir. 2004).

26. 8 C.F.R. § 1240.26(i) (2014). If the non-citizen then departs within 30 days of filing the petition for review and provides DHS with proof of departure and evidence that he or she remains outside the United States, the departure will not be deemed a removal. *Id.*

27. 28 U.S.C. § 1361 (2012).

28. 5 U.S.C. §§ 701, *et seq.* (2012).

Writs of Mandamus

The Mandamus Act authorizes district courts to order a remedy and, as such, can be used to compel administrative agencies to act.[29] However, while a court may compel the government to take some action, it cannot compel the agency to exercise its discretion in a particular manner,[30] nor can it grant the relief that the plaintiff is seeking from the agency. Because delays in adjudication of applications for immigration benefits (e.g., adjustment of status, issuance of employment authorization documents, scheduling of naturalization cases for interview, issuance of non-immigrant visas, etc.) are commonplace and often lengthy, filing a mandamus action can be an effective way to compel the agency to make a decision.[31] As one court has held, "The duty to act is no duty at all if the deadline is eternity."[32]

The plaintiff must demonstrate that he or she has a clear right to the relief requested,[33] that the defendant has a clear duty to perform the act

---

29. The Mandamus Act, codified at 28 U.S.C. § 1361 (2012), provides: "Action to compel an officer of the United States to perform his duty. The district courts shall have original jurisdiction of any action in the nature of mandamus to compel an officer or employee of the United States or any agency thereof to perform a duty owed to the plaintiff."

30. *See, e.g.*, Silveyra v. Moschorak, 989 F.2d 1012, 1015 (9th Cir. 1993) ("Mandamus may not be used to instruct an official how to exercise discretion unless that official has ignored or violated 'statutory or regulatory standards delimiting the scope or manner in which such discretion can be exercised.'") (internal citation omitted); Nigmadzhanov v. Mueller, 550 F. Supp. 2d 540, 546 (S.D.N.Y. 2008) (Attorney General has discretion to grant or deny an application, but does not have discretion to fail to adjudicate an adjustment application).

31. Mandamus also can be an effective means to remedy delays by the U.S. Department of Labor (DOL) in the context of either prevailing wage determinations (PWDs) or labor certifications for permanent resident applications. DOL's own regulations are clear that the agency's statutory responsibility imposes a mandatory duty to decide applications and issue PWDs. 20 C.F.R. §§ 656.17(b), 656.24. Generally, a mandamus suit over the delayed issuance of a PWD or adjudication of a labor certification application will be similar to any other mandamus suit. Both the employer and the employee may sue over the delayed adjudication of the labor certification application, because both are harmed by the delay.

32. Tang v. Chertoff, 493 F. Supp. 2d 148, 150 (D. Mass. 2007).

33. In the adjustment context, courts have found that the INA establishes a clear right to relief. *See, e.g.*, Kamal v. Gonzales, 547 F. Supp. 2d 869, 876 (N.D. Ill. 2008); Deepakkumar Himatlal Soneji v. DHS, 525 F. Supp. 2d 1151, 1155 (N.D. Cal. 2007); Iddir v. INS, 301 F.3d 492, 499–500 (7th Cir. 2002) (affirmed in Ahmed v. DHS, 328 F.3d 383 (7th Cir. 2003)).

in question,[34] and that no other adequate remedy is available.[35] The courts will dismiss a mandamus action where the plaintiff's claim is moot or where one of the statutory bars to review under INA § 242 applies.[36]

Plaintiffs in a mandamus action should allege jurisdiction under both the mandamus statute, 28 U.S.C. § 1361, and the federal question statute, 28 U.S.C. § 1331.[37] Because mandamus is a civil action, the FRCP and the district court's local rules apply. Unless otherwise specified, venue in a mandamus action can be in any judicial district in which the defendant resides, in which a substantial part of the events or omissions giving rise to the claim occurred, or in which the plaintiff resides.[38]

Challenging Agency Decisions under the APA

The APA states that a person is entitled to judicial review where that person has suffered a legal wrong because of agency action, or is adversely affected by agency action within the meaning of a relevant statute.[39] The APA is not an independent basis for subject matter jurisdiction in the federal courts.[40] Rather, jurisdiction in APA cases is based on 28 U.S.C. § 1331, which provides a general grant of subject matter jurisdiction to federal district courts in civil actions over "federal questions."[41]

---

34. *See, e.g., Iddir*, 301 F.3d at 500 (applications under the diversity visa lottery program); Patel v. Reno, 134 F.3d 929, 933 (9th Cir. 1997) (visa application); Aslam v. Mukasey, 531 F. Supp. 2d 736, 742 (E.D. Va. 2008) (adjustment application); Yu v. Brown, 36 F. Supp. 2d 922, 932 (D.N.M. 1999) (Special Immigrant Juvenile application). *But see* Orlov v. Howard, 523 F. Supp. 2d 30, 38 (D.D.C. 2007) (no duty to increase the pace of adjudicating an adjustment application).

35. Some courts have held that the availability of relief under the APA, 5 U.S.C. § 551 *et seq.* (2012), precludes the granting of mandamus relief. *See, e.g.,* Valona v. U.S. Parole Comm'n, 165 F.3d 508, 510 (7th Cir. 1998) ("[The] APA . . . authorizes district courts to 'compel agency action unlawfully withheld or unreasonably delayed' without the need of a separate action seeking mandamus."); Ali v. Frazier, 575 F. Supp. 2d 1084, 1090–91 (D. Minn. 2008); Sawan v. Chertoff, 589 F. Supp. 2d 817, 825–26 (S.D. Tex. 2008).

36. The REAL ID Act of 2005, Pub. L. No. 109-13, 119 Stat. 231 (May 11, 2005), amended INA § 242 to include specific bars to judicial review by mandamus action.

37. In addition, the APA provides a basis for suit where the government unreasonably delays action or fails to act. *See* 5 U.S.C. §§ 555(b), 706(1) (2012). *See also* Geneme v. Holder, 935 F. Supp. 2d 184, 195 (D.D.C. 2013); Villa v. DHS, 607 F. Supp. 2d 359, 365 (N.D.N.Y. 2009) (APA § 555(b) requires USCIS to adjudicate applications within a reasonable time). *See* discussion of actions brought under the APA, *infra*.

38. 28 U.S.C. § 1391(e) (2012).

39. 5 U.S.C. § 702 (2012).

40. *See generally* Califano v. Sanders, 430 U.S. 99 (1977).

41. Reliance on the APA as the sole ground of jurisdiction, without also alleging jurisdiction under 28 U.S.C. § 1331 (2012), can result in dismissal of the case. *See, e.g.,* Figgens v.

Although the APA is not a basis for federal court jurisdiction, it does provide a cause of action for parties who have been adversely affected by "agency action."[42] "Agency action" includes "the whole or a part of an agency rule, order, license, sanction, relief, or the equivalent or denial thereof, or failure to act."[43] Judicial review under the APA is limited: no review is permitted where another statute specifically precludes review, where agency action is committed to agency discretion by law,[44] or where the petitioner has not first exhausted all available administrative remedies.[45]

The APA states that a court can "hold unlawful and set aside agency actions, findings and conclusions" that meet certain criteria.[46] Four of these criteria apply to all cases where the agency action was arbitrary, capricious, an abuse of discretion, or otherwise not in accordance with the law; contrary to constitutional right, power, privilege, or immunity; in excess of statutory jurisdiction, authority, or limitations, or short of statutory right; or without observance of procedures required by law.[47]

To meet the standing requirements under the APA, the plaintiff must not only have suffered injury-in-fact but also demonstrate that the interests to be protected are within the "zone of interests" protected by the

---

USCIS, No. 1:05-CV-107, 2006 U.S. Dist. LEXIS 28734, at *10–15 (N.D. Utah May 8, 2006); Co. Dept. of Soc. Servs. v. Dept. of Health and Human Servs., 558 F. Supp. 337, 339 (D. Colo. 1983).

42. *See* Bennett v. Spear, 520 U.S. 154, 175 (1997) (stating that 5 U.S.C. § 704 provides a cause of action for all "final agency action for which there is no other adequate remedy in a court").

43. 5 U.S.C. § 551(13) (2012).

44. *Id.* § 701(a)(2). The Supreme Court has held that the APA embodies "a basic presumption of judicial review." Abbott Laboratories v. Gardner, 387 U.S. 136, 140 (1967). "[O]nly upon a showing of 'clear and convincing evidence' of a contrary legislative intent should the courts restrict access to judicial review." *Id.* at 141. Under § 701(a)(2) of the APA, this presumption of judicial review over agency action can be overcome where such action is committed to agency discretion by law. However, the Supreme Court has held that such circumstances are "rare," and only occur "where the relevant statute 'is drawn so that a court would have no meaningful standard against which to judge the agency's exercise of discretion.'" Lincoln v. Vigil, 508 U.S. 182, 191 (1993) (quoting Heckler v. Chaney, 470 U.S. 821, 830 (1985)).

45. The Supreme Court has held that there are limits on the requirement to exhaust administrative remedies. Darby v. Cisneros, 509 U.S. 137 (1993). *See* discussion of administrative exhaustion, *supra.*

46. 5 U.S.C. § 706(2) (2012).

47. *Id.* § 706(2)(A)–(D). *See* Citizens to Preserve Overton Park, Inc. v. Volpe, 401 U.S. 402, 413–14 (1971) ("In all cases agency action must be set aside if the action was 'arbitrary, capricious, an abuse of discretion or otherwise not in accordance with law' or if the action failed to meet statutory, procedural, or constitutional requirements.").

statute.[48] Judicial review under the APA is limited to the administrative record that was before the agency when it made its decision, and thus discovery generally is not allowed.[49]

Courts that have ruled on the issue have found that the general six-year statute of limitations for civil actions brought against the United States[50] applies to suits brought against the United States as APA actions.

Writs of Habeas Corpus—Obtaining a Client's Release from Immigration Detention

The writ of habeas corpus historically "has served as a means of reviewing the legality of executive detention."[51] The federal habeas corpus statute, 28 U.S.C. § 2241, grants district courts jurisdiction to grant a writ of habeas corpus to any person who is held in "custody" by the federal government in violation of the Constitution, laws, or treaties of the United States.

In the immigration context, a habeas corpus complaint can be an effective way to obtain a client's release from DHS custody. The REAL ID Act of 2005[52] eliminated habeas corpus jurisdiction over final orders of removal, deportation, and exclusion and consolidated such review in the court of appeals but did not impact the ongoing availability of habeas corpus to challenge the length or conditions of immigration detention.

A petitioner need not be physically detained to file a habeas corpus petition. Section 2241 states that habeas corpus is available only when a person is "in custody," however, courts have found that actual physical restraint is not required where other restrictions on liberty can satisfy the "custody" requirement.[53]

The Supreme Court has held that the actual or immediate custodian of the facility where the petitioner is confined is the only proper defendant in

---

48. 5 U.S.C. § 702 (2012). *See* Ass'n of Data Processing Serv. Orgs., Inc. v. Camp, 397 U.S. 150, 153 (1970).

49. *See* Camp v. Pitts, 411 U.S. 138, 142 (1973) ("[T]he focal point for judicial review [in an APA suit] should be the administrative record already in existence, not some new record made initially in the reviewing court."). *But see* Voyageurs National Park Assoc. v. Norton, 381 F.3d 759, 766 (8th Cir. 2004) (where an incomplete administrative record "will frustrate effective judicial review," the court may allow discovery to supplement the agency record).

50. 28 U.S.C. § 2401(a) (2012).

51. INS v. St. Cyr, 533 U.S. 289, 301 (2001).

52. Pub. L. No. 109-13, 119 Stat. 231 (2005).

53. Rumsfeld v. Padilla, 542 U.S. 426, 437 (2004) ("[O]ur understanding of custody has broadened to include restraints short of physical confinement . . . .").

a habeas corpus action, but the Court did not specify whether a different rule might apply to immigration-related habeas cases.[54]

"1447(b) Actions"—Judicial Relief for a Delayed Naturalization Application

Where an individual faces an unreasonable delay in obtaining action on a naturalization application, federal courts may provide an avenue of relief: Section 336(b) of the INA grants district courts jurisdiction to intervene where USCIS has failed to make a decision on the naturalization application within 120 days of the applicant's "examination" by USCIS.[55] These so-called "Section 1447(b) Actions" require the following:

- USCIS has failed to make a decision on the naturalization application. Section 1447(b) is only a remedy for a delay in adjudication, and it does not apply if a decision already has been issued.
- At least 120 days must have passed since the "examination."[56] A Section 1447(b) Action is ripe only after USCIS has failed to make a decision within 120 days after the "date on which the examination is conducted under [§ 1446]."[57]
- A Section 1447(b) Action must be filed in the federal district court. The statute vests jurisdiction in district court. Courts of appeals and district courts have held that a district court has exclusive jurisdiction upon the filing of a Section 1447(b) Action, and that USCIS

---

54. *Id.*

55. 8 U.S.C. § 1447(b) (2012). Courts have also held that the INA establishes a clear right to relief for delayed naturalization applications where the interview has not yet been conducted. *See* Hadad v. Scharfen, No. 08-22608-CIV, 2009 U.S. Dist. LEXIS 26147, at *6–8 (S.D. Fla. Mar. 12, 2009); Olayan v. Holder, No. 1:08-cv-715, 2009 U.S. Dist. LEXIS 12825, at *11–12 (S.D. Ind. Feb. 17, 2009).

56. Most courts have held that "examination" refers to the initial interview scheduled under 8 U.S.C. § 1446. *See, e.g.,* Walji v. Gonzales, 500 F.3d 432, 435–36 & n.5 (5th Cir. 2007); *see also* 8 C.F.R. § 335.2. The regulations differentiate between an "initial" examination and a "reexamination." 8 C.F.R. § 335.3(b), but even in the context of a request for evidence followed by a reexamination, some courts have held that USCIS still must make its decision within 120 days of the initial examination. *See, e.g.,* Angel v. Ridge, Case No. 2004-cv-4121, 2005 U.S. Dist. LEXIS 10667, at *11 (S.D. Ill. May 25, 2005) (the 120-day period runs from date of first interview, not a rescheduled interview). Other courts have held that the term "examination" encompasses a process that includes both the interview and the investigation of the application, including the completion of pending background security checks. *See, e.g.,* Danilov v. Aguirre, 370 F. Supp. 2d 441, 443–44 (E.D. Va. 2005).

57. 8 U.S.C. § 1447(b) (2012).

consequently is divested of jurisdiction to decide the naturalization application unless the district court remands the case to the agency.[58]

• A Section 1447(b) Action must be filed in the federal district court for the district in which the applicant resides.

The district court may either decide the naturalization application or remand to USCIS for adjudication. Despite the statutory authority either to grant or deny a naturalization application, many district courts are reluctant to do so, particularly when security checks are still pending.[59]

"1421(c) Actions"—Judicial Review of Denial of Naturalization Application

If an application for naturalization is *denied* by USCIS, as opposed to delayed, the applicant has the right to an administrative appeal and a hearing (commonly referred to as an "N-336 hearing") before a different officer than the one who conducted the original examination and issued the denial, within 180 days from the date on which the appeal is filed.[60] If the application is denied after the N-336 hearing, INA § 310(c) specifically provides direct judicial review in U.S. district court.[61]

Petitioners and their attorneys should be aware of the following:

• Review of a naturalization decision under 8 U.S.C. § 1421(c) is not available until after the administrative appeal (N-336) hearing.

• Review of the denial shall be in the district court for the district in which the applicant resides.

• The district court's review shall be *de novo*, where the court will make its own findings of fact and conclusions of law.

• The district court shall conduct a new hearing on the application at the request of the applicant.[62]

---

58. *See, e.g.,* Aljabri v. Holder, 745 F.3d 816, *10 (7th Cir. 2013); Bustamante v. Napolitano, 582 F.3d 403, 409 (2d Cir. 2009); Etape v. Chertoff, 497 F.3d 379, 384–85 (4th Cir. 2007); United States v. Hovsepian, 359 F.3d 1144, 1161 (9th Cir. 2004); Taalebinezhaad v. Chertoff, 581 F. Supp. 2d 243, 245 (D. Mass. 2008); Castracani v. Chertoff, 377 F. Supp. 2d 71, 73–74 (D.D.C. 2005).

59. *See, e.g.,* Hussein v. Gonzales, 474 F. Supp. 2d 1265, 1269 (M.D. Fla. 2007).

60. *See* 8 U.S.C. § 1447 (2012); 8 C.F.R. § 336.2 (2014).

61. 8 U.S.C. § 1421(c) (2012).

62. *Id.*

Challenging Visa Denials—Obtaining Review of Consular Decisions

Though the "doctrine of consular nonreviewability" limits most lawsuits challenging visa denials,[63] a visa applicant may file a writ of mandamus to compel adjudication of an unreasonably delayed visa application. In addition, under certain limited circumstances, a visa denial may be challenged on constitutional grounds notwithstanding the doctrine of consular nonreviewability.[64]

The issuance or denial of visas is the responsibility of consular officers under the INA.[65] The INA and its implementing regulations require that the government demonstrate some basis for applying a particular inadmissibility provision to a visa applicant.[66] In general, a consular officer's decision to grant or deny a visa petition is not subject to judicial review.[67] However, limited judicial review is available "when United States sponsors of a foreign individual claim that the State Department's denial of a visa to an alien violated their constitutional rights."[68]

For example, the courts have recognized that U.S. citizens and lawful residents who have invited a foreign scholar to speak in the United States, and who allege a violation of their First Amendment rights to "hear, speak, and debate with" the excluded visa applicant are parties with standing to challenge a consular visa decision.[69] Under so-called

---

63. *See* Din v. Kerry, 718 F.3d 856, 859–61 (9th Cir. 2013).

64. *See id.* at 860–67 (citing Bustamante v. Mukasey, 531 F.3d 1059 (9th Cir. 2008)).

65. *See id.* §§ 1101(a)(9), (16), 1151(b)(2)(A)(i); *see also* Saavedra Bruno v. Albright, 197 F.3d 1153, 1156 (D.C. Cir. 1999) ("The INA confers upon consular officers the exclusive authority to review applications for visas, precluding even the Secretary of State from controlling their determinations."); Patel v. Reno, 134 F.3d 929, 933 (9th Cir. 1997) ("[I]t is uncontested that only State Department consular officers have the power to issue visas.").

66. *See* 8 U.S.C. § 1201(g) (2012) (no visa shall be issued if "the consular officer knows or has reason to believe that such alien is ineligible to receive a visa"); 22 C.F.R. § 40.6 (2014) ("reason to believe" requires "a determination based upon facts or circumstances which would lead a reasonable person to conclude that the applicant is ineligible to receive a visa"). The INA also contains a provision that authorizes waiver of the terrorism-related inadmissibility grounds. 8 U.S.C. § 1182(d)(3)(B)(i) (2012).

67. *See, e.g., Saavedra Bruno,* 197 F.3d at 1159 ("The doctrine holds that a consular official's decision to issue or withhold a visa is not subject to judicial review, at least unless Congress says otherwise.").

68. *Id.* at 1163.

69. Kleindienst v. Mandel, 408 U.S. 753, 762 (1972). *See also* Am. Acad. of Religion v. Napolitano, 573 F.3d 115, 117 (2d Cir. 2009); Abourezk v. Shultz, 785 F.2d 1043, 1050–51 (D.C. Cir. 1986) ("Unquestionably, [the plaintiffs] are 'aggrieved' by the State Department's [decision] to keep out people they have invited to engage in open discourse with them within the

"*Mandel* review," a court will inquire only into whether the consular official has provided a "facially legitimate and bona fide reason" for the visa
decision.[70] In *Mandel*, the Supreme Court did not define the term "facially
legitimate and bona fide." However, courts have subsequently devised a
three-part inquiry to assess whether a consular official's proffered reason for a particular visa decision is "facially legitimate and bona fide":
(1) whether the government provided a reason for the decision; (2) whether
the government has a statutory basis for its decision; and (3) whether the
cited provision was properly applied to the visa applicant.[71]

Accordingly, to determine whether a consular officer has provided a
facially legitimate and bona fide reason for denying a visa to an applicant
sponsored by a U.S. citizen or lawful permanent resident, the Court must
assess whether the proffered reason has an evidentiary basis.[72] Merely
asserting a general or conclusory justification for a visa denial, without
supplying any evidentiary basis, is insufficient to establish a facially
legitimate and bona fide reason for the denial.[73] The government must do
more than merely cite a particular inadmissibility provision to exclude a
visa applicant; it must demonstrate that the statute relied upon is properly construed—i.e., that it actually applies to the excluded alien and that
the consular officer "has reason to believe" the alien was excludable on
the ground cited.[74]

United States.").

70. *Mandel*, 408 U.S. at 770; *Saavedra Bruno*, 197 F.3d at 1163; Bustamante v. Mukasey, 531
F.3d 1059, 1062 (9th Cir. 2008) ("Joining the First, Second, and D.C. Circuits, we hold that
under *Mandel*, a U.S. citizen raising a constitutional challenge to the denial of a visa is
entitled to a limited judicial inquiry regarding the reason for the decision. As long as the
reason given is facially legitimate and bona fide the decision will not be disturbed.").

71. *See Am. Acad. of Religion*, 573 F.3d at 121.

72. *See, e.g., Abourezk*, 785 F.2d at 1060 (cautioning that, on remand, the district court must
"make certain that plaintiffs are accorded access to the decisive evidence to the fullest
extent possible").

73. *See* Abourezk v. Reagan, 592 F. Supp. 880, 886–88 (D.D.C. 1984) (rejecting justification for
exclusion as "entirely conclusory" and stating that "[t]o find the conclusory statement that
the entry of a particular individual would be contrary to [U.S.] foreign policy objectives to
be a 'facially legitimate' reason would be to surrender to the executive total discretion");
Allende v. Shultz, 605 F. Supp. 1220, 1225 (D. Mass. 1985) (rejecting State Department's justification for exclusion as "entirely conclusory"); El-Werfalli v. Smith, 547 F. Supp. 152, 154
(S.D.N.Y. 1982) (rejecting justification for exclusion which was "so general" that it "fail[ed]
to establish a reasoned basis for action").

74. *See Am. Acad. of Religion*, 573 F.3d at 126 ("[T]he identification of both a properly construed statute that provides a ground of exclusion and the consular officer's assurance that
he or she 'knows or has reason to believe' that the visa applicant has done something fit-
ting within the proscribed category constitutes a facially legitimate reason.").

EAJA Fees—Obtaining Attorney's Fees under the Equal Access to Justice Act

A party that prevails against the government in federal court is authorized to receive payment by the government for attorney's fees and costs for such successful litigation, under the Equal Access to Justice Act (EAJA).[75] An eligible "prevailing party" is entitled to a fee award both for litigating the case and for litigating the fee request. Fees and costs under EAJA can be awarded regardless of what the client paid, and include coverage for cases taken on a pro bono basis.

In the immigration context, EAJA fees generally are available for successful petitions for review, mandamus actions, or habeas corpus actions, because the EAJA statute applies to "any civil action (other than cases sounding in tort), including proceedings for judicial review of agency action, brought by or against the United States in any court having jurisdiction of that action."[76]

The EAJA fee applicant must establish that it is a "prevailing party,"[77] and that he or she has met the appropriate "net worth" requirements. The application must allege that the government's litigation position was not substantially justified and that there are no circumstances that would make an award unjust.[78]

EAJA fees are based upon "prevailing market rates for the kind and quality of the services furnished."[79] Rates may be increased if a "special factor," such as "the limited availability of qualified attorneys for the proceedings involved, justifies a higher fee."[80] Some courts have recognized that a specialized knowledge of immigration law could warrant enhanced

---

75. 28 U.S.C. § 2412(d) (2012); 5 U.S.C. §§ 504 *et seq.* (2012).

76. 28 U.S.C. § 2412(d)(1)(A) (2012).

77. A judicially enforceable court order or settlement agreement memorializing a federal court victory is necessary to establish "prevailing party" status. District courts have held that an order granting mandamus to adjudicate an adjustment application is sufficient to convey prevailing party status. *See, e.g.,* Afghani v. Mukasey, 543 F. Supp. 2d 1252, 1255–56 (W.D. Wash. 2008); Oman v. Mukasey, 553 F. Supp. 2d 1252, 1254–56 (W.D. Wash. 2008); Liu v. Chertoff, 538 F.Supp. 2d. 1116, 1121–24 (D. Minn. 2008); Aboushaban v. Mueller, 475 F. Supp. 943, 946–47 (N.D. Cal. 2007). A court-ordered remand to the agency has been deemed sufficient success on the merits to confer prevailing party status. *See, e.g.,* Shalala v. Schaefer, 509 U.S. 292 (1993).

78. 28 U.S.C. § 2412(d)(2)(D) (2012).

79. 28 U.S.C. § 2412(d)(2)(A) (2012).

80. 28 U.S.C. § 2412(d)(2)(A)(ii) (2012).

attorney rates.[81] Law clerks, paralegals, and expert witnesses also may be compensated under EAJA at the prevailing market rate.

The EAJA fee application must include a statement of the total amount of fees and costs requested and an itemized account of time expended and rates charged. An EAJA fee applicant bears the burden of documenting fees and costs.[82] In general, EAJA will compensate for time that is "reasonably expended on the litigation."[83] The Supreme Court has expressly approved compensation for time spent drafting the initial pleadings and developing the theory of the case,[84] therefore, requesting compensation for time spent preparing litigation is permissible, but the initial work performed before DHS or the immigration court is not compensable.

For district court actions where neither side appealed to the court of appeals, the EAJA fee application is filed in the district court where the action was adjudicated; on a petition for review, an EAJA fee application is filed in the court of appeals that adjudicated the petition.

The fee application must be filed within 30 days of entry of final judgment in the action,[85] i.e., within 30 days after the expiration of the time for filing an appeal or, if an appeal is filed, within 30 days of entry of final judgment by the court of appeals or the U.S. Supreme Court.

CONCLUSION

The purpose of this chapter has been to provide a broad overview and general introduction to a variety of immigration actions that can be

---

81. *See, e.g.,* Muhur v. Ashcroft, 382 F.3d 653, 656 (7th Cir. 2004) ("immigration lawyers are not ipso facto entitled to fees above the statutory ceiling," but immigration expertise, "such as knowledge of foreign cultures or of particular, esoteric nooks and crannies of immigration law" warrants a special factor rate adjustment); Rueda-Menicucci v. INS, 132 F.3d 493, 496 (9th Cir. 1997) ("a specialty in immigration law could be a special factor warranting an enhancement of the statutory rate" if that specialty is "needful for the litigation in question"); Pollgreen v. Morris, 911 F.2d 527, 537 (11th Cir. 1990) (a "special factor" rate adjustment might be appropriate for attorneys with a special expertise in immigration law); Douglas v. Baker, 809 F. Supp. 131, 135 (D.D.C. 1992) (awarding enhanced rate based on extensive experience in immigration law). *But see* Johnson v. Gonzales, 416 F.3d 205, 213 (3d Cir. 2005) (enhancement not warranted where case involved "straightforward application of the substantial evidence and asylum standard"); Perales v. Casillas, 950 F.2d 1066, 1078–79 (5th Cir. 1992) (immigration lawyers not *per se* specialized for "special factor" purposes).
82. Hensley v. Eckerhart, 461 U.S. 424, 437 (1983).
83. *Id.* at 433.
84. *See* Webb v. Board of Education, 471 U.S. 234, 243 (1985).
85. 28 U.S.C. § 2412(d)(1)(B) (2012).

brought in federal court, and to discuss a number of the factors that should be considered and the likely obstacles that may arise. The federal courts offer an invaluable forum to obtain review of adverse agency action and can provide relief to a client who was otherwise unsuccessful in his or her administrative proceedings. An informed and prepared federal court practitioner can be an extremely effective advocate for the immigration client.

23

CREATING AND REPRESENTING EB-5 REGIONAL CENTERS

H. Ronald Klasko and Walter S. Gindin[1]

INTRODUCTION

The EB-5 program was implemented in 1990 as a program to provide legal permanent residence status to investors who invest $500,000 or $1 million (depending on the geographical area) in a business that creates employment for a minimum of ten full-time U.S. citizen or permanent resident employees.[2] For various reasons, especially the fact that most businesses do not commence early operations with ten full-time employees, Congress created the regional center program in 1993. A regional center is "any economic unit, public or private, which is involved with the promotion of economic growth, including export sales, improved regional productivity, job creation, and increased domestic capital investment."[3] Today, regional center pooled EB-5 investments constitute over 80 percent of the total EB-5 petitions.

From the investor's point of view, the major advantage of a regional center investment is that the investor's petition can be approved as long as the regional center project creates ten direct or indirect jobs. This allows regional centers to use economic forecasting models to project indirect and induced employment created as a result of the new project. The main disadvantage of a regional center for an investor is that the investment amount is being put toward a project that the investor does not control and generally the investor will not be working in the project in which he

---

1. H. Ronald Klasko (rklasko@klaskolaw.com) is the Philadelphia-based managing partner at Klasko, Rulon, Stock & Seltzer, LLP. A former national president of the American Immigration Lawyers Association, he presently serves as chair of that organization's EB-5 committee. He and his 20-person EB-5 team represent regional centers, project developers, and investors. His website is www.eb5immigration.com. Walter S. Gindin (wgindin @klaskolaw.com) is an associate in the Philadelphia office of Klasko, Rulon, Stock & Seltzer. Walter concentrates his practice on employment-based immigration matters and is a member of the EB-5 immigrant investor practice.

2. 8 U.S.C. § 1153(b)(5) (2012).

3. 8 C.F.R. § 204.6(e) (2013).

invests. In addition, he will be paying the regional center developer a sum of money (often between $40,000 and $60,000) to cover the developer's expenses and profit.

Most, but not all, of the regional center projects are real estate-based projects. With capital becoming unavailable from traditional sources, EB-5 money has become an important alternative source of capital. As a result, the number of regional centers has increased to over 400.

From the developer's point of view, regional center certification provides an aura of legitimacy that may help in marketing to foreign investors. In addition, a particular regional center project may be preapproved by USCIS. Regional center designation is a one-time designation allowing future projects to be marketed without incurring delays. In addition to funding their own projects, regional centers can profit by sponsoring and overseeing projects developed by others.

However, seeking regional center designation does have some disadvantages. Regional center certification may take a lengthy period of time—presently 6 months or longer. Regional center certification may entail significant expense, including hiring multiple professionals as will be discussed below. Regional center certification is not the same as approval of any particular regional center project. With so many regional centers approved, many regional centers have not been able to attract investors; and some newer regional centers find it difficult to compete in their marketing efforts with long-existing regional centers with a track record of many immigration approvals. Finally, regional centers have ongoing administrative and filing requirements with USCIS in order to avoid decertification.

OTHER OPTIONS FOR RAISING CAPITAL UNDER THE EB-5 PROGRAM

A developer might consider three other options for raising capital under the EB-5 program:

- Having a project "adopted" by a certified regional center;
- Purchasing a certified regional center; or
- Pooling investments with individual EB-5 petitions.

Having a project adopted by an existing regional center saves the time and expense involved in developing a new regional center. The existing regional center may have a marketing plan in place and may even have existing investors ready to invest. Furthermore, project preapproval is available.

However, some of the developer's profit will be siphoned off to the regional center operators. Furthermore, the developer needs to do serious due diligence with respect to the regional center to make certain that the developer is not affiliating with a regional center that may have a bad reputation in the marketplace or that may be at risk of decertification.

Some developers have chosen to purchase an existing (sometimes dormant) regional center. Once an agreeable price is reached, the developer does not need to negotiate away profit or control with respect to any particular project. However, as with purchasing any other business, the developer needs to do serious due diligence regarding potential liabilities and negative good will.

Of course, there is no need for a developer to work through a regional center at all. If the project will directly create ten full-time positions for every investor, the investors can invest without the developer creating a regional center. This eliminates serious time delays and expenses, as well as ongoing administration. However, the option of project preapproval is not currently available. Also, marketing to foreign national investors may be more difficult without the aura of regional center designation.

Creating a Regional Center

In order to create a regional center, it is necessary to put together a team of professionals:

- An EB-5 Economist is a critical professional in performing the economic projection of indirect and induced jobs; helping to establish a targeted employment area (TEA); and helping to determine the geographic bounds of the regional center
- A Securities/Corporate Attorney is necessary because the regional center investment offering is subject to securities laws. The securities attorney will prepare the private placement memorandum, including specific immigration risks of the investment, as well as the Subscription Agreement. Usually the same attorney will create two or three corporate entities—the regional center entity; the "new commercial enterprise"; and sometimes the separate job-creating entity.
- The EB-5 Business Plan Writer will be preparing the comprehensive business plan to present a credible explanation of the project, the use of the capital, the time lines, the job creation, and other aspects of the project. Sometimes, the EB-5 business plan writer will also prepare an operating plan for the regional center that clearly describes, among other things, how the regional center will focus on a geographical region of the United States and how it will promote economic growth

through improved regional productivity, job creation, and increased domestic capital investment.

- The Immigration Attorney generally acts as the "quarterback" of the professional team. He needs to ensure consistency between the business plan and economic report; make certain that the business plan is in conformity with USCIS policy; make certain that job creation is both understandable and credible and consistent with USCIS policy; provide advice regarding immigration risks for the private placement memorandum; review all documents for immigration compliance; prepare and file the regional center designation application; prepare and file any application for project preapproval; and in some cases prepare and file the investors' I-526 EB-5 petitions.
- Marketing Firm/Commissioned Agents are a critical part of the process because all of the work done by the other professionals will be for naught unless the project can be successfully marketed to investors.
- A Bank/Escrow Agent is often a part of the process since many regional centers offer a protection to investors of having the investment amount sit in an escrow account at a bank, not to be released until the EB-5 petition is approved.

Issues for Regional Centers

Two of the most important initial issues to be addressed are:

- How much must investors invest?
- How much capital can be raised?

Virtually all regional center investments are $500,000 investments. The reason is that the projects are in "targeted employment areas" (TEAs).[4] As a practical matter, if a project is not in a TEA, the chances of success for marketing of the project to foreign investors are rather slim.

There are three ways to prove that the investment project is in a TEA:

- If the project is in a "rural" area, which is defined as outside of a metropolitan statistical area or outer boundary of any city or town having a population of 20,000 or more, it qualifies as a TEA;[5]
- If the project is in a census tract with an unemployment rate of at least 150 percent of the national average, it qualifies as a TEA; or
- If the economist is able to aggregate a number of contiguous census tracts which together have an average unemployment rate of at least

---

4. *Id.* § 204.6(e).
5. *Id.* § 204.6(j)(6)(i).

150 percent of the national average, and if the designee of the governor of the state provides a letter designating the aggregated census tract area as a TEA, USCIS will generally defer to the state designation.[6]

It is important to note that the ultimate TEA designation is not made until each investor makes his investment.[7] Therefore, a developer risks the possibility that a project could commence at a time when the geographical area is a TEA; but by the time investors actually invest, it may not be a TEA.

The amount of EB-5 capital that can actually be raised for a project is obviously a critical issue. That amount is based on how many direct, indirect, and induced jobs will be created. Ultimately, the maximum number of investors is determined by dividing the job creation projection by 10. Multiplying that number of investors by $500,000 (assuming a TEA) provides the maximum EB-5 capital raise. As a practical matter, investors will generally want to see that the projected job creation is far more (20–30 percent more) than the minimum required.

It is thus rather obvious that the economic job projection report is a critical document. Generally, economists will use one of four recognized "input-output models"; RIMS2, REDYN, REMY, and IMPLAN. These models project indirect and induced employment generally within the geographic bounds of the regional center. Although USCIS previously equivocated on the issue, it now recognizes that indirect and induced jobs can qualify and be counted as jobs attributable to a regional center, based on reasonable economic methodologies, even if they are located outside the geographical boundaries of a regional center.[8]

The immigration attorney, although presumably not an expert economist, should not just accept the economic report in an unquestioning manner. The immigration attorney should consider the following key issues in his review of the economic report:

- It must be completely consistent with the business plan. The economic report will be premised upon certain input projections, which must come from the business plan, such as expenditures, revenues, direct employees, square footage, occupancy rate, etc.
- The immigration attorney must make certain that the economic report is "transparent." In other words, it should be clear from reading the report how the economist extrapolated job projection from the specific foundation facts.

---

6. *Id.* § 204.6(j)(6)(ii) (2013).
7. 8 U.S.C. § 1153(b)(5)(B)(ii) (2012).
8. USCIS EB-5 Adjudications Policy Memorandum, May 30, 2013, at 18 [hereinafter May 30 Policy Memo].

- The immigration attorney must be concerned with a projected timeline for job creation. USCIS policy is that the requisite employment must be created within two and one-half years of EB-5 petition approval.
- The immigration attorney should be concerned with overly aggressive "inputs." If the aggressive estimates are not met, some or all of the investors may not be able to get their conditions removed (see below).
- The immigration attorney must make certain that the economist understands the difference between a "direct" job as defined by USCIS and what an economist normally considers to be a direct job. An economist may consider an employee of the construction company or of the construction project or target business to be a direct employee. However, the USCIS definition of employee is a W-2 employee of the "new commercial enterprise" in which the investor actually invests.[9] Often, this enterprise is different than the job-creating enterprise.

In reviewing the EB-5 business plan, the immigration attorney should be concerned with whether the plan is comprehensive and credible and whether it is consistent with the economic report. The time lines specified in the business plan are critical. Often, the immigration attorney will advocate for a business plan that is not too specific in order to avoid the possibility that the specifics of the business plan are not adhered to, which can raise issues of "material change" at the condition removal stage (see below).

The geographic scope of the regional center often involves several considerations. If the scope is too large, it may be difficult to get the regional center designation approved, as USCIS may consider the area not to be a definable "region." If it is too small, there may be a need to amend the regional center designation if a future project falls outside of the initially designated area. The economist can assist in determining the largest possible area that can be justified as an economically interdependent region. In this regard, it is important to understand that there is no exclusive jurisdiction for regional centers.

In most cases, there are three different entities involved in the regional center creation process:

- The regional center itself is an administrative entity that applies to USCIS for certification. It has ongoing administrative and compliance responsibilities, sometimes markets for investors, performs due

---

9. 8 C.F.R. § 204.6(e) (2013).

diligence regarding the investor's source of funds and may review the investors' EB-5 petitions. The regional center entity also obtains signed Subscription Agreements and Escrow Agreements; monitors employment creation; tracks infusion of capital into the job-creating enterprises; monitors compliance with the business plan and the foundation facts on which the economic report is based; allocates jobs between investors; prepares an annual reporting for filing with USCIS; oversees the preparation of condition removal packages for approved investors; and decides on new projects. Generally, an operational plan is prepared for the regional center. The operational plan often includes an overview of the regional center; information about marketing plans and recruitment of investors; explanation of the funding and budget for the regional center; explanation of the systems to be used for administrative oversight.

- The "new commercial enterprise" is the entity into which the investor invests. This is generally a limited partnership or LLC. In all cases, the investors make equity investments into the new commercial enterprise. In many cases, the new commercial enterprise is in the business of loaning money to one or more job-creating enterprises. In fewer regional centers, the investors in the new commercial enterprise take an equity stake in the development project.
- The job-creating enterprise is the actual development project or business. In the model where the new commercial enterprise loans money, the job-creating enterprise is the borrower. Repayment of the loan with interest provides the exit strategy and rate of return for the investors.

Regional Center Application Process

With all of that as background, the immigration attorney is ready to prepare the application for regional center designation. The application is made on Form I-924 with a volume of additional documentation. Generally, the documentation will include most or all of the following:

- A detailed map illustrating the contiguous geographical area of the proposed regional center, together with an explanation regarding the economic interdependency of the region;
- Economic projection of job creation;
- Business plan;
- North American Industry Classification System (NAICS) code for each industrial category;
- Documentation of TEA;
- Operational plan for the regional center;

- Marketing plan;
- Organizational structure and budget of the regional center;
- Statement from the principal of the regional center that explains the methodologies that the regional center will use to track the infusion of each investor's capital into the job-creating enterprise and to allocate the jobs created;
- Draft Subscription Agreement;
- Draft Private Placement Memorandum;
- Draft Escrow Agreement;
- Corporate documentation for the regional center;
- Hard copy of any marketing materials;
- Plans to remain in compliance with ongoing USCIS monitoring requirements;
- Proof of the investor's involvement in the business;
- Procedure the regional center will use to perform due diligence on the source of funds of the investors; and
- Documentation of community or political support.

At the same time as the regional center requests designation, it can also file an application for preapproval of its initial project. This procedure is completely optional, and investors can file I-526 EB-5 petitions without project preapproval. Also, project preapproval can be filed independently for subsequent projects. If the regional center opts for project preapproval, it must file a complete package containing everything that would be required in an investor's I-526 petition except the investor's source of funds and path of funds.

The advantages of project preapproval are the possibility of avoiding multiple adjudications of projects and a clear marketing advantage, as USCIS policy requires it to afford deference to a prior favorable determination at a subsequent stage in the EB-5 process. The disadvantage is that project preapproval can add significant time.

Assuming the regional center designation is approved, and the marketing effort is successful, the developers want to know when the money will actually be available for the project. Generally, the investor must invest 100 percent of the investment before the I-526 petition is filed. The offering may provide that the developer can use the money immediately or put the money into escrow to be released upon the occurrence of a condition precedent, such as the approval of the investor's I-526 petition. Either option is fully compliant with EB-5 rules and policies, but the latter certainly provides a marketing advantage.

Because of the substantial processing time to obtain the regional center designation, particular project preapproval (if requested) and approval of the investor's EB-5 petition, developers often obtain interim or bridge financing to enable the project to move forward pending receipt of the EB-5 capital. The EB-5 capital then often replaces the bridge financing. This is normal business practice and should not create an issue for EB-5 petition approval because it is the new commercial enterprise (and not the investor) that must create the jobs. Indeed, USCIS has made clear that if a project commences based on temporary financing or temporary equity prior to the receipt of the EB-5 capital and subsequently replaces it with EB-5 capital, the new commercial enterprise may still receive credit for the job creation under the regulations.[10]

Another sometimes controversial issue involves the requirement that the investment must be "at risk."[11] This principle prevents an investor from being assured of a guaranteed redemption at a specific price. Redemption at fair market value is acceptable. Third-party guarantees of the investment have been allowed. The issue of third-party insurance provided by the regional center is an unresolved one.

In addition to dealing with investors, regional centers have ongoing reporting requirements. Every year, the regional center must file Form I-924 A providing, *inter alia*, the total amount of EB-5 capital invested; the amount of job creation; the industry focus; the number of approved and denied I-526 petitions; and the number of approved and denied I-829 petitions.

Certain changes in regional center operations could result in a need for a regional center to seek an amendment of its designation. Form I-924 provides a list of acceptable amendments, to include changes to organizational structure or administration and capital investment projects. Such formal amendments to the regional center designation, however, are not required when a regional center changes its industries of focus, its geographic boundaries, its business plans, or its economic methodologies. Nevertheless, a regional center may elect to pursue an amendment if it seeks certainty in advance that such changes will be permissible to USCIS before they are adjudicated at the I-526 stage.[12]

Once all of the investors' EB-5 petitions are approved, the regional center's job is not done. Within the window of 21 to 24 months after each investor's conditional permanent residence is approved, the investor must file an I-829 petition to remove the conditions on permanent residence and become a full permanent resident. In order to get that petition

---

10. May 30 Policy Memo at 15.
11. *Matter of Izummi*, 22 I. & N. Dec. 169 (Assoc. Comm'r, Examinations 1998).
12. May 30 Policy Memo at 15.

approved, the investor must prove that he has sustained his investment and that the projected jobs have been created.[13]

The concept of material change is a controversial one. The USCIS position is that when material changes occur after the investor has obtained conditional residency, USCIS will permit the investor to remove conditions notwithstanding the material changes, provided that the investment has been sustained and the jobs have been created. In these circumstances, USCIS will examine the new facts de novo for regulatory compliance.[14]

Conversely, when material changes occur before the investor has obtained conditional residency—for example, during the pendency of USCIS's adjudication of the I-526 petition or following the approval of the I-526 petition—USCIS requires the investor to file a new petition.[15]

In defining the term "material," the Service has borrowed the definition articulated in a U.S. Supreme Court decision analyzing a materiality requirement in the context of willful misrepresentations during judicial denaturalization proceedings—this standard is by many accounts particularly unhelpful.[16]

It is certainly best if the regional center can prove that all of the projected direct jobs have occurred and that all of the foundation facts that provided the input for the economist's projection of indirect and induced jobs have actually occurred. What if all of the jobs have not actually occurred by the time of the filing of the condition removal petition? The USCIS regulation allows for proof that the jobs will be created "within a reasonable time" from the date of filing of the condition removal petition, which the USCIS has interpreted as within one year of the two-year anniversary of the investor obtaining conditional permanent resident status.[17]

The regional center EB-5 option is a classic win-win-win program. Developers are able to move forward with projects that otherwise might not have sufficient financing; jobs are created; and investors get green cards. In 2012, Congress reaffirmed its commitment to the regional center model of investment and job creation by removing the word "pilot" from the now twenty-year-old program and by providing a three-year reauthorization of the regional center model. Efforts are underway to get Congress to make the program permanent, which would likely spur its growth well beyond present levels.

---

13. 8 C.F.R. § 216.6(c) (2013).
14. May 30 Policy Memo at 25–27.
15. *Id.* at 24–25.
16. *Id.* at 23 (referencing Kungys v. United States, 485 U.S. 759 (1988)).
17. *Id.* at 22.

24

TAX RULES FOR IMMIGRATION
LAW PRACTITIONERS

Vlad Frants and Brandon D. Hadley[1]

PREFACE

The presentation of the U.S. federal tax law in this chapter is based substantially on content displayed publicly on the U.S. Internal Revenue
Service (IRS) website (www.IRS.gov). This author hopes to add value to
practicing immigration attorneys through compiling, organizing, and
presenting some important aspects of U.S. taxation law that intersect
immigration, all in one place, so that the immigration attorney will have
a starting point for understanding some of the relevant tax-immigration
issues. Further, the information presented in this chapter is quite general
and mostly devoid of specific detail and should not be exclusively relied
upon. A tax advisor should be consulted on your client's specific situation.

INTRODUCTION

As the IRS aptly points out on the IRS website, while the immigration laws
of the United States refer to aliens as immigrants, non-immigrants, and
undocumented (illegal) aliens, the tax laws of the United States refer only
to resident and nonresident aliens. Generally speaking, the controlling
principle is that "resident aliens" are taxed by the United States in the same
manner as U.S. citizens on their worldwide income whereas "nonresident
aliens" are taxed by the United States according to special rules contained

---

1. Vlad Frants is a tax attorney with a particular interest in international taxation. He
holds an LLM in Taxation from the Georgetown University Law Center, a Master of Science in Taxation from the Fordham University Graduate School of Business, and a JD from
Brooklyn Law School.

   Brandon D. Hadley is a tax attorney with the law firm Katten Muchin Rosenman
LLP. He holds an LLM in Taxation from the Georgetown University Law Center, a JD from
American University, Washington College of Law, and a BA from American University,
School of International Service.

in the Internal Revenue Code of 1986, as amended ("Code"). Generally, a nonresident alien is subject to U.S. federal income tax only on income that is derived from sources within the United States.

The residency rules for U.S. federal tax purposes are found in Section 7701(b) of the Code. What an immigration law practitioner will note almost immediately is that those rules define residency for tax purposes very differently from the immigration laws. Discussed in more detail below, under the residency rules of the Code, any alien who is not a resident alien is a nonresident alien. An alien becomes a resident alien in one of three ways: (1) by being admitted to the United States as, or changing status to, a lawful permanent resident under the immigration laws ("Green Card Test"); (2) by passing the Substantial Presence Test (as defined below), a numerical formula that measures days present in the United States; or (3) by making a "First-Year Choice," which enables an alien to pass the Substantial Presence Test one year earlier than under the normal rules. Interestingly, an undocumented illegal alien under the immigration laws who passes the Substantial Presence Test will be treated for U.S. federal tax purposes as a resident alien.

For nonresident aliens, income is subject to U.S. federal income tax if it either is (i) FDAP income from sources in the United States or (ii) income that is effectively connected with a U.S. trade or business. FDAP income is "fixed or determinable annual or periodical" gains, profits, and income. FDAP income includes interest, dividends, and rents. FDAP income that is U.S. source income generally is subject to a 30 percent withholding tax, or to tax at a lower rate if the nonresident alien is entitled to the benefits of a tax treaty with the United States. An important exception to this 30 percent withholding tax is the "portfolio interest exemption," which generally exempts from U.S. federal income tax most U.S. source interest earned by a nonresident alien.

Income that is effectively connected with a U.S. trade or business is taxed on a net income basis in the same manner as income earned by a U.S. person. A nonresident alien who receives income that is effectively connected with a U.S. trade or business generally is required to file a U.S. tax return.

U.S. Citizens, Resident Aliens, and Nonresident Aliens

Simply put, a person either is a U.S. citizen or national, or is an alien. A U.S. citizen includes (1) an individual born in the United States; (2) an individual whose parent is a U.S. citizen and where certain other conditions are met;[2] (3) a former alien who has been naturalized as a U.S. citi-

---

2. Under the Child Citizenship Act, applicable to both adopted and biological children of

zen; (4) an individual born in Puerto Rico, Guam, or U.S. Virgin Islands. U.S. national refers to an individual who owes his or her sole allegiance to the United States, including all U.S. citizens and some people who are not citizens. For tax purposes the term "U.S. national" refers to individuals who were born in either the Commonwealth of the Northern Mariana Islands or in America Samoa.

There are two kinds of aliens: (1) resident aliens and (2) nonresident aliens. A non-U.S. citizen is a nonresident alien unless he or she satisfies the "Green Card Test" or the "Substantial Presence Test." A non-U.S. citizen who satisfies the Green Card Test or the Substantial Presence Test is a resident alien for U.S. federal tax purposes.

Green Card Test
Under the Green Card Test, a person is treated as a resident alien (i.e., a resident for tax purposes) if he or she is a lawful permanent resident of the United States at any time during the calendar year. Such a person receives the privilege of residing permanently in the United States as an immigrant under the immigration laws. Typically, the U.S. Citizenship and Immigration Services (USCIS) issues an alien registration card, Form I-551. This is also known as a "green card." Resident alien status continues under the Green Card Test unless (1) the individual voluntarily renounces and abandons his or her status in writing to the USCIS; (2) the immigration status is administratively terminated by the USCIS; or (3) the immigration status is judicially terminated by a U.S. federal court. If the Green Card Test is met at any point during the calendar year, but the Substantial Presence Test, discussed below, is not met, the individual's residency starting date is the first day on which the person is present in the United States. An alien who has been present in the United States at any point in a calendar year as a lawful permanent resident is able to choose to be treated as a resident alien for the entire calendar year.

When a person has been both a resident alien and a nonresident alien in the same tax year, then that person is deemed to be a dual status alien. Dual status refers only to one's resident status for tax purposes in the United States; it does not have anything to do with one's citizenship status. In determining U.S. income tax liability for a dual status tax year, different

---

U.S. citizens, there will be automatic acquisition of U.S. citizenship when the following four conditions are met: (1) one parent is a U.S. citizen by birth or through naturalization; (2) the child is under the age of 18; (3) the child is residing in the United States as a lawful permanent resident alien and is in the legal and physical custody of the U.S. citizen parent; and (4) if the child is adopted, the adoption must be final.

rules apply for the part of the year that individual is a resident of the United States than for the part of the year the individual is a nonresident.

Substantial Presence Test

Under the Substantial Presence Test, a person is treated as a resident alien (i.e., a resident for U.S. federal tax purposes) if he or she is physically present in the United States on at least (1) 31 days during the calendar year, and (2) 183 days during the 3-year period that includes the current year and the two years immediately before that, counting: (i) all the days present in the current year; and (ii) 1/3 of the days present in the first year before the current year, and (iii) 1/6 of the days present in the second year before the current year. The IRS website describes the following example:

> You were physically present in the United States on 120 days in each of the years 2007, 2008, and 2009. To determine if you meet the substantial presence test for 2009, count the full 120 days of presence in 2009, 40 days in 2008 (1/3 of 120), and 20 days in 2007 (1/6 of 120). Since the total for the 3-year period is 180 days, you are not considered a resident under the substantial presence test for 2009.

While a person generally is treated as present in the United States on any day he or she is physically present in the country, there are exceptions. The following days do not count as days of presence in the United States for the purposes of the Substantial Presence Test: (i) days the individual commutes to work in the United States from a residence in Canada or Mexico, if the person regularly commutes from Canada or Mexico; (ii) days the individual is in the United States for less than 24 hours, while in transit between two places outside of the United States; (iii) days the individual is in the United States as a crew member of a foreign vessel; (iv) days the individual is unable to leave the United States because of a medical condition that develops while in the United States; and (v) days the individual is exempt.

Certain individuals are exempt from counting days of presence in the United States. The following are categories of people who are exempt: (1) individuals temporarily present in the United States as foreign government-related personnel; (2) teachers or trainees temporarily present in the United States under a "J" or "Q" visa, whom substantially comply with the requirements of the visa; (3) students temporarily present in the United States under an "F," "J," "M" or "Q" visa, who substantially comply with the requirements of the visa; and (4) professional athletes temporarily in the United States to compete in a charitable sports event.

Even if an individual satisfies the Substantial Presence Test, he or she nevertheless can be treated as a nonresident alien if that person qualifies for either of these two exceptions: (1) the closer connection exception available to all aliens under Code § 7701(b)(3)(B) and (C) and Treas. Reg. § 301.7701(b)-2 (1993); or (2) the closer connection exception available only to students under Code § 7701(b)(5)(D) and (E) and in Treas. Reg. § 301.7701(b)-3(b)(7)(iii) (1997).

With respect to the closer connection exception available to all aliens, generally, even if one meets the Substantial Presence Test, he or she can still be treated as a nonresident alien if he or she is present in the United States for less than 183 days during the year, maintains a tax home in a foreign country during the year, and has a closer connection during the year to that other foreign country. For determining whether one has a closer connection to a foreign country, the individual's tax home must also be in existence for the entire current year, and must be located in the same foreign country for which closer connection is claimed.

Despite the fact that a foreign student may pass the Substantial Presence Test, an exception exists in U.S. law that allows the foreign student to continue to be treated as a nonresident alien. The second exception to the Substantial Presence Test for aliens is sometimes referred to as the closer connection exception available only to students. The exception contains four requirements for its application. The student (1) must not intend to reside permanently in the United States; (2) must have substantially complied with the immigration laws and requirements relating to the student's non-immigrant status; (3) must not have taken any steps to change his or her non-immigrant status in the United States toward becoming a permanent resident of the United States; and (4) must have a closer connection to a foreign country than to the United States as evidenced by the factors listed in Treasury Regulation § 301.7701(b)-2(d)(1) (1993). The burden of proof is on the student to prove these four factors and to claim the exception for students on an income tax return; a student should attach Form 8843 to his or her Form 1040NR or 1040NR-EZ.

Taxation of Resident Aliens

Generally, a resident alien is taxed just like a U.S. citizen. A resident alien's U.S. tax return must report all interest, dividends, wages or other compensation for services, income from rental property or royalties, and other income. These amounts should be reported on the U.S. federal income tax return irrespective of whether these amounts are from sources within or outside of the United States. In other words, resident aliens' worldwide income generally is subject to U.S. federal income tax and must be reported.

Income of resident aliens is subject to the same graduated tax rates that apply to U.S. citizens.[3] Resident aliens can use the same filing statuses available to U.S. citizens, such as single, married, and head of household. They can claim the same deductions allowed to U.S. citizens as long as they are resident aliens for the entire tax year. They can claim a spousal exemption on a "married filing separate" return as long as their spouse had no gross income for U.S. tax purposes and was not the dependent of another taxpayer; this spousal exemption may be claimed even if the spouse had not been a resident alien for a full tax year or even if the spouse is an alien who has not even come to the United States. Further, a resident alien can claim an exemption for each person who qualifies as a dependent according to the rules for U.S. citizens.[4] Importantly, the resident alien's spouse and each dependent must have either a Social Security Number or an Individual Taxpayer Identification Number (ITIN) to be claimed as a dependent.

Generally, resident aliens can claim tax credits and report tax payments, including withholding taxes, in accordance with the same rules applicable to U.S. citizens. Some examples of claimable tax credits include child and dependent care credit, foreign tax credit, earned income credit, adoption credit, and education credit. Resident aliens can claim the same itemized deductions as U.S. citizens.[5] These deductions include certain medical and dental expenses, state and local income taxes, real estate taxes, home mortgage interest payments, charitable contributions, casualty and theft losses, and miscellaneous deductions. If the resident alien does not itemize deductions, then he or she can claim the standard deduction applicable to the relevant filing status.

A resident alien living outside of the United States may wonder whether he or she will have to pay taxes to both the United States and the country where he or she is living. Unfortunately, if there is no income tax treaty between the resident alien's country of residence and the United States, then he or she must pay taxes to both countries. Gen-

---

3. See the Tax Table and Tax Rate Schedules applicable to U.S. citizens and found in the instructions for Forms 1040, 1040A, or 1040EZ.

4. The dependent must be a citizen or national of the United States or be a resident of the United States, Canada, or Mexico for some part of the calendar year in which the tax year begins.

5. Resident aliens should use Schedule A of Form 1040 to claim itemized deductions.

erally, however, the resident alien will get a tax credit against either the U.S. federal income taxes or foreign income taxes, depending on the particular circumstances, and so double taxation may be avoided. If the foreign country of residence does have an income tax treaty with the United States, the treaty may contain "tie-breaker rules," which will determine the person's country of residence for income tax purposes. Usually, the location of the individual's permanent home or the center of the individual's most significant interests determines resident status. If the resident alien is deemed to be a resident of the treaty country under the tie-breaker rules, and he or she elects to apply the treaty, then he or she will be considered to be a resident of the treaty country for U.S. federal income tax purposes.[6]

U.S. Federal Income Tax Filing Rules

The relevant U.S. federal income tax return forms include (1) IRS Form 1040EZ, Income Tax Return for Single and Joint Filers With No Dependents; (2) IRS Form 1040A, U.S. Individual Income Tax Return; and (3) IRS Form 1040, U.S. Individual Income Tax Return. The due date for filing the return and paying any tax due is April 15 of the year following the year for which the return will be filed. An automatic extension to June 15 will be provided if the resident alien's main place of business and residence are outside of the United States and Puerto Rico on April 15. An automatic extension of time to file until October 15 can be obtained by filing IRS Form 4868 on or before April 15.

If the resident alien has not filed a U.S. income tax return for one or more years and there is no tax liability for any of those years, then he or she generally should file returns for the current year and the two prior years. However, if the resident alien has not filed a U.S. income tax return for one or more years and U.S. federal income tax is due for any of those years, then he or she generally should file returns for the current year and five previous years.

Taxation of Nonresident Aliens

A nonresident alien is an alien who has not satisfied the Green Card Test or the Substantial Presence Test described above.

---

6. To make this election, a U.S. Nonresident Alien Income Tax Return (IRS Form 1040NR) must be filed in the year of the election; an IRS Form 8833 (Treaty-Based Return Position Disclosure under Section 6114 or 7701(b)) must be attached to the IRS Form 1040NR.

A nonresident alien's income is subject to U.S. federal income tax if it is (1) income that is effectively connected with a trade or business in the United States; or (2) U.S. source FDAP income.

Effectively Connected Income

Effectively connected income (ECI) refers to income that is effectively connected with a trade or business in the United States. In other words, when a non-U.S. person engages in a trade or business in the United States, all income connected with the conduct of that trade or business is considered to be ECI.

After allowable deductions, ECI is taxed at graduated rates; these are the same rates that apply to U.S. citizens and residents.[7]

One must be engaged in a trade or business during the tax year to have ECI that year. Whether a person is engaged in a trade or business in the United States depends upon all the facts and circumstances, and a person generally is considered to be engaged in a U.S. trade or business when he or she performs personal services in the United States. Certain kinds of FDAP income are treated as ECI under the Code if they are connected with a U.S. trade or business. Moreover, certain kinds of investment income can be treated as ECI if it passes certain tests.[8] Further, in limited circumstances, some kinds of foreign source income may be treated as ECI.

The following categories of income usually are considered to be connected with a trade or business in the United States: (1) persons temporarily present in the United States as a non-immigrant on an "F," "J," "M," or "Q" visa are generally considered to be engaged in a trade or business in the United States;[9] (2) members of a partnership that at any time during the tax year is engaged in a trade or business in the United States are considered to be engaged in a trade or business in the United States; (3) individuals performing personal services in the United States are usually engaged in a U.S. trade or business; (4) persons who own and operate a business in the United States that sells services, products, or merchan-

---

7. ECI income should be reported on page one of IRS Form 1040NR.

8. Certain kinds of investment income are treated as ECI if they pass either the Asset-Use Test or the Business Activities Test. Under the Asset-Use Test the income must be associated with U.S. assets used in, or held for use in, the conduct of a U.S. trade or business. Under the Business Activities Test, the activities of that trade or business conducted in the United States are a material factor in the realization of the income.

9. The taxable part of any U.S. source scholarship or fellowship grant received by a non-immigrant in "F," "J," "M," or "Q" status is treated as effectively connected with a trade or business in the United States.

dise, subject to some exceptions, are engaged in a trade or business in the United States; (5) individuals are taxed as if they are engaged in a trade or business in the United States on gains and losses from the sale or exchange of U.S. real property interests; and (6) income from the rental of real property may be treated as ECI if the taxpayer elects to do so. If the individual's only U.S. activity is trading in stocks, securities, or commodities (including hedging transactions) either directly for its own account or through a U.S. resident broker or other agent, then that person is not deemed to be engaging in a trade or business in the United States.

FDAP Income

While FDAP income generally consists of passive investment income, it could consist of other types of income.[10] FDAP income includes very generally income that is fixed, determinable, and periodic. Income is "fixed" when it is paid in amounts known ahead of time, "determinable" whenever there is a basis for figuring the amount to be paid, and "periodic" if it is paid from time to time. Income does not have to be paid annually or at regular intervals.[11] Income can be determinable or periodic, irrespective of whether the length of time during which the payments are made is increased or decreased.

FDAP income is taxed for U.S. federal income tax purposes at a flat 30 percent (or lower treaty rate, if applicable) and no deductions are allowed against such income. This tax rate applies to FDAP income or gains from U.S. sources, but only if they are not effectively connected with the taxpayer's U.S. trade or business.

The following items are examples of FDAP income: (i) dividends; (ii) interest; (iii) pensions and annuities; (iv) alimony; (v) real property income, such as rents, other than gains from the sale of real property; (vi) royalties; (vii) scholarships and fellowship grants; (viii) other grants, prizes, and awards;[12] (ix) a sales commission paid or credited monthly; (x) a commission paid for a single transaction; (xi) the distributable net income of an estate or trust that is FDAP income, and that must be distributed currently, or has been paid or credited during the tax year, to a

---

10. FDAP income should be reported on page four of IRS Form 1040NR, if a return is required.

11. Income can be FDAP income whether it is paid in a series of repeated payments or in a single lump sum.

12. Racing purses are FDAP income and racetrack operators must withhold 30 percent on any purse paid to a nonresident alien racehorse owner in the absence of definite information contained in a statement provided with an IRS Form W-8BEN that the owner has not raced, or does not intend to enter, a horse in another race in the United States during the tax year.

nonresident alien beneficiary;[13] (xii) a distribution or allocation from a U.S. partnership of FDAP income; (xiii) taxes, mortgage interest, or insurance premiums paid to, or for the account of, a nonresident alien landlord by a tenant under the terms of a lease; (xiv) prizes awarded to nonresident alien artists for pictures exhibited in the United States; (xv) purses paid to nonresident alien boxers for prize fights in the United States; and (xvi) prizes awarded to nonresident alien professional golfers in golfing tournaments in the United States.

Capital Gains

If the nonresident alien was present in the United States for less than 183 days during the tax year then he or she will not be taxed on capital gains, except for the following types of gains: (1) gains that are effectively connected with a trade or business in the United States during the tax year; (2) gains on the disposal of timber, coal, or domestic iron ore with a retained economic interest; (3) gains on certain transfers of all substantial rights to, or an undivided interest in, patents;[14] and (4) gains on the sale or exchange of original issue discount obligations. It is important to note that this 183-day test is not the same as the 183-day test used in the Substantial Presence Test. Tax treaties may contain provisions that reduce or eliminate taxation on capital gains.

U.S. Federal Income Tax Filing Rules

Nonresident aliens who are required to file an income tax return must use IRS Form 1040NR or IRS Form 1040NR-EZ. If required to file, there are specific rules on when to file. If the nonresident alien is an employee or self-employed person, and receives wages or non-employee compensation subject to U.S. income tax withholding, or if he or she has an office or place of business in the United States, then he or she generally must file by the fifteenth day of the fourth month after the tax year ends. For a person filing using a calendar year this is generally April 15. If the nonresident alien is not an employee or self-employed person who receives wages or non-employee compensation subject to U.S. income tax with-

---

13. Income derived by an insured nonresident alien from the surrender of, or at the maturity of, a life insurance policy can be FDAP income and subject to withholding tax. The proceeds are income to the extent they exceed the cost of the policy. However, certain payments received under a life insurance contract on the life of a terminally or chronically ill individual before death may not be subject to tax. This also applies to certain payments received for the sale or assignment of any portion of the death benefit under contract to a viatical settlement provider.

14. If the transfers were made before October 5, 1966.

holding, or if he or she does not have an office or place of business in the United States, then he or she must file by the fifteenth day of the sixth month after the tax year ends. For a person filing using a calendar year this is generally June 15.

Where the nonresident alien cannot file the return by the due date, he or she should file IRS Form 4868 by the regular due date of the return to request an automatic extension of time to file. It is very important that the return not be filed late. To be entitled to get any allowable deductions or credits, a true and accurate income tax return must be timely filed.

The following nonresident alien individuals, or other relevant persons, generally must file a U.S. federal income tax return: (1) nonresident alien individuals engaged or considered to be engaged in a trade or business in the United States during the year;[15] (2) nonresident alien individuals not engaged in a trade or business in the United States but that have U.S. income on which the tax liability was not satisfied by the withholding of tax at the source; (3) representatives or agents responsible for filing the return of an individual described in categories one or two above; (4) fiduciaries for a nonresident alien estate or trust; or (5) residents or domestic fiduciaries, or other persons, charged with the care of the person or property of a nonresident alien individual.[16] An income tax return also must be filed to claim a refund of overwithheld or overpaid tax or to claim the benefit of any deductions or credits. For instance, if the nonresident alien had no U.S. business activities but had income from real property that he or she chose to treat as effectively connected income, then he or she must timely file a true and accurate return to take any allowable deductions against that income.

If the nonresident alien was a student, teacher, or trainee temporarily present in the United States on an "F," "J," "M," or "Q" visa, then that person is deemed to have engaged in a trade or business in the United States. They must file IRS Form 1040NR (or IRS Form 1040NR-EZ) only if they had income that is subject to tax, such as wages, tips, scholarship and fellowship grants, dividends, etc. See discussion on foreign students and scholars below.

---

15. These individuals must file even if (i) their income did not come from a trade or business conducted in the United States; (ii) they had no income from U.S. sources; or (iii) their income is exempt from income tax. However, if their only U.S. source income is wages in an amount less than the personal exemption amount, then they are not required to file.

16. *See* Treas. Reg. § 1.6012-3(b) (1960).

Taxation of Foreign Students and Scholars

Foreign scholars, teachers, researchers, trainees, physicians, au pairs, summer camp workers, and other non-students in J-1, Q-1, or Q-2 non-immigrant status who have been in the United States less than two calendar years are considered nonresident aliens and are exempt from U.S. Social Security and Medicare taxes that normally are imposed on wage income and certain business income. However, foreign scholars, teachers, researchers, trainees, physicians, au pairs, summer camp workers, and other non-students in J-1, Q-1, or Q-2 non-immigrant status who have been in the United States for more than two calendar years are considered resident aliens and are therefore liable for U.S. Social Security and Medicare taxes on such income. When measuring an alien's date of entry for the purposes of determining the five calendar years or the two calendar years, the actual date of entry is not important. It is the calendar year of entry that is counted toward the two or five calendar years respectively. Thus, for example, a foreign student who enters the United States on December 31, 2008, counts 2008 as the first of his five years as an "exempt individual."

The IRS has issued regulations that clearly stipulate that the spouses and dependents of alien students, scholars, trainees, teachers, or researchers temporarily present in the United States in F-2, J-2, or M-2 status are not exempt from U.S. Social Security and Medicare taxes, and are fully liable for U.S. Social Security and Medicare taxes on any wages they earn in the United States because these aliens have not entered into the United States for the primary purpose of engaging in study, training, teaching, or research.

Alien students, scholars, trainees, teachers, or researchers in F-1, J-1, M-1, Q-1, or Q-2 status who change to a non-immigrant status other than F-1, J-1, M-1, Q-1, or Q-2 will become liable for U.S. Social Security and Medicare taxes in most cases on the day of the change of status. Teachers, trainees, and researchers in H-1b status, and alien nurses in H-1a status, are liable for U.S. Social Security and Medicare taxes from the first day of U.S. employment, regardless of whether they are nonresident or resident aliens, and regardless of whether their wages may or may not be exempt from U.S. federal income taxes under an applicable income tax treaty.

Foreign scholars, teachers, researchers, or trainees who arrive in the United States in O-1 status or TN status (from Canada or Mexico under the NAFTA treaty) are fully liable for U.S. Social Security and Medicare taxes if they are employed on the payroll of the university or other employer, regardless of whether or not they are resident or nonresident aliens unless the provisions of a Totalization Agreement relieve such aliens from liability for U.S. Social Security and Medicare taxes.

Under the rules pertaining to the Substantial Presence Test, foreign scholars, teachers, researchers, trainees (including medical interns), physicians, au pairs, summer camp workers, and other non-immigrants who arrive in the United States on J-1, Q-1, and Q-2 visas are considered to be "exempt individuals" (i.e., exempt from counting days of presence in the United States under the Substantial Presence Test) during the first two calendar years of their physical presence in the United States; and foreign students who arrive in the United States on F-1, J-1, M-1, Q-1 or Q-2 visas are considered to be exempt individuals during the first five calendar years of their physical presence in the United States. This means that foreign scholars, teachers, researchers, trainees, physicians, au pairs, summer camp workers, and other non-students who enter the United States on J-1, Q-1, or Q-2 visas are considered to be nonresident aliens during their first two calendar years in the United States; and foreign students who enter the United States on F-1, J-1, M-1, Q-1, or Q-2 visas are considered to be nonresident during their first five calendar years in the United States. Foreign scholars, teachers, researchers, trainees, physicians, au pairs, summer camp workers, and other non-students who enter the United States on J-1, Q-1, or Q-2 visas usually become resident aliens on January 1 of their third calendar year in the United States; and foreign students who enter the United States on F-1, J-1, M-1, Q-1 or Q-2 visas usually become resident aliens on January 1 of their sixth calendar year in the United States.

After an alien student, scholar, teacher, researcher, trainee, physician, au pair, summer camp worker, or other non-immigrant in F, J, M, or Q status has become a resident alien under the residency rules of the Code, then he or she loses the nonresident alien exemption from U.S. Social Security and Medicare taxes provided by the Code, and will become fully liable for such taxes.

Departing Alien

Prior to departing from the United States, aliens generally must obtain a certificate of compliance. This document, also popularly known as the sailing permit or departure permit must be secured from the IRS before leaving the United States. One will receive a sailing or departure permit after filing an IRS Form 1040-C or IRS Form 2063. Even upon leaving the United States and filing the requisite form, on departure, a departing alien must file an annual U.S. federal income tax return.

25
‾‾

THE "DESERVING VICTIM" IN IMMIGRATION LAW: VISAS FOR VICTIMS OF CRIME

Julie Dahlstrom[1]

OVERVIEW

Immigration law provides for a variety of mechanisms for victims of crime to receive lawful immigration status, regardless of whether the crime occurred in the United States or abroad. The law originally embodied a limited concept of victimization, both geographically and substantively, confining status to those who were victimized abroad and subject to the most egregious crimes, such as torture and persecution. Over time, the law has gradually expanded to embrace a more generous definition, providing status to individuals victimized in the United States and subject to a wider variety of crimes. This chapter will briefly review the historical treatment of victims in immigration law and then provide an introduction for practitioners to victim-based immigration relief, including U and T visas.[2]

BACKGROUND

Although immigration law has long embodied certain general discretionary relief provisions, the current regime derives largely from the Refugee Act of 1980, which established a statutory right to asylum for individuals who had suffered past persecution or who had a "well-founded fear of persecution on account of race, religion, nationality, membership in a

---

1. Julie Dahlstrom is the Managing Attorney of the Immigration Legal Assistance Program at Lutheran Social Services of New England. She is also Lecturer in Law and Director of the Human Trafficking Clinic at Boston University School of Law. Many thanks to Faustino Mora for his excellent research assistance.
2. For the purpose of simplification, the term "visa" is used throughout this chapter to refer to both nonimmigrant status and the visa. Generally, "non-immigrant status" refers to an immigration benefit provided to principal applicants in the United States whereas a "visa" is issued by U.S. Consulates and Embassies abroad.

509

particular social group or political opinion."[3] Refugee and asylum law
has evolved over time to embody a more expansive definition and protect
victims of domestic violence and persecution based on sexual orientation.
But few, if any, protections were available for individuals victimized by
crime in the United States until more recently.

Acknowledging the limitations of this approach, Congress passed the
Violence Against Women Act (VAWA) in 1994 and offered new forms of
immigration relief to victims of domestic violence in the United States.[4]
The legislation allowed battered spouses to apply for immigration status
or to "self-petition" if married to a lawful permanent resident or U.S. citizen spouse, along with certain other criteria. VAWA also created a similar
form of relief called Cancellation of Removal for battered spouses who
were in removal (i.e., deportation) proceedings. While a momentous victory, this important legislation still tied immigration status to marriage to
a qualifying relative and extended protection only to victims of domestic
violence, not other crimes.

In an effort to address these gaps, the 2000 Victims of Trafficking and
Violence Prevention Act (TVPA) significantly expanded immigration relief
by creating the U and T visa.[5] T visas were aimed at protecting victims of
human trafficking while U visas focused on victims of a wider variety of
crimes. A key feature of TVPA was the mandate that non-citizen crime
victims cooperate with law enforcement in order to qualify for immigration relief. Additionally, the TVPA created a more generous waiver available to victims of violent crime who may have triggered certain grounds
of inadmissibility. Thus, the legislation combined prosecutorial and
humanitarian goals in a novel way, leaving attorneys and applicants to
explore their limits.

U Visa for Victims of Violent Crime

To qualify for a U visa, the applicant must establish that she:[6]

1. suffered substantial physical or mental abuse as a result of having been a victim of a qualifying criminal activity;
2. has information concerning that criminal activity;

---

3. Immigration and Nationality Act (INA) § 208(a), 8 U.S.C. § 1158(a) (2012).
4. Violent Crime Control and Law Enforcement Act of 1994, Pub. L. No. 103-322, 108 Stat.
1796, 1902–55 (1994).
5. Victims of Trafficking and Violence Prevention Act, Pub. L. No. 106-386 Division A, 114
Stat. 1464 (2000).
6. Feminine pronouns have been used throughout this chapter for simplification, but victim-
based immigration relief is available to individuals regardless of gender, sexual identity, or
sexual orientation.

3. has been helpful, is being helpful, or is likely to be helpful in the investigation or prosecution of the crime;
4. that the criminal activity violated the laws of the United States or occurred in the United States (including in Indian country and military institutions) or the territories and possessions of the United States;[7] and
5. is admissible in the United States.

If the application is approved, the U visa provides for permission to remain and work in the United States for four years,[8] a pathway to lawful permanent residence,[9] and a way for derivative family members to apply for legal status.[10] Ten thousand U visas may be issued annually with additional visas available for derivative family members.[11] When the cap is reached, applicants are placed on a wait list and may qualify for deferred action and employment authorization until a visa becomes available.[12]

As the U visa is a fairly new immigration benefit, there remain many questions about its implementation. Although the TVPA passed in 2000, federal regulations were not promulgated until January 12, 2009.[13] In the interim, U.S. Citizenship and Immigration Services (USCIS) offered "interim relief" to those establishing prima facie eligibility, requiring all applicants to reapply for a U visa after the regulations took effect. USCIS did not adjudicate U visa applications until after January 2009, and the visa remains a somewhat novel form of relief.

Qualifying Criminal Activity

When evaluating eligibility for a U visa, the first question is whether the individual was a victim of "qualifying criminal activity."[14] The criminal activity must have either violated the laws of the United States or occurred within the United States, its territories, or its possessions. Crimes occurring outside of the United States generally do not qualify unless they otherwise violated the laws of the United States.

"Qualifying criminal activity" involves one or more of the following crimes: (1) rape, (2) torture, (3) trafficking, (4) incest, (5) domestic

---

7. INA § 101(a)(15)(U)(i), 8 U.S.C. § 1101(a)(15)(U)(i).
8. INA § 245(m), 8 U.S.C. § 1255(m) (2013).
9. 8 C.F.R. § 214.14(c)(7) (2013).
10. *Id.* § 214.14(f).
11. *Id.* § 214.14(d)(1).
12. *Id.* § 214.14(d)(2).
13. *Id.* § 214.14; USCIS Interim Final Rule, New Classification for Victims of Criminal Activity; Eligibility for 'U' Nonimmigrant Status, 72 Fed. Reg. 53014 (Sept. 17, 2007).
14. INA § 101(a)(15)(U)(iii), 8 U.S.C. § 1101(a)(15)(U)(iii); 8 C.F.R. § 214.14(a)(9).

violence, (6) sexual assault, (7) abusive sexual contact, (8) prostitution, (9) sexual exploitation, (10) female genital mutilation, (11) being held hostage, (12) peonage, (13) involuntary servitude, (14) slave trade, (15) kidnapping or abduction, (16) unlawful criminal restraint, (17) false imprisonment, (18) blackmail or extortion, (19) murder or manslaughter, (20) felonious assault, (21) witness tampering, (22) obstruction of justice, (23) perjury, (24) stalking, and (25) foreign labor contracting fraud.[15] Qualifying crimes also include the attempt, conspiracy, or solicitation to commit such crimes as well as "substantially similar" crimes, especially if the crime targets a vulnerable immigrant population.[16]

Practitioners should look to relevant state and federal criminal law to determine eligibility. It is not required that the perpetrator of the crime be charged with a qualifying crime but rather that the elements of the crime are met. For example, while robbery is not a recognized qualifying crime, an applicant may qualify if the applicant can show that the robbery involved the elements of qualifying crimes, such as felonious assault or attempted murder.

Direct and Indirect Victims

The TVPA adopts an expansive definition of who may be a victim, allowing both direct and indirect victims to qualify for U visas. A direct victim is a person who has suffered direct harm or who is directly or proximately harmed due to the criminal activity. This may include bystander victims, if they suffered unusually severe harm that resulted from witnessing the criminal activity. For example, if an applicant had a heart attack after witnessing a murder, she may qualify as a direct victim.[17]

Indirect victims may include:

1. qualifying family members of murder victims, manslaughter victims, and victims who are incapacitated or incompetent;[18] and
2. a "next friend," defined as a person who appears in a lawsuit to act for the benefit of an immigrant victim who is incapacitated, incompetent, or under the age of 16, and who has suffered sub-

---

15. INA § 101(a)(15)(U)(iii), 8 U.S.C. § 1101(a)(15)(U)(iii).

16. USCIS Fact Sheet, USCIS Publishes Rule for Nonimmigrant Victims of Criminal Activity (Sep. 7, 2007), *available at* http://www.uscis.gov/sites/default/files/files/pressrelease/U -VisaFS_05Sep07.pdf (emphasizing that USCIS will focus on the "myriad types of behavior that can constitute domestic violence, sexual abuse, trafficking, or other crimes [with] which vulnerable immigrants are often targeted").

17. USCIS Interim Final Rule, New Classification for Victims of Criminal Activity; Eligibility for 'U' Nonimmigrant Status, 72 Fed. Reg. 53014 (Sept. 17, 2007).

18. 8 C.F.R. § 214.14(a)(14)(i).

stantial physical or mental abuse as a result of being a victim of qualifying criminal activity.[19]

According to the Vermont Service Center, which adjudicates victim-based petitions, U.S. citizen children are considered incompetent or incapacitated and, therefore, parents may qualify as indirect victims if their child was a victim of a qualifying crime.[20] A common example is the parent of a child victim of sexual abuse.

Cooperation in the Investigation or Prosecution of the Crime

To qualify for a U visa, an individual must show that she "is helpful, is being helpful, or is likely to be helpful in the investigation or prosecution of the crime."[21] As evidence of cooperation, the applicant must receive a "U Non-immigrant Status Certification," on Form I-918, Supplement B, signed by a certifying official investigating or prosecuting the criminal activity.[22] Absent a signed Form I-918, Supplement B, the applicant cannot qualify for relief. Please note that the cooperation requirement continues beyond receipt of the U visa. The regulations specify that an applicant cannot refuse or fail to provide information that is "reasonably requested," and law enforcement retains the authority to withdraw certification at any time.[23]

A variety of agencies are empowered to issue U visa certifications, including federal, state, or local law enforcement agencies, prosecutors, judges, and other agency that investigates or prosecutes criminal activity.[24] Other potential certifying agencies include Child Protective Services, the Equal Employment Opportunity Commission, the U.S. Department of Labor, and the National Labor Relations Board. Some agencies have issued formal protocols establishing their internal procedure for issuing U visa certification.[25] Others may designate a contact person for certification requests.

---

19. *Id.* § 214.14(a)(7).
20. AILA VSC Liaison Committee's Minutes of VSC Stakeholders Meeting (August 20, 2009), *available at* www.aila.org. AILA InfoNet Doc. No. 09090265 (posted 9/2/09).
21. INA § 101(a)(15)(U)(i)(III), 8 U.S.C. § 1101(a)(15)(U)(i)(III).
22. 8 C.F.R. § 214.14(c)(2)(i).
23. *Id.* § 214.14(b)(3).
24. *Id.* § 214.14(c)(2)(i).
25. *See, e.g.*, U.S. Department of Labor, Certification of Supplement B Forms of U Nonimmigrant Visa Applications, Field Assistance Bulletin No. 2011-1 (April 28, 2011), *available at* http://www.dol.gov/whd/FieldBulletins/fab2011_1.htm; U.S. Equal Employment Opportunity Commission, EEOC Procedures for U Nonimmigrant Classification Certification

When requesting U visa certification, it is recommended that practitioners complete a draft Form I-918, Supplement B, and submit it to the certifying officer with a letter or memorandum outlining eligibility for certification. Every agency approaches certification differently, so it may be helpful to speak with practitioners in your area to find out tips for interacting with certifiers. If you encounter resistance, there are a variety of resources to educate law enforcement, including the "Tool Kit for Law Enforcement Use of the U-Visa" prepared by VERA Institute of Justice and Legal Momentum as well as the "U Visa Law Enforcement Certification Resource Guide" prepared by the Department of Homeland Security.[26] USCIS's Office of Policy and Strategy and the Vermont Service Center also offers training to law enforcement personnel, which can be requested by e-mail at T-U-VAWATraining@uscis.dhs.gov. Furthermore, Scott Whelan, USCIS Adjudications Officer with Office of Policy and Strategy, is available to answer questions from law enforcement agencies about the U visa certification process at (202) 272-8137 or via e-mail at Scott.Whelan@dhs.gov.

Substantial Physical or Mental Abuse

The applicant must establish that she suffered substantial physical or mental abuse as a result of the qualifying criminal activity.[27] Physical or mental abuse is defined as an "injury or harm to the victim's physical person, or harm or impairment of the emotional or psychological soundness of the victim."[28] While "no single factor is a prerequisite to establish that the abuse suffered was substantial," one act or a series of acts taken together may constitute physical or mental abuse. Emotional harm alone may be sufficient. In such cases, it is essential to clearly document the nature of psychological harm through the applicant's declaration and supporting documents, such as a psychological evaluation, and/or letters of support from witnesses or victim service providers.

(July 3, 2008), *available at* http://iwp.legalmomentum.org/immigration/u-visa/government-memoranda-and-factsheets/U%20VISA_EEOC%20Certification%20Memo_7.3.08.pdf.

26. VERA Institute of Justice and Legal Momentum, Tool Kit for Law Enforcement Use of the U-Visa (Nov. 2010), *available at* http://www.acasa.us/pdfs/U-Visa-Toolkit%20%20FINAL.pdf; U.S. Department of Homeland Security, U Visa Law Enforcement Certification Resource Guide for Federal, State, Local, Tribal and Territorial Law Enforcement (2011), *available at* http://www.dhs.gov/xlibrary/assets/dhs_u_visa_certification_guide.pdf.

27. INA § 101(a)(15)(U)(i)(I), 8 U.S.C. § 1101(a)(15)(U)(i)(I).

28. 8 C.F.R. § 214.14(a)(8). "Substantial" refers to both the severity of the injury and of the overall scheme of abuse inflicted by the perpetrator. *See id.* § 214.14(b)(1).

Application Process

To apply for a U visa, applicants must complete Form I-918, Application for U Non-immigrant Status, and attach two passport-sized photographs. In support of the application, an applicant must submit the original, signed Form I-918, Supplement B, Law Enforcement Certification, in addition to his or her declaration and any supporting evidence. If she is inadmissible for reasons discussed in section V(A) below, the applicant may also submit a waiver application on Form I-192, Application for Advance Permission to Enter as Non-immigrant, and attach the filing fee or a request for fee waiver on Form I-912. Furthermore, the applicant may submit Form I-918, Supplement A, to apply for any derivative family members. Derivative applications may be submitted concurrently with the U visa application or after approval.

T VISAS FOR VICTIMS OF HUMAN TRAFFICKING

The Victims of Trafficking and Violence Prevention Act (TVPA) of 2000 also established a separate form of immigration relief for victims of severe forms of human trafficking.[29] Recognizing that human trafficking investigations are heavily dependent on victim cooperation, the T visa was designed to provide protection to victims while creating an additional incentive for victims to cooperate with law enforcement. In order to be eligible for the T visa, each applicant must demonstrate that she:

1. is or has been a victim of a severe form of trafficking in person;
2. is physically present in the United States due to trafficking;
3. has complied with any reasonable request for assistance in the investigation or prosecution of acts of trafficking in persons (if they are over 18);
4. would suffer extreme hardship involving unusual and severe harm if removed from the United States;[30] and
5. is admissible in the United States.

The T visa provides for permission to remain and work in the United States for a maximum of four years,[31] a pathway to lawful permanent residence,[32] and a means for derivatives to apply for status and eventual

---

29. INA § 101(a)(15)(T), 8 U.S.C. § 1101(a)(15)(T).
30. INA § 101(a)(15)(T), 8 U.S.C. § 1101(a)(15)(T); 8 C.F.R. § 214.11(b).
31. INA § 101(i)(2), 8 U.S.C. § 1101(i)(2).
32. INA § 245(l), 8 U.S.C. § 1255(l).

permanent residence.[33] Five thousand T visas may be issued annually to principal applicants, but this cap has never been reached.[34]

Victims of human trafficking may be eligible for both U and T visas. Therefore, it is important to keep in mind that there are certain benefits afforded to recipients of T visas that are unavailable for U visa recipients. First, T visa approval will trigger the issuance of a certification letter from the U.S. Department of Health and Human Services. This allows the applicant to qualify for the Match Grant program or certain public benefits, including food stamps and refugee cash assistance.[35] This can be an enormous benefit to your client. Second, T visa recipients may be eligible to adjust status more quickly than U visa recipients if the investigation or prosecution of human trafficking is complete. Third, since the cap for T visas has never been reached, a visa may be more readily available. In addition, the T and U visa have different eligibility and waiver requirements that should be considered before deciding whether to submit a T or U visa application.

Victim of Human Trafficking

"Human trafficking" is defined as "severe forms of trafficking in persons," meaning:

1. sex trafficking in which a commercial sex act is induced by force, fraud, or coercion, or in which the person induced to perform such act has not attained 18 years of age; or
2. the recruitment, harboring, transportation, provision, or obtaining of a person for labor or services, through the use of force, fraud, or coercion for the purpose of subjection to involuntary servitude, peonage, debt bondage, or slavery.[36]

Common examples of sex trafficking include individuals involved in brothels, massage parlors, nail salons, and other industries wherein sexual services are provided. In the labor context, cases are found in a variety of industries, including hospitality, agriculture, factories, and seasonal work, as well as more traditional settings such as domestic work. Human traf-

---

33. INA § 101(a)(15)(T)(ii), 8 U.S.C. § 1101(a)(15)(T)(ii); 8 C.F.R. § 214.11(o)(1).
34. INA § 245(l)(4), 8 U.S.C. § 1255(l)(4).
35. This certification letter may also be issued upon the grant of continued presence, a temporary form of immigration relief for victims of human trafficking who are potential witnesses in a trafficking prosecution, or upon application to the Office for Refugee Resettlement for child victims. If the applicant has already received a certification letter from the Department of Health and Human Services, she will not receive the letter again after the T visa is granted.
36. 22 U.S.C. § 7102(8); 8 C.F.R. § 214.11(a).

ficking differs from human smuggling. Human trafficking is generally a crime against the person, whereas human smuggling is a crime against the border, which involves individuals entering the United States unlawfully.

When evaluating whether the applicant is a victim of trafficking, it is important to gather facts and conduct a careful legal analysis to see if the standard is met. Keep in mind that physical violence is not required, and there need not be transportation across borders (state or international) to qualify. Furthermore, traffickers often use more subtle forms of coercion, such as threats of deportation, connections to law enforcement, and knowledge about the location of the individual's family, to instill fear.[37] Therefore, it is essential to build trust with your client and to elicit information related to her relationship with the trafficker, including any cultural considerations, to determine whether she meets the definition. It is often helpful to work with survivor-led or survivor-informed programs to build trust and ensure that a survivor's needs are met during the legal process.

Presence in the United States

A visa applicant must be physically present in the United States, American Samoa, or the Commonwealth of the Northern Mariana Islands to qualify.[38] Therefore, individuals who are outside of the United States do not qualify. Furthermore, the applicant must show that she is in the United States "on account of" human trafficking. According to the regulations, the physical presence requirement includes applicants who (1) are present because they are being held in some sort of severe form of trafficking in persons situation, (2) were recently liberated from a severe form of trafficking in persons, or (3) were subject to severe forms of trafficking in persons at some point in the past and remain present in the United States for reasons directly related to the original trafficking in persons. It is not required that the applicant's entry be related to the human trafficking. However, in such cases, it is important to highlight facts related to human trafficking that make it difficult for the applicant to return to her country, such as the importance of continued cooperation with law enforcement, need for access to medical and mental health treatment to heal from human trafficking, and the fear of retaliation from traffickers in the applicant's home country.[39]

---

37. 8 C.F.R. § 214.11(a).

38. *Id.* § 214.11(g).

39. *See id.* § 214.11(f)(4)(g). When the trafficking survivor has been liberated from the trafficking situation, the applicant must demonstrate that there has not been a "clear chance to leave" and return to her country of origin since exiting the trafficking situation. USCIS has considered relevant factors to explain why the applicant has not returned to her home country, including traumatization resulting from the trafficking, risk of re-victimization

Compliance with Any Reasonable Request for Assistance

Similar to the U visa context, adult applicants must comply with "any reasonable requests for assistance" from law enforcement agencies and prosecutors in the investigation or prosecution of human trafficking.[40] A law enforcement agency is defined as a law enforcement agency that has the responsibility and authority for the detection, investigation, or prosecution of severe forms of trafficking in persons. Qualified law enforcement agencies may include the U.S. Department of Justice, the offices of the United States Attorneys, the Federal Bureau of Investigation, USCIS, Immigration and Customs Enforcement, United States Marshals Service, and the Diplomatic Security Service of the United States Department of State.[41]

If the applicant has not yet cooperated with law enforcement, practitioners may be in the position to initiate contact. Prior to making a referral, one should explain to the client clearly what cooperation may entail, including the risks of alerting law enforcement to the applicant's presence in the United States. This could include the issuance of a Notice to Appear if the client is undocumented or potential criminal liability if the client engaged in prostitution or other crimes. If the client consents, the practitioner should report the trafficking incident to any appropriate federal, state, and local law enforcement agency. In addition, it is recommended to contact the DOJ Civil Rights Division's Trafficking in Persons and Worker Exploitation Task Force complaint hotline and/or fax a request for investigation to the DOJ Civil Rights Division's Trafficking Unit. After reporting to law enforcement, officers may seek to interview the applicant to investigate the human trafficking case.[42] Throughout this process, whenever possible, practitioners should express to law enforcement the applicant's willingness to cooperate and request T visa certification. It is very important to carefully document any communication with law enforcement, especially requests for certification.

---

in home country, and lack of access to vital victim services in her country of origin. Also, if the applicant has returned to her country after the trafficking occurred, she will need to explain affirmatively about trips made and why travel was related to human trafficking. *See id.* § 214.11(g)(3).

40. Minors under the age of 18 are exempt from this requirement. INA § 101(a)(15)(T), 8 USC § 1101(a)(15)(T).

41. 8 C.F.R. § 214.11(a).

42. It is important to note that the applicant can still qualify for a T visa even if law enforcement chooses not to investigate the human trafficking incident. In such cases, it is important to carefully document any reports made to law enforcement to submit as secondary evidence of the applicant's cooperation.

Unlike in the U visa context, certification from law enforcement is not required to receive a T visa. However, Form I-914, Law Enforcement Declaration, signed by federal law enforcement, is the best primary evidence of cooperation.[43] Certification by state and local law enforcement, while probative, is secondary evidence of cooperation.[44] If unable to obtain certification, practitioners should document any attempts to cooperate and can submit any credible secondary evidence, including:

1. evidence that the victim received continued presence, a temporary form of immigration status for victims of human trafficking who are potential witnesses in a trafficking prosecution;[45]
2. a letter from U.S. Department of Health and Human Services, certifying that the applicant is a victim of human trafficking and eligible for public benefits;
3. any other "credible and relevant evidence" of cooperation, including a copy of investigation request sent to the U.S. Department of Justice, e-mail correspondence with law enforcement, and a copy of business cards for law enforcement agents.

Please note that there is a limited cooperation exception for those who are unable to assist law enforcement "due to psychological or physical trauma."[46] While there are not clear guidelines regarding the trauma exception, an exception will only be granted in exceptional circumstances. Therefore, if attempting to qualify for the exception, it is very important to clearly document any evidence of trauma through the applicant's declaration, medical or psychological evaluations, medical records, and/or letters of support.

Hardship

T visa applicants must establish "extreme hardship involving unusual and severe harm upon removal" to their country of origin. This is a heightened standard, unlike the "extreme hardship" often used in immigration

---

43. 8 C.F.R. § 214.11(f)(1).

44. TVPA mandated that the definition of qualified law enforcement agency be broadened to encompass state and local law enforcement, but USCIS has not yet implemented this section of the law. Pursuant to the policy articulated in an April 15, 2004, memorandum, USCIS is awaiting further guidance prior to implementation.

45. Continued presence is available if "after an assessment, it is determined [by federal law enforcement] that such individual is a victim of a severe form of trafficking and a potential witness to such trafficking in order to effectuate prosecution of those responsible." 28 C.F.R. § 1100.35.

46. INA § 1101(a)(15)(T)(iii), 8 U.S.C. § 1101(a)(15)(T)(iii).

law.[47] Therefore, it is important to carefully assess any considerations making return difficult, including a history of domestic violence in his/her country of origin and the effect of losing access to medical or psychological services not available in home country. Although economic need is not a factor when considering hardship, it may be relevant if it makes the applicant particularly susceptible to revictimization.

Application Process

To apply for a T visa, applicants must complete Form I-914, Application for T Non-immigrant Status, and attach three passport-sized photographs.[48] In support of the application, an applicant must submit the original, signed Form I-914, Supplement B, Law Enforcement Certification, and/or any secondary evidence of cooperation, unless the applicant is a minor or the trauma exception applies. If she is inadmissible for reasons discussed below, the applicant also should submit a waiver application on Form I-192, Application for Advance Permission to Enter as Non-immigrant, and the filing fee or a request for a fee waiver. Furthermore, the applicant may submit Form I-914, Supplement A, to apply for any derivative family members at the time of filing or when the visa is approved.

GENERAL ISSUES FOR U AND T VISA APPLICANTS

Admissibility

To qualify for a U or T visa, the applicant generally must be "admissible." Certain grounds of inadmissibility may result in the denial of an application for entry or extension of status.[49] Common grounds include: (1) entry without inspection, (2) certain criminal convictions, (3) prostitution, (4) unlawful presence bars, (5) material misrepresentation to obtain an immigration benefit, (6) false claims to U.S. citizenship, and (7) prior removal orders. The TVPA provides for a very expansive waiver of many grounds of inadmissibility. In fact, the U and T visa waiver is more gener-

---

47. USCIS considers a variety of factors, looking to the totality of circumstances, when determining whether the hardship standard is met. Considerations include but are not limited to the applicant's age and personal circumstances; serious physical or mental illness of the applicant that requires medical or psychological attention not reasonably available in the foreign country; the physical and psychological consequences of the trafficking activity; and the impact on the applicant of loss of access to U.S. courts and criminal justice system for purposes such as protection of the applicant and criminal and civil redress for the acts of trafficking. 8 C.F.R. § 214.11(i).

48. *See id.* INA § 214.11(d)(2).

49. INA § 212, 8 U.S.C. § 1182.

ous than many forms of immigration relief, waiving certain grounds of inadmissibility, such as false claims of U.S. citizenship and aggravated felonies, which are clear bars to status in other contexts.[50]

In order to apply, the applicant must complete Form I-192 with the required fee or Form I-912, Request for Fee Waiver. In addition, the applicant should submit supporting documentation, including her statement, establishing why it is in the public interest for her to remain in the United States.[51] When deciding the waiver, USCIS will evaluate social and humanitarian concerns in light of any adverse factors of inadmissibility. In the T visa context unlike the U visa context, the applicant must additionally prove that the inadmissibility grounds were caused by or incident to the victimization.

Derivative Family Members

Certain qualified family members are eligible to accompany or follow to join U or T principal applicants, regardless of whether they are living in the United States or overseas.[52] Whether a family member is "qualified" depends on his or her relationship to the principal, the age of the principal at filing, and the age of the derivative.[53] U and T principal applicants who are over 21 years at the age of filing may file for their spouses and unmarried children under 21. If under 21 years of age, U and T principals

---

50. The U and T visa have different guidelines regarding which grounds of inadmissibility may be waived and the standard for granting a waiver. For T visa applicants, all grounds of inadmissibility may be waived with the exception of certain security and terrorism grounds, international child abduction, and renouncing U.S. citizenship to avoid taxes. Such grounds may be waived if it is in the "national interest" *and* the activities triggering inadmissibility were caused by or incident to the victimization. In the U visa context, the waiver is even more generous, pardoning all inadmissibility grounds except for those who are Nazis, participants in genocide, or persons who committed, ordered, incited, assisted or otherwise participated in torture or extrajudicial killings. INA § 212(d)(14), 8 U.S.C. § 1182(d)(14). Furthermore, the applicant need only establish that it is in the "public or national interest." The activities triggering the waiver need not be tied to the applicant's victimization.

51. 8 C.F.R. § 212.17(b)(1).

52. INA § 101(a)(15)(U)(ii), 8 U.S.C. § 1101(a)(15)(U)(ii); INA § 101(a)(15)(T)(ii), 8 U.S.C. § 1101(a)(15)(T)(ii).

53. The qualifying relationship must exist at the time of filing and at the date of adjudication. 8 C.F.R. § 214.14(f)(4). Also, the age of the principal and beneficiary is fixed at the time of filing. USCIS issued interim guidance regarding age-out protection for derivative U non-immigrant status holders on October 24, 2012, and practitioners should consult this memorandum for more detailed advice regarding the aging out of derivative beneficiaries. *See* USCIS Interim Policy Memorandum, Age-Out Protection for Derivative U Nonimmigrant Status Holders: Pending Petitions, Initial Approvals, and Extensions of Status (Oct. 24, 2012).

may file for their spouse, children under 21, parents, and unmarried siblings under age 18. Derivative family members who are perpetrators of the qualifying crime are not eligible to receive U or T visas.[54]

Travel

While U and T visa recipients theoretically are eligible to travel overseas, great caution should be exercised when advising clients to travel. Overseas travel is risky for a variety of reasons. First, if the individual has accrued more than six months out of status prior to issuance of the visa, she may trigger the three- or ten-year bar, preventing reentry into the United States. While this ground of inadmissibility may be waived, the individual will not know whether the application is approved until after exiting from the United States, and there is a risk that she cannot reenter. Second, to remain eligible for U or T visa adjustment of status, an applicant must establish continuous physical presence in the United States. Given that continuous presence is interrupted by "any period in excess of 90 days or for any periods in the aggregate of 180 days," the visa recipient may be ineligible to adjust status if travel is longer than the authorized period.[55]

Adjustment of Status

U and T visa holders may adjust to permanent residence after three years of continuous physical presence in the United States.[56] T visa holders may be able to adjust their status even earlier if they can demonstrate that the human trafficking investigation or prosecution is complete. In the U visa context, qualifying family members who never held a U visa can also apply for status at the green card stage.[57] In such cases, the qualifying family member must establish that she was never admitted in U non-immigrant status, and that either family member or the U-1 principal applicant would suffer extreme hardship if the qualifying family member is not allowed to remain in or be admitted to the United States. To apply for such family members, the principal must file an immigrant petition on Form I-929, Petition for Qualifying Family Member of a U-1 Nonimmigrant, concurrently or subsequent to filing their Form I-485, Application for Adjustment of Status.

---

54. INA § 214(o)(1), 8 U.S.C. § 1184(o)(1); 8 C.F.R. § 214.11(c). Applicants for U and T visas also cannot file a non-immigrant or immigrant visa petition for the person who abused their child. INA § 204(a)(1)(L).
55. 8 C.F.R. § 245.24(a)(1).
56. *Id.*
57. *Id.* § 245.24(g).

TABLE OF CASES

Alwan v. Ashcroft, 388 F.3d 507 (5th Cir. 2004)   473 n.25
Am. Acad. of Religion v. Napolitano, 573 F.3d 115 (2d Cir. 2009)   480 n.69, 481 n.71, 481 n.74
Matter of A-M-E- & J-G-U-, 24 I. & N. Dec. 69 (B.I.A. 2007)   329 n.99, 330 n.103
Amfani v. Ashcroft, 328 F.3d 719 (3d Cir. 2003)   329 n.94
Amilcar-Orellana v. Mukasey, 551 F.3d 86 (1st Cir. 2008)   331 n.108
Amtel Group of Florida v. Yongmahapakorn, ARB Case No. 04-087, 2004-LCA-00006, slip op. (Sept. 29, 2006)   166 n.83
Angel v. Ridge, Case No. 2004-cv-4121, 2005 U.S. Dist. LEXIS 10667 (S.D. Ill. May 25, 2005)   478 n.56
Apartment Management Co., 88-INA-215 (Feb. 2, 1989)   245 n.22
Aragon-Ayon v. INS, 206 F.3d 847 (9th Cir. 2000)   384 n.54
Matter of Aramark Corporation, 2008-PER-00181 (BALCA Jan. 8, 2009)   175 n.18
Arizona, United States v., No. 2:10-cv-01413-SRB (9th Cir. 2011)   60 n.19
Arizona v. United States, 132 S. Ct. 2492 (2012)   44 n.53
Matter of Arjani, 12 I. & N. Dec. 649 (R.C. 1967)   153 n.17
Arteaga v. INS, 863 F.2d 1227 (9th Cir. 1988)   332 n.114
Arteaga v. Mukasey, 511 F.3d 940 (9th Cir. 2007)   331 n.108
Matter of Arturo, 24 I. & N. Dec. 459 (B.I.A. 2008)   405
Matter of Aruna, 24 I. & N. Dec. 492 (B.I.A. 2008)   393 n.118, 394
Matter of A-S-B-, 24 I. & N. Dec. 493 (B.I.A. 2008)   461 n.86
Asere v. Gonzales, 439 F.3d 378 (7th Cir. 2006)   463 n.97
Aslam v. Mukasey, 531 F. Supp. 2d 736 (E.D. Va. 2008)   475 n.34
Matter of Assaad, 23 I. & N. Dec. 553 (B.I.A. 2003)   463 n.96
Ass'n of Data Processing Serv. Orgs., Inc. v. Camp, 397 U.S. 150 (1970)   477 n.48
Matter of A-T-, 24 I. & N. Dec. 296 (B.I.A. 2007)   324 n.50, 330 n.107

B
Matter of B-, 20 I. & N. Dec. 427 (B.I.A. 1991)   333 n.124
Matter of B-, 21 I. & N. Dec. 66 (B.I.A. 1995)   346 n.224
Matter of B-, 21 I. & N. Dec. 287 (B.I.A. 1996)   387 n.69
Matter of Babaisakov, 24 I. & N. Dec. 306 (B.I.A. 2007)   390 n.100, 401 n.155, 402
Bah v. Gonzales, 462 F.3d 637 (6th Cir. 2006)   330 n.107
Matter of Bahta, 22 I. & N. Dec. 1381 (B.I.A. 2000)   388 n.82
Balazoski v. INS, 932 F.2d 638 (7th Cir. 1991)   323 n.42
Balliu v. Gonzales, 467 F.3d 609 (7th Cir. 2006)   324 n.49, 342 n.195
Balogun v. U.S. Att'y Gen., 425 F.3d 1356 (11th Cir. 2005)   391 n.103
Baron-Medina, United States v., 187 F.3d 1144 (9th Cir. 1999)   399 n.147
Matter of Barrett, 20 I. & N. Dec. 171 (B.I.A. 1990)   392
Matter of Beckford, 22 I. & N. Dec. 1216 (B.I.A. 2000)   458 n.67
Bell v. Reno, 218 F.3d 86 (2d Cir. 2000)   384 n.54
Benitez-Ramos v. Holder, 589 F.3d 426 (7th Cir. 2009)   329 n.98, 330 n.106, 331 n.108
Bennett v. Spear, 520 U.S. 154 (1997)   476 n.42
Bernal v. Fainter, 467 U.S. 216 (1984)   60 n.19
Berroteran-Melendez v. INS, 955 F.2d 1251 (9th Cir. 1992)   325 n.60, 325 n.61
Biwot v. Gonzales, 403 F.3d 1094 (9th Cir. 2005)   72 n.83

T
Taalebinezhaad v. Chertoff, 581 F. Supp. 2d 243 (D. Mass. 2008)   479 n.58
Tang v. Chertoff, 493 F. Supp. 2d 148 (D. Mass. 2007)   474 n.32
Tapia-Martinez v. Gonzalez, 482 F.3d 417 (6th Cir. 2007)   463 n.97
Tapiero de Orjuela v. Gonzales, 423 F.3d 666 (7th Cir. 2005)   329 n.97
Taylor v. United States, 495 U.S. 575 (1990)   389, 399 n.146
Matter of Tekkote, a division of Jen-Coat, Inc., 2008-PER-00218 (BALCA Jan. 5, 2009)   175 n.18
Matter of Terixeira, 21 I. & N. Dec. 316 (B.I.A. 1996)   409 n.197
Terrace v. Thompson, 263 U.S. 197 (1923)   59 n.18
Tewabe v. Gonzales, 446 F.3d 533 (4th Cir. 2006)   341 n.187
Matter of Tijerina-Villarreal, 13 I. & N. Dec. 327 (B.I.A. 1969)   355 n.12
Matter of Toboso-Alfonso, 20 I. & N. Dec. 819 (A.G. 1994)   329 n.94
Tokatly v. Ashcroft, 371 F.3d 613 (9th Cir. 2004)   400 n.152
Matter of Toro, 17 I. & N. Dec. 340 (B.I.A. 1980)   66, 66 n.56
Matter of Tran, 21 I. & N. Dec. 291 (B.I.A. 1996)   395 n.129
Travis v. Reno, 12 F. Supp. 2d. 921 (W.D. Wis. 1998)   60 n.25
Troxel v. Granville, 530 U.S. 57 (2000)   64, 64 n.40, 64 n.43
Truax v. Raich, 239 U.S. 33 (1915)   59 n.18
Tunis v. Gonzales, 447 F.3d 547 (7th Cir. 2006)   339 n.168
Matter of T-Z-, 24 I. & N. Dec. 163 (B.I.A. 2007)   323 n.35

U
Ucelo-Gomez v. Mukasey, 509 F.3d 70 (2d Cir. 2007)   331 n.108
Uddin v. USCIS, 437 F. App'x 196 (3d Cir. 2011)   471 n.20
Umana-Ramos v. Holder, 724 F.3d 667 (6th Cir. 2013)   330 n.105
Umanzor-Alvarado v. INS, 896 F.2d 14 (1st Cir. 1990)   332 n.114
Un v. Gonzales, 415 F.3d 205 (1st Cir. 2005)   324 n.49, 342 n.195
United Parcel Service, 90-INA-90 (Mar. 28, 1991)   255 n.79
Urbina-Mejia v. Holder, 597 F.3d 360 (6th Cir. 2010)   331 n.108
Uzama v. Holder, 629 F.3d 440 (4th Cir. 2011)   331 n.108

V
Valansi v. Ashcroft, 278 F.3d 203 (3d Cir. 2002)   390 n.94
Valdiviezo-Galdamez v. Att'y Gen. of U.S., 663 F.3d 582 (3d Cir. 2011)   330 n.105, 331 n.108, 333 n.119
Valenzuela-Bernal, United States v., 458 U.S. 858 (1982)   40 n.34
Valona v. U.S. Parole Comm'n, 165 F.3d 508 (7th Cir. 1998)   475 n.35
Vance v. Terrazas, 444 U.S. 252 (1980)   56 n.6
Matter of Vasquez-Munoz, 23 I. & N. Dec. 207 (B.I.A. 2001)   397 n.141, 398 n.143
Vazquez-Flores, United States v., 265 F.3d 1122 (10th Cir. 2001)   388 n.85
Matter of Velasquez, 25 I. & N. Dec. 278 (B.I.A. 2010)   396 n.133
Velazquez v. Ashcroft, 103 F. App'x 142 (9th Cir. 2004)   348 n.243
Matter of V-F-D-, 23 I. & N. Dec. 859 (B.I.A. 2006)   384 n.55
Matter of Vigil, 19 I. & N. Dec. 572 (B.I.A. 1988)   332 n.114
Villa v. DHS, 607 F. Supp. 2d 359 (N.D.N.Y. 2009)   475 n.37

INDEX

Insanity, 23–24
Inter-Governmental Service
    Agreement (IGSA), 68
Internal Revenue Service (IRS), no-
    match letters and, 221. *See also*
    Tax
International cultural exchange visa,
    134, 143–145, 204
International organization visas,
    123–126
Interns, 134–135
Interpreter, right to, 73, 454–455
Interview
    immigrant visa application,
        102–103, 102 n.51
    naturalization, 368–370
    non-immigrant visa application,
        87–88, 89–90
Intracompany transferee, 138–141, 271
Investor visa, treaty, 117–118, 119–121,
    214, 268–269, 269–270. *See also*
    EB-5 regional centers
IRCA. *See* Immigration Reform and
    Control Act (IRCA)
IRS. *See* Internal Revenue Service (IRS)
ITIN. *See* Individual Taxpayer
    Identification Number (ITIN)

J
J-1 program sponsorship, 135–136
J-1 visa, 9, 92 n.34, 134–136, 418
    for medical graduates, 204–208
    taxes and, 498–499, 505, 506, 507
J-2 visa, 92 n.34, 418, 506
Japanese immigrants, 21–22
Job description, for Labor Certification,
    243–249
Job Zones, 246–247
Joseph hearings, 447
Journalism, 133–134
Judges
    discretion of, with immigration
        consequences of criminal
        conviction, 376
    federal court, 465–466
    immigration court, 440
Judicial branch. *See* Supreme Court

Jurisdiction
    Administrative Procedure Act and,
        475–476, 475 n.41
    with appeals, 470–471
    bars to, in federal court, 466–467,
        470–471
    foreign, over military, 434 n.56
    Mandamus Act and, 474 n.29, 475
Jus sanguinis, 354
Jus soli, 354
Justice Department, 5–8
Juvenile delinquency adjudications,
    407–408
Juveniles. *See* Children

K
K visa, 62, 81 n.16, 82, 82 n.18, 84 n.15,
    108 n.5, 136–138, 313–315, 418
K-1 visa, 136–137, 313–314
K-3 visas, 137–138
Kidnapping, 387
Korean War, 428

L
L visa, 82 n.19, 94 n.37, 271–273, 418
L-1 visa, 138–140
    corporate restructuring and,
        186–187
    layoffs and, 193–194
L-1A visa, 139–140
L-1B visa, 140
Labor Certification (LC)
    applicant evaluation in, 254–256
    audit file, 256–259
    audits, 173–180
    corporate restructuring and, 189
    debarment with, 173, 178, 180
    determination, 261
    enforcement actions with, 178–180
    experience gained with employer
        in, 176, 245–246
    foreign-language requirement in,
        176
    history of, 241–243
    investigation, 178–179
    job description for, 243–249
    job requirements in, abnormal, 177

Representation
  dual, 49–50, 53
  vesting of, 52
Required recruitment effort, 251–254
Research, by medical graduates
  B-1 visa for, 204
  J-1 visa for, 207
Research Scholar, 207
Researchers, 277–278
Residence
  asylum and, 321–323
  continuous, 298–299, 359–360
  defined, 359 n.34
  for naturalization, maintenance of,
    297–300
  naturalization and, 359–360
  in tax code, 495–496
Respondents, in federal court, 467–468
Respondent's Answering Brief, 473
Restructuring, corporate
  adjustment of status and, 190, 196,
    198–199
  E visa and, 187–188, 193–194
  H-1B visa and, 184–186
  L-1 visa and, 186–187, 193–194
  Labor Certification and, 177, 189,
    194–195
  labor condition application and,
    185–186
  name changes in, 186–187
  permanent residence process and,
    188–189
Return, intent to, 289–290
Returning resident visa, 296–297
Rights. *See* Alien rights
RIR. *See* Reduction in recruitment
  (RIR)
Rural EB-5 center, 488

S
S visa, 81 n.16, 84 n.15, 108 n.5, 146,
  309, 418
Sailing permit, 507
SB-1 visa, 296–297
Search and seizure, unlawful, 64–65
Seasonal workers, 27, 130–131
Securities attorney, in EB-5 regional
  centers, 487

Security clearance, 368, 421, 423, 424
  n.57, 438
Selective Service registration, 364,
  365–366, 379, 413–414, 415, 421
Senate Homeland Security and
  Government Accountability
  Committee, 12
Senate Subcommittee on Immigration,
  Refugees, and Border Security, 12
Sentence modification, 407
September 11 attacks, 2, 89 n.31, 425,
  428, 430, 433
SESAs. *See* State Employment Security
  Agencies (SESAs)
SEVIS. *See* Student Exchange Visitor
  Information System (SEVIS)
Sex offender registration, 379
Sexual abuse, of minor, 384, 387
Short-Term Research Scholar, 207
Sixth Amendment, 51, 73, 375, 450 n.35
Smuggling, 380
"Snitch" visa, 146. *See also* S visa
Social distinction, asylum and, 329–330
Social group membership, asylum and,
  328–331
Social Security Administration (SSA),
  no-match letters and, 221
Social Security number. *See also* No-
  match letter(s)
  marriage and, 62–63
  recognizing invalid, 231
  taxes and, 500
Social Security tax, 506
Specialized knowledge professionals,
  140, 272
Specialty occupation position, 152–153,
  164–165
Specialty worker visa, 117–118,
  126–128. *See also* H-1B visa
Specific Vocational Preparation (SVP),
  246
SSA. *See* Social Security
  Administration (SSA)
Staff
  embassy, 110–111
  household, of international
    organization representatives,
    123–124, 125–126

Stalking, 380–381, 395
Standard Occupational Classification
    System, 158
Standard Vocational Preparation code,
    158
State Department, 8–9
State Employment Security Agencies
    (SESAs), 242
State health department waivers, for
    medical graduates, 208–209
State immigration law, 34–35, 35–38,
    41–43, 59–60
State Workforce Agency (SWA), 242,
    253
Student Exchange Visitor Information
    System (SEVIS), 87, 122
Student visa, 87, 98, 122–123, 141,
    506–507. *See also* F-1 visa; J-1 visa
Subsidiary, in L-1 classification, 139
Substantial Presence Test, for tax,
    498–499, 507
Succession plan, 54
Summary affirmance, 461–462
Supervised recruitment, 177–178,
    259–260
Support Our Law Enforcement and
    Safe Neighborhoods Act, 44 n.53
Supremacy Clause, 37
Supreme Court, 12–13
SVP. *See* Specific Vocational
    Preparation (SVP)
SWA. *See* State Workforce Agency
    (SWA)
Swains Island, 355 n.7

T
T visa, 84 n.15, 147, 418
TA. *See* Trial attorney (TA)
Targeted employment area (TEA), 487,
    488–489
Tax
    Asset-Use Test for, 502 n.8
    avoidance of, by renunciation of
        citizenship, 94
    Business Activities Test for, 502 n.8
    capital gains, 504
    credits, 500
    for departing alien, 507

dual, 500–501
effectively connected income in,
    502–503, 502 n.8
evasion, 385
failure to file, 366–367
FDAP, 496, 502, 503–504, 503 n.11,
    503 n.12, 504 n.13
filing, 501, 504–505
for foreign students and scholars,
    506–507
Green Card Test for, 497–498
head, 35, 35 n.12
Individual Taxpayer Identification
    Number and, 500
individuals subject to, 495–497
Medicare, 506, 507
nonresident filing of, 293, 501–504
on resident aliens, 495–496, 499–501,
    506–507
returns, 501
Social Security, 506
Social Security number and, 500
Substantial Presence Test for,
    498–499, 507
treaties with other countries on, 501
TC visa, 418
TCN. *See* Third country national
    (TCN)
TD visa, 418
TEA. *See* Targeted employment area
    (TEA)
Television. *See* O-1 visa
Temporary visit abroad, 289–290
Temporary workers, 130–131
Tenth Amendment, 35
Term of imprisonment, 404
Termination date, 291
Terrorism
    asylum and, 334, 334 n.126
    inadmissibility for, 381
    non-immigrant visas and, 104
    personal appearance waiver and,
        89 n.31
    REAL ID Act and, 61
    removal for, 381
    S visa and, 81 n.16, 146, 309
    September 11 attacks, 2, 89 n.31,
        425, 428, 430, 433